International Trade Law

Documents Supplement to the Second Edition

International Trade Law

Documents Supplement to the Second Edition

Andrew T. Guzman
Professor of Law
Berkeley Law School
University of California, Berkeley

Joost H.B. Pauwelyn
Professor of International Law
Graduate Institute of International and
Development Studies, Geneva, and
Senior Advisor, King & Spalding LLP

Published by Wolters Kluwer Law & Business in New York.

Wolters Kluwer Law & Business serves customers worldwide with CCH, Aspen Publishers, and Kluwer Law International products. (www.wolterskluwerlb.com)

To contact Customer Service, e-mail customer.service@wolterskluwer.com, call 1-800-234-1660, fax 1-800-901-9075, or mail correspondence to:

Wolters Kluwer Law & Business
Attn: Order Department
PO Box 990
Frederick, MD 21705

Printed in the United States of America.

1 2 3 4 5 6 7 8 9 0

ISBN 978-0-7355-0801-9

About Wolters Kluwer Law & Business

Wolters Kluwer Law & Business is a leading global provider of intelligent information and digital solutions for legal and business professionals in key specialty areas, and respected educational resources for professors and law students. Wolters Kluwer Law & Business connects legal and business professionals as well as those in the education market with timely, specialized authoritative content and information-enabled solutions to support success through productivity, accuracy and mobility.

Serving customers worldwide, Wolters Kluwer Law & Business products include those under the Aspen Publishers, CCH, Kluwer Law International, Loislaw, Best Case, ftwilliam.com and MediRegs family of products.

CCH products have been a trusted resource since 1913, and are highly regarded resources for legal, securities, antitrust and trade regulation, government contracting, banking, pension, payroll, employment and labor, and healthcare reimbursement and compliance professionals.

Aspen Publishers products provide essential information to attorneys, business professionals and law students. Written by preeminent authorities, the product line offers analytical and practical information in a range of specialty practice areas from securities law and intellectual property to mergers and acquisitions and pension/benefits. Aspen's trusted legal education resources provide professors and students with high-quality, up-to-date and effective resources for successful instruction and study in all areas of the law.

Kluwer Law International products provide the global business community with reliable international legal information in English. Legal practitioners, corporate counsel and business executives around the world rely on Kluwer Law journals, looseleafs, books, and electronic products for comprehensive information in many areas of international legal practice.

Loislaw is a comprehensive online legal research product providing legal content to law firm practitioners of various specializations. Loislaw provides attorneys with the ability to quickly and efficiently find the necessary legal information they need, when and where they need it, by facilitating access to primary law as well as state-specific law, records, forms and treatises.

Best Case Solutions is the leading bankruptcy software product to the bankruptcy industry. It provides software and workflow tools to flawlessly streamline petition preparation and the electronic filing process, while timely incorporating ever-changing court requirements.

ftwilliam.com offers employee benefits professionals the highest quality plan documents (retirement, welfare and non-qualified) and government forms (5500/PBGC, 1099 and IRS) software at highly competitive prices.

MediRegs products provide integrated health care compliance content and software solutions for professionals in healthcare, higher education and life sciences, including professionals in accounting, law and consulting.

Wolters Kluwer Law & Business, a division of Wolters Kluwer, is headquartered in New York. Wolters Kluwer is a market-leading global information services company focused on professionals.

Contents

Preface

This volume is a companion to the second edition of *International Trade Law*. It only includes publicly available documents. Its added value is that it brings together a series of agreements, declarations, and statutes that are dispersed in several places and that were concluded both at the creation of the WTO and afterwards. The bulk of the volume sets out WTO agreements. We included most but not all of the agreements concluded in April 1994, at the close of the Uruguay Round (not, for example, the now defunct Textiles and Clothing Agreement, nor the plurilateral Agreement on Trade in Civil Aircraft). You can find the complete series of WTO agreements and declarations on the WTO website (www.wto.org).

Not included in this volume, but very important to figure out specific commitments engaged in at the WTO by specific WTO members are the tariff schedules and services commitments of each WTO member that form an integral part of the WTO Agreement. They account for thousands of pages and are available on the WTO website: *Goods*: http://www.wto.org/english/tratop_e/schedules_e/goods_schedules_table_e.htm/. *Services*: http://www.wto.org/english/tratop_e/serv_e/serv_commitments_e.htm/.

We do find it useful, however, for students and practitioners to have the main WTO agreements in hard copy, in a volume like this one. The WTO Secretariat published its own volume with *The Legal Texts*. However, the often frustrating thing about that volume is that it does not include certain crucial documents such as the Enabling Clause or the Government Procurement Agreement, or any of the post-1994 agreements or declarations (such as the Doha Declaration or the TRIPS amendment).

In addition, besides WTO agreements and declarations, we have also included U.S. and EU domestic regulations setting out internal procedures on how to initiate WTO disputes. Another important document for both students and practitioners that we decided to include, which is not in the WTO *Legal Texts*, is China's Accession Protocol.

Several improvements have been made since the supplement to the first edition of *International Trade Law*. We included subheadings (e.g., documents on "dispute settlement," "trade in goods," "selected accession documents and protocols," etc.) to make the supplement more user-friendly. To make the supplement more complete we have also added a number of documents even though they already existed when the first edition of *International Trade Law* was published. We did so because some of these documents (such as the Customs Valuation Agreement or the Decision of the TBT Committee on international standards) have only recently been referred to in WTO dispute settlement. We also expanded the documents related to dispute settlement to include the Working Procedures for Appellate Review and the Rules of Conduct under the DSU. In addition, we substantially expanded the documents on intellectual property rights by including the relevant provisions of the Paris and Berne Conventions. Finally, we added the Revised Government Procurement Agreement as well as Russia's Accession Protocol (both agreed upon in December 2011) and updated the list of members and observers to the WTO, as well as the lists of signatories to the Government Procurement Agreement and the Information Technology Agreement, to make it up to date as of May 2012. In this way, we hope that this supplement will be an even better guide to facilitate your study of the casebook and may also assist practitioners beyond the confines of *International Trade Law*.

Joost H.B. Pauwelyn
Andrew T. Guzman

July 2012

PART I

WTO Membership and Structure

Document 1

LIST OF WTO MEMBERS AND OBSERVERS

Current 10 May 2012, with Dates of Membership

Albania (8 September 2000);
Angola (23 November 1996);
Antigua and Barbuda (1 January 1995);
Argentina (1 January 1995);
Armenia (5 February 2003);
Australia (1January 1995);
Austria (1 January 1995);
Bahrain, Kingdom of (1 January 1995);
Bangladesh (1 January 1995);
Barbados (1 January 1995);
Belgium (1 January 1995);
Belize (1 January 1995);
Benin (22 February 1996);
Bolivia (12 September 1995);
Botswana (31 May 1995);
Brazil (1 January 1995)
Brunei Darussalam (1 January 1995);
Bulgaria (1 December 1996);
Burkina Faso (3 June 1995);
Burundi (23 July 1995);
Cambodia (13 October 2004);
Cameroon (13 December 1995);
Canada (1 January 1995);
Cape Verde (23 July 2008);
Central African Republic (31 May 1995);
Chad (19 October 1996);
Chile (1 January 1995);

China (11 December 2001);
Colombia (30 April 1995);
Congo (27 March 1997);
Costa Rica (1 January 1995);
Côte d'Ivoire (1 January 1995);
Croatia (30 November 2000);
Cuba (20 April 1995);
Cyprus (30 July 1995);
Czech Republic (1 January 1995);
Democratic Republic of the Congo (1 January 1997);
Denmark (1January 1995);
Djibouti (31 May 1995);
Dominica (1 January 1995);
Dominican Republic (9 March 1995);
Ecuador (21 January 1996);
Egypt (30 June 1995);
El Salvador (7 May 1995);
Estonia (13 November 1999);
European Communities (1 January 1995);
Fiji (14 January 1996);
Finland (1 January 1995);
Former Yugoslav Republic of Macedonia (FYROM) (4 April 2003);
France (1 January 1995);
Gabon (1 January 1995);
The Gambia (23 October 1996);
Georgia (14 June 2000);
Germany (1 January 1995);
Ghana (1January 1995);
Greece (1 January 1995);
Grenada (22 February 1996);
Guatemala (21 July 1995);
Guinea (25 October 1995);
Guinea Bissau (31 May 1995);
Guyana (1 January 1995);
Haiti (30 January 1996);
Honduras (1 January 1995);
Hong Kong, China (1 January 1995);
Hungary (1 January 1995);
Iceland (1 January 1995);
India (1 January 1995);
Indonesia (1 January 1995);
Ireland (1 January 1995);
Israel (21 April 1995);
Italy (1 January 1995);
Jamaica (9 March 1995);
Japan (1 January 1995);

Jordan (11April 2000);
Kenya (1 January 1995);
Korea, Republic of (1January 1995);
Kuwait (1 January 1995);
Kyrgyz Republic (20 December 1998);
Latvia (10 February 1999);
Lesotho (31 May 1995);
Liechtenstein (1 September 1995);
Lithuania (31 May 2001);
Luxembourg (1 January 1995);
Macao, China (1 January 1995);
Madagascar (17 November 1995);
Malawi (31 May 1995);
Malaysia (1 January 1995);
Maldives (31 May 1995);
Mali (31 May 1995);
Malta (1 January 1995);
Mauritania (31 May 1995);
Mauritius (1 January 1995);
Mexico (1 January 1995);
Moldova (26 July 2001);
Mongolia (29 January 1997);
Montenegro (29 April 2012);
Morocco (1 January 1995);
Mozambique (26 August 1995);
Myanmar (1 January 1995);
Namibia (1 January 1995);
Nepal (23 April 2004);
Netherlands—For the Kingdom in Europe and for the Netherlands Antilles (1 January 1995);
New Zealand (1 January 1995);
Nicaragua (3 September 1995);
Niger (13 December 1996);
Nigeria (1 January 1995);
Norway (1 January 1995);
Oman (9 November 2000);
Pakistan (1 January 1995);
Panama (6 September 1997);
Papua New Guinea (9 June 1996);
Paraguay (1 January 1995);
Peru (1 January 1995);
Philippines (1 January 1995);
Poland (1 July 1995);
Portugal (1 January 1995);
Qatar (13 January 1996);
Romania (1 January 1995);

Russia (waiting for ratification, but Accession Package approved on 16 December 2011);
Rwanda (22 May 1996);
Saint Kitts and Nevis (21 February 1996);
Saint Lucia (1 January 1995);
Saint Vincent & the Grenadines (1 January 1995);
Samoa (10 May 2012);
Saudi Arabia (11 December 2005);
Senegal (1 January 1995);
Sierra Leone (23 July 1995);
Singapore (1 January 1995);
Slovak Republic (1 January 1995);
Slovenia (30 July 1995);
Solomon Islands (26 July 1996);
South Africa (1 January 1995);
Spain (1 January 1995);
Sri Lanka (1 January 1995);
Suriname (1 January 1995);
Swaziland (1 January 1995);
Sweden (1 January 1995);
Switzerland (1 July 1995);
Chinese Taipei (1 January 2002);
Tanzania (1 January 1995);
Thailand (1 January 1995);
Togo (31 May 1995);
Tonga (27 July 2007);
Trinidad and Tobago (1 March 1995);
Tunisia (29 March 1995);
Turkey (26 March 1995);
Uganda (1 January 1995);
Ukraine (16 May 2008);
United Arab Emirates (10 April 1996);
United Kingdom (1 January 1995);
United States of America (1January 1995);
Uruguay (1 January 1995);
Venezuela (Bolivarian Republic of) (1January 1995);
Viet Nam (11January 2007);
Zambia (1 January 1995);
Zimbabwe (5 March 1995).

Observer governments:

Afghanistan;
Algeria;
Andorra;
Azerbaijan;

Bahamas;
Belarus;
Bhutan;
Bosnia and Herzegovina;
Comoros;
Equatorial Guinea;
Ethiopia;
Holy See (Vatican);
Iran;
Iraq;
Kazakhstan;
Lao People's Democratic Republic;
Lebanese Republic;
Liberia,
Republic of; Libya;
Sao Tomé and Principe;
Serbia;
Seychelles;
Sudan;
Syrian Arab Republic;
Tajikistan;
Uzbekistan;
Vanuatu;
Yemen.

Document 2

WTO STRUCTURE

WTO structure

All WTO members may participate in all councils, committees, etc, except Appellate Body, Dispute Settlement panels, and plurilateral committees.

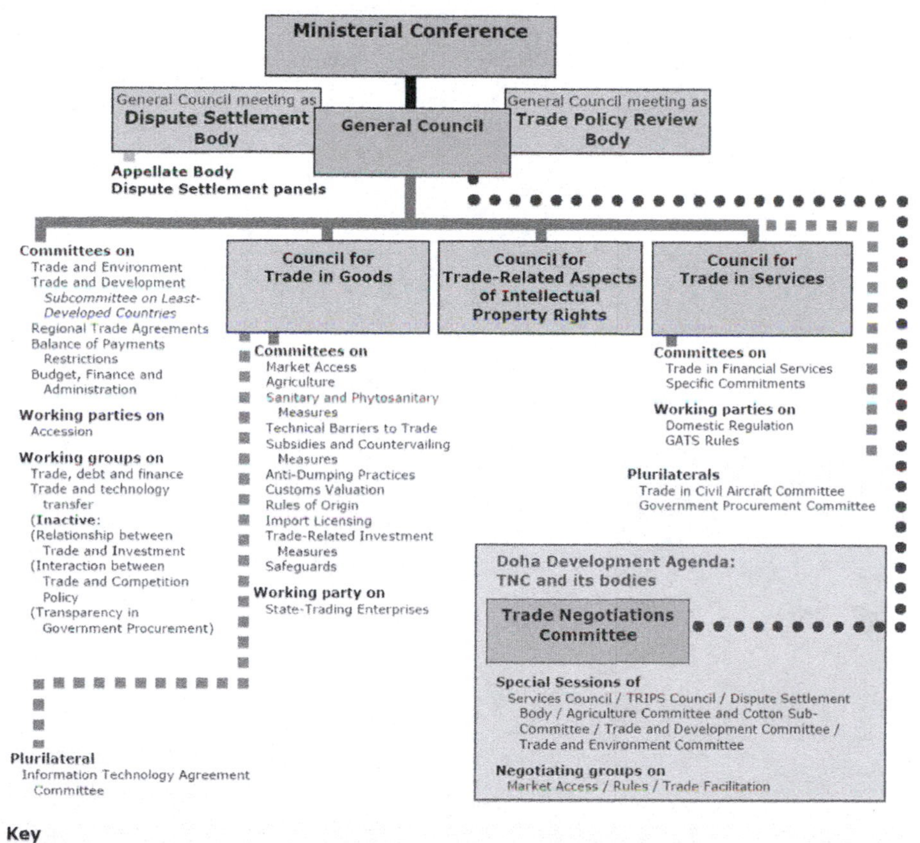

Key

- Reporting to General Council (or a subsidiary)
- Reporting to Dispute Settlement Body
- Plurilateral committees inform the General Council or Goods Council of their activities, although these agreements are not signed by all WTO members
- Trade Negotiations Committee reports to General Council

The General Council also meets as the Trade Policy Review Body and Dispute Settlement Body

PART II

Marrakesh Agreement Establishing the WTO

Document 3

MARRAKESH DECLARATION OF 15 APRIL 1994

Ministers,

Representing the 124 Governments and the European Communities participating in the Uruguay Round of Multilateral Trade Negotiations, on the occasion of the final session of the Trade Negotiations Committee at Ministerial level held at Marrakesh, Morocco from 12 to 15 April 1994,

Recalling the Ministerial Declaration adopted at Punta del Este, Uruguay on 20 September 1986 to launch the Uruguay Round of Multilateral Trade Negotiations,

Recalling the progress achieved at the Ministerial meetings held at Montreal, Canada and Brussels, Belgium in December of 1988 and 1990 respectively,

Noting that the negotiations were substantially concluded on 15 December 1993,

Determined to build upon the success of the Uruguay Round through the participation of their economies in the world trading system, based upon open, market-oriented policies and the commitments set out in the Uruguay Round Agreements and Decisions,

Have today *adopted* the following:

DECLARATION

1. Ministers salute the historic achievement represented by the conclusion of the Round, which they believe will strengthen the world economy and lead to more trade, investment, employment and income growth throughout the world. In particular, they welcome:

- the stronger and clearer legal framework they have adopted for the conduct of international trade, including a more effective and reliable dispute settlement mechanism,
- the global reduction by 40 per cent of tariffs and wider market-opening agreements on goods, and the increased predictability and security represented by a major expansion in the scope of tariff commitments, and
- the establishment of a multilateral framework of disciplines for trade in services and for the protection of trade-related intellectual property rights, as well as the reinforced multilateral trade provisions in agriculture and in textiles and clothing.

2. Ministers affirm that the establishment of the World Trade Organization (WTO) ushers in a new era of global economic cooperation, reflecting the widespread desire to operate in a fairer and more open multilateral trading system for the benefit and welfare of their peoples. Ministers express their determination to resist protectionist pressures of all kinds. They believe that the trade liberalization and strengthened rules achieved in the Uruguay Round will lead to a progressively more open world trading environment. Ministers undertake, with immediate effect and until the entry into force of the WTO, not to take any trade measures that would undermine or adversely affect the results of the Uruguay Round negotiations or their implementation.

3. Ministers confirm their resolution to strive for greater global coherence of policies in the fields of trade, money and finance, including cooperation between the WTO, the IMF and the World Bank for that purpose.

4. Ministers welcome the fact that participation in the Uruguay Round was considerably wider than in any previous multilateral trade negotiation and, in particular, that developing countries played a notably active rôle in it. This has marked a historic step towards a more balanced and integrated global trade partnership. Ministers note that during the period these negotiations were underway significant measures of economic reform and autonomous trade liberalization were implemented in many developing countries and formerly centrally planned economies.

5. Ministers recall that the results of the negotiations embody provisions conferring differential and more favourable treatment for developing

economies, including special attention to the particular situation of least-developed countries. Ministers recognize the importance of the implementation of these provisions for the least- developed countries and declare their intention to continue to assist and facilitate the expansion of their trade and investment opportunities. They agree to keep under regular review by the Ministerial Conference and the appropriate organs of the WTO the impact of the results of the Round on the least-developed countries as well as on the net food-importing developing countries, with a view to fostering positive measures to enable them to achieve their development objectives. Ministers recognize the need for strengthening the capability of the GATT and the WTO to provide increased technical assistance in their areas of competence, and in particular to substantially expand its provision to the least-developed countries.

6. Ministers declare that their signature of the "Final Act Embodying the Results of the Uruguay Round of Multilateral Trade Negotiations" and their adoption of associated Ministerial Decisions initiates the transition from the GATT to the WTO. They have in particular established a Preparatory Committee to lay the ground for the entry into force of the WTO Agreement and commit themselves to seek to complete all steps necessary to ratify the WTO Agreement so that it can enter into force by 1 January 1995 or as early as possible thereafter. Ministers have furthermore adopted a Decision on Trade and Environment.

7. Ministers express their sincere gratitude to His Majesty King Hassan II for his personal contribution to the success of this Ministerial Meeting, and to his Government and the people of Morocco for their warm hospitality and the excellent organization they have provided. The fact that this final Ministerial Meeting of the Uruguay Round has been held at Marrakesh is an additional manifestation of Morocco's commitment to an open world trading system and to its fullest integration to the global economy.

8. With the adoption and signature of the Final Act and the opening for acceptance of the WTO Agreement, Ministers declare the work of the Trade Negotiations Committee to be complete and the Uruguay Round formally concluded.

Document 4

FINAL ACT EMBODYING THE RESULTS OF THE URUGUAY ROUND OF MULTILATERAL TRADE NEGOTIATIONS

1. Having met in order to conclude the Uruguay Round of Multilateral Trade Negotiations, representatives of the governments and of the European Communities, members of the Trade Negotiations Committee, *agree* that the Agreement Establishing the World Trade Organization (referred to in this Final Act as the "WTO Agreement"), the Ministerial Declarations and Decisions, and the Understanding on Commitments in Financial Services, as annexed hereto, embody the results of their negotiations and form an integral part of this Final Act.

2. By signing the present Final Act, the representatives *agree*

(a) to submit, as appropriate, the WTO Agreement for the consideration of their respective competent authorities with a view to seeking approval of the Agreement in accordance with their procedures; and

(b) to adopt the Ministerial Declarations and Decisions.

3. The representatives *agree* on the desirability of acceptance of the WTO Agreement by all participants in the Uruguay Round of Multilateral Trade Negotiations (hereinafter referred to as "participants") with a view to its entry into force by 1 January 1995, or as early as possible thereafter. Not later than late 1994, Ministers will meet, in accordance with the final paragraph of the Punta del Este Ministerial Declaration, to decide on the international implementation of the results, including the timing of their entry into force.

4. The representatives *agree* that the WTO Agreement shall be open for acceptance as a whole, by signature or otherwise, by all participants pursuant to Article XIV thereof. The acceptance and entry into force of a Plurilateral Trade Agreement included in Annex 4 of the WTO Agreement shall be governed by the provisions of that Plurilateral Trade Agreement.

5. Before accepting the WTO Agreement, participants which are not contracting parties to the General Agreement on Tariffs and Trade must first have concluded negotiations for their accession to the General Agreement and become contracting parties thereto. For participants which are not contracting parties to the General Agreement as of the date of the Final Act, the Schedules are not definitive and shall be subsequently completed for the purpose of their accession to the General Agreement and acceptance of the WTO Agreement.

6. This Final Act and the texts annexed hereto shall be deposited with the Director-General to the CONTRACTING PARTIES to the General Agreement on Tariffs and Trade who shall promptly furnish to each participant a certified copy thereof.

DONE at Marrakesh this fifteenth day of April one thousand nine hundred and ninety-four, in a single copy, in the English, French and Spanish languages, each text being authentic.

[List of signatures to be included in the treaty copy of the Final Act for signature]

Document 5

WTO AGREEMENT

Official name: Marrakesh Agreement Establishing the World Trade Organization

The *Parties* to this Agreement,

Recognizing that their relations in the field of trade and economic endeavour should be conducted with a view to raising standards of living, ensuring full employment and a large and steadily growing volume of real income and effective demand, and expanding the production of and trade in goods and services, while allowing for the optimal use of the world's resources in accordance with the objective of sustainable development, seeking both to protect and preserve the environment and to enhance the means for doing so in a manner consistent with their respective needs and concerns at different levels of economic development,

Recognizing further that there is need for positive efforts designed to ensure that developing countries, and especially the least developed among them, secure a share in the growth in international trade commensurate with the needs of their economic development,

Being desirous of contributing to these objectives by entering into reciprocal and mutually advantageous arrangements directed to the substantial reduction of tariffs and other barriers to trade and to the elimination of discriminatory treatment in international trade relations,

Resolved, therefore, to develop an integrated, more viable and durable multilateral trading system encompassing the General Agreement on Tariffs and Trade, the results of past trade liberalization efforts, and all of the results of the Uruguay Round of Multilateral Trade Negotiations,

Determined to preserve the basic principles and to further the objectives underlying this multilateral trading system,

Agree as follows:

Article I

Establishment of the Organization

The World Trade Organization (hereinafter referred to as "the WTO") is hereby established.

Article II

Scope of the WTO

1. The WTO shall provide the common institutional framework for the conduct of trade relations among its Members in matters related to the agreements and associated legal instruments included in the Annexes to this Agreement.

2. The agreements and associated legal instruments included in Annexes 1, 2 and 3 (hereinafter referred to as "Multilateral Trade Agreements") are integral parts of this Agreement, binding on all Members.

3. The agreements and associated legal instruments included in Annex 4 (hereinafter referred to as "Plurilateral Trade Agreements") are also part of this Agreement for those Members that have accepted them, and are binding on those Members. The Plurilateral Trade Agreements do not create either obligations or rights for Members that have not accepted them.

4. The General Agreement on Tariffs and Trade 1994 as specified in Annex 1A (hereinafter referred to as "GATT 1994") is legally distinct from the General Agreement on Tariffs and Trade, dated 30 October 1947, annexed to the Final Act Adopted at the Conclusion of the Second Session of the Preparatory Committee of the United Nations Conference on Trade and Employment, as subsequently rectified, amended or modified (hereinafter referred to as "GATT 1947").

Article III

Functions of the WTO

1. The WTO shall facilitate the implementation, administration and operation, and further the objectives, of this Agreement and of the Multilateral Trade Agreements, and shall also provide the framework for the implementation, administration and operation of the Plurilateral Trade Agreements.

2. The WTO shall provide the forum for negotiations among its Members concerning their multilateral trade relations in matters dealt with under the agreements in the Annexes to this Agreement. The WTO may also provide a forum for further negotiations among its Members concerning their multilateral trade relations, and a framework for the implementation of the results of such negotiations, as may be decided by the Ministerial Conference.

3. The WTO shall administer the Understanding on Rules and Procedures Governing the Settlement of Disputes (hereinafter referred to as the "Dispute Settlement Understanding" or "DSU") in Annex 2 to this Agreement.

4. The WTO shall administer the Trade Policy Review Mechanism (hereinafter referred to as the "TPRM") provided for in Annex 3 to this Agreement.

5. With a view to achieving greater coherence in global economic policy-making, the WTO shall cooperate, as appropriate, with the International Monetary Fund and with the International Bank for Reconstruction and Development and its affiliated agencies.

Article IV

Structure of the WTO

1. There shall be a Ministerial Conference composed of representatives of all the Members, which shall meet at least once every two years. The Ministerial Conference shall carry out the functions of the WTO and take actions necessary to this effect. The Ministerial Conference shall have the authority to take decisions on all matters under any of the Multilateral Trade Agreements, if so requested by a Member, in accordance with the specific requirements for decision-making in this Agreement and in the relevant Multilateral Trade Agreement.

2. There shall be a General Council composed of representatives of all the Members, which shall meet as appropriate. In the intervals between meetings of the Ministerial Conference, its functions shall be conducted by the General Council. The General Council shall also carry out the functions assigned to it by this Agreement. The General Council shall establish its rules of procedure and approve the rules of procedure for the Committees provided for in paragraph 7.

3. The General Council shall convene as appropriate to discharge the responsibilities of the Dispute Settlement Body provided for in the Dispute Settlement Understanding. The Dispute Settlement Body may have its own chairman and shall establish such rules of procedure as it deems necessary for the fulfilment of those responsibilities.

4. The General Council shall convene as appropriate to discharge the responsibilities of the Trade Policy Review Body provided for in the TPRM. The Trade Policy Review Body may have its own chairman and shall establish such rules of procedure as it deems necessary for the fulfilment of those responsibilities.

5. There shall be a Council for Trade in Goods, a Council for Trade in Services and a Council for Trade-Related Aspects of Intellectual Property Rights (hereinafter referred to as the "Council for TRIPS"), which shall operate under the general guidance of the General Council. The Council for Trade in Goods shall oversee the functioning of the Multilateral Trade Agreements in Annex 1A. The Council for Trade in Services shall oversee the functioning of the General Agreement on Trade in Services (hereinafter referred to as "GATS"). The Council for TRIPS shall oversee the functioning of the Agreement on Trade-Related Aspects of Intellectual Property Rights (hereinafter referred to as the "Agreement on TRIPS"). These Councils shall carry out the functions assigned to them by their respective agreements and by the General Council. They shall establish their respective rules of procedure subject to the approval of the General Council. Membership in these Councils shall be open to representatives of all Members. These Councils shall meet as necessary to carry out their functions.

6. The Council for Trade in Goods, the Council for Trade in Services and the Council for TRIPS shall establish subsidiary bodies as required. These subsidiary bodies shall establish their respective rules of procedure subject to the approval of their respective Councils.

7. The Ministerial Conference shall establish a Committee on Trade and Development, a Committee on Balance-of-Payments Restrictions and a Committee on Budget, Finance and Administration, which shall carry out the functions assigned to them by this Agreement and by the Multilateral Trade Agreements, and any additional functions assigned to them by the General Council, and may establish such additional Committees with such functions as it may deem appropriate. As part of its functions, the Committee on Trade and Development shall periodically review the special provisions in the Multilateral Trade Agreements in favour of the least-developed country Members and report to the General Council for appropriate action. Membership in these Committees shall be open to representatives of all Members.

8. The bodies provided for under the Plurilateral Trade Agreements shall carry out the functions assigned to them under those Agreements and shall operate within the institutional framework of the WTO. These bodies shall keep the General Council informed of their activities on a regular basis.

Article V

Relations with Other Organizations

1. The General Council shall make appropriate arrangements for effective cooperation with other intergovernmental organizations that have responsibilities related to those of the WTO.

2. The General Council may make appropriate arrangements for consultation and cooperation with non-governmental organizations concerned with matters related to those of the WTO.

Article VI

The Secretariat

1. There shall be a Secretariat of the WTO (hereinafter referred to as "the Secretariat") headed by a Director-General.

2. The Ministerial Conference shall appoint the Director-General and adopt regulations setting out the powers, duties, conditions of service and term of office of the Director-General.

3. The Director-General shall appoint the members of the staff of the Secretariat and determine their duties and conditions of service in accordance with regulations adopted by the Ministerial Conference.

4. The responsibilities of the Director-General and of the staff of the Secretariat shall be exclusively international in character. In the discharge of their duties, the Director-General and the staff of the Secretariat shall not seek or accept instructions from any government or any other authority external to the WTO. They shall refrain from any action which might adversely reflect on their position as international officials. The Members of the WTO shall respect the international character of the responsibilities of the Director-General and of the staff of the Secretariat and shall not seek to influence them in the discharge of their duties.

Article VII

Budget and Contributions

1. The Director-General shall present to the Committee on Budget, Finance and Administration the annual budget estimate and financial statement of the WTO. The Committee on Budget, Finance and Administration shall review the annual budget estimate and the financial statement presented by the Director-General and make recommendations thereon to

the General Council. The annual budget estimate shall be subject to approval by the General Council.

2. The Committee on Budget, Finance and Administration shall propose to the General Council financial regulations which shall include provisions setting out:

(a) the scale of contributions apportioning the expenses of the WTO among its Members; and

(b) the measures to be taken in respect of Members in arrears.

The financial regulations shall be based, as far as practicable, on the regulations and practices of GATT 1947.

3. The General Council shall adopt the financial regulations and the annual budget estimate by a two-thirds majority comprising more than half of the Members of the WTO.

4. Each Member shall promptly contribute to the WTO its share in the expenses of the WTO in accordance with the financial regulations adopted by the General Council.

Article VIII

Status of the WTO

1. The WTO shall have legal personality, and shall be accorded by each of its Members such legal capacity as may be necessary for the exercise of its functions.

2. The WTO shall be accorded by each of its Members such privileges and immunities as are necessary for the exercise of its functions.

3. The officials of the WTO and the representatives of the Members shall similarly be accorded by each of its Members such privileges and immunities as are necessary for the independent exercise of their functions in connection with the WTO.

4. The privileges and immunities to be accorded by a Member to the WTO, its officials, and the representatives of its Members shall be similar to the privileges and immunities stipulated in the Convention on the Privileges and Immunities of the Specialized Agencies, approved by the General Assembly of the United Nations on 21 November 1947.

5. The WTO may conclude a headquarters agreement.

Article IX

Decision-Making

1. The WTO shall continue the practice of decision-making by consensus followed under GATT 1947.[1] Except as otherwise provided, where a decision cannot be arrived at by consensus, the matter at issue shall be decided by voting. At meetings of the Ministerial Conference and the General Council, each Member of the WTO shall have one vote. Where the European Communities exercise their right to vote, they shall have a number of votes equal to the number of their member States[2] which are Members of the WTO. Decisions of the Ministerial Conference and the General Council shall be taken by a majority of the votes cast, unless otherwise provided in this Agreement or in the relevant Multilateral Trade Agreement.[3]

2. The Ministerial Conference and the General Council shall have the exclusive authority to adopt interpretations of this Agreement and of the Multilateral Trade Agreements. In the case of an interpretation of a Multilateral Trade Agreement in Annex 1, they shall exercise their authority on the basis of a recommendation by the Council overseeing the functioning of that Agreement. The decision to adopt an interpretation shall be taken by a three-fourths majority of the Members. This paragraph shall not be used in a manner that would undermine the amendment provisions in Article X.

3. In exceptional circumstances, the Ministerial Conference may decide to waive an obligation imposed on a Member by this Agreement or any of the Multilateral Trade Agreements, provided that any such decision shall be taken by three fourths[4] of the Members unless otherwise provided for in this paragraph.

(a) A request for a waiver concerning this Agreement shall be submitted to the Ministerial Conference for consideration pursuant to the practice of decision-making by consensus. The Ministerial Conference shall establish a time-period, which shall not exceed 90 days, to consider the request. If consensus is not reached during the time-period, any decision to grant a waiver shall be taken by three fourths4 of the Members.

(b) A request for a waiver concerning the Multilateral Trade Agreements in Annexes 1A or 1B or 1C and their annexes shall be submitted

1. The body concerned shall be deemed to have decided by consensus on a matter submitted for its consideration, if no Member, present at the meeting when the decision is taken, formally objects to the proposed decision.

2. The number of votes of the European Communities and their member States shall in no case exceed the number of the member States of the European Communities.

3. Decisions by the General Council when convened as the Dispute Settlement Body shall be taken only in accordance with the provisions of paragraph 4 of Article 2 of the Dispute Settlement Understanding.

4. A decision to grant a waiver in respect of any obligation subject to a transition period or a period for staged implementation that the requesting Member has not performed by the end of the relevant period shall be taken only by consensus.

initially to the Council for Trade in Goods, the Council for Trade in Services or the Council for TRIPS, respectively, for consideration during a time-period which shall not exceed 90 days. At the end of the time-period, the relevant Council shall submit a report to the Ministerial Conference.

4. A decision by the Ministerial Conference granting a waiver shall state the exceptional circumstances justifying the decision, the terms and conditions governing the application of the waiver, and the date on which the waiver shall terminate. Any waiver granted for a period of more than one year shall be reviewed by the Ministerial Conference not later than one year after it is granted, and thereafter annually until the waiver terminates. In each review, the Ministerial Conference shall examine whether the exceptional circumstances justifying the waiver still exist and whether the terms and conditions attached to the waiver have been met. The Ministerial Conference, on the basis of the annual review, may extend, modify or terminate the waiver.

5. Decisions under a Plurilateral Trade Agreement, including any decisions on interpretations and waivers, shall be governed by the provisions of that Agreement.

Article X

Amendments

1. Any Member of the WTO may initiate a proposal to amend the provisions of this Agreement or the Multilateral Trade Agreements in Annex 1 by submitting such proposal to the Ministerial Conference. The Councils listed in paragraph 5 of Article IV may also submit to the Ministerial Conference proposals to amend the provisions of the corresponding Multilateral Trade Agreements in Annex 1 the functioning of which they oversee. Unless the Ministerial Conference decides on a longer period, for a period of 90 days after the proposal has been tabled formally at the Ministerial Conference any decision by the Ministerial Conference to submit the proposed amendment to the Members for acceptance shall be taken by consensus. Unless the provisions of paragraphs 2, 5 or 6 apply, that decision shall specify whether the provisions of paragraphs 3 or 4 shall apply. If consensus is reached, the Ministerial Conference shall forthwith submit the proposed amendment to the Members for acceptance. If consensus is not reached at a meeting of the Ministerial Conference within the established period, the Ministerial Conference shall decide by a two-thirds majority of the Members whether to submit the proposed amendment to the Members for acceptance. Except as provided in paragraphs 2, 5 and 6, the provisions of paragraph 3 shall apply to the proposed amendment, unless the Ministerial Conference

decides by a three-fourths majority of the Members that the provisions of paragraph 4 shall apply.

2. Amendments to the provisions of this Article and to the provisions of the following Articles shall take effect only upon acceptance by all Members:

Article IX of this Agreement;
Articles I and II of GATT 1994;
Article II:1 of GATS;
Article 4 of the Agreement on TRIPS.

3. Amendments to provisions of this Agreement, or of the Multilateral Trade Agreements in Annexes 1A and 1C, other than those listed in paragraphs 2 and 6, of a nature that would alter the rights and obligations of the Members, shall take effect for the Members that have accepted them upon acceptance by two thirds of the Members and thereafter for each other Member upon acceptance by it. The Ministerial Conference may decide by a three-fourths majority of the Members that any amendment made effective under this paragraph is of such a nature that any Member which has not accepted it within a period specified by the Ministerial Conference in each case shall be free to withdraw from the WTO or to remain a Member with the consent of the Ministerial Conference.

4. Amendments to provisions of this Agreement or of the Multilateral Trade Agreements in Annexes 1A and 1C, other than those listed in paragraphs 2 and 6, of a nature that would not alter the rights and obligations of the Members, shall take effect for all Members upon acceptance by two thirds of the Members.

5. Except as provided in paragraph 2 above, amendments to Parts I, II and III of GATS and the respective annexes shall take effect for the Members that have accepted them upon acceptance by two thirds of the Members and thereafter for each Member upon acceptance by it. The Ministerial Conference may decide by a three-fourths majority of the Members that any amendment made effective under the preceding provision is of such a nature that any Member which has not accepted it within a period specified by the Ministerial Conference in each case shall be free to withdraw from the WTO or to remain a Member with the consent of the Ministerial Conference. Amendments to Parts IV, V and VI of GATS and the respective annexes shall take effect for all Members upon acceptance by two thirds of the Members.

6. Notwithstanding the other provisions of this Article, amendments to the Agreement on TRIPS meeting the requirements of paragraph 2 of Article 71 thereof may be adopted by the Ministerial Conference without further formal acceptance process.

7. Any Member accepting an amendment to this Agreement or to a Multilateral Trade Agreement in Annex 1 shall deposit an instrument of acceptance with the Director-General of the WTO within the period of acceptance specified by the Ministerial Conference.

8. Any Member of the WTO may initiate a proposal to amend the provisions of the Multilateral Trade Agreements in Annexes 2 and 3 by submitting such proposal to the Ministerial Conference. The decision to approve amendments to the Multilateral Trade Agreement in Annex 2 shall be made by consensus and these amendments shall take effect for all Members upon approval by the Ministerial Conference. Decisions to approve amendments to the Multilateral Trade Agreement in Annex 3 shall take effect for all Members upon approval by the Ministerial Conference.

9. The Ministerial Conference, upon the request of the Members parties to a trade agreement, may decide exclusively by consensus to add that agreement to Annex 4. The Ministerial Conference, upon the request of the Members parties to a Plurilateral Trade Agreement, may decide to delete that Agreement from Annex 4.

10. Amendments to a Plurilateral Trade Agreement shall be governed by the provisions of that Agreement.

Article XI

Original Membership

1. The contracting parties to GATT 1947 as of the date of entry into force of this Agreement, and the European Communities, which accept this Agreement and the Multilateral Trade Agreements and for which Schedules of Concessions and Commitments are annexed to GATT 1994 and for which Schedules of Specific Commitments are annexed to GATS shall become original Members of the WTO.

2. The least-developed countries recognized as such by the United Nations will only be required to undertake commitments and concessions to the extent consistent with their individual development, financial and trade needs or their administrative and institutional capabilities.

Article XII

Accession

1. Any State or separate customs territory possessing full autonomy in the conduct of its external commercial relations and of the other matters provided for in this Agreement and the Multilateral Trade Agreements may accede to this Agreement, on terms to be agreed between it and the WTO.

Such accession shall apply to this Agreement and the Multilateral Trade Agreements annexed thereto.

2. Decisions on accession shall be taken by the Ministerial Conference. The Ministerial Conference shall approve the agreement on the terms of accession by a two-thirds majority of the Members of the WTO.

3. Accession to a Plurilateral Trade Agreement shall be governed by the provisions of that Agreement.

Article XIII

Non-Application of Multilateral Trade Agreements Between Particular Members

1. This Agreement and the Multilateral Trade Agreements in Annexes 1 and 2 shall not apply as between any Member and any other Member if either of the Members, at the time either becomes a Member, does not consent to such application.

2. Paragraph 1 may be invoked between original Members of the WTO which were contracting parties to GATT 1947 only where Article XXXV of that Agreement had been invoked earlier and was effective as between those contracting parties at the time of entry into force for them of this Agreement.

3. Paragraph 1 shall apply between a Member and another Member which has acceded under Article XII only if the Member not consenting to the application has so notified the Ministerial Conference before the approval of the agreement on the terms of accession by the Ministerial Conference.

4. The Ministerial Conference may review the operation of this Article in particular cases at the request of any Member and make appropriate recommendations.

5. Non-application of a Plurilateral Trade Agreement between parties to that Agreement shall be governed by the provisions of that Agreement.

Article XIV

Acceptance, Entry into Force and Deposit

1. This Agreement shall be open for acceptance, by signature or otherwise, by contracting parties to GATT 1947, and the European Communities, which are eligible to become original Members of the WTO in accordance with Article XI of this Agreement. Such acceptance shall apply to

this Agreement and the Multilateral Trade Agreements annexed hereto. This Agreement and the Multilateral Trade Agreements annexed hereto shall enter into force on the date determined by Ministers in accordance with paragraph 3 of the Final Act Embodying the Results of the Uruguay Round of Multilateral Trade Negotiations and shall remain open for acceptance for a period of two years following that date unless the Ministers decide otherwise. An acceptance following the entry into force of this Agreement shall enter into force on the 30th day following the date of such acceptance.

2. A Member which accepts this Agreement after its entry into force shall implement those concessions and obligations in the Multilateral Trade Agreements that are to be implemented over a period of time starting with the entry into force of this Agreement as if it had accepted this Agreement on the date of its entry into force.

3. Until the entry into force of this Agreement, the text of this Agreement and the Multilateral Trade Agreements shall be deposited with the Director-General to the CONTRACTING PARTIES to GATT 1947. The Director-General shall promptly furnish a certified true copy of this Agreement and the Multilateral Trade Agreements, and a notification of each acceptance thereof, to each government and the European Communities having accepted this Agreement. This Agreement and the Multilateral Trade Agreements, and any amendments thereto, shall, upon the entry into force of this Agreement, be deposited with the Director-General of the WTO.

4. The acceptance and entry into force of a Plurilateral Trade Agreement shall be governed by the provisions of that Agreement. Such Agreements shall be deposited with the Director-General to the CONTRACTING PARTIES to GATT 1947. Upon the entry into force of this Agreement, such Agreements shall be deposited with the Director-General of the WTO.

Article XV

Withdrawal

1. Any Member may withdraw from this Agreement. Such withdrawal shall apply both to this Agreement and the Multilateral Trade Agreements and shall take effect upon the expiration of six months from the date on which written notice of withdrawal is received by the Director-General of the WTO.

2. Withdrawal from a Plurilateral Trade Agreement shall be governed by the provisions of that Agreement.

Article XVI

Miscellaneous Provisions

1. Except as otherwise provided under this Agreement or the Multilateral Trade Agreements, the WTO shall be guided by the decisions, procedures and customary practices followed by the CONTRACTING PARTIES to GATT 1947 and the bodies established in the framework of GATT 1947.

2. To the extent practicable, the Secretariat of GATT 1947 shall become the Secretariat of the WTO, and the Director-General to the CONTRACTING PARTIES to GATT 1947, until such time as the Ministerial Conference has appointed a Director-General in accordance with paragraph 2 of Article VI of this Agreement, shall serve as Director-General of the WTO.

3. In the event of a conflict between a provision of this Agreement and a provision of any of the Multilateral Trade Agreements, the provision of this Agreement shall prevail to the extent of the conflict.

4. Each Member shall ensure the conformity of its laws, regulations and administrative procedures with its obligations as provided in the annexed Agreements.

5. No reservations may be made in respect of any provision of this Agreement. Reservations in respect of any of the provisions of the Multilateral Trade Agreements may only be made to the extent provided for in those Agreements. Reservations in respect of a provision of a Plurilateral Trade Agreement shall be governed by the provisions of that Agreement.

6. This Agreement shall be registered in accordance with the provisions of Article 102 of the Charter of the United Nations.

DONE at Marrakesh this fifteenth day of April one thousand nine hundred and ninety-four, in a single copy, in the English, French and Spanish languages, each text being authentic.

Explanatory Notes:

The terms "country" or "countries" as used in this Agreement and the Multilateral Trade Agreements are to be understood to include any separate customs territory Member of the WTO.

In the case of a separate customs territory Member of the WTO, where an expression in this Agreement and the Multilateral Trade Agreements is qualified by the term "national," such expression shall be read as pertaining to that customs territory, unless otherwise specified.

LIST OF ANNEXES

Annex 1

ANNEX 1A: Multilateral Agreements on Trade in Goods
General Agreement on Tariffs and Trade 1994
Agreement on Agriculture
Agreement on the Application of Sanitary and Phytosanitary Measures
Agreement on Textiles and Clothing
Agreement on Technical Barriers to Trade
Agreement on Trade-Related Investment Measures
Agreement on Implementation of Article VI of the General Agreement on Tariffs and Trade 1994
Agreement on Implementation of Article VII of the General Agreement on Tariffs and Trade 1994
Agreement on Preshipment Inspection
Agreement on Rules of Origin
Agreement on Import Licensing Procedures
Agreement on Subsidies and Countervailing Measures
Agreement on Safeguards

ANNEX 1B: General Agreement on Trade in Services and Annexes

ANNEX 1C: Agreement on Trade-Related Aspects of Intellectual Property Rights

Annex 2

Understanding on Rules and Procedures Governing the Settlement of Disputes

Annex 3

Trade Policy Review Mechanism

Annex 4

Plurilateral Trade Agreements

Agreement on Trade in Civil Aircraft
Agreement on Government Procurement
International Dairy Agreement
International Bovine Meat Agreement

Document 6

TRADE POLICY REVIEW MECHANISM

Annex 3, Agreement Establishing the World Trade Organization

Members hereby *agree* as follows:

A. Objectives

(i) The purpose of the Trade Policy Review Mechanism ("TPRM") is to contribute to improved adherence by all Members to rules, disciplines and commitments made under the Multilateral Trade Agreements and, where applicable, the Plurilateral Trade Agreements, and hence to the smoother functioning of the multilateral trading system, by achieving greater transparency in, and understanding of, the trade policies and practices of Members. Accordingly, the review mechanism enables the regular collective appreciation and evaluation of the full range of individual Members' trade policies and practices and their impact on the functioning of the multilateral trading system. It is not, however, intended to serve as a basis for the enforcement of specific obligations under the Agreements or for dispute settlement procedures, or to impose new policy commitments on Members.

(ii) The assessment carried out under the review mechanism takes place, to the extent relevant, against the background of the wider economic and developmental needs, policies and objectives of the Member concerned, as well as of its external environment. However, the function of the review mechanism is to examine the impact of a Member's trade policies and practices on the multilateral trading system.

B. Domestic transparency

Members recognize the inherent value of domestic transparency of government decision-making on trade policy matters for both Members' economies and the multilateral trading system, and agree to encourage and promote greater transparency within their own systems, acknowledging that the implementation of domestic transparency must be on a voluntary basis and take account of each Member's legal and political systems.

C. Procedures for review

(i) The Trade Policy Review Body (referred to herein as the "TPRB") is hereby established to carry out trade policy reviews.

(ii) The trade policies and practices of all Members shall be subject to periodic review. The impact of individual Members on the functioning of the multilateral trading system, defined in terms of their share of world trade in a recent representative period, will be the determining factor in deciding on the frequency of reviews. The first four trading entities so identified (counting the European Communities as one) shall be subject to review every two years. The next 16 shall be reviewed every four years. Other Members shall be reviewed every six years, except that a longer period may be fixed for least-developed country Members. It is understood that the review of entities having a common external policy covering more than one Member shall cover all components of policy affecting trade including relevant policies and practices of the individual Members. Exceptionally, in the event of changes in a Member's trade policies or practices that may have a significant impact on its trading partners, the Member concerned may be requested by the TPRB, after consultation, to bring forward its next review.

(iii) Discussions in the meetings of the TPRB shall be governed by the objectives set forth in paragraph A. The focus of these discussions shall be on the Member's trade policies and practices, which are the subject of the assessment under the review mechanism.

(iv) The TPRB shall establish a basic plan for the conduct of the reviews. It may also discuss and take note of update reports from Members. The TPRB shall establish a programme of reviews for each year in consultation with the Members directly concerned. In consultation with the Member or Members under review, the Chairman may choose discussants who, acting in their personal capacity, shall introduce the discussions in the TPRB.

(v) The TPRB shall base its work on the following documentation:

(a) a full report, referred to in paragraph D, supplied by the Member or Members under review;

(b) a report, to be drawn up by the Secretariat on its own responsibility, based on the information available to it and that provided by the Member or Members concerned. The Secretariat should seek clarification from the Member or Members concerned of their trade policies and practices.

(vi) The reports by the Member under review and by the Secretariat, together with the minutes of the respective meeting of the TPRB, shall be published promptly after the review.

(vii) These documents will be forwarded to the Ministerial Conference, which shall take note of them.

D. Reporting

In order to achieve the fullest possible degree of transparency, each Member shall report regularly to the TPRB. Full reports shall describe the trade policies and practices pursued by the Member or Members concerned, based on an agreed format to be decided upon by the TPRB. This format shall initially be based on the Outline Format for Country Reports established by the Decision of 19 July 1989 (BISD 36S/406-409), amended as necessary to extend the coverage of reports to all aspects of trade policies covered by the Multilateral Trade Agreements in Annex 1 and, where applicable, the Plurilateral Trade Agreements. This format may be revised by the TPRB in the light of experience. Between reviews, Members shall provide brief reports when there are any significant changes in their trade policies; an annual update of statistical information will be provided according to the agreed format. Particular account shall be taken of difficulties presented to least-developed country Members in compiling their reports. The Secretariat shall make available technical assistance on request to developing country Members, and in particular to the least-developed country Members. Information contained in reports should to the greatest extent possible be coordinated with notifications made under provisions of the Multilateral Trade Agreements and, where applicable, the Plurilateral Trade Agreements.

E. Relationship with the balance-of-payments provisions of GATT 1994 and GATS

Members recognize the need to minimize the burden for governments also subject to full consultations under the balance-of-payments provisions of GATT 1994 or GATS. To this end, the Chairman of the TPRB shall, in consultation with the Member or Members concerned, and with the Chairman of the Committee on Balance-of-Payments Restrictions, devise administrative arrangements that harmonize the normal rhythm of the trade policy reviews with the timetable for balance-of-payments consultations but do not postpone the trade policy review by more than 12 months.

F. Appraisal of the Mechanism

The TPRB shall undertake an appraisal of the operation of the TPRM not more than five years after the entry into force of the Agreement Establishing the WTO. The results of the appraisal will be presented to the Ministerial Conference. It may subsequently undertake appraisals of the TPRM at intervals to be determined by it or as requested by the Ministerial Conference.

G. Overview of Developments in the International Trading Environment

An annual overview of developments in the international trading environment which are having an impact on the multilateral trading system shall also be undertaken by the TPRB. The overview is to be assisted by an annual report by the Director-General setting out major activities of the WTO and highlighting significant policy issues affecting the trading system.

PART III

Dispute Settlement

Document 7

DISPUTE SETTLEMENT UNDERSTANDING

Official name: Understanding on Rules and Procedures Governing the Settlement of Disputes (Annex 2, Agreement Establishing the World Trade Organization)

Members hereby *agree* as follows:

Article 1

Coverage and Application

1. The rules and procedures of this Understanding shall apply to disputes brought pursuant to the consultation and dispute settlement provisions of the agreements listed in Appendix 1 to this Understanding (referred to in this Understanding as the "covered agreements"). The rules and procedures of this Understanding shall also apply to consultations and the settlement of disputes between Members concerning their rights and obligations under the provisions of the Agreement Establishing the World Trade Organization (referred to in this Understanding as the "WTO Agreement") and of this Understanding taken in isolation or in combination with any other covered agreement.

2. The rules and procedures of this Understanding shall apply subject to such special or additional rules and procedures on dispute settlement contained in the covered agreements as are identified in Appendix 2 to this Understanding. To the extent that there is a difference between the rules and procedures of this Understanding and the special or additional rules and procedures set forth in Appendix 2, the special or additional rules and procedures in Appendix 2 shall prevail. In disputes involving rules and

procedures under more than one covered agreement, if there is a conflict between special or additional rules and procedures of such agreements under review, and where the parties to the dispute cannot agree on rules and procedures within 20 days of the establishment of the panel, the Chairman of the Dispute Settlement Body provided for in paragraph 1 of Article 2 (referred to in this Understanding as the "DSB"), in consultation with the parties to the dispute, shall determine the rules and procedures to be followed within 10 days after a request by either Member. The Chairman shall be guided by the principle that special or additional rules and procedures should be used where possible, and the rules and procedures set out in this Understanding should be used to the extent necessary to avoid conflict.

Article 2

Administration

1. The Dispute Settlement Body is hereby established to administer these rules and procedures and, except as otherwise provided in a covered agreement, the consultation and dispute settlement provisions of the covered agreements. Accordingly, the DSB shall have the authority to establish panels, adopt panel and Appellate Body reports, maintain surveillance of implementation of rulings and recommendations, and authorize suspension of concessions and other obligations under the covered agreements. With respect to disputes arising under a covered agreement which is a Plurilateral Trade Agreement, the term "Member" as used herein shall refer only to those Members that are parties totherelevant Plurilateral Trade Agreement. Where the DSB administers the dispute settlement provisions of a Plurilateral Trade Agreement, only those Members that are parties to that Agreement may participate in decisions or actions taken by the DSB with respect to that dispute.

2. The DSB shall inform the relevant WTO Councils and Committees of any developments in disputes related to provisions of the respective covered agreements.

3. The DSB shall meet as often as necessary to carry out its functions within the time-frames provided in this Understanding.

4. Where the rules and procedures of this Understanding provide for the DSB to take a decision, it shall do so by consensus.[1]

1. The DSB shall be deemed to have decided by consensus on a matter submitted for its consideration, if no Member, present at the meeting of the DSB when the decision is taken, formally objects to the proposed decision.

Article 3

General Provisions

1. Members affirm their adherence to the principles for the management of disputes heretofore applied under Articles XXII and XXIII of GATT 1947, and the rules and procedures as further elaborated and modified herein.

2. The dispute settlement system of the WTO is a central element in providing security and predictability to the multilateral trading system. The Members recognize that it serves to preserve the rights and obligations of Members under the covered agreements, and to clarify the existing provisions of those agreements in accordance with customary rules of interpretation of public international law. Recommendations and rulings of the DSB cannot add to or diminish the rights and obligations provided in the covered agreements.

3. The prompt settlement of situations in which a Member considers that any benefits accruing to it directly or indirectly under the covered agreements are being impaired by measures taken by another Member is essential to the effective functioning of the WTO and the maintenance of a proper balance between the rights and obligations of Members.

4. Recommendations or rulings made by the DSB shall be aimed at achieving a satisfactory settlement of the matter in accordance with the rights and obligations under this Understanding and under the covered agreements.

5. All solutions to matters formally raised under the consultation and dispute settlement provisions of the covered agreements, including arbitration awards, shall be consistent with those agreements and shall not nullify or impair benefits accruing to any Member under those agreements, nor impede the attainment of any objective of those agreements.

6. Mutually agreed solutions to matters formally raised under the consultation and dispute settlement provisions of the covered agreements shall be notified to the DSB and the relevant Councils and Committees, where any Member may raise any point relating thereto.

7. Before bringing a case, a Member shall exercise its judgement as to whether action under these procedures would be fruitful. The aim of the dispute settlement mechanism is to secure a positive solution to a dispute. A solution mutually acceptable to the parties to a dispute and consistent with the covered agreements is clearly to be preferred. In the absence of a mutually agreed solution, the first objective of the dispute settlement mechanism is usually to secure the withdrawal of the measures concerned if these

are found to be inconsistent with the provisions of any of the covered agreements. The provision of compensation should be resorted to only if the immediate withdrawal of the measure is impracticable and as a temporary measure pending the withdrawal of the measure which is inconsistent with a covered agreement. The last resort which this Understanding provides to the Member invoking the dispute settlement procedures is the possibility of suspending the application of concessions or other obligations under the covered agreements on a discriminatory basis vis-à-vis the other Member, subject to authorization by the DSB of such measures.

8. In cases where there is an infringement of the obligations assumed under a covered agreement, the action is considered *prima facie* to constitute a case of nullification or impairment. This means that there is normally a presumption that a breach of the rules has an adverse impact on other Members parties to that covered agreement, and in such cases, it shall be up to the Member against whom the complaint has been brought to rebut the charge.

9. The provisions of this Understanding are without prejudice to the rights of Members to seek authoritative interpretation of provisions of a covered agreement through decision-making under the WTO Agreement or a covered agreement which is a Plurilateral Trade Agreement.

10. It is understood that requests for conciliation and the use of the dispute settlement procedures should not be intended or considered as contentious acts and that, if a dispute arises, all Members will engage in these procedures in good faith in an effort to resolve the dispute. It is also understood that complaints and counter-complaints in regard to distinct matters should not be linked.

11. This Understanding shall be applied only with respect to new requests for consultations under the consultation provisions of the covered agreements made on or after the date of entry into force of the WTO Agreement. With respect to disputes for which the request for consultations was made under GATT 1947 or under any other predecessor agreement to the covered agreements before the date of entry into force of the WTO Agreement, the relevant dispute settlement rules and procedures in effect immediately prior to the date of entry into force of the WTO Agreement shall continue to apply.[2]

12. Notwithstanding paragraph 11, if a complaint based on any of the covered agreements is brought by a developing country Member against a developed country Member, the complaining party shall have the right to

2. This paragraph shall also be applied to disputes on which panel reports have not been adopted or fully implemented.

invoke, as an alternative to the provisions contained in Articles 4, 5, 6 and 12 of this Understanding, the corresponding provisions of the Decision of 5 April 1966 (BISD 14S/18), except that where the Panel considers that the time-frame provided for in paragraph 7 of that Decision is insufficient to provide its report and with the agreement of the complaining party, that time-frame may be extended. To the extent that there is a difference between the rules and procedures of Articles 4, 5, 6 and 12 and the corresponding rules and procedures of the Decision, the latter shall prevail.

Article 4

Consultations

1. Members affirm their resolve to strengthen and improve the effectiveness of the consultation procedures employed by Members.

2. Each Member undertakes to accord sympathetic consideration to and afford adequate opportunity for consultation regarding any representations made by another Member concerning measures affecting the operation of any covered agreement taken within the territory of the former.[3]

3. If a request for consultations is made pursuant to a covered agreement, the Member to which the request is made shall, unless otherwise mutually agreed, reply to the request within 10 days after the date of its receipt and shall enter into consultations in good faith within a period of no more than 30 days after the date of receipt of the request, with a view to reaching a mutually satisfactory solution. If the Member does not respond within 10 days after the date of receipt of the request, or does not enter into consultations within a period of no more than 30 days, or a period otherwise mutually agreed, after the date of receipt of the request, then the Member that requested the holding of consultations may proceed directly to request the establishment of a panel.

4. All such requests for consultations shall be notified to the DSB and the relevant Councils and Committees by the Member which requests consultations. Any request for consultations shall be submitted in writing and shall give the reasons for the request, including identification of the measures at issue and an indication of the legal basis for the complaint.

5. In the course of consultations in accordance with the provisions of a covered agreement, before resorting to further action under this

3. Where the provisions of any other covered agreement concerning measures taken by regional or local governments or authorities within the territory of a Member contain provisions different from the provisions of this paragraph, the provisions of such other covered agreement shall prevail.

Understanding, Members should attempt to obtain satisfactory adjustment of the matter.

6. Consultations shall be confidential, and without prejudice to the rights of any Member in any further proceedings.

7. If the consultations fail to settle a dispute within 60 days after the date of receipt of the request for consultations, the complaining party may request the establishment of a panel. The complaining party may request a panel during the 60-day period if the consulting parties jointly consider that consultations have failed to settle the dispute.

8. In cases of urgency, including those which concern perishable goods, Members shall enter into consultations within a period of no more than 10 days after the date of receipt of the request. If the consultations have failed to settle the dispute within a period of 20 days after the date of receipt of the request, the complaining party may request the establishment of a panel.

9. In cases of urgency, including those which concern perishable goods, the parties to the dispute, panels and the Appellate Body shall make every effort to accelerate the proceedings to the greatest extent possible.

10. During consultations Members should give special attention to the particular problems and interests of developing country Members.

11. Whenever a Member other than the consulting Members considers that it has a substantial trade interest in consultations being held pursuant to paragraph 1 of Article XXII of GATT 1994, paragraph 1 of Article XXII of GATS, or the corresponding provisions in other covered agreements[4], such Member may notify the consulting Members and the DSB, within 10 days after the date of the circulation of the request for consultations under said Article, of its desire to be joined in the consultations. Such Member shall be joined in the consultations, provided that the Member to which the request for consultations was addressed agrees that the claim of substantial interest is well-founded. In that event they shall so inform the DSB. If the request to be

4. The corresponding consultation provisions in the covered agreements are listed hereunder: Agreement on Agriculture, Article 19; Agreement on the Application of Sanitary and Phytosanitary Measures, paragraph 1 of Article 11; Agreement on Textiles and Clothing, paragraph 4 of Article 8; Agreement on Technical Barriers to Trade, paragraph 1 of Article 14; Agreement on Trade-Related Investment Measures, Article 8; Agreement on Implementation of Article VI of GATT 1994, paragraph 2 of Article 17; Agreement on Implementation of Article VII of GATT 1994, paragraph 2 of Article 19; Agreement on Preshipment Inspection, Article 7; Agreement on Rules of Origin, Article 7; Agreement on Import Licensing Procedures, Article 6; Agreement on Subsidies and Countervailing Measures, Article 30; Agreement on Safeguards, Article 14; Agreement on Trade-Related Aspects of Intellectual Property Rights, Article 64.1; and any corresponding consultation provisions in Plurilateral Trade Agreements as determined by the competent bodies of each Agreement and as notified to the DSB.

joined in the consultations is not accepted, the applicant Member shall be free to request consultations under paragraph 1 of Article XXII or paragraph 1 of Article XXIII of GATT 1994, paragraph 1 of Article XXII or paragraph 1 of Article XXIII of GATS, or the corresponding provisions in other covered agreements.

Article 5

Good Offices, Conciliation and Mediation

1. Good offices, conciliation and mediation are procedures that are undertaken voluntarily if the parties to the dispute so agree.

2. Proceedings involving good offices, conciliation and mediation, and in particular positions taken by the parties to the dispute during these proceedings, shall be confidential, and without prejudice to the rights of either party in any further proceedings under these procedures.

3. Good offices, conciliation or mediation may be requested at any time by any party to a dispute. They may begin at any time and be terminated at any time. Once procedures for good offices, conciliation or mediation are terminated, a complaining party may then proceed with a request for the establishment of a panel.

4. When good offices, conciliation or mediation are entered into within 60 days after the date of receipt of a request for consultations, the complaining party must allow a period of 60 days after the date of receipt of the request for consultations before requesting the establishment of a panel. The complaining party may request the establishment of a panel during the 60-day period if the parties to the dispute jointly consider that the good offices, conciliation or mediation process has failed to settle the dispute.

5. If the parties to a dispute agree, procedures for good offices, conciliation or mediation may continue while the panel process proceeds.

6. The Director-General may, acting in an *ex officio* capacity, offer good offices, conciliation or mediation with the view to assisting Members to settle a dispute.

Article 6

Establishment of Panels

1. If the complaining party so requests, a panel shall be established at the latest at the DSB meeting following that at which the request first

appears as an item on the DSB's agenda, unless at that meeting the DSB decides by consensus not to establish a panel.[5]

2. The request for the establishment of a panel shall be made in writing. It shall indicate whether consultations were held, identify the specific measures at issue and provide a brief summary of the legal basis of the complaint sufficient to present the problem clearly. In case the applicant requests the establishment of a panel with other than standard terms of reference, the written request shall include the proposed text of special terms of reference.

Article 7

Terms of Reference of Panels

1. Panels shall have the following terms of reference unless the parties to the dispute agree otherwise within 20 days from the establishment of the panel:

> "To examine, in the light of the relevant provisions in (name of the covered agreement(s) cited by the parties to the dispute), the matter referred to the DSB by (name of party) in document . . . and to make such findings as will assist the DSB in making the recommendations or in giving the rulings provided for in that/those agreement(s)."

2. Panels shall address the relevant provisions in any covered agreement or agreements cited by the parties to the dispute.

3. In establishing a panel, the DSB may authorize its Chairman to draw up the terms of reference of the panel in consultation with the parties to the dispute, subject to the provisions of paragraph 1. The terms of reference thus drawn up shall be circulated to all Members. If other than standard terms of reference are agreed upon, any Member may raise any point relating thereto in the DSB.

Article 8

Composition of Panels

1. Panels shall be composed of well-qualified governmental and/or non-governmental individuals, including persons who have served on or presented a case to a panel, served as a representative of a Member or of a contracting party to GATT 1947 or as a representative to the Council or Committee of any covered agreement or its predecessor agreement, or in

5. If the complaining party so requests, a meeting of the DSB shall be convened for this purpose within 15 days of the request, provided that at least 10 days' advance notice of the meeting is given.

the Secretariat, taught or published on international trade law or policy, or served as a senior trade policy official of a Member.

2. Panel members should be selected with a view to ensuring the independence of the members, a sufficiently diverse background and a wide spectrum of experience.

3. Citizens of Members whose governments[6] are parties to the dispute or third parties as defined in paragraph 2 of Article 10 shall not serve on a panel concerned with that dispute, unless the parties to the dispute agree otherwise.

4. To assist in the selection of panelists, the Secretariat shall maintain an indicative list of governmental and non-governmental individuals possessing the qualifications outlined in paragraph 1, from which panelists may be drawn as appropriate. That list shall include the roster of non-governmental panelists established on 30 November 1984 (BISD 31S/9), and other rosters and indicative lists established under any of the covered agreements, and shall retain the names of persons on those rosters and indicative lists at the time of entry into force of the WTO Agreement. Members may periodically suggest names of governmental and non-governmental individuals for inclusion on the indicative list, providing relevant information on their knowledge of international trade and of the sectors or subject matter of the covered agreements, and those names shall be added to the list upon approval by the DSB. For each of the individuals on the list, the list shall indicate specific areas of experience or expertise of the individuals in the sectors or subject matter of the covered agreements.

5. Panels shall be composed of three panelists unless the parties to the dispute agree, within 10 days from the establishment of the panel, to a panel composed of five panelists. Members shall be informed promptly of the composition of the panel.

6. The Secretariat shall propose nominations for the panel to the parties to the dispute. The parties to the dispute shall not oppose nominations except for compelling reasons.

7. If there is no agreement on the panelists within 20 days after the date of the establishment of a panel, at the request of either party, the Director-General, in consultation with the Chairman of the DSB and the Chairman of the relevant Council or Committee, shall determine the composition of the panel by appointing the panelists whom the Director-General considers most appropriate in accordance with any relevant special or additional rules

6. In the case where customs unions or common markets are parties to a dispute, this provision applies to citizens of all member countries of the customs unions or common markets.

or procedures of the covered agreement or covered agreements which are at issue in the dispute, after consulting with the parties to the dispute. The Chairman of the DSB shall inform the Members of the composition of the panel thus formed no later than 10 days after the date the Chairman receives such a request.

8. Members shall undertake, as a general rule, to permit their officials to serve as panelists.

9. Panelists shall serve in their individual capacities and not as government representatives, nor as representatives of any organization. Members shall therefore not give them instructions nor seek to influence them as individuals with regard to matters before a panel.

10. When a dispute is between a developing country Member and a developed country Member the panel shall, if the developing country Member so requests, include at least one panelist from a developing country Member.

11. Panelists' expenses, including travel and subsistence allowance, shall be met from the WTO budget in accordance with criteria to be adopted by the General Council, based on recommendations of the Committee on Budget, Finance and Administration.

Article 9

Procedures for Multiple Complainants

1. Where more than one Member requests the establishment of a panel related to the same matter, a single panel may be established to examine these complaints taking into account the rights of all Members concerned. A single panel should be established to examine such complaints whenever feasible.

2. The single panel shall organize its examination and present its findings to the DSB in such a manner that the rights which the parties to the dispute would have enjoyed had separate panels examined the complaints are in no way impaired. If one of the parties to the dispute so requests, the panel shall submit separate reports on the dispute concerned. The written submissions by each of the complainants shall be made available to the other complainants, and each complainant shall have the right to be present when any one of the other complainants presents its views to the panel.

3. If more than one panel is established to examine the complaints related to the same matter, to the greatest extent possible the same persons shall serve as panelists on each of the separate panels and the timetable for the panel process in such disputes shall be harmonized.

Article 10

Third Parties

1. The interests of the parties to a dispute and those of other Members under a covered agreement at issue in the dispute shall be fully taken into account during the panel process.

2. Any Member having a substantial interest in a matter before a panel and having notified its interest to the DSB (referred to in this Understanding as a "third party") shall have an opportunity to be heard by the panel and to make written submissions to the panel. These submissions shall also be given to the parties to the dispute and shall be reflected in the panel report.

3. Third parties shall receive the submissions of the parties to the dispute to the first meeting of the panel.

4. If a third party considers that a measure already the subject of a panel proceeding nullifies or impairs benefits accruing to it under any covered agreement, that Member may have recourse to normal dispute settlement procedures under this Understanding. Such a dispute shall be referred to the original panel wherever possible.

Article 11

Function of Panels

The function of panels is to assist the DSB in discharging its responsibilities under this Understanding and the covered agreements. Accordingly, a panel should make an objective assessment of the matter before it, including an objective assessment of the facts of the case and the applicability of and conformity with the relevant covered agreements, and make such other findings as will assist the DSB in making the recommendations or in giving the rulings provided for in the covered agreements. Panels should consult regularly with the parties to the dispute and give them adequate opportunity to develop a mutually satisfactory solution.

Article 12

Panel Procedures

1. Panels shall follow the Working Procedures in Appendix 3 unless the panel decides otherwise after consulting the parties to the dispute.

2. Panel procedures should provide sufficient flexibility so as to ensure high-quality panel reports, while not unduly delaying the panel process.

3. After consulting the parties to the dispute, the panelists shall, as soon as practicable and whenever possible within one week after the composition and terms of reference of the panel have been agreed upon, fix the timetable for the panel process, taking into account the provisions of paragraph 9 of Article 4, if relevant.

4. In determining the timetable for the panel process, the panel shall provide sufficient time for the parties to the dispute to prepare their submissions.

5. Panels should set precise deadlines for written submissions by the parties and the parties should respect those deadlines.

6. Each party to the dispute shall deposit its written submissions with the Secretariat for immediate transmission to the panel and to the other party or parties to the dispute. The complaining party shall submit its first submission in advance of the responding party's first submission unless the panel decides, in fixing the timetable referred to in paragraph 3 and after consultations with the parties to the dispute, that the parties should submit their first submissions simultaneously. When there are sequential arrangements for the deposit of first submissions, the panel shall establish a firm time-period for receipt of the responding party's submission. Any subsequent written submissions shall be submitted simultaneously.

7. Where the parties to the dispute have failed to develop a mutually satisfactory solution, the panel shall submit its findings in the form of a written report to the DSB. In such cases, the report of a panel shall set out the findings of fact, the applicability of relevant provisions and the basic rationale behind any findings and recommendations that it makes. Where a settlement of the matter among the parties to the dispute has been found, the report of the panel shall be confined to a brief description of the case and to reporting that a solution has been reached.

8. In order to make the procedures more efficient, the period in which the panel shall conduct its examination, from the date that the composition and terms of reference of the panel have been agreed upon until the date the final report is issued to the parties to the dispute, shall, as a general rule, not exceed six months. In cases of urgency, including those relating to perishable goods, the panel shall aim to issue its report to the parties to the dispute within three months.

9. When the panel considers that it cannot issue its report within six months, or within three months in cases of urgency, it shall inform the DSB in writing of the reasons for the delay together with an estimate of the period within which it will issue its report. In no case should the period from the establishment of the panel to the circulation of the report to the Members exceed nine months.

10. In the context of consultations involving a measure taken by a developing country Member, the parties may agree to extend the periods established in paragraphs 7 and 8 of Article 4. If, after the relevant period has elapsed, the consulting parties cannot agree that the consultations have concluded, the Chairman of the DSB shall decide, after consultation with the parties, whether to extend the relevant period and, if so, for how long. In addition, in examining a complaint against a developing country Member, the panel shall accord sufficient time for the developing country Member to prepare and present its argumentation. The provisions of paragraph 1 of Article 20 and paragraph 4 of Article 21 are not affected by any action pursuant to this paragraph.

11. Where one or more of the parties is a developing country Member, the panel's report shall explicitly indicate the form in which account has been taken of relevant provisions on differential and more-favourable treatment for developing country Members that form part of the covered agreements which have been raised by the developing country Member in the course of the dispute settlement procedures.

12. The panel may suspend its work at any time at the request of the complaining party for a period not to exceed 12 months. In the event of such a suspension, the time-frames set out in paragraphs 8 and 9 of this Article, paragraph 1 of Article 20, and paragraph 4 of Article 21 shall be extended by the amount of time that the work was suspended. If the work of the panel has been suspended for more than 12 months, the authority for establishment of the panel shall lapse.

Article 13

Right to Seek Information

1. Each panel shall have the right to seek information and technical advice from any individual or body which it deems appropriate. However, before a panel seeks such information or advice from any individual or body within the jurisdiction of a Member it shall inform the authorities of that Member. A Member should respond promptly and fully to any request by a panel for such information as the panel considers necessary and appropriate. Confidential information which is provided shall not be revealed without formal authorization from the individual, body, or authorities of the Member providing the information.

2. Panels may seek information from any relevant source and may consult experts to obtain their opinion on certain aspects of the matter. With respect to a factual issue concerning a scientific or other technical matter raised by a party to a dispute, a panel may request an advisory report in writing from an expert review group. Rules for the establishment of such a group and its procedures are set forth in Appendix 4.

Article 14

Confidentiality

1. Panel deliberations shall be confidential.

2. The reports of panels shall be drafted without the presence of the parties to the dispute in the light of the information provided and the statements made.

3. Opinions expressed in the panel report by individual panelists shall be anonymous.

Article 15

Interim Review Stage

1. Following the consideration of rebuttal submissions and oral arguments, the panel shall issue the descriptive (factual and argument) sections of its draft report to the parties to the dispute. Within a period of time set by the panel, the parties shall submit their comments in writing.

2. Following the expiration of the set period of time for receipt of comments from the parties to the dispute, the panel shall issue an interim report to the parties, including both the descriptive sections and the panel's findings and conclusions. Within a period of time set by the panel, a party may submit a written request for the panel to review precise aspects of the interim report prior to circulation of the final report to the Members. At the request of a party, the panel shall hold a further meeting with the parties on the issues identified in the written comments. If no comments are received from any party within the comment period, the interim report shall be considered the final panel report and circulated promptly to the Members.

3. The findings of the final panel report shall include a discussion of the arguments made at the interim review stage. The interim review stage shall be conducted within the time-period set out in paragraph 8 of Article 12.

Article 16

Adoption of Panel Reports

1. In order to provide sufficient time for the Members to consider panel reports, the reports shall not be considered for adoption by the DSB until 20 days after the date they have been circulated to the Members.

2. Members having objections to a panel report shall give written reasons to explain their objections for circulation at least 10 days prior to the DSB meeting at which the panel report will be considered.

3. The parties to a dispute shall have the right to participate fully in the consideration of the panel report by the DSB, and their views shall be fully recorded.

4. Within 60 days after the date of circulation of a panel report to the Members, the report shall be adopted at a DSB meeting[7] unless a party to the dispute formally notifies the DSB of its decision to appeal or the DSB decides by consensus not to adopt the report. If a party has notified its decision to appeal, the report by the panel shall not be considered for adoption by the DSB until after completion of the appeal. This adoption procedure is without prejudice to the right of Members to express their views on a panel report.

Article 17

Appellate Review Standing Appellate Body

1. A standing Appellate Body shall be established by the DSB. The Appellate Body shall hear appeals from panel cases. It shall be composed of seven persons, three of whom shall serve on any one case. Persons serving on the Appellate Body shall serve in rotation. Such rotation shall be determined in the working procedures of the Appellate Body.

2. The DSB shall appoint persons to serve on the Appellate Body for a four-year term, and each person may be reappointed once. However, the terms of three of the seven persons appointed immediately after the entry into force of the WTO Agreement shall expire at the end of two years, to be determined by lot. Vacancies shall be filled as they arise. A person appointed to replace a person whose term of office has not expired shall hold office for the remainder of the predecessor's term.

3. The Appellate Body shall comprise persons of recognized authority, with demonstrated expertise in law, international trade and the subject matter of the covered agreements generally. They shall be unaffiliated with any government. The Appellate Body membership shall be broadly representative of membership in the WTO. All persons serving on the Appellate Body shall be available at all times and on short notice, and shall stay abreast of dispute settlement activities and other relevant activities of the WTO. They shall not participate in the consideration of any disputes that would create a direct or indirect conflict of interest.

4. Only parties to the dispute, not third parties, may appeal a panel report. Third parties which have notified the DSB of a substantial interest in

7. If a meeting of the DSB is not scheduled within this period at a time that enables the requirements of paragraphs 1 and 4 of Article 16 to be met, a meeting of the DSB shall be held for this purpose.

the matter pursuant to paragraph 2 of Article 10 may make written submissions to, and be given an opportunity to be heard by, the Appellate Body.

5. As a general rule, the proceedings shall not exceed 60 days from the date a party to the dispute formally notifies its decision to appeal to the date the Appellate Body circulates its report. In fixing its timetable the Appellate Body shall take into account the provisions of paragraph 9 of Article 4, if relevant. When the Appellate Body considers that it cannot provide its report within 60 days, it shall inform the DSB in writing of the reasons for the delay together with an estimate of the period within which it will submit its report. In no case shall the proceedings exceed 90 days.

6. An appeal shall be limited to issues of law covered in the panel report and legal interpretations developed by the panel.

7. The Appellate Body shall be provided with appropriate administrative and legal support as it requires.

8. The expenses of persons serving on the Appellate Body, including travel and subsistence allowance, shall be met from the WTO budget in accordance with criteria to be adopted by the General Council, based on recommendations of the Committee on Budget, Finance and Administration.

Procedures for Appellate Review

9. Working procedures shall be drawn up by the Appellate Body in consultation with the Chairman of the DSB and the Director-General, and communicated to the Members for their information.

10. The proceedings of the Appellate Body shall be confidential. The reports of the Appellate Body shall be drafted without the presence of the parties to the dispute and in the light of the information provided and the statements made.

11. Opinions expressed in the Appellate Body report by individuals serving on the Appellate Body shall be anonymous.

12. The Appellate Body shall address each of the issues raised in accordance with paragraph 6 during the appellate proceeding.

13. The Appellate Body may uphold, modify or reverse the legal findings and conclusions of the panel.

Adoption of Appellate Body Reports

14. An Appellate Body report shall be adopted by the DSB and unconditionally accepted by the parties to the dispute unless the DSB decides by consensus not to adopt the Appellate Body report within 30 days following its circulation to the Members.[8] This adoption procedure is without prejudice to the right of Members to express their views on an Appellate Body report.

Article 18

Communications with the Panel or Appellate Body

1. There shall be no *ex parte* communications with the panel or Appellate Body concerning matters under consideration by the panel or Appellate Body.

2. Written submissions to the panel or the Appellate Body shall be treated as confidential, but shall be made available to the parties to the dispute. Nothing in this Understanding shall preclude a party to a dispute from disclosing statements of its own positions to the public. Members shall treat as confidential information submitted by another Member to the panel or the Appellate Body which that Member has designated as confidential. A party to a dispute shall also, upon request of a Member, provide a non-confidential summary of the information contained in its written submissions that could be disclosed to the public.

Article 19

Panel and Appellate Body Recommendations

1. Where a panel or the Appellate Body concludes that a measure is inconsistent with a covered agreement, it shall recommend that the Member concerned[9] bring the measure into conformity with that agreement.[10] In addition to its recommendations, the panel or Appellate Body may suggest ways in which the Member concerned could implement the recommendations.

2. In accordance with paragraph 2 of Article 3, in their findings and recommendations, the panel and Appellate Body cannot add to or diminish the rights and obligations provided in the covered agreements.

8. If a meeting of the DSB is not scheduled during this period, such a meeting of the DSB shall be held for this purpose.

9. The "Member concerned" is the party to the dispute to which the panel or Appellate Body recommendations are directed.

10. With respect to recommendations in cases not involving a violation of GATT 1994 or any other covered agreement, see Article 26.

Article 20

Time-Frame for DSB Decisions

Unless otherwise agreed to by the parties to the dispute, the period from the date of establishment of the panel by the DSB until the date the DSB considers the panel or appellate report for adoption shall as a general rule not exceed nine months where the panel report is not appealed or 12 months where the report is appealed. Where either the panel or the Appellate Body has acted, pursuant to paragraph 9 of Article 12 or paragraph 5 of Article 17, to extend the time for providing its report, the additional time taken shall be added to the above periods.

Article 21

Surveillance of Implementation of Recommendations and Rulings

1. Prompt compliance with recommendations or rulings of the DSB is essential in order to ensure effective resolution of disputes to the benefit of all Members.

2. Particular attention should be paid to matters affecting the interests of developing country Members with respect to measures which have been subject to dispute settlement.

3. At a DSB meeting held within 30 days[11] after the date of adoption of the panel or Appellate Body report, the Member concerned shall inform the DSB of its intentions in respect of implementation of the recommendations and rulings of the DSB. If it is impracticable to comply immediately with the recommendations and rulings, the Member concerned shall have a reasonable period of time in which to do so. The reasonable period of time shall be:

(a) the period of time proposed by the Member concerned, provided that such period is approved by the DSB; or, in the absence of such approval,

(b) a period of time mutually agreed by the parties to the dispute within 45 days after the date of adoption of the recommendations and rulings; or, in the absence of such agreement,

(c) a period of time determined through binding arbitration within 90 days after the date of adoption of the recommendations and rulings.[12] In

11. If a meeting of the DSB is not scheduled during this period, such a meeting of the DSB shall be held for this purpose.

12. If the parties cannot agree on an arbitrator within ten days after referring the matter to arbitration, the arbitrator shall be appointed by the Director-General within ten days, after consulting the parties.

such arbitration, a guideline for the arbitrator[13] should be that the reasonable period of time to implement panel or Appellate Body recommendations should not exceed 15 months from the date of adoption of a panel or Appellate Body report. However, that time may be shorter or longer, depending upon the particular circumstances.

4. Except where the panel or the Appellate Body has extended, pursuant to paragraph 9 of Article 12 or paragraph 5 of Article 17, the time of providing its report, the period from the date of establishment of the panel by the DSB until the date of determination of the reasonable period of time shall not exceed 15 months unless the parties to the dispute agree otherwise. Where either the panel or the Appellate Body has acted to extend the time of providing its report, the additional time taken shall be added to the 15-month period; provided that unless the parties to the dispute agree that there are exceptional circumstances, the total time shall not exceed 18 months.

5. Where there is disagreement as to the existence or consistency with a covered agreement of measures taken to comply with the recommendations and rulings such dispute shall be decided through recourse to these dispute settlement procedures, including wherever possible resort to the original panel. The panel shall circulate its report within 90 days after the date of referral of the matter to it. When the panel considers that it cannot provide its report within this time frame, it shall inform the DSB in writing of the reasons for the delay together with an estimate of the period within which it will submit its report.

6. The DSB shall keep under surveillance the implementation of adopted recommendations or rulings. The issue of implementation of the recommendations or rulings may be raised at the DSB by any Member at any time following their adoption. Unless the DSB decides otherwise, the issue of implementation of the recommendations or rulings shall be placed on the agenda of the DSB meeting after six months following the date of establishment of the reasonable period of time pursuant to paragraph 3 and shall remain on the DSB's agenda until the issue is resolved. At least 10 days prior to each such DSB meeting, the Member concerned shall provide the DSB with a status report in writing of its progress in the implementation of the recommendations or rulings.

7. If the matter is one which has been raised by a developing country Member, the DSB shall consider what further action it might take which would be appropriate to the circumstances.

13. The expression "arbitrator" shall be interpreted as referring either to an individual or a group.

8. If the case is one brought by a developing country Member, in considering what appropriate action might be taken, the DSB shall take into account not only the trade coverage of measures complained of, but also their impact on the economy of developing country Members concerned.

Article 22

Compensation and the Suspension of Concessions

1. Compensation and the suspension of concessions or other obligations are temporary measures available in the event that the recommendations and rulings are not implemented within a reasonable period of time. However, neither compensation nor the suspension of concessions or other obligations is preferred to full implementation of a recommendation to bring a measure into conformity with the covered agreements. Compensation is voluntary and, if granted, shall be consistent with the covered agreements.

2. If the Member concerned fails to bring the measure found to be inconsistent with a covered agreement into compliance therewith or otherwise comply with the recommendations and rulings within the reasonable period of time determined pursuant to paragraph 3 of Article 21, such Member shall, if so requested, and no later than the expiry of the reasonable period of time, enter into negotiations with any party having invoked the dispute settlement procedures, with a view to developing mutually acceptable compensation. If no satisfactory compensation has been agreed within 20 days after the date of expiry of the reasonable period of time, any party having invoked the dispute settlement procedures may request authorization from the DSB to suspend the application to the Member concerned of concessions or other obligations under the covered agreements.

3. In considering what concessions or other obligations to suspend, the complaining party shall apply the following principles and procedures:

(a) the general principle is that the complaining party should first seek to suspend concessions or other obligations with respect to the same sector(s) as that in which the panel or Appellate Body has found a violation or other nullification or impairment;

(b) if that party considers that it is not practicable or effective to suspend concessions or other obligations with respect to the same sector(s), it may seek to suspend concessions or other obligations in other sectors under the same agreement;

(c) if that party considers that it is not practicable or effective to suspend concessions or other obligations with respect to other sectors under the same agreement, and that the circumstances are serious enough, it may seek to suspend concessions or other obligations under another covered agreement;

(d) in applying the above principles, that party shall take into account:

(i) the trade in the sector or under the agreement under which the panel or Appellate Body has found a violation or other nullification or impairment, and the importance of such trade to that party;

(ii) the broader economic elements related to the nullification or impairment and the broader economic consequences of the suspension of concessions or other obligations;

(e) if that party decides to request authorization to suspend concessions or other obligations pursuant to subparagraphs (b) or (c), it shall state the reasons therefor in its request. At the same time as the request is forwarded to the DSB, it also shall be forwarded to the relevant Councils and also, in the case of a request pursuant to subparagraph (b), the relevant sectoral bodies;

(f) for purposes of this paragraph, "sector" means:

(i) with respect to goods, all goods;

(ii) with respect to services, a principal sector as identified in the current "Services Sectoral Classification List" which identifies such sectors;[14]

(iii) with respect to trade-related intellectual property rights, each of the categories of intellectual property rights covered in Section 1, or Section 2, or Section 3, or Section 4, or Section 5, or Section 6, or Section 7 of Part II, or the obligations under Part III, or Part IV of the Agreement on TRIPS;

(g) for purposes of this paragraph, "agreement" means:

(i) with respect to goods, the agreements listed in Annex 1A of the WTO Agreement, taken as a whole as well as the Plurilateral Trade Agreements in so far as the relevant parties to the dispute are parties to these agreements;

(ii) with respect to services, the GATS;

14. The list in document MTN.GNS/W/120 identifies eleven sectors.

(iii) with respect to intellectual property rights, the Agreement on TRIPS.

4. The level of the suspension of concessions or other obligations authorized by the DSB shall be equivalent to the level of the nullification or impairment.

5. The DSB shall not authorize suspension of concessions or other obligations if a covered agreement prohibits such suspension.

6. When the situation described in paragraph 2 occurs, the DSB, upon request, shall grant authorization to suspend concessions or other obligations within 30 days of the expiry of the reasonable period of time unless the DSB decides by consensus to reject the request. However, if the Member concerned objects to the level of suspension proposed, or claims that the principles and procedures set forth in paragraph 3 have not been followed where a complaining party has requested authorization to suspend concessions or other obligations pursuant to paragraph 3(b) or (c), the matter shall be referred to arbitration. Such arbitration shall be carried out by the original panel, if members are available, or by an arbitrator[15] appointed by the Director-General and shall be completed within 60 days after the date of expiry of the reasonable period of time. Concessions or other obligations shall not be suspended during the course of the arbitration.

7. The arbitrator[16] acting pursuant to paragraph 6 shall not examine the nature of the concessions or other obligations to be suspended but shall determine whether the level of such suspension is equivalent to the level of nullification or impairment. The arbitrator may also determine if the proposed suspension of concessions or other obligations is allowed under the covered agreement. However, if the matter referred to arbitration includes a claim that the principles and procedures set forth in paragraph 3 have not been followed, the arbitrator shall examine that claim. In the event the arbitrator determines that those principles and procedures have not been followed, the complaining party shall apply them consistent with paragraph 3. The parties shall accept the arbitrator's decision as final and the parties concerned shall not seek a second arbitration. The DSB shall be informed promptly of the decision of the arbitrator and shall upon request, grant authorization to suspend concessions or other obligations where the request is consistent with the decision of the arbitrator, unless the DSB decides by consensus to reject the request.

15. The expression "arbitrator" shall be interpreted as referring either to an individual or a group.

16. The expression "arbitrator" shall be interpreted as referring either to an individual or a group or to the members of the original panel when serving in the capacity of arbitrator.

8. The suspension of concessions or other obligations shall be temporary and shall only be applied until such time as the measure found to be inconsistent with a covered agreement has been removed, or the Member that must implement recommendations or rulings provides a solution to the nullification or impairment of benefits, or a mutually satisfactory solution is reached. In accordance with paragraph 6 of Article 21, the DSB shall continue to keep under surveillance the implementation of adopted recommendations or rulings, including those cases where compensation has been provided or concessions or other obligations have been suspended but the recommendations to bring a measure into conformity with the covered agreements have not been implemented.

9. The dispute settlement provisions of the covered agreements may be invoked in respect of measures affecting their observance taken by regional or local governments or authorities within the territory of a Member. When the DSB has ruled that a provision of a covered agreement has not been observed, the responsible Member shall take such reasonable measures as may be available to it to ensure its observance. The provisions of the covered agreements and this Understanding relating to compensation and suspension of concessions or other obligations apply in cases where it has not been possible to secure such observance.[17]

Article 23

Strengthening of the Multilateral System

1. When Members seek the redress of a violation of obligations or other nullification or impairment of benefits under the covered agreements or an impediment to the attainment of any objective of the covered agreements, they shall have recourse to, and abide by, the rules and procedures of this Understanding.

2. In such cases, Members shall:

(a) not make a determination to the effect that a violation has occurred, that benefits have been nullified or impaired or that the attainment of any objective of the covered agreements has been impeded, except through recourse to dispute settlement in accordance with the rules and procedures of this Understanding, and shall make any such determination consistent with the findings contained in the panel or Appellate Body report adopted by the DSB or an arbitration award rendered under this Understanding;

17. Where the provisions of any covered agreement concerning measures taken by regional or local governments or authorities within the territory of a Member contain provisions different from the provisions of this paragraph, the provisions of such covered agreement shall prevail.

(b) follow the procedures set forth in Article 21 to determine the reasonable period of time for the Member concerned to implement the recommendations and rulings; and

(c) follow the procedures set forth in Article 22 to determine the level of suspension of concessions or other obligations and obtain DSB authorization in accordance with those procedures before suspending concessions or other obligations under the covered agreements in response to the failure of the Member concerned to implement the recommendations and rulings within that reasonable period of time.

Article 24

Special Procedures Involving Least-Developed Country Members

1. At all stages of the determination of the causes of a dispute and of dispute settlement procedures involving a least-developed country Member, particular consideration shall be given to the special situation of least-developed country Members. In this regard, Members shall exercise due restraint in raising matters under these procedures involving a least-developed country Member. If nullification or impairment is found to result from a measure taken by a least-developed country Member, complaining parties shall exercise due restraint in asking for compensation or seeking authorization to suspend the application of concessions or other obligations pursuant to these procedures.

2. In dispute settlement cases involving a least-developed country Member, where a satisfactory solution has not been found in the course of consultations the Director-General or the Chairman of the DSB shall, upon request by a least-developed country Member offer their good offices, conciliation and mediation with a view to assisting the parties to settle the dispute, before a request for a panel is made. The Director-General or the Chairman of the DSB, in providing the above assistance, may consult any source which either deems appropriate.

Article 25

Arbitration

1. Expeditious arbitration within the WTO as an alternative means of dispute settlement can facilitate the solution of certain disputes that concern issues that are clearly defined by both parties.

2. Except as otherwise provided in this Understanding, resort to arbitration shall be subject to mutual agreement of the parties which shall agree on the procedures to be followed. Agreements to resort to arbitration shall be notified to all Members sufficiently in advance of the actual commencement of the arbitration process.

3. Other Members may become party to an arbitration proceeding only upon the agreement of the parties which have agreed to have recourse to arbitration. The parties to the proceeding shall agree to abide by the arbitration award. Arbitration awards shall be notified to the DSB and the Council or Committee of any relevant agreement where any Member may raise any point relating thereto.

4. Articles 21 and 22 of this Understanding shall apply *mutatis mutandis* to arbitration awards.

Article 26

1. Non-Violation Complaints of the Type Described in Paragraph 1(b) of Article XXIII of GATT 1994

Where the provisions of paragraph 1(b) of Article XXIII of GATT 1994 are applicable to a covered agreement, a panel or the Appellate Body may only make rulings and recommendations where a party to the dispute considers that any benefit accruing to it directly or indirectly under the relevant covered agreement is being nullified or impaired or the attainment of any objective of that Agreement is being impeded as a result of the application by a Member of any measure, whether or not it conflicts with the provisions of that Agreement. Where and to the extent that such party considers and a panel or the Appellate Body determines that a case concerns a measure that does not conflict with the provisions of a covered agreement to which the provisions of paragraph 1(b) of Article XXIII of GATT 1994 are applicable, the procedures in this Understanding shall apply, subject to the following:

(a) the complaining party shall present a detailed justification in support of any complaint relating to a measure which does not conflict with the relevant covered agreement;

(b) where a measure has been found to nullify or impair benefits under, or impede the attainment of objectives, of the relevant covered agreement without violation thereof, there is no obligation to withdraw the measure. However, in such cases, the panel or the Appellate Body shall recommend that the Member concerned make a mutually satisfactory adjustment;

(c) notwithstanding the provisions of Article 21, the arbitration provided for in paragraph 3 of Article 21, upon request of either party, may include a determination of the level of benefits which have been nullified or impaired, and may also suggest ways and means of reaching a mutually satisfactory adjustment; such suggestions shall not be binding upon the parties to the dispute;

(d) notwithstanding the provisions of paragraph 1 of Article 22, compensation may be part of a mutually satisfactory adjustment as final settlement of the dispute.

2. Complaints of the Type Described in Paragraph 1(c) of Article XXIII of GATT 1994

Where the provisions of paragraph 1(c) of Article XXIII of GATT 1994 are applicable to a covered agreement, a panel may only make rulings and recommendations where a party considers that any benefit accruing to it directly or indirectly under the relevant covered agreement is being nullified or impaired or the attainment of any objective of that Agreement is being impeded as a result of the existence of any situation other than those to which the provisions of paragraphs 1(a) and 1(b) of Article XXIII of GATT 1994 are applicable. Where and to the extent that such party considers and a panel determines that the matter is covered by this paragraph, the procedures of this Understanding shall apply only up to and including the point in the proceedings where the panel report has been circulated to the Members. The dispute settlement rules and procedures contained in the Decision of 12 April 1989 (BISD 36S/61-67) shall apply to consideration for adoption, and surveillance and implementation of recommendations and rulings. The following shall also apply:

(a) the complaining party shall present a detailed justification in support of any argument made with respect to issues covered under this paragraph;

(b) in cases involving matters covered by this paragraph, if a panel finds that cases also involve dispute settlement matters other than those covered by this paragraph, the panel shall circulate a report to the DSB addressing any such matters and a separate report on matters falling under this paragraph.

Article 27

Responsibilities of the Secretariat

1. The Secretariat shall have the responsibility of assisting panels, especially on the legal, historical and procedural aspects of the matters dealt with, and of providing secretarial and technical support.

2. While the Secretariat assists Members in respect of dispute settlement at their request, there may also be a need to provide additional legal advice and assistance in respect of dispute settlement to developing country Members. To this end, the Secretariat shall make available a qualified legal expert from the WTO technical cooperation services to any developing

country Member which so requests. This expert shall assist the developing country Member in a manner ensuring the continued impartiality of the Secretariat.

3. The Secretariat shall conduct special training courses for interested Members concerning these dispute settlement procedures and practices so as to enable Members' experts to be better informed in this regard.

Appendix 1
Agreements Covered by the Understanding

(A) Agreement Establishing the World Trade Organization
(B) Multilateral Trade Agreements
  Annex 1A: Multilateral Agreements on Trade in Goods
  Annex 1B: General Agreement on Trade in Services
  Annex 1C: Agreement on Trade-Related Aspects of Intellectual Property Rights
  Annex 2: Understanding on Rules and Procedures Governing the Settlement of Disputes
(C) Plurilateral Trade Agreements
  Annex 4: Agreement on Trade in Civil Aircraft
  Agreement on Government Procurement
  International Dairy Agreement
  International Bovine Meat Agreement

The applicability of this Understanding to the Plurilateral Trade Agreements shall be subject to the adoption of a decision by the parties to each agreement setting out the terms for the application of the Understanding to the individual agreement, including any special or additional rules or procedures for inclusion in Appendix 2, as notified to the DSB.

Appendix 2
Special or Additional Rules and Procedures Contained in the Covered Agreements

Agreement	*Rules and Procedures*
Agreement on the Application of Sanitary and Phytosanitary Measures	11.2
Agreement on Textiles and Clothing	2.14, 2.21, 4.4, 5.2, 5.4, 5.6, 6.9, 6.10, 6.11, 8.1 through 8.12
Agreement on Technical Barriers to Trade	14.2 through 14.4, Annex 2

Agreement	*Rules and Procedures*
Agreement on Implementation of Article VI of GATT 1994	17.4 through 17.7
Agreement on Implementation of Article VII of GATT 1994	19.3 through 19.5, Annex II.2(f), 3, 9, 21
Agreement on Subsidies and Countervailing Measures	4.2 through 4.12, 6.6, 7.2 through 7.10, 8.5, footnote 35, 24.4, 27.7, Annex V
General Agreement on Trade in Services	XXII:3, XXIII:3
Annex on Financial Services	4
Annex on Air Transport Services	4
Decision on Certain Dispute	1 through 5
Settlement Procedures for the GATS	

The list of rules and procedures in this Appendix includes provisions where only a part of the provision may be relevant in this context.

Any special or additional rules or procedures in the Plurilateral Trade Agreements as determined by the competent bodies of each agreement and as notified to the DSB.

Appendix 3
Working Procedures

1. In its proceedings the panel shall follow the relevant provisions of this Understanding. In addition, the following working procedures shall apply.

2. The panel shall meet in closed session. The parties to the dispute, and interested parties, shall be present at the meetings only when invited by the panel to appear before it.

3. The deliberations of the panel and the documents submitted to it shall be kept confidential. Nothing in this Understanding shall preclude a party to a dispute from disclosing statements of its own positions to the public. Members shall treat as confidential information submitted by another Member to the panel which that Member has designated as confidential. Where a party to a dispute submits a confidential version of its written submissions to the panel, it shall also, upon request of a Member, provide a non-confidential summary of the information contained in its submissions that could be disclosed to the public.

4. Before the first substantive meeting of the panel with the parties, the parties to the dispute shall transmit to the panel written submissions in which they present the facts of the case and their arguments.

5. At its first substantive meeting with the parties, the panel shall ask the party which has brought the complaint to present its case. Subsequently, and still at the same meeting, the party against which the complaint has been brought shall be asked to present its point of view.

6. All third parties which have notified their interest in the dispute to the DSB shall be invited in writing to present their views during a session of the first substantive meeting of the panel set aside for that purpose. All such third parties may be present during the entirety of this session.

7. Formal rebuttals shall be made at a second substantive meeting of the panel. The party complained against shall have the right to take the floor first to be followed by the complaining party. The parties shall submit, prior to that meeting, written rebuttals to the panel.

8. The panel may at any time put questions to the parties and ask them for explanations either in the course of a meeting with the parties or in writing.

9. The parties to the dispute and any third party invited to present its views in accordance with Article 10 shall make available to the panel a written version of their oral statements.

10. In the interest of full transparency, the presentations, rebuttals and statements referred to in paragraphs 5 to 9 shall be made in the presence of the parties. Moreover, each party's written submissions, including any comments on the descriptive part of the report and responses to questions put by the panel, shall be made available to the other party or parties.

11. Any additional procedures specific to the panel.

12. Proposed timetable for panel work:

(a) Receipt of first written submissions of the parties:
 (1) complaining Party: ________3-6 weeks
 (2) Party complained against: ________2-3 weeks
(b) Date, time and place of first substantive meeting with the parties; third party session: ________1-2 weeks
(c) Receipt of written rebuttals of the parties: ________2-3 weeks
(d) Date, time and place of second substantive meeting with the parties: ________1-2 weeks
(e) Issuance of descriptive part of the report to the parties: ________2-4 weeks

(f)	Receipt of comments by the parties on the descriptive part of the report:	________2 weeks
(g)	Issuance of the interim report, including the findings and conclusions, to the parties:	________2-4 weeks
(h)	Deadline for party to request review of part(s) of report:	________1 week
(i)	Period of review by panel, including possible additional meeting with parties:	________2 weeks
(j)	Issuance of final report to parties to dispute:	________2 weeks
(k)	Circulation of the final report to the Members:	________3 weeks

The above calendar may be changed in the light of unforeseen developments. Additional meetings with the parties shall be scheduled if required.

Appendix 4
Expert Review Groups

The following rules and procedures shall apply to expert review groups established in accordance with the provisions of paragraph 2 of Article 13.

1. Expert review groups are under the panel's authority. Their terms of reference and detailed working procedures shall be decided by the panel, and they shall report to the panel.

2. Participation in expert review groups shall be restricted to persons of professional standing and experience in the field in question.

3. Citizens of parties to the dispute shall not serve on an expert review group without the joint agreement of the parties to the dispute, except in exceptional circumstances when the panel considers that the need for specialized scientific expertise cannot be fulfilled otherwise. Government officials of parties to the dispute shall not serve on an expert review group. Members of expert review groups shall serve in their individual capacities and not as government representatives, nor as representatives of any organization. Governments or organizations shall therefore not give them instructions with regard to matters before an expert review group.

4. Expert review groups may consult and seek information and technical advice from any source they deem appropriate. Before an expert review group seeks such information or advice from a source within the jurisdiction of a Member, it shall inform the government of that Member. Any Member shall respond promptly and fully to any request by an expert review group for such information as the expert review group considers necessary and appropriate.

5. The parties to a dispute shall have access to all relevant information provided to an expert review group, unless it is of a confidential nature. Confidential information provided to the expert review group shall not be released without formal authorization from the government, organization or person providing the information. Where such information is requested from the expert review group but release of such information by the expert review group is not authorized, a non-confidential summary of the information will be provided by the government, organization or person supplying the information.

6. The expert review group shall submit a draft report to the parties to the dispute with a view to obtaining their comments, and taking them into account, as appropriate, in the final report, which shall also be issued to the parties to the dispute when it is submitted to the panel. The final report of the expert review group shall be advisory only.

Document 8

WORKING PROCEDURES FOR APPELLATE REVIEW

WT/AB/WP/6, 16 August 2010

Definitions

1. In these *Working Procedures for Appellate Review*,

"appellant"

means any party to the dispute that has filed a Notice of Appeal pursuant to Rule 20;

"appellate report"

means an Appellate Body report as described in Article 17 of the DSU;

"appellee"

means any party to the dispute that has filed a submission pursuant to Rule 22 or paragraph 4 of Rule 23;

"consensus"

a decision is deemed to be made by consensus if no Member formally objects to it;

"covered agreements"

has the same meaning as "covered agreements" in paragraph 1 of Article 1 of the DSU;

"division"

means the three Members who are selected to serve on any one appeal in accordance with paragraph 1 of Article 17 of the DSU and paragraph 2 of Rule 6;

"documents"

means the Notice of Appeal, any Notice of Other Appeal and the submissions and other written statements presented by the participants or third participants;

"DSB"

means the Dispute Settlement Body established under Article 2 of the DSU;

"DSU"

means the *Understanding on Rules and Procedures Governing the Settlement of Disputes* which is Annex 2 to the *WTO Agreement*;

"Member"

means a Member of the Appellate Body who has been appointed by the DSB in accordance with Article 17 of the DSU;

"other appellant"

means any party to the dispute that has filed a Notice of Other Appeal pursuant to paragraph 1 of Rule 23;

"participant"

means any party to the dispute that has filed a Notice of Appeal pursuant to Rule 20, a Notice of Other Appeal pursuant to Rule 23 or a submission pursuant to Rule 22 or paragraph 4 of Rule 23;

"party to the dispute"

means any WTO Member who was a complaining or defending party in the panel dispute, but does not include a third party;

"proof of service"

means a letter or other written acknowledgement that a document has been delivered, as required, to the parties to the dispute, participants, third parties or third participants, as the case may be;

"Rules"

means these *Working Procedures for Appellate Review;*

"*Rules of Conduct*"

means the *Rules of Conduct for the Understanding on Rules and Procedures Governing the Settlement of Disputes* as attached in Annex II to these Rules;

"*SCM Agreement*"

means the *Agreement on Subsidies and Countervailing Measures* which is in Annex 1A to the *WTO Agreement;*

"Secretariat"

means the Appellate Body Secretariat;

"service address"

means the address of the party to the dispute, participant, third party or third participant as generally used in WTO dispute settlement proceedings, unless the party to the dispute, participant, third party or third participant has clearly indicated another address;

"third participant"

means any third party that has filed a written submission pursuant to Rule 24(1); or any third party that appears at the oral hearing, whether or not it makes an oral statement at that hearing;

"third party"

means any WTO Member who has notified the DSB of its substantial interest in the matter before the panel pursuant to paragraph 2 of Article 10 of the DSU;

"WTO"

means the World Trade Organization;

"*WTO Agreement*"

means the *Marrakesh Agreement Establishing the World Trade Organization*, done at Marrakesh, Morocco on 15 April 1994;

"WTO Member"

means any State or separate customs territory possessing full autonomy in the conduct of its external commercial relations that has accepted or acceded to the WTO in accordance with Articles XI, XII or XIV of the *WTO Agreement;* and

"WTO Secretariat"

means the Secretariat of the World Trade Organization.

Part I

MEMBERS

Duties and Responsibilities

2. (1) A Member shall abide by the terms and conditions of the DSU, these Rules and any decisions of the DSB affecting the Appellate Body.

(2) During his/her term, a Member shall not accept any employment nor pursue any professional activity that is inconsistent with his/her duties and responsibilities.

(3) A Member shall exercise his/her office without accepting or seeking instructions from any international, governmental, or non-governmental organization or any private source.

(4) A Member shall be available at all times and on short notice and, to this end, shall keep the Secretariat informed of his/her whereabouts at all times.

Decision-Making

3. (1) In accordance with paragraph 1 of Article 17 of the DSU, decisions relating to an appeal shall be taken solely by the division assigned to that appeal. Other decisions shall be taken by the Appellate Body as a whole.

(2) The Appellate Body and its divisions shall make every effort to take their decisions by consensus. Where, nevertheless, a decision cannot be arrived at by consensus, the matter at issue shall be decided by a majority vote.

Collegiality

4. (1) To ensure consistency and coherence in decision-making, and to draw on the individual and collective expertise of the Members, the Members shall convene on a regular basis to discuss matters of policy, practice and procedure.

(2) The Members shall stay abreast of dispute settlement activities and other relevant activities of the WTO and, in particular, each Member shall receive all documents filed in an appeal.

(3) In accordance with the objectives set out in paragraph 1, the division responsible for deciding each appeal shall exchange views with the other Members before the division finalizes the appellate report for circulation to the WTO Members. This paragraph is subject to paragraphs 2 and 3 of Rule 11.

(4) Nothing in these Rules shall be interpreted as interfering with a division's full authority and freedom to hear and decide an appeal assigned to it in accordance with paragraph 1 of Article 17 of the DSU.

Chairman

5. (1) There shall be a Chairman of the Appellate Body who shall be elected by the Members.

(2) The term of office of the Chairman of the Appellate Body shall be one year. The Appellate Body Members may decide to extend the term of office for an additional period of up to one year. However, in order to ensure rotation of the Chairmanship, no Member shall serve as Chairman for more than two consecutive terms.

(3) The Chairman shall be responsible for the overall direction of the Appellate Body business, and in particular, his/her responsibilities shall include:

(a) the supervision of the internal functioning of the Appellate Body; and

(b) any such other duties as the Members may agree to entrust to him/her.

(4) Where the office of the Chairman becomes vacant due to permanent incapacity as a result of illness or death or by resignation or expiration of his/her term, the Members shall elect a new Chairman who shall serve a full term in accordance with paragraph 2.

(5) In the event of a temporary absence or incapacity of the Chairman, the Appellate Body shall authorize another Member to act as Chairman *ad interim*, and the Member so authorized shall temporarily exercise all the powers, duties and functions of the Chairman until the Chairman is capable of resuming his/her functions.

Divisions

6. (1) In accordance with paragraph 1 of Article 17 of the DSU, a division consisting of three Members shall be established to hear and decide an appeal.

(2) The Members constituting a division shall be selected on the basis of rotation, while taking into account the principles of random selection, unpredictability and opportunity for all Members to serve regardless of their national origin.

(3) A Member selected pursuant to paragraph 2 to serve on a division shall serve on that division, unless:

(a) he/she is excused from that division pursuant to Rule 9 or 10;

(b) he/she has notified the Chairman and the Presiding Member that he/she is prevented from serving on the division because of illness or other serious reasons pursuant to Rule 12; or

(c) he/she has notified his/her intentions to resign pursuant to Rule 14.

Presiding Member of the Division

7. (1) Each division shall have a Presiding Member, who shall be elected by the Members of that division.

(2) The responsibilities of the Presiding Member shall include:

(a) coordinating the overall conduct of the appeal proceeding;

(b) chairing all oral hearings and meetings related to that appeal; and

(c) coordinating the drafting of the appellate report.

(3) In the event that a Presiding Member becomes incapable of performing his/her duties, the other Members serving on that division and the Member selected as a replacement pursuant to Rule 13 shall elect one of their number to act as the Presiding Member.

Rules of Conduct

8. (1) On a provisional basis, the Appellate Body adopts those provisions of the *Rules of Conduct for the Understanding on Rules and Procedures Governing the Settlement of Disputes*, attached in Annex II to these Rules, which are applicable to it, until *Rules of Conduct* are approved by the DSB.

(2) Upon approval of *Rules of Conduct* by the DSB, such *Rules of Conduct* shall be directly incorporated and become part of these Rules and shall supersede Annex II.

9. (1) Upon the filing of a Notice of Appeal, each Member shall take the steps set out in Article VI:4(b)(i) of Annex II, and a Member may consult with the other Members prior to completing the disclosure form.

(2) Upon the filing of a Notice of Appeal, the professional staff of the Secretariat assigned to that appeal shall take the steps set out in Article VI:4(b)(ii) of Annex II.

(3) Where information has been submitted pursuant to Article VI:4(b)(i) or (ii) of Annex II, the Appellate Body shall consider whether further action is necessary.

(4) As a result of the Appellate Body's consideration of the matter pursuant to paragraph 3, the Member or the professional staff member concerned may continue to be assigned to the division or may be excused from the division.

10. (1) Where evidence of a material violation is filed by a participant pursuant to Article VIII of Annex II, such evidence shall be confidential and shall be supported by affidavits made by persons having actual knowledge or a reasonable belief as to the truth of the facts stated.

(2) Any evidence filed pursuant to Article VIII:1 of Annex II shall be filed at the earliest practicable time: that is, forthwith after the participant submitting it knew or reasonably could have known of the facts supporting it. In no case shall such evidence be filed after the appellate report is circulated to the WTO Members.

(3) Where a participant fails to submit such evidence at the earliest practicable time, it shall file an explanation in writing of the reasons why it did not do so earlier, and the Appellate Body may decide to consider or not to consider such evidence, as appropriate.

(4) While taking fully into account paragraph 5 of Article 17 of the DSU, where evidence has been filed pursuant to Article VIII of Annex II, an appeal shall be suspended for fifteen days or until the procedure referred to in Article VIII:14-16 of Annex II is completed, whichever is earlier.

(5) As a result of the procedure referred to in Article VIII:14-16 of Annex II, the Appellate Body may decide to dismiss the allegation, to excuse the Member or professional staff member concerned from being assigned to the division or make such other order as it deems necessary in accordance with Article VIII of Annex II.

11. (1) A Member who has submitted a disclosure form with information attached pursuant to Article VI:4(b)(i) or is the subject of evidence of a material

violation pursuant to Article VIII:1 of Annex II, shall not participate in any decision taken pursuant to paragraph 4 of Rule 9 or paragraph 5 of Rule 10.

(2) A Member who is excused from a division pursuant to paragraph 4 of Rule 9 or paragraph 5 of Rule 10 shall not take part in the exchange of views conducted in that appeal pursuant to paragraph 3 of Rule 4.

(3) A Member who, had he/she been a Member of a division, would have been excused from that division pursuant to paragraph 4 of Rule 9, shall not take part in the exchange of views conducted in that appeal pursuant to paragraph 3 of Rule 4.

Incapacity

12. (1) A Member who is prevented from serving on a division by illness or for other serious reasons shall give notice and duly explain such reasons to the Chairman and to the Presiding Member.

(2) Upon receiving such notice, the Chairman and the Presiding Member shall forthwith inform the Appellate Body.

Replacement

13. Where a Member is unable to serve on a division for a reason set out in paragraph 3 of Rule 6, another Member shall be selected forthwith pursuant to paragraph 2 of Rule 6 to replace the Member originally selected for that division.

Resignation

14. (1) A Member who intends to resign from his/her office shall notify his/her intentions in writing to the Chairman of the Appellate Body who shall immediately inform the Chairman of the DSB, the Director-General and the other Members of the Appellate Body.

(2) The resignation shall take effect 90 days after the notification has been made pursuant to paragraph 1, unless the DSB, in consultation with the Appellate Body, decides otherwise.

Transition

15. A person who ceases to be a Member of the Appellate Body may, with the authorization of the Appellate Body and upon notification to the DSB, complete the disposition of any appeal to which that person was assigned while a Member, and that person shall, for that purpose only, be deemed to continue to be a Member of the Appellate Body.

Part II

PROCESS

General Provisions

16. (1) In the interests of fairness and orderly procedure in the conduct of an appeal, where a procedural question arises that is not covered by these Rules, a division may adopt an appropriate procedure for the purposes of that appeal only, provided that it is not inconsistent with the DSU, the other covered agreements and these Rules. Where such a procedure is adopted, the division shall immediately notify the parties to the dispute, participants, third parties and third participants as well as the other Members of the Appellate Body.

(2) In exceptional circumstances, where strict adherence to a time-period set out in these Rules would result in a manifest unfairness, a party to the dispute, a participant, a third party or a third participant may request that a division modify a time-period set out in these Rules for the filing of documents or the date set out in the working schedule for the oral hearing. Where such a request is granted by a division, any modification of time shall be notified to the parties to the dispute, participants, third parties and third participants in a revised working schedule.

17. (1) Unless the DSB decides otherwise, in computing any time-period stipulated in the DSU or in the special or additional provisions of the covered agreements, or in these Rules, within which a communication must be made or an action taken by a WTO Member to exercise or preserve its rights, the day from which the time-period begins to run shall be excluded and, subject to paragraph 2, the last day of the time-period shall be included.

(2) The DSB Decision on "Expiration of Time-Periods in the DSU", WT/DSB/M/7, shall apply to appeals heard by divisions of the Appellate Body.

Documents

18. (1) No document is considered filed with the Appellate Body unless the document is received by the Secretariat within the time-period set out for filing in accordance with these Rules.

Official versions of documents shall be submitted in paper form to the Appellate Body Secretariat by 17:00 Geneva time on the day that the document is due. Participants, parties, third participants and third parties shall, by the same deadline, also provide to the Appellate Body Secretariat an electronic copy of each document. Such electronic copy may be sent via electronic mail to the Appellate Body Secretariat's electronic mail address, or brought to the Appellate Body Secretariat on a data storage device such as a CD-ROM or USB flash drive.

(2) Except as otherwise provided in these Rules, every document filed by a party to the dispute, a participant, a third party or a third participant shall on the same day be served on each of the other parties to the dispute, participants, third parties and third participants in the appeal, in accordance with paragraph 4.

(3) A proof of service on the other parties to the dispute, participants, third parties and third participants shall appear on, or be affixed to, each document filed with the Secretariat under paragraph 1 above.

(4) A document shall be served by the most expeditious means of delivery or communication available, including by:

(a) delivering a copy of the document to the service address of the party to the dispute, participant, third party or third participant; or

(b) sending a copy of the document to the service address of the party to the dispute, participant, third party or third participant by facsimile transmission, expedited delivery courier or expedited mail service.

Electronic copies of documents served shall also be provided on the same day, either by electronic mail, or through physical delivery of a data storage device containing an electronic copy of the document.

(5) Upon authorization by the division, a participant or a third participant may correct clerical errors in any of its documents (including typographical mistakes, errors of grammar, or words or numbers placed in the wrong order). The request to correct clerical errors shall identify the specific errors to be corrected and shall be filed with the Secretariat no later than 30 days after the date of the filing of the Notice of Appeal. A copy of the request shall be served upon the other parties to the dispute, participants, third parties and third participants, each of whom shall be given an opportunity to comment in writing on the request. The division shall notify the parties to the dispute, participants, third parties and third participants of its decision.

Ex Parte Communications

19. (1) Neither a division nor any of its Members shall meet with or contact one party to the dispute, participant, third party or third participant in the absence of the other parties to the dispute, participants, third parties and third participants.

(2) No Member of the division may discuss any aspect of the subject matter of an appeal with any party to the dispute, participant, third party or third participant in the absence of the other Members of the division.

(3) A Member who is not assigned to the division hearing the appeal shall not discuss any aspect of the subject matter of the appeal with any party to the dispute, participant, third party or third participant.

Commencement of Appeal

20. (1) An appeal shall be commenced by notification in writing to the DSB in accordance with paragraph 4 of Article 16 of the DSU and simultaneous filing of a Notice of Appeal with the Secretariat.

(2) A Notice of Appeal shall include the following information:

(a) the title of the panel report under appeal;

(b) the name of the party to the dispute filing the Notice of Appeal;

(c) the service address, telephone and facsimile numbers of the party to the dispute; and

(d) a brief statement of the nature of the appeal, including:

(i) identification of the alleged errors in the issues of law covered in the panel report and legal interpretations developed by the panel;

(ii) a list of the legal provision(s) of the covered agreements that the panel is alleged to have erred in interpreting or applying; and

(iii) without prejudice to the ability of the appellant to refer to other paragraphs of the panel report in the context of its appeal, an indicative list of the paragraphs of the panel report containing the alleged errors.

Appellant's Submission

21. (1) The appellant shall, on the same day as the date of the filing of the Notice of Appeal, file with the Secretariat a written submission prepared in accordance with paragraph 2 and serve a copy of the submission on the other parties to the dispute and third parties.

(2) A written submission referred to in paragraph 1 shall:

(a) be dated and signed by the appellant; and

(b) set out:

(i) a precise statement of the grounds for the appeal, including the specific allegations of errors in the issues of law covered in the panel report and legal interpretations developed by the panel, and the legal arguments in support thereof;

(ii) a precise statement of the provisions of the covered agreements and other legal sources relied on; and

(iii) the nature of the decision or ruling sought.

Appellee's Submission

22. (1) Any party to the dispute that wishes to respond to allegations raised in an appellant's submission filed pursuant to Rule 21 may, within 18 days after the date of the filing of the Notice of Appeal, file with the Secretariat a written submission prepared in accordance with paragraph 2 and serve a copy of the submission on the appellant, other parties to the dispute and third parties.

(2) A written submission referred to in paragraph 1 shall:

(a) be dated and signed by the appellee; and

(b) set out:

(i) a precise statement of the grounds for opposing the specific allegations of errors in the issues of law covered in the panel report and legal interpretations developed by the panel raised in the appellant's submission, and the legal arguments in support thereof;

(ii) an acceptance of, or opposition to, each ground set out in the appellant's submission;

(iii) a precise statement of the provisions of the covered agreements and other legal sources relied on; and

(iv) the nature of the decision or ruling sought.

Multiple Appeals

23. (1) Within 5 days after the date of the filing of the Notice of Appeal, a party to the dispute other than the original appellant may join in that appeal or appeal on the basis of other alleged errors in the issues of law

covered in the panel report and legal interpretations developed by the panel. That party shall notify the DSB in writing of its appeal and shall simultaneously file a Notice of Other Appeal with the Secretariat.

(2) A Notice of Other Appeal shall include the following information:

(a) the title of the panel report under appeal;

(b) the name of the party to the dispute filing the Notice of Other Appeal;

(c) the service address, telephone and facsimile numbers of the party to the dispute; and either

(i) a statement of the issues raised on appeal by another participant with which the party joins; or

(ii) a brief statement of the nature of the other appeal, including:

(A) identification of the alleged errors in the issues of law covered in the panel report and legal interpretations developed by the panel;

(B) a list of the legal provision(s) of the covered agreements that the panel is alleged to have erred in interpreting or applying; and

(C) without prejudice to the ability of the other appellant to refer to other paragraphs of the panel report in the context of its appeal, an indicative list of the paragraphs of the panel report containing the alleged errors.

(3) The other appellant shall, within 5 days after the date of the filing of the Notice of Appeal, file with the Secretariat a written submission prepared in accordance with paragraph 2 of Rule 21 and serve a copy of the submission on the other parties to the dispute and third parties.

(4) The appellant, any appellee and any other party to the dispute that wishes to respond to a submission filed pursuant to paragraph 3 may file a written submission within 18 days after the date of the filing of the Notice of Appeal, and any such submission shall be in the format required by paragraph 2 of Rule 22.

(5) This Rule does not preclude a party to the dispute which has not filed a submission under Rule 21 or a Notice of Other Appeal under paragraph 1 of this Rule from exercising its right of appeal pursuant to paragraph 4 of Article 16 of the DSU.

(6) Where a party to the dispute which has not filed a submission under Rule 21 or a Notice of Other Appeal under paragraph 1 of this Rule exercises its right to appeal as set out in paragraph 5, a single division shall examine the appeals.

Amending Notices of Appeal

23*bis*. (1) The division may authorize an original appellant to amend a Notice of Appeal or an other appellant to amend a Notice of Other Appeal.

(2) A request to amend a Notice of Appeal or a Notice of Other Appeal shall be made as soon as possible in writing and shall state the reason(s) for the request and identify precisely the specific amendments that the appellant or other appellant wishes to make to the Notice. A copy of the request shall be served on the other parties to the dispute, participants, third participants and third parties, each of whom shall be given an opportunity to comment in writing on the request.

(3) In deciding whether to authorize, in full or in part, a request to amend a Notice of Appeal or Notice of Other Appeal, the division shall take into account:

(a) the requirement to circulate the appellate report within the time-period set out in Article 17.5 of the DSU or, as appropriate, Article 4.9 of the *SCM Agreement*; and,

(b) the interests of fairness and orderly procedure, including the nature and extent of the proposed amendment, the timing of the request to amend a Notice of Appeal or Notice of Other Appeal, any reasons why the proposed amended Notice of Appeal or Notice of Other Appeal was not or could not have been filed on its original date, and any other considerations that may be appropriate.

(4) The division shall notify the parties to the dispute, participants, third participants, and third parties of its decision. In the event that the division authorizes an amendment to a Notice of Appeal or a Notice of Other Appeal, it shall provide an amended copy of the Notice to the DSB.

Third Participants

24. (1) Any third party may file a written submission containing the grounds and legal arguments in support of its position. Such submission shall be filed within 21 days after the date of the filing of the Notice of Appeal.

(2) A third party not filing a written submission shall, within the same period of 21 days, notify the Secretariat in writing if it intends to appear at the oral hearing, and, if so, whether it intends to make an oral statement.

(3) Third participants are encouraged to file written submissions to facilitate their positions being taken fully into account by the division hearing the appeal and in order that participants and other third participants will have notice of positions to be taken at the oral hearing.

(4) Any third party that has neither filed a written submission pursuant to paragraph 1, nor notified the Secretariat pursuant to paragraph 2, may notify the Secretariat that it intends to appear at the oral hearing, and may request to make an oral statement at the hearing. Such notifications and requests should be notified to the Secretariat in writing at the earliest opportunity.

Transmittal of Record

25. (1) Upon the filing of a Notice of Appeal, the Director-General of the WTO shall transmit forthwith to the Appellate Body the complete record of the panel proceeding.

(2) The complete record of the panel proceeding includes, but is not limited to:

(a) written submissions, rebuttal submissions, and supporting evidence attached thereto by the parties to the dispute and the third parties;

(b) written arguments submitted at the panel meetings with the parties to the dispute and the third parties, the recordings of such panel meetings, and any written answers to questions posed at such panel meetings;

(c) the correspondence relating to the panel dispute between the panel or the WTO Secretariat and the parties to the dispute or the third parties; and

(d) any other documentation submitted to the panel.

Working Schedule

26. (1) Forthwith after the commencement of an appeal, the division shall draw up an appropriate working schedule for that appeal in accordance with the time-periods stipulated in these Rules.

(2) The working schedule shall set forth precise dates for the filing of documents and a timetable for the division's work, including where possible, the date for the oral hearing.

(3) In accordance with paragraph 9 of Article 4 of the DSU, in appeals of urgency, including those which concern perishable goods, the Appellate Body shall make every effort to accelerate the appellate proceedings to the greatest extent possible. A division shall take this into account in drawing up its working schedule for that appeal.

(4) The Secretariat shall serve forthwith a copy of the working schedule on the appellant, the parties to the dispute and any third parties.

Oral Hearing

27. (1) A division shall hold an oral hearing, which shall be held, as a general rule, between 30 and 45 days after the date of the filing of a Notice of Appeal.

(2) Where possible in the working schedule or otherwise at the earliest possible date, the Secretariat shall notify all parties to the dispute, participants, third parties and third participants of the date for the oral hearing.

(3) (a) Any third party that has filed a submission pursuant to Rule 24(1), or has notified the Secretariat pursuant to Rule 24(2) that it intends to appear at the oral hearing, may appear at the oral hearing, make an oral statement at the hearing, and respond to questions posed by the division.

(b) Any third party that has notified the Secretariat pursuant to Rule 24(4) that it intends to appear at the oral hearing may appear at the oral hearing.

(c) Any third party that has made a request pursuant to Rule 24(4) may, at the discretion of the division hearing the appeal, taking into account the requirements of due process, make an oral statement at the hearing, and respond to questions posed by the division.

(4) The Presiding Member may set time-limits for oral arguments.

Written Responses

28. (1) At any time during the appellate proceeding, including, in particular, during the oral hearing, the division may address questions orally or in writing to, or request additional memoranda from, any participant or third participant, and specify the time-periods by which written responses or memoranda shall be received.

(2) Any such questions, responses or memoranda shall be made available to the other participants and third participants in the appeal, who shall be given an opportunity to respond.

(3) When the questions or requests for memoranda are made prior to the oral hearing, then the questions or requests, as well as the responses or memoranda, shall also be made available to the third parties, who shall also be given an opportunity to respond.

Failure to Appear

29. Where a participant fails to file a submission within the required time-periods or fails to appear at the oral hearing, the division shall, after hearing the views of the participants, issue such order, including dismissal of the appeal, as it deems appropriate.

Withdrawal of Appeal

30. (1) At any time during an appeal, the appellant may withdraw its appeal by notifying the Appellate Body, which shall forthwith notify the DSB.

(2) Where a mutually agreed solution to a dispute which is the subject of an appeal has been notified to the DSB pursuant to paragraph 6 of Article 3 of the DSU, it shall be notified to the Appellate Body.

Prohibited Subsidies

31. (1) Subject to Article 4 of the *SCM Agreement*, the general provisions of these Rules shall apply to appeals relating to panel reports concerning prohibited subsidies under Part II of that *Agreement*.

(2) The working schedule for an appeal involving prohibited subsidies under Part II of the *SCM Agreement* shall be as set out in Annex I to these Rules.

Entry into Force and Amendment

32. (1) These Rules entered into force on 15 February 1996, and have subsequently been amended as indicated in Annex III.

(2) The Appellate Body may amend these Rules in compliance with the procedures set forth in paragraph 9 of Article 17 of the DSU. The Appellate Body will announce the date on which such amendments come into force. The document number for each revised version of these Rules, and the date upon which each version entered into force and succeeded the previous version, are indicated in Annex III.

(3) Whenever there is an amendment to the DSU or to the special or additional rules and procedures of the covered agreements, the Appellate Body shall examine whether amendments to these Rules are necessary.

Annex I

TIMETABLE FOR APPEALS[1]

	General Appeals	Prohibited Subsidies Appeals
	Day	Day
Notice of Appeal[2]	0	0
Appellant's Submission[3]	0	0
Notice of Other Appeal[4]	5	2
Other Appellant's Submission[5]	5	2
Appellee's Submission[6]	18	9
Third Participant's Submission[7]	21	10
Third Participant's Notification[8]	21	10
Oral Hearing[9]	30–45	15–23
Circulation of Appellate Report	60–90[10]	30–60[11]
DSB Meeting for Adoption	90–120[12]	50–80[13]

1. Rule 17 applies to the computation of the time-periods below.
2. Rule 20.
3. Rule 21(1).
4. Rule 23(1).
5. Rule 23(3).
6. Rules 22 and 23(4).
7. Rule 24(1).
8. Rule 24(2).
9. Rule 27.
10. Article 17.5, DSU.
11. Article 4.9, *SCM Agreement*.
12. Article 17.14, DSU.
13. Article 4.9, *SCM Agreement*.

Annex II

RULES OF CONDUCT FOR THE UNDERSTANDING ON RULES AND PROCEDURES GOVERNING THE SETTLEMENT OF DISPUTES

I. Preamble

Members,

Recalling that on 15 April 1994 in Marrakesh, Ministers welcomed the stronger and clearer legal framework they had adopted for the conduct of international trade, including a more effective and reliable dispute settlement mechanism;

Recognizing the importance of full adherence to the Understanding on Rules and Procedures Governing the Settlement of Disputes ("DSU") and the principles for the management of disputes applied under Articles XXII and XXIII of GATT 1947, as further elaborated and modified by the DSU;

Affirming that the operation of the DSU would be strengthened by rules of conduct designed to maintain the integrity, impartiality and confidentiality of proceedings conducted under the DSU thereby enhancing confidence in the new dispute settlement mechanism;

Hereby establish the following Rules of Conduct.

II. Governing Principle

1. Each person covered by these Rules (as defined in paragraph 1 of Section IV below and hereinafter called "covered person") shall be independent and impartial, shall avoid direct or indirect conflicts of interest and shall respect the confidentiality of proceedings of bodies pursuant to the dispute settlement mechanism, so that through the observance of such standards of conduct the integrity and impartiality of that mechanism are preserved. These Rules shall in no way modify the rights and obligations of Members under the DSU nor the rules and procedures therein.

III. Observance of the Governing Principle

1. To ensure the observance of the Governing Principle of these Rules, each covered person is expected (1) to adhere strictly to the provisions of the DSU; (2) to disclose the existence or development of any interest, relationship or matter that that person could reasonably be expected to know and that is likely to affect, or give rise to justifiable doubts as to, that person's independence or impartiality; and (3) to take due care in the performance of their duties to fulfil these expectations, including through avoidance of any direct or indirect conflicts of interest in respect of the subject matter of the proceedings.

2. Pursuant to the Governing Principle, each covered person, shall be independent and impartial, and shall maintain confidentiality. Moreover, such persons shall consider only issues raised in, and necessary to fulfil their responsibilities within, the dispute settlement proceeding and shall not delegate this responsibility to any other person. Such person shall not incur any obligation or accept any benefit that would in anyway interfere with, or which could give rise to, justifiable doubts as to the proper performance of that person's dispute settlement duties.

IV. Scope

1. These Rules shall apply, as specified in the text, to each person serving: (a) on a panel; (b) on the Standing Appellate Body; (c) as an arbitrator pursuant to the provisions mentioned in Annex "1a"; or (d) as an expert participating in the dispute settlement mechanism pursuant to the provisions mentioned in Annex "1b". These Rules shall also apply, as specified in this text and the relevant provisions of the Staff Regulations, to those members of the Secretariat called upon to assist the panel in accordance with Article 27.1 of the DSU or to assist in formal arbitration proceedings pursuant to Annex "1a"; to the Chairman of the Textiles Monitoring Body (hereinafter called "TMB") and other members of the TMB Secretariat called upon to assist the TMB in formulating recommendations, findings or observations pursuant to the WTO Agreement on Textiles and Clothing; and to Standing Appellate Body support staff called upon to provide the Standing Appellate Body with administrative or legal support in accordance with Article 17.7 of the DSU (hereinafter "Member of the Secretariat or Standing Appellate Body support staff"), reflecting their acceptance of established norms regulating the conduct of such persons as international civil servants and the Governing Principle of these Rules.

2. The application of these Rules shall not in any way impede the Secretariat's discharge of its responsibility to continue to respond to Members' requests for assistance and information.

3. These Rules shall apply to the members of the TMB to the extent prescribed in Section V.

V. Textiles Monitoring Body

1. Members of the TMB shall discharge their functions on an *ad personam* basis, in accordance with the requirement of Article 8.1 of the Agreement on Textiles and Clothing, as further elaborated in the working procedures of the TMB, so as to preserve the integrity and impartiality of its proceedings.[1]

VI. Self-Disclosure Requirements by Covered Persons

1. (a) Each person requested to serve on a panel, on the Standing Appellate Body, as an arbitrator, or as an expert shall, at the time of the request, receive from the Secretariat these Rules, which include an Illustrative List (Annex 2) of examples of the matters subject to disclosure.

(b) Any member of the Secretariat described in paragraph IV:1, who may expect to be called upon to assist in a dispute, and Standing Appellate Body support staff, shall be familiar with these Rules.

2. As set out in paragraph VI:4 below, all covered persons described in paragraph VI.1(a) and VI.1(b) shall disclose any information that could reasonably be expected to be known to them at the time which, coming within the scope of the Governing Principle of these Rules, is likely to affect or give rise to justifiable doubts as to their independence or impartiality. These disclosures include the type of information described in the Illustrative List, if relevant.

1. These working procedures, as adopted by the TMB on 26 July 1995 (G/TMB/R/1), currently include, *inter alia*, the following language in paragraph 1.4: "In discharging their functions in accordance with paragraph 1.1 above, the TMB members and alternates shall undertake not to solicit, accept or act upon instructions from governments, nor to be influenced by any other organisations or undue extraneous factors. They shall disclose to the Chairman any information that they may consider likely to impede their capacity to discharge their functions on an *ad personam* basis. Should serious doubts arise during the deliberations of the TMB regarding the ability of a TMB member to act on an *ad personam* basis, they shall be communicated to the Chairman. The Chairman shall deal with the particular matter as necessary".

3. These disclosure requirements shall not extend to the identification of matters whose relevance to the issues to be considered in the proceedings would be insignificant. They shall take into account the need to respect the personal privacy of those to whom these Rules apply and shall not be so administratively burdensome as to make it impracticable for otherwise qualified persons to serve on panels, the Standing Appellate Body, or in other dispute settlement roles.

4. (a) All panelists, arbitrators and experts, prior to confirmation of their appointment, shall complete the form at Annex 3 of these Rules. Such information would be disclosed to the Chair of the Dispute Settlement Body ("DSB") for consideration by the parties to the dispute.

(b)(i) Persons serving on the Standing Appellate Body who, through rotation, are selected to hear the appeal of a particular panel case, shall review the factual portion of the Panel report and complete the form at Annex 3. Such information would be disclosed to the Standing Appellate Body for its consideration whether the member concerned should hear a particular appeal.

(ii) Standing Appellate Body support staff shall disclose any relevant matter to the Standing Appellate Body, for its consideration in deciding on the assignment of staff to assist in a particular appeal.

(c) When considered to assist in a dispute, members of the Secretariat shall disclose to the Director-General of the WTO the information required under paragraph VI:2 of these Rules and any other relevant information required under the Staff Regulations, including the information described in the footnote.**

**Pending adoption of the Staff Regulations, members of the Secretariat shall make disclosures to the Director-General in accordance with the following draft provision to be included in the Staff Regulations:

"When paragraph VI:4(c) of the Rules of Conduct for the DSU is applicable, members of the Secretariat would disclose to the Director-General of the WTO the information required in paragraph VI:2 of those Rules, as well as any information regarding their participation in earlier formal consideration of the specific measure at issue in a dispute under any provisions of the WTO Agreement, including through formal legal advice under Article 27.2 of the DSU, as well as any involvement with the dispute as an official of a WTO Member government or otherwise professionally, before having joined the Secretariat.

The Director-General shall consider any such disclosures in deciding on the assignment of members of the Secretariat to assist in a dispute.

When the Director-General, in the light of his consideration, including of available Secretariat resources, decides that a potential conflict of interest is not sufficiently material to warrant non-assignment of a particular member of the Secretariat to assist in a dispute, the Director-General shall inform the panel of his decision and of the relevant supporting information."

5. During a dispute, each covered person shall also disclose any new information relevant to paragraph VI:2 above at the earliest time they become aware of it.

6. The Chair of the DSB, the Secretariat, parties to the dispute, and other individuals involved in the dispute settlement mechanism shall maintain the confidentiality of any information revealed through this disclosure process, even after the panel process and its enforcement procedures, if any, are completed.

VII. Confidentiality

1. Each covered person shall at all times maintain the confidentiality of dispute settlement deliberations and proceedings together with any information identified by a party as confidential. No covered person shall at any time use such information acquired during such deliberations and proceedings to gain personal advantage or advantage for others.

2. During the proceedings, no covered person shall engage in *ex parte* contacts concerning matters under consideration. Subject to paragraph VII:1, no covered person shall make any statements on such proceedings or the issues in dispute in which that person is participating, until the report of the panel or the Standing Appellate Body has been derestricted.

VIII. Procedures Concerning Subsequent Disclosure and Possible Material Violations

1. Any party to a dispute, conducted pursuant to the WTO Agreement, who possesses or comes into possession of evidence of a material violation of the obligations of independence, impartiality or confidentiality or the avoidance of direct or indirect conflicts of interest by covered persons which may impair the integrity, impartiality or confidentiality of the dispute settlement mechanism, shall at the earliest possible time and on a confidential basis, submit such evidence to the Chair of the DSB, the Director-General or the Standing Appellate Body, as appropriate according to the respective procedures detailed in paragraphs VIII:5 to VIII:17 below, in a written statement specifying the relevant facts and circumstances. Other Members who possess or come into possession of such evidence, may provide such evidence to the parties to the dispute in the interest of maintaining the integrity and impartiality of the dispute settlement mechanism.

2. When evidence as described in paragraph VIII:1 is based on an alleged failure of a covered person to disclose a relevant interest, relationship

or matter, that failure to disclose, as such, shall not be a sufficient ground for disqualification unless there is also evidence of a material violation of the obligations of independence, impartiality, confidentiality or the avoidance of direct or indirect conflicts of interests and that the integrity, impartiality or confidentiality of the dispute settlement mechanism would be impaired thereby.

3. When such evidence is not provided at the earliest practicable time, the party submitting the evidence shall explain why it did not do so earlier and this explanation shall be taken into account in the procedures initiated in paragraph VIII:1.

4. Following the submission of such evidence to the Chair of the DSB, the Director-General of the WTO or the Standing Appellate Body, as specified below, the procedures outlined in paragraphs VIII:5 to VIII:17 below shall be completed within fifteen working days.

Panelists, Arbitrators, Experts

5. If the covered person who is the subject of the evidence is a panelist, an arbitrator or an expert, the party shall provide such evidence to the Chair of the DSB.

6. Upon receipt of the evidence referred to in paragraphs VIII:1 and VIII:2, the Chair of the DSB shall forthwith provide the evidence to the person who is the subject of such evidence, for consideration by the latter.

7. If, after having consulted with the person concerned, the matter is not resolved, the Chair of the DSB shall forthwith provide all the evidence, and any additional information from the person concerned, to the parties to the dispute. If the person concerned resigns, the Chair of the DSB shall inform the parties to the dispute and, as the case may be, the panelists, the arbitrator(s) or experts.

8. In all cases, the Chair of the DSB, in consultation with the Director-General and a sufficient number of Chairs of the relevant Council or Councils to provide an odd number, and after having provided a reasonable opportunity for the views of the person concerned and the parties to the dispute to be heard, would decide whether a material violation of these Rules as referred to in paragraphs VIII:1 and VIII:2 above has occurred. Where the parties agree that a material violation of these Rules has occurred, it would be expected that, consistent with maintaining the integrity of the dispute settlement mechanism, the disqualification of the person concerned would be confirmed.

9. The person who is the subject of the evidence shall continue to participate in the consideration of the dispute unless it is decided that a material violation of these Rules has occurred.

10. The Chair of the DSB shall thereafter take the necessary steps for the appointment of the person who is the subject of the evidence to be formally revoked, or excused from the dispute as the case may be, as of that time.

Secretariat

11. If the covered person who is the subject of the evidence is a member of the Secretariat, the party shall only provide the evidence to the Director-General of the WTO, who shall forthwith provide the evidence to the person who is the subject of such evidence and shall further inform the other party or parties to the dispute and the panel.

12. It shall be for the Director-General to take any appropriate action in accordance with the Staff Regulations.***

13. The Director-General shall inform the parties to the dispute, the panel and the Chair of the DSB of his decision, together with relevant supporting information.

Standing Appellate Body

14. If the covered person who is the subject of the evidence is a member of the Standing Appellate Body or of the Standing Appellate Body support staff, the party shall provide the evidence to the other party to the dispute and the evidence shall thereafter be provided to the Standing Appellate Body.

15. Upon receipt of the evidence referred to in paragraphs VIII:1 and VIII:2 above, the Standing Appellate Body shall forthwith provide it to the person who is the subject of such evidence, for consideration by the latter.

16. It shall be for the Standing Appellate Body to take any appropriate action after having provided a reasonable opportunity for the views of the person concerned and the parties to the dispute to be heard.

***Pending adoption of the Staff Regulations, the Director-General would act in accordance with the following draft provision for the Staff Regulations: "If paragraph VIII:11 of the Rules of Conduct for the DSU governing the settlement of disputes is invoked, the Director-General shall consult with the person who is the subject of the evidence and the panel and shall, if necessary, take appropriate disciplinary action".

17. The Standing Appellate Body shall inform the parties to the dispute and the Chair of the DSB of its decision, together with relevant supporting information.

***

18. Following completion of the procedures in paragraphs VIII:5 to VIII:17, if the appointment of a covered person, other than a member of the Standing Appellate Body, is revoked or that person is excused or resigns, the procedures specified in the DSU for initial appointment shall be followed for appointment of a replacement, but the time-periods shall be half those specified in the DSU.**** The member of the Standing Appellate Body who, under that Body's rules, would next be selected through rotation to consider the dispute, would automatically be assigned to the appeal. The panel, members of the Standing Appellate Body hearing the appeal, or the arbitrator, as the case may be, may then decide after consulting with the parties to the dispute, on any necessary modifications to their working procedures or proposed timetable.

19. All covered persons and Members concerned shall resolve matters involving possible material violations of these Rules as expeditiously as possible so as not to delay the completion of proceedings, as provided in the DSU.

20. Except to the extent strictly necessary to carry out this decision, all information concerning possible or actual material violations of these Rules shall be kept confidential.

IX. Review

1.These Rules of Conduct shall be reviewed within two years of their adoption and a decision shall be taken by the DSB as to whether to continue, modify or terminate these Rules.

Annex 1a

Arbitrators acting pursuant to the following provisions:

—Articles 21.3(c); 22.6 and 22.7; 26.1(c) and 25 of the DSU;

**** Appropriate adjustments would be made in the case of appointments pursuant to the Agreement on Subsidies and Countervailing Measures.

—Article 8.5 of the Agreement on Subsidies and Countervailing Measures;

—Articles XXI.3 and XXII.3 of the General Agreement on Trade in Services.

Annex 1b

Experts advising or providing information pursuant to the following provisions:

—Article 13.1; 13.2 of the DSU;

—Article 4.5 of the Agreement on Subsidies and Countervailing Measures;

—Article 11.2 of the Agreement on the Application of Sanitary and Phytosanitary Measures;

—Article 14.2; 14.3 of the Agreement on Technical Barriers to Trade.

Annex 2

ILLUSTRATIVE LIST OF INFORMATION TO BE DISCLOSED

This list contains examples of information of the type that a person called upon to serve in a dispute should disclose pursuant to the Rules of Conduct for the Understanding on Rules and Procedures Governing the Settlement of Disputes.

Each covered person, as defined in Section IV:1 of these Rules of Conduct has a continuing duty to disclose the information described in Section VI:2 of these Rules which may include the following:

(a) financial interests (e.g. investments, loans, shares, interests, other debts); business interests (e.g. directorship or other contractual interests); and property interests relevant to the dispute in question;

(b) professional interests (e.g. a past or present relationship with private clients, or any interests the person may have in domestic or international proceedings, and their implications, where these involve issues similar to those addressed in the dispute in question);

(c) other active interests (e.g. active participation in public interest groups or other organisations which may have a declared agenda relevant to the dispute in question);

(d) considered statements of personal opinion on issues relevant to the dispute in question (e.g. publications, public statements);

(e) employment or family interests (e.g. the possibility of any indirect advantage or any likelihood of pressure which could arise from their employer, business associates or immediate family members).

Annex 3

Dispute Number: ____

WORLD TRADE ORGANIZATION DISCLOSURE FORM

I have read the Understanding on Rules and Procedures Governing the Settlement of Disputes (DSU) and the Rules of Conduct for the DSU. I understand my continuing duty, while participating in the dispute settlement mechanism, and until such time as the Dispute Settlement Body (DSB) makes a decision on adoption of a report relating to the proceeding or notes its settlement, to disclose herewith and in future any information likely to affect my independence or impartiality, or which could give rise to justifiable doubts as to the integrity and impartiality of the dispute settlement mechanism; and to respect my obligations regarding the confidentiality of dispute settlement proceedings.

Signed: Dated:

Annex III

Table of Consolidated and Revised Versions of the *Working Procedures for Appellate Review*

Document Number	Effective Date	Rules Amended	Working Documents/ Explanatory Texts	Minutes of Principal DSB Meeting(s) at which Amendments were Discussed
WT/AB/WP/1	15 February 1996	N/A	WT/AB/WP/W/1	31 January 1996, WT/DSB/M/10 and 21 February 1996, WT/DSB/M/11
WT/AB/WP/2	28 February 1997	Rule 5(2) and Annex II	WT/AB/WP/W/2, WT/AB/WP/W/3	25 February 1997, WT/DSB/M/29
WT/AB/WP/3	24 January 2002	Rule 5(2)	WT/AB/WP/W/4, WT/AB/WP/W/5	24 July 2001, WT/DSB/M/107
WT/AB/WP/4	1 May 2003	Rules 24 and 27(3), with consequential amendments to Rules 1, 16, 18, 19, and 28, and Annex I	WT/AB/WP/W/6, WT/AB/WP/W/7	23 October 2002, WT/DSB/M/134
WT/AB/WP/5	1 January 2005	Rules 1, 18, 20, 21, 23, 23 *bis*, and 27, and Annexes I and III	WT/AB/WP/W/8, WT/AB/WP/W/9	19 May 2004, WT/DSB/M/169
WT/AB/WP/6	15 September 2010	Rules 6(3), 18(1), 18(2), 18(4), 21(1), 22(1), 23(1), 23(3), 23(4), 24(1), 24(2), 27(1), 32(1), and 32(2), and Annexes I and III; additional technical amendments to Spanish and French versions only	WT/AB/WP/W/10, WT/AB/WP/W/11	18 May 2010, WT/DSB/M/283

Document 9

RULES OF CONDUCT FOR THE UNDERSTANDING ON RULES AND PROCEDURES GOVERNING THE SETTLEMENT OF DISPUTES

WT/DSB/RC/1, 11 December 1996

I. Preamble

Members,

Recalling that on 15 April 1994 in Marrakesh, Ministers welcomed the stronger and clearer legal framework they had adopted for the conduct of international trade, including a more effective and reliable dispute settlement mechanism;

Recognizing the importance of full adherence to the Understanding on Rules and Procedures Governing the Settlement of Disputes ("DSU") and the principles for the management of disputes applied under Articles XXII and XXIII of GATT 1947, as further elaborated and modified by the DSU;

Affirming that the operation of the DSU would be strengthened by rules of conduct designed to maintain the integrity, impartiality and confidentiality of proceedings conducted under the DSU thereby enhancing confidence in the new dispute settlement mechanism;

Hereby establish the following Rules of Conduct.

II. Governing Principle

1. Each person covered by these Rules (as defined in paragraph 1 of Section IV below and hereinafter called "covered person") shall be

independent and impartial, shall avoid direct or indirect conflicts of interest and shall respect the confidentiality of proceedings of bodies pursuant to the dispute settlement mechanism, so that through the observance of such standards of conduct the integrity and impartiality of that mechanism are preserved. These Rules shall in no way modify the rights and obligations of Members under the DSU nor the rules and procedures therein.

III. Observance of the Governing Principle

1. To ensure the observance of the Governing Principle of these Rules, each covered person is expected (1) to adhere strictly to the provisions of the DSU; (2) to disclose the existence or development of any interest, relationship or matter that that person could reasonably be expected to know and that is likely to affect, or give rise to justifiable doubts as to, that person's independence or impartiality; and (3) to take due care in the performance of their duties to fulfil these expectations, including through avoidance of any direct or indirect conflicts of interest in respect of the subject matter of the proceedings.

2. Pursuant to the Governing Principle, each covered person, shall be independent and impartial, and shall maintain confidentiality. Moreover, such persons shall consider only issues raised in, and necessary to fulfil their responsibilities within, the dispute settlement proceeding and shall not delegate this responsibility to any other person. Such person shall not incur any obligation or accept any benefit that would in anyway interfere with, or which could give rise to, justifiable doubts as to the proper performance of that person's dispute settlement duties.

IV. Scope

1. These Rules shall apply, as specified in the text, to each person serving: (a) on a panel; (b) on the Standing Appellate Body; (c) as an arbitrator pursuant to the provisions mentioned in Annex "1a"; or (d) as an expert participating in the dispute settlement mechanism pursuant to the provisions mentioned in Annex "1b". These Rules shall also apply, as specified in this text and the relevant provisions of the Staff Regulations, to those members of the Secretariat called upon to assist the panel in accordance with Article 27.1 of the DSU or to assist in formal arbitration proceedings pursuant to Annex "1a"; to the Chairman of the Textiles Monitoring Body (hereinafter called "TMB") and other members of the TMB Secretariat called upon to assist the TMB in formulating recommendations, findings or observations pursuant to the WTO Agreement on Textiles and Clothing; and to Standing Appellate Body support staff called

upon to provide the Standing Appellate Body with administrative or legal support in accordance with Article 17.7 of the DSU (hereinafter "Member of the Secretariat or Standing Appellate Body support staff"), reflecting their acceptance of established norms regulating the conduct of such persons as international civil servants and the Governing Principle of these Rules.

2. The application of these Rules shall not in any way impede the Secretariat's discharge of its responsibility to continue to respond to Members' requests for assistance and information.

3. These Rules shall apply to the members of the TMB to the extent prescribed in Section V.

V. Textiles Monitoring Body

1. Members of the TMB shall discharge their functions on an *ad personam* basis, in accordance with the requirement of Article 8.1 of the Agreement on Textiles and Clothing, as further elaborated in the working procedures of the TMB, so as to preserve the integrity and impartiality of its proceedings.[1]

VI. Self-Disclosure Requirements by Covered Persons

1. (a) Each person requested to serve on a panel, on the Standing Appellate Body, as an arbitrator, or as an expert shall, at the time of the request, receive from the Secretariat these Rules, which include an Illustrative List (Annex 2) of examples of the matters subject to disclosure.

(b) Any member of the Secretariat described in paragraph IV:1, who may expect to be called upon to assist in a dispute, and Standing Appellate Body support staff, shall be familiar with these Rules.

2. As set out in paragraph VI:4 below, all covered persons described in paragraph VI.1(a) and VI.1(b) shall disclose any information that could

1. These working procedures, as adopted by the TMB on 26 July 1995 (G/TMB/R/1), currently include, *inter alia*, the following language in paragraph 1.4: "In discharging their functions in accordance with paragraph 1.1 above, the TMB members and alternates shall undertake not to solicit, accept or act upon instructions from governments, nor to be influenced by any other organisations or undue extraneous factors. They shall disclose to the Chairman any information that they may consider likely to impede their capacity to discharge their functions on an *ad personam* basis. Should serious doubts arise during the deliberations of the TMB regarding the ability of a TMB member to act on an *ad personam* basis, they shall be communicated to the Chairman. The Chairman shall deal with the particular matter as necessary".

reasonably be expected to be known to them at the time which, coming within the scope of the Governing Principle of these Rules, is likely to affect or give rise to justifiable doubts as to their independence or impartiality. These disclosures include the type of information described in the Illustrative List, if relevant.

3. These disclosure requirements shall not extend to the identification of matters whose relevance to the issues to be considered in the proceedings would be insignificant. They shall take into account the need to respect the personal privacy of those to whom these Rules apply and shall not be so administratively burdensome as to make it impracticable for otherwise qualified persons to serve on panels, the Standing Appellate Body, or in other dispute settlement roles.

4. (a) All panelists, arbitrators and experts, prior to confirmation of their appointment, shall complete the form at Annex 3 of these Rules. Such information would be disclosed to the Chair of the Dispute Settlement Body ("DSB") for consideration by the parties to the dispute.

(b) (i) Persons serving on the Standing Appellate Body who, through rotation, are selected to hear the appeal of a particular panel case, shall review the factual portion of the Panel report and complete the form at Annex 3. Such information would be disclosed to the Standing Appellate Body for its consideration whether the member concerned should hear a particular appeal.

(ii) Standing Appellate Body support staff shall disclose any relevant matter to the Standing Appellate Body, for its consideration in deciding on the assignment of staff to assist in a particular appeal.

(c) When considered to assist in a dispute, members of the Secretariat shall disclose to the Director-General of the WTO the information required under paragraph VI:2 of these Rules and any other relevant information required under the Staff Regulations, including the information described in the footnote.[2]

2. Pending adoption of the Staff Regulations, members of the Secretariat shall make disclosures to the Director-General in accordance with the following draft provision to be included in the Staff Regulations: "When paragraph VI:4(c) of the Rules of Conduct for the DSU is applicable, members of the Secretariat would disclose to the Director-General of the WTO the information required in paragraph VI:2 of those Rules, as well as any information regarding their participation in earlier formal consideration of the specific measure at issue in a dispute under any provisions of the WTO Agreement, including through formal legal advice under Article 27.2 of the DSU, as well as any involvement with the dispute as an official of a WTO Member government or otherwise professionally, before having joined the Secretariat. The Director-General shall consider any such disclosures in deciding on the assignment of members of the Secretariat to assist in a dispute. When the Director-General, in the light of his consideration, including of available Secretariat resources, decides that a potential conflict of interest is not sufficiently material to warrant non-assignment of a particular member of the

5. During a dispute, each covered person shall also disclose any new information relevant to paragraph VI:2 above at the earliest time they become aware of it.

6. The Chair of the DSB, the Secretariat, parties to the dispute, and other individuals involved in the dispute settlement mechanism shall maintain the confidentiality of any information revealed through this disclosure process, even after the panel process and its enforcement procedures, if any, are completed.

VII. Confidentiality

1. Each covered person shall at all times maintain the confidentiality of dispute settlement deliberations and proceedings together with any information identified by a party as confidential. No covered person shall at any time use such information acquired during such deliberations and proceedings to gain personal advantage or advantage for others.

2. During the proceedings, no covered person shall engage in *ex parte* contacts concerning matters under consideration. Subject to paragraph VII:1, no covered person shall make any statements on such proceedings or the issues in dispute in which that person is participating, until the report of the panel or the Standing Appellate Body has been derestricted.

VIII. Procedures Concerning Subsequent Disclosure and Possible Material Violations

1. Any party to a dispute, conducted pursuant to the WTO Agreement, who possesses or comes into possession of evidence of a material violation of the obligations of independence, impartiality or confidentiality or the avoidance of direct or indirect conflicts of interest by covered persons which may impair the integrity, impartiality or confidentiality of the dispute settlement mechanism, shall at the earliest possible time and on a confidential basis, submit such evidence to the Chair of the DSB, the Director-General or the Standing Appellate Body, as appropriate according to the respective procedures detailed in paragraphs VIII:5 to VIII:17 below, in a written statement specifying the relevant facts and circumstances. Other Members who possess or come into possession of such evidence, may provide such evidence to the parties to the dispute in the interest of maintaining the integrity and impartiality of the dispute settlement mechanism.

Secretariat to assist in a dispute, the Director-General shall inform the panel of his decision and of the relevant supporting information."

2. When evidence as described in paragraph VIII:1 is based on an alleged failure of a covered person to disclose a relevant interest, relationship or matter, that failure to disclose, as such, shall not be a sufficient ground for disqualification unless there is also evidence of a material violation of the obligations of independence, impartiality, confidentiality or the avoidance of direct or indirect conflicts of interests and that the integrity, impartiality or confidentiality of the dispute settlement mechanism would be impaired thereby.

3. When such evidence is not provided at the earliest practicable time, the party submitting the evidence shall explain why it did not do so earlier and this explanation shall be taken into account in the procedures initiated in paragraph VIII:1.

4. Following the submission of such evidence to the Chair of the DSB, the Director-General of the WTO or the Standing Appellate Body, as specified below, the procedures outlined in paragraphs VIII:5 to VIII:17 below shall be completed within fifteen working days.

Panelists, Arbitrators, Experts

5. If the covered person who is the subject of the evidence is a panelist, an arbitrator or an expert, the party shall provide such evidence to the Chair of the DSB.

6. Upon receipt of the evidence referred to in paragraphs VIII:1 and VIII:2, the Chair of the DSB shall forthwith provide the evidence to the person who is the subject of such evidence, for consideration by the latter.

7. If, after having consulted with the person concerned, the matter is not resolved, the Chair of the DSB shall forthwith provide all the evidence, and any additional information from the person concerned, to the parties to the dispute. If the person concerned resigns, the Chair of the DSB shall inform the parties to the dispute and, as the case may be, the panelists, the arbitrator(s) or experts.

8. In all cases, the Chair of the DSB, in consultation with the Director-General and a sufficient number of Chairs of the relevant Council or Councils to provide an odd number, and after having provided a reasonable opportunity for the views of the person concerned and the parties to the dispute to be heard, would decide whether a material violation of these Rules as referred to in paragraphs VIII:1 and VIII:2 above has occurred. Where the parties agree that a material violation of these Rules has occurred, it would be expected that, consistent with maintaining the integrity of the dispute settlement mechanism, the disqualification of the person concerned would be confirmed.

9. The person who is the subject of the evidence shall continue to participate in the consideration of the dispute unless it is decided that a material violation of these Rules has occurred.

10. The Chair of the DSB shall thereafter take the necessary steps for the appointment of the person who is the subject of the evidence to be formally revoked, or excused from the dispute as the case may be, as of that time.

Secretariat

11. If the covered person who is the subject of the evidence is a member of the Secretariat, the party shall only provide the evidence to the Director-General of the WTO, who shall forthwith provide the evidence to the person who is the subject of such evidence and shall further inform the other party or parties to the dispute and the panel.

12. It shall be for the Director-General to take any appropriate action in accordance with the Staff Regulations.[3]

13. The Director-General shall inform the parties to the dispute, the panel and the Chair of the DSB of his decision, together with relevant supporting information.

Standing Appellate Body

14. If the covered person who is the subject of the evidence is a member of the Standing Appellate Body or of the Standing Appellate Body support staff, the party shall provide the evidence to the other party to the dispute and the evidence shall thereafter be provided to the Standing Appellate Body.

15. Upon receipt of the evidence referred to in paragraphs VIII:1 and VIII:2 above, the Standing Appellate Body shall forthwith provide it to the person who is the subject of such evidence, for consideration by the latter.

16. It shall be for the Standing Appellate Body to take any appropriate action after having provided a reasonable opportunity for the views of the person concerned and the parties to the dispute to be heard.

3. Pending adoption of the Staff Regulations, the Director-General would act in accordance with the following draft provision for the Staff Regulations: "If paragraph VIII:11 of the Rules of Conduct for the DSU governing the settlement of disputes is invoked, the Director-General shall consult with the person who is the subject of the evidence and the panel and shall, if necessary, take appropriate disciplinary action".

17. The Standing Appellate Body shall inform the parties to the dispute and the Chair of the DSB of its decision, together with relevant supporting information.

18. Following completion of the procedures in paragraphs VIII:5 to VIII:17, if the appointment of a covered person, other than a member of the Standing Appellate Body, is revoked or that person is excused or resigns, the procedures specified in the DSU for initial appointment shall be followed for appointment of a replacement, but the time periods shall be half those specified in the DSU.[4] The member of the Standing Appellate Body who, under that Body's rules, would next be selected through rotation to consider the dispute, would automatically be assigned to the appeal. The panel, members of the Standing Appellate Body hearing the appeal, or the arbitrator, as the case may be, may then decide after consulting with the parties to the dispute, on any necessary modifications to their working procedures or proposed timetable.

19. All covered persons and Members concerned shall resolve matters involving possible material violations of these Rules as expeditiously as possible so as not to delay the completion of proceedings, as provided in the DSU.

20. Except to the extent strictly necessary to carry out this decision, all information concerning possible or actual material violations of these Rules shall be kept confidential.

IX. Review

1. These Rules of Conduct shall be reviewed within two years of their adoption and a decision shall be taken by the DSB as to whether to continue, modify or terminate these Rules.

Annex 1a

Arbitrators acting pursuant to the following provisions:

- Articles 21.3(c); 22.6 and 22.7; 26.1(c) and 25 of the DSU;
- Article 8.5 of the Agreement on Subsidies and Countervailing Measures;
- Articles XXI.3 and XXII.3 of the General Agreement on Trade in Services.

4. Appropriate adjustments would be made in the case of appointments pursuant to the Agreement on Subsidies and Countervailing Measures.

Annex 1b

Experts advising or providing information pursuant to the following provisions:

- Article 13.1; 13.2 of the DSU;
- Article 4.5 of the Agreement on Subsidies and Countervailing Measures;
- Article 11.2 of the Agreement on the Application of Sanitary and Phytosanitary Measures;
- Article 14.2; 14.3 of the Agreement on Technical Barriers to Trade.

Annex 2

ILLUSTRATIVE LIST OF INFORMATION TO BE DISCLOSED

This list contains examples of information of the type that a person called upon to serve in a dispute should disclose pursuant to the Rules of Conduct for the Understanding on Rules and Procedures Governing the Settlement of Disputes.

Each covered person, as defined in Section IV:1 of these Rules of Conduct has a continuing duty to disclose the information described in Section VI:2 of these Rules which may include the following:

(a) financial interests (e.g. investments, loans, shares, interests, other debts); business interests (e.g. directorship or other contractual interests); and property interests relevant to the dispute in question;

(b) professional interests (e.g. a past or present relationship with private clients, or any interests the person may have in domestic or international proceedings, and their implications, where these involve issues similar to those addressed in the dispute in question);

(c) other active interests (e.g. active participation in public interest groups or other organisations which may have a declared agenda relevant to the dispute in question);

(d) considered statements of personal opinion on issues relevant to the dispute in question (e.g. publications, public statements);

(e) employment or family interests (e.g. the possibility of any indirect advantage or any likelihood of pressure which could arise from their employer, business associates or immediate family members).

Annex 3

Dispute Number: ________

WORLD TRADE ORGANIZATION
DISCLOSURE FORM

I have read the Understanding on Rules and Procedures Governing the Settlement of Disputes (DSU) and the Rules of Conduct for the DSU. I understand my continuing duty, while participating in the dispute settlement mechanism, and until such time as the Dispute Settlement Body (DSB) makes a decision on adoption of a report relating to the proceeding or notes its settlement, to disclose herewith and in future any information likely to affect my independence or impartiality, or which could give rise to justifiable doubts as to the integrity and impartiality of the dispute settlement mechanism; and to respect my obligations regarding the confidentiality of dispute settlement proceedings.

Signed: Dated:

Document 10

SECTIONS 301-310 OF THE U.S. TRADE ACT OF 1974 (as amended)

19 USCA Ch. 12, Subch. III, §2411-2420

§2411. Actions by United States Trade Representative

(a) Mandatory action

(1) If the United States Trade Representative determines under section 2414(a)(1) of this title that—

(A) the rights of the United States under any trade agreement are being denied; or

(B) an act, policy, or practice of a foreign country—

(i) violates, or is inconsistent with, the provisions of, or otherwise denies benefits to the United States under, any trade agreement, or

(ii) is unjustifiable and burdens or restricts United States commerce;

the Trade Representative shall take action authorized in subsection (c) of this section, subject to the specific direction, if any, of the President regarding any such action, and shall take all other appropriate and feasible action within the power of the President that the President may direct the Trade Representative to take under this subsection, to enforce such rights or to obtain the elimination of such act, policy, or practice. Actions may be taken that are within the power of the President with respect to trade in any goods or services, or with respect to any other area of pertinent relations with the foreign country.

(2) The Trade Representative is not required to take action under paragraph (1) in any case in which—

(A) The Dispute Settlement Body (as defined in section 3531(5) of this title) has adopted a report, or a ruling issued under the formal dispute settlement proceeding provided under any other trade agreement finds, that—

(i) the rights of the United States under a trade agreement are not being denied, or

(ii) the act, policy, or practice—

(I) is not a violation of, or inconsistent with, the rights of the United States, or

(II) does not deny, nullify, or impair benefits to the United States under any trade agreement; or

(B) the Trade Representative finds that—

(i) the foreign country is taking satisfactory measures to grant the rights of the United States under a trade agreement,

(ii) the foreign country has—

(I) agreed to eliminate or phase out the act, policy, or practice, or

(II) agreed to an imminent solution to the burden or restriction on United States commerce that is satisfactory to the Trade Representative,

(iii) it is impossible for the foreign country to achieve the results described in clause (i) or (ii), as appropriate, but the foreign country agrees to provide to the United States compensatory trade benefits that are satisfactory to the Trade Representative,

(iv) in extraordinary cases, where the taking of action under this subsection would have an adverse impact on the United States economy substantially out of proportion to the benefits of such action, taking into account the impact of not taking such action on the credibility of the provisions of this subchapter, or

(v) the taking of action under this subsection would cause serious harm to the national security of the United States.

(3) Any action taken under paragraph (1) to eliminate an act, policy, or practice shall be devised so as to affect goods or services of the foreign country in an amount that is equivalent in value to the burden or restriction being imposed by that country on United States commerce.

(b) Discretionary action

If the Trade Representative determines under section 2414(a)(1) of this title that—

(1) an act, policy, or practice of a foreign country is unreasonable or discriminatory and burdens or restricts United States commerce, and

(2) action by the United States is appropriate, the Trade Representative shall take all appropriate and feasible action authorized under subsection (c) of this section, subject to the specific direction, if any, of the President regarding any such action, and all other appropriate and feasible action within the power of the President that the President may direct the Trade Representative to take under this subsection, to obtain the elimination of that act, policy, or practice. Actions may be taken that are within the power of the President with respect to trade in any goods or services, or with respect to any other area of pertinent relations with the foreign country.

(c) Scope of authority

(1) For purposes of carrying out the provisions of subsection (a) or (b) of this section, the Trade Representative is authorized to—

(A) suspend, withdraw, or prevent the application of, benefits of trade agreement concessions to carry out a trade agreement with the foreign country referred to in such subsection;

(B) impose duties or other import restrictions on the goods of, and, notwithstanding any other provision of law, fees or restrictions on the services of, such foreign country for such time as the Trade Representative determines appropriate;

(C) in a case in which the act, policy, or practice also fails to meet the eligibility criteria for receiving duty-free treatment under subsections (b) and (c) of section 2462 of this title, subsections (b) and (c) of section 2702 of this title, or subsections (c) and (d) of section 3202 of this title, withdraw, limit, or suspend such treatment under such provisions, notwithstanding the provisions of subsection (a)(3) of this section; or

(D) enter into binding agreements with such foreign country that commit such foreign country to—

(i) eliminate, or phase out, the act, policy, or practice that is the subject of the action to be taken under subsection (a) or (b) of this section,

(ii) eliminate any burden or restriction on United States commerce resulting from such act, policy, or practice, or

(iii) provide the United States with compensatory trade benefits that—

(I) are satisfactory to the Trade Representative, and

(II) meet the requirements of paragraph (4).

(2)(A) Notwithstanding any other provision of law governing any service sector access authorization, and in addition to the authority conferred in paragraph (1), the Trade Representative may, for purposes of carrying out the provisions of subsection (a) or (b) of this section—

(i) restrict, in the manner and to the extent the Trade Representative determines appropriate, the terms and conditions of any such authorization, or

(ii) deny the issuance of any such authorization.

(B) Actions described in subparagraph (A) may only be taken under this section with respect to service sector access authorizations granted, or applications therefor pending, on or after the date on which—

(i) a petition is filed under section 2412(a) of this title, or

(ii) a determination to initiate an investigation is made by the Trade Representative under section 2412(b) of this title.

(C) Before the Trade Representative takes any action under this section involving the imposition of fees or other restrictions on the services of a foreign country, the Trade Representative shall, if the services involved are subject to regulation by any agency of the Federal Government or of any State, consult, as appropriate, with the head of the agency concerned.

(3) The actions the Trade Representative is authorized to take under subsection (a) or (b) of this section may be taken against any goods or economic sector—

(A) on a nondiscriminatory basis or solely against the foreign country described in such subsection, and

(B) without regard to whether or not such goods or economic sector were involved in the act, policy, or practice that is the subject of such action.

(4) Any trade agreement described in paragraph (1)(D)(iii) shall provide compensatory trade benefits that benefit the economic sector which includes the domestic industry that would benefit from the elimination of the act, policy, or practice that is the subject of the action to be taken under subsection (a) or (b) of this section, or benefit the economic sector as closely related as possible to such economic sector, unless—

(A) the provision of such trade benefits is not feasible, or

(B) trade benefits that benefit any other economic sector would be more satisfactory than such trade benefits.

(5) If the Trade Representative determines that actions to be taken under subsection (a) or (b) of this section are to be in the form of import restrictions, the Trade Representative shall—

(A) give preference to the imposition of duties over the imposition of other import restrictions, and

(B) if an import restriction other than a duty is imposed, consider substituting, on an incremental basis, an equivalent duty for such other import restriction.

(6) Any action taken by the Trade Representative under this section with respect to export targeting shall, to the extent possible, reflect the full benefit level of the export targeting to the beneficiary over the period during which the action taken has an effect.

(d) Definitions and special rules

For purposes of this chapter—

(1) The term "commerce" includes, but is not limited to—

(A) services (including transfers of information) associated with international trade, whether or not such services are related to specific goods, and

(B) foreign direct investment by United States persons with implications for trade in goods or services.

(2) An act, policy, or practice of a foreign country that burdens or restricts United States commerce may include the provision, directly or indirectly, by that foreign country of subsidies for the construction of vessels used in the commercial transportation by water of goods between foreign countries and the United States.

(3)(A) An act, policy, or practice is unreasonable if the act, policy, or practice, while not necessarily in violation of, or inconsistent with, the international legal rights of the United States, is otherwise unfair and inequitable.

(B) Acts, policies, and practices that are unreasonable include, but are not limited to, any act, policy, or practice, or any combination of acts, policies, or practices, which—

(i) denies fair and equitable—

(I) opportunities for the establishment of an enterprise,

(II) provision of adequate and effective protection of intellectual property rights notwithstanding the fact that the foreign country may be in compliance with the specific obligations of the Agreement on Trade-Related Aspects of Intellectual Property Rights referred to in section 3511(d)(15) of this title,

(III) nondiscriminatory market access opportunities for United States persons that rely upon intellectual property protection, or

(IV) market opportunities, including the toleration by a foreign government of systematic anticompetitive activities by enterprises or among enterprises in the foreign country that have the effect of restricting, on a basis that is inconsistent with commercial considerations, access of United States goods or services to a foreign market,

(ii) constitutes export targeting, or

(iii) constitutes a persistent pattern of conduct that—

(I) denies workers the right of association,

(II) denies workers the right to organize and bargain collectively,

(III) permits any form of forced or compulsory labor,

(IV) fails to provide a minimum age for the employment of children, or

(V) fails to provide standards for minimum wages, hours of work, and occupational safety and health of workers.

(C)(i) Acts, policies, and practices of a foreign country described in subparagraph (B)(iii) shall not be treated as being unreasonable if the Trade Representative determines that—

(I) the foreign country has taken, or is taking, actions that demonstrate a significant and tangible overall advancement in providing throughout the foreign country (including any designated zone within the foreign country) the rights and other standards described in the subclauses of subparagraph (B)(iii), or

(II) such acts, policies, and practices are not inconsistent with the level of economic development of the foreign country.

(ii) The Trade Representative shall publish in the Federal Register any determination made under clause (i), together with a description of the facts on which such determination is based.

(D) For purposes of determining whether any act, policy, or practice is unreasonable, reciprocal opportunities in the United States for foreign nationals and firms shall be taken into account, to the extent appropriate.

(E) The term "export targeting" means any government plan or scheme consisting of a combination of coordinated actions (whether carried out severally or jointly) that are bestowed on a specific enterprise, industry, or group thereof, the effect of which is to assist the enterprise, industry, or group to become more competitive in the export of a class or kind of merchandise.

(F)(i) For the purposes of subparagraph (B)(i)(II), adequate and effective protection of intellectual property rights includes adequate and effective means under the laws of the foreign country for persons who are not citizens or nationals of such country to secure, exercise, and enforce rights and enjoy commercial benefits relating to patents, trademarks, copyrights and related rights, mask works, trade secrets, and plant breeder's rights.

(ii) For purposes of subparagraph (B)(i)(IV), the denial of fair and equitable nondiscriminatory market access opportunities includes restrictions on market access related to the use, exploitation, or enjoyment of commercial benefits derived from exercising intellectual property rights in protected works or fixations or products embodying protected works.

(4)(A) An act, policy, or practice is unjustifiable if the act, policy, or practice is in violation of, or inconsistent with, the international legal rights of the United States.

(B) Acts, policies, and practices that are unjustifiable include, but are not limited to, any act, policy, or practice described in subparagraph (A) which denies national or most-favored-nation treatment or the right of establishment or protection of intellectual property rights.

(5) Acts, policies, and practices that are discriminatory include, when appropriate, any act, policy, and practice which denies national or most-favored-nation treatment to United States goods, services, or investment.

(6) The term "service sector access authorization" means any license, permit, order, or other authorization, issued under the authority of Federal law, that permits a foreign supplier of services access to the United States market in a service sector concerned.

(7) The term "foreign country" includes any foreign instrumentality. Any possession or territory of a foreign country that is administered separately for customs purposes shall be treated as a separate foreign country.

(8) The term "Trade Representative" means the United States Trade Representative.

(9) The term "interested persons," only for purposes of sections 2412(a)(4)(B), 2414(b)(1)(A), 2416(c)(2), and 2417(a)(2) of this title, includes, but is not limited to, domestic firms and workers, representatives of consumer interests, United States product exporters, and any industrial user of any goods or services that may be affected by actions taken under subsection (a) or (b) of this section.

§2412. Initiation of investigations

(a) Petitions

(1) Any interested person may file a petition with the Trade Representative requesting that action be taken under section 2411 of this title and setting forth the allegations in support of the request.

(2) The Trade Representative shall review the allegations in any petition filed under paragraph (1) and, not later than 45 days after the date on which the Trade Representative received the petition, shall determine whether to initiate an investigation.

(3) If the Trade Representative determines not to initiate an investigation with respect to a petition, the Trade Representative shall inform the petitioner of the reasons therefor and shall publish notice of the determination, together with a summary of such reasons, in the Federal Register.

(4) If the Trade Representative makes an affirmative determination under paragraph (2) with respect to a petition, the Trade Representative shall initiate an investigation regarding the issues raised in the petition. The Trade Representative shall publish a summary of the petition in the Federal Register and shall, as soon as possible, provide opportunity for the presentation of views concerning the issues, including a public hearing—

(A) within the 30-day period beginning on the date of the affirmative determination (or on a date after such period if agreed to by the petitioner) if a public hearing within such period is requested in the petition, or

(B) at such other time if a timely request therefor is made by the petitioner or by any interested person.

(b) Initiation of investigation by means other than petition

(1)(A) If the Trade Representative determines that an investigation should be initiated under this subchapter with respect to any matter in order to determine whether the matter is actionable under section 2411 of this title, the Trade Representative shall publish such determination in the Federal Register and shall initiate such investigation.

(B) The Trade Representative shall, before making any determination under subparagraph (A), consult with appropriate committees established pursuant to section 2155 of this title.

(2)(A) By no later than the date that is 30 days after the date on which a country is identified under section 2242(a)(2) of this title, the Trade Representative shall initiate an investigation under this subchapter with respect to any act, policy, or practice of that country that—

(i) was the basis for such identification, and

(ii) is not at that time the subject of any other investigation or action under this subchapter.

(B) The Trade Representative is not required under subparagraph (A) to initiate an investigation under this subchapter with respect to any act, policy, or practice of a foreign country if the Trade Representative determines that the initiation of the investigation would be detrimental to United States economic interests.

(C) If the Trade Representative makes a determination under subparagraph (B) not to initiate an investigation, the Trade Representative shall submit to the Congress a written report setting forth, in detail—

(i) the reasons for the determination, and

(ii) the United States economic interests that would be adversely affected by the investigation.

(D) The Trade Representative shall, from time to time, consult with the Register of Copyrights, the Under Secretary of Commerce for Intellectual Property and Director of the United States Patent and Trademark Office, and other appropriate officers of the Federal Government, during any investigation initiated under this subchapter by reason of subparagraph (A).

(c) Discretion

In determining whether to initiate an investigation under subsection (a) or (b) of this section of any act, policy, or practice that is enumerated in any provision of section 2411(d) of this title, the Trade Representative shall have discretion to determine whether action under section 2411 of this title would be effective in addressing such act, policy, or practice.

§2413. Consultation upon initiation of investigation

(a) In general

(1) On the date on which an investigation is initiated under section 2412 of this title, the Trade Representative, on behalf of the United States, shall request consultations with the foreign country concerned regarding the issues involved in such investigation.

(2) If the investigation initiated under section 2412 of this title involves a trade agreement and a mutually acceptable resolution is not reached before the earlier of—

(A) the close of the consultation period, if any, specified in the trade agreement, or

(B) the 150th day after the day on which consultation was commenced,

the Trade Representative shall promptly request proceedings on the matter under the formal dispute settlement procedures provided under such agreement.

(3) The Trade Representative shall seek information and advice from the petitioner (if any) and the appropriate committees established pursuant to section 2155 of this title in preparing United States presentations for consultations and dispute settlement proceedings.

(b) Delay of request for consultations

(1) Notwithstanding the provisions of subsection (a) of this section—

(A) the United States Trade Representative may, after consulting with the petitioner (if any), delay for up to 90 days any request for consultations under subsection (a) of this section for the purpose of verifying or improving the petition to ensure an adequate basis for consultation, and

(B) if such consultations are delayed by reason of subparagraph (A), each time limitation under section 2414 of this title shall be extended for the period of such delay.

(2) The Trade Representative shall—

(A) publish notice of any delay under paragraph (1) in the Federal Register, and

(B) report to Congress on the reasons for such delay in the report required under section 2419(a)(3) of this title.

§2414. Determinations by Trade Representative

(a) In general

(1) On the basis of the investigation initiated under section 2412 of this title and the consultations (and the proceedings, if applicable) under section 2413 of this title, the Trade Representative shall—

(A) determine whether—

(i) the rights to which the United States is entitled under any trade agreement are being denied, or

(ii) any act, policy, or practice described in subsection (a)(1)(B) or (b)(1) of section 2411 of this title exists, and

(B) if the determination made under subparagraph (A) is affirmative, determine what action, if any, the Trade Representative should take under subsection (a) or (b) of section 2411 of this title.

(2) The Trade Representative shall make the determinations required under paragraph (1) on or before—

(A) in the case of an investigation involving a trade agreement, except an investigation initiated pursuant to section 2412(b)(2)(A) of this title involving rights under the Agreement on Trade-Related Aspects of Intellectual Property Rights (referred to in section 3511(d)(15) of this title) or the GATT 1994 (as defined in section 3501(1)(B) of this title) relating to products subject to intellectual property protection, the earlier of—

(i) the date that is 30 days after the date on which the dispute settlement procedure is concluded, or

(ii) the date that is 18 months after the date on which the investigation is initiated, or

(B) in all cases not described in subparagraph (A) or paragraph (3), the date that is 12 months after the date on which the investigation is initiated.

(3)(A) If an investigation is initiated under this subchapter by reason of section 2412(b)(2) of this title and—

(i) the Trade Representative considers that rights under the Agreement on Trade-Related Aspects of Intellectual Property Rights or the GATT 1994 relating to products subject to intellectual property protection are involved, the Trade Representative shall make the determination required under paragraph (1) not later than 30 days after the date on which the dispute settlement procedure is concluded; or

(ii) the Trade Representative does not consider that a trade agreement, including the Agreement on Trade-Related Aspects of Intellectual Property Rights, is involved or does not make a determination described in subparagraph (B) with respect to such investigation, the Trade Representative shall make the determinations required under paragraph (1) with respect to such investigation not later than the date that is 6 months after the date on which such investigation is initiated.

(B) If the Trade Representative determines with respect to an investigation initiated by reason of section 2412(b)(2) of this title (other than an investigation involving a trade agreement) that—

(i) complex or complicated issues are involved in the investigation that require additional time,

(ii) the foreign country involved in the investigation is making substantial progress in drafting or implementing legislative or administrative measures that will provide adequate and effective protection of intellectual property rights, or

(iii) such foreign country is undertaking enforcement measures to provide adequate and effective protection of intellectual property rights,

the Trade Representative shall publish in the Federal Register notice of such determination and shall make the determinations required under paragraph (1) with respect to such investigation by no later than the date that is 9 months after the date on which such investigation is initiated.

(4) In any case in which a dispute is not resolved before the close of the minimum dispute settlement period provided for in a trade agreement, the Trade Representative, within 15 days after the close of such dispute settlement period, shall submit a report to Congress setting forth the reasons why the dispute was not resolved within the minimum dispute settlement period, the status of the case at the close of the period, and the prospects for resolution. For purposes of this paragraph, the minimum dispute settlement period provided for under any such trade agreement is the total period of time that results if all stages of the formal dispute settlement procedures are carried out within the time limitations specified in the agreement, but computed without regard to any extension authorized under the agreement at any stage.

(b) Consultation before determinations

(1) Before making the determinations required under subsection (a)(1) of this section, the Trade Representative, unless expeditious action is required—

(A) shall provide an opportunity (after giving not less than 30 days notice thereof) for the presentation of views by interested persons, including a public hearing if requested by any interested person,

(B) shall obtain advice from the appropriate committees established pursuant to section 2155 of this title, and

(C) may request the views of the United States International Trade Commission regarding the probable impact on the economy of the United States of the taking of action with respect to any goods or service.

(2) If the Trade Representative does not comply with the requirements of subparagraphs (A) and (B) of paragraph (1) because expeditious action is required, the Trade Representative shall, after making the determinations under subsection (a)(1) of this section, comply with such subparagraphs.

(c) Publication

The Trade Representative shall publish in the Federal Register any determination made under subsection (a)(1) of this section, together with a description of the facts on which such determination is based.

§2415. Implementation of actions

(a) Actions to be taken under section 2411

(1) Except as provided in paragraph (2), the Trade Representative shall implement the action the Trade Representative determines under section 2414(a)(1)(B) of this title to take under section 2411 of this title, subject to the specific direction, if any, of the President regarding any such action, by no later than the date that is 30 days after the date on which such determination is made.

(2)(A) Except as otherwise provided in this paragraph, the Trade Representative may delay, by not more than 180 days, the implementation of any action that is to be taken under section 2411 of this title—

(i) if—

(I) in the case of an investigation initiated under section 2412(a) of this title, the petitioner requests a delay, or

(II) in the case of an investigation initiated under section 2412(b)(1) of this title or to which section 2414(a)(3)(B) of this title applies, a delay is requested by a majority of the representatives of the domestic industry that would benefit from the action, or

(ii) if the Trade Representative determines that substantial progress is being made, or that a delay is necessary or desirable, to obtain United States rights or a satisfactory solution with respect to the acts, policies, or practices that are the subject of the action.

(B) The Trade Representative may not delay under subparagraph (A) the implementation of any action that is to be taken under section 2411 of this title with respect to any investigation to which section 2414(a)(3)(A)(ii) of this title applies.

(C) The Trade Representative may not delay under subparagraph (A) the implementation of any action that is to be taken under section 2411 of this title with respect to any investigation to which section 2414(a)(3)(B) of this title applies by more than 90 days.

(b) Alternative actions in certain cases of export targeting

(1) If the Trade Representative makes an affirmative determination under section 2414(a)(1)(A) of this title involving export targeting by a foreign country and determines to take no action under section 2411 of this title with respect to such affirmation determination, the Trade Representative—

(A) shall establish an advisory panel to recommend measures which will promote the competitiveness of the domestic industry affected by the export targeting,

(B) on the basis of the report of such panel submitted under paragraph (2)(B) and subject to the specific direction, if any, of the President, may take any administrative actions authorized under any other provision of law, and, if necessary, propose legislation to implement any other actions, that would restore or improve the international competitiveness of the domestic industry affected by the export targeting, and

(C) shall, by no later than the date that is 30 days after the date on which the report of such panel is submitted under paragraph (2)(B), submit a report to the Congress on the administrative actions taken, and legislative proposals made, under subparagraph (B) with respect to the domestic industry affected by the export targeting.

(2)(A) The advisory panels established under paragraph (1)(A) shall consist of individuals appointed by the Trade Representative who—

(i) earn their livelihood in the private sector of the economy, including individuals who represent management and labor in the domestic industry affected by the export targeting that is the subject of the affirmative determination made under section 2414(a)(1)(A) of this title, and

(ii) by education or experience, are qualified to serve on the advisory panel.

(B) By no later than the date that is 6 months after the date on which an advisory panel is established under paragraph (1)(A), the advisory panel shall submit to the Trade Representative and to the Congress a report on measures that the advisory panel recommends be taken by the United States to promote the competitiveness of the domestic industry affected by the export targeting that is the subject of the affirmative determination made under section 2414(a)(1)(A) of this title.

§2416. Monitoring of foreign compliance

(a) In general

The Trade Representative shall monitor the implementation of each measure undertaken, or agreement that is entered into, by a foreign country to provide a satisfactory resolution of a matter subject to investigation under this subchapter or subject to dispute settlement proceedings to enforce the rights of the United States under a trade agreement providing for such proceedings.

(b) Further action

(1) In general

If, on the basis of the monitoring carried out under subsection (a) of this section, the Trade Representative considers that a foreign country is not satisfactorily implementing a measure or agreement referred to in subsection (a) of this section, the Trade Representative shall determine what further action the Trade Representative shall take under section 2411(a) of this title. For purposes of section 2411 of this title, any such determination shall be treated as a determination made under section 2414(a)(1) of this title.

(2) WTO dispute settlement recommendations

(A) Failure to implement recommendation

If the measure or agreement referred to in subsection (a) of this section concerns the implementation of a recommendation made pursuant to dispute settlement proceedings under the World Trade Organization, and the Trade Representative considers that the foreign country has failed to implement it, the Trade Representative shall make the determination in paragraph (1) no later than 30 days after the expiration of the reasonable period of time provided for such implementation under paragraph 21 of the Understanding on Rules and Procedures Governing the Settlement of Disputes that is referred to in section 3511(d)(16) of this title.

(B) Revision of retaliation list and action

(i) In general

Except as provided in clause (ii), in the event that the United States initiates a retaliation list or takes any other action described in section 2411(c)(1)(A) or (B) of this title against the goods of a foreign country or countries because of the failure of such country or countries to implement the recommendation made pursuant to a dispute settlement proceeding under the World Trade Organization, the Trade Representative shall periodically revise the list or action to affect other goods of the country or countries that have failed to implement the recommendation.

(ii) Exception

The Trade Representative is not required to revise the retaliation list or the action described in clause (i) with respect to a country, if—

(I) the Trade Representative determines that implementation of a recommendation made pursuant to a dispute settlement proceeding described in clause (i) by the country is imminent; or

(II) the Trade Representative together with the petitioner involved in the initial investigation under this subchapter (or if no petition was filed, the affected United States industry) agree that it is unnecessary to revise the retaliation list.

(C) Schedule for revising list or action

The Trade Representative shall, 120 days after the date the retaliation list or other section 2411(a) action is first taken, and every 180 days thereafter, review the list or action taken and revise, in whole or in part, the list or action to affect other goods of the subject country or countries.

(D) Standards for revising list or action

In revising any list or action against a country or countries under this subsection, the Trade Representative shall act in a manner that is most likely to result in the country or countries implementing the recommendations adopted in the dispute settlement proceeding or in achieving a mutually satisfactory solution to the issue that gave rise to the dispute settlement proceeding. The Trade Representative shall consult with the petitioner, if any, involved in the initial investigation under this subchapter.

(E) Retaliation list

The term "retaliation list" means the list of products of a foreign country or countries that have failed to comply with the report of the panel or Appellate Body of the WTO and with respect to which the Trade Representative is imposing duties above the level that would otherwise be imposed under the Harmonized Tariff Schedule of the United States.

(F) Requirement to include reciprocal goods on retaliation list

The Trade Representative shall include on the retaliation list, and on any revised lists, reciprocal goods of the industries affected by the failure of the foreign country or countries to implement the recommendation made pursuant to a dispute settlement proceeding under the World Trade Organization, except in cases where existing retaliation and its corresponding preliminary retaliation list do not already meet this requirement.

(c) Consultations

Before making any determination under subsection (b) of this section, the Trade Representative shall—

(1) consult with the petitioner, if any, involved in the initial investigation under this subchapter and with representatives of the domestic industry concerned; and

(2) provide an opportunity for the presentation of views by interested persons.

§2417. Modification and termination of actions

(a) In general

(1) The Trade Representative may modify or terminate any action, subject to the specific direction, if any, of the President with respect to such action, that is being taken under section 2411 of this title if—

(A) any of the conditions described in section 2411(a)(2) of this title exist,

(B) the burden or restriction on United States commerce of the denial rights, or of the acts, policies, and practices, that are the subject of such action has increased or decreased, or

(C) such action is being taken under section 2411(b) of this title and is no longer appropriate.

(2) Before taking any action under paragraph (1) to modify or terminate any action taken under section 2411 of this title, the Trade Representative shall consult with the petitioner, if any, and with representatives of the domestic industry concerned, and shall provide opportunity for the presentation of views by other interested persons affected by the proposed modification or termination concerning the effects of the modification or termination and whether any modification or termination of the action is appropriate.

(b) Notice; report to Congress

The Trade Representative shall promptly publish in the Federal Register notice of, and report in writing to the Congress with respect to, any modification or termination of any action taken under section 2411 of this title and the reasons therefor.

(c) Review of necessity

(1) If—

(A) a particular action has been taken under section 2411 of this title during any 4-year period, and

(B) neither the petitioner nor any representative of the domestic industry which benefits from such action has submitted to the Trade Representative during the last 60 days of such 4-year period a written request for the continuation of such action,

such action shall terminate at the close of such 4-year period.

(2) The Trade Representative shall notify by mail the petitioner and representatives of the domestic industry described in paragraph (1)(B) of any termination of action by reason of paragraph (1) at least 60 days before the date of such termination.

(3) If a request is submitted to the Trade Representative under paragraph (1)(B) to continue taking a particular action under section 2411 of this title, the Trade Representative shall conduct a review of—

(A) the effectiveness in achieving the objectives of section 2411 of this title of—

(i) such action, and

(ii) other actions that could be taken (including actions against other products or services), and

(B) the effects of such actions on the United States economy, including consumers.

§2418. Request for information

(a) In general

Upon receipt of written request therefor from any person, the Trade Representative shall make available to that person information (other than that to which confidentiality applies) concerning—

(1) the nature and extent of a specific trade policy or practice of a foreign country with respect to particular goods, services, investment, or intellectual property rights, to the extent that such information is available to the Trade Representative or other Federal agencies;

(2) United States rights under any trade agreement and the remedies which may be available under that agreement and under the laws of the United States; and

(3) past and present domestic and international proceedings or actions with respect to the policy or practice concerned.

(b) If information not available

If information that is requested by a person under subsection (a) of this section is not available to the Trade Representative or other Federal agencies, the Trade Representative shall, within 30 days after receipt of the request—

(1) request the information from the foreign government; or

(2) decline to request the information and inform the person in writing of the reasons for refusal.

(c) Certain business information not made available

(1) Except as provided in paragraph (2), and notwithstanding any other provision of law (including section 552 of Title 5), no information requested and received by the Trade Representative in aid of any investigation under this subchapter shall be made available to any person if—

(A) the person providing such information certifies that—

(i) such information is business confidential,

(ii) the disclosure of such information would endanger trade secrets or profitability, and

(iii) such information is not generally available;

(B) the Trade Representative determines that such certification is well-founded; and

(C) to the extent required in regulations prescribed by the Trade Representative, the person providing such information provides an adequate nonconfidential summary of such information.

(2) The Trade Representative may—

(A) use such information, or make such information available (in his own discretion) to any employee of the Federal Government for use, in any investigation under this subchapter, or

(B) may make such information available to any other person in a form which cannot be associated with, or otherwise identify, the person providing the information.

§2419. Administration

The Trade Representative shall—

(1) issue regulations concerning the filing of petitions and the conduct of investigations and hearings under this subchapter,

(2) keep the petitioner regularly informed of all determinations and developments regarding the investigation conducted with respect to the petition under this subchapter, including the reasons for any undue delays, and

(3) submit a report to the House of Representatives and the Senate semiannually describing—

(A) the petitions filed and the determinations made (and reasons therefor) under section 2412 of this title,

(B) developments in, and the current status of, each investigation or proceeding under this subchapter,

(C) the actions taken, or the reasons for no action, by the Trade Representative under section 2411 of this title with respect to investigations conducted under this subchapter, and

(D) the commercial effects of actions taken under section 2411 of this title.

§2420. Identification of trade expansion priorities

(a) Identification

(1) Within 180 days after the submission in calendar year 1995 of the report required by section 2241(b) of this title, the Trade Representative shall—

(A) review United States trade expansion priorities,

(B) identify priority foreign country practices, the elimination of which is likely to have the most significant potential to increase United States exports, either directly or through the establishment of a beneficial precedent, and

(C) submit to the Committee on Finance of the Senate and the Committee on Ways and Means of the House of Representatives and publish in the Federal Register a report on the priority foreign country practices identified.

(2) In identifying priority foreign country practices under paragraph (1) of this section, the Trade Representative shall take into account all relevant factors, including—

(A) the major barriers and trade distorting practices described in the National Trade Estimate Report required under section 2241(b) of this title;

(B) the trade agreements to which a foreign country is a party and its compliance with those agreements;

(C) the medium- and long-term implications of foreign government procurement plans; and

(D) the international competitive position and export potential of United States products and services.

(3) The Trade Representative may include in the report, if appropriate—

(A) a description of foreign country practices that may in the future warrant identification as priority foreign country practices; and

(B) a statement about other foreign country practices that were not identified because they are already being addressed by provisions of United States trade law, by existing bilateral trade agreements, or as part of trade negotiations with other countries and progress is being made toward the elimination of such practices.

(b) Initiation of investigations

By no later than the date which is 21 days after the date on which a report is submitted to the appropriate congressional committees under subsection (a)(1) of this section, the Trade Representative shall initiate under section 2412(b)(1) of this title investigations under this subchapter with respect to all of the priority foreign country practices identified.

(c) Agreements for elimination of barriers

In the consultations with a foreign country that the Trade Representative is required to request under section 2413(a) of this title with respect to an investigation initiated by reason of subsection (b) of this section, the Trade Representative shall seek to negotiate an agreement that provides for the elimination of the practices that are the subject of the investigation as quickly as possible or, if elimination of the practices is not feasible, an agreement that provides for compensatory trade benefits.

(d) Reports

The Trade Representative shall include in the semiannual report required by section 2419 of this title a report on the status of any investigations initiated pursuant to subsection (b) of this section and, where appropriate, the extent to which such investigations have led to increased opportunities for the export of products and services of the United States.

Document 11

EC TRADE BARRIERS REGULATION*

Official name: COUNCIL REGULATION (EC) No 3286/94 of 22 December 1994 laying down Community procedures in the field of the common commercial policy in order to ensure the exercise of the Community's rights under international trade rules, in particular those established under the auspices of the World Trade Organization

THE COUNCIL OF THE EUROPEAN UNION,

Having regard to the Treaty establishing the European Community, and in particular Article 113 thereof,

Having regard to the rules establishing the common organization of agricultural markets and the rules adopted pursuant to Article 235 of the Treaty, applicable to goods processed from agricultural products, and in particular those provisions thereof, which allow for derogation from the general principle that any quantitative restriction or measure having equivalent effect may be replaced solely by the measures provided for in those instruments,

Having regard to the proposal from the Commission,

Having regard to the opinion of the European Parliament,

Whereas the common commercial policy must be based on uniform principles, in particular with regard to commercial defence

*As ammended, current through 5 March 2008. Originally printed at OJ 1994, L349/71.

Whereas Council Regulation (EEC) No 2641/84 of 17 September 1984 on the strengthening of the common commercial policy with regard in particular to protection against illicit commercial practices provided the Community with procedures enabling it:

— to respond to any illicit commercial practice with a view to removing the injury resulting therefrom, and

— to ensure full exercise of the Community's rights with regard to the commercial practices of third countries

Whereas experience in the application of Regulation (EEC) No 2641/84 has shown that the need to deal with obstacles to trade adopted or maintained by third countries remains, and whereas the approach followed in Regulation (EEC) No 2641/84 has not proved to be entirely effective

Whereas it appears necessary, therefore, to establish new and improved Community procedures to ensure the effective exercise of the rights of the Community under international trade rules

Whereas international trade rules are primarily those established under the auspices of the WTO and laid down in the Annexes to the WTO Agreement, but they can also be those laid down in any other agreement to which the Community is a party and which sets out rules applicable to trade between the Community and third countries, and whereas it is appropriate to give a clear idea of the types of agreements to which the term 'international trade rules. Refers

Whereas the abovementioned Community procedures should be based on a legal mechanism under Community law which would be fully transparent, and would ensure that the decision to invoke the Community's rights under international trade rules is taken on the basis of accurate factual information and legal analysis

Whereas this mechanism aims to provide procedural means to request that the Community institutions react to obstacles to trade adopted or maintained by third countries which cause injury or otherwise adverse trade effects, provided that a right of action exists, in respect of such obstacles, under applicable international trade rules

Whereas the right of Member States to resort to this mechanism should be without prejudice to their possibility to raise the same or similar matters through other existing Community procedures, and in particular before the committee established by Article 113 of the Treaty

Whereas regard should be paid to the institutional role of the committee established by Article 113 of the Treaty in formulating advice for the institutions of the Community on all issues of commercial policy whereas, therefore, this committee should be kept informed of the development of individual cases, in order to enable it to consider their broader policy implications

Whereas, moreover, to the extent that an agreement with a third country appears to be the most appropriate means to resolve a dispute arising from an obstacle to trade, negotiations to this end shall be conducted according to the procedures established in Article 113 of the Treaty, in particular in consultation with the committee established thereby

Whereas it is appropriate to confirm that the Community must act in compliance with its international obligations and, where such obligations result from agreements, maintain the balance of rights and obligations which it is the purpose of those agreements to establish

Whereas it is also appropriate to confirm that any measures taken under the procedures in question should also be in conformity with the Community's international obligations, as well as being without prejudice to other measures in cases not covered by this Regulation which might be adopted directly pursuant to Article 113 of the Treaty

Whereas the rules of procedures to be followed during the examination procedure provided for in this Regulation should also be confirmed, in particular as regards the rights and obligations of the Community authorities and the parties involved, and the conditions under which interested parties may have access to information and may ask to be informed of the essential facts and considerations resulting from the examination procedure

Whereas in acting pursuant to this Regulation the Community has to bear in mind the need for rapid and effective action, through the application of the decision-making procedures provided for in the Regulation

Whereas it is incumbent on the Commission and the Council to act in respect of obstacles to trade adopted or maintained by third countries, within the framework of the Community's international rights and obligations, only when the interests of the Community call for intervention, and whereas, when assessing such interests, the Commission and the Council should give due consideration to the views by all interested parties in the proceedings

HAS ADOPTED THIS REGULATION:

Article 1

Aims

This Regulation establishes Community procedures in the field of the common commercial policy in order to ensure the exercise of the Community's rights under international trade rules, in particular those established under the auspices of the World Trade Organization which, subject to compliance with existing international obligations and procedures, are aimed at:

(a) responding to obstacles to trade that have an effect on the market of the Community, with a view to removing the injury resulting therefrom

(b) responding to obstacles to trade that have an effect on the market of a third country, with a view to removing the adverse trade effects resulting therefrom.

These procedures shall be applied in particular to the initiation and subsequent conduct and termination of international dispute settlement procedures in the area of common commercial policy.

Article 2

Definitions

1. For the purposes of this Regulation, "obstacles to trade" shall be any trade practice adopted or maintained by a third country in respect of which international trade rules establish a right of action. Such a right of action exists when international trade rules either prohibit a practice outright, or give another party affected by the practice a right to seek elimination of the effect of the practice in question.

2. For the purposes of this Regulation and subject to paragraph 8, "the Community's rights" shall be those international trade rights of which it may avail itself under international trade rules. In this context, 'international trade rules. are primarily those established under the auspices of the WTO and laid down in the Annexes to the WTO Agreement, but they can also be those laid down in any other agreement to which the Community is a party and which sets out rules applicable to trade between the Community and third countries.

3. For the purposes of this Regulation, "injury" shall be any material injury which an obstacle to trade causes or threatens to cause, in respect of a product or service, to a Community industry on the market of the Community.

4. For the purposes of this Regulation, "adverse trade effects" shall be those which an obstacle to trade causes or threatens to cause, in respect of a product or service, to Community enterprises on the market of any third

country, and which have a material impact on the economy of the Community or of a region of the Community, or on a sector of economic activity therein. The fact that the complainant suffers from such adverse effects shall not be considered sufficient to justify, on its own, that the Community institutions proceed with any action.

5. The term "Community industry" shall be taken to mean all Community producers or providers, respectively:

— of products or services identical or similar to the product or service which is the subject of an obstacle to trade, or

— of products or services competing directly with that product or service, or

— who are consumers or processors of the product or consumers or users of the service which is the subject of an obstacle to trade,

or all those producers or providers whose combined output constitutes a major proportion of total Community production of the products or services in question however:

(a) when producers or providers are related to the exporters or importers or are themselves importers of the product or service alleged to be the subject of obstacles to trade, the term "Community industry" may be interpreted as referring to the rest of the producers or providers

(b) in particular circumstances, the producers or providers within a region of the Community may be regarded as the Community industry if their collective output constitutes the major proportion of the output of the product or service in question in the Member State or Member States within which the region is located provided that the effect of the obstacle to trade is concentrated in that Member State or those Member States.

6. The term "Community enterprise" shall be taken to mean a company or firm formed in accordance with the law of a Member State and having its registered office, central administration or principal place of business within the Community, directly concerned by the production of goods or the provision of services which are the subject of the obstacle to trade.

7. For the purposes of this Regulation, the notion of 'providers of services. in the context of both the term "Community industry" as defined in paragraph 5, and the term "Community enterprises" as defined in paragraph 6, is without prejudice to the non-commercial nature which the provision of any particular service may have according to the legislation or regulation of a Member State.

8. For the purposes of this Regulation, the term "services" shall be taken to mean those services in respect of which international agreements can be concluded by the Community on the basis of Article 113 of the Treaty.

Article 3

Complaint on behalf of the Community industry

1. Any natural or legal person, or any association not having legal personality, acting on behalf of a Community industry which considers that it has suffered injury as a result of obstacles to trade that have an effect on the market of the Community may lodge a written complaint.

2. The complaint must contain sufficient evidence of the existence of the obstacles to trade and of the injury resulting therefrom. Evidence of injury must be given on the basis of the illustrative list of factors indicated in Article 10, where applicable.

Article 4

Complaint on behalf of Community enterprises

1. Any Community enterprise, or any association, having or not legal personality, acting on behalf of one or more Community enterprises, which considers that such Community enterprises have suffered adverse trade effects as a result of obstacles to trade that have an effect on the market of a third country may lodge a written complaint. Such complaint, however, shall only be admissible if the obstacle to trade alleged therein is the subject of a right of action established under international trade rules laid down in a multilateral or plurilateral trade agreement.

2. The complaint must contain sufficient evidence of the existence of the obstacles to trade and of the adverse trade effects, resulting therefrom. Evidence of adverse trade effects must be given on the basis of the illustrative list of factors indicated in Article 10, where applicable.

Article 5

Complaint procedures

1. The complaint shall be submitted to the Commission, which shall send a copy thereof to the Member States.

2. The complaint may be withdrawn, in which case the procedure may be terminated unless such termination would not be in the interests of the Community.

3. Where it becomes apparent after consultation that the complaint does not provide sufficient evidence to justify initiating an investigation, then the complainant shall be so informed.

4. The Commission shall take a decision as soon as possible on the opening of a Community examination procedure following any complaint made in accordance with Articles 3 or 4 the decision shall normally be taken within 45 days of the lodging of the complaint this period may be suspended at the request, or with the agreement, of the complainant, in order to allow the provision of complementary information which may be needed to fully assess the validity of the complainant's case.

Article 6

Referral by a Member State

1. Any Member State may ask the Commission to initiate the procedures referred to in Article 1.

2. It shall supply the Commission with sufficient evidence to support its request, as regards obstacles to trade and of any effects resulting therefrom. Where evidence of injury or of adverse trade effects is appropriate, is must be given on the basis of the illustrative list of factors indicated in Article 10, where applicable.

3. The Commission shall notify the other Member States of the requests without delay.

4. Where it becomes apparent after consultation that the request does not provide sufficient evidence to justify initiating an investigation, then the Member State shall be so informed.

5. The Commission shall take a decision as soon as possible on the opening of a Community examination procedure following any referral by a Member State made in accordance with Article 6 the decision shall normally be taken with 45 days of the referral this period may be suspended at the request, or with the agreement, of the referring Member State, in order to allow the provision of complementary information which may be needed to fully assess the validity of the case presented by the referring Member State.

Article 7

Consultation procedure

1. For the purpose of consultations pursuant to this Regulation, an Advisory Committee, hereinafter referred to as "the Committee," is hereby

set up and shall consist of representatives of each Member State, with a representative of the Commission as chairman.

2. Consultations shall be held immediately at the request of a Member State or on the initiative of the Commission, and in any event within a time frame which allows the time limits set by this Regulation to be respected. The chairman of the Committee shall provide the Member States, as promptly as possible, with all relevant information in his possession. The Commission shall also refer such information to the committee established by Article 113 of the Treaty so that it can consider any wider implications for the common commercial policy.

3. The Committee shall meet when convened by its chairman.

4. Where necessary, consultations may be in writing. In such case the Commission shall notify in writing the Member States who, within a period of eight working days from such notification, shall be entitled to express their opinions in writing or to request oral consultations which the chairman shall arrange, provided that such oral consultations can be held within a time frame which allows the time limits set by this Regulation to be respected.

Article 8

Community examination procedure

1. Where, after consultation, it is apparent to the Commission that there is sufficient evidence to justify initiating an examination procedure and that it is necessary in the interest of the Community, the Commission shall act as follows:

(a) it shall announce the initiation of an examination procedure in the Official Journal of the European Communities such announcement shall indicate the product or service and countries concerned, give a summary of the information received, and provide that all relevant information is to be communicated to the Commission it shall state the period within which interested parties may apply to be heard orally by the Commission in accordance with paragraph 5

(b) it shall officially notify the representatives of the country or countries which are the subject of the procedure, with whom, where appropriate, consultations may be held

(c) it shall conduct the examination at Community level, acting in co-operation with the Member States.

2. (a) If necessary the Commission shall seek all the information it deems necessary and attempt to check this information with the importers,

traders, agents, producers, trade associations and organizations, provided that the undertakings or organizations concerned give their consent.

(b) Where necessary, the Commission shall carry out investigations in the territory of third countries, provided that the governments of the countries have been officially notified and raise no objection within a reasonable period.

(c) The Commission shall be assisted in its investigation by officials of the Member State in whose territory the checks are carried out, provided that the Member State in question so requests.

3. Member States shall supply the Commission, upon request, with all information necessary for the examination, in accordance with the detailed arrangements laid down by the Commission.

4. (a) The complainants and the exporters and importers concerned, as well as the representatives of the country or countries concerned, may inspect all information made available to the Commission except for internal documents for the use of the Commission and the administrations, provided that such information is relevant to the protection of their interests and not confidential within the meaning of Article 9 and that it is used by the Commission in its examination procedure. The persons concerned shall address a reasoned request in writing to the Commission, indicating the information required.

(b) The complainants and the exporters and importers concerned and the representatives of the country or countries concerned may ask to be informed of the principal facts and considerations resulting from the examination procedure.

5. The Commission may hear the parties concerned. It shall hear them if they have, within the period prescribed in the notice published in the Official Journal of the European Communities, made a written request for a hearing showing that they are a party primarily concerned by the result of the procedure.

6. Furthermore, the Commission shall, on request, give the parties primarily concerned an opportunity to meet, so that opposing views may be presented and any rebuttal argument put forward. In providing this opportunity the Commission shall take account of the wishes of the parties and of the need to preserve confidentiality. There shall be no obligation on any party to attend a meeting and failure to do so shall not be prejudicial to that party's case.

7. When the information requested by the Commission is not supplied within a reasonable time or where the investigation is significantly impeded, findings may be made on the basis of the facts available.

8. When it has concluded its examination the Commission shall report to the Committee. The report should normally be presented within five months of the announcement of initiation of the procedure, unless the complexity of the examination is such that the Commission extends the period to seven months.

Article 9

Confidentiality

1. Information received pursuant to this Regulation shall be used only for the purpose for which it was requested.

2. (a) Neither the Council, nor the Commission, nor Member States, nor the officials of any of these, shall reveal any information of a confidential nature received pursuant to this Regulation, or any information provided on a confidential basis by a party to an examination procedure, without specific permission from the party submitting such information.

(b) Each request for confidential treatment shall indicate why the information is confidential and shall be accompanied by a non-confidential summary of the information or a statement of the reasons why the information is not susceptible of such summary.

3. Information will normally be considered to be confidential if its disclosure is likely to have a significantly adverse effect upon the supplier or the source of such information.

4. However, if it appears that a request for confidentiality is not warranted and if the supplier is either unwilling to make the information public or to authorize its disclosure in generalized or summary form, the information in question may be disregarded.

5. This Article shall not preclude the disclosure of general information by the Community authorities and in particular of the reasons on which decisions taken pursuant to this Regulation are based. Such disclosure must take into account the legitimate interest of the parties concerned that their business secrets should not be divulged.

Article 10

Evidence

1. An examination of injury shall involve where applicable the following factors:

(a) the volume of Community imports or exports concerned, notably where there has been a significant increase or decrease, either in absolute terms or relative to production or consumption on the market in question

(b) the prices of the Community industry's competitors, in particular in order to determine whether there has been, either in the Community or on third country markets, significant undercutting of the prices of the Community industry

(c) the consequent impact on the Community industry and as indicated by trends in certain economic factors such as: production, utilization of capacity, stocks, sales, market share, prices (that is depression of prices or prevention of price increases which would normally have occurred), profits, return on capital, investment, employment.

2. Where a threat of injury is alleged, the Commission shall also examine whether it is clearly foreseeable that a particular situation is likely to develop into actual injury. In this regard, account may also be taken of factors such as:

(a) the rate of increase of exports to the market where the competition with Community products is taking place

(b) export capacity in the country of origin or export, which is already in existence or will be operational in the foreseeable future, and the likelihood that the exports resulting from that capacity will be to the market referred to in point (a).

3. Injury caused by other factors which, either individually or in combination, are also adversely affecting Community industry must not be attributed to the practices under consideration.

4. Where adverse trade effects are alleged, the Commission shall examine the impact of such adverse effects on the economy of the Community or of a region of the Community, or on a sector of economic activity therein. To this effect, the Commission may take into account, where relevant, factors of the type listed in paragraphs 1 and 2. Adverse trade effects may arise, inter alia, in situations in which trade flows concerning a product or service are prevented, impeded or diverted as a result of any obstacle to trade, or from situations in which obstacles to trade have materially affected the supply or inputs (e.g. parts and components or raw materials) to Community enterprises. Where a threat of adverse trade effects is alleged, the Commission shall also examine whether it is clearly foreseeable that a particular situation is likely to develop into actual adverse trade effects.

5. The Commission shall also, in examining evidence of adverse trade effects, have regard to the provisions, principles or practice which

govern the right of action under relevant international rules referred to in Article 2 (1).

6. The Commission shall further examine any other relevant evidence contained in the complaint or in the referral. In this respect, the list of factors and the indications given in paragraphs 1 to 5 are not exhaustive, nor can one or several of such factors and indications necessarily give decisive guidance as to the existence of injury or of adverse trade effects.

Article 11

Termination and suspension of the procedure

1. When it is found as a result of the examination procedure that the interests of the Community do not require any action to be taken, the procedure shall be terminated in accordance with Article 14.

2. (a) When, after an examination procedure, the third country or countries concerned take(s) measures which are considered satisfactory, and therefore no action by the Community is required, the procedure may be suspended in accordance with the provisions of Article 14.

(b) The Commission shall supervise the application of these measures, where appropriate on the basis of information supplied at intervals, which it may request from the third countries concerned and check as necessary.

(c) Where the measures taken by the third country or countries concerned have been rescinded, suspended or improperly implemented or where the Commission has grounds for believing this to be the case or, finally, where a request for information made by the Commission as provided for by point (b) has not been granted, the Commission shall inform the Member States, and where necessary and justified by the results of the investigation and the new facts available any measures shall be taken in accordance with Article 13 (3).

3. Where, either after an examination procedure, or at any time before, during and after an international dispute settlement procedure, it appears that the most appropriate means to resolve a dispute arising from an obstacle to trade is the conclusion of an agreement with the third country or countries concerned, which may change the substantive rights of the Community and of the third country or countries concerned, the procedure shall be suspended according to the provisions of Article 14, and negotiations shall be carried out according to the provisions of Article 113 of the Treaty.

Article 12

Adoption of commercial policy measures

1. Where it is found (as a result of the examination procedure, unless the factual and legal situation is such that an examination procedure may not be required) that action is necessary in the interests of the Community in order to ensure the exercise of the Community's rights under international trade rules, with a view to removing the injury or the adverse trade effects resulting from obstacles to trade adopted or maintained by third countries, the appropriate measures shall be determined in accordance with the procedure set out in Article 13.3

2. Where the Community's international obligations require the prior discharge of an international procedure for consultation or for the settlement of disputes, the measures referred to in paragraph 3 shall only be decided on after that procedure has been terminated, and taking account of the results of the procedure. In particular, where the Community has requested an international dispute settlement body to indicate and authorize the measures which are appropriate for the implementation of the results of an international dispute settlement procedure, the Community commercial policy measures which may be needed in consequence of such authorization shall be in accordance with the recommendation of such international dispute settlement body.

3. Any commercial policy measures may be taken which are compatible with existing international obligations and procedures, notably:

(a) suspension or withdrawal of any concession resulting from commercial policy negotiations

(b) the raising of existing customs duties or the introduction of any other charge on imports

(c) the introduction of quantitative restrictions or any other measures modifying import or export conditions or otherwise affecting trade with the third country concerned.

4. The corresponding decisions shall state the reasons on which they are based and shall be published in the Official Journal of the European Communities. Publication shall also be deemed to constitute notification to the countries and parties primarily concerned.

Article 13

Decision-making procedures

1. The decisions referred to in Article 11 (1) and (2) (a) shall be adopted in accordance with the provisions of Article 14.

2. Where the Community, as a result of a complaint pursuant to Articles 3 or 4, or of a referral pursuant to Article 6, follows formal international consultation or dispute settlement procedures, decisions relating to the initiation, conduct or termination of such procedures shall be taken in accordance with Article 14.

3. Where the Community, having acted in accordance with Article 12 (2), has to take a decision on the measures of commercial policy to be adopted pursuant to Article 11 (2) (c) or pursuant to Article 12 the Council shall act, in accordance with Article 113 of the Treaty, by a qualified majority, not later than 30 working days after receiving the proposal.

Article 14

Committee procedure

1. Should reference be made to the procedure provided for in this Article, the matter shall be brought before the Committee by its chairman.

2. The Commission representative shall submit to the Committee a draft of the decision to be taken. The Committee shall discuss the matter within a period to be fixed by the chairman, depending on the urgency of the matter.

3. The Commission shall adopt a decision which it shall communicate to the Member States and which shall apply after a period of 10 days if during this period no Member State has referred the matter to the Council.

4. The Council may, at the request of a Member State and acting by a qualified majority revise the Commission's decision.

5. The Commission's decision shall apply after a period of 30 days if the Council has not given a ruling within this period, calculated from the day on which the matter was referred to the Council.

Article 15

General provisions

1. This Regulation shall not apply in cases covered by other existing rules in the common commercial policy field. It shall operate by way of complement to:

— the rules establishing the common organization of agricultural markets and their implementing provisions, and

— the specific rules adopted pursuant to Article 235 of the Treaty, applicable to goods processed from agricultural products.

It shall be without prejudice to other measures which may be taken pursuant to Article 113 of the Treaty, as well as to Community procedures for dealing with matters concerning obstacles to trade raised by Member States in the committee established by Article 113 of the Treaty.

2. Regulation (EEC) No 2641/84 is hereby repealed. References to the repealed Regulation shall be construed as references to this Regulation.

Article 16

Entry into force

This Regulation shall enter into force on 1 January 1996. It shall apply to proceedings initiated after that date.

This Regulation shall be binding in its entirety and directly applicable in all Member States.

Done at Brussels, 22 December 1994.

Document 12

MODEL TBR COMPLAINT

1. TITLE

Complaint Pursuant to Article 4 of Council Regulation No. 3286/94 ("Trade Barriers Regulation") concerning obstacles to exports of TV sets to Wonderland

TBR Complaints may be brought by Community industries or by Community enterprises.
*Community enterprises, or their associations, may lodge a complaint under **Article 4** of the TBR. Article 4 complaints refer to cases where "adverse trade effects" are felt on a third country market.*
*Community industries may lodge a complaint under **Article 3** of the TBR. Industry complaints refer to cases where economic damage ("injury") takes place on the market of the Community. Such complaints are admissible if they are brought on behalf of EC producers or service providers whose combined output constitutes a major proportion of total Community production of the products or services in question.*

2. IDENTITY OF COMPLAINANT

The Complainant in this case is the European Association of TV set producers (EATV). The EATV registered office is located at 200, Rue de la Loi, 1040 Brussels (Belgium), Tel. +32-255555, Fax. +32-2-66666, E-mail: contact@EATV.org.

The EATV was established in 1987 as the representative association of European manufacturers of TV sets. Its 43 member companies are manufacturers and assemblers of TV sets established in the 25 Member States of the European Union and together they represent around 80% of the EU manufacturing capacity in that sector. Our member companies account for approximately 90% of EU exports of TV sets to third countries. A list of member companies is attached at Annex A.

If the complain is lodged under Article 3 of the TBR (i.e. complaints against trade practices affecting the Community market), the complaining industry must certify that has been authorised to act on behalf of EC producers or service providers whose combined output constitutes a major proportion of total Community production of the products or services in question.

3. PRODUCT AT ISSUE

The products affected by the contested trade practices are reception apparatus for television, whether or not incorporating radio-broadcast receivers or sound or video recording or reproducing apparatus (hereinafter, "TV sets") manufactured in the EU and classified within Chapter 85 of the Harmonised Customs Nomenclature under HS Sub Headings 8528.12 (colour) and 8528.13 (black and white or other monochrome).

The complaint must contain an accurate description of the product, service or intellectual property right affected by the challenged trade practice. (In some cases, all goods, services or intellectual property rights may be affected, e.g. restrictions on payments.) In the case of goods or services, the customs classification of the product may in some cases not be enough, in particular if the problem affects a very specific sub-category of goods or services. In the case of intellectual property rights, reference should be made to the international rule which recognises the right in question.

4. DESCRIPTION OF THE MARKET

Wonderland's market for TV sets is one of the most important markets in the world both in terms of size (1 million units were sold on average every year during the period 2001-2004) and growth potential (it is expected that both the number of households and their disposable income will double over the next 20 years).

EU exports of TV sets to Wonderland have grown steadily over the past decade to reach an outstanding level in the past few years: in 2003, 500.000 units were sold for a value of €45 million F.O.B. In that year, EU exports accounted for 50% of the market and 60% of total imports of TV sets into Wonderland. Other exporter countries include Japan, China and Mexico.

However, in 2004, following the introduction of a number of measures by Wonderland's Government, EU exports of TV sets have plummeted, as we shall describe in the following sections of this Complaint.

EU-manufactured TV sets are typically imported by independent importers who have entered into long-term exclusivity contracts with EU exporters. Imports from other countries are carried out on a similar basis.

The domestic industry was historically important in the past, but it has undergone a serious crisis starting in the early 90s which is mainly due to a combination of inferior technology and high production costs. At present there is only one manufacturer in Wonderland – WonderTelly Inc. – whose estimated market share had declined till 2003 (17%) but it is now rapidly growing.

A list of the main importers and domestic manufacturers, with the corresponding TV set brands, is attached at Annex B.

A statistical overview of the market is attached at Annex C.

Complaints must include a basic description of the Community market (for Article 3 complaints) or of the third country market (for Article 4 complaints) in order to enable an initial assessment of the economic effects of the alleged obstacles to trade, and to identify the main economic operators who the Commission may need to contact in the course of its investigation. Such description can be presented as a stand-alone section, as suggested in this model complaint, or as part of the section on "injury"/"adverse trade effects".

5. OBSTACLE TO TRADE

Through this Complaint EATV is challenging a set of measures adopted by Wonderland's Government in 2004 which negatively affect imports of TV sets. EATV believes that those measures were adopted with the aim of providing protection to the only domestic producer against external competition, in a manner inconsistent with international trade principles.

4.1. Description of the challenged trade practice

On 17 March 2004, the Government adopted Decree No. 242/04 laying down technical specifications for TV sets and other electrical appliances (Annex D). The aim of the new rules is to ensure that such articles are designed to minimise the risks arising from electrical malfunctions for consumers and their properties.

In so far as TV sets are concerned, Decree No. 242/04 follows quite closely the substantive contents of the relevant international standards. This was actually a welcome step that does not represent a problem for EU manufacturers. However, the Decree also laid down a procedure to test the conformity of TV sets with the compulsory technical specifications, which is further specified in a Customs Circular dated 24 March 2004 (Annex E). In particular:

- A testing facility has been created in Furthertown, a small port located in an island off the coast of Wonderland, where imported articles must be shipped for the purposes of assessing their conformity with Decree No. 242/04. Once in Furthertown, samples are selected and they are sent to the laboratory in order to ascertain whether the design and composition of the articles conform to Wonderland's technical specifications. Consignments must remain in a bonded warehouse at the port while tests are conducted in the laboratory, which may take up to 15 days. The fact that a given model of TV set has already been tested with a satisfactory outcome does not exempt future consignments of that model from further testing. As a result of these practices, Furthertown has become the only port of entry for imported TV sets.
- Importers are supposed to pay for the conformity assessment procedure. Customs in Furthertown charge a service fee equivalent to 1% of the customs value of each consignment. There is also the cost of the bonded warehouse, which amounts to 0.25% of the customs value for periods of less than two weeks (up to 14 days), and 0.75% for periods of more than two weeks (15 days or more), regardless of the actual number of days which the goods spend in the warehouse.

WonderTelly, the only domestic manufacturer, is in principle subject to the same conformity assessment requirement. However: the sampling takes place at their factory in mainland Wonderland (with a frequency that we have not been able to determine but that we suspect to be very low); only the selected items are shipped to the laboratory in Furthertown; the service fee is calculated on the basis of the number of articles actually tested.

The main features of the third country's trade practice should be explained in sufficient detail, in order to understand its operation and impact on EC operators.

Where the practice is codified in a legal rule (a regulation, decree, administrative notice . . .) the relevant texts should be provided with the complaint. If the problem is related to administrative practices under a regulation, specific evidence on the way the

regulation is applied will be needed (e.g. examples of individual decisions adopted by the third country authorities).
If the obstacle to trade consists of an unwritten practice, complainants should endeavour to provide sufficient direct and/or indirect evidence of its existence.

In cases where discrimination vis-à-vis EC products is alleged, it is important to explain in detail which are the rules or practices that apply to the products of the third country at hand.

4.2. Right of action under international trade rules

EATV is of the view that the trade practices described above constitute a breach of the WTO Agreement (specifically Article 5 of the WTO Agreement on Technical Barriers to Trade (TBT) and Article VIII of the General Agreement on Tariffs and Trade 1994 (GATT)), in so far as:

- the laboratory facilities have been set up in a port out of the common commercial routes for international trade into and out of Wonderland;
- service and storage fees that are different in the case of domestic manufacturers and importers, and are not commensurate with the cost of the service rendered;
- in general, the conformity assessment procedure unduly and unnecessarily penalises imports.

Complainants should put the emphasis on the factual description of the alleged obstacle to trade rather than on its legal characterisation under the relevant trade rules. As regards this latter aspect, it is enough to explain ***clearly but briefly*** *which are the legal provisions that are being breached (or which otherwise give the EC a right of action under international trade rules) and in which way they are breached. Provided that the basis for the complaint is clear enough, it is by no means necessary to engage into an exhaustive legal analysis. For instance, the fact that the complaint fails to identify some legal provisions that may be relevant does* ***not*** *have any negative consequences for its admissibility.*

6. ADVERSE TRADE EFFECTS OR INJURY

Since the introduction of the new rules in March 2004, EATV members' exports to Wonderland have significantly declined. The new rules entail important additional transport and logistics costs, as well as delays in customs clearance. The new regulatory environment had an immediate effect on imports of TV sets, which for several weeks were actually brought to a halt. The industry had to adjust rapidly to the new situation, but at a very high cost. As a result, the competitive position of imported TV sets has been seriously impaired in Wonderland. In this regard, EU exports statistics are most telling:

EU exports to Wonderland (F.O.B.)	Year
€ 38,975,000	2001
€ 42,500,000	2002
€ 45,000,000	2003
€ 23,050,000	2004
€ 33,750,000 (forecast)	2005

Imports into Wonderland from the other main exporting countries have experienced a similar trend. On the other hand, the market share of the only domestic manufacturer has rapidly increased (from 17% in 2003 to a forecasted 40% in 2005), as it has been able to use its excess capacity to fill in the gap left by imports.

A full statistical outlook is enclosed as Annex F.

The decrease in exports to Wonderland has a serious impact on the TV manufacturing industry, which employ 50,000 people in the EU. Wonderland is the industry's second largest export market and the first one in terms of future potential. Exports to Wonderland used to account for 16% of the industry's total output and 46% of its total exports.

TBR complaints can be aimed at a trade practice maintained by a third country which causes economic damage within the EU market ("injury"), or at trade practices whose effects are felt in third country markets ("adverse trade effects").

In cases of "injury" -or "threat of injury"- to an EU industry on the EU market, complainants should aim at providing sufficient evidence relating to: (a) the volume of Community imports or exports; (b) the prices of the Community industry's competitors; (c) the impact on the EU industry, measured in terms of output, stocks, sales, market share etc. The relevant economic factors are described in more detail in Article 10 of the TBR.

In cases of "adverse trade effects" - or "threat of adverse trade effects" - on a third country market, complainants must provide sufficient evidence of such adverse effects on the economy of the EU or of a region of the EU, or on a specific sector of activity. Complainants may rely, inter alia, on import/export statistics, market shares or price statistics to show that, for instance, trade flows between the EU and the third country concerned are being restricted or prevented as a result of an obstacle to trade. Restrictions on access to raw materials from third countries may also be the subject matter of TBR complaints. Where direct evidence relating to trade flows is not decisive or unclear, it may be necessary to complement the economic data through information on the actual monetary costs of the trade practice and estimates of potential export increases if the practice was eliminated.

7. CONCLUSION

On the basis of the above elements, EATV requests the European Commission to open an investigation pursuant to the Trade Barriers Regulation on Wonderland's trade practices affecting EU exports of TV sets.

PART IV

Trade in Goods: GATT

Document 13

THE GENERAL AGREEMENT ON TARIFFS AND TRADE 1947

The Governments of the Commonwealth of Australia, the Kingdom of Belgium, the United States of Brazil, Burma, Canada, Ceylon, the Republic of Chile, the Republic of China, the Republic of Cuba, the Czechoslovak Republic, the French Republic, India, Lebanon, the Grand-Duchy of Luxemburg, the Kingdom of the Netherlands, New Zealand, the Kingdom of Norway, Pakistan, Southern Rhodesia, Syria, the Union of South Africa, the United Kingdom of Great Britain and Northern Ireland, and the United States of America:

Recognizing that their relations in the field of trade and economic endeavour should be conducted with a view to raising standards of living, ensuring full employment and a large and steadily growing volume of real income and effective demand, developing the full use of the resources of the world and expanding the production and exchange of goods,

Being desirous of contributing to these objectives by entering into reciprocal and mutually advantageous arrangements directed to the substantial reduction of tariffs and other barriers to trade and to the elimination of discriminatory treatment in international commerce,

Have through their Representatives agreed as follows:

Part I

Article I

General Most-Favoured-Nation Treatment

1. With respect to customs duties and charges of any kind imposed on or in connection with importation or exportation or imposed on the international transfer of payments for imports or exports, and with respect to the method of levying such duties and charges, and with respect to all rules and formalities in connection with importation and exportation, and with respect to all matters referred to in paragraphs 2 and 4 of Article III,* [asterisks refer to Ad Articles beginning on page 161] any advantage, favour, privilege or immunity granted by any contracting party to any product originating in or destined for any other country shall be accorded immediately and unconditionally to the like product originating in or destined for the territories of all other contracting parties.

2. The provisions of paragraph 1 of this Article shall not require the elimination of any preferences in respect of import duties or charges which do not exceed the levels provided for in paragraph 4 of this Article and which fall within the following descriptions:

(*a*) Preferences in force exclusively between two or more of the territories listed in Annex A, subject to the conditions set forth therein;

(*b*) Preferences in force exclusively between two or more territories which on July 1, 1939, were connected by common sovereignty or relations of protection or suzerainty and which are listed in Annexes B, C and D, subject to the conditions set forth therein;

(*c*) Preferences in force exclusively between the United States of America and the Republic of Cuba;

(*d*) Preferences in force exclusively between neighbouring countries listed in Annexes E and F.

3. The provisions of paragraph 1 shall not apply to preferences between the countries formerly a part of the Ottoman Empire and detached from it on July 24, 1923, provided such preferences are approved under paragraph 5,[1] of Article XXV which shall be applied in this respect in the light of paragraph 1 of Article XXIX.

4. The margin of preference* on any product in respect of which a preference is permitted under paragraph 2 of this Article but is not

1. The authentic text erroneously reads "subparagraph 5 (a)."

specifically set forth as a maximum margin of preference in the appropriate Schedule annexed to this Agreement shall not exceed:

(*a*) in respect of duties or charges on any product described in such Schedule, the difference between the most-favoured-nation and preferential rates provided for therein; if no preferential rate is provided for, the preferential rate shall for the purposes of this paragraph be taken to be that in force on April 10, 1947, and, if no most-favoured-nation rate is provided for, the margin shall not exceed the difference between the most-favoured-nation and preferential rates existing on April 10, 1947;

(*b*) in respect of duties or charges on any product not described in the appropriate Schedule, the difference between the most-favoured-nation and preferential rates existing on April 10, 1947.

In the case of the contracting parties named in Annex G, the date of April 10, 1947, referred to in subparagraph (*a*) and (*b*) of this paragraph shall be replaced by the respective dates set forth in that Annex.

Article II

Schedules of Concessions

1. (*a*) Each contracting party shall accord to the commerce of the other contracting parties treatment no less favourable than that provided for in the appropriate Part of the appropriate Schedule annexed to this Agreement.

(*b*) The products described in Part I of the Schedule relating to any contracting party, which are the products of territories of other contracting parties, shall, on their importation into the territory to which the Schedule relates, and subject to the terms, conditions or qualifications set forth in that Schedule, be exempt from ordinary customs duties in excess of those set forth and provided therein. Such products shall also be exempt from all other duties or charges of any kind imposed on or in connection with the importation in excess of those imposed on the date of this Agreement or those directly and mandatorily required to be imposed thereafter by legislation in force in the importing territory on that date.

(*c*) The products described in Part II of the Schedule relating to any contracting party which are the products of territories entitled under Article I to receive preferential treatment upon importation into the territory to which the Schedule relates shall, on their importation into such territory, and subject to the terms, conditions or qualifications set forth in that Schedule, be exempt from ordinary customs duties in excess of those set forth and provided for in Part II of that Schedule. Such products shall also be exempt from all other duties or charges of any kind imposed on or in connection with importation in excess of those imposed on the date of this Agreement or those directly or mandatorily required to be imposed thereafter by legislation in force in the importing territory on that date. Nothing in this Article shall prevent any contracting party from maintaining its requirements existing on the date of this Agreement as to the eligibility of goods for entry at preferential rates of duty.

2. Nothing in this Article shall prevent any contracting party from imposing at any time on the importation of any product:

(*a*) a charge equivalent to an internal tax imposed consistently with the provisions of paragraph 2 of Article III* in respect of the like domestic product or in respect of an article from which the imported product has been manufactured or produced in whole or in part;

(*b*) any anti-dumping or countervailing duty applied consistently with the provisions of Article VI;*

(*c*) fees or other charges commensurate with the cost of services rendered.

3. No contracting party shall alter its method of determining dutiable value or of converting currencies so as to impair the value of any of the concessions provided for in the appropriate Schedule annexed to this Agreement.

4. If any contracting party establishes, maintains or authorizes, formally or in effect, a monopoly of the importation of any product described in the appropriate Schedule annexed to this Agreement, such monopoly shall not, except as provided for in that Schedule or as otherwise agreed between the parties which initially negotiated the concession, operate so as to afford protection on the average in excess of the amount of protection provided for in that Schedule. The provisions of this paragraph shall not limit the use by contracting parties of any form of assistance to domestic producers permitted by other provisions of this Agreement.*

5. If any contracting party considers that a product is not receiving from another contracting party the treatment which the first contracting party believes to have been contemplated by a concession provided for in the appropriate Schedule annexed to this Agreement, it shall bring the matter directly to the attention of the other contracting party. If the latter agrees that the treatment contemplated was that claimed by the first contracting party, but declares that such treatment cannot be accorded because a court or other proper authority has ruled to the effect that the product involved cannot be classified under the tariff laws of such contracting party so as to permit the treatment contemplated in this Agreement, the two contracting

parties, together with any other contracting parties substantially interested, shall enter promptly into further negotiations with a view to a compensatory adjustment of the matter.

6. (*a*) The specific duties and charges included in the Schedules relating to contracting parties members of the International Monetary Fund, and margins of preference in specific duties and charges maintained by such contracting parties, are expressed in the appropriate currency at the par value accepted or provisionally recognized by the Fund at the date of this Agreement. Accordingly, in case this par value is reduced consistently with the Articles of Agreement of the International Monetary Fund by more than twenty per centum, such specific duties and charges and margins of preference may be adjusted to take account of such reduction; *provided* that the CONTRACTING PARTIES (*i.e.*, the contracting parties acting jointly as provided for in Article XXV) concur that such adjustments will not impair the value of the concessions provided for in the appropriate Schedule or elsewhere in this Agreement, due account being taken of all factors which may influence the need for, or urgency of, such adjustments.

(*b*) Similar provisions shall apply to any contracting party not a member of the Fund, as from the date on which such contracting party becomes a member of the Fund or enters into a special exchange agreement in pursuance of Article XV.

7. The Schedules annexed to this Agreement are hereby made an integral part of Part I of this Agreement.

Part II

*Article III**

National Treatment on Internal Taxation and Regulation

1. The contracting parties recognize that internal taxes and other internal charges, and laws, regulations and requirements affecting the internal sale, offering for sale, purchase, transportation, distribution or use of products, and internal quantitative regulations requiring the mixture, processing or use of products in specified amounts or proportions, should not be applied to imported or domestic products so as to afford protection to domestic production.*

2. The products of the territory of any contracting party imported into the territory of any other contracting party shall not be subject, directly or indirectly, to internal taxes or other internal charges of any kind in excess of those applied, directly or indirectly, to like domestic products. Moreover, no

contracting party shall otherwise apply internal taxes or other internal charges to imported or domestic products in a manner contrary to the principles set forth in paragraph 1.*

3. With respect to any existing internal tax which is inconsistent with the provisions of paragraph 2, but which is specifically authorized under a trade agreement, in force on April 10, 1947, in which the import duty on the taxed product is bound against increase, the contracting party imposing the tax shall be free to postpone the application of the provisions of paragraph 2 to such tax until such time as it can obtain release from the obligations of such trade agreement in order to permit the increase of such duty to the extent necessary to compensate for the elimination of the protective element of the tax.

4. The products of the territory of any contracting party imported into the territory of any other contracting party shall be accorded treatment no less favourable than that accorded to like products of national origin in respect of all laws, regulations and requirements affecting their internal sale, offering for sale, purchase, transportation, distribution or use. The provisions of this paragraph shall not prevent the application of differential internal transportation charges which are based exclusively on the economic operation of the means of transport and not on the nationality of the product.

5. No contracting party shall establish or maintain any internal quantitative regulation relating to the mixture, processing or use of products in specified amounts or proportions which requires, directly or indirectly, that any specified amount or proportion of any product which is the subject of the regulation must be supplied from domestic sources. Moreover, no contracting party shall otherwise apply internal quantitative regulations in a manner contrary to the principles set forth in paragraph 1.*

6. The provisions of paragraph 5 shall not apply to any internal quantitative regulation in force in the territory of any contracting party on July 1, 1939, April 10, 1947, or March 24, 1948, at the option of that contracting party; *Provided* that any such regulation which is contrary to the provisions of paragraph 5 shall not be modified to the detriment of imports and shall be treated as a customs duty for the purpose of negotiation.

7. No internal quantitative regulation relating to the mixture, processing or use of products in specified amounts or proportions shall be applied in such a manner as to allocate any such amount or proportion among external sources of supply.

8. (*a*) The provisions of this Article shall not apply to laws, regulations or requirements governing the procurement by governmental agencies of

products purchased for governmental purposes and not with a view to commercial resale or with a view to use in the production of goods for commercial sale.

(*b*) The provisions of this Article shall not prevent the payment of subsidies exclusively to domestic producers, including payments to domestic producers derived from the proceeds of internal taxes or charges applied consistently with the provisions of this Article and subsidies effected through governmental purchases of domestic products.

9. The contracting parties recognize that internal maximum price control measures, even though conforming to the other provisions of this Article, can have effects prejudicial to the interests of contracting parties supplying imported products. Accordingly, contracting parties applying such measures shall take account of the interests of exporting contracting parties with a view to avoiding to the fullest practicable extent such prejudicial effects.

10. The provisions of this Article shall not prevent any contracting party from establishing or maintaining internal quantitative regulations relating to exposed cinematograph films and meeting the requirements of Article IV.

Article IV

Special Provisions relating to Cinematograph Films

If any contracting party establishes or maintains internal quantitative regulations relating to exposed cinematograph films, such regulations shall take the form of screen quotas which shall conform to the following requirements:

(*a*) Screen quotas may require the exhibition of cinematograph films of national origin during a specified minimum proportion of the total screen time actually utilized, over a specified period of not less than one year, in the commercial exhibition of all films of whatever origin, and shall be computed on the basis of screen time per theatre per year or the equivalent thereof;

(*b*) With the exception of screen time reserved for films of national origin under a screen quota, screen time including that released by administrative action from screen time reserved for films of national origin, shall not be allocated formally or in effect among sources of supply;

(*c*) Notwithstanding the provisions of subparagraph (*b*) of this Article, any contracting party may maintain screen quotas conforming to the requirements of subparagraph (*a*) of this Article which reserve a minimum proportion of screen time for films of a specified origin other than that of the contracting party imposing such screen quotas; *Provided* that no such minimum proportion of screen time shall be increased above the level in effect on April 10, 1947;

(*d*) Screen quotas shall be subject to negotiation for their limitation, liberalization or elimination.

Article V

Freedom of Transit

1. Goods (including baggage), and also vessels and other means of transport, shall be deemed to be in transit across the territory of a contracting party when the passage across such territory, with or without transshipment, warehousing, breaking bulk, or change in the mode of transport, is only a portion of a complete journey beginning and terminating beyond the frontier of the contracting party across whose territory the traffic passes. Traffic of this nature is termed in this article "traffic in transit."

2. There shall be freedom of transit through the territory of each contracting party, via the routes most convenient for international transit, for traffic in transit to or from the territory of other contracting parties. No distinction shall be made which is based on the flag of vessels, the place of origin, departure, entry, exit or destination, or on any circumstances relating to the ownership of goods, of vessels or of other means of transport.

3. Any contracting party may require that traffic in transit through its territory be entered at the proper custom house, but, except in cases of failure to comply with applicable customs laws and regulations, such traffic coming from or going to the territory of other contracting parties shall not be subject to any unnecessary delays or restrictions and shall be exempt from customs duties and from all transit duties or other charges imposed in respect of transit, except charges for transportation or those commensurate with administrative expenses entailed by transit or with the cost of services rendered.

4. All charges and regulations imposed by contracting parties on traffic in transit to or from the territories of other contracting parties shall be reasonable, having regard to the conditions of the traffic.

5. With respect to all charges, regulations and formalities in connection with transit, each contracting party shall accord to traffic in transit to or from the territory of any other contracting party treatment no less favourable than the treatment accorded to traffic in transit to or from any third country.*

6. Each contracting party shall accord to products which have been in transit through the territory of any other contracting party treatment no less favourable than that which would have been accorded to such products had they been transported from their place of origin to their destination without going through the territory of such other contracting party. Any contracting party shall, however, be free to maintain its requirements of direct consignment existing on the date of this Agreement, in respect of any goods in regard to which such direct consignment is a requisite condition of eligibility for entry of the goods at preferential rates of duty or has relation to the contracting party's prescribed method of valuation for duty purposes.

7. The provisions of this Article shall not apply to the operation of aircraft in transit, but shall apply to air transit of goods (including baggage).

Article VI

Anti-Dumping and Countervailing Duties

1. The contracting parties recognize that dumping, by which products of one country are introduced into the commerce of another country at less than the normal value of the products, is to be condemned if it causes or threatens material injury to an established industry in the territory of a contracting party or materially retards the establishment of a domestic industry. For the purposes of this Article, a product is to be considered as being introduced into the commerce of an importing country at less than its normal value, if the price of the product exported from one country to another

(*a*) is less than the comparable price, in the ordinary course of trade, for the like product when destined for consumption in the exporting country, or,

(*b*) in the absence of such domestic price, is less than either

(i) the highest comparable price for the like product for export to any third country in the ordinary course of trade, or

(ii) the cost of production of the product in the country of origin plus a reasonable addition for selling cost and profit.

Due allowance shall be made in each case for differences in conditions and terms of sale, for differences in taxation, and for other differences affecting price comparability.*

2. In order to offset or prevent dumping, a contracting party may levy on any dumped product an anti-dumping duty not greater in amount than the margin of dumping in respect of such product. For the purposes of this

Article, the margin of dumping is the price difference determined in accordance with the provisions of paragraph 1.*

3. No countervailing duty shall be levied on any product of the territory of any contracting party imported into the territory of another contracting party in excess of an amount equal to the estimated bounty or subsidy determined to have been granted, directly or indirectly, on the manufacture, production or export of such product in the country of origin or exportation, including any special subsidy to the transportation of a particular product. The term "countervailing duty" shall be understood to mean a special duty levied for the purpose of offsetting any bounty or subsidy bestowed, directly, or indirectly, upon the manufacture, production or export of any merchandise.*

4. No product of the territory of any contracting party imported into the territory of any other contracting party shall be subject to anti-dumping or countervailing duty by reason of the exemption of such product from duties or taxes borne by the like product when destined for consumption in the country of origin or exportation, or by reason of the refund of such duties or taxes.

5. No product of the territory of any contracting party imported into the territory of any other contracting party shall be subject to both anti-dumping and countervailing duties to compensate for the same situation of dumping or export subsidization.

6. (*a*) No contracting party shall levy any anti-dumping or countervailing duty on the importation of any product of the territory of another contracting party unless it determines that the effect of the dumping or subsidization, as the case may be, is such as to cause or threaten material injury to an established domestic industry, or is such as to retard materially the establishment of a domestic industry.

(*b*) The CONTRACTING PARTIES may waive the requirement of subparagraph (*a*) of this paragraph so as to permit a contracting party to levy an anti-dumping or countervailing duty on the importation of any product for the purpose of offsetting dumping or subsidization which causes or threatens material injury to an industry in the territory of another contracting party exporting the product concerned to the territory of the importing contracting party. The CONTRACTING PARTIES shall waive the requirements of subparagraph (*a*) of this paragraph, so as to permit the levying of a countervailing duty, in cases in which they find that a subsidy is causing or threatening material injury to an industry in the territory of another contracting party exporting the product concerned to the territory of the importing contracting party.*

(*c*) In exceptional circumstances, however, where delay might cause damage which would be difficult to repair, a contracting party may levy a countervailing duty for the purpose referred to in subparagraph (*b*) of this paragraph without the prior approval of the CONTRACTING PARTIES; *Provided* that such action shall be reported immediately to the CONTRACTING PARTIES and that the countervailing duty shall be withdrawn promptly if the CONTRACTING PARTIES disapprove.

7. A system for the stabilization of the domestic price or of the return to domestic producers of a primary commodity, independently of the movements of export prices, which results at times in the sale of the commodity for export at a price lower than the comparable price charged for the like commodity to buyers in the domestic market, shall be presumed not to result in material injury within the meaning of paragraph 6 if it is determined by consultation among the contracting parties substantially interested in the commodity concerned that:

(*a*) the system has also resulted in the sale of the commodity for export at a price higher than the comparable price charged for the like commodity to buyers in the domestic market, and

(*b*) the system is so operated, either because of the effective regulation of production, or otherwise, as not to stimulate exports unduly or otherwise seriously prejudice the interests of other contracting parties.

Article VII

Valuation for Customs Purposes

1. The contracting parties recognize the validity of the general principles of valuation set forth in the following paragraphs of this Article, and they undertake to give effect to such principles, in respect of all products subject to duties or other charges* or restrictions on importation and exportation based upon or regulated in any manner by value. Moreover, they shall, upon a request by another contracting party review the operation of any of their laws or regulations relating to value for customs purposes in the light of these principles. The CONTRACTING PARTIES may request from contracting parties reports on steps taken by them in pursuance of the provisions of this Article.

2. (*a*) The value for customs purposes of imported merchandise should be based on the actual value of the imported merchandise on which duty is assessed, or of like merchandise, and should not be based on the value of merchandise of national origin or on arbitrary or fictitious values.*

(*b*) "Actual value" should be the price at which, at a time and place determined by the legislation of the country of importation, such or like merchandise is sold or offered for sale in the ordinary course of trade under fully competitive conditions. To the extent to which the price of such or like merchandise is governed by the quantity in a particular transaction, the price to be considered should uniformly be related to either (i) comparable quantities, or (ii) quantities not less favourable to importers than those in which the greater volume of the merchandise is sold in the trade between the countries of exportation and importation.*

(*c*) When the actual value is not ascertainable in accordance with subparagraph (*b*) of this paragraph, the value for customs purposes should be based on the nearest ascertainable equivalent of such value.*

3. The value for customs purposes of any imported product should not include the amount of any internal tax, applicable within the country of origin or export, from which the imported product has been exempted or has been or will be relieved by means of refund.

4. (*a*) Except as otherwise provided for in this paragraph, where it is necessary for the purposes of paragraph 2 of this Article for a contracting party to convert into its own currency a price expressed in the currency of another country, the conversion rate of exchange to be used shall be based, for each currency involved, on the par value as established pursuant to the Articles of Agreement of the International Monetary Fund or on the rate of exchange recognized by the Fund, or on the par value established in accordance with a special exchange agreement entered into pursuant to Article XV of this Agreement.

(*b*) Where no such established par value and no such recognized rate of exchange exist, the conversion rate shall reflect effectively the current value of such currency in commercial transactions.

(*c*) The CONTRACTING PARTIES, in agreement with the International Monetary Fund, shall formulate rules governing the conversion by contracting parties of any foreign currency in respect of which multiple rates of exchange are maintained consistently with the Articles of Agreement of the International Monetary Fund. Any contracting party may apply such rules in respect of such foreign currencies for the purposes of paragraph 2 of this Article as an alternative to the use of par values. Until such rules are adopted by the Contracting Parties, any contracting party may employ, in respect of any such foreign currency, rules of conversion for the purposes of paragraph 2 of this Article which are designed to reflect effectively the value of such foreign currency in commercial transactions.

(*d*) Nothing in this paragraph shall be construed to require any contracting party to alter the method of converting currencies for customs purposes which is applicable in its territory on the date of this Agreement, if such alteration would have the effect of increasing generally the amounts of duty payable.

5. The bases and methods for determining the value of products subject to duties or other charges or restrictions based upon or regulated in any manner by value should be stable and should be given sufficient publicity to enable traders to estimate, with a reasonable degree of certainty, the value for customs purposes.

Article VIII

*Fees and Formalities Connected with Importation and Exportation**

1. (*a*) All fees and charges of whatever character (other than import and export duties and other than taxes within the purview of Article III) imposed by contracting parties on or in connection with importation or exportation shall be limited in amount to the approximate cost of services rendered and shall not represent an indirect protection to domestic products or a taxation of imports or exports for fiscal purposes.

(*b*) The contracting parties recognize the need for reducing the number and diversity of fees and charges referred to in subparagraph (*a*).

(*c*) The contracting parties also recognize the need for minimizing the incidence and complexity of import and export formalities and for decreasing and simplifying import and export documentation requirements.*

2. A contracting party shall, upon request by another contracting party or by the CONTRACTING PARTIES, review the operation of its laws and regulations in the light of the provisions of this Article.

3. No contracting party shall impose substantial penalties for minor breaches of customs regulations or procedural requirements. In particular, no penalty in respect of any omission or mistake in customs documentation which is easily rectifiable and obviously made without fraudulent intent or gross negligence shall be greater than necessary to serve merely as a warning.

4. The provisions of this Article shall extend to fees, charges, formalities and requirements imposed by governmental authorities in connection with importation and exportation, including those relating to:

(*a*) consular transactions, such as consular invoices and certificates;

(*b*) quantitative restrictions;

(*c*) licensing;

(*d*) exchange control;

(*e*) statistical services;

(*f*) documents, documentation and certification;

(*g*) analysis and inspection; and

(*h*) quarantine, sanitation and fumigation.

Article IX

Marks of Origin

1. Each contracting party shall accord to the products of the territories of other contracting parties treatment with regard to marking requirements no less favourable than the treatment accorded to like products of any third country.

2. The contracting parties recognize that, in adopting and enforcing laws and regulations relating to marks of origin, the difficulties and inconveniences which such measures may cause to the commerce and industry of exporting countries should be reduced to a minimum, due regard being had to the necessity of protecting consumers against fraudulent or misleading indications.

3. Whenever it is administratively practicable to do so, contracting parties should permit required marks of origin to be affixed at the time of importation.

4. The laws and regulations of contracting parties relating to the marking of imported products shall be such as to permit compliance without seriously damaging the products, or materially reducing their value, or unreasonably increasing their cost.

5. As a general rule, no special duty or penalty should be imposed by any contracting party for failure to comply with marking requirements prior to importation unless corrective marking is unreasonably delayed or deceptive marks have been affixed or the required marking has been intentionally omitted.

6. The contracting parties shall co-operate with each other with a view to preventing the use of trade names in such manner as to misrepresent the true origin of a product, to the detriment of such distinctive regional or

geographical names of products of the territory of a contracting party as are protected by its legislation. Each contracting party shall accord full and sympathetic consideration to such requests or representations as may be made by any other contracting party regarding the application of the undertaking set forth in the preceding sentence to names of products which have been communicated to it by the other contracting party.

Article X

Publication and Administration of Trade Regulations

1. Laws, regulations, judicial decisions and administrative rulings of general application, made effective by any contracting party, pertaining to the classification or the valuation of products for customs purposes, or to rates of duty, taxes or other charges, or to requirements, restrictions or prohibitions on imports or exports or on the transfer of payments therefor, or affecting their sale, distribution, transportation, insurance, warehousing inspection, exhibition, processing, mixing or other use, shall be published promptly in such a manner as to enable governments and traders to become acquainted with them. Agreements affecting international trade policy which are in force between the government or a governmental agency of any contracting party and the government or governmental agency of any other contracting party shall also be published. The provisions of this paragraph shall not require any contracting party to disclose confidential information which would impede law enforcement or otherwise be contrary to the public interest or would prejudice the legitimate commercial interests of particular enterprises, public or private.

2. No measure of general application taken by any contracting party effecting an advance in a rate of duty or other charge on imports under an established and uniform practice, or imposing a new or more burdensome requirement, restriction or prohibition on imports, or on the transfer of payments therefor, shall be enforced before such measure has been officially published.

3. (*a*) Each contracting party shall administer in a uniform, impartial and reasonable manner all its laws, regulations, decisions and rulings of the kind described in paragraph 1 of this Article.

(*b*) Each contracting party shall maintain, or institute as soon as practicable, judicial, arbitral or administrative tribunals or procedures for the purpose, *inter alia*, of the prompt review and correction of administrative action relating to customs matters. Such tribunals or procedures shall be independent of the agencies entrusted with administrative enforcement and their decisions shall be implemented by, and shall govern the practice of, such agencies unless an appeal is lodged with a court or tribunal of superior jurisdiction within the time prescribed for appeals to be lodged by importers; *Provided* that the central administration of such agency may take steps to obtain a review of the matter in another proceeding if there is good cause to believe that the decision is inconsistent with established principles of law or the actual facts.

(*c*) The provisions of subparagraph (*b*) of this paragraph shall not require the elimination or substitution of procedures in force in the territory of a contracting party on the date of this Agreement which in fact provide for an objective and impartial review of administrative action even though such procedures are not fully or formally independent of the agencies entrusted with administrative enforcement. Any contracting party employing such procedures shall, upon request, furnish the CONTRACTING PARTIES with full information thereon in order that they may determine whether such procedures conform to the requirements of this subparagraph.

*Article XI**

General Elimination of Quantitative Restrictions

1. No prohibitions or restrictions other than duties, taxes or other charges, whether made effective through quotas, import or export licences or other measures, shall be instituted or maintained by any contracting party on the importation of any product of the territory of any other contracting party or on the exportation or sale for export of any product destined for the territory of any other contracting party.

2. The provisions of paragraph 1 of this Article shall not extend to the following:

(*a*) Export prohibitions or restrictions temporarily applied to prevent or relieve critical shortages of foodstuffs or other products essential to the exporting contracting party;

(*b*) Import and export prohibitions or restrictions necessary to the application of standards or regulations for the classification, grading or marketing of commodities in international trade;

(*c*) Import restrictions on any agricultural or fisheries product, imported in any form,* necessary to the enforcement of governmental measures which operate:

(i) to restrict the quantities of the like domestic product permitted to be marketed or produced, or, if there is no substantial domestic production of the like product, of a domestic product for which the imported product can be directly substituted; or

(ii) to remove a temporary surplus of the like domestic product, or, if there is no substantial domestic production of the like product, of a domestic product for which the imported product can be directly substituted, by making the surplus available to certain groups of domestic consumers free of charge or at prices below the current market level; or

(iii) to restrict the quantities permitted to be produced of any animal product the production of which is directly dependent, wholly or mainly, on the imported commodity, if the domestic production of that commodity is relatively negligible.

Any contracting party applying restrictions on the importation of any product pursuant to subparagraph (*c*) of this paragraph shall give public notice of the total quantity or value of the product permitted to be imported during a specified future period and of any change in such quantity or value. Moreover, any restrictions applied under (i) above shall not be such as will reduce the total of imports relative to the total of domestic production, as compared with the proportion which might reasonably be expected to rule between the two in the absence of restrictions. In determining this proportion, the contracting party shall pay due regard to the proportion prevailing during a previous representative period and to any special factors* which may have affected or may be affecting the trade in the product concerned.

*Article XII**

Restrictions to Safeguard the Balance of Payments

1. Notwithstanding the provisions of paragraph 1 of Article XI, any contracting party, in order to safeguard its external financial position and its balance of payments, may restrict the quantity or value of merchandise permitted to be imported, subject to the provisions of the following paragraphs of this Article.

2. (*a*) Import restrictions instituted, maintained or intensified by a contracting party under this Article shall not exceed those necessary:

(i) to forestall the imminent threat of, or to stop, a serious decline in its monetary reserves; or

(ii) in the case of a contracting party with very low monetary reserves, to achieve a reasonable rate of increase in its reserves.

Due regard shall be paid in either case to any special factors which may be affecting the reserves of such contracting party or its need for reserves, including, where special external credits or other resources are available to it, the need to provide for the appropriate use of such credits or resources.

(*b*) Contracting parties applying restrictions under sub-paragraph (*a*) of this paragraph shall progressively relax them as such conditions improve, maintaining them only to the extent that the conditions specified in that sub-paragraph still justify their application. They shall eliminate the restrictions when conditions would no longer justify their institution or maintenance under that subparagraph.

3. (*a*) Contracting parties undertake, in carrying out their domestic policies, to pay due regard to the need for maintaining or restoring equilibrium in their balance of payments on a sound and lasting basis and to the desirability of avoiding an uneconomic employment of productive resources. They recognize that, in order to achieve these ends, it is desirable so far as possible to adopt measures which expand rather than contract international trade.

(*b*) Contracting parties applying restrictions under this Article may determine the incidence of the restrictions on imports of different products or classes of products in such a way as to give priority to the importation of those products which are more essential.

(*c*) Contracting parties applying restrictions under this Article undertake:

(i) to avoid unnecessary damage to the commercial or economic interests of any other contracting party;*

(ii) not to apply restrictions so as to prevent unreasonably the importation of any description of goods in minimum commercial quantities the exclusion of which would impair regular channels of trade; and

(iii) not to apply restrictions which would prevent the importations of commercial samples or prevent compliance with patent, trade mark, copyright, or similar procedures.

(*d*) The contracting parties recognize that, as a result of domestic policies directed towards the achievement and maintenance of full and productive employment or towards the development of economic resources, a contracting party may experience a high level of demand for imports involving a threat to its monetary reserves of the sort referred to in paragraph 2 (*a*) of this Article. Accordingly, a contracting party otherwise complying with the provisions of this Article shall not be required to withdraw or modify restrictions on the ground that a change in those policies would render unnecessary restrictions which it is applying under this Article.

4. (*a*) Any contracting party applying new restrictions or raising the general level of its existing restrictions by a substantial intensification of the measures applied under this Article shall immediately after instituting or intensifying such restrictions (or, in circumstances in which prior consultation is practicable, before doing so) consult with the CONTRACTING PARTIES as to the nature of its balance of payments difficulties, alternative corrective measures which may be available, and the possible effect of the restrictions on the economies of other contracting parties.

(*b*) On a date to be determined by them,* the CONTRACTING PARTIES shall review all restrictions still applied under this Article on that date. Beginning one year after that date, contracting parties applying import restrictions under this Article shall enter into consultations of the type provided for in subparagraph (*a*) of this paragraph with the CONTRACTING PARTIES annually.

(*c*) (i) If, in the course of consultations with a contracting party under subparagraph (*a*) or (*b*) above, the CONTRACTING PARTIES find that the restrictions are not consistent with provisions of this Article or with those of Article XIII (subject to the provisions of Article XIV), they shall indicate the nature of the inconsistency and may advise that the restrictions be suitably modified.

(ii) If, however, as a result of the consultations, the CONTRACTING PARTIES determine that the restrictions are being applied in a manner involving an inconsistency of a serious nature with the provisions of this Article or with those of Article XIII (subject to the provisions of Article XIV) and that damage to the trade of any contracting party is caused or threatened thereby, they shall so inform the contracting party applying the restrictions and shall make appropriate recommendations for securing conformity with such provisions within the specified period of time. If such contracting party does not comply with these recommendations within the specified period, the CONTRACTING PARTIES may release any contracting party the trade of which is adversely affected by the restrictions from such obligations under this Agreement towards the contracting party applying the restrictions as they determine to be appropriate in the circumstances.

(*d*) The CONTRACTING PARTIES shall invite any contracting party which is applying restrictions under this Article to enter into consultations with them at the request of any contracting party which can establish a *prima facie* case that the restrictions are inconsistent with the provisions of this Article or with those of Article XIII (subject to the provisions of Article XIV) and that its trade is adversely affected thereby. However, no such invitation shall be issued unless the CONTRACTING PARTIES have ascertained that direct discussions between the contracting parties concerned have not been successful. If, as a result of the consultations with the CONTRACTING PARTIES, no agreement is reached and they determine that the restrictions are being applied inconsistently with such provisions, and that damage to the trade of the contracting party initiating the procedure is caused or threatened thereby, they shall recommend the withdrawal or modification of the restrictions. If the restrictions are not withdrawn or modified within such time as the CONTRACTING PARTIES may prescribe, they may release the contracting party initiating the procedure from such obligations under this Agreement towards the contracting party applying the restrictions as they determine to be appropriate in the circumstances.

(*e*) In proceeding under this paragraph, the CONTRACTING PARTIES shall have due regard to any special external factors adversely affecting the export trade of the contracting party applying the restrictions.*

(*f*) Determinations under this paragraph shall be rendered expeditiously and, if possible, within sixty days of the initiation of the consultations.

5. If there is a persistent and widespread application of import restrictions under this Article, indicating the existence of a general disequilibrium which is restricting international trade, the CONTRACTING PARTIES shall initiate discussions to consider whether other measures might be taken, either by those contracting parties the balance of payments of which are under pressure or by those the balance of payments of which are tending to be exceptionally favourable, or by any appropriate intergovernmental organization, to remove the underlying causes of the disequilibrium. On the invitation of the CONTRACTING PARTIES, contracting parties shall participate in such discussions.

*Article XIII**

Non-Discriminatory Administration of Quantitative Restrictions

1. No prohibition or restriction shall be applied by any contracting party on the importation of any product of the territory of any other contracting party or on the exportation of any product destined for the territory of any other contracting party, unless the importation of the like product of all third countries or the exportation of the like product to all third countries is similarly prohibited or restricted.

2. In applying import restrictions to any product, contracting parties shall aim at a distribution of trade in such product approaching as closely as

possible the shares which the various contracting parties might be expected to obtain in the absence of such restrictions and to this end shall observe the following provisions:

(*a*) Wherever practicable, quotas representing the total amount of permitted imports (whether allocated among supplying countries or not) shall be fixed, and notice given of their amount in accordance with paragraph 3 (*b*) of this Article;

(*b*) In cases in which quotas are not practicable, the restrictions may be applied by means of import licences or permits without a quota;

(*c*) Contracting parties shall not, except for purposes of operating quotas allocated in accordance with subparagraph (*d*) of this paragraph, require that import licences or permits be utilized for the importation of the product concerned from a particular country or source;

(*d*) In cases in which a quota is allocated among supplying countries the contracting party applying the restrictions may seek agreement with respect to the allocation of shares in the quota with all other contracting parties having a substantial interest in supplying the product concerned. In cases in which this method is not reasonably practicable, the contracting party concerned shall allot to contracting parties having a substantial interest in supplying the product shares based upon the proportions, supplied by such contracting parties during a previous representative period, of the total quantity or value of imports of the product, due account being taken of any special factors which may have affected or may be affecting the trade in the product. No conditions or formalities shall be imposed which would prevent any contracting party from utilizing fully the share of any such total quantity or value which has been allotted to it, subject to importation being made within any prescribed period to which the quota may relate.*

3. (*a*) In cases in which import licences are issued in connection with import restrictions, the contracting party applying the restrictions shall provide, upon the request of any contracting party having an interest in the trade in the product concerned, all relevant information concerning the administration of the restrictions, the import licences granted over a recent period and the distribution of such licences among supplying countries; *Provided* that there shall be no obligation to supply information as to the names of importing or supplying enterprises.

(*b*) In the case of import restrictions involving the fixing of quotas, the contracting party applying the restrictions shall give public notice of the total quantity or value of the product or products which will be permitted to be imported during a specified future period and of any change in such quantity or value. Any supplies of the product in question which were *en route* at the time at which public notice was given shall not be excluded from entry; *Provided* that they may be counted so far as practicable, against the quantity permitted to be imported in the period in question, and also, where necessary, against the quantities permitted to be imported in the next following period or periods; and *Provided* further that if any contracting party customarily exempts from such restrictions products entered for consumption or withdrawn from warehouse for consumption during a period of thirty days after the day of such public notice, such practice shall be considered full compliance with this subparagraph.

(*c*) In the case of quotas allocated among supplying countries, the contracting party applying the restrictions shall promptly inform all other contracting parties having an interest in supplying the product concerned of the shares in the quota currently allocated, by quantity or value, to the various supplying countries and shall give public notice thereof.

4. With regard to restrictions applied in accordance with paragraph 2 (*d*) of this Article or under paragraph 2 (*c*) of Article XI, the selection of a representative period for any product and the appraisal of any special factors* affecting the trade in the product shall be made initially by the contracting party applying the restriction; *Provided* that such contracting party shall, upon the request of any other contracting party having a substantial interest in supplying that product or upon the request of the CONTRACTING PARTIES, consult promptly with the other contracting party or the CONTRACTING PARTIES regarding the need for an adjustment of the proportion determined or of the base period selected, or for the reappraisal of the special factors involved, or for the elimination of conditions, formalities or any other provisions established unilaterally relating to the allocation of an adequate quota or its unrestricted utilization.

5. The provisions of this Article shall apply to any tariff quota instituted or maintained by any contracting party, and, in so far as applicable, the principles of this Article shall also extend to export restrictions.

*Article XIV**

Exceptions to the Rule of Non-Discrimination

1. A contracting party which applies restrictions under Article XII or under Section B of Article XVIII may, in the application of such restrictions, deviate from the provisions of Article XIII in a manner having equivalent effect to restrictions on payments and transfers for current international transactions which that contracting party may at that time apply under Article VIII or XIV of the Articles of Agreement of the International

Monetary Fund, or under analogous provisions of a special exchange agreement entered into pursuant to paragraph 6 of Article XV.*

2. A contracting party which is applying import restrictions under Article XII or under Section B of Article XVIII may, with the consent of the CONTRACTING PARTIES, temporarily deviate from the provisions of Article XIII in respect of a small part of its external trade where the benefits to the contracting party or contracting parties concerned substantially outweigh any injury which may result to the trade of other contracting parties.*

3. The provisions of Article XIII shall not preclude a group of territories having a common quota in the International Monetary Fund from applying against imports from other countries, but not among themselves, restrictions in accordance with the provisions of Article XII or of Section B of Article XVIII on condition that such restrictions are in all other respects consistent with the provisions of Article XIII.

4. A contracting party applying import restrictions under Article XII or under Section B of Article XVIII shall not be precluded by Articles XI to XV or Section B of Article XVIII of this Agreement from applying measures to direct its exports in such a manner as to increase its earnings of currencies which it can use without deviation from the provisions of Article XIII.

5. A contracting party shall not be precluded by Articles XI to XV, inclusive, or by Section B of Article XVIII, of this Agreement from applying quantitative restrictions:

(*a*) having equivalent effect to exchange restrictions authorized under Section 3 (*b*) of Article VII of the Articles of Agreement of the International Monetary Fund, or

(*b*) under the preferential arrangements provided for in Annex A of this Agreement, pending the outcome of the negotiations referred to therein.

Article XV

Exchange Arrangements

1. The CONTRACTING PARTIES shall seek co-operation with the International Monetary Fund to the end that the CONTRACTING PARTIES and the Fund may pursue a co-ordinated policy with regard to exchange questions within the jurisdiction of the Fund and questions of quantitative restrictions and other trade measures within the jurisdiction of the CONTRACTING PARTIES.

2. In all cases in which the CONTRACTING PARTIES are called upon to consider or deal with problems concerning monetary reserves, balances of payments or foreign exchange arrangements, they shall consult fully with the International Monetary Fund. In such consultations, the CONTRACTING PARTIES shall accept all findings of statistical and other facts presented by the Fund relating to foreign exchange, monetary reserves and balances of payments, and shall accept the determination of the Fund as to whether action by a contracting party in exchange matters is in accordance with the Articles of Agreement of the International Monetary Fund, or with the terms of a special exchange agreement between that contracting party and the CONTRACTING PARTIES. The CONTRACTING PARTIES in reaching their final decision in cases involving the criteria set forth in paragraph 2 (*a*) of Article XII or in paragraph 9 of Article XVIII, shall accept the determination of the Fund as to what constitutes a serious decline in the contracting party's monetary reserves, a very low level of its monetary reserves or a reasonable rate of increase in its monetary reserves, and as to the financial aspects of other matters covered in consultation in such cases.

3. The CONTRACTING PARTIES shall seek agreement with the Fund regarding procedures for consultation under paragraph 2 of this Article.

4. Contracting parties shall not, by exchange action, frustrate* the intent of the provisions of this Agreement, nor, by trade action, the intent of the provisions of the Articles of Agreement of the International Monetary Fund.

5. If the CONTRACTING PARTIES consider, at any time, that exchange restrictions on payments and transfers in connection with imports are being applied by a contracting party in a manner inconsistent with the exceptions provided for in this Agreement for quantitative restrictions, they shall report thereon to the Fund.

6. Any contracting party which is not a member of the Fund shall, within a time to be determined by the CONTRACTING PARTIES after consultation with the Fund, become a member of the Fund, or, failing that, enter into a special exchange agreement with the CONTRACTING PARTIES. A contracting party which ceases to be a member of the Fund shall forthwith enter into a special exchange agreement with the CONTRACTING PARTIES. Any special exchange agreement entered into by a contracting party under this paragraph shall thereupon become part of its obligations under this Agreement.

7. (*a*) A special exchange agreement between a contracting party and the CONTRACTING PARTIES under paragraph 6 of this Article shall provide to the satisfaction of the CONTRACTING PARTIES that the

objectives of this Agreement will not be frustrated as a result of action in exchange matters by the contracting party in question.

(*b*) The terms of any such agreement shall not impose obligations on the contracting party in exchange matters generally more restrictive than those imposed by the Articles of Agreement of the International Monetary Fund on members of the Fund.

8. A contracting party which is not a member of the Fund shall furnish such information within the general scope of section 5 of Article VIII of the Articles of Agreement of the International Monetary Fund as the CONTRACTING PARTIES may require in order to carry out their functions under this Agreement.

9. Nothing in this Agreement shall preclude:

(*a*) the use by a contracting party of exchange controls or exchange restrictions in accordance with the Articles of Agreement of the International Monetary Fund or with that contracting party's special exchange agreement with the CONTRACTING PARTIES, or

(*b*) the use by a contracting party of restrictions or controls in imports or exports, the sole effect of which, additional to the effects permitted under Articles XI, XII, XIII and XIV, is to make effective such exchange controls or exchange restrictions.

*Article XVI**

Subsidies

Section A—Subsidies in General

1. If any contracting party grants or maintains any subsidy, including any form of income or price support, which operates directly or indirectly to increase exports of any product from, or to reduce imports of any product into, its territory, it shall notify the CONTRACTING PARTIES in writing of the extent and nature of the subsidization, of the estimated effect of the subsidization on the quantity of the affected product or products imported into or exported from its territory and of the circumstances making the subsidization necessary. In any case in which it is determined that serious prejudice to the interests of any other contracting party is caused or threatened by any such subsidization, the contracting party granting the subsidy shall, upon request, discuss with the other contracting party or parties concerned, or with the CONTRACTING PARTIES, the possibility of limiting the subsidization.

Section B—Additional Provisions on Export Subsidies*

2. The contracting parties recognize that the granting by a contracting party of a subsidy on the export of any product may have harmful effects for other contracting parties, both importing and exporting, may cause undue disturbance to their normal commercial interests, and may hinder the achievement of the objectives of this Agreement.

3. Accordingly, contracting parties should seek to avoid the use of subsidies on the export of primary products. If, however, a contracting party grants directly or indirectly any form of subsidy which operates to increase the export of any primary product from its territory, such subsidy shall not be applied in a manner which results in that contracting party having more than an equitable share of world export trade in that product, account being taken of the shares of the contracting parties in such trade in the product during a previous representative period, and any special factors which may have affected or may be affecting such trade in the product.*

4. Further, as from 1 January 1958 or the earliest practicable date thereafter, contracting parties shall cease to grant either directly or indirectly any form of subsidy on the export of any product other than a primary product which subsidy results in the sale of such product for export at a price lower than the comparable price charged for the like product to buyers in the domestic market. Until 31 December 1957 no contracting party shall extend the scope of any such subsidization beyond that existing on 1 January 1955 by the introduction of new, or the extension of existing, subsidies.*

5. The CONTRACTING PARTIES shall review the operation of the provisions of this Article from time to time with a view to examining its effectiveness, in the light of actual experience, in promoting the objectives of this Agreement and avoiding subsidization seriously prejudicial to the trade or interests of contracting parties.

Article XVII

State Trading Enterprises

1.* (*a*) Each contracting party undertakes that if it establishes or maintains a State enterprise, wherever located, or grants to any enterprise, formally or in effect, exclusive or special privileges,* such enterprise shall, in its purchases or sales involving either imports or exports, act in a manner consistent with the general principles of non-discriminatory treatment prescribed in this Agreement for governmental measures affecting imports or exports by private traders.

(*b*) The provisions of subparagraph (*a*) of this paragraph shall be understood to require that such enterprises shall, having due regard to the other provisions of this Agreement, make any such purchases or sales solely in accordance with commercial considerations,* including price, quality, availability, marketability, transportation and other conditions of purchase or sale, and shall afford the enterprises of the other contracting parties adequate opportunity, in accordance with customary business practice, to compete for participation in such purchases or sales.

(*c*) No contracting party shall prevent any enterprise (whether or not an enterprise described in subparagraph (*a*) of this paragraph) under its jurisdiction from acting in accordance with the principles of subparagraphs (*a*) and (*b*) of this paragraph.

2. The provisions of paragraph 1 of this Article shall not apply to imports of products for immediate or ultimate consumption in governmental use and not otherwise for resale or use in the production of goods* for sale. With respect to such imports, each contracting party shall accord to the trade of the other contracting parties fair and equitable treatment.

3. The contracting parties recognize that enterprises of the kind described in paragraph 1 (*a*) of this Article might be operated so as to create serious obstacles to trade; thus negotiations on a reciprocal and mutually advantageous basis designed to limit or reduce such obstacles are of importance to the expansion of international trade.*

4. (*a*) Contracting parties shall notify the CONTRACTING PARTIES of the products which are imported into or exported from their territories by enterprises of the kind described in paragraph 1 (*a*) of this Article.

(*b*) A contracting party establishing, maintaining or authorizing an import monopoly of a product, which is not the subject of a concession under Article II, shall, on the request of another contracting party having a substantial trade in the product concerned, inform the CONTRACTING PARTIES of the import mark-up* on the product during a recent representative period, or, when it is not possible to do so, of the price charged on the resale of the product.

(*c*) The CONTRACTING PARTIES may, at the request of a contracting party which has reason to believe that its interest under this Agreement are being adversely affected by the operations of an enterprise of the kind described in paragraph 1 (*a*), request the contracting party establishing, maintaining or authorizing such enterprise to supply information about its operations related to the carrying out of the provisions of this Agreement.

(*d*) The provisions of this paragraph shall not require any contracting party to disclose confidential information which would impede law enforcement or otherwise be contrary to the public interest or would prejudice the legitimate commercial interests of particular enterprises.

*Article XVIII**

Governmental Assistance to Economic Development

1. The contracting parties recognize that the attainment of the objectives of this Agreement will be facilitated by the progressive development of their economies, particularly of those contracting parties the economies of which can only support low standards of living* and are in the early stages of development.*

2. The contracting parties recognize further that it may be necessary for those contracting parties, in order to implement programmes and policies of economic development designed to raise the general standard of living of their people, to take protective or other measures affecting imports, and that such measures are justified in so far as they facilitate the attainment of the objectives of this Agreement. They agree, therefore, that those contracting parties should enjoy additional facilities to enable them (*a*) to maintain sufficient flexibility in their tariff structure to be able to grant the tariff protection required for the establishment of a particular industry* and (*b*) to apply quantitative restrictions for balance of payments purposes in a manner which takes full account of the continued high level of demand for imports likely to be generated by their programmes of economic development.

3. The contracting parties recognize finally that, with those additional facilities which are provided for in Sections A and B of this Article, the provisions of this Agreement would normally be sufficient to enable contracting parties to meet the requirements of their economic development. They agree, however, that there may be circumstances where no measure consistent with those provisions is practicable to permit a contracting party in the process of economic development to grant the governmental assistance required to promote the establishment of particular industries* with a view to raising the general standard of living of its people. Special procedures are laid down in Sections C and D of this Article to deal with those cases.

4. (*a*) Consequently, a contracting party, the economy of which can only support low standards of living* and is in the early stages of development,* shall be free to deviate temporarily from the provisions of the other Articles of this Agreement, as provided in Sections A, B and C of this Article.

(*b*) A contracting party, the economy of which is in the process of development, but which does not come within the scope of subparagraph (*a*) above, may submit applications to the CONTRACTING PARTIES under Section D of this Article.

5. The contracting parties recognize that the export earnings of contracting parties, the economies of which are of the type described in paragraph 4 (*a*) and (*b*) above and which depend on exports of a small number of primary commodities, may be seriously reduced by a decline in the sale of such commodities. Accordingly, when the exports of primary commodities by such a contracting party are seriously affected by measures taken by another contracting party, it may have resort to the consultation provisions of Article XXII of this Agreement.

6. The CONTRACTING PARTIES shall review annually all measures applied pursuant to the provisions of Sections C and D of this Article.

Section A

7. (*a*) If a contracting party coming within the scope of paragraph 4 (*a*) of this Article considers it desirable, in order to promote the establishment of a particular industry* with a view to raising the general standard of living of its people, to modify or withdraw a concession included in the appropriate Schedule annexed to this Agreement, it shall notify the CONTRACTING PARTIES to this effect and enter into negotiations with any contracting party with which such concession was initially negotiated, and with any other contracting party determined by the CONTRACTING PARTIES to have a substantial interest therein. If agreement is reached between such contracting parties concerned, they shall be free to modify or withdraw concessions under the appropriate Schedules to this Agreement in order to give effect to such agreement, including any compensatory adjustments involved.

(*b*) If agreement is not reached within sixty days after the notification provided for in subparagraph (*a*) above, the contracting party which proposes to modify or withdraw the concession may refer the matter to the CONTRACTING PARTIES which shall promptly examine it. If they find that the contracting party which proposes to modify or withdraw the concession has made every effort to reach an agreement and that the compensatory adjustment offered by it is adequate, that contracting party shall be free to modify or withdraw the concession if, at the same time, it gives effect to the compensatory adjustment. If the CONTRACTING PARTIES do not find that the compensation offered by a contracting party proposing to modify or withdraw the concession is adequate, but find that it has made every reasonable effort to offer adequate compensation, that contracting party shall be free to proceed with such modification or withdrawal. If such action is taken, any other contracting party referred to in subparagraph (*a*) above shall be free to modify or withdraw substantially equivalent concessions initially negotiated with the contracting party which has taken the action.*

Section B

8. The contracting parties recognize that contracting parties coming within the scope of paragraph 4 (*a*) of this Article tend, when they are in rapid process of development, to experience balance of payments difficulties arising mainly from efforts to expand their internal markets as well as from the instability in their terms of trade.

9. In order to safeguard its external financial position and to ensure a level of reserves adequate for the implementation of its programme of economic development, a contracting party coming within the scope of paragraph 4 (*a*) of this Article may, subject to the provisions of paragraphs 10 to 12, control the general level of its imports by restricting the quantity or value of merchandise permitted to be imported; *Provided* that the import restrictions instituted, maintained or intensified shall not exceed those necessary:

(*a*) to forestall the threat of, or to stop, a serious decline in its monetary reserves, or

(*b*) in the case of a contracting party with inadequate monetary reserves, to achieve a reasonable rate of increase in its reserves.

Due regard shall be paid in either case to any special factors which may be affecting the reserves of the contracting party or its need for reserves, including, where special external credits or other resources are available to it, the need to provide for the appropriate use of such credits or resources.

10. In applying these restrictions, the contracting party may determine their incidence on imports of different products or classes of products in such a way as to give priority to the importation of those products which are more essential in the light of its policy of economic development; *Provided* that the restrictions are so applied as to avoid unnecessary damage to the commercial or economic interests of any other contracting party and not to prevent unreasonably the importation of any description of goods in minimum commercial quantities the exclusion of which would impair regular channels of trade; and *Provided* further that the restrictions are not so applied as to prevent the importation of commercial samples or to prevent compliance with patent, trade mark, copyright or similar procedures.

11. In carrying out its domestic policies, the contracting party concerned shall pay due regard to the need for restoring equilibrium in its balance of payments on a sound and lasting basis and to the desirability of assuring an economic employment of productive resources. It shall progressively relax any restrictions applied under this Section as conditions improve, maintaining them only to the extent necessary under the terms of paragraph 9 of this Article and shall eliminate them when conditions no

longer justify such maintenance; *Provided* that no contracting party shall be required to withdraw or modify restrictions on the ground that a change in its development policy would render unnecessary the restrictions which it is applying under this Section.*

12. (*a*) Any contracting party applying new restrictions or raising the general level of its existing restrictions by a substantial intensification of the measures applied under this Section, shall immediately after instituting or intensifying such restrictions (or, in circumstances in which prior consultation is practicable, before doing so) consult with the CONTRACTING PARTIES as to the nature of its balance of payments difficulties, alternative corrective measures which may be available, and the possible effect of the restrictions on the economies of other contracting parties.

(*b*) On a date to be determined by them* the CONTRACTING PARTIES shall review all restrictions still applied under this Section on that date. Beginning two years after that date, contracting parties applying restrictions under this Section shall enter into consultations of the type provided for in subparagraph (*a*) above with the CONTRACTING PARTIES at intervals of approximately, but not less than, two years according to a programme to be drawn up each year by the CONTRACTING PARTIES; *Provided* that no consultation under this subparagraph shall take place within two years after the conclusion of a consultation of a general nature under any other provision of this paragraph.

(*c*) (i) If, in the course of consultations with a contracting party under subparagraph (*a*) or (*b*) of this paragraph, the CONTRACTING PARTIES find that the restrictions are not consistent with the provisions of this Section or with those of Article XIII (subject to the provisions of Article XIV), they shall indicate the nature of the inconsistency and may advise that the restrictions be suitably modified.

(ii) If, however, as a result of the consultations, the CONTRACTING PARTIES determine that the restrictions are being applied in a manner involving an inconsistency of a serious nature with the provisions of this Section or with those of Article XIII (subject to the provisions of Article XIV) and that damage to the trade of any contracting party is caused or threatened thereby, they shall so inform the contracting party applying the restrictions and shall make appropriate recommendations for securing conformity with such provisions within a specified period. If such contracting party does not comply with these recommendations within the specified period, the CONTRACTING PARTIES may release any contracting party the trade of which is adversely affected by the restrictions from such obligations under this Agreement towards the contracting party applying the restrictions as they determine to be appropriate in the circumstances.

(*d*) The CONTRACTING PARTIES shall invite any contracting party which is applying restrictions under this Section to enter into consultations with them at the request of any contracting party which can establish a *prima facie* case that the restrictions are inconsistent with the provisions of this Section or with those of Article XIII (subject to the provisions of Article XIV) and that its trade is adversely affected thereby. However, no such invitation shall be issued unless the CONTRACTING PARTIES have ascertained that direct discussions between the contracting parties concerned have not been successful. If, as a result of the consultations with the CONTRACTING PARTIES no agreement is reached and they determine that the restrictions are being applied inconsistently with such provisions, and that damage to the trade of the contracting party initiating the procedure is caused or threatened thereby, they shall recommend the withdrawal or modification of the restrictions. If the restrictions are not withdrawn or modified within such time as the CONTRACTING PARTIES may prescribe, they may release the contracting party initiating the procedure from such obligations under this Agreement towards the contracting party applying the restrictions as they determine to be appropriate in the circumstances.

(*e*) If a contracting party against which action has been taken in accordance with the last sentence of subparagraph (*c*) (ii) or (*d*) of this paragraph, finds that the release of obligations authorized by the CONTRACTING PARTIES adversely affects the operation of its programme and policy of economic development, it shall be free, not later than sixty days after such action is taken, to give written notice to the Executive Secretary[2] to the Contracting Parties of its intention to withdraw from this Agreement and such withdrawal shall take effect on the sixtieth day following the day on which the notice is received by him.

(*f*) In proceeding under this paragraph, the CONTRACTING PARTIES shall have due regard to the factors referred to in paragraph 2 of this Article. Determinations under this paragraph shall be rendered expeditiously and, if possible, within sixty days of the initiation of the consultations.

Section C

13. If a contracting party coming within the scope of paragraph 4 (*a*) of this Article finds that governmental assistance is required to promote the establishment of a particular industry* with a view to raising the general standard of living of its people, but that no measure consistent with the other

2. By the Decision of 23 March 1965, the CONTRACTING PARTIES changed the title of the head of the GATT secretariat from "Executive Secretary" to "Director-General."

provisions of this Agreement is practicable to achieve that objective, it may have recourse to the provisions and procedures set out in this Section.*

14. The contracting party concerned shall notify the CONTRACTING PARTIES of the special difficulties which it meets in the achievement of the objective outlined in paragraph 13 of this Article and shall indicate the specific measure affecting imports which it proposes to introduce in order to remedy these difficulties. It shall not introduce that measure before the expiration of the time-limit laid down in paragraph 15 or 17, as the case may be, or if the measure affects imports of a product which is the subject of a concession included in the appropriate Schedule annexed to this Agreement, unless it has secured the concurrence of the CONTRACTING PARTIES in accordance with provisions of paragraph 18; *Provided* that, if the industry receiving assistance has already started production, the contracting party may, after informing the CONTRACTING PARTIES, take such measures as may be necessary to prevent, during that period, imports of the product or products concerned from increasing substantially above a normal level.*

15. If, within thirty days of the notification of the measure, the CONTRACTING PARTIES do not request the contracting party concerned to consult with them,* that contracting party shall be free to deviate from the relevant provisions of the other Articles of this Agreement to the extent necessary to apply the proposed measure.

16. If it is requested by the CONTRACTING PARTIES to do so,* the contracting party concerned shall consult with them as to the purpose of the proposed measure, as to alternative measures which may be available under this Agreement, and as to the possible effect of the measure proposed on the commercial and economic interests of other contracting parties. If, as a result of such consultation, the CONTRACTING PARTIES agree that there is no measure consistent with the other provisions of this Agreement which is practicable in order to achieve the objective outlined in paragraph 13 of this Article, and concur* in the proposed measure, the contracting party concerned shall be released from its obligations under the relevant provisions of the other Articles of this Agreement to the extent necessary to apply that measure.

17. If, within ninety days after the date of the notification of the proposed measure under paragraph 14 of this Article, the CONTRACTING PARTIES have not concurred in such measure, the contracting party concerned may introduce the measure proposed after informing the CONTRACTING PARTIES.

18. If the proposed measure affects a product which is the subject of a concession included in the appropriate Schedule annexed to this

Agreement, the contracting party concerned shall enter into consultations with any other contracting party with which the concession was initially negotiated, and with any other contracting party determined by the CONTRACTING PARTIES to have a substantial interest therein. The CONTRACTING PARTIES shall concur* in the measure if they agree that there is no measure consistent with the other provisions of this Agreement which is practicable in order to achieve the objective set forth in paragraph 13 of this Article, and if they are satisfied:

(*a*) that agreement has been reached with such other contracting parties as a result of the consultations referred to above, or

(*b*) if no such agreement has been reached within sixty days after the notification provided for in paragraph 14 has been received by the CONTRACTING PARTIES, that the contracting party having recourse to this Section has made all reasonable efforts to reach an agreement and that the interests of other contracting parties are adequately safeguarded.*

The contracting party having recourse to this Section shall thereupon be released from its obligations under the relevant provisions of the other Articles of this Agreement to the extent necessary to permit it to apply the measure.

19. If a proposed measure of the type described in paragraph 13 of this Article concerns an industry the establishment of which has in the initial period been facilitated by incidental protection afforded by restrictions imposed by the contracting party concerned for balance of payments purposes under the relevant provisions of this Agreement, that contracting party may resort to the provisions and procedures of this Section; *Provided* that it shall not apply the proposed measure without the concurrence* of the CONTRACTING PARTIES.*

20. Nothing in the preceding paragraphs of this Section shall authorize any deviation from the provisions of Articles I, II and XIII of this Agreement. The provisos to paragraph 10 of this Article shall also be applicable to any restriction under this Section.

21. At any time while a measure is being applied under paragraph 17 of this Article any contracting party substantially affected by it may suspend the application to the trade of the contracting party having recourse to this Section of such substantially equivalent concessions or other obligations under this Agreement the suspension of which the CONTRACTING PARTIES do not disapprove;* *Provided* that sixty days' notice of such suspension is given to the CONTRACTING PARTIES not later than six months after the measure has been introduced or changed substantially to the detriment of the contracting party affected. Any such contracting party shall afford

adequate opportunity for consultation in accordance with the provisions of Article XXII of this Agreement.

Section D

22. A contracting party coming within the scope of subparagraph 4 (*b*) of this Article desiring, in the interest of the development of its economy, to introduce a measure of the type described in paragraph 13 of this Article in respect of the establishment of a particular industry* may apply to the CONTRACTING PARTIES for approval of such measure. The CONTRACTING PARTIES shall promptly consult with such contracting party and shall, in making their decision, be guided by the considerations set out in paragraph 16. If the CONTRACTING PARTIES concur* in the proposed measure the contracting party concerned shall be released from its obligations under the relevant provisions of the other Articles of this Agreement to the extent necessary to permit it to apply the measure. If the proposed measure affects a product which is the subject of a concession included in the appropriate Schedule annexed to this Agreement, the provisions of paragraph 18 shall apply.*

23. Any measure applied under this Section shall comply with the provisions of paragraph 20 of this Article.

Article XIX

Emergency Action on Imports of Particular Products

1. (*a*) If, as a result of unforeseen developments and of the effect of the obligations incurred by a contracting party under this Agreement, including tariff concessions, any product is being imported into the territory of that contracting party in such increased quantities and under such conditions as to cause or threaten serious injury to domestic producers in that territory of like or directly competitive products, the contracting party shall be free, in respect of such product, and to the extent and for such time as may be necessary to prevent or remedy such injury, to suspend the obligation in whole or in part or to withdraw or modify the concession.

(*b*) If any product, which is the subject of a concession with respect to a preference, is being imported into the territory of a contracting party in the circumstances set forth in subparagraph (*a*) of this paragraph, so as to cause or threaten serious injury to domestic producers of like or directly competitive products in the territory of a contracting party which receives or received such preference, the importing contracting party shall be free, if that other contracting party so requests, to suspend the relevant obligation in whole or in part or to withdraw or modify the concession in respect of the product, to the extent and for such time as may be necessary to prevent or remedy such injury.

2. Before any contracting party shall take action pursuant to the provisions of paragraph 1 of this Article, it shall give notice in writing to the CONTRACTING PARTIES as far in advance as may be practicable and shall afford the CONTRACTING PARTIES and those contracting parties having a substantial interest as exporters of the product concerned an opportunity to consult with it in respect of the proposed action. When such notice is given in relation to a concession with respect to a preference, the notice shall name the contracting party which has requested the action. In critical circumstances, where delay would cause damage which it would be difficult to repair, action under paragraph 1 of this Article may be taken provisionally without prior consultation, on the condition that consultation shall be effected immediately after taking such action.

3. (*a*) If agreement among the interested contracting parties with respect to the action is not reached, the contracting party which proposes to take or continue the action shall, nevertheless, be free to do so, and if such action is taken or continued, the affected contracting parties shall then be free, not later than ninety days after such action is taken, to suspend, upon the expiration of thirty days from the day on which written notice of such suspension is received by the CONTRACTING PARTIES, the application to the trade of the contracting party taking such action, or, in the case envisaged in paragraph 1 (*b*) of this Article, to the trade of the contracting party requesting such action, of such substantially equivalent concessions or other obligations under this Agreement the suspension of which the CONTRACTING PARTIES do not disapprove.

(*b*) Notwithstanding the provisions of subparagraph (*a*) of this paragraph, where action is taken under paragraph 2 of this Article without prior consultation and causes or threatens serious injury in the territory of a contracting party to the domestic producers of products affected by the action, that contracting party shall, where delay would cause damage difficult to repair, be free to suspend, upon the taking of the action and throughout the period of consultation, such concessions or other obligations as may be necessary to prevent or remedy the injury.

Article XX

General Exceptions

Subject to the requirement that such measures are not applied in a manner which would constitute a means of arbitrary or unjustifiable discrimination between countries where the same conditions prevail, or a disguised restriction on international trade, nothing in this Agreement shall be construed to prevent the adoption or enforcement by any contracting party of measures:

(*a*) necessary to protect public morals;

(*b*) necessary to protect human, animal or plant life or health;

(*c*) relating to the importations or exportations of gold or silver;

(*d*) necessary to secure compliance with laws or regulations which are not inconsistent with the provisions of this Agreement, including those relating to customs enforcement, the enforcement of monopolies operated under paragraph 4 of Article II and Article XVII, the protection of patents, trade marks and copyrights, and the prevention of deceptive practices;

(*e*) relating to the products of prison labour;

(*f*) imposed for the protection of national treasures of artistic, historic or archaeological value;

(*g*) relating to the conservation of exhaustible natural resources if such measures are made effective in conjunction with restrictions on domestic production or consumption;

(*h*) undertaken in pursuance of obligations under any intergovernmental commodity agreement which conforms to criteria submitted to the CONTRACTING PARTIES and not disapproved by them or which is itself so submitted and not so disapproved;*

(*i*) involving restrictions on exports of domestic materials necessary to ensure essential quantities of such materials to a domestic processing industry during periods when the domestic price of such materials is held below the world price as part of a governmental stabilization plan; *Provided* that such restrictions shall not operate to increase the exports of or the protection afforded to such domestic industry, and shall not depart from the provisions of this Agreement relating to non-discrimination;

(*j*) essential to the acquisition or distribution of products in general or local short supply; *Provided* that any such measures shall be consistent with the principle that all contracting parties are entitled to an equitable share of the international supply of such products, and that any such measures, which are inconsistent with the other provisions of the Agreement shall be discontinued as soon as the conditions giving rise to them have ceased to exist. The CONTRACTING PARTIES shall review the need for this sub-paragraph not later than 30 June 1960.

Article XXI

Security Exceptions

Nothing in this Agreement shall be construed

(*a*) to require any contracting party to furnish any information the disclosure of which it considers contrary to its essential security interests; or

(*b*) to prevent any contracting party from taking any action which it considers necessary for the protection of its essential security interests

(i) relating to fissionable materials or the materials from which they are derived;

(ii) relating to the traffic in arms, ammunition and implements of war and to such traffic in other goods and materials as is carried on directly or indirectly for the purpose of supplying a military establishment;

(iii) taken in time of war or other emergency in international relations; or

(*c*) to prevent any contracting party from taking any action in pursuance of its obligations under the United Nations Charter for the maintenance of international peace and security.

Article XXII

Consultation

1. Each contracting party shall accord sympathetic consideration to, and shall afford adequate opportunity for consultation regarding, such representations as may be made by another contracting party with respect to any matter affecting the operation of this Agreement.

2. The CONTRACTING PARTIES may, at the request of a contracting party, consult with any contracting party or parties in respect of any matter for which it has not been possible to find a satisfactory solution through consultation under paragraph 1.

Article XXIII

Nullification or Impairment

1. If any contracting party should consider that any benefit accruing to it directly or indirectly under this Agreement is being nullified or impaired or

that the attainment of any objective of the Agreement is being impeded as the result of

(*a*) the failure of another contracting party to carry out its obligations under this Agreement, or

(*b*) the application by another contracting party of any measure, whether or not it conflicts with the provisions of this Agreement, or

(*c*) the existence of any other situation,

the contracting party may, with a view to the satisfactory adjustment of the matter, make written representations or proposals to the other contracting party or parties which it considers to be concerned. Any contracting party thus approached shall give sympathetic consideration to the representations or proposals made to it.

2. If no satisfactory adjustment is effected between the contracting parties concerned within a reasonable time, or if the difficulty is of the type described in paragraph 1 (*c*) of this Article, the matter may be referred to the CONTRACTING PARTIES. The CONTRACTING PARTIES shall promptly investigate any matter so referred to them and shall make appropriate recommendations to the contracting parties which they consider to be concerned, or give a ruling on the matter, as appropriate. The CONTRACTING PARTIES may consult with contracting parties, with the Economic and Social Council of the United Nations and with any appropriate inter-governmental organization in cases where they consider such consultation necessary. If the CONTRACTING PARTIES consider that the circumstances are serious enough to justify such action, they may authorize a contracting party or parties to suspend the application to any other contracting party or parties of such concessions or other obligations under this Agreement as they determine to be appropriate in the circumstances. If the application to any contracting party of any concession or other obligation is in fact suspended, that contracting party shall then be free, not later than sixty days after such action is taken, to give written notice to the Executive Secretary[3] to the Contracting Parties of its intention to withdraw from this Agreement and such withdrawal shall take effect upon the sixtieth day following the day on which such notice is received by him.

3. By the Decision of 23 March 1965, the CONTRACTING PARTIES changed the title of the head of the GATT secretariat from "Executive Secretary" to "Director-General."

Part III

Article XXIV

Territorial Application—Frontier Traffic—Customs Unions and Free-Trade Areas

1. The provisions of this Agreement shall apply to the metropolitan customs territories of the contracting parties and to any other customs territories in respect of which this Agreement has been accepted under Article XXVI or is being applied under Article XXXIII or pursuant to the Protocol of Provisional Application. Each such customs territory shall, exclusively for the purposes of the territorial application of this Agreement, be treated as though it were a contracting party; *Provided* that the provisions of this paragraph shall not be construed to create any rights or obligations as between two or more customs territories in respect of which this Agreement has been accepted under Article XXVI or is being applied under Article XXXIII or pursuant to the Protocol of Provisional Application by a single contracting party.

2. For the purposes of this Agreement a customs territory shall be understood to mean any territory with respect to which separate tariffs or other regulations of commerce are maintained for a substantial part of the trade of such territory with other territories.

3. The provisions of this Agreement shall not be construed to prevent:

(*a*) Advantages accorded by any contracting party to adjacent countries in order to facilitate frontier traffic;

(*b*) Advantages accorded to the trade with the Free Territory of Trieste by countries contiguous to that territory, provided that such advantages are not in conflict with the Treaties of Peace arising out of the Second World War.

4. The contracting parties recognize the desirability of increasing freedom of trade by the development, through voluntary agreements, of closer integration between the economies of the countries parties to such agreements. They also recognize that the purpose of a customs union or of a free-trade area should be to facilitate trade between the constituent territories and not to raise barriers to the trade of other contracting parties with such territories.

5. Accordingly, the provisions of this Agreement shall not prevent, as between the territories of contracting parties, the formation of a customs union or of a free-trade area or the adoption of an interim agreement

necessary for the formation of a customs union or of a free-trade area; *Provided* that:

(*a*) with respect to a customs union, or an interim agreement leading to a formation of a customs union, the duties and other regulations of commerce imposed at the institution of any such union or interim agreement in respect of trade with contracting parties not parties to such union or agreement shall not on the whole be higher or more restrictive than the general incidence of the duties and regulations of commerce applicable in the constituent territories prior to the formation of such union or the adoption of such interim agreement, as the case may be;

(*b*) with respect to a free-trade area, or an interim agreement leading to the formation of a free-trade area, the duties and other regulations of commerce maintained in each of the constituent territories and applicable at the formation of such free-trade area or the adoption of such interim agreement to the trade of contracting parties not included in such area or not parties to such agreement shall not be higher or more restrictive than the corresponding duties and other regulations of commerce existing in the same constituent territories prior to the formation of the free-trade area, or interim agreement as the case may be; and

(*c*) any interim agreement referred to in subparagraphs (*a*) and (*b*) shall include a plan and schedule for the formation of such a customs union or of such a free-trade area within a reasonable length of time.

6. If, in fulfilling the requirements of subparagraph 5 (*a*), a contracting party proposes to increase any rate of duty inconsistently with the provisions of Article II, the procedure set forth in Article XXVIII shall apply. In providing for compensatory adjustment, due account shall be taken of the compensation already afforded by the reduction brought about in the corresponding duty of the other constituents of the union.

7. (*a*) Any contracting party deciding to enter into a customs union or free-trade area, or an interim agreement leading to the formation of such a union or area, shall promptly notify the CONTRACTING PARTIES and shall make available to them such information regarding the proposed union or area as will enable them to make such reports and recommendations to contracting parties as they may deem appropriate.

(*b*) If, after having studied the plan and schedule included in an interim agreement referred to in paragraph 5 in consultation with the parties to that agreement and taking due account of the information made available in accordance with the provisions of subparagraph (*a*), the CONTRACTING PARTIES find that such agreement is not likely to result in the formation of a customs union or of a free-trade area within the period contemplated by the parties to the agreement or that such period is not a reasonable one, the CONTRACTING PARTIES shall make recommendations to the parties to the agreement. The parties shall not maintain or put into force, as the case may be, such agreement if they are not prepared to modify it in accordance with these recommendations.

(*c*) Any substantial change in the plan or schedule referred to in paragraph 5 (*c*) shall be communicated to the CONTRACTING PARTIES, which may request the contracting parties concerned to consult with them if the change seems likely to jeopardize or delay unduly the formation of the customs union or of the free-trade area.

8. For the purposes of this Agreement:

(*a*) A customs union shall be understood to mean the substitution of a single customs territory for two or more customs territories, so that

(i) duties and other restrictive regulations of commerce (except, where necessary, those permitted under Articles XI, XII, XIII, XIV, XV and XX) are eliminated with respect to substantially all the trade between the constituent territories of the union or at least with respect to substantially all the trade in products originating in such territories, and,

(ii) subject to the provisions of paragraph 9, substantially the same duties and other regulations of commerce are applied by each of the members of the union to the trade of territories not included in the union;

(*b*) A free-trade area shall be understood to mean a group of two or more customs territories in which the duties and other restrictive regulations of commerce (except, where necessary, those permitted under Articles XI, XII, XIII, XIV, XV and XX) are eliminated on substantially all the trade between the constituent territories in products originating in such territories.

9. The preferences referred to in paragraph 2 of Article I shall not be affected by the formation of a customs union or of a free-trade area but may be eliminated or adjusted by means of negotiations with contracting parties affected.* This procedure of negotiations with affected contracting parties shall, in particular, apply to the elimination of preferences required to conform with the provisions of paragraph 8 (*a*)(i) and paragraph 8 (*b*).

10. The CONTRACTING PARTIES may by a two-thirds majority approve proposals which do not fully comply with the requirements of paragraphs 5 to 9 inclusive, provided that such proposals lead to

the formation of a customs union or a free-trade area in the sense of this Article.

11. Taking into account the exceptional circumstances arising out of the establishment of India and Pakistan as independent States and recognizing the fact that they have long constituted an economic unit, the contracting parties agree that the provisions of this Agreement shall not prevent the two countries from entering into special arrangements with respect to the trade between them, pending the establishment of their mutual trade relations on a definitive basis.*

12. Each contracting party shall take such reasonable measures as may be available to it to ensure observance of the provisions of this Agreement by the regional and local governments and authorities within its territories.

Article XXV

Joint Action by the Contracting Parties

1. Representatives of the contracting parties shall meet from time to time for the purpose of giving effect to those provisions of this Agreement which involve joint action and, generally, with a view to facilitating the operation and furthering the objectives of this Agreement. Wherever reference is made in this Agreement to the contracting parties acting jointly they are designated as the CONTRACTING PARTIES.

2. The Secretary-General of the United Nations is requested to convene the first meeting of the CONTRACTING PARTIES, which shall take place not later than March 1, 1948.

3. Each contracting party shall be entitled to have one vote at all meetings of the CONTRACTING PARTIES.

4. Except as otherwise provided for in this Agreement, decisions of the CONTRACTING PARTIES shall be taken by a majority of the votes cast.

5. In exceptional circumstances not elsewhere provided for in this Agreement, the CONTRACTING PARTIES may waive an obligation imposed upon a contracting party by this Agreement; *Provided* that any such decision shall be approved by a two-thirds majority of the votes cast and that such majority shall comprise more than half of the contracting parties. The CONTRACTING PARTIES may also by such a vote

(i) define certain categories of exceptional circumstances to which other voting requirements shall apply for the waiver of obligations, and

(ii) prescribe such criteria as may be necessary for the application of this paragraph.[4]

Article XXVI

Acceptance, Entry into Force and Registration

1. The date of this Agreement shall be 30 October 1947.

2. This Agreement shall be open for acceptance by any contracting party which, on 1 March 1955, was a contracting party or was negotiating with a view to accession to this Agreement.

3. This Agreement, done in a single English original and a single French original, both texts authentic, shall be deposited with the Secretary-General of the United Nations, who shall furnish certified copies thereof to all interested governments.

4. Each government accepting this Agreement shall deposit an instrument of acceptance with the Executive Secretary[5] to the Contracting Parties, who will inform all interested governments of the date of deposit of each instrument of acceptance and of the day on which this Agreement enters into force under paragraph 6 of this Article.

5. (*a*) Each government accepting this Agreement does so in respect of its metropolitan territory and of the other territories for which it has international responsibility, except such separate customs territories as it shall notify to the Executive Secretary[5] to the CONTRACTING PARTIES at the time of its own acceptance.

(*b*) Any government, which has so notified the Executive Secretary[5] under the exceptions in subparagraph (*a*) of this paragraph, may at any time give notice to the Executive Secretary[5] that its acceptance shall be effective in respect of any separate customs territory or territories so excepted and such notice shall take effect on the thirtieth day following the day on which it is received by the Executive Secretary.[5]

(*c*) If any of the customs territories, in respect of which a contracting party has accepted this Agreement, possesses or acquires full autonomy in the conduct of its external commercial relations and of the other matters provided for in this Agreement, such territory shall, upon sponsorship

4. The authentic text erroneously reads "sub-paragraph."

5. By the Decision of 23 March 1965, the CONTRACTING PARTIES changed the title of the head of the GATT secretariat from "Executive Secretary" to "Director-General."

through a declaration by the responsible contracting party establishing the above-mentioned fact, be deemed to be a contracting party.

6. This Agreement shall enter into force, as among the governments which have accepted it, on the thirtieth day following the day on which instruments of acceptance have been deposited with Executive Secretary[6] to the Contracting Parties on behalf of governments named in Annex H, the territories of which account for 85 per centum of the total external trade of the territories of such governments, computed in accordance with the applicable column of percentages set forth therein. The instrument of acceptance of each other government shall take effect on the thirtieth day following the day on which such instrument has been deposited.

7. The United Nations is authorized to effect registration of this Agreement as soon as it enters into force.

Article XXVII

Withholding or Withdrawal of Concessions

Any contracting party shall at any time be free to withhold or to withdraw in whole or in part any concession, provided for in the appropriate Schedule annexed to this Agreement, in respect of which such contracting party determines that it was initially negotiated with a government which has not become, or has ceased to be, a contracting party. A contracting party taking such action shall notify the CONTRACTING PARTIES and, upon request, consult with contracting parties which have a substantial interest in the product concerned.

*Article XXVIII**

Modification of Schedules

1. On the first day of each three-year period, the first period beginning on 1 January 1958 (or on the first day of any other period* that may be specified by the CONTRACTING PARTIES by two-thirds of the votes cast) a contracting party (hereafter in this Article referred to as the "applicant contracting party") may, by negotiation and agreement with any contracting party with which such concession was initially negotiated and with any other contracting party determined by the CONTRACTING PARTIES to have a principal supplying interest* (which two preceding categories of contracting parties, together with the applicant contracting party, are in this Article hereinafter referred to as the "contracting parties primarily concerned"), and subject to consultation with any other contracting party determined by

6. By the Decision of 23 March 1965, the CONTRACTING PARTIES changed the title of the head of the GATT secretariat from "Executive Secretary" to "Director-General."

the CONTRACTING PARTIES to have a substantial interest* in such concession, modify or withdraw a concession* included in the appropriate schedule annexed to this Agreement.

2. In such negotiations and agreement, which may include provision for compensatory adjustment with respect to other products, the contracting parties concerned shall endeavour to maintain a general level of reciprocal and mutually advantageous concessions not less favourable to trade than that provided for in this Agreement prior to such negotiations.

3. (*a*) If agreement between the contracting parties primarily concerned cannot be reached before 1 January 1958 or before the expiration of a period envisaged in paragraph 1 of this Article, the contracting party which proposes to modify or withdraw the concession shall, nevertheless, be free to do so and if such action is taken any contracting party with which such concession was initially negotiated, any contracting party determined under paragraph 1 to have a principal supplying interest and any contracting party determined under paragraph 1 to have a substantial interest shall then be free not later than six months after such action is taken, to withdraw, upon the expiration of thirty days from the day on which written notice of such withdrawal is received by the CONTRACTING PARTIES, substantially equivalent concessions initially negotiated with the applicant contracting party.

(*b*) If agreement between the contracting parties primarily concerned is reached but any other contracting party determined under paragraph 1 of this Article to have a substantial interest is not satisfied, such other contracting party shall be free, not later than six months after action under such agreement is taken, to withdraw, upon the expiration of thirty days from the day on which written notice of such withdrawal is received by the CONTRACTING PARTIES, substantially equivalent concessions initially negotiated with the applicant contracting party.

4. The CONTRACTING PARTIES may, at any time, in special circumstances, authorize* a contracting party to enter into negotiations for modification or withdrawal of a concession included in the appropriate Schedule annexed to this Agreement subject to the following procedures and conditions:

(*a*) Such negotiations* and any related consultations shall be conducted in accordance with the provisions of paragraph 1 and 2 of this Article.

(*b*) If agreement between the contracting parties primarily concerned is reached in the negotiations, the provisions of paragraph 3 (*b*) of this Article shall apply.

(*c*) If agreement between the contracting parties primarily concerned is not reached within a period of sixty days* after negotiations have been authorized, or within such longer period as the CONTRACTING PARTIES may have prescribed, the applicant contracting party may refer the matter to the CONTRACTING PARTIES.

(*d*) Upon such reference, the CONTRACTING PARTIES shall promptly examine the matter and submit their views to the contracting parties primarily concerned with the aim of achieving a settlement. If a settlement is reached, the provisions of paragraph 3 (*b*) shall apply as if agreement between the contracting parties primarily concerned had been reached. If no settlement is reached between the contracting parties primarily concerned, the applicant contracting party shall be free to modify or withdraw the concession, unless the CONTRACTING PARTIES determine that the applicant contracting party has unreasonably failed to offer adequate compensation.* If such action is taken, any contracting party with which the concession was initially negotiated, any contracting party determined under paragraph 4 (*a*) to have a principal supplying interest and any contracting party determined under paragraph 4 (*a*) to have a substantial interest, shall be free, not later than six months after such action is taken, to modify or withdraw, upon the expiration of thirty days from the day on which written notice of such withdrawal is received by the CONTRACTING PARTIES, substantially equivalent concessions initially negotiated with applicant contracting party.

5. Before 1 January 1958 and before the end of any period envisaged in paragraph 1 a contracting party may elect by notifying the CONTRACTING PARTIES to reserve the right, for the duration of the next period, to modify the appropriate Schedule in accordance with the procedures of paragraph 1 to 3. If a contracting party so elects, other contracting parties shall have the right, during the same period, to modify or withdraw, in accordance with the same procedures, concessions initially negotiated with that contracting party.

Article XXVIII bis

Tariff Negotiations

1. The contracting parties recognize that customs duties often constitute serious obstacles to trade; thus negotiations on a reciprocal and mutually advantageous basis, directed to the substantial reduction of the general level of tariffs and other charges on imports and exports and in particular to the reduction of such high tariffs as discourage the importation even of minimum quantities, and conducted with due regard to the objectives of this Agreement and the varying needs of individual contracting parties, are of great importance

to the expansion of international trade. The CONTRACTING PARTIES may therefore sponsor such negotiations from time to time.

2. (*a*) Negotiations under this Article may be carried out on a selective product-by-product basis or by the application of such multilateral procedures as may be accepted by the contracting parties concerned. Such negotiations may be directed towards the reduction of duties, the binding of duties at then existing levels or undertakings that individual duties or the average duties on specified categories of products shall not exceed specified levels. The binding against increase of low duties or of duty-free treatment shall, in principle, be recognized as a concession equivalent in value to the reduction of high duties.

(*b*) The contracting parties recognize that in general the success of multilateral negotiations would depend on the participation of all contracting parties which conduct a substantial proportion of their external trade with one another.

3. Negotiations shall be conducted on a basis which affords adequate opportunity to take into account:

(*a*) the needs of individual contracting parties and individual industries;

(*b*) the needs of less-developed countries for a more flexible use of tariff protection to assist their economic development and the special needs of these countries to maintain tariffs for revenue purposes; and

(*c*) all other relevant circumstances, including the fiscal,* developmental, strategic and other needs of the contracting parties concerned.

Article XXIX

The Relation of this Agreement to the Havana Charter

1. The contracting parties undertake to observe to the fullest extent of their executive authority the general principles of Chapters I to VI inclusive and of Chapter IX of the Havana Charter pending their acceptance of it in accordance with their constitutional procedures.*

2. Part II of this Agreement shall be suspended on the day on which the Havana Charter enters into force.

3. If by September 30, 1949, the Havana Charter has not entered into force, the contracting parties shall meet before December 31, 1949, to agree whether this Agreement shall be amended, supplemented or maintained.

4. If at any time the Havana Charter should cease to be in force, the CONTRACTING PARTIES shall meet as soon as practicable thereafter to agree whether this Agreement shall be supplemented, amended or maintained. Pending such agreement, Part II of this Agreement shall again enter into force; *Provided* that the provisions of Part II other than Article XXIII shall be replaced, *mutatis mutandis,* in the form in which they then appeared in the Havana Charter; and *Provided* further that no contracting party shall be bound by any provisions which did not bind it at the time when the Havana Charter ceased to be in force.

5. If any contracting party has not accepted the Havana Charter by the date upon which it enters into force, the CONTRACTING PARTIES shall confer to agree whether, and if so in what way, this Agreement in so far as it affects relations between such contracting party and other contracting parties, shall be supplemented or amended. Pending such agreement the provisions of Part II of this Agreement shall, notwithstanding the provisions of paragraph 2 of this Article, continue to apply as between such contracting party and other contracting parties.

6. Contracting parties which are Members of the International Trade Organization shall not invoke the provisions of this Agreement so as to prevent the operation of any provision of the Havana Charter. The application of the principle underlying this paragraph to any contracting party which is not a Member of the International Trade Organization shall be the subject of an agreement pursuant to paragraph 5 of this Article.

Article XXX

Amendments

1. Except where provision for modification is made elsewhere in this Agreement, amendments to the provisions of Part I of this Agreement or the provisions of Article XXIX or of this Article shall become effective upon acceptance by all the contracting parties, and other amendments to this Agreement shall become effective, in respect of those contracting parties which accept them, upon acceptance by two-thirds of the contracting parties and thereafter for each other contracting party upon acceptance by it.

2. Any contracting party accepting an amendment to this Agreement shall deposit an instrument of acceptance with the Secretary-General of the United Nations within such period as the CONTRACTING PARTIES may specify. The CONTRACTING PARTIES may decide that any amendment made effective under this Article is of such a nature that any contracting party which has not accepted it within a period specified by the CONTRACTING PARTIES shall be free to withdraw from this Agreement, or to remain a contracting party with the consent of the CONTRACTING PARTIES.

Article XXXI

Withdrawal

Without prejudice to the provisions of paragraph 12 of Article XVIII, of Article XXIII or of paragraph 2 of Article XXX, any contracting party may withdraw from this Agreement, or may separately withdraw on behalf of any of the separate customs territories for which it has international responsibility and which at the time possesses full autonomy in the conduct of its external commercial relations and of the other matters provided for in this Agreement. The withdrawal shall take effect upon the expiration of six months from the day on which written notice of withdrawal is received by the Secretary-General of the United Nations.

Article XXXII

Contracting Parties

1. The contracting parties to this Agreement shall be understood to mean those governments which are applying the provisions of this Agreement under Articles XXVI or XXXIII or pursuant to the Protocol of Provisional Application.

2. At any time after the entry into force of this Agreement pursuant to paragraph 6 of Article XXVI, those contracting parties which have accepted this Agreement pursuant to paragraph 4 of Article XXVI may decide that any contracting party which has not so accepted it shall cease to be a contracting party.

Article XXXIII

Accession

A government not party to this Agreement, or a government acting on behalf of a separate customs territory possessing full autonomy in the conduct of its external commercial relations and of the other matters provided for in this Agreement, may accede to this Agreement, on its own behalf or on behalf of that territory, on terms to be agreed between such government and the CONTRACTING PARTIES. Decisions of the CONTRACTING PARTIES under this paragraph shall be taken by a two-thirds majority.

Article XXXIV

Annexes

The annexes to this Agreement are hereby made an integral part of this Agreement.

Article XXXV

Non-Application of the Agreement Between Particular Contracting Parties

1. This Agreement, or alternatively Article II of this Agreement, shall not apply as between any contracting party and any other contracting party if:

(*a*) the two contracting parties have not entered into tariff negotiations with each other, and

(*b*) either of the contracting parties, at the time either becomes a contracting party, does not consent to such application.

2. The CONTRACTING PARTIES may review the operation of this Article in particular cases at the request of any contracting party and make appropriate recommendations.

Part IV*

TRADE AND DEVELOPMENT

Article XXXVI

Principles and Objectives

1.* The contracting parties,

(*a*) recalling that the basic objectives of this Agreement include the raising of standards of living and the progressive development of the economies of all contracting parties, and considering that the attainment of these objectives is particularly urgent for less-developed contracting parties;

(*b*) considering that export earnings of the less-developed contracting parties can play a vital part in their economic development and that the extent of this contribution depends on the prices paid by the less-developed contracting parties for essential imports, the volume of their exports, and the prices received for these exports;

(*c*) noting, that there is a wide gap between standards of living in less-developed countries and in other countries;

(*d*) recognizing that individual and joint action is essential to further the development of the economies of less-developed contracting parties and to bring about a rapid advance in the standards of living in these countries;

(*e*) recognizing that international trade as a means of achieving economic and social advancement should be governed by such rules and procedures—and measures in conformity with such rules and procedures—as are consistent with the objectives set forth in this Article;

(*f*) noting that the CONTRACTING PARTIES may enable less-developed contracting parties to use special measures to promote their trade and development;

agree as follows.

2. There is need for a rapid and sustained expansion of the export earnings of the less-developed contracting parties.

3. There is need for positive efforts designed to ensure that less-developed contracting parties secure a share in the growth in international trade commensurate with the needs of their economic development.

4. Given the continued dependence of many less-developed contracting parties on the exportation of a limited range of primary products,* there is need to provide in the largest possible measure more favourable and acceptable conditions of access to world markets for these products, and wherever appropriate to devise measures designed to stabilize and improve conditions of world markets in these products, including in particular measures designed to attain stable, equitable and remunerative prices, thus permitting an expansion of world trade and demand and a dynamic and steady growth of the real export earnings of these countries so as to provide them with expanding resources for their economic development.

5. The rapid expansion of the economies of the less-developed contracting parties will be facilitated by a diversification* of the structure of their economies and the avoidance of an excessive dependence on the export of primary products. There is, therefore, need for increased access in the largest possible measure to markets under favourable conditions for processed and manufactured products currently or potentially of particular export interest to less-developed contracting parties.

6. Because of the chronic deficiency in the export proceeds and other foreign exchange earnings of less-developed contracting parties, there are important inter-relationships between trade and financial assistance to development. There is, therefore, need for close and continuing collaboration between the CONTRACTING PARTIES and the international lending agencies so that they can contribute most effectively to alleviating the burdens these less-developed contracting parties assume in the interest of their economic development.

7. There is need for appropriate collaboration between the CONTRACTING PARTIES, other intergovernmental bodies and the organs and agencies of the United Nations system, whose activities relate to the trade and economic development of less-developed countries.

8. The developed contracting parties do not expect reciprocity for commitments made by them in trade negotiations to reduce or remove tariffs and other barriers to the trade of less-developed contracting parties.*

9. The adoption of measures to give effect to these principles and objectives shall be a matter of conscious and purposeful effort on the part of the contracting parties both individually and jointly.

Article XXXVII

Commitments

1. The developed contracting parties shall to the fullest extent possible —that is, except when compelling reasons, which may include legal reasons, make it impossible—give effect to the following provisions:

(*a*) accord high priority to the reduction and elimination of barriers to products currently or potentially of particular export interest to less-developed contracting parties, including customs duties and other restrictions which differentiate unreasonably between such products in their primary and in their processed forms;*

(*b*) refrain from introducing, or increasing the incidence of, customs duties or non-tariff import barriers on products currently or potentially of particular export interest to less-developed contracting parties; and

(*c*) (i) refrain from imposing new fiscal measures, and

(ii) in any adjustments of fiscal policy accord high priority to the reduction and elimination of fiscal measures, which would hamper, or which hamper, significantly the growth of consumption of primary products, in raw or processed form, wholly or mainly produced in the territories of less-developed contracting parties, and which are applied specifically to those products.

2. (*a*) Whenever it is considered that effect is not being given to any of the provisions of subparagraph (*a*), (*b*) or (*c*) of paragraph 1, the matter shall be reported to the CONTRACTING PARTIES either by the contracting party not so giving effect to the relevant provisions or by any other interested contracting party.

(b) (i) The CONTRACTING PARTIES shall, if requested so to do by any interested contracting party, and without prejudice to any bilateral consultations that may be undertaken, consult with the contracting party concerned and all interested contracting parties with respect to the matter with a view to reaching solutions satisfactory to all contracting parties concerned in order to further the objectives set forth in Article XXXVI. In the course of these consultations, the reasons given in cases where effect was not being given to the provisions of subparagraph *(a)*, *(b)* or *(c)* of paragraph 1 shall be examined.

(ii) As the implementation of the provisions of subparagraph *(a)*, *(b)* or *(c)* of paragraph 1 by individual contracting parties may in some cases be more readily achieved where action is taken jointly with other developed contracting parties, such consultation might, where appropriate, be directed towards this end.

(iii) The consultations by the CONTRACTING PARTIES might also, in appropriate cases, be directed towards agreement on joint action designed to further the objectives of this Agreement as envisaged in paragraph 1 of Article XXV.

3. The developed contracting parties shall:

(a) make every effort, in cases where a government directly or indirectly determines the resale price of products wholly or mainly produced in the territories of less-developed contracting parties, to maintain trade margins at equitable levels;

(b) give active consideration to the adoption of other measures* designed to provide greater scope for the development of imports from less-developed contracting parties and collaborate in appropriate international action to this end;

(c) have special regard to the trade interests of less-developed contracting parties when considering the application of other measures permitted under this Agreement to meet particular problems and explore all possibilities of constructive remedies before applying such measures where they would affect essential interests of those contracting parties.

4. Less-developed contracting parties agree to take appropriate action in implementation of the provisions of Part IV for the benefit of the trade of other less-developed contracting parties, in so far as such action is consistent with their individual present and future development, financial and trade needs taking into account past trade developments as well as the trade interests of less-developed contracting parties as a whole.

5. In the implementation of the commitments set forth in paragraph 1 to 4 each contracting party shall afford to any other interested contracting party or contracting parties full and prompt opportunity for consultations under the normal procedures of this Agreement with respect to any matter or difficulty which may arise.

Article XXXVIII

Joint Action

1. The contracting parties shall collaborate jointly, with the framework of this Agreement and elsewhere, as appropriate, to further the objectives set forth in Article XXXVI.

2. In particular, the CONTRACTING PARTIES shall:

(*a*) where appropriate, take action, including action through international arrangements, to provide improved and acceptable conditions of access to world markets for primary products of particular interest to less-developed contracting parties and to devise measures designed to stabilize and improve conditions of world markets in these products including measures designed to attain stable, equitable and remunerative prices for exports of such products;

(*b*) seek appropriate collaboration in matters of trade and development policy with the United Nations and its organs and agencies, including any institutions that may be created on the basis of recommendations by the United Nations Conference on Trade and Development;

(*c*) collaborate in analysing the development plans and policies of individual less-developed contracting parties and in examining trade and aid relationships with a view to devising concrete measures to promote the development of export potential and to facilitate access to export markets for the products of the industries thus developed and, in this connection, seek appropriate collaboration with governments and international organizations, and in particular with organizations having competence in relation to financial assistance for economic development, in systematic studies of trade and aid relationships in individual less-developed contracting parties aimed at obtaining a clear analysis of export potential, market prospects and any further action that may be required;

(*d*) keep under continuous review the development of world trade with special reference to the rate of growth of the trade of less-developed contracting parties and make such recommendations to contracting parties as may, in the circumstances, be deemed appropriate;

(*e*) collaborate in seeking feasible methods to expand trade for the purpose of economic development, through international harmonization and adjustment of national policies and regulations, through technical and commercial standards affecting production, transportation and marketing, and through export promotion by the establishment of facilities for the increased flow of trade information and the development of market research; and

(*f*) establish such institutional arrangements as may be necessary to further the objectives set forth in Article XXXVI and to give effect to the provision of this Part.

Annex A

LIST OF TERRITORIES REFERRED TO IN PARAGRAPH 2 (a) OF ARTICLE I

United Kingdom of Great Britain and Northern Ireland
Dependent territories of the United Kingdom of Great Britain and Northern Ireland
Canada
Commonwealth of Australia
Dependent territories of the Commonwealth of Australia
New Zealand
Dependent territories of New Zealand
Union of South Africa including South West Africa
Ireland
India (as on April 10, 1947)
Newfoundland
Southern Rhodesia
Burma
Ceylon

Certain of the territories listed above have two or more preferential rates in force for certain products. Any such territory may, by agreement with the other contracting parties which are principal suppliers of such products at the most-favoured-nation rate, substitute for such preferential rates a single preferential rate which shall not on the whole be less favourable to suppliers at the most-favoured-nation rate than the preferences in force prior to such substitution.

The imposition of an equivalent margin of tariff preference to replace a margin of preference in an internal tax existing on April 10, 1947 exclusively between two or more of the territories listed in this Annex or to replace the preferential quantitative arrangements described in the following paragraph, shall not be deemed to constitute an increase in a margin of tariff preference.

The preferential arrangements referred to in paragraph 5 (*b*) of Article XIV are those existing in the United Kingdom on 10 April 1947, under contractual agreements with the Governments of Canada, Australia and New Zealand, in respect of chilled and frozen beef and veal, frozen mutton and lamb, chilled and frozen pork and bacon. It is the intention, without prejudice to any action taken under subparagraph (*h*)[7] of Article XX, that these arrangements shall be eliminated or replaced by tariff preferences, and that negotiations to this end shall take place as soon as practicable among the countries substantially concerned or involved.

The film hire tax in force in New Zealand on 10 April 1947, shall, for the purposes of this Agreement, be treated as a customs duty under Article I. The renters' film quota in force in New Zealand on April 10, 1947, shall, for the purposes of this Agreement, be treated as a screen quota under Article IV.

The Dominions of India and Pakistan have not been mentioned separately in the above list since they had not come into existence as such on the base date of April 10, 1947.

Annex B

LIST OF TERRITORIES OF THE FRENCH UNION REFERRED TO IN PARAGRAPH 2 (*b*) OF ARTICLE I

France
French Equatorial Africa (Treaty Basin of the Congo[8] and other territories)
French West Africa
Cameroons under French Trusteeship[8]
French Somali Coast and Dependencies
French Establishments in Oceania
French Establishments in the Condominium of the New Hebrides[8]

7. The authentic text erroneously reads "part I (*h*)."
8. For imports into Metropolitan France and Territories of the French Union.

Indo-China
Madagascar and Dependencies
Morocco (French zone)[8]
New Caledonia and Dependencies
Saint-Pierre and Miquelon
Togo under French Trusteeship[8]
Tunisia

Annex C

LIST OF TERRITORIES REFERRED TO IN PARAGRAPH 2 (*b*) OF ARTICLE I AS RESPECTS THE CUSTOMS UNION OF BELGIUM, LUXEMBURG AND THE NETHERLANDS

The Economic Union of Belgium and Luxemburg
Belgian Congo
Ruanda Urundi
Netherlands
New Guinea
Surinam
Netherlands Antilles
Republic of Indonesia
For imports into the territories constituting the Customs Union only.

Annex D

LIST OF TERRITORIES REFERRED TO IN PARAGRAPH 2 (*b*) OF ARTICLE I AS RESPECTS THE UNITED STATES OF AMERICA

United States of America (customs territory)
Dependent territories of the United States of America
Republic of the Philippines

The imposition of an equivalent margin of tariff preference to replace a margin of preference in an internal tax existing on 10 April, 1947, exclusively between two or more of the territories listed in this Annex shall not be deemed to constitute an increase in a margin of tariff preference.

Annex E

LIST OF TERRITORIES COVERED BY PREFERENTIAL ARRANGEMENTS BETWEEN CHILE AND NEIGHBOURING COUNTRIES REFERRED TO IN PARAGRAPH 2 (*d*) OF ARTICLE I

Preferences in force exclusively between Chile on the one hand, and

1. Argentina

2. Bolivia

3. Peru

on the other hand.

Annex F

LIST OF TERRITORIES COVERED BY PREFERENTIAL ARRANGEMENTS BETWEEN LEBANON AND SYRIA AND NEIGHBOURING COUNTRIES REFERRED TO IN PARAGRAPH 2 (*d*) OF ARTICLE I

Preferences in force exclusively between the Lebano-Syrian Customs Union, on the one hand, and

1. Palestine

2. Transjordan

on the other hand.

Annex G

DATES ESTABLISHING MAXIMUM MARGINS OF PREFERENCE REFERRED TO IN PARAGRAPH 4[9] OF ARTICLE I

Australia .... October 15, 1946

Canada .... July 1, 1939

France .... January 1, 1939

9. The authentic text erroneously reads "Paragraph 3."

Lebano-Syrian Customs Union..November 30, 1938

Union of South Africa...July 1, 1938

Southern Rhodesia...May 1, 1941

Annex H

PERCENTAGE SHARES OF TOTAL EXTERNAL TRADE TO BE USED FOR THE PURPOSE OF MAKING THE DETERMINATION REFERRED TO IN ARTICLE XXVI (BASED ON THE AVERAGE OF 1949-1953)

If, prior to the accession of the Government of Japan to the General Agreement, the present Agreement has been accepted by contracting parties the external trade of which under Column I accounts for the percentage of such trade specified in paragraph 6 of Article XXVI, column I shall be applicable for the purposes of that paragraph. If the present Agreement has not been so accepted prior to the accession of the Government of Japan, column II shall be applicable for the purposes of that paragraph.

	Column I (Contracting parties on 1 March 1955)	Column II (Contracting parties on 1 March 1955 and Japan)
Australia	3.1	3.0
Austria	0.9	0.8
Belgium-Luxemburg	4.3	4.2
Brazil	2.5	2.4
Burma	0.3	0.3
Canada	6.7	6.5
Ceylon	0.5	0.5
Chile	0.6	0.6
Cuba	1.1	1.1
Czechoslovakia	1.4	1.4
Denmark	1.4	1.4
Dominican Republic	0.1	0.1
Finland	1.0	1.0
France	8.7	8.5
Germany, Federal Republic of	5.3	5.2
Greece	0.4	0.4
Haiti	0.1	0.1
India	2.4	2.4
Indonesia	1.3	1.3
Italy	2.9	2.8

	Column I (Contracting parties on 1 March 1955)	Column II (Contracting parties on 1 March 1955 and Japan)
Netherlands, Kingdom of the	4.7	4.6
New Zealand	1.0	1.0
Nicaragua	0.1	0.1
Norway	1.1	1.1
Pakistan	0.9	0.8
Peru	0.4	0.4
Rhodesia and Nyasaland	0.6	0.6
Sweden	2.5	2.4
Turkey	0.6	0.6
Union of South Africa	1.8	1.8
United Kingdom	20.3	19.8
United States of America	20.6	20.1
Uruguay	0.4	0.4
Japan	-	2.3
	100.0	100.0

Note: These percentages have been computed taking into account the trade of all territories in respect of which the General Agreement on Tariffs and Trade is applied.

Annex I

NOTES AND SUPPLEMENTARY PROVISIONS

Ad Article I

Paragraph 1

The obligations incorporated in paragraph 1 of Article I by reference to paragraphs 2 and 4 of Article III and those incorporated in paragraph 2 *(b)* of Article II by reference to Article VI shall be considered as falling within Part II for the purposes of the Protocol of Provisional Application.

The cross-references, in the paragraph immediately above and in paragraph 1 of Article I, to paragraphs 2 and 4 of Article III shall only apply after Article III has been modified by the entry into force of the amendment provided for in the Protocol Modifying Part II and Article XXVI of the General Agreement on Tariffs and Trade, dated September 14, 1948.[10]

10. This Protocol entered into force on 14 December 1948.

Paragraph 4

The term "margin of preference" means the absolute difference between the most-favoured-nation rate of duty and the preferential rate of duty for the like product, and not the proportionate relation between those rates. As examples:

(1) If the most-favoured-nation rate were 36 per cent *ad valorem* and the preferential rate were 24 per cent *ad valorem*, the margin of preference would be 12 per cent *ad valorem*, and not one-third of the most-favoured-nation rate;

(2) If the most-favoured-nation rate were 36 per cent *ad valorem* and the preferential rate were expressed as two-thirds of the most-favoured-nation rate, the margin of preference would be 12 per cent *ad valorem*;

(3) If the most-favoured-nation rate were 2 francs per kilogramme and the preferential rate were 1.50 francs per kilogramme, the margin of preference would be 0.50 franc per kilogramme.

The following kinds of customs action, taken in accordance with established uniform procedures, would not be contrary to a general binding of margins of preference:

(i) The re-application to an imported product of a tariff classification or rate of duty, properly applicable to such product, in cases in which the application of such classification or rate to such product was temporarily suspended or inoperative on April 10, 1947; and

(ii) The classification of a particular product under a tariff item other than that under which importations of that product were classified on April 10, 1947, in cases in which the tariff law clearly contemplates that such product may be classified under more than one tariff item.

Ad Article II

***Paragraph 2* (a)**

The cross-reference, in paragraph 2 (*a*) of Article II, to paragraph 2 of Article III shall only apply after Article III has been modified by the entry into force of the amendment provided for in the Protocol Modifying Part II and Article XXVI of the General Agreement on Tariffs and Trade, dated September 14, 1948.[11]

11. This Protocol entered into force on 14 December 1948.

Paragraph 2 (b)

See the note relating to paragraph 1 of Article I.

Paragraph 4

Except where otherwise specifically agreed between the contracting parties which initially negotiated the concession, the provisions of this paragraph will be applied in the light of the provisions of Article 31 of the Havana Charter.

Ad Article III

Any internal tax or other internal charge, or any law, regulation or requirement of the kind referred to in paragraph 1 which applies to an imported product and to the like domestic product and is collected or enforced in the case of the imported product at the time or point of importation, is nevertheless to be regarded as an internal tax or other internal charge, or a law, regulation or requirement of the kind referred to in paragraph 1, and is accordingly subject to the provisions of Article III.

Paragraph 1

The application of paragraph 1 to internal taxes imposed by local governments and authorities with the territory of a contracting party is subject to the provisions of the final paragraph of Article XXIV. The term "reasonable measures" in the last-mentioned paragraph would not require, for example, the repeal of existing national legislation authorizing local governments to impose internal taxes which, although technically inconsistent with the letter of Article III, are not in fact inconsistent with its spirit, if such repeal would result in a serious financial hardship for the local governments or authorities concerned. With regard to taxation by local governments or authorities which is inconsistent with both the letter and spirit of Article III, the term "reasonable measures" would permit a contracting party to eliminate the inconsistent taxation gradually over a transition period, if abrupt action would create serious administrative and financial difficulties.

Paragraph 2

A tax conforming to the requirements of the first sentence of paragraph 2 would be considered to be inconsistent with the provisions of the second sentence only in cases where competition was involved between, on the one hand, the taxed product and, on the other hand, a directly competitive or substitutable product which was not similarly taxed.

Paragraph 5

Regulations consistent with the provisions of the first sentence of paragraph 5 shall not be considered to be contrary to the provisions of the second sentence in any case in which all of the products subject to the regulations are produced domestically in substantial quantities. A regulation cannot be justified as being consistent with the provisions of the second sentence on the ground that the proportion or amount allocated to each of the products which are the subject of the regulation constitutes an equitable relationship between imported and domestic products.

Ad Article V

Paragraph 5

With regard to transportation charges, the principle laid down in paragraph 5 refers to like products being transported on the same route under like conditions.

Ad Article VI

Paragraph 1

1. Hidden dumping by associated houses (that is, the sale by an importer at a price below that corresponding to the price invoiced by an exporter with whom the importer is associated, and also below the price in the exporting country) constitutes a form of price dumping with respect to which the margin of dumping may be calculated on the basis of the price at which the goods are resold by the importer.

2. It is recognized that, in the case of imports from a country which has a complete or substantially complete monopoly of its trade and where all domestic prices are fixed by the State, special difficulties may exist in determining price comparability for the purposes of paragraph 1, and in such cases importing contracting parties may find it necessary to take into account the possibility that a strict comparison with domestic prices in such a country may not always be appropriate.

Paragraphs 2 and 3

1. As in many other cases in customs administration, a contracting party may require reasonable security (bond or cash deposit) for the payment of anti-dumping or countervailing duty pending final determination of the facts in any case of suspected dumping or subsidization.

2. Multiple currency practices can in certain circumstances constitute a subsidy to exports which may be met by countervailing duties under paragraph 3 or can constitute a form of dumping by means of a partial

depreciation of a country's currency which may be met by action under paragraph 2. By "multiple currency practices" is meant practices by governments or sanctioned by governments.

Paragraph 6 (b)

Waivers under the provisions of this subparagraph shall be granted only on application by the contracting party proposing to levy an anti-dumping or countervailing duty, as the case may be.

Ad Article VII

Paragraph 1

The expression "or other charges" is not to be regarded as including internal taxes or equivalent charges imposed on or in connection with imported products.

Paragraph 2

1. It would be in conformity with Article VII to presume that "actual value" may be represented by the invoice price, plus any non-included charges for legitimate costs which are proper elements of "actual value" and plus any abnormal discount or other reduction from the ordinary competitive price.

2. It would be in conformity with Article VII, paragraph 2 *(b)*, for a contracting party to construe the phrase "in the ordinary course of trade . . . under fully competitive conditions", as excluding any transaction wherein the buyer and seller are not independent of each other and price is not the sole consideration.

3. The standard of "fully competitive conditions" permits a contracting party to exclude from consideration prices involving special discounts limited to exclusive agents.

4. The wording of subparagraphs *(a)* and *(b)* permits a contracting party to determine the value for customs purposes uniformly either (1) on the basis of a particular exporter's prices of the imported merchandise, or (2) on the basis of the general price level of like merchandise.

Ad Article VIII

1. While Article VIII does not cover the use of multiple rates of exchange as such, paragraphs 1 and 4 condemn the use of exchange taxes or fees as a device for implementing multiple currency practices; if, however, a contracting party is using multiple currency exchange fees for balance of

payments reasons with the approval of the International Monetary Fund, the provisions of paragraph 9 *(a)* of Article XV fully safeguard its position.

2. It would be consistent with paragraph 1 if, on the importation of products from the territory of a contracting party into the territory of another contracting party, the production of certificates of origin should only be required to the extent that is strictly indispensable.

Ad Articles XI, XII, XIII, XIV and XVIII

Throughout Articles XI, XII, XIII, XIV and XVIII, the terms "import restrictions" or "export restrictions" include restrictions made effective through state-trading operations.

Ad Article XI

Paragraph 2 (c)

The term "in any form" in this paragraph covers the same products when in an early stage of processing and still perishable, which compete directly with the fresh product and if freely imported would tend to make the restriction on the fresh product ineffective.

Paragraph 2, last subparagraph

The term "special factors" includes changes in relative productive efficiency as between domestic and foreign producers, or as between different foreign producers, but not changes artificially brought about by means not permitted under the Agreement.

Ad Article XII

The CONTRACTING PARTIES shall make provision for the utmost secrecy in the conduct of any consultation under the provisions of this Article.

Paragraph 3 (c)*(i)*

Contracting parties applying restrictions shall endeavour to avoid causing serious prejudice to exports of a commodity on which the economy of a contracting party is largely dependent.

Paragraph 4 (b)

It is agreed that the date shall be within ninety days after the entry into force of the amendments of this Article effected by the Protocol Amending the Preamble and Parts II and III of this Agreement. However, should the CONTRACTING PARTIES find that conditions were not suitable for the application of the provisions of this subparagraph at the time envisaged, they may determine a later date; *Provided* that such date is not more than thirty days after such time as the obligations of Article VIII, Sections 2, 3 and 4, of the Articles of Agreement of the International Monetary Fund become applicable to contracting parties, members of the Fund, the combined foreign trade of which constitutes at least fifty per centum of the aggregate foreign trade of all contracting parties.

Paragraph 4 (e)

It is agreed that paragraph 4 *(e)* does not add any new criteria for the imposition or maintenance of quantitative restrictions for balance of payments reasons. It is solely intended to ensure that all external factors such as changes in the terms of trade, quantitative restrictions, excessive tariffs and subsidies, which may be contributing to the balance of payments difficulties of the contracting party applying restrictions, will be fully taken into account.

Ad Article XIII

Paragraph 2 (d)

No mention was made of "commercial considerations" as a rule for the allocation of quotas because it was considered that its application by governmental authorities might not always be practicable. Moreover, in cases where it is practicable, a contracting party could apply these considerations in the process of seeking agreement, consistently with the general rule laid down in the opening sentence of paragraph 2.

Paragraph 4

See note relating to "special factors" in connection with the last subparagraph of paragraph 2 of Article XI.

Ad Article XIV

Paragraph 1

The provisions of this paragraph shall not be so construed as to preclude full consideration by the CONTRACTING PARTIES, in the consultations provided for in paragraph 4 of Article XII and in paragraph 12 of Article XVIII, of the nature, effects and reasons for discrimination in the field of import restrictions.

Paragraph 2

One of the situations contemplated in paragraph 2 is that of a contracting party holding balances acquired as a result of current transactions which it finds itself unable to use without a measure of discrimination.

Ad Article XV

Paragraph 4

The word "frustrate" is intended to indicate, for example, that infringements of the letter of any Article of this Agreement by exchange action shall not be regarded as a violation of that Article if, in practice, there is no appreciable departure from the intent of the Article. Thus, a contracting party which, as part of its exchange control operated in accordance with the Articles of Agreement of the International Monetary Fund, requires payment to be received for its exports in its own currency or in the currency of one or more members of the International Monetary Fund will not thereby be deemed to contravene Article XI or Article XIII. Another example would be that of a contracting party which specifies on an import licence the country from which the goods may be imported, for the purpose not of introducing any additional element of discrimination in its import licensing system but of enforcing permissible exchange controls.

Ad Article XVI

The exemption of an exported product from duties or taxes borne by the like product when destined for domestic consumption, or the remission of such duties or taxes in amounts not in excess of those which have accrued, shall not be deemed to be a subsidy.

Section B

1. Nothing in Section B shall preclude the use by a contracting party of multiple rates of exchange in accordance with the Articles of Agreement of the International Monetary Fund.

2. For the purposes of Section B, a "primary product" is understood to be any product of farm, forest or fishery, or any mineral, in its natural form or which has undergone such processing as is customarily required to prepare it for marketing in substantial volume in international trade.

Paragraph 3

1. The fact that a contracting party has not exported the product in question during the previous representative period would not in itself preclude that contracting party from establishing its right to obtain a share of the trade in the product concerned.

2. A system for the stabilization of the domestic price or of the return to domestic producers of a primary product independently of the movements of export prices, which results at times in the sale of the product for export at a price lower than the comparable price charged for the like product to buyers in the domestic market, shall be considered not to involve a subsidy

on exports within the meaning of paragraph 3 if the CONTRACTING PARTIES determine that:

(a) the system has also resulted, or is so designed as to result, in the sale of the product for export at a price higher than the comparable price charged for the like product to buyers in the domestic market; and

(b) the system is so operated, or is designed so to operate, either because of the effective regulation of production or otherwise, as not to stimulate exports unduly or otherwise seriously to prejudice the interests of other contracting parties.

Notwithstanding such determination by the CONTRACTING PARTIES, operations under such a system shall be subject to the provisions of paragraph 3 where they are wholly or partly financed out of government funds in addition to the funds collected from producers in respect of the product concerned.

Paragraph 4

The intention of paragraph 4 is that the contracting parties should seek before the end of 1957 to reach agreement to abolish all remaining subsidies as from 1 January 1958; or, failing this, to reach agreement to extend the application of the standstill until the earliest date thereafter by which they can expect to reach such agreement.

Ad Article XVII

Paragraph 1

The operations of Marketing Boards, which are established by contracting parties and are engaged in purchasing or selling, are subject to the provisions of subparagraphs *(a)* and *(b)*.

The activities of Marketing Boards which are established by contracting parties and which do not purchase or sell but lay down regulations covering private trade are governed by the relevant Articles of this Agreement.

The charging by a state enterprise of different prices for its sales of a product in different markets is not precluded by the provisions of this Article, provided that such different prices are charged for commercial reasons, to meet conditions of supply and demand in export markets.

Paragraph 1 **(a)**

Governmental measures imposed to insure standards of quality and efficiency in the operation of external trade, or privileges granted for the exploitation of national natural resources but which do not empower the government to exercise control over the trading activities of the enterprise in question, do not constitute "exclusive or special privileges."

Paragraph 1 **(b)**

A country receiving a "tied loan" is free to take this loan into account as a "commercial consideration" when purchasing requirements abroad.

Paragraph 2

The term "goods" is limited to products as understood in commercial practice, and is not intended to include the purchase or sale of services.

Paragraph 3

Negotiations which contracting parties agree to conduct under this paragraph may be directed towards the reduction of duties and other charges on imports and exports or towards the conclusion of any other mutually satisfactory arrangement consistent with the provisions of this Agreement. (See paragraph 4 of Article II and the note to that paragraph.)

Paragraph 4 **(b)**

The term "import mark-up" in this paragraph shall represent the margin by which the price charged by the import monopoly for the imported product (exclusive of internal taxes within the purview of Article III, transportation, distribution, and other expenses incident to the purchase, sale or further processing, and a reasonable margin of profit) exceeds the landed cost.

Ad Article XVIII

The CONTRACTING PARTIES and the contracting parties concerned shall preserve the utmost secrecy in respect of matters arising under this Article.

Paragraphs 1 and 4

1. When they consider whether the economy of a contracting party "can only support low standards of living," the CONTRACTING PARTIES shall take into consideration the normal position of that economy and shall not base their determination on exceptional circumstances such as those which may result from the temporary existence of exceptionally favourable conditions for the staple export product or products of such contracting party.

2. The phrase "in the early stages of development" is not meant to apply only to contracting parties which have just started their economic

development, but also to contracting parties the economies of which are undergoing a process of industrialization to correct an excessive dependence on primary production.

Paragraphs 2, 3, 7, 13 and 22

The reference to the establishment of particular industries shall apply not only to the establishment of a new industry, but also to the establishment of a new branch of production in an existing industry and to the substantial transformation of an existing industry, and to the substantial expansion of an existing industry supplying a relatively small proportion of the domestic demand. It shall also cover the reconstruction of an industry destroyed or substantially damaged as a result of hostilities or natural disasters.

Paragraph 7 (b)

A modification or withdrawal, pursuant to paragraph 7 *(b)*, by a contracting party, other than the applicant contracting party, referred to in paragraph 7 *(a)*, shall be made within six months of the day on which the action is taken by the applicant contracting party, and shall become effective on the thirtieth day following the day on which such modification or withdrawal has been notified to the CONTRACTING PARTIES.

Paragraph 11

The second sentence in paragraph 11 shall not be interpreted to mean that a contracting party is required to relax or remove restrictions if such relaxation or removal would thereupon produce conditions justifying the intensification or institution, respectively, of restrictions under paragraph 9 of Article XVIII.

Paragraph 12 (b)

The date referred to in paragraph 12 *(b)* shall be the date determined by the CONTRACTING PARTIES in accordance with the provisions of paragraph 4 *(b)* of Article XII of this Agreement.

Paragraphs 13 and 14

It is recognized that, before deciding on the introduction of a measure and notifying the CONTRACTING PARTIES in accordance with paragraph 14, a contracting party may need a reasonable period of time to assess the competitive position of the industry concerned.

Paragraphs 15 and 16

It is understood that the CONTRACTING PARTIES shall invite a contracting party proposing to apply a measure under Section C to consult with them pursuant to paragraph 16 if they are requested to do so by a contracting party the trade of which would be appreciably affected by the measure in question.

Paragraphs 16, 18, 19 and 22

1. It is understood that the CONTRACTING PARTIES may concur in a proposed measure subject to specific conditions or limitations. If the measure as applied does not conform to the terms of the concurrence it will to that extent be deemed a measure in which the CONTRACTING PARTIES have not concurred. In cases in which the CONTRACTING PARTIES have concurred in a measure for a specified period, the contracting party concerned, if it finds that the maintenance of the measure for a further period of time is required to achieve the objective for which the measure was originally taken, may apply to the CONTRACTING PARTIES for an extension of that period in accordance with the provisions and procedures of Section C or D, as the case may be.

2. It is expected that the CONTRACTING PARTIES will, as a rule, refrain from concurring in a measure which is likely to cause serious prejudice to exports of a commodity on which the economy of a contracting party is largely dependent.

Paragraph 18 and 22

The phrase "that the interests of other contracting parties are adequately safeguarded" is meant to provide latitude sufficient to permit consideration in each case of the most appropriate method of safeguarding those interests. The appropriate method may, for instance, take the form of an additional concession to be applied by the contracting party having recourse to Section C or D during such time as the deviation from the other Articles of the Agreement would remain in force or of the temporary suspension by any other contracting party referred to in paragraph 18 of a concession substantially equivalent to the impairment due to the introduction of the measure in question. Such contracting party would have the right to safeguard its interests through such a temporary suspension of a concession; *Provided* that this right will not be exercised when, in the case of a measure imposed by a contracting party coming within the scope of paragraph 4 *(a)*, the CONTRACTING PARTIES have determined that the extent of the compensatory concession proposed was adequate.

Paragraph 19

The provisions of paragraph 19 are intended to cover the cases where an industry has been in existence beyond the "reasonable period of time" referred to in the note to paragraphs 13 and 14, and should not be so construed as to deprive a contracting party coming within the scope of paragraph 4 *(a)* of Article XVIII, of its right to resort to the other provisions of Section C, including paragraph 17, with regard to a newly established industry even though it has benefited from incidental protection afforded by balance of payments import restrictions.

Paragraph 21

Any measure taken pursuant to the provisions of paragraph 21 shall be withdrawn forthwith if the action taken in accordance with paragraph 17 is withdrawn or if the CONTRACTING PARTIES concur in the measure proposed after the expiration of the ninety-day time limit specified in paragraph 17.

Ad Article XX

Subparagraph **(h)**

The exception provided for in this subparagraph extends to any commodity agreement which conforms to the principles approved by the Economic and Social Council in its resolution 30 (IV) of 28 March 1947.

Ad Article XXIV

Paragraph 9

It is understood that the provisions of Article I would require that, when a product which has been imported into the territory of a member of a customs union or free-trade area at a preferential rate of duty is re-exported to the territory of another member of such union or area, the latter member should collect a duty equal to the difference between the duty already paid and any higher duty that would be payable if the product were being imported directly into its territory.

Paragraph 11

Measures adopted by India and Pakistan in order to carry out definitive trade arrangements between them, once they have been agreed upon, might depart from particular provisions of this Agreement, but these measures would in general be consistent with the objectives of the Agreement.

Ad Article XXVIII

The CONTRACTING PARTIES and each contracting party concerned should arrange to conduct the negotiations and consultations with the greatest possible secrecy in order to avoid premature disclosure of details of prospective tariff changes. The CONTRACTING PARTIES shall be informed immediately of all changes in national tariffs resulting from recourse to this Article.

Paragraph 1

1. If the CONTRACTING PARTIES specify a period other than a three-year period, a contracting party may act pursuant to paragraph 1 or paragraph 3 of Article XXVIII on the first day following the expiration of such other period and, unless the CONTRACTING PARTIES have again specified another period, subsequent periods will be three-year periods following the expiration of such specified period.

2. The provision that on 1 January 1958, and on other days determined pursuant to paragraph 1, a contracting party "may . . . modify or withdraw a concession" means that on such day, and on the first day after the end of each period, the legal obligation of such contracting party under Article II is altered; it does not mean that the changes in its customs tariff should necessarily be made effective on that day. If a tariff change resulting from negotiations undertaken pursuant to this Article is delayed, the entry into force of any compensatory concessions may be similarly delayed.

3. Not earlier than six months, nor later than three months, prior to 1 January 1958, or to the termination date of any subsequent period, a contracting party wishing to modify or withdraw any concession embodied in the appropriate Schedule, should notify the CONTRACTING PARTIES to this effect. The CONTRACTING PARTIES shall then determine the contracting party or contracting parties with which the negotiations or consultations referred to in paragraph 1 shall take place. Any contracting party so determined shall participate in such negotiations or consultations with the applicant contracting party with the aim of reaching agreement before the end of the period. Any extension of the assured life of the Schedules shall relate to the Schedules as modified after such negotiations, in accordance with paragraphs 1, 2, and 3 of Article XXVIII. If the CONTRACTING PARTIES are arranging for multilateral tariff negotiations to take place within the period of six months before 1 January 1958, or before any other day determined pursuant to paragraph 1, they shall include in the arrangements for such negotiations suitable procedures for carrying out the negotiations referred to in this paragraph.

4. The object of providing for the participation in the negotiation of any contracting party with a principle supplying interest, in addition to any contracting party with which the concession was originally negotiated, is to ensure that a contracting party with a larger share in the trade affected by the concession than a contracting party with which the concession was originally negotiated shall have an effective opportunity to protect the contractual right which it enjoys under this Agreement. On the other hand, it is not intended that the scope of the negotiations should be such as to make negotiations and agreement under Article XXVIII unduly difficult nor to create complications in the application of this Article in the future to

concessions which result from negotiations thereunder. Accordingly, the CONTRACTING PARTIES should only determine that a contracting party has a principal supplying interest if that contracting party has had, over a reasonable period of time prior to the negotiations, a larger share in the market of the applicant contracting party than a contracting party with which the concession was initially negotiated or would, in the judgement of the CONTRACTING PARTIES, have had such a share in the absence of discriminatory quantitative restrictions maintained by the applicant contracting party. It would therefore not be appropriate for the CONTRACTING PARTIES to determine that more than one contracting party, or in those exceptional cases where there is near equality more than two contracting parties, had a principal supplying interest.

5. Notwithstanding the definition of a principal supplying interest in note 4 to paragraph 1, the CONTRACTING PARTIES may exceptionally determine that a contracting party has a principal supplying interest if the concession in question affects trade which constitutes a major part of the total exports of such contracting party.

6. It is not intended that provision for participation in the negotiations of any contracting party with a principal supplying interest, and for consultation with any contracting party having a substantial interest in the concession which the applicant contracting party is seeking to modify or withdraw, should have the effect that it should have to pay compensation or suffer retaliation greater than the withdrawal or modification sought, judged in the light of the conditions of trade at the time of the proposed withdrawal or modification, making allowance for any discriminatory quantitative restrictions maintained by the applicant contracting party.

7. The expression "substantial interest" is not capable of a precise definition and accordingly may present difficulties for the CONTRACTING PARTIES. It is, however, intended to be construed to cover only those contracting parties which have, or in the absence of discriminatory quantitative restrictions affecting their exports could reasonably be expected to have, a significant share in the market of the contracting party seeking to modify or withdraw the concession.

Paragraph 4

1. Any request for authorization to enter into negotiations shall be accompanied by all relevant statistical and other data. A decision on such request shall be made within thirty days of its submission.

2. It is recognized that to permit certain contracting parties, depending in large measure on a relatively small number of primary commodities and relying on the tariff as an important aid for furthering diversification of their

economies or as an important source of revenue, normally to negotiate for the modification or withdrawal of concessions only under paragraph 1 of Article XXVIII, might cause them at such time to make modifications or withdrawals which in the long run would prove unnecessary. To avoid such a situation the CONTRACTING PARTIES shall authorize any such contracting party, under paragraph 4, to enter into negotiations unless they consider this would result in, or contribute substantially towards, such an increase in tariff levels as to threaten the stability of the Schedules to this Agreement or lead to undue disturbance of international trade.

3. It is expected that negotiations authorized under paragraph 4 for modification or withdrawal of a single item, or a very small group of items, could normally be brought to a conclusion in sixty days. It is recognized, however, that such a period will be inadequate for cases involving negotiations for the modification or withdrawal of a larger number of items and in such cases, therefore, it would be appropriate for the CONTRACTING PARTIES to prescribe a longer period.

4. The determination referred to in paragraph 4 *(d)* shall be made by the CONTRACTING PARTIES within thirty days of the submission of the matter to them unless the applicant contracting party agrees to a longer period.

5. In determining under paragraph 4 *(d)* whether an applicant contracting party has unreasonably failed to offer adequate compensation, it is understood that the CONTRACTING PARTIES will take due account of the special position of a contracting party which has bound a high proportion of its tariffs at very low rates of duty and to this extent has less scope than other contracting parties to make compensatory adjustment.

Ad Article XXVIII bis

Paragraph 3

It is understood that the reference to fiscal needs would include the revenues aspect of duties and particularly duties imposed primarily for revenue purpose, or duties imposed on products which can be substituted for products subject to revenue duties to prevent the avoidance of such duties.

Ad Article XXIX

Paragraph 1

Chapters VII and VIII of the Havana Charter have been excluded from paragraph 1 because they generally deal with the organization, functions and procedures of the International Trade Organization.

Ad Part IV

The words "developed contracting parties" and the words "less-developed contracting parties" as used in Part IV are to be understood to refer to developed and less-developed countries which are parties to the General Agreement on Tariffs and Trade.

Ad Article XXXVI

Paragraph 1

This Article is based upon the objectives set forth in Article I as it will be amended by Section A of paragraph 1 of the Protocol Amending Part I and Articles XXIX and XXX when that Protocol enters into force.[12]

Paragraph 4

The term "primary products" includes agricultural products, *vide* paragraph 2 of the note *ad* Article XVI, Section B.

Paragraph 5

A diversification programme would generally include the intensification of activities for the processing of primary products and the development of manufacturing industries, taking into account the situation of the particular contracting party and the world outlook for production and consumption of different commodities.

Paragraph 8

It is understood that the phrase "do not expect reciprocity" means, in accordance with the objectives set forth in this Article, that the less-developed contracting parties should not be expected, in the course of trade negotiations, to make contributions which are inconsistent with their individual development, financial and trade needs, taking into consideration past trade developments.

This paragraph would apply in the event of action under Section A of Article XVIII, Article XXVIII, Article XXVIII *bis* (Article XXIX after the amendment set forth in Section A of paragraph 1 of the Protocol Amending Part I and Articles XXIX and XXX shall have become effective[13]), Article XXXIII, or any other procedure under this Agreement.

12. This Protocol was abandoned on 1 January 1968.
13. This Protocol was abandoned on 1 January 1968.

Ad Article XXXVII

Paragraph 1 (a)

This paragraph would apply in the event of negotiations for reduction or elimination of tariffs or other restrictive regulations of commerce under Articles XXVIII, XXVIII *bis* (XXIX after the amendment set forth in Section A of paragraph 1 of the Protocol Amending Part I and Articles XXIX and XXX shall have become effective[13]), and Article XXXIII, as well as in connection with other action to effect such reduction or elimination which contracting parties may be able to undertake.

Paragraph 3 (b)

The other measures referred to in this paragraph might include steps to promote domestic structural changes, to encourage the consumption of particular products, or to introduce measures of trade promotion.

Document 14

GENERAL AGREEMENT ON TARIFFS AND TRADE 1994

1. The General Agreement on Tariffs and Trade 1994 ("GATT 1994") shall consist of:

(a) the provisions in the General Agreement on Tariffs and Trade, dated 30 October 1947, annexed to the Final Act Adopted at the Conclusion of the Second Session of the Preparatory Committee of the United Nations Conference on Trade and Employment (excluding the Protocol of Provisional Application), as rectified, amended or modified by the terms of legal instruments which have entered into force before the date of entry into force of the WTO Agreement;

(b) the provisions of the legal instruments set forth below that have entered into force under the GATT 1947 before the date of entry into force of the WTO Agreement:

(i) protocols and certifications relating to tariff concessions;

(ii) protocols of accession (excluding the provisions (*a*) concerning provisional application and withdrawal of provisional application and (*b*) providing that Part II of GATT 1947 shall be applied provisionally to the fullest extent not inconsistent with legislation existing on the date of the Protocol);

(iii) decisions on waivers granted under Article XXV of GATT 1947 and still in force on the date of entry into force of the WTO Agreement[1];

(iv) other decisions of the CONTRACTING PARTIES to GATT 1947;

(c) the Understandings set forth below:

(i) Understanding on the Interpretation of Article II:1(b) of the General Agreement on Tariffs and Trade 1994;

(ii) Understanding on the Interpretation of Article XVII of the General Agreement on Tariffs and Trade 1994;

(iii) Understanding on Balance-of-Payments Provisions of the General Agreement on Tariffs and Trade 1994;

(iv) Understanding on the Interpretation of Article XXIV of the General Agreement on Tariffs and Trade 1994;

(v) Understanding in Respect of Waivers of Obligations under the General Agreement on Tariffs and Trade 1994;

(vi) Understanding on the Interpretation of Article XXVIII of the General Agreement on Tariffs and Trade 1994; and

(d) the Marrakesh Protocol to GATT 1994.

2. Explanatory Notes

(a) The references to "contracting party" in the provisions of GATT 1994 shall be deemed to read "Member." The references to "less-developed contracting party" and "developed contracting party" shall be deemed to read "developing country Member" and "developed country Member." The references to "Executive Secretary" shall be deemed to read "Director-General of the WTO."

(b) The references to the CONTRACTING PARTIES acting jointly in Articles XV:1, XV:2, XV:8, XXXVIII and the Notes *Ad* Article XII and

1. The waivers covered by this provision are listed in footnote 7 on pages 11 and 12 in Part II of document MTN/FA of 15 December 1993 and in MTN/FA/Corr.6 of 21 March 1994. The Ministerial Conference shall establish at its first session a revised list of waivers covered by this provision that adds any waivers granted under GATT 1947 after 15 December 1993 and before the date of entry into force of the WTO Agreement, and deletes the waivers which will have expired by that time.

XVIII; and in the provisions on special exchange agreements in Articles XV:2, XV:3, XV:6, XV:7 and XV:9 of GATT 1994 shall be deemed to be references to the WTO. The other functions that the provisions of GATT 1994 assign to the CONTRACTING PARTIES acting jointly shall be allocated by the Ministerial Conference.

(c) (i) The text of GATT 1994 shall be authentic in English, French and Spanish.

(ii) The text of GATT 1994 in the French language shall be subject to the rectifications of terms indicated in Annex A to document MTN. TNC/41.

(iii) The authentic text of GATT 1994 in the Spanish language shall be the text in Volume IV of the Basic Instruments and Selected Documents series, subject to the rectifications of terms indicated in Annex B to document MTN.TNC/41.

3. (a) The provisions of Part II of GATT 1994 shall not apply to measures taken by a Member under specific mandatory legislation, enacted by that Member before it became a contracting party to GATT 1947, that prohibits the use, sale or lease of foreign-built or foreign-reconstructed vessels in commercial applications between points in national waters or the waters of an exclusive economic zone. This exemption applies to: (*a*) the continuation or prompt renewal of a non-conforming provision of such legislation; and (*b*) the amendment to a non-conforming provision of such legislation to the extent that the amendment does not decrease the conformity of the provision with Part II of GATT 1947. This exemption is limited to measures taken under legislation described above that is notified and specified prior to the date of entry into force of the WTO Agreement. If such legislation is subsequently modified to decrease its conformity with Part II of GATT 1994, it will no longer qualify for coverage under this paragraph.

(b) The Ministerial Conference shall review this exemption not later than five years after the date of entry into force of the WTO Agreement and thereafter every two years for as long as the exemption is in force for the purpose of examining whether the conditions which created the need for the exemption still prevail.

(c) A Member whose measures are covered by this exemption shall annually submit a detailed statistical notification consisting of a five-year moving average of actual and expected deliveries of relevant vessels as well as additional information on the use, sale, lease or repair of relevant vessels covered by this exemption.

(d) A Member that considers that this exemption operates in such a manner as to justify a reciprocal and proportionate limitation on the use, sale, lease or repair of vessels constructed in the territory of the Member invoking the exemption shall be free to introduce such a limitation subject to prior notification to the Ministerial Conference.

(e) This exemption is without prejudice to solutions concerning specific aspects of the legislation covered by this exemption negotiated in sectoral agreements or in other fora.

Document 15

MARRAKESH PROTOCOL TO THE GENERAL AGREEMENT ON TARIFFS AND TRADE 1994

Members,

Having carried out negotiations within the framework of GATT 1947, pursuant to the Ministerial Declaration on the Uruguay Round,

Hereby *agree* as follows:

1. The schedule annexed to this Protocol relating to a Member shall become a Schedule to GATT 1994 relating to that Member on the day on which the WTO Agreement enters into force for that Member. Any schedule submitted in accordance with the Ministerial Decision on measures in favour of least-developed countries shall be deemed to be annexed to this Protocol.

2. The tariff reductions agreed upon by each Member shall be implemented in five equal rate reductions, except as may be otherwise specified in a Member's Schedule. The first such reduction shall be made effective on the date of entry into force of the WTO Agreement, each successive reduction shall be made effective on 1 January of each of the following years, and the final rate shall become effective no later than the date four years after the date of entry into force of the WTO Agreement, except as may be otherwise specified in that Member's Schedule. Unless otherwise specified in its Schedule, a Member that accepts the WTO Agreement after its entry into force shall, on the date that Agreement enters into force for it, make effective all rate reductions that have already taken place together with the reductions which it would under the preceding sentence have been obligated to make effective on 1 January of the year following, and shall make effective all

remaining rate reductions on the schedule specified in the previous sentence. The reduced rate should in each stage be rounded off to the first decimal. For agricultural products, as defined in Article 2 of the Agreement on Agriculture, the staging of reductions shall be implemented as specified in the relevant parts of the schedules.

3. The implementation of the concessions and commitments contained in the schedules annexed to this Protocol shall, upon request, be subject to multilateral examination by the Members. This would be without prejudice to the rights and obligations of Members under Agreements in Annex 1A of the WTO Agreement.

4. After the schedule annexed to this Protocol relating to a Member has become a Schedule to GATT 1994 pursuant to the provisions of paragraph 1, such Member shall be free at any time to withhold or to withdraw in whole or in part the concession in such Schedule with respect to any product for which the principal supplier is any other Uruguay Round participant the schedule of which has not yet become a Schedule to GATT 1994. Such action can, however, only be taken after written notice of any such withholding or withdrawal of a concession has been given to the Council for Trade in Goods and after consultations have been held, upon request, with any Member, the relevant schedule relating to which has become a Schedule to GATT 1994 and which has a substantial interest in the product involved. Any concessions so withheld or withdrawn shall be applied on and after the day on which the schedule of the Member which has the principal supplying interest becomes a Schedule to GATT 1994.

5. (a) Without prejudice to the provisions of paragraph 2 of Article 4 of the Agreement on Agriculture, for the purpose of the reference in paragraphs 1:(b) and 1(c) of Article II of GATT 1994 to the date of that Agreement, the applicable date in respect of each product which is the subject of a concession provided for in a schedule of concessions annexed to this Protocol shall be the date of this Protocol.

(b) For the purpose of the reference in paragraph 6(a) of Article II of GATT 1994 to the date of that Agreement, the applicable date in respect of a schedule of concessions annexed to this Protocol shall be the date of this Protocol.

6. In cases of modification or withdrawal of concessions relating to non-tariff measures as contained in Part III of the schedules, the provisions of Article XXVIII of GATT 1994 and the "Procedures for Negotiations under Article XXVIII" adopted on 10 November 1980 (BISD 27S/26-28) shall apply. This would be without prejudice to the rights and obligations of Members under GATT 1994.

7. In each case in which a schedule annexed to this Protocol results for any product in treatment less favourable than was provided for such product in the Schedules of GATT 1947 prior to the entry into force of the WTO Agreement, the Member to whom the schedule relates shall be deemed to have taken appropriate action as would have been otherwise necessary under the relevant provisions of Article XXVIII of GATT 1947 or 1994. The provisions of this paragraph shall apply only to Egypt, Peru, South Africa and Uruguay.

8. The Schedules annexed hereto are authentic in the English, French or Spanish language as specified in each Schedule.

9. The date of this Protocol is 15 April 1994.

[The agreed schedules of participants will be annexed to the Marrakesh Protocol in the treaty copy of the WTO Agreement.]

Document 16

UNDERSTANDING ON THE INTERPRETATION OF ARTICLE II:1(b) OF THE GENERAL AGREEMENT ON TARIFFS AND TRADE 1994

Members hereby *agree* as follows:

1. In order to ensure transparency of the legal rights and obligations deriving from paragraph 1(b) of Article II, the nature and level of any "other duties or charges" levied on bound tariff items, as referred to in that provision, shall be recorded in the Schedules of concessions annexed to GATT 1994 against the tariff item to which they apply. It is understood that such recording does not change the legal character of "other duties or charges."

2. The date as of which "other duties or charges" are bound, for the purposes of Article II, shall be 15 April 1994. "Other duties or charges" shall therefore be recorded in the Schedules at the levels applying on this date. At each subsequent renegotiation of a concession or negotiation of a new concession the applicable date for the tariff item in question shall become the date of the incorporation of the new concession in the appropriate Schedule. However, the date of the instrument by which a concession on any particular tariff item was first incorporated into GATT 1947 or GATT 1994 shall also continue to be recorded in column 6 of the Loose-Leaf Schedules.

3. "Other duties or charges" shall be recorded in respect of all tariff bindings.

4. Where a tariff item has previously been the subject of a concession, the level of "other duties or charges" recorded in the appropriate Schedule shall not be higher than the level obtaining at the time of the first incor-

poration of the concession in that Schedule. It will be open to any Member to challenge the existence of an "other duty or charge," on the ground that no such "other duty or charge" existed at the time of the original binding of the item in question, as well as the consistency of the recorded level of any "other duty or charge" with the previously bound level, for a period of three years after the date of entry into force of the WTO Agreement or three years after the date of deposit with the Director-General of the WTO of the instrument incorporating the Schedule in question into GATT 1994, if that is a later date.

5. The recording of "other duties or charges" in the Schedules is without prejudice to their consistency with rights and obligations under GATT 1994 other than those affected by paragraph 4. All Members retain the right to challenge, at any time, the consistency of any "other duty or charge" with such obligations.

6. For the purposes of this Understanding, the provisions of Articles XXII and XXIII of GATT 1994 as elaborated and applied by the Dispute Settlement Understanding shall apply.

7. "Other duties or charges" omitted from a Schedule at the time of deposit of the instrument incorporating the Schedule in question into GATT 1994 with, until the date of entry into force of the WTO Agreement, the Director-General to the CONTRACTING PARTIES to GATT 1947 or, thereafter, with the Director-General of the WTO, shall not subsequently be added to it and any "other duty or charge" recorded at a level lower than that prevailing on the applicable date shall not be restored to that level unless such additions or changes are made within six months of the date of deposit of the instrument.

8. The decision in paragraph 2 regarding the date applicable to each concession for the purposes of paragraph 1(b) of Article II of GATT 1994 supersedes the decision regarding the applicable date taken on 26 March 1980 (BISD 27S/24).

Document 17

UNDERSTANDING ON THE INTERPRETATION OF ARTICLE XVII OF THE GENERAL AGREEMENT ON TARIFFS AND TRADE 1994

Members,

Noting that Article XVII provides for obligations on Members in respect of the activities of the state trading enterprises referred to in paragraph 1 of Article XVII, which are required to be consistent with the general principles of non-discriminatory treatment prescribed in GATT 1994 for governmental measures affecting imports or exports by private traders;

Noting further that Members are subject to their GATT 1994 obligations in respect of those governmental measures affecting state trading enterprises;

Recognizing that this Understanding is without prejudice to the substantive disciplines prescribed in Article XVII;

Hereby *agree* as follows:

1. In order to ensure the transparency of the activities of state trading enterprises, Members shall notify such enterprises to the Council for Trade in Goods, for review by the working party to be set up under paragraph 5, in accordance with the following working definition:

> "Governmental and non-governmental enterprises, including marketing boards, which have been granted exclusive or special rights or privileges, including statutory or constitutional powers, in the exercise of which they

> influence through their purchases or sales the level or direction of imports or exports."

This notification requirement does not apply to imports of products for immediate or ultimate consumption in governmental use or in use by an enterprise as specified above and not otherwise for resale or use in the production of goods for sale.

2. Each Member shall conduct a review of its policy with regard to the submission of notifications on state trading enterprises to the Council for Trade in Goods, taking account of the provisions of this Understanding. In carrying out such a review, each Member should have regard to the need to ensure the maximum transparency possible in its notifications so as to permit a clear appreciation of the manner of operation of the enterprises notified and the effect of their operations on international trade.

3. Notifications shall be made in accordance with the questionnaire on state trading adopted on 24 May 1960 (BISD 9S/184-185), it being understood that Members shall notify the enterprises referred to in paragraph 1 whether or not imports or exports have in fact taken place.

4. Any Member which has reason to believe that another Member has not adequately met its notification obligation may raise the matter with the Member concerned. If the matter is not satisfactorily resolved it may make a counter-notification to the Council for Trade in Goods, for consideration by the working party set up under paragraph 5, simultaneously informing the Member concerned.

5. A working party shall be set up, on behalf of the Council for Trade in Goods, to review notifications and counter-notifications. In the light of this review and without prejudice to paragraph 4(c) of Article XVII, the Council for Trade in Goods may make recommendations with regard to the adequacy of notifications and the need for further information. The working party shall also review, in the light of the notifications received, the adequacy of the above-mentioned questionnaire on state trading and the coverage of state trading enterprises notified under paragraph 1. It shall also develop an illustrative list showing the kinds of relationships between governments and enterprises, and the kinds of activities, engaged in by these enterprises, which may be relevant for the purposes of Article XVII. It is understood that the Secretariat will provide a general background paper for the working party on the operations of state trading enterprises as they relate to international trade. Membership of the working party shall be open to all Members indicating their wish to serve on it. It shall meet within a year of the date of entry into force of the WTO Agreement and thereafter

at least once a year. It shall report annually to the Council for Trade in Goods.[1]

1. The activities of this working party shall be coordinated with those of the working group provided for in Section III of the Ministerial Decision on Notification Procedures adopted on 15 April 1994.

Document 18

UNDERSTANDING ON THE BALANCE-OF-PAYMENTS PROVISIONS OF THE GENERAL AGREEMENT ON TARIFFS AND TRADE 1994

Members,

Recognizing the provisions of Articles XII and XVIII:B of GATT 1994 and of the Declaration on Trade Measures Taken for Balance-of-Payments Purposes adopted on 28 November 1979 (BISD 26S/205-209, referred to in this Understanding as the "1979 Declaration") and in order to clarify such provisions;[1]

Hereby *agree* as follows:

Application of Measures

1. Members confirm their commitment to announce publicly, as soon as possible, time-schedules for the removal of restrictive import measures taken for balance-of-payments purposes. It is understood that such time-schedules may be modified as appropriate to take into account changes in the balance-of-payments situation. Whenever a time-schedule is not publicly announced

1. Nothing in this Understanding is intended to modify the rights and obligations of Members under Articles XII or XVIII:B of GATT 1994. The provisions of Articles XXII and XXIII of GATT 1994 as elaborated and applied by the Dispute Settlement Understanding may be invoked with respect to any matters arising from the application of restrictive import measures taken for balance-of-payments purposes.

by a Member, that Member shall provide justification as to the reasons therefor.

2. Members confirm their commitment to give preference to those measures which have the least disruptive effect on trade. Such measures (referred to in this Understanding as "price-based measures") shall be understood to include import surcharges, import deposit requirements or other equivalent trade measures with an impact on the price of imported goods. It is understood that, notwithstanding the provisions of Article II, price-based measures taken for balance-of-payments purposes may be applied by a Member in excess of the duties inscribed in the Schedule of that Member. Furthermore, that Member shall indicate the amount by which the price-based measure exceeds the bound duty clearly and separately under the notification procedures of this Understanding.

3. Members shall seek to avoid the imposition of new quantitative restrictions for balance-of-payments purposes unless, because of a critical balance-of-payments situation, price-based measures cannot arrest a sharp deterioration in the external payments position. In those cases in which a Member applies quantitative restrictions, it shall provide justification as to the reasons why price-based measures are not an adequate instrument to deal with the balance-of-payments situation. A Member maintaining quantitative restrictions shall indicate in successive consultations the progress made in significantly reducing the incidence and restrictive effect of such measures. It is understood that not more than one type of restrictive import measure taken for balance-of-payments purposes may be applied on the same product.

4. Members confirm that restrictive import measures taken for balance-of-payments purposes may only be applied to control the general level of imports and may not exceed what is necessary to address the balance-of-payments situation. In order to minimize any incidental protective effects, a Member shall administer restrictions in a transparent manner. The authorities of the importing Member shall provide adequate justification as to the criteria used to determine which products are subject to restriction. As provided in paragraph 3 of Article XII and paragraph 10 of Article XVIII, Members may, in the case of certain essential products, exclude or limit the application of surcharges applied across the board or other measures applied for balance-of-payments purposes. The term "essential products" shall be understood to mean products which meet basic consumption needs or which contribute to the Member's effort to improve its balance-of-payments situation, such as capital goods or inputs needed for production. In the administration of quantitative restrictions, a Member shall use discretionary licensing only when unavoidable and shall phase it out progressively. Appropriate justification shall be provided as to the criteria used to determine allowable import quantities or values.

Procedures for Balance-of-Payments Consultations

5. The Committee on Balance-of-Payments Restrictions (referred to in this Understanding as the "Committee") shall carry out consultations in order to review all restrictive import measures taken for balance-of-payments purposes. The membership of the Committee is open to all Members indicating their wish to serve on it. The Committee shall follow the procedures for consultations on balance-of-payments restrictions approved on 28 April 1970 (BISD 18S/48-53, referred to in this Understanding as "full consultation procedures"), subject to the provisions set out below.

6. A Member applying new restrictions or raising the general level of its existing restrictions by a substantial intensification of the measures shall enter into consultations with the Committee within four months of the adoption of such measures. The Member adopting such measures may request that a consultation be held under paragraph 4(a) of Article XII or paragraph 12(a) of Article XVIII as appropriate. If no such request has been made, the Chairman of the Committee shall invite the Member to hold such a consultation. Factors that may be examined in the consultation would include, *inter alia*, the introduction of new types of restrictive measures for balance-of-payments purposes, or an increase in the level or product coverage of restrictions.

7. All restrictions applied for balance-of-payments purposes shall be subject to periodic review in the Committee under paragraph 4(b) of Article XII or under paragraph 12(b) of Article XVIII, subject to the possibility of altering the periodicity of consultations in agreement with the consulting Member or pursuant to any specific review procedure that may be recommended by the General Council.

8. Consultations may be held under the simplified procedures approved on 19 December 1972 (BISD 20S/47-49, referred to in this Understanding as "simplified consultation procedures") in the case of least-developed country Members or in the case of developing country Members which are pursuing liberalization efforts in conformity with the schedule presented to the Committee in previous consultations. Simplified consultation procedures may also be used when the Trade Policy Review of a developing country Member is scheduled for the same calendar year as the date fixed for the consultations. In such cases the decision as to whether full consultation procedures should be used will be made on the basis of the factors enumerated in paragraph 8 of the 1979 Declaration. Except in the case of least-developed country Members, no more than two successive consultations may be held under simplified consultation procedures.

Notification and Documentation

9. A Member shall notify to the General Council the introduction of or any changes in the application of restrictive import measures taken for balance-of-payments purposes, as well as any modifications in time-schedules for the removal of such measures as announced under paragraph 1. Significant changes shall be notified to the General Council prior to or not later than 30 days after their announcement. On a yearly basis, each Member shall make available to the Secretariat a consolidated notification, including all changes in laws, regulations, policy statements or public notices, for examination by Members. Notifications shall include full information, as far as possible, at the tariff-line level, on the type of measures applied, the criteria used for their administration, product coverage and trade flows affected.

10. At the request of any Member, notifications may be reviewed by the Committee. Such reviews would be limited to the clarification of specific issues raised by a notification or examination of whether a consultation under paragraph 4(a) of Article XII or paragraph 12(a) of Article XVIII is required. Members which have reasons to believe that a restrictive import measure applied by another Member was taken for balance-of-payments purposes may bring the matter to the attention of the Committee. The Chairman of the Committee shall request information on the measure and make it available to all Members. Without prejudice to the right of any member of the Committee to seek appropriate clarifications in the course of consultations, questions may be submitted in advance for consideration by the consulting Member.

11. The consulting Member shall prepare a Basic Document for the consultations which, in addition to any other information considered to be relevant, should include: *(a)* an overview of the balance-of-payments situation and prospects, including a consideration of the internal and external factors having a bearing on the balance-of-payments situation and the domestic policy measures taken in order to restore equilibrium on a sound and lasting basis; *(b)* a full description of the restrictions applied for balance-of-payments purposes, their legal basis and steps taken to reduce incidental protective effects; *(c)* measures taken since the last consultation to liberalize import restrictions, in the light of the conclusions of the Committee; *(d)* a plan for the elimination and progressive relaxation of remaining restrictions. References may be made, when relevant, to the information provided in other notifications or reports made to the WTO. Under simplified consultation procedures, the consulting Member shall submit a written statement containing essential information on the elements covered by the Basic Document.

12. The Secretariat shall, with a view to facilitating the consultations in the Committee, prepare a factual background paper dealing with the

different aspects of the plan for consultations. In the case of developing country Members, the Secretariat document shall include relevant background and analytical material on the incidence of the external trading environment on the balance-of-payments situation and prospects of the consulting Member. The technical assistance services of the Secretariat shall, at the request of a developing country Member, assist in preparing the documentation for the consultations.

Conclusions of Balance-of-Payments Consultations

13. The Committee shall report on its consultations to the General Council. When full consultation procedures have been used, the report should indicate the Committee's conclusions on the different elements of the plan for consultations, as well as the facts and reasons on which they are based. The Committee shall endeavour to include in its conclusions proposals for recommendations aimed at promoting the implementation of Articles XII and XVIII:B, the 1979 Declaration and this Understanding. In those cases in which a time-schedule has been presented for the removal of restrictive measures taken for balance-of-payments purposes, the General Council may recommend that, in adhering to such a time-schedule, a Member shall be deemed to be in compliance with its GATT 1994 obligations. Whenever the General Council has made specific recommendations, the rights and obligations of Members shall be assessed in the light of such recommendations. In the absence of specific proposals for recommendations by the General Council, the Committee's conclusions should record the different views expressed in the Committee. When simplified consultation procedures have been used, the report shall include a summary of the main elements discussed in the Committee and a decision on whether full consultation procedures are required.

Document 19

UNDERSTANDING ON THE INTERPRETATION OF ARTICLE XXIV OF THE GENERAL AGREEMENT ON TARIFFS AND TRADE 1994

Members,

Having regard to the provisions of Article XXIV of GATT 1994;

Recognizing that customs unions and free trade areas have greatly increased in number and importance since the establishment of GATT 1947 and today cover a significant proportion of world trade;

Recognizing the contribution to the expansion of world trade that may be made by closer integration between the economies of the parties to such agreements;

Recognizing also that such contribution is increased if the elimination between the constituent territories of duties and other restrictive regulations of commerce extends to all trade, and diminished if any major sector of trade is excluded;

Reaffirming that the purpose of such agreements should be to facilitate trade between the constituent territories and not to raise barriers to the trade of other Members with such territories; and that in their formation or enlargement the parties to them should to the greatest possible extent avoid creating adverse effects on the trade of other Members;

Convinced also of the need to reinforce the effectiveness of the role of the Council for Trade in Goods in reviewing agreements notified under Article

XXIV, by clarifying the criteria and procedures for the assessment of new or enlarged agreements, and improving the transparency of all Article XXIV agreements;

Recognizing the need for a common understanding of the obligations of Members under paragraph 12 of Article XXIV;

Hereby *agree* as follows:

1. Customs unions, free-trade areas, and interim agreements leading to the formation of a customs union or free-trade area, to be consistent with Article XXIV, must satisfy, *inter alia*, the provisions of paragraphs 5, 6, 7 and 8 of that Article.

Article XXIV:5

2. The evaluation under paragraph 5(a) of Article XXIV of the general incidence of the duties and other regulations of commerce applicable before and after the formation of a customs union shall in respect of duties and charges be based upon an overall assessment of weighted average tariff rates and of customs duties collected. This assessment shall be based on import statistics for a previous representative period to be supplied by the customs union, on a tariff-line basis and in values and quantities, broken down by WTO country of origin. The Secretariat shall compute the weighted average tariff rates and customs duties collected in accordance with the methodology used in the assessment of tariff offers in the Uruguay Round of Multilateral Trade Negotiations. For this purpose, the duties and charges to be taken into consideration shall be the applied rates of duty. It is recognized that for the purpose of the overall assessment of the incidence of other regulations of commerce for which quantification and aggregation are difficult, the examination of individual measures, regulations, products covered and trade flows affected may be required.

3. The "reasonable length of time" referred to in paragraph 5(c) of Article XXIV should exceed 10 years only in exceptional cases. In cases where Members parties to an interim agreement believe that 10 years would be insufficient they shall provide a full explanation to the Council for Trade in Goods of the need for a longer period.

Article XXIV:6

4. Paragraph 6 of Article XXIV establishes the procedure to be followed when a Member forming a customs union proposes to increase a bound rate of duty. In this regard Members reaffirm that the procedure set forth in Article XXVIII, as elaborated in the guidelines adopted on 10 November 1980 (BISD 27S/26-28) and in the Understanding on the Interpretation of

Article XXVIII of GATT 1994, must be commenced before tariff concessions are modified or withdrawn upon the formation of a customs union or an interim agreement leading to the formation of a customs union.

5. These negotiations will be entered into in good faith with a view to achieving mutually satisfactory compensatory adjustment. In such negotiations, as required by paragraph 6 of Article XXIV, due account shall be taken of reductions of duties on the same tariff line made by other constituents of the customs union upon its formation. Should such reductions not be sufficient to provide the necessary compensatory adjustment, the customs union would offer compensation, which may take the form of reductions of duties on other tariff lines. Such an offer shall be taken into consideration by the Members having negotiating rights in the binding being modified or withdrawn. Should the compensatory adjustment remain unacceptable, negotiations should be continued. Where, despite such efforts, agreement in negotiations on compensatory adjustment under Article XXVIII as elaborated by the Understanding on the Interpretation of Article XXVIII of GATT 1994 cannot be reached within a reasonable period from the initiation of negotiations, the customs union shall, nevertheless, be free to modify or withdraw the concessions; affected Members shall then be free to withdraw substantially equivalent concessions in accordance with Article XXVIII.

6. GATT 1994 imposes no obligation on Members benefiting from a reduction of duties consequent upon the formation of a customs union, or an interim agreement leading to the formation of a customs union, to provide compensatory adjustment to its constituents.

Review of Customs Unions and Free-Trade Areas

7. All notifications made under paragraph 7(a) of Article XXIV shall be examined by a working party in the light of the relevant provisions of GATT 1994 and of paragraph 1 of this Understanding. The working party shall submit a report to the Council for Trade in Goods on its findings in this regard. The Council for Trade in Goods may make such recommendations to Members as it deems appropriate.

8. In regard to interim agreements, the working party may in its report make appropriate recommendations on the proposed time-frame and on measures required to complete the formation of the customs union or free-trade area. It may if necessary provide for further review of the agreement.

9. Members parties to an interim agreement shall notify substantial changes in the plan and schedule included in that agreement to the Council for Trade in Goods and, if so requested, the Council shall examine the changes.

10. Should an interim agreement notified under paragraph 7(a) of Article XXIV not include a plan and schedule, contrary to paragraph 5(c) of Article XXIV, the working party shall in its report recommend such a plan and schedule. The parties shall not maintain or put into force, as the case may be, such agreement if they are not prepared to modify it in accordance with these recommendations. Provision shall be made for subsequent review of the implementation of the recommendations.

11. Customs unions and constituents of free-trade areas shall report periodically to the Council for Trade in Goods, as envisaged by the CONTRACTING PARTIES to GATT 1947 in their instruction to the GATT 1947 Council concerning reports on regional agreements (BISD 18S/38), on the operation of the relevant agreement. Any significant changes and/or developments in the agreements should be reported as they occur.

Dispute Settlement

12. The provisions of Articles XXII and XXIII of GATT 1994 as elaborated and applied by the Dispute Settlement Understanding may be invoked with respect to any matters arising from the application of those provisions of Article XXIV relating to customs unions, free-trade areas or interim agreements leading to the formation of a customs union or free-trade area.

Article XXIV:12

13. Each Member is fully responsible under GATT 1994 for the observance of all provisions of GATT 1994, and shall take such reasonable measures as may be available to it to ensure such observance by regional and local governments and authorities within its territory.

14. The provisions of Articles XXII and XXIII of GATT 1994 as elaborated and applied by the Dispute Settlement Understanding may be invoked in respect of measures affecting its observance taken by regional or local governments or authorities within the territory of a Member. When the Dispute Settlement Body has ruled that a provision of GATT 1994 has not been observed, the responsible Member shall take such reasonable measures as may be available to it to ensure its observance. The provisions relating to compensation and suspension of concessions or other obligations apply in cases where it has not been possible to secure such observance.

15. Each Member undertakes to accord sympathetic consideration to and afford adequate opportunity for consultation regarding any representations made by another Member concerning measures affecting the operation of GATT 1994 taken within the territory of the former.

Document 20

UNDERSTANDING IN RESPECT OF WAIVERS OF OBLIGATIONS UNDER THE GENERAL AGREEMENT ON TARIFFS AND TRADE 1994

Members hereby *agree* as follows:

1. A request for a waiver or for an extension of an existing waiver shall describe the measures which the Member proposes to take, the specific policy objectives which the Member seeks to pursue and the reasons which prevent the Member from achieving its policy objectives by measures consistent with its obligations under GATT 1994.

2. Any waiver in effect on the date of entry into force of the WTO Agreement shall terminate, unless extended in accordance with the procedures above and those of Article IX of the WTO Agreement, on the date of its expiry or two years from the date of entry into force of the WTO Agreement, whichever is earlier.

3. Any Member considering that a benefit accruing to it under GATT 1994 is being nullified or impaired as a result of:

(a) the failure of the Member to whom a waiver was granted to observe the terms or conditions of the waiver, or

(b) the application of a measure consistent with the terms and conditions of the waiver

may invoke the provisions of Article XXIII of GATT 1994 as elaborated and applied by the Dispute Settlement Understanding.

Document 21

UNDERSTANDING ON THE INTERPRETATION OF ARTICLE XXVIII OF THE GENERAL AGREEMENT ON TARIFFS AND TRADE 1994

Members hereby *agree* as follows:

1. For the purposes of modification or withdrawal of a concession, the Member which has the highest ratio of exports affected by the concession (i.e. exports of the product to the market of the Member modifying or withdrawing the concession) to its total exports shall be deemed to have a principal supplying interest if it does not already have an initial negotiating right or a principal supplying interest as provided for in paragraph 1 of Article XXVIII. It is however agreed that this paragraph will be reviewed by the Council for Trade in Goods five years from the date of entry into force of the WTO Agreement with a view to deciding whether this criterion has worked satisfactorily in securing a redistribution of negotiating rights in favour of small and medium-sized exporting Members. If this is not the case, consideration will be given to possible improvements, including, in the light of the availability of adequate data, the adoption of a criterion based on the ratio of exports affected by the concession to exports to all markets of the product in question.

2. Where a Member considers that it has a principal supplying interest in terms of paragraph 1, it should communicate its claim in writing, with supporting evidence, to the Member proposing to modify or withdraw a concession, and at the same time inform the Secretariat. Paragraph 4 of the "Procedures for Negotiations under Article XXVIII" adopted on 10 November 1980 (BISD 27S/26-28) shall apply in these cases.

3. In the determination of which Members have a principal supplying interest (whether as provided for in paragraph 1 above or in paragraph 1 of Article XXVIII) or substantial interest, only trade in the affected product which has taken place on an MFN basis shall be taken into consideration. However, trade in the affected product which has taken place under non-contractual preferences shall also be taken into account if the trade in question has ceased to benefit from such preferential treatment, thus becoming MFN trade, at the time of the negotiation for the modification or withdrawal of the concession, or will do so by the conclusion of that negotiation.

4. When a tariff concession is modified or withdrawn on a new product (i.e. a product for which three years' trade statistics are not available) the Member possessing initial negotiating rights on the tariff line where the product is or was formerly classified shall be deemed to have an initial negotiating right in the concession in question. The determination of principal supplying and substantial interests and the calculation of compensation shall take into account, *inter alia,* production capacity and investment in the affected product in the exporting Member and estimates of export growth, as well as forecasts of demand for the product in the importing Member. For the purposes of this paragraph, "new product" is understood to include a tariff item created by means of a breakout from an existing tariff line.

5. Where a Member considers that it has a principal supplying or a substantial interest in terms of paragraph 4, it should communicate its claim in writing, with supporting evidence, to the Member proposing to modify or withdraw a concession, and at the same time inform the Secretariat. Paragraph 4 of the above-mentioned "Procedures for Negotiations under Article XXVIII" shall apply in these cases.

6. When an unlimited tariff concession is replaced by a tariff rate quota, the amount of compensation provided should exceed the amount of the trade actually affected by the modification of the concession. The basis for the calculation of compensation should be the amount by which future trade prospects exceed the level of the quota. It is understood that the calculation of future trade prospects should be based on the greater of:

(a) the average annual trade in the most recent representative three-year period, increased by the average annual growth rate of imports in that same period, or by 10 per cent, whichever is the greater; or

(b) trade in the most recent year increased by 10 per cent.

In no case shall a Member's liability for compensation exceed that which would be entailed by complete withdrawal of the concession.

7. Any Member having a principal supplying interest, whether as provided for in paragraph 1 above or in paragraph 1 of Article XXVIII, in a concession which is modified or withdrawn shall be accorded an initial negotiating right in the compensatory concessions, unless another form of compensation is agreed by the Members concerned.

PART V

Trade in Goods: Other Agreements and Decisions

Document 22

CONFLICTS BETWEEN GATT 1994 AND OTHER MULTILATERAL AGREEMENTS ON TRADE IN GOODS

General interpretative note to Annex 1A:

In the event of conflict between a provision of the General Agreement on Tariffs and Trade 1994 and a provision of another agreement in Annex 1A to the Agreement Establishing the World Trade Organization (referred to in the agreements in Annex 1A as the "WTO Agreement"), the provision of the other agreement shall prevail to the extent of the conflict.

Document 23

AGREEMENT ON AGRICULTURE

Members,

Having decided to establish a basis for initiating a process of reform of trade in agriculture in line with the objectives of the negotiations as set out in the Punta del Este Declaration;

Recalling that their long-term objective as agreed at the Mid-Term Review of the Uruguay Round "is to establish a fair and market-oriented agricultural trading system and that a reform process should be initiated through the negotiation of commitments on support and protection and through the establishment of strengthened and more operationally effective GATT rules and disciplines";

Recalling further that "the above-mentioned long-term objective is to provide for substantial progressive reductions in agricultural support and protection sustained over an agreed period of time, resulting in correcting and preventing restrictions and distortions in world agricultural markets";

Committed to achieving specific binding commitments in each of the following areas: market access; domestic support; export competition; and to reaching an agreement on sanitary and phytosanitary issues;

Having agreed that in implementing their commitments on market access, developed country Members would take fully into account the particular needs and conditions of developing country Members by providing for a greater improvement of opportunities and terms of access for agricultural products of particular interest to these Members, including the fullest liberalization of trade in tropical agricultural products as agreed at the

Mid-Term Review, and for products of particular importance to the diversification of production from the growing of illicit narcotic crops;

Noting that commitments under the reform programme should be made in an equitable way among all Members, having regard to non-trade concerns, including food security and the need to protect the environment; having regard to the agreement that special and differential treatment for developing countries is an integral element of the negotiations, and taking into account the possible negative effects of the implementation of the reform programme on least-developed and net food-importing developing countries;

Hereby *agree* as follows:

Part I

Article 1

Definition of Terms

In this Agreement, unless the context otherwise requires:

(a) "Aggregate Measurement of Support" and "AMS" mean the annual level of support, expressed in monetary terms, provided for an agricultural product in favour of the producers of the basic agricultural product or non-product-specific support provided in favour of agricultural producers in general, other than support provided under programmes that qualify as exempt from reduction under Annex 2 to this Agreement, which is:

(i) with respect to support provided during the base period, specified in the relevant tables of supporting material incorporated by reference in Part IV of a Member's Schedule; and

(ii) with respect to support provided during any year of the implementation period and thereafter, calculated in accordance with the provisions of Annex 3 of this Agreement and taking into account the constituent data and methodology used in the tables of supporting material incorporated by reference in Part IV of the Member's Schedule;

(b) "basic agricultural product" in relation to domestic support commitments is defined as the product as close as practicable to the point of first sale as specified in a Member's Schedule and in the related supporting material;

(c) "budgetary outlays" or "outlays" includes revenue foregone;

(d) "Equivalent Measurement of Support" means the annual level of support, expressed in monetary terms, provided to producers of a basic agricultural product through the application of one or more measures, the calculation of which in accordance with the AMS methodology is impracticable, other than support provided under programmes that qualify as exempt from reduction under Annex 2 to this Agreement, and which is:

(i) with respect to support provided during the base period, specified in the relevant tables of supporting material incorporated by reference in Part IV of a Member's Schedule; and

(ii) with respect to support provided during any year of the implementation period and thereafter, calculated in accordance with the provisions of Annex 4 of this Agreement and taking into account the constituent data and methodology used in the tables of supporting material incorporated by reference in Part IV of the Member's Schedule;

(e) "export subsidies" refers to subsidies contingent upon export performance, including the export subsidies listed in Article 9 of this Agreement;

(f) "implementation period" means the six-year period commencing in the year 1995, except that, for the purposes of Article 13, it means the nine-year period commencing in 1995;

(g) "market access concessions" includes all market access commitments undertaken pursuant to this Agreement;

(h) "Total Aggregate Measurement of Support" and "Total AMS" mean the sum of all domestic support provided in favour of agricultural producers, calculated as the sum of all aggregate measurements of support for basic agricultural products, all non-product-specific aggregate measurements of support and all equivalent measurements of support for agricultural products, and which is:

(i) with respect to support provided during the base period (i.e. the "Base Total AMS") and the maximum support permitted to be provided during any year of the implementation period or thereafter (i.e. the "Annual and Final Bound Commitment Levels"), as specified in Part IV of a Member's Schedule; and

(ii) with respect to the level of support actually provided during any year of the implementation period and thereafter (i.e. the "Current Total AMS"), calculated in accordance with the provisions of this Agreement, including Article 6, and with the constituent data and methodology used in the tables of supporting material incorporated by reference in Part IV of the Member's Schedule;

(i) "year" in paragraph (f) above and in relation to the specific commitments of a Member refers to the calendar, financial or marketing year specified in the Schedule relating to that Member.

Article 2

Product Coverage

This Agreement applies to the products listed in Annex 1 to this Agreement, hereinafter referred to as agricultural products.

Part II

Article 3

Incorporation of Concessions and Commitments

1. The domestic support and export subsidy commitments in Part IV of each Member's Schedule constitute commitments limiting subsidization and are hereby made an integral part of GATT 1994.

2. Subject to the provisions of Article 6, a Member shall not provide support in favour of domestic producers in excess of the commitment levels specified in Section I of Part IV of its Schedule.

3. Subject to the provisions of paragraphs 2(b) and 4 of Article 9, a Member shall not provide export subsidies listed in paragraph 1 of Article 9 in respect of the agricultural products or groups of products specified in Section II of Part IV of its Schedule in excess of the budgetary outlay and quantity commitment levels specified therein and shall not provide such subsidies in respect of any agricultural product not specified in that Section of its Schedule.

Part III

Article 4

Market Access

1. Market access concessions contained in Schedules relate to bindings and reductions of tariffs, and to other market access commitments as specified therein.

2. Members shall not maintain, resort to, or revert to any measures of the kind which have been required to be converted into ordinary customs duties,[1] except as otherwise provided for in Article 5 and Annex 5.

Article 5

Special Safeguard Provisions

1. Notwithstanding the provisions of paragraph 1(b) of Article II of GATT 1994, any Member may take recourse to the provisions of paragraphs 4 and 5 below in connection with the importation of an agricultural product, in respect of which measures referred to in paragraph 2 of Article 4 of this Agreement have been converted into an ordinary customs duty and which is designated in its Schedule with the symbol "SSG" as being the subject of a concession in respect of which the provisions of this Article may be invoked, if:

(a) the volume of imports of that product entering the customs territory of the Member granting the concession during any year exceeds a trigger level which relates to the existing market access opportunity as set out in paragraph 4; or, but not concurrently:

(b) the price at which imports of that product may enter the customs territory of the Member granting the concession, as determined on the basis of the c.i.f. import price of the shipment concerned expressed in terms of its domestic currency, falls below a trigger price equal to the average 1986 to 1988 reference price[2] for the product concerned.

2. Imports under current and minimum access commitments established as part of a concession referred to in paragraph 1 above shall be counted for the purpose of determining the volume of imports required for invoking the provisions of subparagraph 1(a) and paragraph 4, but imports under such commitments shall not be affected by any additional duty imposed under either subparagraph 1(a) and paragraph 4 or subparagraph 1(b) and paragraph 5 below.

1. These measures include quantitative import restrictions, variable import levies, minimum import prices, discretionary import licensing, non-tariff measures maintained through state-trading enterprises, voluntary export restraints, and similar border measures other than ordinary customs duties, whether or not the measures are maintained under country-specific derogations from the provisions of GATT 1947, but not measures maintained under balance-of-payments provisions or under other general, non-agriculture-specific provisions of GATT 1994 or of the other Multilateral Trade Agreements in Annex 1A to the WTO Agreement.

2. The reference price used to invoke the provisions of this subparagraph shall, in general, be the average c.i.f. unit value of the product concerned, or otherwise shall be an appropriate price in terms of the quality of the product and its stage of processing. It shall, following its initial use, be publicly specified and available to the extent necessary to allow other Members to assess the additional duty that may be levied.

3. Any supplies of the product in question which were *en route* on the basis of a contract settled before the additional duty is imposed under subparagraph 1(a) and paragraph 4 shall be exempted from any such additional duty, provided that they may be counted in the volume of imports of the product in question during the following year for the purposes of triggering the provisions of subparagraph 1(a) in that year.

4. Any additional duty imposed under subparagraph 1(a) shall only be maintained until the end of the year in which it has been imposed, and may only be levied at a level which shall not exceed one third of the level of the ordinary customs duty in effect in the year in which the action is taken. The trigger level shall be set according to the following schedule based on market access opportunities defined as imports as a percentage of the corresponding domestic consumption[3] during the three preceding years for which data are available:

(a) where such market access opportunities for a product are less than or equal to 10 per cent, the base trigger level shall equal 125 per cent;

(b) where such market access opportunities for a product are greater than 10 per cent but less than or equal to 30 per cent, the base trigger level shall equal 110 per cent;

(c) where such market access opportunities for a product are greater than 30 per cent, the base trigger level shall equal 105 per cent.

In all cases the additional duty may be imposed in any year where the absolute volume of imports of the product concerned entering the customs territory of the Member granting the concession exceeds the sum of (*x*) the base trigger level set out above multiplied by the average quantity of imports during the three preceding years for which data are available and (*y*) the absolute volume change in domestic consumption of the product concerned in the most recent year for which data are available compared to the preceding year, provided that the trigger level shall not be less than 105 per cent of the average quantity of imports in (*x*) above.

5. The additional duty imposed under subparagraph 1(b) shall be set according to the following schedule:

(a) if the difference between the c.i.f. import price of the shipment expressed in terms of the domestic currency (hereinafter referred to as the "import price") and the trigger price as defined under that subparagraph is

3. Where domestic consumption is not taken into account, the base trigger level under subparagraph 4(a) shall apply.

less than or equal to 10 per cent of the trigger price, no additional duty shall be imposed;

(b) if the difference between the import price and the trigger price (hereinafter referred to as the "difference") is greater than 10 per cent but less than or equal to 40 per cent of the trigger price, the additional duty shall equal 30 per cent of the amount by which the difference exceeds 10 per cent;

(c) if the difference is greater than 40 per cent but less than or equal to 60 per cent of the trigger price, the additional duty shall equal 50 per cent of the amount by which the difference exceeds 40 per cent, plus the additional duty allowed under (b);

(d) if the difference is greater than 60 per cent but less than or equal to 75 per cent, the additional duty shall equal 70 per cent of the amount by which the difference exceeds 60 per cent of the trigger price, plus the additional duties allowed under (b) and (c);

(e) if the difference is greater than 75 per cent of the trigger price, the additional duty shall equal 90 per cent of the amount by which the difference exceeds 75 per cent, plus the additional duties allowed under (b), (c) and (d).

6. For perishable and seasonal products, the conditions set out above shall be applied in such a manner as to take account of the specific characteristics of such products. In particular, shorter time periods under subparagraph 1(a) and paragraph 4 may be used in reference to the corresponding periods in the base period and different reference prices for different periods may be used under subparagraph 1(b).

7. The operation of the special safeguard shall be carried out in a transparent manner. Any Member taking action under subparagraph 1(a) above shall give notice in writing, including relevant data, to the Committee on Agriculture as far in advance as may be practicable and in any event within 10 days of the implementation of such action. In cases where changes in consumption volumes must be allocated to individual tariff lines subject to action under paragraph 4, relevant data shall include the information and methods used to allocate these changes. A Member taking action under paragraph 4 shall afford any interested Members the opportunity to consult with it in respect of the conditions of application of such action. Any Member taking action under subparagraph 1(b) above shall give notice in writing, including relevant data, to the Committee on Agriculture within 10 days of the implementation of the first such action or, for perishable and seasonal products, the first action in any period. Members undertake, as far as practicable, not to take recourse to the provisions of subparagraph 1(b)

where the volume of imports of the products concerned are declining. In either case a Member taking such action shall afford any interested Members the opportunity to consult with it in respect of the conditions of application of such action.

8. Where measures are taken in conformity with paragraphs 1 through 7 above, Members undertake not to have recourse, in respect of such measures, to the provisions of paragraphs 1(a) and 3 of Article XIX of GATT 1994 or paragraph 2 of Article 8 of the Agreement on Safeguards.

9. The provisions of this Article shall remain in force for the duration of the reform process as determined under Article 20.

Part IV

Article 6

Domestic Support Commitments

1. The domestic support reduction commitments of each Member contained in Part IV of its Schedule shall apply to all of its domestic support measures in favour of agricultural producers with the exception of domestic measures which are not subject to reduction in terms of the criteria set out in this Article and in Annex 2 to this Agreement. The commitments are expressed in terms of Total Aggregate Measurement of Support and "Annual and Final Bound Commitment Levels."

2. In accordance with the Mid-Term Review Agreement that government measures of assistance, whether direct or indirect, to encourage agricultural and rural development are an integral part of the development programmes of developing countries, investment subsidies which are generally available to agriculture in developing country Members and agricultural input subsidies generally available to low-income or resource-poor producers in developing country Members shall be exempt from domestic support reduction commitments that would otherwise be applicable to such measures, as shall domestic support to producers in developing country Members to encourage diversification from growing illicit narcotic crops. Domestic support meeting the criteria of this paragraph shall not be required to be included in a Member's calculation of its Current Total AMS.

3. A Member shall be considered to be in compliance with its domestic support reduction commitments in any year in which its domestic support in favour of agricultural producers expressed in terms of Current Total AMS does not exceed the corresponding annual or final bound commitment level specified in Part IV of the Member's Schedule.

4. (a) A Member shall not be required to include in the calculation of its Current Total AMS and shall not be required to reduce:

(i) product-specific domestic support which would otherwise be required to be included in a Member's calculation of its Current AMS where such support does not exceed 5 per cent of that Member's total value of production of a basic agricultural product during the relevant year; and

(ii) non-product-specific domestic support which would otherwise be required to be included in a Member's calculation of its Current AMS where such support does not exceed 5 per cent of the value of that Member's total agricultural production.

(b) For developing country Members, the *de minimis* percentage under this paragraph shall be 10 per cent.

5. (a) Direct payments under production-limiting programmes shall not be subject to the commitment to reduce domestic support if:

(i) such payments are based on fixed area and yields; or

(ii) such payments are made on 85 per cent or less of the base level of production; or

(iii) livestock payments are made on a fixed number of head.

(b) The exemption from the reduction commitment for direct payments meeting the above criteria shall be reflected by the exclusion of the value of those direct payments in a Member's calculation of its Current Total AMS.

Article 7

General Disciplines on Domestic Support

1. Each Member shall ensure that any domestic support measures in favour of agricultural producers which are not subject to reduction commitments because they qualify under the criteria set out in Annex 2 to this Agreement are maintained in conformity therewith.

2. (a) Any domestic support measure in favour of agricultural producers, including any modification to such measure, and any measure that is subsequently introduced that cannot be shown to satisfy the criteria in Annex 2 to this Agreement or to be exempt from reduction by reason of any other provision of this Agreement shall be included in the Member's calculation of its Current Total AMS.

(b) Where no Total AMS commitment exists in Part IV of a Member's Schedule, the Member shall not provide support to agricultural producers in excess of the relevant *de minimis* level set out in paragraph 4 of Article 6.

Part V

Article 8

Export Competition Commitments

Each Member undertakes not to provide export subsidies otherwise than in conformity with this Agreement and with the commitments as specified in that Member's Schedule.

Article 9

Export Subsidy Commitments

1. The following export subsidies are subject to reduction commitments under this Agreement:

(a) the provision by governments or their agencies of direct subsidies, including payments-in-kind, to a firm, to an industry, to producers of an agricultural product, to a cooperative or other association of such producers, or to a marketing board, contingent on export performance;

(b) the sale or disposal for export by governments or their agencies of non-commercial stocks of agricultural products at a price lower than the comparable price charged for the like product to buyers in the domestic market;

(c) payments on the export of an agricultural product that are financed by virtue of governmental action, whether or not a charge on the public account is involved, including payments that are financed from the proceeds of a levy imposed on the agricultural product concerned or on an agricultural product from which the exported product is derived;

(d) the provision of subsidies to reduce the costs of marketing exports of agricultural products (other than widely available export promotion and advisory services) including handling, upgrading and other processing costs, and the costs of international transport and freight;

(e) internal transport and freight charges on export shipments, provided or mandated by governments, on terms more favourable than for domestic shipments;

(f) subsidies on agricultural products contingent on their incorporation in exported products.

2. (a) Except as provided in subparagraph (b), the export subsidy commitment levels for each year of the implementation period, as specified in a Member's Schedule, represent with respect to the export subsidies listed in paragraph 1 of this Article:

(i) in the case of budgetary outlay reduction commitments, the maximum level of expenditure for such subsidies that may be allocated or incurred in that year in respect of the agricultural product, or group of products, concerned; and

(ii) in the case of export quantity reduction commitments, the maximum quantity of an agricultural product, or group of products, in respect of which such export subsidies may be granted in that year.

(b) In any of the second through fifth years of the implementation period, a Member may provide export subsidies listed in paragraph 1 above in a given year in excess of the corresponding annual commitment levels in respect of the products or groups of products specified in Part IV of the Member's Schedule, provided that:

(i) the cumulative amounts of budgetary outlays for such subsidies, from the beginning of the implementation period through the year in question, does not exceed the cumulative amounts that would have resulted from full compliance with the relevant annual outlay commitment levels specified in the Member's Schedule by more than 3 per cent of the base period level of such budgetary outlays;

(ii) the cumulative quantities exported with the benefit of such export subsidies, from the beginning of the implementation period through the year in question, does not exceed the cumulative quantities that would have resulted from full compliance with the relevant annual quantity commitment levels specified in the Member's Schedule by more than 1.75 per cent of the base period quantities;

(iii) the total cumulative amounts of budgetary outlays for such export subsidies and the quantities benefiting from such export subsidies over the entire implementation period are no greater than the totals that would have resulted from full compliance with the relevant annual commitment levels specified in the Member's Schedule; and

(iv) the Member's budgetary outlays for export subsidies and the quantities benefiting from such subsidies, at the conclusion of the implementation period, are no greater than 64 per cent and 79 per cent of the

1986-1990 base period levels, respectively. For developing country Members these percentages shall be 76 and 86 per cent, respectively.

3. Commitments relating to limitations on the extension of the scope of export subsidization are as specified in Schedules.

4. During the implementation period, developing country Members shall not be required to undertake commitments in respect of the export subsidies listed in subparagraphs (d) and (e) of paragraph 1 above, provided that these are not applied in a manner that would circumvent reduction commitments.

Article 10

Prevention of Circumvention of Export Subsidy Commitments

1. Export subsidies not listed in paragraph 1 of Article 9 shall not be applied in a manner which results in, or which threatens to lead to, circumvention of export subsidy commitments; nor shall non-commercial transactions be used to circumvent such commitments.

2. Members undertake to work toward the development of internationally agreed disciplines to govern the provision of export credits, export credit guarantees or insurance programmes and, after agreement on such disciplines, to provide export credits, export credit guarantees or insurance programmes only in conformity therewith.

3. Any Member which claims that any quantity exported in excess of a reduction commitment level is not subsidized must establish that no export subsidy, whether listed in Article 9 or not, has been granted in respect of the quantity of exports in question.

4. Members donors of international food aid shall ensure:

(a) that the provision of international food aid is not tied directly or indirectly to commercial exports of agricultural products to recipient countries;

(b) that international food aid transactions, including bilateral food aid which is monetized, shall be carried out in accordance with the FAO "Principles of Surplus Disposal and Consultative Obligations," including, where appropriate, the system of Usual Marketing Requirements (UMRs); and

(c) that such aid shall be provided to the extent possible in fully grant form or on terms no less concessional than those provided for in Article IV of the Food Aid Convention 1986.

Article 11

Incorporated Products

In no case may the per-unit subsidy paid on an incorporated agricultural primary product exceed the per-unit export subsidy that would be payable on exports of the primary product as such.

Part VI

Article 12

Disciplines on Export Prohibitions and Restrictions

1. Where any Member institutes any new export prohibition or restriction on foodstuffs in accordance with paragraph 2(a) of Article XI of GATT 1994, the Member shall observe the following provisions:

(a) the Member instituting the export prohibition or restriction shall give due consideration to the effects of such prohibition or restriction on importing Members' food security;

(b) before any Member institutes an export prohibition or restriction, it shall give notice in writing, as far in advance as practicable, to the Committee on Agriculture comprising such information as the nature and the duration of such measure, and shall consult, upon request, with any other Member having a substantial interest as an importer with respect to any matter related to the measure in question. The Member instituting such export prohibition or restriction shall provide, upon request, such a Member with necessary information.

2. The provisions of this Article shall not apply to any developing country Member, unless the measure is taken by a developing country Member which is a net-food exporter of the specific foodstuff concerned.

Part VII

Article 13

Due Restraint

During the implementation period, notwithstanding the provisions of GATT 1994 and the Agreement on Subsidies and Countervailing Measures (referred to in this Article as the "Subsidies Agreement"):

(a) domestic support measures that conform fully to the provisions of Annex 2 to this Agreement shall be:

(i) non-actionable subsidies for purposes of countervailing duties[4];

(ii) exempt from actions based on Article XVI of GATT 1994 and Part III of the Subsidies Agreement; and

(iii) exempt from actions based on non-violation nullification or impairment of the benefits of tariff concessions accruing to another Member under Article II of GATT 1994, in the sense of paragraph 1(b) of Article XXIII of GATT 1994;

(b) domestic support measures that conform fully to the provisions of Article 6 of this Agreement including direct payments that conform to the requirements of paragraph 5 thereof, as reflected in each Member's Schedule, as well as domestic support within *de minimis* levels and in conformity with paragraph 2 of Article 6, shall be:

(i) exempt from the imposition of countervailing duties unless a determination of injury or threat thereof is made in accordance with Article VI of GATT 1994 and Part V of the Subsidies Agreement, and due restraint shall be shown in initiating any countervailing duty investigations;

(ii) exempt from actions based on paragraph 1 of Article XVI of GATT 1994 or Articles 5 and 6 of the Subsidies Agreement, provided that such measures do not grant support to a specific commodity in excess of that decided during the 1992 marketing year; and

(iii) exempt from actions based on non-violation nullification or impairment of the benefits of tariff concessions accruing to another Member under Article II of GATT 1994, in the sense of paragraph 1(b) of Article XXIII of GATT 1994, provided that such measures do not grant support to a specific commodity in excess of that decided during the 1992 marketing year;

(c) export subsidies that conform fully to the provisions of Part V of this Agreement, as reflected in each Member's Schedule, shall be:

(i) subject to countervailing duties only upon a determination of injury or threat thereof based on volume, effect on prices, or consequent impact in accordance with Article VI of GATT 1994 and Part V of the Subsidies Agreement, and due restraint shall be shown in initiating any countervailing duty investigations; and

4. "Countervailing duties" where referred to in this Article are those covered by Article VI of GATT 1994 and Part V of the Agreement on Subsidies and Countervailing Measures.

(ii) exempt from actions based on Article XVI of GATT 1994 or Articles 3, 5 and 6 of the Subsidies Agreement.

Part VIII

Article 14

Sanitary and Phytosanitary Measures

Members agree to give effect to the Agreement on the Application of Sanitary and Phytosanitary Measures.

Part IX

Article 15

Special and Differential Treatment

1. In keeping with the recognition that differential and more favourable treatment for developing country Members is an integral part of the negotiation, special and differential treatment in respect of commitments shall be provided as set out in the relevant provisions of this Agreement and embodied in the Schedules of concessions and commitments.

2. Developing country Members shall have the flexibility to implement reduction commitments over a period of up to 10 years. Least-developed country Members shall not be required to undertake reduction commitments.

Part X

Article 16

Least-Developed and Net Food-Importing Developing Countries

1. Developed country Members shall take such action as is provided for within the framework of the Decision on Measures Concerning the Possible Negative Effects of the Reform Programme on Least-Developed and Net Food-Importing Developing Countries.

2. The Committee on Agriculture shall monitor, as appropriate, the follow-up to this Decision.

Part XI

Article 17

Committee on Agriculture

A Committee on Agriculture is hereby established.

Article 18

Review of the Implementation of Commitments

1. Progress in the implementation of commitments negotiated under the Uruguay Round reform programme shall be reviewed by the Committee on Agriculture.

2. The review process shall be undertaken on the basis of notifications submitted by Members in relation to such matters and at such intervals as shall be determined, as well as on the basis of such documentation as the Secretariat may be requested to prepare in order to facilitate the review process.

3. In addition to the notifications to be submitted under paragraph 2, any new domestic support measure, or modification of an existing measure, for which exemption from reduction is claimed shall be notified promptly. This notification shall contain details of the new or modified measure and its conformity with the agreed criteria as set out either in Article 6 or in Annex 2.

4. In the review process Members shall give due consideration to the influence of excessive rates of inflation on the ability of any Member to abide by its domestic support commitments.

5. Members agree to consult annually in the Committee on Agriculture with respect to their participation in the normal growth of world trade in agricultural products within the framework of the commitments on export subsidies under this Agreement.

6. The review process shall provide an opportunity for Members to raise any matter relevant to the implementation of commitments under the reform programme as set out in this Agreement.

7. Any Member may bring to the attention of the Committee on Agriculture any measure which it considers ought to have been notified by another Member.

Article 19

Consultation and Dispute Settlement

The provisions of Articles XXII and XXIII of GATT 1994, as elaborated and applied by the Dispute Settlement Understanding, shall apply to consultations and the settlement of disputes under this Agreement.

Part XII

Article 20

Continuation of the Reform Process

Recognizing that the long-term objective of substantial progressive reductions in support and protection resulting in fundamental reform is an ongoing process, Members agree that negotiations for continuing the process will be initiated one year before the end of the implementation period, taking into account:

(a) the experience to that date from implementing the reduction commitments;

(b) the effects of the reduction commitments on world trade in agriculture;

(c) non-trade concerns, special and differential treatment to developing country Members, and the objective to establish a fair and market-oriented agricultural trading system, and the other objectives and concerns mentioned in the preamble to this Agreement; and

(d) what further commitments are necessary to achieve the above mentioned long-term objectives.

Part XIII

Article 21

Final Provisions

1. The provisions of GATT 1994 and of other Multilateral Trade Agreements in Annex 1A to the WTO Agreement shall apply subject to the provisions of this Agreement.

2. The Annexes to this Agreement are hereby made an integral part of this Agreement.

Annex 1

PRODUCT COVERAGE

1. This Agreement shall cover the following products:

(i)	HS Chapters 1 to 24 less fish and fish products, plus*		
(ii)	HS Code	2905.43	(mannitol)
	HS Code	2905.44	(sorbitol)
	HS Heading	33.01	(essential oils)
	HS Headings	35.01 to 35.05	(albuminoidal substances, modified starches, glues)
	HS Code	3809.10	(finishing agents)
	HS Code	3823.60	(sorbitol n.e.p.)
	HS Headings	41.01 to 41.03	(hides and skins)
	HS Heading	43.01	(raw furskins)
	HS Headings	50.01 to 50.03	(raw silk and silk waste)
	HS Headings	51.01 to 51.03	(wool and animal hair)
	HS Headings	52.01 to 52.03	(raw cotton, waste and cotton carded or combed)
	HS Heading	53.01	(raw flax)
	HS Heading	53.02	(raw hemp)

2. The foregoing shall not limit the product coverage of the Agreement on the Application of Sanitary and Phytosanitary Measures.

*The product descriptions in round brackets are not necessarily exhaustive.

Annex 2

DOMESTIC SUPPORT: THE BASIS FOR EXEMPTION FROM THE REDUCTION COMMITMENTS

1. Domestic support measures for which exemption from the reduction commitments is claimed shall meet the fundamental requirement that they have no, or at most minimal, trade-distorting effects or effects on production. Accordingly, all measures for which exemption is claimed shall conform to the following basic criteria:

(a) the support in question shall be provided through a publicly-funded government programme (including government revenue fore-gone) not involving transfers from consumers; and,

(b) the support in question shall not have the effect of providing price support to producers;

plus policy-specific criteria and conditions as set out below.

Government Service Programmes

2. General services

Policies in this category involve expenditures (or revenue foregone) in relation to programmes which provide services or benefits to agriculture or the rural community. They shall not involve direct payments to producers or processors. Such programmes, which include but are not restricted to the following list, shall meet the general criteria in paragraph 1 above and policy-specific conditions where set out below:

(a) research, including general research, research in connection with environmental programmes, and research programmes relating to particular products;

(b) pest and disease control, including general and product-specific pest and disease control measures, such as early-warning systems, quarantine and eradication;

(c) training services, including both general and specialist training facilities;

(d) extension and advisory services, including the provision of means to facilitate the transfer of information and the results of research to producers and consumers;

(e) inspection services, including general inspection services and the inspection of particular products for health, safety, grading or standardization purposes;

(f) marketing and promotion services, including market information, advice and promotion relating to particular products but excluding expenditure for unspecified purposes that could be used by sellers to reduce their selling price or confer a direct economic benefit to purchasers; and

(g) infrastructural services, including: electricity reticulation, roads and other means of transport, market and port facilities, water supply facilities, dams and drainage schemes, and infrastructural works associated with environmental programmes. In all cases the expenditure shall be directed to the provision or construction of capital works only, and shall exclude the subsidized provision of on-farm facilities other than for the reticulation of generally available public utilities. It shall not include subsidies to inputs or operating costs, or preferential user charges.

3. Public stockholding for food security purposes[5]

Expenditures (or revenue foregone) in relation to the accumulation and holding of stocks of products which form an integral part of a food security programme identified in national legislation. This may include government aid to private storage of products as part of such a programme.

The volume and accumulation of such stocks shall correspond to predetermined targets related solely to food security. The process of stock accumulation and disposal shall be financially transparent. Food purchases by the government shall be made at current market prices and sales from food security stocks shall be made at no less than the current domestic market price for the product and quality in question.

4. Domestic food aid[6]

Expenditures (or revenue foregone) in relation to the provision of domestic food aid to sections of the population in need.

Eligibility to receive the food aid shall be subject to clearly-defined criteria related to nutritional objectives. Such aid shall be in the form of direct provision of food to those concerned or the provision of means to allow eligible recipients to buy food either at market or at subsidized prices. Food purchases by the government shall be made at current market prices and the financing and administration of the aid shall be transparent.

5. Direct payments to producers

Support provided through direct payments (or revenue foregone, including payments in kind) to producers for which exemption from reduction commitments is claimed shall meet the basic criteria set out in paragraph 1 above, plus specific criteria applying to individual types of direct payment as set out in paragraphs 6 through 13 below. Where exemption from reduction is claimed for any existing or new type of direct payment other than those

5. For the purposes of paragraph 3 of this Annex, governmental stockholding programmes for food security purposes in developing countries whose operation is transparent and conducted in accordance with officially published objective criteria or guidelines shall be considered to be in conformity with the provisions of this paragraph, including programmes under which stocks of foodstuffs for food security purposes are acquired and released at administered prices, provided that the difference between the acquisition price and the external reference price is accounted for in the AMS.

6. For the purposes of paragraphs 3 and 4 of this Annex, the provision of foodstuffs at subsidized prices with the objective of meeting food requirements of urban and rural poor in developing countries on a regular basis at reasonable prices shall be considered to be in conformity with the provisions of this paragraph.

specified in paragraphs 6 through 13, it shall conform to criteria (b) through (e) in paragraph 6, in addition to the general criteria set out in paragraph 1.

6. Decoupled income support

(a) Eligibility for such payments shall be determined by clearly-defined criteria such as income, status as a producer or landowner, factor use or production level in a defined and fixed base period.

(b) The amount of such payments in any given year shall not be related to, or based on, the type or volume of production (including livestock units) undertaken by the producer in any year after the base period.

(c) The amount of such payments in any given year shall not be related to, or based on, the prices, domestic or international, applying to any production undertaken in any year after the base period.

(d) The amount of such payments in any given year shall not be related to, or based on, the factors of production employed in any year after the base period.

(e) No production shall be required in order to receive such payments.

7. Government financial participation in income insurance and income safety-net programmes

(a) Eligibility for such payments shall be determined by an income loss, taking into account only income derived from agriculture, which exceeds 30 per cent of average gross income or the equivalent in net income terms (excluding any payments from the same or similar schemes) in the preceding three-year period or a three-year average based on the preceding five-year period, excluding the highest and the lowest entry. Any producer meeting this condition shall be eligible to receive the payments.

(b) The amount of such payments shall compensate for less than 70 per cent of the producer's income loss in the year the producer becomes eligible to receive this assistance.

(c) The amount of any such payments shall relate solely to income; it shall not relate to the type or volume of production (including livestock units) undertaken by the producer; or to the prices, domestic or international, applying to such production; or to the factors of production employed.

(d) Where a producer receives in the same year payments under this paragraph and under paragraph 8 (relief from natural disasters), the total of such payments shall be less than 100 per cent of the producer's total loss.

8. Payments (made either directly or by way of government financial participation in crop insurance schemes) for relief from natural disasters

(a) Eligibility for such payments shall arise only following a formal recognition by government authorities that a natural or like disaster (including disease outbreaks, pest infestations, nuclear accidents, and war on the territory of the Member concerned) has occurred or is occurring; and shall be determined by a production loss which exceeds 30 per cent of the average of production in the preceding three-year period or a three-year average based on the preceding five-year period, excluding the highest and the lowest entry.

(b) Payments made following a disaster shall be applied only in respect of losses of income, livestock (including payments in connection with the veterinary treatment of animals), land or other production factors due to the natural disaster in question.

(c) Payments shall compensate for not more than the total cost of replacing such losses and shall not require or specify the type or quantity of future production.

(d) Payments made during a disaster shall not exceed the level required to prevent or alleviate further loss as defined in criterion (b) above.

(e) Where a producer receives in the same year payments under this paragraph and under paragraph 7 (income insurance and income safety-net programmes), the total of such payments shall be less than 100 per cent of the producer's total loss.

9. Structural adjustment assistance provided through producer retirement programmes

(a) Eligibility for such payments shall be determined by reference to clearly defined criteria in programmes designed to facilitate the retirement of persons engaged in marketable agricultural production, or their movement to non-agricultural activities.

(b) Payments shall be conditional upon the total and permanent retirement of the recipients from marketable agricultural production.

10. Structural adjustment assistance provided through resource retirement programmes

(a) Eligibility for such payments shall be determined by reference to clearly defined criteria in programmes designed to remove land or other resources, including livestock, from marketable agricultural production.

(b) Payments shall be conditional upon the retirement of land from marketable agricultural production for a minimum of three years, and in the case of livestock on its slaughter or definitive permanent disposal.

(c) Payments shall not require or specify any alternative use for such land or other resources which involves the production of marketable agricultural products.

(d) Payments shall not be related to either the type or quantity of production or to the prices, domestic or international, applying to production undertaken using the land or other resources remaining in production.

11. Structural adjustment assistance provided through investment aids

(a) Eligibility for such payments shall be determined by reference to clearly-defined criteria in government programmes designed to assist the financial or physical restructuring of a producer's operations in response to objectively demonstrated structural disadvantages. Eligibility for such programmes may also be based on a clearly-defined government programme for the reprivatization of agricultural land.

(b) The amount of such payments in any given year shall not be related to, or based on, the type or volume of production (including livestock units) undertaken by the producer in any year after the base period other than as provided for under criterion (e) below.

(c) The amount of such payments in any given year shall not be related to, or based on, the prices, domestic or international, applying to any production undertaken in any year after the base period.

(d) The payments shall be given only for the period of time necessary for the realization of the investment in respect of which they are provided.

(e) The payments shall not mandate or in any way designate the agricultural products to be produced by the recipients except to require them not to produce a particular product.

(f) The payments shall be limited to the amount required to compensate for the structural disadvantage.

12. Payments under environmental programmes

(a) Eligibility for such payments shall be determined as part of a clearly-defined government environmental or conservation programme and be dependent on the fulfilment of specific conditions under the government programme, including conditions related to production methods or inputs.

(b) The amount of payment shall be limited to the extra costs or loss of income involved in complying with the government programme.

13. Payments under regional assistance programmes

(a) Eligibility for such payments shall be limited to producers in disadvantaged regions. Each such region must be a clearly designated contiguous geographical area with a definable economic and administrative identity, considered as disadvantaged on the basis of neutral and objective criteria clearly spelt out in law or regulation and indicating that the region's difficulties arise out of more than temporary circumstances.

(b) The amount of such payments in any given year shall not be related to, or based on, the type or volume of production (including livestock units) undertaken by the producer in any year after the base period other than to reduce that production.

(c) The amount of such payments in any given year shall not be related to, or based on, the prices, domestic or international, applying to any production undertaken in any year after the base period.

(d) Payments shall be available only to producers in eligible regions, but generally available to all producers within such regions.

(e) Where related to production factors, payments shall be made at a degressive rate above a threshold level of the factor concerned.

(f) The payments shall be limited to the extra costs or loss of income involved in undertaking agricultural production in the prescribed area.

Annex 3

DOMESTIC SUPPORT: CALCULATION OF AGGREGATE MEASUREMENT OF SUPPORT

1. Subject to the provisions of Article 6, an Aggregate Measurement of Support (AMS) shall be calculated on a product-specific basis for each basic agricultural product receiving market price support, non-exempt direct

payments, or any other subsidy not exempted from the reduction commitment ("other non-exempt policies"). Support which is non-product specific shall be totalled into one non-product-specific AMS in total monetary terms.

2. Subsidies under paragraph 1 shall include both budgetary outlays and revenue foregone by governments or their agents.

3. Support at both the national and sub-national level shall be included.

4. Specific agricultural levies or fees paid by producers shall be deducted from the AMS.

5. The AMS calculated as outlined below for the base period shall constitute the base level for the implementation of the reduction commitment on domestic support.

6. For each basic agricultural product, a specific AMS shall be established, expressed in total monetary value terms.

7. The AMS shall be calculated as close as practicable to the point of first sale of the basic agricultural product concerned. Measures directed at agricultural processors shall be included to the extent that such measures benefit the producers of the basic agricultural products.

8. Market price support: market price support shall be calculated using the gap between a fixed external reference price and the applied administered price multiplied by the quantity of production eligible to receive the applied administered price. Budgetary payments made to maintain this gap, such as buying-in or storage costs, shall not be included in the AMS.

9. The fixed external reference price shall be based on the years 1986 to 1988 and shall generally be the average f.o.b. unit value for the basic agricultural product concerned in a net exporting country and the average c.i.f. unit value for the basic agricultural product concerned in a net importing country in the base period. The fixed reference price may be adjusted for quality differences as necessary.

10. Non-exempt direct payments: non-exempt direct payments which are dependent on a price gap shall be calculated either using the gap between the fixed reference price and the applied administered price multiplied by the quantity of production eligible to receive the administered price, or using budgetary outlays.

11. The fixed reference price shall be based on the years 1986 to 1988 and shall generally be the actual price used for determining payment rates.

12. Non-exempt direct payments which are based on factors other than price shall be measured using budgetary outlays.

13. Other non-exempt measures, including input subsidies and other measures such as marketing-cost reduction measures: the value of such measures shall be measured using government budgetary outlays or, where the use of budgetary outlays does not reflect the full extent of the subsidy concerned, the basis for calculating the subsidy shall be the gap between the price of the subsidized good or service and a representative market price for a similar good or service multiplied by the quantity of the good or service.

Annex 4

DOMESTIC SUPPORT: CALCULATION OF EQUIVALENT MEASUREMENT OF SUPPORT

1. Subject to the provisions of Article 6, equivalent measurements of support shall be calculated in respect of all basic agricultural products where market price support as defined in Annex 3 exists but for which calculation of this component of the AMS is not practicable. For such products the base level for implementation of the domestic support reduction commitments shall consist of a market price support component expressed in terms of equivalent measurements of support under paragraph 2 below, as well as any non-exempt direct payments and other non-exempt support, which shall be evaluated as provided for under paragraph 3 below. Support at both national and sub-national level shall be included.

2. The equivalent measurements of support provided for in paragraph 1 shall be calculated on a product-specific basis for all basic agricultural products as close as practicable to the point of first sale receiving market price support and for which the calculation of the market price support component of the AMS is not practicable. For those basic agricultural products, equivalent measurements of market price support shall be made using the applied administered price and the quantity of production eligible to receive that price or, where this is not practicable, on budgetary outlays used to maintain the producer price.

3. Where basic agricultural products falling under paragraph 1 are the subject of non-exempt direct payments or any other product-specific subsidy not exempted from the reduction commitment, the basis for equivalent measurements of support concerning these measures shall be calculations as for the corresponding AMS components (specified in paragraphs 10 through 13 of Annex 3).

4. Equivalent measurements of support shall be calculated on the amount of subsidy as close as practicable to the point of first sale of the basic agricultural product concerned. Measures directed at agricultural processors shall be included to the extent that such measures benefit the producers of the basic agricultural products. Specific agricultural levies or fees paid by producers shall reduce the equivalent measurements of support by a corresponding amount.

Annex 5

SPECIAL TREATMENT WITH RESPECT TO PARAGRAPH 2 OF ARTICLE 4

Section A

1. The provisions of paragraph 2 of Article 4 shall not apply with effect from the entry into force of the WTO Agreement to any primary agricultural product and its worked and/or prepared products ("designated products") in respect of which the following conditions are complied with (hereinafter referred to as "special treatment"):

(a) imports of the designated products comprised less than 3 per cent of corresponding domestic consumption in the base period 1986-1988 ("the base period");

(b) no export subsidies have been provided since the beginning of the base period for the designated products;

(c) effective production-restricting measures are applied to the primary agricultural product;

(d) such products are designated with the symbol "ST-Annex 5" in Section I-B of Part I of a Member's Schedule annexed to the Marrakesh Protocol, as being subject to special treatment reflecting factors of non-trade concerns, such as food security and environmental protection; and

(e) minimum access opportunities in respect of the designated products correspond, as specified in Section I-B of Part I of the Schedule of the Member concerned, to 4 per cent of base period domestic consumption of the designated products from the beginning of the first year of the implementation period and, thereafter, are increased by 0.8 per cent of corresponding domestic consumption in the base period per year for the remainder of the implementation period.

2. At the beginning of any year of the implementation period a Member may cease to apply special treatment in respect of the designated products by complying with the provisions of paragraph 6. In such a case, the Member concerned shall maintain the minimum access opportunities already in effect at such time and increase the minimum access opportunities by 0.4 per cent of corresponding domestic consumption in the base period per year for the remainder of the implementation period. Thereafter, the level of minimum access opportunities resulting from this formula in the final year of the implementation period shall be maintained in the Schedule of the Member concerned.

3. Any negotiation on the question of whether there can be a continuation of the special treatment as set out in paragraph 1 after the end of the implementation period shall be completed within the time-frame of the implementation period itself as a part of the negotiations set out in Article 20 of this Agreement, taking into account the factors of non-trade concerns.

4. If it is agreed as a result of the negotiation referred to in paragraph 3 that a Member may continue to apply the special treatment, such Member shall confer additional and acceptable concessions as determined in that negotiation.

5. Where the special treatment is not to be continued at the end of the implementation period, the Member concerned shall implement the provisions of paragraph 6. In such a case, after the end of the implementation period the minimum access opportunities for the designated products shall be maintained at the level of 8 per cent of corresponding domestic consumption in the base period in the Schedule of the Member concerned.

6. Border measures other than ordinary customs duties maintained in respect of the designated products shall become subject to the provisions of paragraph 2 of Article 4 with effect from the beginning of the year in which the special treatment ceases to apply. Such products shall be subject to ordinary customs duties, which shall be bound in the Schedule of the Member concerned and applied, from the beginning of the year in which special treatment ceases and thereafter, at such rates as would have been applicable had a reduction of at least 15 per cent been implemented over the implementation period in equal annual instalments. These duties shall be established on the basis of tariff equivalents to be calculated in accordance with the guidelines prescribed in the attachment hereto.

Section B

7. The provisions of paragraph 2 of Article 4 shall also not apply with effect from the entry into force of the WTO Agreement to a primary agricultural product that is the predominant staple in the traditional diet of a

developing country Member and in respect of which the following conditions, in addition to those specified in paragraph 1(a) through 1(d), as they apply to the products concerned, are complied with:

(a) minimum access opportunities in respect of the products concerned, as specified in Section I-B of Part I of the Schedule of the developing country Member concerned, correspond to 1 per cent of base period domestic consumption of the products concerned from the beginning of the first year of the implementation period and are increased in equal annual instalments to 2 per cent of corresponding domestic consumption in the base period at the beginning of the fifth year of the implementation period. From the beginning of the sixth year of the implementation period, minimum access opportunities in respect of the products concerned correspond to 2 per cent of corresponding domestic consumption in the base period and are increased in equal annual instalments to 4 per cent of corresponding domestic consumption in the base period until the beginning of the 10th year. Thereafter, the level of minimum access opportunities resulting from this formula in the 10th year shall be maintained in the Schedule of the developing country Member concerned;

(b) appropriate market access opportunities have been provided for in other products under this Agreement.

8. Any negotiation on the question of whether there can be a continuation of the special treatment as set out in paragraph 7 after the end of the 10th year following the beginning of the implementation period shall be initiated and completed within the time-frame of the 10th year itself following the beginning of the implementation period.

9. If it is agreed as a result of the negotiation referred to in paragraph 8 that a Member may continue to apply the special treatment, such Member shall confer additional and acceptable concessions as determined in that negotiation.

10. In the event that special treatment under paragraph 7 is not to be continued beyond the 10th year following the beginning of the implementation period, the products concerned shall be subject to ordinary customs duties, established on the basis of a tariff equivalent to be calculated in accordance with the guidelines prescribed in the attachment hereto, which shall be bound in the Schedule of the Member concerned. In other respects, the provisions of paragraph 6 shall apply as modified by the relevant special and differential treatment accorded to developing country Members under this Agreement.

Attachment to Annex 5

GUIDELINES FOR THE CALCULATION OF TARIFF EQUIVALENTS FOR THE SPECIFIC PURPOSE SPECIFIED IN PARAGRAPHS 6 AND 10 OF THIS ANNEX

1. The calculation of the tariff equivalents, whether expressed as *ad valorem* or specific rates, shall be made using the actual difference between internal and external prices in a transparent manner. Data used shall be for the years 1986 to 1988. Tariff equivalents:

(a) shall primarily be established at the four-digit level of the HS;

(b) shall be established at the six-digit or a more detailed level of the HS wherever appropriate;

(c) shall generally be established for worked and/or prepared products by multiplying the specific tariff equivalent(s) for the primary agricultural product(s) by the proportion(s) in value terms or in physical terms as appropriate of the primary agricultural product(s) in the worked and/or prepared products, and take account, where necessary, of any additional elements currently providing protection to industry.

2. External prices shall be, in general, actual average c.i.f. unit values for the importing country. Where average c.i.f. unit values are not available or appropriate, external prices shall be either:

(a) appropriate average c.i.f. unit values of a near country; or

(b) estimated from average f.o.b. unit values of (an) appropriate major exporter(s) adjusted by adding an estimate of insurance, freight and other relevant costs to the importing country.

3. The external prices shall generally be converted to domestic currencies using the annual average market exchange rate for the same period as the price data.

4. The internal price shall generally be a representative wholesale price ruling in the domestic market or an estimate of that price where adequate data is not available.

5. The initial tariff equivalents may be adjusted, where necessary, to take account of differences in quality or variety using an appropriate coefficient.

6. Where a tariff equivalent resulting from these guidelines is negative or lower than the current bound rate, the initial tariff equivalent may be established at the current bound rate or on the basis of national offers for that product.

7. Where an adjustment is made to the level of a tariff equivalent which would have resulted from the above guidelines, the Member concerned shall afford, on request, full opportunities for consultation with a view to negotiating appropriate solutions.

Document 24

AGREEMENT ON THE APPLICATION OF SANITARY AND PHYTOSANITARY MEASURES

Members,

Reaffirming that no Member should be prevented from adopting or enforcing measures necessary to protect human, animal or plant life or health, subject to the requirement that these measures are not applied in a manner which would constitute a means of arbitrary or unjustifiable discrimination between Members where the same conditions prevail or a disguised restriction on international trade;

Desiring to improve the human health, animal health and phytosanitary situation in all Members;

Noting that sanitary and phytosanitary measures are often applied on the basis of bilateral agreements or protocols;

Desiring the establishment of a multilateral framework of rules and disciplines to guide the development, adoption and enforcement of sanitary and phytosanitary measures in order to minimize their negative effects on trade;

Recognizing the important contribution that international standards, guidelines and recommendations can make in this regard;

Desiring to further the use of harmonized sanitary and phytosanitary measures between Members, on the basis of international standards, guidelines and recommendations developed by the relevant international organizations, including the Codex Alimentarius Commission, the International Office of Epizootics, and the relevant international and regional organizations operating within the framework of the International Plant Protection Convention, without requiring Members to change their appropriate level of protection of human, animal or plant life or health;

Recognizing that developing country Members may encounter special difficulties in complying with the sanitary or phytosanitary measures of importing Members, and as a consequence in access to markets, and also in the formulation and application of sanitary or phytosanitary measures in their own territories, and desiring to assist them in their endeavours in this regard;

Desiring therefore to elaborate rules for the application of the provisions of GATT 1994 which relate to the use of sanitary or phytosanitary measures, in particular the provisions of Article XX(b);[1]

Hereby agree as follows:

Article 1

General Provisions

1. This Agreement applies to all sanitary and phytosanitary measures which may, directly or indirectly, affect international trade. Such measures shall be developed and applied in accordance with the provisions of this Agreement.

2. For the purposes of this Agreement, the definitions provided in Annex A shall apply.

3. The annexes are an integral part of this Agreement.

4. Nothing in this Agreement shall affect the rights of Members under the Agreement on Technical Barriers to Trade with respect to measures not within the scope of this Agreement.

Article 2

Basic Rights and Obligations

1. Members have the right to take sanitary and phytosanitary measures necessary for the protection of human, animal or plant life or health, provided that such measures are not inconsistent with the provisions of this Agreement.

2. Members shall ensure that any sanitary or phytosanitary measure is applied only to the extent necessary to protect human, animal or plant life or

1. In this Agreement, reference to Article XX(b) includes also the chapeau of that Article.

health, is based on scientific principles and is not maintained without sufficient scientific evidence, except as provided for in paragraph 7 of Article 5.

3. Members shall ensure that their sanitary and phytosanitary measures do not arbitrarily or unjustifiably discriminate between Members where identical or similar conditions prevail, including between their own territory and that of other Members. Sanitary and phytosanitary measures shall not be applied in a manner which would constitute a disguised restriction on international trade.

4. Sanitary or phytosanitary measures which conform to the relevant provisions of this Agreement shall be presumed to be in accordance with the obligations of the Members under the provisions of GATT 1994 which relate to the use of sanitary or phytosanitary measures, in particular the provisions of Article XX(b).

Article 3

Harmonization

1. To harmonize sanitary and phytosanitary measures on as wide a basis as possible, Members shall base their sanitary or phytosanitary measures on international standards, guidelines or recommendations, where they exist, except as otherwise provided for in this Agreement, and in particular in paragraph 3.

2. Sanitary or phytosanitary measures which conform to international standards, guidelines or recommendations shall be deemed to be necessary to protect human, animal or plant life or health, and presumed to be consistent with the relevant provisions of this Agreement and of GATT 1994.

3. Members may introduce or maintain sanitary or phytosanitary measures which result in a higher level of sanitary or phytosanitary protection than would be achieved by measures based on the relevant international standards, guidelines or recommendations, if there is a scientific justification, or as a consequence of the level of sanitary or phytosanitary protection a Member determines to be appropriate in accordance with the relevant provisions of paragraphs 1 through 8 of Article 5.[2] Notwithstanding the above, all measures which result in a level of sanitary or phytosanitary protection different from that which would be achieved by measures based

2. For the purposes of paragraph 3 of Article 3, there is a scientific justification if, on the basis of an examination and evaluation of available scientific information in conformity with the relevant provisions of this Agreement, a Member determines that the relevant international standards, guidelines or recommendations are not sufficient to achieve its appropriate level of sanitary or phytosanitary protection.

on international standards, guidelines or recommendations shall not be inconsistent with any other provision of this Agreement.

4. Members shall play a full part, within the limits of their resources, in the relevant international organizations and their subsidiary bodies, in particular the Codex Alimentarius Commission, the International Office of Epizootics, and the international and regional organizations operating within the framework of the International Plant Protection Convention, to promote within these organizations the development and periodic review of standards, guidelines and recommendations with respect to all aspects of sanitary and phytosanitary measures.

5. The Committee on Sanitary and Phytosanitary Measures provided for in paragraphs 1 and 4 of Article 12 (referred to in this Agreement as the "Committee") shall develop a procedure to monitor the process of international harmonization and coordinate efforts in this regard with the relevant international organizations.

Article 4

Equivalence

1. Members shall accept the sanitary or phytosanitary measures of other Members as equivalent, even if these measures differ from their own or from those used by other Members trading in the same product, if the exporting Member objectively demonstrates to the importing Member that its measures achieve the importing Member's appropriate level of sanitary or phytosanitary protection. For this purpose, reasonable access shall be given, upon request, to the importing Member for inspection, testing and other relevant procedures.

2. Members shall, upon request, enter into consultations with the aim of achieving bilateral and multilateral agreements on recognition of the equivalence of specified sanitary or phytosanitary measures.

Article 5

Assessment of Risk and Determination of the Appropriate Level of Sanitary or Phytosanitary Protection

1. Members shall ensure that their sanitary or phytosanitary measures are based on an assessment, as appropriate to the circumstances, of the risks to human, animal or plant life or health, taking into account risk assessment techniques developed by the relevant international organizations.

2. In the assessment of risks, Members shall take into account available scientific evidence; relevant processes and production methods; relevant inspection, sampling and testing methods; prevalence of specific diseases or

pests; existence of pest- or disease-free areas; relevant ecological and environmental conditions; and quarantine or other treatment.

3. In assessing the risk to animal or plant life or health and determining the measure to be applied for achieving the appropriate level of sanitary or phytosanitary protection from such risk, Members shall take into account as relevant economic factors: the potential damage in terms of loss of production or sales in the event of the entry, establishment or spread of a pest or disease; the costs of control or eradication in the territory of the importing Member; and the relative cost-effectiveness of alternative approaches to limiting risks.

4. Members should, when determining the appropriate level of sanitary or phytosanitary protection, take into account the objective of minimizing negative trade effects.

5. With the objective of achieving consistency in the application of the concept of appropriate level of sanitary or phytosanitary protection against risks to human life or health, or to animal and plant life or health, each Member shall avoid arbitrary or unjustifiable distinctions in the levels it considers to be appropriate in different situations, if such distinctions result in discrimination or a disguised restriction on international trade. Members shall cooperate in the Committee, in accordance with paragraphs 1, 2 and 3 of Article 12, to develop guidelines to further the practical implementation of this provision. In developing the guidelines, the Committee shall take into account all relevant factors, including the exceptional character of human health risks to which people voluntarily expose themselves.

6. Without prejudice to paragraph 2 of Article 3, when establishing or maintaining sanitary or phytosanitary measures to achieve the appropriate level of sanitary or phytosanitary protection, Members shall ensure that such measures are not more trade-restrictive than required to achieve their appropriate level of sanitary or phytosanitary protection, taking into account technical and economic feasibility.[3]

7. In cases where relevant scientific evidence is insufficient, a Member may provisionally adopt sanitary or phytosanitary measures on the basis of available pertinent information, including that from the relevant international organizations as well as from sanitary or phytosanitary measures applied by other Members. In such circumstances, Members shall seek to obtain the additional information necessary for a more objective assessment

3. For purposes of paragraph 6 of Article 5, a measure is not more trade-restrictive than required unless there is another measure, reasonably available taking into account technical and economic feasibility, that achieves the appropriate level of sanitary or phytosanitary protection and is significantly less restrictive to trade.

of risk and review the sanitary or phytosanitary measure accordingly within a reasonable period of time.

8. When a Member has reason to believe that a specific sanitary or phytosanitary measure introduced or maintained by another Member is constraining, or has the potential to constrain, its exports and the measure is not based on the relevant international standards, guidelines or recommendations, or such standards, guidelines or recommendations do not exist, an explanation of the reasons for such sanitary or phytosanitary measure may be requested and shall be provided by the Member maintaining the measure.

Article 6

Adaptation to Regional Conditions, Including Pest- or Disease-Free Areas and Areas of Low Pest or Disease Prevalence

1. Members shall ensure that their sanitary or phytosanitary measures are adapted to the sanitary or phytosanitary characteristics of the area—whether all of a country, part of a country, or all or parts of several countries—from which the product originated and to which the product is destined. In assessing the sanitary or phytosanitary characteristics of a region, Members shall take into account, *inter alia,* the level of prevalence of specific diseases or pests, the existence of eradication or control programmes, and appropriate criteria or guidelines which may be developed by the relevant international organizations.

2. Members shall, in particular, recognize the concepts of pest- or disease-free areas and areas of low pest or disease prevalence. Determination of such areas shall be based on factors such as geography, ecosystems, epidemiological surveillance, and the effectiveness of sanitary or phytosanitary controls.

3. Exporting Members claiming that areas within their territories are pest- or disease-free areas or areas of low pest or disease prevalence shall provide the necessary evidence thereof in order to objectively demonstrate to the importing Member that such areas are, and are likely to remain, pest- or disease-free areas or areas of low pest or disease prevalence, respectively. For this purpose, reasonable access shall be given, upon request, to the importing Member for inspection, testing and other relevant procedures.

Article 7

Transparency

Members shall notify changes in their sanitary or phytosanitary measures and shall provide information on their sanitary or phytosanitary measures in accordance with the provisions of Annex B.

Article 8

Control, Inspection and Approval Procedures

Members shall observe the provisions of Annex C in the operation of control, inspection and approval procedures, including national systems for approving the use of additives or for establishing tolerances for contaminants in foods, beverages or feedstuffs, and otherwise ensure that their procedures are not inconsistent with the provisions of this Agreement.

Article 9

Technical Assistance

1. Members agree to facilitate the provision of technical assistance to other Members, especially developing country Members, either bilaterally or through the appropriate international organizations. Such assistance may be, *inter alia,* in the areas of processing technologies, research and infrastructure, including in the establishment of national regulatory bodies, and may take the form of advice, credits, donations and grants, including for the purpose of seeking technical expertise, training and equipment to allow such countries to adjust to, and comply with, sanitary or phytosanitary measures necessary to achieve the appropriate level of sanitary or phytosanitary protection in their export markets.

2. Where substantial investments are required in order for an exporting developing country Member to fulfil the sanitary or phytosanitary requirements of an importing Member, the latter shall consider providing such technical assistance as will permit the developing country Member to maintain and expand its market access opportunities for the product involved.

Article 10

Special and Differential Treatment

1. In the preparation and application of sanitary or phytosanitary measures, Members shall take account of the special needs of developing country Members, and in particular of the least-developed country Members.

2. Where the appropriate level of sanitary or phytosanitary protection allows scope for the phased introduction of new sanitary or phytosanitary measures, longer time-frames for compliance should be accorded on products of interest to developing country Members so as to maintain opportunities for their exports.

3. With a view to ensuring that developing country Members are able to comply with the provisions of this Agreement, the Committee is enabled to grant to such countries, upon request, specified, time-limited exceptions in

whole or in part from obligations under this Agreement, taking into account their financial, trade and development needs.

4. Members should encourage and facilitate the active participation of developing country Members in the relevant international organizations.

Article 11

Consultations and Dispute Settlement

1. The provisions of Articles XXII and XXIII of GATT 1994 as elaborated and applied by the Dispute Settlement Understanding shall apply to consultations and the settlement of disputes under this Agreement, except as otherwise specifically provided herein.

2. In a dispute under this Agreement involving scientific or technical issues, a panel should seek advice from experts chosen by the panel in consultation with the parties to the dispute. To this end, the panel may, when it deems it appropriate, establish an advisory technical experts group, or consult the relevant international organizations, at the request of either party to the dispute or on its own initiative.

3. Nothing in this Agreement shall impair the rights of Members under other international agreements, including the right to resort to the good offices or dispute settlement mechanisms of other international organizations or established under any international agreement.

Article 12

Administration

1. A Committee on Sanitary and Phytosanitary Measures is hereby established to provide a regular forum for consultations. It shall carry out the functions necessary to implement the provisions of this Agreement and the furtherance of its objectives, in particular with respect to harmonization. The Committee shall reach its decisions by consensus.

2. The Committee shall encourage and facilitate ad hoc consultations or negotiations among Members on specific sanitary or phytosanitary issues. The Committee shall encourage the use of international standards, guidelines or recommendations by all Members and, in this regard, shall sponsor technical consultation and study with the objective of increasing coordination and integration between international and national systems and approaches for approving the use of food additives or for establishing tolerances for contaminants in foods, beverages or feedstuffs.

3. The Committee shall maintain close contact with the relevant international organizations in the field of sanitary and phytosanitary protection, especially with the Codex Alimentarius Commission, the International Office of Epizootics, and the Secretariat of the International Plant Protection Convention, with the objective of securing the best available scientific and technical advice for the administration of this Agreement and in order to ensure that unnecessary duplication of effort is avoided.

4. The Committee shall develop a procedure to monitor the process of international harmonization and the use of international standards, guidelines or recommendations. For this purpose, the Committee should, in conjunction with the relevant international organizations, establish a list of international standards, guidelines or recommendations relating to sanitary or phytosanitary measures which the Committee determines to have a major trade impact. The list should include an indication by Members of those international standards, guidelines or recommendations which they apply as conditions for import or on the basis of which imported products conforming to these standards can enjoy access to their markets. For those cases in which a Member does not apply an international standard, guideline or recommendation as a condition for import, the Member should provide an indication of the reason therefor, and, in particular, whether it considers that the standard is not stringent enough to provide the appropriate level of sanitary or phytosanitary protection. If a Member revises its position, following its indication of the use of a standard, guideline or recommendation as a condition for import, it should provide an explanation for its change and so inform the Secretariat as well as the relevant international organizations, unless such notification and explanation is given according to the procedures of Annex B.

5. In order to avoid unnecessary duplication, the Committee may decide, as appropriate, to use the information generated by the procedures, particularly for notification, which are in operation in the relevant international organizations.

6. The Committee may, on the basis of an initiative from one of the Members, through appropriate channels invite the relevant international organizations or their subsidiary bodies to examine specific matters with respect to a particular standard, guideline or recommendation, including the basis of explanations for non-use given according to paragraph 4.

7. The Committee shall review the operation and implementation of this Agreement three years after the date of entry into force of the WTO Agreement, and thereafter as the need arises. Where appropriate, the Committee may submit to the Council for Trade in Goods proposals to amend the text of this Agreement having regard, *inter alia*, to the experience gained in its implementation.

Article 13

Implementation

Members are fully responsible under this Agreement for the observance of all obligations set forth herein. Members shall formulate and implement positive measures and mechanisms in support of the observance of the provisions of this Agreement by other than central government bodies. Members shall take such reasonable measures as may be available to them to ensure that non-governmental entities within their territories, as well as regional bodies in which relevant entities within their territories are members, comply with the relevant provisions of this Agreement. In addition, Members shall not take measures which have the effect of, directly or indirectly, requiring or encouraging such regional or non-governmental entities, or local governmental bodies, to act in a manner inconsistent with the provisions of this Agreement. Members shall ensure that they rely on the services of non-governmental entities for implementing sanitary or phytosanitary measures only if these entities comply with the provisions of this Agreement.

Article 14

Final Provisions

The least-developed country Members may delay application of the provisions of this Agreement for a period of five years following the date of entry into force of the WTO Agreement with respect to their sanitary or phytosanitary measures affecting importation or imported products. Other developing country Members may delay application of the provisions of this Agreement, other than paragraph 8 of Article 5 and Article 7, for two years following the date of entry into force of the WTO Agreement with respect to their existing sanitary or phytosanitary measures affecting importation or imported products, where such application is prevented by a lack of technical expertise, technical infrastructure or resources.

Annex A

DEFINITIONS[4]

1. *Sanitary or phytosanitary measure*—Any measure applied:

(a) to protect animal or plant life or health within the territory of the Member from risks arising from the entry, establishment or spread of pests, diseases, disease-carrying organisms or disease-causing organisms;

4. For the purpose of these definitions, "animal" includes fish and wild fauna; "plant" includes forests and wild flora; "pests" include weeds; and "contaminants" include pesticide and veterinary drug residues and extraneous matter.

(b) to protect human or animal life or health within the territory of the Member from risks arising from additives, contaminants, toxins or disease-causing organisms in foods, beverages or feedstuffs;

(c) to protect human life or health within the territory of the Member from risks arising from diseases carried by animals, plants or products thereof, or from the entry, establishment or spread of pests; or

(d) to prevent or limit other damage within the territory of the Member from the entry, establishment or spread of pests.

Sanitary or phytosanitary measures include all relevant laws, decrees, regulations, requirements and procedures including, *inter alia*, end product criteria; processes and production methods; testing, inspection, certification and approval procedures; quarantine treatments including relevant requirements associated with the transport of animals or plants, or with the materials necessary for their survival during transport; provisions on relevant statistical methods, sampling procedures and methods of risk assessment; and packaging and labelling requirements directly related to food safety.

2. *Harmonization*—The establishment, recognition and application of common sanitary and phytosanitary measures by different Members.

3. *International standards, guidelines and recommendations*

(a) for food safety, the standards, guidelines and recommendations established by the Codex Alimentarius Commission relating to food additives, veterinary drug and pesticide residues, contaminants, methods of analysis and sampling, and codes and guidelines of hygienic practice;

(b) for animal health and zoonoses, the standards, guidelines and recommendations developed under the auspices of the International Office of Epizootics;

(c) for plant health, the international standards, guidelines and recommendations developed under the auspices of the Secretariat of the International Plant Protection Convention in cooperation with regional organizations operating within the framework of the International Plant Protection Convention; and

(d) for matters not covered by the above organizations, appropriate standards, guidelines and recommendations promulgated by other relevant international organizations open for membership to all Members, as identified by the Committee.

4. *Risk assessment*—The evaluation of the likelihood of entry, establishment or spread of a pest or disease within the territory of an importing Member according to the sanitary or phytosanitary measures which might be

applied, and of the associated potential biological and economic consequences; or the evaluation of the potential for adverse effects on human or animal health arising from the presence of additives, contaminants, toxins or disease-causing organisms in food, beverages or feedstuffs.

5. *Appropriate level of sanitary or phytosanitary protection*—The level of protection deemed appropriate by the Member establishing a sanitary or phytosanitary measure to protect human, animal or plant life or health within its territory.

NOTE: Many Members otherwise refer to this concept as the "acceptable level of risk."

6. *Pest- or disease-free area*—An area, whether all of a country, part of a country, or all or parts of several countries, as identified by the competent authorities, in which a specific pest or disease does not occur.

NOTE: A pest- or disease-free area may surround, be surrounded by, or be adjacent to an area—whether within part of a country or in a geographic region which includes parts of or all of several countries—in which a specific pest or disease is known to occur but is subject to regional control measures such as the establishment of protection, surveillance and buffer zones which will confine or eradicate the pest or disease in question.

7. *Area of low pest or disease prevalence*—An area, whether all of a country, part of a country, or all or parts of several countries, as identified by the competent authorities, in which a specific pest or disease occurs at low levels and which is subject to effective surveillance, control or eradication measures.

Annex B

TRANSPARENCY OF SANITARY AND
PHYTOSANITARY REGULATIONS

Publication of regulations

1. Members shall ensure that all sanitary and phytosanitary regulations[5] which have been adopted are published promptly in such a manner as to enable interested Members to become acquainted with them.

2. Except in urgent circumstances, Members shall allow a reasonable interval between the publication of a sanitary or phytosanitary regulation

5. Sanitary and phytosanitary measures such as laws, decrees or ordinances which are applicable generally.

and its entry into force in order to allow time for producers in exporting Members, and particularly in developing country Members, to adapt their products and methods of production to the requirements of the importing Member.

Enquiry points

3. Each Member shall ensure that one enquiry point exists which is responsible for the provision of answers to all reasonable questions from interested Members as well as for the provision of relevant documents regarding:

(a) any sanitary or phytosanitary regulations adopted or proposed within its territory;

(b) any control and inspection procedures, production and quarantine treatment, pesticide tolerance and food additive approval procedures, which are operated within its territory;

(c) risk assessment procedures, factors taken into consideration, as well as the determination of the appropriate level of sanitary or phytosanitary protection;

(d) the membership and participation of the Member, or of relevant bodies within its territory, in international and regional sanitary and phytosanitary organizations and systems, as well as in bilateral and multilateral agreements and arrangements within the scope of this Agreement, and the texts of such agreements and arrangements.

4. Members shall ensure that where copies of documents are requested by interested Members, they are supplied at the same price (if any), apart from the cost of delivery, as to the nationals[6] of the Member concerned.

Notification procedures

5. Whenever an international standard, guideline or recommendation does not exist or the content of a proposed sanitary or phytosanitary regulation is not substantially the same as the content of an international standard, guideline or recommendation, and if the regulation may have a significant effect on trade of other Members, Members shall:

6. When "nationals" are referred to in this Agreement, the term shall be deemed, in the case of a separate customs territory Member of the WTO, to mean persons, natural or legal, who are domiciled or who have a real and effective industrial or commercial establishment in that customs territory.

(a) publish a notice at an early stage in such a manner as to enable interested Members to become acquainted with the proposal to introduce a particular regulation;

(b) notify other Members, through the Secretariat, of the products to be covered by the regulation together with a brief indication of the objective and rationale of the proposed regulation. Such notifications shall take place at an early stage, when amendments can still be introduced and comments taken into account;

(c) provide upon request to other Members copies of the proposed regulation and, whenever possible, identify the parts which in substance deviate from international standards, guidelines or recommendations;

(d) without discrimination, allow reasonable time for other Members to make comments in writing, discuss these comments upon request, and take the comments and the results of the discussions into account.

6. However, where urgent problems of health protection arise or threaten to arise for a Member, that Member may omit such of the steps enumerated in paragraph 5 of this Annex as it finds necessary, provided that the Member:

(a) immediately notifies other Members, through the Secretariat, of the particular regulation and the products covered, with a brief indication of the objective and the rationale of the regulation, including the nature of the urgent problem(s);

(b) provides, upon request, copies of the regulation to other Members;

(c) allows other Members to make comments in writing, discusses these comments upon request, and takes the comments and the results of the discussions into account.

7. Notifications to the Secretariat shall be in English, French or Spanish.

8. Developed country Members shall, if requested by other Members, provide copies of the documents or, in case of voluminous documents, summaries of the documents covered by a specific notification in English, French or Spanish.

9. The Secretariat shall promptly circulate copies of the notification to all Members and interested international organizations and draw the attention of developing country Members to any notifications relating to products of particular interest to them.

10. Members shall designate a single central government authority as responsible for the implementation, on the national level, of the provisions concerning notification procedures according to paragraphs 5, 6, 7 and 8 of this Annex.

General reservations

11. Nothing in this Agreement shall be construed as requiring:

(a) the provision of particulars or copies of drafts or the publication of texts other than in the language of the Member except as stated in paragraph 8 of this Annex; or

(b) Members to disclose confidential information which would impede enforcement of sanitary or phytosanitary legislation or which would prejudice the legitimate commercial interests of particular enterprises.

Annex C

CONTROL, INSPECTION AND APPROVAL PROCEDURES[7]

1. Members shall ensure, with respect to any procedure to check and ensure the fulfilment of sanitary or phytosanitary measures, that:

(a) such procedures are undertaken and completed without undue delay and in no less favourable manner for imported products than for like domestic products;

(b) the standard processing period of each procedure is published or that the anticipated processing period is communicated to the applicant upon request; when receiving an application, the competent body promptly examines the completeness of the documentation and informs the applicant in a precise and complete manner of all deficiencies; the competent body transmits as soon as possible the results of the procedure in a precise and complete manner to the applicant so that corrective action may be taken if necessary; even when the application has deficiencies, the competent body proceeds as far as practicable with the procedure if the applicant so requests; and that upon request, the

7. Control, inspection and approval procedures include, *inter alia*, procedures for sampling, testing and certification.

applicant is informed of the stage of the procedure, with any delay being explained;

(c) information requirements are limited to what is necessary for appropriate control, inspection and approval procedures, including for approval of the use of additives or for the establishment of tolerances for contaminants in food, beverages or feedstuffs;

(d) the confidentiality of information about imported products arising from or supplied in connection with control, inspection and approval is respected in a way no less favourable than for domestic products and in such a manner that legitimate commercial interests are protected;

(e) any requirements for control, inspection and approval of individual specimens of a product are limited to what is reasonable and necessary;

(f) any fees imposed for the procedures on imported products are equitable in relation to any fees charged on like domestic products or products originating in any other Member and should be no higher than the actual cost of the service;

(g) the same criteria should be used in the siting of facilities used in the procedures and the selection of samples of imported products as for domestic products so as to minimize the inconvenience to applicants, importers, exporters or their agents;

(h) whenever specifications of a product are changed subsequent to its control and inspection in light of the applicable regulations, the procedure for the modified product is limited to what is necessary to determine whether adequate confidence exists that the product still meets the regulations concerned; and

(i) a procedure exists to review complaints concerning the operation of such procedures and to take corrective action when a complaint is justified.

Where an importing Member operates a system for the approval of the use of food additives or for the establishment of tolerances for contaminants in food, beverages or feedstuffs which prohibits or restricts access to its domestic markets for products based on the absence of an approval, the importing Member shall consider the use of a relevant international standard as the basis for access until a final determination is made.

2. Where a sanitary or phytosanitary measure specifies control at the level of production, the Member in whose territory the production takes place shall provide the necessary assistance to facilitate such control and the work of the controlling authorities.

3. Nothing in this Agreement shall prevent Members from carrying out reasonable inspection within their own territories.

Document 25

AGREEMENT ON TECHNICAL BARRIERS TO TRADE

Members,

Having regard to the Uruguay Round of Multilateral Trade Negotiations;

Desiring to further the objectives of GATT 1994;

Recognizing the important contribution that international standards and conformity assessment systems can make in this regard by improving efficiency of production and facilitating the conduct of international trade;

Desiring therefore to encourage the development of such international standards and conformity assessment systems;

Desiring however to ensure that technical regulations and standards, including packaging, marking and labelling requirements, and procedures for assessment of conformity with technical regulations and standards do not create unnecessary obstacles to international trade;

Recognizing that no country should be prevented from taking measures necessary to ensure the quality of its exports, or for the protection of human, animal or plant life or health, of the environment, or for the prevention of deceptive practices, at the levels it considers appropriate, subject to the requirement that they are not applied in a manner which would constitute a means of arbitrary or unjustifiable discrimination between countries where the same conditions prevail or a disguised restriction on international trade, and are otherwise in accordance with the provisions of this Agreement;

Recognizing that no country should be prevented from taking measures necessary for the protection of its essential security interest;

Recognizing the contribution which international standardization can make to the transfer of technology from developed to developing countries;

Recognizing that developing countries may encounter special difficulties in the formulation and application of technical regulations and standards and procedures for assessment of conformity with technical regulations and standards, and desiring to assist them in their endeavours in this regard;

Hereby *agree* as follows:

Article 1

General Provisions

1.1 General terms for standardization and procedures for assessment of conformity shall normally have the meaning given to them by definitions adopted within the United Nations system and by international standardizing bodies taking into account their context and in the light of the object and purpose of this Agreement.

1.2 However, for the purposes of this Agreement the meaning of the terms given in Annex 1 applies.

1.3 All products, including industrial and agricultural products, shall be subject to the provisions of this Agreement.

1.4 Purchasing specifications prepared by governmental bodies for production or consumption requirements of governmental bodies are not subject to the provisions of this Agreement but are addressed in the Agreement on Government Procurement, according to its coverage.

1.5 The provisions of this Agreement do not apply to sanitary and phytosanitary measures as defined in Annex A of the Agreement on the Application of Sanitary and Phytosanitary Measures.

1.6 All references in this Agreement to technical regulations, standards and conformity assessment procedures shall be construed to include any amendments thereto and any additions to the rules or the product coverage thereof, except amendments and additions of an insignificant nature.

Technical Regulations and Standards

Article 2

Preparation, Adoption and Application of Technical Regulations by Central Government Bodies

With respect to their central government bodies:

2.1 Members shall ensure that in respect of technical regulations, products imported from the territory of any Member shall be accorded treatment no less favourable than that accorded to like products of national origin and to like products originating in any other country.

2.2 Members shall ensure that technical regulations are not prepared, adopted or applied with a view to or with the effect of creating unnecessary obstacles to international trade. For this purpose, technical regulations shall not be more trade-restrictive than necessary to fulfil a legitimate objective, taking account of the risks non-fulfilment would create. Such legitimate objectives are, *inter alia:* national security requirements; the prevention of deceptive practices; protection of human health or safety, animal or plant life or health, or the environment. In assessing such risks, relevant elements of consideration are, *inter alia:* available scientific and technical information, related processing technology or intended end-uses of products.

2.3 Technical regulations shall not be maintained if the circumstances or objectives giving rise to their adoption no longer exist or if the changed circumstances or objectives can be addressed in a less trade-restrictive manner.

2.4 Where technical regulations are required and relevant international standards exist or their completion is imminent, Members shall use them, or the relevant parts of them, as a basis for their technical regulations except when such international standards or relevant parts would be an ineffective or inappropriate means for the fulfilment of the legitimate objectives pursued, for instance because of fundamental climatic or geographical factors or fundamental technological problems.

2.5 A Member preparing, adopting or applying a technical regulation which may have a significant effect on trade of other Members shall, upon the request of another Member, explain the justification for that technical regulation in terms of the provisions of paragraphs 2 to 4. Whenever a technical regulation is prepared, adopted or applied for one of the legitimate objectives explicitly mentioned in paragraph 2, and is in accordance with relevant international standards, it shall be rebuttably presumed not to create an unnecessary obstacle to international trade.

2.6 With a view to harmonizing technical regulations on as wide a basis as possible, Members shall play a full part, within the limits of their resources, in the preparation by appropriate international standardizing bodies of international standards for products for which they either have adopted, or expect to adopt, technical regulations.

2.7 Members shall give positive consideration to accepting as equivalent technical regulations of other Members, even if these regulations differ from their own, provided they are satisfied that these regulations adequately fulfil the objectives of their own regulations.

2.8 Wherever appropriate, Members shall specify technical regulations based on product requirements in terms of performance rather than design or descriptive characteristics.

2.9 Whenever a relevant international standard does not exist or the technical content of a proposed technical regulation is not in accordance with the technical content of relevant international standards, and if the technical regulation may have a significant effect on trade of other Members, Members shall:

2.9.1 publish a notice in a publication at an early appropriate stage, in such a manner as to enable interested parties in other Members to become acquainted with it, that they propose to introduce a particular technical regulation;

2.9.2 notify other Members through the Secretariat of the products to be covered by the proposed technical regulation, together with a brief indication of its objective and rationale. Such notifications shall take place at an early appropriate stage, when amendments can still be introduced and comments taken into account;

2.9.3 upon request, provide to other Members particulars or copies of the proposed technical regulation and, whenever possible, identify the parts which in substance deviate from relevant international standards;

2.9.4 without discrimination, allow reasonable time for other Members to make comments in writing, discuss these comments upon request, and take these written comments and the results of these discussions into account.

2.10 Subject to the provisions in the lead-in to paragraph 9, where urgent problems of safety, health, environmental protection or national security arise or threaten to arise for a Member, that Member may omit such of the steps enumerated in paragraph 9 as it finds necessary, provided that the Member, upon adoption of a technical regulation, shall:

2.10.1 notify immediately other Members through the Secretariat of the particular technical regulation and the products covered, with a brief indication of the objective and the rationale of the technical regulation, including the nature of the urgent problems;

2.10.2 upon request, provide other Members with copies of the technical regulation;

2.10.3 without discrimination, allow other Members to present their comments in writing, discuss these comments upon request, and take these written comments and the results of these discussions into account.

2.11 Members shall ensure that all technical regulations which have been adopted are published promptly or otherwise made available in such a manner as to enable interested parties in other Members to become acquainted with them.

2.12 Except in those urgent circumstances referred to in paragraph 10, Members shall allow a reasonable interval between the publication of technical regulations and their entry into force in order to allow time for producers in exporting Members, and particularly in developing country Members, to adapt their products or methods of production to the requirements of the importing Member.

Article 3

Preparation, Adoption and Application of Technical Regulations by Local Government Bodies and Non-Governmental Bodies

With respect to their local government and non-governmental bodies within their territories:

3.1 Members shall take such reasonable measures as may be available to them to ensure compliance by such bodies with the provisions of Article 2, with the exception of the obligation to notify as referred to in paragraphs 9.2 and 10.1 of Article 2.

3.2 Members shall ensure that the technical regulations of local governments on the level directly below that of the central government in Members are notified in accordance with the provisions of paragraphs 9.2 and 10.1 of Article 2, noting that notification shall not be required for technical regulations the technical content of which is substantially the same as that of previously notified technical regulations of central government bodies of the Member concerned.

3.3 Members may require contact with other Members, including the notifications, provision of information, comments and discussions referred to in paragraphs 9 and 10 of Article 2, to take place through the central government.

3.4 Members shall not take measures which require or encourage local government bodies or non-governmental bodies within their territories to act in a manner inconsistent with the provisions of Article 2.

3.5 Members are fully responsible under this Agreement for the observance of all provisions of Article 2. Members shall formulate and implement positive measures and mechanisms in support of the observance of the provisions of Article 2 by other than central government bodies.

Article 4

Preparation, Adoption and Application of Standards

4.1 Members shall ensure that their central government standardizing bodies accept and comply with the Code of Good Practice for the Preparation, Adoption and Application of Standards in Annex 3 to this Agreement (referred to in this Agreement as the "Code of Good Practice"). They shall take such reasonable measures as may be available to them to ensure that local government and non-governmental standardizing bodies within their territories, as well as regional standardizing bodies of which they or one or more bodies within their territories are members, accept and comply with this Code of Good Practice. In addition, Members shall not take measures which have the effect of, directly or indirectly, requiring or encouraging such standardizing bodies to act in a manner inconsistent with the Code of Good Practice. The obligations of Members with respect to compliance of standardizing bodies with the provisions of the Code of Good Practice shall apply irrespective of whether or not a standardizing body has accepted the Code of Good Practice.

4.2 Standardizing bodies that have accepted and are complying with the Code of Good Practice shall be acknowledged by the Members as complying with the principles of this Agreement.

Conformity with Technical Regulations and Standards

Article 5

Procedures for Assessment of Conformity by Central Government Bodies

5.1 Members shall ensure that, in cases where a positive assurance of conformity with technical regulations or standards is required, their central government bodies apply the following provisions to products originating in the territories of other Members:

5.1.1 conformity assessment procedures are prepared, adopted and applied so as to grant access for suppliers of like products originating in the territories of other Members under conditions no less favourable than those accorded to suppliers of like products of national origin or originating in any other country, in a comparable situation; access entails suppliers' right to an assessment of conformity under the rules of the procedure, including, when foreseen by this procedure, the possibility to have conformity assessment activities undertaken at the site of facilities and to receive the mark of the system;

5.1.2 conformity assessment procedures are not prepared, adopted or applied with a view to or with the effect of creating unnecessary obstacles to international trade. This means, *inter alia*, that conformity assessment procedures shall not be more strict or be applied more strictly than is necessary to give the importing Member adequate confidence that products conform with the applicable technical regulations or standards, taking account of the risks non-conformity would create.

5.2 When implementing the provisions of paragraph 1, Members shall ensure that:

5.2.1 conformity assessment procedures are undertaken and completed as expeditiously as possible and in a no less favourable order for products originating in the territories of other Members than for like domestic products;

5.2.2 the standard processing period of each conformity assessment procedure is published or that the anticipated processing period is communicated to the applicant upon request; when receiving an application, the competent body promptly examines the completeness of the documentation and informs the applicant in a precise and complete manner of all deficiencies; the competent body transmits as soon as possible the results of the assessment in a precise and complete manner to the applicant so that corrective action may be taken if necessary; even when the application has deficiencies, the competent body proceeds as far as practicable with the conformity assessment if the applicant so requests; and that, upon request, the applicant is informed of the stage of the procedure, with any delay being explained;

5.2.3 information requirements are limited to what is necessary to assess conformity and determine fees;

5.2.4 the confidentiality of information about products originating in the territories of other Members arising from or supplied in connection with such conformity assessment procedures is respected in the same way as for domestic products and in such a manner that legitimate commercial interests are protected;

5.2.5 any fees imposed for assessing the conformity of products originating in the territories of other Members are equitable in relation to any fees chargeable for assessing the conformity of like products of national origin or originating in any other country, taking into account communication, transportation and other costs arising from differences between location of facilities of the applicant and the conformity assessment body;

5.2.6 the siting of facilities used in conformity assessment procedures and the selection of samples are not such as to cause unnecessary inconvenience to applicants or their agents;

5.2.7 whenever specifications of a product are changed subsequent to the determination of its conformity to the applicable technical regulations or standards, the conformity assessment procedure for the modified product is limited to what is necessary to determine whether adequate confidence exists that the product still meets the technical regulations or standards concerned;

5.2.8 a procedure exists to review complaints concerning the operation of a conformity assessment procedure and to take corrective action when a complaint is justified.

5.3 Nothing in paragraphs 1 and 2 shall prevent Members from carrying out reasonable spot checks within their territories.

5.4 In cases where a positive assurance is required that products conform with technical regulations or standards, and relevant guides or recommendations issued by international standardizing bodies exist or their completion is imminent, Members shall ensure that central government bodies use them, or the relevant parts of them, as a basis for their conformity assessment procedures, except where, as duly explained upon request, such guides or recommendations or relevant parts are inappropriate for the Members concerned, for, *inter alia*, such reasons as: national security requirements; the prevention of deceptive practices; protection of human health or safety, animal or plant life or health, or the environment; fundamental climatic or other geographical factors; fundamental technological or infrastructural problems.

5.5 With a view to harmonizing conformity assessment procedures on as wide a basis as possible, Members shall play a full part, within the limits of their resources, in the preparation by appropriate international standardizing bodies of guides and recommendations for conformity assessment procedures.

5.6 Whenever a relevant guide or recommendation issued by an international standardizing body does not exist or the technical content of a proposed conformity assessment procedure is not in accordance with relevant guides and recommendations issued by international standardizing bodies, and if the conformity assessment procedure may have a significant effect on trade of other Members, Members shall:

5.6.1 publish a notice in a publication at an early appropriate stage, in such a manner as to enable interested parties in other Members to become acquainted with it, that they propose to introduce a particular conformity assessment procedure;

5.6.2 notify other Members through the Secretariat of the products to be covered by the proposed conformity assessment procedure, together with a brief indication of its objective and rationale. Such notifications shall take place at an early appropriate stage, when amendments can still be introduced and comments taken into account;

5.6.3 upon request, provide to other Members particulars or copies of the proposed procedure and, whenever possible, identify the parts which in substance deviate from relevant guides or recommendations issued by international standardizing bodies;

5.6.4 without discrimination, allow reasonable time for other Members to make comments in writing, discuss these comments upon request, and take these written comments and the results of these discussions into account.

5.7 Subject to the provisions in the lead-in to paragraph 6, where urgent problems of safety, health, environmental protection or national security arise or threaten to arise for a Member, that Member may omit such of the steps enumerated in paragraph 6 as it finds necessary, provided that the Member, upon adoption of the procedure, shall:

5.7.1 notify immediately other Members through the Secretariat of the particular procedure and the products covered, with a brief indication of the objective and the rationale of the procedure, including the nature of the urgent problems;

5.7.2 upon request, provide other Members with copies of the rules of the procedure;

5.7.3 without discrimination, allow other Members to present their comments in writing, discuss these comments upon request, and take these written comments and the results of these discussions into account.

5.8 Members shall ensure that all conformity assessment procedures which have been adopted are published promptly or otherwise made available in such a manner as to enable interested parties in other Members to become acquainted with them.

5.9 Except in those urgent circumstances referred to in paragraph 7, Members shall allow a reasonable interval between the publication of requirements concerning conformity assessment procedures and their entry into force in order to allow time for producers in exporting Members, and particularly in developing country Members, to adapt their products or methods of production to the requirements of the importing Member.

Article 6

Recognition of Conformity Assessment by Central Government Bodies

With respect to their central government bodies:

6.1 Without prejudice to the provisions of paragraphs 3 and 4, Members shall ensure, whenever possible, that results of conformity assessment procedures in other Members are accepted, even when those procedures differ from their own, provided they are satisfied that those procedures offer an assurance of conformity with applicable technical regulations or standards equivalent to their own procedures. It is recognized that prior consultations may be necessary in order to arrive at a mutually satisfactory understanding regarding, in particular:

6.1.1 adequate and enduring technical competence of the relevant conformity assessment bodies in the exporting Member, so that confidence in the continued reliability of their conformity assessment results can exist; in this regard, verified compliance, for instance through accreditation, with relevant guides or recommendations issued by international standardizing bodies shall be taken into account as an indication of adequate technical competence;

6.1.2 limitation of the acceptance of conformity assessment results to those produced by designated bodies in the exporting Member.

6.2 Members shall ensure that their conformity assessment procedures permit, as far as practicable, the implementation of the provisions in paragraph 1.

6.3 Members are encouraged, at the request of other Members, to be willing to enter into negotiations for the conclusion of agreements for the mutual recognition of results of each other's conformity assessment procedures. Members may require that such agreements fulfil the criteria of paragraph 1 and give mutual satisfaction regarding their potential for facilitating trade in the products concerned.

6.4 Members are encouraged to permit participation of conformity assessment bodies located in the territories of other Members in their conformity assessment procedures under conditions no less favourable than those accorded to bodies located within their territory or the territory of any other country.

Article 7

Procedures for Assessment of Conformity by Local Government Bodies

With respect to their local government bodies within their territories:

7.1 Members shall take such reasonable measures as may be available to them to ensure compliance by such bodies with the provisions of Articles 5 and 6, with the exception of the obligation to notify as referred to in paragraphs 6.2 and 7.1 of Article 5.

7.2 Members shall ensure that the conformity assessment procedures of local governments on the level directly below that of the central government in Members are notified in accordance with the provisions of paragraphs 6.2 and 7.1 of Article 5, noting that notifications shall not be required for conformity assessment procedures the technical content of which is substantially the same as that of previously notified conformity assessment procedures of central government bodies of the Members concerned.

7.3 Members may require contact with other Members, including the notifications, provision of information, comments and discussions referred to in paragraphs 6 and 7 of Article 5, to take place through the central government.

7.4 Members shall not take measures which require or encourage local government bodies within their territories to act in a manner inconsistent with the provisions of Articles 5 and 6.

7.5 Members are fully responsible under this Agreement for the observance of all provisions of Articles 5 and 6. Members shall formulate and implement positive measures and mechanisms in support of the observance of the provisions of Articles 5 and 6 by other than central government bodies.

Article 8

Procedures for Assessment of Conformity by Non-Governmental Bodies

8.1 Members shall take such reasonable measures as may be available to them to ensure that non-governmental bodies within their territories which operate conformity assessment procedures comply with the provisions of

Articles 5 and 6, with the exception of the obligation to notify proposed conformity assessment procedures. In addition, Members shall not take measures which have the effect of, directly or indirectly, requiring or encouraging such bodies to act in a manner inconsistent with the provisions of Articles 5 and 6.

8.2 Members shall ensure that their central government bodies rely on conformity assessment procedures operated by non-governmental bodies only if these latter bodies comply with the provisions of Articles 5 and 6, with the exception of the obligation to notify proposed conformity assessment procedures.

Article 9

International and Regional Systems

9.1 Where a positive assurance of conformity with a technical regulation or standard is required, Members shall, wherever practicable, formulate and adopt international systems for conformity assessment and become members thereof or participate therein.

9.2 Members shall take such reasonable measures as may be available to them to ensure that international and regional systems for conformity assessment in which relevant bodies within their territories are members or participants comply with the provisions of Articles 5 and 6. In addition, Members shall not take any measures which have the effect of, directly or indirectly, requiring or encouraging such systems to act in a manner inconsistent with any of the provisions of Articles 5 and 6.

9.3 Members shall ensure that their central government bodies rely on international or regional conformity assessment systems only to the extent that these systems comply with the provisions of Articles 5 and 6, as applicable.

Information and ASsistance

Article 10

Information About Technical Regulations, Standards and Conformity Assessment Procedures

10.1 Each Member shall ensure that an enquiry point exists which is able to answer all reasonable enquiries from other Members and interested parties in other Members as well as to provide the relevant documents regarding:

10.1.1 any technical regulations adopted or proposed within its territory by central or local government bodies, by non-governmental bodies which have legal power to enforce a technical regulation, or by regional standardizing bodies of which such bodies are members or participants;

10.1.2 any standards adopted or proposed within its territory by central or local government bodies, or by regional standardizing bodies of which such bodies are members or participants;

10.1.3 any conformity assessment procedures, or proposed conformity assessment procedures, which are operated within its territory by central or local government bodies, or by non-governmental bodies which have legal power to enforce a technical regulation, or by regional bodies of which such bodies are members or participants;

10.1.4 the membership and participation of the Member, or of relevant central or local government bodies within its territory, in international and regional standardizing bodies and conformity assessment systems, as well as in bilateral and multilateral arrangements within the scope of this Agreement; it shall also be able to provide reasonable information on the provisions of such systems and arrangements;

10.1.5 the location of notices published pursuant to this Agreement, or the provision of information as to where such information can be obtained; and

10.1.6 the location of the enquiry points mentioned in paragraph 3.

10.2 If, however, for legal or administrative reasons more than one enquiry point is established by a Member, that Member shall provide to the other Members complete and unambiguous information on the scope of responsibility of each of these enquiry points. In addition, that Member shall ensure that any enquiries addressed to an incorrect enquiry point shall promptly be conveyed to the correct enquiry point.

10.3 Each Member shall take such reasonable measures as may be available to it to ensure that one or more enquiry points exist which are able to answer all reasonable enquiries from other Members and interested parties in other Members as well as to provide the relevant documents or information as to where they can be obtained regarding:

10.3.1 any standards adopted or proposed within its territory by non-governmental standardizing bodies, or by regional standardizing bodies of which such bodies are members or participants; and

10.3.2 any conformity assessment procedures, or proposed conformity assessment procedures, which are operated within its territory by non-governmental bodies, or by regional bodies of which such bodies are members or participants;

10.3.3 the membership and participation of relevant non-governmental bodies within its territory in international and regional standardizing bodies and conformity assessment systems, as well as in bilateral and multilateral arrangements within the scope of this Agreement; they shall also be able to provide reasonable information on the provisions of such systems and arrangements.

10.4 Members shall take such reasonable measures as may be available to them to ensure that where copies of documents are requested by other Members or by interested parties in other Members, in accordance with the provisions of this Agreement, they are supplied at an equitable price (if any) which shall, apart from the real cost of delivery, be the same for the nationals[1] of the Member concerned or of any other Member.

10.5 Developed country Members shall, if requested by other Members, provide, in English, French or Spanish, translations of the documents covered by a specific notification or, in case of voluminous documents, of summaries of such documents.

10.6 The Secretariat shall, when it receives notifications in accordance with the provisions of this Agreement, circulate copies of the notifications to all Members and interested international standardizing and conformity assessment bodies, and draw the attention of developing country Members to any notifications relating to products of particular interest to them.

10.7 Whenever a Member has reached an agreement with any other country or countries on issues related to technical regulations, standards or conformity assessment procedures which may have a significant effect on trade, at least one Member party to the agreement shall notify other Members through the Secretariat of the products to be covered by the agreement and include a brief description of the agreement. Members concerned are encouraged to enter, upon request, into consultations with other Members for the purposes of concluding similar agreements or of arranging for their participation in such agreements.

10.8 Nothing in this Agreement shall be construed as requiring:

10.8.1 the publication of texts other than in the language of the Member;

10.8.2 the provision of particulars or copies of drafts other than in the language of the Member except as stated in paragraph 5; or

1. "Nationals" here shall be deemed, in the case of a separate customs territory Member of the WTO, to mean persons, natural or legal, who are domiciled or who have a real and effective industrial or commercial establishment in that customs territory.

10.8.3 Members to furnish any information, the disclosure of which they consider contrary to their essential security interests.

10.9 Notifications to the Secretariat shall be in English, French or Spanish.

10.10 Members shall designate a single central government authority that is responsible for the implementation on the national level of the provisions concerning notification procedures under this Agreement except those included in Annex 3.

10.11 If, however, for legal or administrative reasons the responsibility for notification procedures is divided among two or more central government authorities, the Member concerned shall provide to the other Members complete and unambiguous information on the scope of responsibility of each of these authorities.

Article 11

Technical Assistance to Other Members

11.1 Members shall, if requested, advise other Members, especially the developing country Members, on the preparation of technical regulations.

11.2 Members shall, if requested, advise other Members, especially the developing country Members, and shall grant them technical assistance on mutually agreed terms and conditions regarding the establishment of national standardizing bodies, and participation in the international standardizing bodies, and shall encourage their national standardizing bodies to do likewise.

11.3 Members shall, if requested, take such reasonable measures as may be available to them to arrange for the regulatory bodies within their territories to advise other Members, especially the developing country Members, and shall grant them technical assistance on mutually agreed terms and conditions regarding:

11.3.1 the establishment of regulatory bodies, or bodies for the assessment of conformity with technical regulations; and

11.3.2 the methods by which their technical regulations can best be met.

11.4 Members shall, if requested, take such reasonable measures as may be available to them to arrange for advice to be given to other Members, especially the developing country Members, and shall grant them technical assistance on mutually agreed terms and conditions regarding the establishment of bodies for the assessment of conformity with standards adopted within the territory of the requesting Member.

11.5 Members shall, if requested, advise other Members, especially the developing country Members, and shall grant them technical assistance on mutually agreed terms and conditions regarding the steps that should be taken by their producers if they wish to have access to systems for conformity assessment operated by governmental or non-governmental bodies within the territory of the Member receiving the request.

11.6 Members which are members or participants of international or regional systems for conformity assessment shall, if requested, advise other Members, especially the developing country Members, and shall grant them technical assistance on mutually agreed terms and conditions regarding the establishment of the institutions and legal framework which would enable them to fulfil the obligations of membership or participation in such systems.

11.7 Members shall, if so requested, encourage bodies within their territories which are members or participants of international or regional systems for conformity assessment to advise other Members, especially the developing country Members, and should consider requests for technical assistance from them regarding the establishment of the institutions which would enable the relevant bodies within their territories to fulfil the obligations of membership or participation.

11.8 In providing advice and technical assistance to other Members in terms of paragraphs 1 to 7, Members shall give priority to the needs of the least-developed country Members.

Article 12

Special and Differential Treatment of Developing Country Members

12.1 Members shall provide differential and more favourable treatment to developing country Members to this Agreement, through the following provisions as well as through the relevant provisions of other Articles of this Agreement.

12.2 Members shall give particular attention to the provisions of this Agreement concerning developing country Members' rights and obligations and shall take into account the special development, financial and trade needs of developing country Members in the implementation of this Agreement, both nationally and in the operation of this Agreement's institutional arrangements.

12.3 Members shall, in the preparation and application of technical regulations, standards and conformity assessment procedures, take account of the special development, financial and trade needs of developing country Members, with a view to ensuring that such technical regulations, standards and conformity assessment procedures do not create unnecessary obstacles to exports from developing country Members.

12.4 Members recognize that, although international standards, guides or recommendations may exist, in their particular technological and socio-economic conditions, developing country Members adopt certain technical regulations, standards or conformity assessment procedures aimed at preserving indigenous technology and production methods and processes compatible with their development needs. Members therefore recognize that developing country Members should not be expected to use international standards as a basis for their technical regulations or standards, including test methods, which are not appropriate to their development, financial and trade needs.

12.5 Members shall take such reasonable measures as may be available to them to ensure that international standardizing bodies and international systems for conformity assessment are organized and operated in a way which facilitates active and representative participation of relevant bodies in all Members, taking into account the special problems of developing country Members.

12.6 Members shall take such reasonable measures as may be available to them to ensure that international standardizing bodies, upon request of developing country Members, examine the possibility of, and, if practicable, prepare international standards concerning products of special interest to developing country Members.

12.7 Members shall, in accordance with the provisions of Article 11, provide technical assistance to developing country Members to ensure that the preparation and application of technical regulations, standards and conformity assessment procedures do not create unnecessary obstacles to the expansion and diversification of exports from developing country Members. In determining the terms and conditions of the technical assistance, account shall be taken of the stage of development of the requesting Members and in particular of the least-developed country Members.

12.8 It is recognized that developing country Members may face special problems, including institutional and infrastructural problems, in the field of preparation and application of technical regulations, standards and conformity assessment procedures. It is further recognized that the special development and trade needs of developing country Members, as well as their stage of technological development, may hinder their ability to discharge fully their obligations under this Agreement. Members, therefore, shall take this fact fully into account. Accordingly, with a view to ensuring that developing country Members are able to comply with this Agreement, the Committee on Technical Barriers to Trade provided for in Article 13 (referred to in this Agreement as the "Committee") is enabled to grant, upon request, specified, time-limited exceptions in whole or in part from obligations under this Agreement. When considering such requests the Committee shall take into account the special problems, in the field of preparation and application of technical regulations, standards and conformity assessment procedures, and the special development and trade needs of the developing country Member, as well as its stage of technological development, which may hinder its ability to discharge fully its obligations under this Agreement. The Committee shall, in particular, take into account the special problems of the least-developed country Members.

12.9 During consultations, developed country Members shall bear in mind the special difficulties experienced by developing country Members in formulating and implementing standards and technical regulations and conformity assessment procedures, and in their desire to assist developing country Members with their efforts in this direction, developed country Members shall take account of the special needs of the former in regard to financing, trade and development.

12.10 The Committee shall examine periodically the special and differential treatment, as laid down in this Agreement, granted to developing country Members on national and international levels.

Institutions, Consultation and Dispute Settlement

Article 13

The Committee on Technical Barriers to Trade

13.1 A Committee on Technical Barriers to Trade is hereby established, and shall be composed of representatives from each of the Members. The Committee shall elect its own Chairman and shall meet as necessary, but no less than once a year, for the purpose of affording Members the opportunity of consulting on any matters relating to the operation of this Agreement or the furtherance of its objectives, and shall carry out such responsibilities as assigned to it under this Agreement or by the Members.

13.2 The Committee shall establish working parties or other bodies as may be appropriate, which shall carry out such responsibilities as may be assigned to them by the Committee in accordance with the relevant provisions of this Agreement.

13.3 It is understood that unnecessary duplication should be avoided between the work under this Agreement and that of governments in other technical bodies. The Committee shall examine this problem with a view to minimizing such duplication.

Article 14

Consultation and Dispute Settlement

14.1 Consultations and the settlement of disputes with respect to any matter affecting the operation of this Agreement shall take place under the auspices of the Dispute Settlement Body and shall follow, *mutatis mutandis*, the provisions of Articles XXII and XXIII of GATT 1994, as elaborated and applied by the Dispute Settlement Understanding.

14.2 At the request of a party to a dispute, or at its own initiative, a panel may establish a technical expert group to assist in questions of a technical nature, requiring detailed consideration by experts.

14.3 Technical expert groups shall be governed by the procedures of Annex 2.

14.4 The dispute settlement provisions set out above can be invoked in cases where a Member considers that another Member has not achieved satisfactory results under Articles 3, 4, 7, 8 and 9 and its trade interests are significantly affected. In this respect, such results shall be equivalent to those as if the body in question were a Member.

Final Provisions

Article 15

Final Provisions

Reservations

15.1 Reservations may not be entered in respect of any of the provisions of this Agreement without the consent of the other Members.

Review

15.2 Each Member shall, promptly after the date on which the WTO Agreement enters into force for it, inform the Committee of measures in existence or taken to ensure the implementation and administration of this Agreement. Any changes of such measures thereafter shall also be notified to the Committee.

15.3 The Committee shall review annually the implementation and operation of this Agreement taking into account the objectives thereof.

15.4 Not later than the end of the third year from the date of entry into force of the WTO Agreement and at the end of each three-year period thereafter, the Committee shall review the operation and implementation of this Agreement, including the provisions relating to transparency, with a view to recommending an adjustment of the rights and obligations of this Agreement where necessary to ensure mutual economic advantage and balance of rights and obligations, without prejudice to the provisions of Article 12. Having regard, *inter alia,* to the experience gained in the implementation of the Agreement, the Committee shall, where appropriate, submit proposals for amendments to the text of this Agreement to the Council for Trade in Goods.

Annexes

15.5 The annexes to this Agreement constitute an integral part thereof.

Annex 1

TERMS AND THEIR DEFINITIONS FOR THE PURPOSE OF THIS AGREEMENT

The terms presented in the sixth edition of the ISO/IEC Guide 2: 1991, General Terms and Their Definitions Concerning Standardization and Related Activities, shall, when used in this Agreement, have the same meaning as given in the definitions in the said Guide taking into account that services are excluded from the coverage of this Agreement.

For the purpose of this Agreement, however, the following definitions shall apply:

1. *Technical regulation*

Document which lays down product characteristics or their related processes and production methods, including the applicable administrative provisions, with which compliance is mandatory. It may also include or deal exclusively with terminology, symbols, packaging, marking or labelling requirements as they apply to a product, process or production method.

Explanatory note

The definition in ISO/IEC Guide 2 is not self-contained, but based on the so-called "building block" system.

2. *Standard*

Document approved by a recognized body, that provides, for common and repeated use, rules, guidelines or characteristics for products or related processes and production methods, with which compliance is not mandatory. It may also include or deal exclusively with terminology, symbols, packaging, marking or labelling requirements as they apply to a product, process or production method.

Explanatory note

The terms as defined in ISO/IEC Guide 2 cover products, processes and services. This Agreement deals only with technical regulations, standards and conformity assessment procedures related to products or processes and production methods. Standards as defined by ISO/IEC Guide 2 may be mandatory or voluntary. For the purpose of this Agreement standards are defined as voluntary and technical regulations as mandatory documents. Standards prepared by the international standardization community are based on consensus. This Agreement covers also documents that are not based on consensus.

3. *Conformity assessment procedures*

Any procedure used, directly or indirectly, to determine that relevant requirements in technical regulations or standards are fulfilled.

Explanatory note

Conformity assessment procedures include, *inter alia*, procedures for sampling, testing and inspection; evaluation, verification and assurance of conformity; registration, accreditation and approval as well as their combinations.

4. *International body or system*

Body or system whose membership is open to the relevant bodies of at least all Members.

5. *Regional body or system*

Body or system whose membership is open to the relevant bodies of only some of the Members.

6. *Central government body*

Central government, its ministries and departments or any body subject to the control of the central government in respect of the activity in question.

Explanatory note:

In the case of the European Communities the provisions governing central government bodies apply. However, regional bodies or conformity assessment systems may be established within the European Communities, and in such cases would be subject to the provisions of this Agreement on regional bodies or conformity assessment systems.

7. *Local government body*

Government other than a central government (e.g. states, provinces, Länder, cantons, municipalities, etc.), its ministries or departments or any body subject to the control of such a government in respect of the activity in question.

8. *Non-governmental body*

Body other than a central government body or a local government body, including a non-governmental body which has legal power to enforce a technical regulation.

Annex 2

TECHNICAL EXPERT GROUPS

The following procedures shall apply to technical expert groups established in accordance with the provisions of Article 14.

1. Technical expert groups are under the panel's authority. Their terms of reference and detailed working procedures shall be decided by the panel, and they shall report to the panel.

2. Participation in technical expert groups shall be restricted to persons of professional standing and experience in the field in question.

3. Citizens of parties to the dispute shall not serve on a technical expert group without the joint agreement of the parties to the dispute, except in exceptional circumstances when the panel considers that the need for specialized scientific expertise cannot be fulfilled otherwise. Government officials of parties to the dispute shall not serve on a technical expert group. Members of technical expert groups shall serve in their individual capacities and not as government representatives, nor as representatives of any organization. Governments or organizations shall therefore not give them instructions with regard to matters before a technical expert group.

4. Technical expert groups may consult and seek information and technical advice from any source they deem appropriate. Before a technical expert group seeks such information or advice from a source within the jurisdiction of a Member, it shall inform the government of that Member. Any Member shall respond promptly and fully to any request by a technical expert group for such information as the technical expert group considers necessary and appropriate.

5. The parties to a dispute shall have access to all relevant information provided to a technical expert group, unless it is of a confidential nature. Confidential information provided to the technical expert group shall not be released without formal authorization from the government, organization or person providing the information. Where such information is requested from the technical expert group but release of such information by the technical expert group is not authorized, a non-confidential summary of the information will be provided by the government, organization or person supplying the information.

6. The technical expert group shall submit a draft report to the Members concerned with a view to obtaining their comments, and taking them into account, as appropriate, in the final report, which shall also be circulated to the Members concerned when it is submitted to the panel.

Annex 3

CODE OF GOOD PRACTICE FOR THE PREPARATION, ADOPTION AND APPLICATION OF STANDARDS

General Provisions

A. For the purposes of this Code the definitions in Annex 1 of this Agreement shall apply.

B. This Code is open to acceptance by any standardizing body within the territory of a Member of the WTO, whether a central government body, a local government body, or a non-governmental body; to any governmental regional standardizing body one or more members of which are Members of the WTO; and to any non-governmental regional standardizing body one or more members of which are situated within the territory of a Member of the WTO (referred to in this Code collectively as "standardizing bodies" and individually as "the standardizing body").

C. Standardizing bodies that have accepted or withdrawn from this Code shall notify this fact to the ISO/IEC Information Centre in Geneva. The notification shall include the name and address of the body concerned and the scope of its current and expected standardization activities. The notification may be sent either directly to the ISO/IEC Information Centre, or through the national member body of ISO/IEC or, preferably, through the relevant national member or international affiliate of ISONET, as appropriate.

SUBSTANTIVE PROVISIONS

D. In respect of standards, the standardizing body shall accord treatment to products originating in the territory of any other Member of the WTO no less favourable than that accorded to like products of national origin and to like products originating in any other country.

E. The standardizing body shall ensure that standards are not prepared, adopted or applied with a view to, or with the effect of, creating unnecessary obstacles to international trade.

F. Where international standards exist or their completion is imminent, the standardizing body shall use them, or the relevant parts of them, as a basis for the standards it develops, except where such international standards or relevant parts would be ineffective or inappropriate, for instance, because of an insufficient level of protection or fundamental climatic or geographical factors or fundamental technological problems.

G. With a view to harmonizing standards on as wide a basis as possible, the standardizing body shall, in an appropriate way, play a full part, within the limits of its resources, in the preparation by relevant international standardizing bodies of international standards regarding subject matter for which it either has adopted, or expects to adopt, standards. For standardizing bodies within the territory of a Member, participation in a particular international standardization activity shall, whenever possible, take place through one delegation representing all standardizing bodies in the territory that have adopted, or expect to adopt, standards for the subject matter to which the international standardization activity relates.

H. The standardizing body within the territory of a Member shall make every effort to avoid duplication of, or overlap with, the work of other standardizing bodies in the national territory or with the work of relevant international or regional standardizing bodies. They shall also make every effort to achieve a national consensus on the standards they develop. Likewise the regional standardizing body shall make every effort to avoid duplication of, or overlap with, the work of relevant international standardizing bodies.

I. Wherever appropriate, the standardizing body shall specify standards based on product requirements in terms of performance rather than design or descriptive characteristics.

J. At least once every six months, the standardizing body shall publish a work programme containing its name and address, the standards it is currently preparing and the standards which it has adopted in the preceding period. A standard is under preparation from the moment a decision has been taken to develop a standard until that standard has been adopted. The titles of specific draft standards shall, upon request, be provided in English, French or Spanish. A notice of the existence of the work programme shall be published in a national or, as the case may be, regional publication of standardization activities.

The work programme shall for each standard indicate, in accordance with any ISONET rules, the classification relevant to the subject matter, the stage attained in the standard's development, and the references of any international standards taken as a basis. No later than at the time of publication of its work programme, the standardizing body shall notify the existence thereof to the ISO/IEC Information Centre in Geneva.

The notification shall contain the name and address of the standardizing body, the name and issue of the publication in which the work programme is published, the period to which the work programme applies, its price (if any), and how and where it can be obtained. The notification may be sent directly to the ISO/IEC Information Centre, or, preferably, through the relevant national member or international affiliate of ISONET, as appropriate.

K. The national member of ISO/IEC shall make every effort to become a member of ISONET or to appoint another body to become a member as well as to acquire the most advanced membership type possible for the ISONET member. Other standardizing bodies shall make every effort to associate themselves with the ISONET member.

L. Before adopting a standard, the standardizing body shall allow a period of at least 60 days for the submission of comments on the draft standard by interested parties within the territory of a Member of the WTO. This period may, however, be shortened in cases where urgent problems of safety, health or environment arise or threaten to arise. No later than at the start of the comment period, the standardizing body shall publish a notice announcing the period for commenting in the publication referred to in paragraph J. Such notification shall include, as far as practicable, whether the draft standard deviates from relevant international standards.

M. On the request of any interested party within the territory of a Member of the WTO, the standardizing body shall promptly provide, or arrange to provide, a copy of a draft standard which it has submitted for comments. Any fees charged for this service shall, apart from the real cost of delivery, be the same for foreign and domestic parties.

N. The standardizing body shall take into account, in the further processing of the standard, the comments received during the period for commenting. Comments received through standardizing bodies that have accepted this Code of Good Practice shall, if so requested, be replied to as promptly as possible. The reply shall include an explanation why a deviation from relevant international standards is necessary.

O. Once the standard has been adopted, it shall be promptly published.

P. On the request of any interested party within the territory of a Member of the WTO, the standardizing body shall promptly provide, or arrange to provide, a copy of its most recent work programme or of a standard which it produced. Any fees charged for this service shall, apart from the real cost of delivery, be the same for foreign and domestic parties.

Q. The standardizing body shall afford sympathetic consideration to, and adequate opportunity for, consultation regarding representations with respect to the operation of this Code presented by standardizing bodies that have accepted this Code of Good Practice. It shall make an objective effort to solve any complaints.

Document 26

DECISION OF THE COMMITTEE ON PRINCIPLES FOR THE DEVELOPMENT OF INTERNATIONAL STANDARDS, GUIDES AND RECOMMENDATIONS WITH RELATION TO ARTICLES 2, 5 AND ANNEX 3 OF THE AGREEMENT

Decision[1]

1. The following principles and procedures should be observed, when international standards, guides and recommendations (as mentioned under Articles 2, 5 and Annex 3 of the TBT Agreement for the preparation of mandatory technical regulations, conformity assessment procedures and voluntary standards) are elaborated, to ensure transparency, openness, impartiality and consensus, effectiveness and relevance, coherence, and to address the concerns of developing countries.

2. The same principles should also be observed when technical work or a part of the international standard development is delegated under agreements or contracts by international standardizing bodies to other relevant organizations, including regional bodies.

1. Transparency

3. All essential information regarding current work programmes, as well as on proposals for standards, guides and recommendations under consideration and on the final results should be made easily accessible to at least all

1. G/TBT/9, 13 November 2000, para. 20 and Annex 4.

interested parties in the territories of at least all WTO Members. Procedures should be established so that adequate time and opportunities are provided for written comments. The information on these procedures should be effectively disseminated.

4. In providing the essential information, the transparency procedures should, at a minimum, include:

(a) the publication of a notice at an early appropriate stage, in such a manner as to enable interested parties to become acquainted with it, that the international standardizing body proposes to develop a particular standard;

(b) the notification or other communication through established mechanisms to members of the international standardizing body, providing a brief description of the scope of the draft standard, including its objective and rationale. Such communications shall take place at an early appropriate stage, when amendments can still be introduced and comments taken into account;

(c) upon request, the prompt provision to members of the international standardizing body of the text of the draft standard;

(d) the provision of an adequate period of time for interested parties in the territory of at least all members of the international standardizing body to make comments in writing and take these written comments into account in the further consideration of the standard;

(e) the prompt publication of a standard upon adoption; and

(f) to publish periodically a work programme containing information on the standards currently being prepared and adopted.

5. It is recognized that the publication and communication of notices, notifications, draft standards, comments, adopted standards or work programmes electronically, via the Internet, where feasible, can provide a useful means of ensuring the timely provision of information. At the same time, it is also recognized that the requisite technical means may not be available in some cases, particularly with regard to developing countries. Accordingly, it is important that procedures are in place to enable hard copies of such documents to be made available upon request.

2. Openness

6. Membership of an international standardizing body should be open on a non-discriminatory basis to relevant bodies of at least all WTO Mem-

bers. This would include openness without discrimination with respect to the participation at the policy development level and at every stage of standards development, such as the:

(a) proposal and acceptance of new work items;

(b) technical discussion on proposals;

(c) submission of comments on drafts in order that they can be taken into account;

(d) reviewing existing standards;

(e) voting and adoption of standards; and

(f) dissemination of the adopted standards.

7. Any interested member of the international standardizing body, including especially developing country Members, with an interest in a specific standardization activity should be provided with meaningful opportunities to participate at all stages of standard development. It is noted that with respect to standardizing bodies within the territory of a WTO Member that have accepted the Code of Good Practice for the Preparation, Adoption and Application of Standards by Standardizing Bodies (Annex 3 of the TBT Agreement) participation in a particular international standardization activity takes place, wherever possible, through one delegation representing all standardizing bodies in the territory that have adopted, or expected to adopt, standards for the subject-matter to which the international standardization activity relates. This is illustrative of the importance of participation in the international standardizing process accommodating all relevant interests.

3. Impartiality and Consensus

8. All relevant bodies of WTO Members should be provided with meaningful opportunities to contribute to the elaboration of an international standard so that the standard development process will not give privilege to, or favour the interests of, a particular supplier/s, country/ies or region/s. Consensus procedures should be established that seek to take into account the views of all parties concerned and to reconcile any conflicting arguments.

9. Impartiality should be accorded throughout all the standards development process with respect to, among other things:

(a) access to participation in work;

(b) submission of comments on drafts;

(c) consideration of views expressed and comments made;

(d) decision-making through consensus;

(e) obtaining of information and documents;

(f) dissemination of the international standard;

(g) fees charged for documents;

(h) right to transpose the international standard into a regional or national standard; and

(i) revision of the international standard.

4. Effectiveness and Relevance

10. In order to serve the interests of the WTO membership in facilitating international trade and preventing unnecessary trade barriers, international standards need to be relevant and to effectively respond to regulatory and market needs, as well as scientific and technological developments in various countries. They should not distort the global market, have adverse effects on fair competition, or stifle innovation and technological development. In addition, they should not give preference to the characteristics or requirements of specific countries or regions when different needs or interests exist in other countries or regions. Whenever possible, international standards should be performance based rather than based on design or descriptive characteristics.

11. Accordingly, it is important that international standardizing bodies:

(a) take account of relevant regulatory or market needs, as feasible and appropriate, as well as scientific and technological developments in the elaboration of standards;

(b) put in place procedures aimed at identifying and reviewing standards that have become obsolete, inappropriate or ineffective for various reasons; and

(c) put in place procedures aimed at improving communication with the World Trade Organization.

5. Coherence

12. In order to avoid the development of conflicting international standards, it is important that international standardizing bodies avoid duplication of, or overlap with, the work of other international standardizing bodies. In this respect, cooperation and coordination with other relevant international bodies is essential.

6. Development Dimension

13. Constraints on developing countries, in particular, to effectively participate in standards development, should be taken into consideration in the standards development process. Tangible ways of facilitating developing countries' participation in international standards development should be sought. The impartiality and openness of any international standardization process requires that developing countries are not excluded de facto from the process. With respect to improving participation by developing countries, it may be appropriate to use technical assistance, in line with Article 11 of the TBT Agreement. Provisions for capacity building and technical assistance within international standardizing bodies are important in this context.

Document 27

AGREEMENT ON TRADE-RELATED INVESTMENT MEASURES

Members,

Considering that Ministers agreed in the Punta del Este Declaration that "Following an examination of the operation of GATT Articles related to the trade restrictive and distorting effects of investment measures, negotiations should elaborate, as appropriate, further provisions that may be necessary to avoid such adverse effects on trade";

Desiring to promote the expansion and progressive liberalisation of world trade and to facilitate investment across international frontiers so as to increase the economic growth of all trading partners, particularly developing country Members, while ensuring free competition;

Taking into account the particular trade, development and financial needs of developing country Members, particularly those of the least-developed country Members;

Recognizing that certain investment measures can cause trade-restrictive and distorting effects;

Hereby *agree* as follows:

Article 1

Coverage

This Agreement applies to investment measures related to trade in goods only (referred to in this Agreement as "TRIMs").

Article 2

National Treatment and Quantitative Restrictions

1. Without prejudice to other rights and obligations under GATT 1994, no Member shall apply any TRIM that is inconsistent with the provisions of Article III or Article XI of GATT 1994.

2. An illustrative list of TRIMs that are inconsistent with the obligation of national treatment provided for in paragraph 4 of Article III of GATT 1994 and the obligation of general elimination of quantitative restrictions provided for in paragraph 1 of Article XI of GATT 1994 is contained in the Annex to this Agreement.

Article 3

Exceptions

All exceptions under GATT 1994 shall apply, as appropriate, to the provisions of this Agreement.

Article 4

Developing Country Members

A developing country Member shall be free to deviate temporarily from the provisions of Article 2 to the extent and in such a manner as Article XVIII of GATT 1994, the Understanding on the Balance-of-Payments Provisions of GATT 1994, and the Declaration on Trade Measures Taken for Balance-of-Payments Purposes adopted on 28 November 1979 (BISD 26S/205-209) permit the Member to deviate from the provisions of Articles III and XI of GATT 1994.

Article 5

Notification and Transitional Arrangements

1. Members, within 90 days of the date of entry into force of the WTO Agreement, shall notify the Council for Trade in Goods of all TRIMs they are applying that are not in conformity with the provisions of this Agreement. Such TRIMs of general or specific application shall be notified, along with their principal features.[1]

1. In the case of TRIMs applied under discretionary authority, each specific application shall be notified. Information that would prejudice the legitimate commercial interests of particular enterprises need not be disclosed.

2. Each Member shall eliminate all TRIMs which are notified under paragraph 1 within two years of the date of entry into force of the WTO Agreement in the case of a developed country Member, within five years in the case of a developing country Member, and within seven years in the case of a least-developed country Member.

3. On request, the Council for Trade in Goods may extend the transition period for the elimination of TRIMs notified under paragraph 1 for a developing country Member, including a least-developed country Member, which demonstrates particular difficulties in implementing the provisions of this Agreement. In considering such a request, the Council for Trade in Goods shall take into account the individual development, financial and trade needs of the Member in question.

4. During the transition period, a Member shall not modify the terms of any TRIM which it notifies under paragraph 1 from those prevailing at the date of entry into force of the WTO Agreement so as to increase the degree of inconsistency with the provisions of Article 2. TRIMs introduced less than 180 days before the date of entry into force of the WTO Agreement shall not benefit from the transitional arrangements provided in paragraph 2.

5. Notwithstanding the provisions of Article 2, a Member, in order not to disadvantage established enterprises which are subject to a TRIM notified under paragraph 1, may apply during the transition period the same TRIM to a new investment (*i*) where the products of such investment are like products to those of the established enterprises, and (*ii*) where necessary to avoid distorting the conditions of competition between the new investment and the established enterprises. Any TRIM so applied to a new investment shall be notified to the Council for Trade in Goods. The terms of such a TRIM shall be equivalent in their competitive effect to those applicable to the established enterprises, and it shall be terminated at the same time.

Article 6

Transparency

1. Members reaffirm, with respect to TRIMs, their commitment to obligations on transparency and notification in Article X of GATT 1994, in the undertaking on "Notification" contained in the Understanding Regarding Notification, Consultation, Dispute Settlement and Surveillance adopted on 28 November 1979 and in the Ministerial Decision on Notification Procedures adopted on 15 April 1994.

2. Each Member shall notify the Secretariat of the publications in which TRIMs may be found, including those applied by regional and local governments and authorities within their territories.

3. Each Member shall accord sympathetic consideration to requests for information, and afford adequate opportunity for consultation, on any matter arising from this Agreement raised by another Member. In conformity with Article X of GATT 1994 no Member is required to disclose information the disclosure of which would impede law enforcement or otherwise be contrary to the public interest or would prejudice the legitimate commercial interests of particular enterprises, public or private.

Article 7

Committee on Trade-Related Investment Measures

1. A Committee on Trade-Related Investment Measures (referred to in this Agreement as the "Committee") is hereby established, and shall be open to all Members. The Committee shall elect its own Chairman and Vice-Chairman, and shall meet not less than once a year and otherwise at the request of any Member.

2. The Committee shall carry out responsibilities assigned to it by the Council for Trade in Goods and shall afford Members the opportunity to consult on any matters relating to the operation and implementation of this Agreement.

3. The Committee shall monitor the operation and implementation of this Agreement and shall report thereon annually to the Council for Trade in Goods.

Article 8

Consultation and Dispute Settlement

The provisions of Articles XXII and XXIII of GATT 1994, as elaborated and applied by the Dispute Settlement Understanding, shall apply to consultations and the settlement of disputes under this Agreement.

Article 9

Review by the Council for Trade in Goods

Not later than five years after the date of entry into force of the WTO Agreement, the Council for Trade in Goods shall review the operation of this Agreement and, as appropriate, propose to the Ministerial Conference amendments to its text. In the course of this review, the Council for Trade in Goods shall consider whether the Agreement should be complemented with provisions on investment policy and competition policy.

Annex

Illustrative List

1. TRIMs that are inconsistent with the obligation of national treatment provided for in paragraph 4 of Article III of GATT 1994 include those which are mandatory or enforceable under domestic law or under administrative rulings, or compliance with which is necessary to obtain an advantage, and which require:

(a) the purchase or use by an enterprise of products of domestic origin or from any domestic source, whether specified in terms of particular products, in terms of volume or value of products, or in terms of a proportion of volume or value of its local production; or

(b) that an enterprise's purchases or use of imported products be limited to an amount related to the volume or value of local products that it exports.

2. TRIMs that are inconsistent with the obligation of general elimination of quantitative restrictions provided for in paragraph 1 of Article XI of GATT 1994 include those which are mandatory or enforceable under domestic law or under administrative rulings, or compliance with which is necessary to obtain an advantage, and which restrict:

(a) the importation by an enterprise of products used in or related to its local production, generally or to an amount related to the volume or value of local production that it exports;

(b) the importation by an enterprise of products used in or related to its local production by restricting its access to foreign exchange to an amount related to the foreign exchange inflows attributable to the enterprise; or

(c) the exportation or sale for export by an enterprise of products, whether specified in terms of particular products, in terms of volume or value of products, or in terms of a proportion of volume or value of its local production.

Document 28

ANTI-DUMPING AGREEMENT

Official name: Agreement on Implementation of Article VI of the General Agreement on Tariffs and Trade 1994

Members hereby *agree* as follows:

Part I

Article 1

Principles

An anti-dumping measure shall be applied only under the circumstances provided for in Article VI of GATT 1994 and pursuant to investigations initiated[1] and conducted in accordance with the provisions of this Agreement. The following provisions govern the application of Article VI of GATT 1994 in so far as action is taken under anti-dumping legislation or regulations.

Article 2

Determination of Dumping

2.1 For the purpose of this Agreement, a product is to be considered as being dumped, i.e. introduced into the commerce of another country at less than its normal value, if the export price of the product exported from one country to another is less than the comparable price, in the ordinary course

1. The term "initiated" as used in this Agreement means the procedural action by which a Member formally commences an investigation as provided in Article 5.

of trade, for the like product when destined for consumption in the exporting country.

2.2 When there are no sales of the like product in the ordinary course of trade in the domestic market of the exporting country or when, because of the particular market situation or the low volume of the sales in the domestic market of the exporting country,[2] such sales do not permit a proper comparison, the margin of dumping shall be determined by comparison with a comparable price of the like product when exported to an appropriate third country, provided that this price is representative, or with the cost of production in the country of origin plus a reasonable amount for administrative, selling and general costs and for profits.

2.2.1 Sales of the like product in the domestic market of the exporting country or sales to a third country at prices below per unit (fixed and variable) costs of production plus administrative, selling and general costs may be treated as not being in the ordinary course of trade by reason of price and may be disregarded in determining normal value only if the authorities[3] determine that such sales are made within an extended period of time[4] in substantial quantities[5] and are at prices which do not provide for the recovery of all costs within a reasonable period of time. If prices which are below per unit costs at the time of sale are above weighted average per unit costs for the period of investigation, such prices shall be considered to provide for recovery of costs within a reasonable period of time.

2.2.1.1 For the purpose of paragraph 2, costs shall normally be calculated on the basis of records kept by the exporter or producer under investigation, provided that such records are in accordance with the generally accepted accounting principles of the exporting country and reasonably reflect the costs associated with the production and sale of the product under consideration. Authorities shall consider all available evidence on the proper allocation of costs, including that

2. Sales of the like product destined for consumption in the domestic market of the exporting country shall normally be considered a sufficient quantity for the determination of the normal value if such sales constitute 5 per cent or more of the sales of the product under consideration to the importing Member, provided that a lower ratio should be acceptable where the evidence demonstrates that domestic sales at such lower ratio are nonetheless of sufficient magnitude to provide for a proper comparison.

3. When in this Agreement the term "authorities" is used, it shall be interpreted as meaning authorities at an appropriate senior level.

4. The extended period of time should normally be one year but shall in no case be less than six months.

5. Sales below per unit costs are made in substantial quantities when the authorities establish that the weighted average selling price of the transactions under consideration for the determination of the normal value is below the weighted average per unit costs, or that the volume of sales below per unit costs represents not less than 20 per cent of the volume sold in transactions under consideration for the determination of the normal value.

which is made available by the exporter or producer in the course of the investigation provided that such allocations have been historically utilized by the exporter or producer, in particular in relation to establishing appropriate amortization and depreciation periods and allowances for capital expenditures and other development costs. Unless already reflected in the cost allocations under this sub-paragraph, costs shall be adjusted appropriately for those non-recurring items of cost which benefit future and/or current production, or for circumstances in which costs during the period of investigation are affected by start-up operations.[6]

2.2.2 For the purpose of paragraph 2, the amounts for administrative, selling and general costs and for profits shall be based on actual data pertaining to production and sales in the ordinary course of trade of the like product by the exporter or producer under investigation. When such amounts cannot be determined on this basis, the amounts may be determined on the basis of:

(i) the actual amounts incurred and realized by the exporter or producer in question in respect of production and sales in the domestic market of the country of origin of the same general category of products;

(ii) the weighted average of the actual amounts incurred and realized by other exporters or producers subject to investigation in respect of production and sales of the like product in the domestic market of the country of origin;

(iii) any other reasonable method, provided that the amount for profit so established shall not exceed the profit normally realized by other exporters or producers on sales of products of the same general category in the domestic market of the country of origin.

2.3 In cases where there is no export price or where it appears to the authorities concerned that the export price is unreliable because of association or a compensatory arrangement between the exporter and the importer or a third party, the export price may be constructed on the basis of the price at which the imported products are first resold to an independent buyer, or if the products are not resold to an independent buyer, or not resold in the condition as imported, on such reasonable basis as the authorities may determine.

6. The adjustment made for start-up operations shall reflect the costs at the end of the start-up period or, if that period extends beyond the period of investigation, the most recent costs which can reasonably be taken into account by the authorities during the investigation.

2.4 A fair comparison shall be made between the export price and the normal value. This comparison shall be made at the same level of trade, normally at the ex-factory level, and in respect of sales made at as nearly as possible the same time. Due allowance shall be made in each case, on its merits, for differences which affect price comparability, including differences in conditions and terms of sale, taxation, levels of trade, quantities, physical characteristics, and any other differences which are also demonstrated to affect price comparability.[7] In the cases referred to in paragraph 3, allowances for costs, including duties and taxes, incurred between importation and resale, and for profits accruing, should also be made. If in these cases price comparability has been affected, the authorities shall establish the normal value at a level of trade equivalent to the level of trade of the constructed export price, or shall make due allowance as warranted under this paragraph. The authorities shall indicate to the parties in question what information is necessary to ensure a fair comparison and shall not impose an unreasonable burden of proof on those parties.

2.4.1 When the comparison under paragraph 4 requires a conversion of currencies, such conversion should be made using the rate of exchange on the date of sale,[8] provided that when a sale of foreign currency on forward markets is directly linked to the export sale involved, the rate of exchange in the forward sale shall be used. Fluctuations in exchange rates shall be ignored and in an investigation the authorities shall allow exporters at least 60 days to have adjusted their export prices to reflect sustained movements in exchange rates during the period of investigation.

2.4.2 Subject to the provisions governing fair comparison in paragraph 4, the existence of margins of dumping during the investigation phase shall normally be established on the basis of a comparison of a weighted average normal value with a weighted average of prices of all comparable export transactions or by a comparison of normal value and export prices on a transaction-to-transaction basis. A normal value established on a weighted average basis may be compared to prices of individual export transactions if the authorities find a pattern of export prices which differ significantly among different purchasers, regions or time periods, and if an explanation is provided as to why such differences cannot be taken into account appropriately by the use of a weighted average-to-weighted average or transaction-to-transaction comparison.

2.5 In the case where products are not imported directly from the country of origin but are exported to the importing Member from an

7. It is understood that some of the above factors may overlap, and authorities shall ensure that they do not duplicate adjustments that have been already made under this provision.

8. Normally, the date of sale would be the date of contract, purchase order, order confirmation, or invoice, whichever establishes the material terms of sale.

intermediate country, the price at which the products are sold from the country of export to the importing Member shall normally be compared with the comparable price in the country of export. However, comparison may be made with the price in the country of origin, if, for example, the products are merely transshipped through the country of export, or such products are not produced in the country of export, or there is no comparable price for them in the country of export.

2.6 Throughout this Agreement the term "like product" ("produit similaire") shall be interpreted to mean a product which is identical, i.e. alike in all respects to the product under consideration, or in the absence of such a product, another product which, although not alike in all respects, has characteristics closely resembling those of the product under consideration.

2.7 This Article is without prejudice to the second Supplementary Provision to paragraph 1 of Article VI in Annex I to GATT 1994.

Article 3

Determination of Injury[9]

3.1 A determination of injury for purposes of Article VI of GATT 1994 shall be based on positive evidence and involve an objective examination of both *(a)* the volume of the dumped imports and the effect of the dumped imports on prices in the domestic market for like products, and *(b)* the consequent impact of these imports on domestic producers of such products.

3.2 With regard to the volume of the dumped imports, the investigating authorities shall consider whether there has been a significant increase in dumped imports, either in absolute terms or relative to production or consumption in the importing Member. With regard to the effect of the dumped imports on prices, the investigating authorities shall consider whether there has been a significant price undercutting by the dumped imports as compared with the price of a like product of the importing Member, or whether the effect of such imports is otherwise to depress prices to a significant degree or prevent price increases, which otherwise would have occurred, to a significant degree. No one or several of these factors can necessarily give decisive guidance.

3.3 Where imports of a product from more than one country are simultaneously subject to anti-dumping investigations, the investigating authorities may cumulatively assess the effects of such imports only if they

9. Under this Agreement the term "injury" shall, unless otherwise specified, be taken to mean material injury to a domestic industry, threat of material injury to a domestic industry or material retardation of the establishment of such an industry and shall be interpreted in accordance with the provisions of this Article.

determine that *(a)* the margin of dumping established in relation to the imports from each country is more than *de minimis* as defined in paragraph 8 of Article 5 and the volume of imports from each country is not negligible and *(b)* a cumulative assessment of the effects of the imports is appropriate in light of the conditions of competition between the imported products and the conditions of competition between the imported products and the like domestic product.

3.4 The examination of the impact of the dumped imports on the domestic industry concerned shall include an evaluation of all relevant economic factors and indices having a bearing on the state of the industry, including actual and potential decline in sales, profits, output, market share, productivity, return on investments, or utilization of capacity; factors affecting domestic prices; the magnitude of the margin of dumping; actual and potential negative effects on cash flow, inventories, employment, wages, growth, ability to raise capital or investments. This list is not exhaustive, nor can one or several of these factors necessarily give decisive guidance.

3.5 It must be demonstrated that the dumped imports are, through the effects of dumping, as set forth in paragraphs 2 and 4, causing injury within the meaning of this Agreement. The demonstration of a causal relationship between the dumped imports and the injury to the domestic industry shall be based on an examination of all relevant evidence before the authorities. The authorities shall also examine any known factors other than the dumped imports which at the same time are injuring the domestic industry, and the injuries caused by these other factors must not be attributed to the dumped imports. Factors which may be relevant in this respect include, *inter alia*, the volume and prices of imports not sold at dumping prices, contraction in demand or changes in the patterns of consumption, trade restrictive practices of and competition between the foreign and domestic producers, developments in technology and the export performance and productivity of the domestic industry.

3.6 The effect of the dumped imports shall be assessed in relation to the domestic production of the like product when available data permit the separate identification of that production on the basis of such criteria as the production process, producers' sales and profits. If such separate identification of that production is not possible, the effects of the dumped imports shall be assessed by the examination of the production of the narrowest group or range of products, which includes the like product, for which the necessary information can be provided.

3.7 A determination of a threat of material injury shall be based on facts and not merely on allegation, conjecture or remote possibility. The change in circumstances which would create a situation in which the dumping would cause injury must be clearly foreseen and imminent.[10] In making a determination regarding the existence of a threat of material injury, the authorities should consider, *inter alia*, such factors as:

(i) a significant rate of increase of dumped imports into the domestic market indicating the likelihood of substantially increased importation;

(ii) sufficient freely disposable, or an imminent, substantial increase in, capacity of the exporter indicating the likelihood of substantially increased dumped exports to the importing Member's market, taking into account the availability of other export markets to absorb any additional exports;

(iii) whether imports are entering at prices that will have a significant depressing or suppressing effect on domestic prices, and would likely increase demand for further imports; and

(iv) inventories of the product being investigated.

No one of these factors by itself can necessarily give decisive guidance but the totality of the factors considered must lead to the conclusion that further dumped exports are imminent and that, unless protective action is taken, material injury would occur.

3.8 With respect to cases where injury is threatened by dumped imports, the application of anti-dumping measures shall be considered and decided with special care.

Article 4

Definition of Domestic Industry

4.1 For the purposes of this Agreement, the term "domestic industry" shall be interpreted as referring to the domestic producers as a whole of the like products or to those of them whose collective output of the products constitutes a major proportion of the total domestic production of those products, except that:

(i) when producers are related[11] to the exporters or importers or are themselves importers of the allegedly dumped product, the term

10. One example, though not an exclusive one, is that there is convincing reason to believe that there will be, in the near future, substantially increased importation of the product at dumped prices.

11. For the purpose of this paragraph, producers shall be deemed to be related to exporters or importers only if *(a)* one of them directly or indirectly controls the other; or *(b)* both of them are directly or indirectly controlled by a third person; or *(c)* together they directly

"domestic industry" may be interpreted as referring to the rest of the producers;

(ii) in exceptional circumstances the territory of a Member may, for the production in question, be divided into two or more competitive markets and the producers within each market may be regarded as a separate industry if *(a)* the producers within such market sell all or almost all of their production of the product in question in that market, and *(b)* the demand in that market is not to any substantial degree supplied by producers of the product in question located elsewhere in the territory. In such circumstances, injury may be found to exist even where a major portion of the total domestic industry is not injured, provided there is a concentration of dumped imports into such an isolated market and provided further that the dumped imports are causing injury to the producers of all or almost all of the production within such market.

4.2 When the domestic industry has been interpreted as referring to the producers in a certain area, i.e. a market as defined in paragraph 1(ii), anti-dumping duties shall be levied[12] only on the products in question consigned for final consumption to that area. When the constitutional law of the importing Member does not permit the levying of anti-dumping duties on such a basis, the importing Member may levy the anti-dumping duties without limitation only if *(a)* the exporters shall have been given an opportunity to cease exporting at dumped prices to the area concerned or otherwise give assurances pursuant to Article 8 and adequate assurances in this regard have not been promptly given, and *(b)* such duties cannot be levied only on products of specific producers which supply the area in question.

4.3 Where two or more countries have reached under the provisions of paragraph 8(a) of Article XXIV of GATT 1994 such a level of integration that they have the characteristics of a single, unified market, the industry in the entire area of integration shall be taken to be the domestic industry referred to in paragraph 1.

4.4 The provisions of paragraph 6 of Article 3 shall be applicable to this Article.

---

or indirectly control a third person, provided that there are grounds for believing or suspecting that the effect of the relationship is such as to cause the producer concerned to behave differently from non-related producers. For the purpose of this paragraph, one shall be deemed to control another when the former is legally or operationally in a position to exercise restraint or direction over the latter.

12. As used in this Agreement "levy" shall mean the definitive or final legal assessment or collection of a duty or tax.

Article 5

Initiation and Subsequent Investigation

5.1 Except as provided for in paragraph 6, an investigation to determine the existence, degree and effect of any alleged dumping shall be initiated upon a written application by or on behalf of the domestic industry.

5.2 An application under paragraph 1 shall include evidence of *(a)* dumping, *(b)* injury within the meaning of Article VI of GATT 1994 as interpreted by this Agreement and *(c)* a causal link between the dumped imports and the alleged injury. Simple assertion, unsubstantiated by relevant evidence, cannot be considered sufficient to meet the requirements of this paragraph. The application shall contain such information as is reasonably available to the applicant on the following:

(i) the identity of the applicant and a description of the volume and value of the domestic production of the like product by the applicant. Where a written application is made on behalf of the domestic industry, the application shall identify the industry on behalf of which the application is made by a list of all known domestic producers of the like product (or associations of domestic producers of the like product) and, to the extent possible, a description of the volume and value of domestic production of the like product accounted for by such producers;

(ii) a complete description of the allegedly dumped product, the names of the country or countries of origin or export in question, the identity of each known exporter or foreign producer and a list of known persons importing the product in question;

(iii) information on prices at which the product in question is sold when destined for consumption in the domestic markets of the country or countries of origin or export (or, where appropriate, information on the prices at which the product is sold from the country or countries of origin or export to a third country or countries, or on the constructed value of the product) and information on export prices or, where appropriate, on the prices at which the product is first resold to an independent buyer in the territory of the importing Member;

(iv) information on the evolution of the volume of the allegedly dumped imports, the effect of these imports on prices of the like product in the domestic market and the consequent impact of the imports on the domestic industry, as demonstrated by relevant factors and indices having a bearing on the state of the domestic industry, such as those listed in paragraphs 2 and 4 of Article 3.

5.3 The authorities shall examine the accuracy and adequacy of the evidence provided in the application to determine whether there is sufficient evidence to justify the initiation of an investigation.

5.4 An investigation shall not be initiated pursuant to paragraph 1 unless the authorities have determined, on the basis of an examination of the degree of support for, or opposition to, the application expressed[13] by domestic producers of the like product, that the application has been made by or on behalf of the domestic industry.[14] The application shall be considered to have been made "by or on behalf of the domestic industry" if it is supported by those domestic producers whose collective output constitutes more than 50 per cent of the total production of the like product produced by that portion of the domestic industry expressing either support for or opposition to the application. However, no investigation shall be initiated when domestic producers expressly supporting the application account for less than 25 per cent of total production of the like product produced by the domestic industry.

5.5 The authorities shall avoid, unless a decision has been made to initiate an investigation, any publicizing of the application for the initiation of an investigation. However, after receipt of a properly documented application and before proceeding to initiate an investigation, the authorities shall notify the government of the exporting Member concerned.

5.6 If, in special circumstances, the authorities concerned decide to initiate an investigation without having received a written application by or on behalf of a domestic industry for the initiation of such investigation, they shall proceed only if they have sufficient evidence of dumping, injury and a causal link, as described in paragraph 2, to justify the initiation of an investigation.

5.7 The evidence of both dumping and injury shall be considered simultaneously *(a)* in the decision whether or not to initiate an investigation, and *(b)* thereafter, during the course of the investigation, starting on a date not later than the earliest date on which in accordance with the provisions of this Agreement provisional measures may be applied.

5.8 An application under paragraph 1 shall be rejected and an investigation shall be terminated promptly as soon as the authorities concerned are satisfied that there is not sufficient evidence of either dumping or of

13. In the case of fragmented industries involving an exceptionally large number of producers, authorities may determine support and opposition by using statistically valid sampling techniques.

14. Members are aware that in the territory of certain Members employees of domestic producers of the like product or representatives of those employees may make or support an application for an investigation under paragraph 1.

injury to justify proceeding with the case. There shall be immediate termination in cases where the authorities determine that the margin of dumping is *de minimis*, or that the volume of dumped imports, actual or potential, or the injury, is negligible. The margin of dumping shall be considered to be *de minimis* if this margin is less than 2 per cent, expressed as a percentage of the export price. The volume of dumped imports shall normally be regarded as negligible if the volume of dumped imports from a particular country is found to account for less than 3 per cent of imports of the like product in the importing Member, unless countries which individually account for less than 3 per cent of the imports of the like product in the importing Member collectively account for more than 7 per cent of imports of the like product in the importing Member.

5.9 An anti-dumping proceeding shall not hinder the procedures of customs clearance.

5.10 Investigations shall, except in special circumstances, be concluded within one year, and in no case more than 18 months, after their initiation.

Article 6

Evidence

6.1 All interested parties in an anti-dumping investigation shall be given notice of the information which the authorities require and ample opportunity to present in writing all evidence which they consider relevant in respect of the investigation in question.

6.1.1 Exporters or foreign producers receiving questionnaires used in an anti-dumping investigation shall be given at least 30 days for reply.[15] Due consideration should be given to any request for an extension of the 30-day period and, upon cause shown, such an extension should be granted whenever practicable.

6.1.2 Subject to the requirement to protect confidential information, evidence presented in writing by one interested party shall be made available promptly to other interested parties participating in the investigation.

6.1.3 As soon as an investigation has been initiated, the authorities shall provide the full text of the written application received under

15. As a general rule, the time-limit for exporters shall be counted from the date of receipt of the questionnaire, which for this purpose shall be deemed to have been received one week from the date on which it was sent to the respondent or transmitted to the appropriate diplomatic representative of the exporting Member or, in the case of a separate customs territory Member of the WTO, an official representative of the exporting territory.

paragraph 1 of Article 5 to the known exporters[16] and to the authorities of the exporting Member and shall make it available, upon request, to other interested parties involved. Due regard shall be paid to the requirement for the protection of confidential information, as provided for in paragraph 5.

6.2 Throughout the anti-dumping investigation all interested parties shall have a full opportunity for the defence of their interests. To this end, the authorities shall, on request, provide opportunities for all interested parties to meet those parties with adverse interests, so that opposing views may be presented and rebuttal arguments offered. Provision of such opportunities must take account of the need to preserve confidentiality and of the convenience to the parties. There shall be no obligation on any party to attend a meeting, and failure to do so shall not be prejudicial to that party's case. Interested parties shall also have the right, on justification, to present other information orally.

6.3 Oral information provided under paragraph 2 shall be taken into account by the authorities only in so far as it is subsequently reproduced in writing and made available to other interested parties, as provided for in subparagraph 1.2.

6.4 The authorities shall whenever practicable provide timely opportunities for all interested parties to see all information that is relevant to the presentation of their cases, that is not confidential as defined in paragraph 5, and that is used by the authorities in an anti-dumping investigation, and to prepare presentations on the basis of this information.

6.5 Any information which is by nature confidential (for example, because its disclosure would be of significant competitive advantage to a competitor or because its disclosure would have a significantly adverse effect upon a person supplying the information or upon a person from whom that person acquired the information), or which is provided on a confidential basis by parties to an investigation shall, upon good cause shown, be treated as such by the authorities. Such information shall not be disclosed without specific permission of the party submitting it.[17]

6.5.1 The authorities shall require interested parties providing confidential information to furnish non-confidential summaries thereof. These summaries shall be in sufficient detail to permit a reasonable

16. It being understood that, where the number of exporters involved is particularly high, the full text of the written application should instead be provided only to the authorities of the exporting Member or to the relevant trade association.

17. Members are aware that in the territory of certain Members disclosure pursuant to a narrowly-drawn protective order may be required.

understanding of the substance of the information submitted in confidence. In exceptional circumstances, such parties may indicate that such information is not susceptible of summary. In such exceptional circumstances, a statement of the reasons why summarization is not possible must be provided.

6.5.2 If the authorities find that a request for confidentiality is not warranted and if the supplier of the information is either unwilling to make the information public or to authorize its disclosure in generalized or summary form, the authorities may disregard such information unless it can be demonstrated to their satisfaction from appropriate sources that the information is correct.[18]

6.6 Except in circumstances provided for in paragraph 8, the authorities shall during the course of an investigation satisfy themselves as to the accuracy of the information supplied by interested parties upon which their findings are based.

6.7 In order to verify information provided or to obtain further details, the authorities may carry out investigations in the territory of other Members as required, provided they obtain the agreement of the firms concerned and notify the representatives of the government of the Member in question, and unless that Member objects to the investigation. The procedures described in Annex I shall apply to investigations carried out in the territory of other Members. Subject to the requirement to protect confidential information, the authorities shall make the results of any such investigations available, or shall provide disclosure thereof pursuant to paragraph 9, to the firms to which they pertain and may make such results available to the applicants.

6.8 In cases in which any interested party refuses access to, or otherwise does not provide, necessary information within a reasonable period or significantly impedes the investigation, preliminary and final determinations, affirmative or negative, may be made on the basis of the facts available. The provisions of Annex II shall be observed in the application of this paragraph.

6.9 The authorities shall, before a final determination is made, inform all interested parties of the essential facts under consideration which form the basis for the decision whether to apply definitive measures. Such disclosure should take place in sufficient time for the parties to defend their interests.

6.10 The authorities shall, as a rule, determine an individual margin of dumping for each known exporter or producer concerned of the product under investigation. In cases where the number of exporters, producers,

18. Members agree that requests for confidentiality should not be arbitrarily rejected.

importers or types of products involved is so large as to make such a determination impracticable, the authorities may limit their examination either to a reasonable number of interested parties or products by using samples which are statistically valid on the basis of information available to the authorities at the time of the selection, or to the largest percentage of the volume of the exports from the country in question which can reasonably be investigated.

6.10.1 Any selection of exporters, producers, importers or types of products made under this paragraph shall preferably be chosen in consultation with and with the consent of the exporters, producers or importers concerned.

6.10.2 In cases where the authorities have limited their examination, as provided for in this paragraph, they shall nevertheless determine an individual margin of dumping for any exporter or producer not initially selected who submits the necessary information in time for that information to be considered during the course of the investigation, except where the number of exporters or producers is so large that individual examinations would be unduly burdensome to the authorities and prevent the timely completion of the investigation. Voluntary responses shall not be discouraged.

6.11 For the purposes of this Agreement, "interested parties" shall include:

(i) an exporter or foreign producer or the importer of a product subject to investigation, or a trade or business association a majority of the members of which are producers, exporters or importers of such product;

(ii) the government of the exporting Member; and

(iii) a producer of the like product in the importing Member or a trade and business association a majority of the members of which produce the like product in the territory of the importing Member.

This list shall not preclude Members from allowing domestic or foreign parties other than those mentioned above to be included as interested parties.

6.12 The authorities shall provide opportunities for industrial users of the product under investigation, and for representative consumer organizations in cases where the product is commonly sold at the retail level, to provide information which is relevant to the investigation regarding dumping, injury and causality.

6.13 The authorities shall take due account of any difficulties experienced by interested parties, in particular small companies, in supplying information requested, and shall provide any assistance practicable.

6.14 The procedures set out above are not intended to prevent the authorities of a Member from proceeding expeditiously with regard to initiating an investigation, reaching preliminary or final determinations, whether affirmative or negative, or from applying provisional or final measures, in accordance with relevant provisions of this Agreement.

Article 7

Provisional Measures

7.1 Provisional measures may be applied only if:

(i) an investigation has been initiated in accordance with the provisions of Article 5, a public notice has been given to that effect and interested parties have been given adequate opportunities to submit information and make comments;

(ii) a preliminary affirmative determination has been made of dumping and consequent injury to a domestic industry; and

(iii) the authorities concerned judge such measures necessary to prevent injury being caused during the investigation.

7.2 Provisional measures may take the form of a provisional duty or, preferably, a security—by cash deposit or bond—equal to the amount of the anti-dumping duty provisionally estimated, being not greater than the provisionally estimated margin of dumping. Withholding of appraisement is an appropriate provisional measure, provided that the normal duty and the estimated amount of the anti-dumping duty be indicated and as long as the withholding of appraisement is subject to the same conditions as other provisional measures.

7.3 Provisional measures shall not be applied sooner than 60 days from the date of initiation of the investigation.

7.4 The application of provisional measures shall be limited to as short a period as possible, not exceeding four months or, on decision of the authorities concerned, upon request by exporters representing a significant percentage of the trade involved, to a period not exceeding six months. When authorities, in the course of an investigation, examine whether a duty lower than the margin of dumping would be sufficient to remove injury, these periods may be six and nine months, respectively.

7.5 The relevant provisions of Article 9 shall be followed in the application of provisional measures.

Article 8

Price Undertakings

8.1 Proceedings may[19] be suspended or terminated without the imposition of provisional measures or anti-dumping duties upon receipt of satisfactory voluntary undertakings from any exporter to revise its prices or to cease exports to the area in question at dumped prices so that the authorities are satisfied that the injurious effect of the dumping is eliminated. Price increases under such undertakings shall not be higher than necessary to eliminate the margin of dumping. It is desirable that the price increases be less than the margin of dumping if such increases would be adequate to remove the injury to the domestic industry.

8.2 Price undertakings shall not be sought or accepted from exporters unless the authorities of the importing Member have made a preliminary affirmative determination of dumping and injury caused by such dumping.

8.3 Undertakings offered need not be accepted if the authorities consider their acceptance impractical, for example, if the number of actual or potential exporters is too great, or for other reasons, including reasons of general policy. Should the case arise and where practicable, the authorities shall provide to the exporter the reasons which have led them to consider acceptance of an undertaking as inappropriate, and shall, to the extent possible, give the exporter an opportunity to make comments thereon.

8.4 If an undertaking is accepted, the investigation of dumping and injury shall nevertheless be completed if the exporter so desires or the authorities so decide. In such a case, if a negative determination of dumping or injury is made, the undertaking shall automatically lapse, except in cases where such a determination is due in large part to the existence of a price undertaking. In such cases, the authorities may require that an undertaking be maintained for a reasonable period consistent with the provisions of this Agreement. In the event that an affirmative determination of dumping and injury is made, the undertaking shall continue consistent with its terms and the provisions of this Agreement.

8.5 Price undertakings may be suggested by the authorities of the importing Member, but no exporter shall be forced to enter into such undertakings. The fact that exporters do not offer such undertakings, or do not accept an invitation to do so, shall in no way prejudice the consideration of the case. However, the authorities are free to determine that a threat of injury is more likely to be realized if the dumped imports continue.

19. The word "may" shall not be interpreted to allow the simultaneous continuation of proceedings with the implementation of price undertakings except as provided in paragraph 4.

8.6 Authorities of an importing Member may require any exporter from whom an undertaking has been accepted to provide periodically information relevant to the fulfilment of such an undertaking and to permit verification of pertinent data. In case of violation of an undertaking, the authorities of the importing Member may take, under this Agreement in conformity with its provisions, expeditious actions which may constitute immediate application of provisional measures using the best information available. In such cases, definitive duties may be levied in accordance with this Agreement on products entered for consumption not more than 90 days before the application of such provisional measures, except that any such retroactive assessment shall not apply to imports entered before the violation of the undertaking.

Article 9

Imposition and Collection of Anti-Dumping Duties

9.1 The decision whether or not to impose an anti-dumping duty in cases where all requirements for the imposition have been fulfilled, and the decision whether the amount of the anti-dumping duty to be imposed shall be the full margin of dumping or less, are decisions to be made by the authorities of the importing Member. It is desirable that the imposition be permissive in the territory of all Members, and that the duty be less than the margin if such lesser duty would be adequate to remove the injury to the domestic industry.

9.2 When an anti-dumping duty is imposed in respect of any product, such anti-dumping duty shall be collected in the appropriate amounts in each case, on a non-discriminatory basis on imports of such product from all sources found to be dumped and causing injury, except as to imports from those sources from which price undertakings under the terms of this Agreement have been accepted. The authorities shall name the supplier or suppliers of the product concerned. If, however, several suppliers from the same country are involved, and it is impracticable to name all these suppliers, the authorities may name the supplying country concerned. If several suppliers from more than one country are involved, the authorities may name either all the suppliers involved, or, if this is impracticable, all the supplying countries involved.

9.3 The amount of the anti-dumping duty shall not exceed the margin of dumping as established under Article 2.

9.3.1 When the amount of the anti-dumping duty is assessed on a retrospective basis, the determination of the final liability for payment of anti-dumping duties shall take place as soon as possible, normally within 12 months, and in no case more than 18 months, after the date on which a request for a final assessment of the amount of the anti-dumping duty has been made.[20] Any refund shall be made promptly and normally in not more than 90 days following the determination of final liability made pursuant to this sub-paragraph. In any case, where a refund is not made within 90 days, the authorities shall provide an explanation if so requested.

9.3.2 When the amount of the anti-dumping duty is assessed on a prospective basis, provision shall be made for a prompt refund, upon request, of any duty paid in excess of the margin of dumping. A refund of any such duty paid in excess of the actual margin of dumping shall normally take place within 12 months, and in no case more than 18 months, after the date on which a request for a refund, duly supported by evidence, has been made by an importer of the product subject to the anti-dumping duty. The refund authorized should normally be made within 90 days of the above-noted decision.

9.3.3 In determining whether and to what extent a reimbursement should be made when the export price is constructed in accordance with paragraph 3 of Article 2, authorities should take account of any change in normal value, any change in costs incurred between importation and resale, and any movement in the resale price which is duly reflected in subsequent selling prices, and should calculate the export price with no deduction for the amount of anti-dumping duties paid when conclusive evidence of the above is provided.

9.4 When the authorities have limited their examination in accordance with the second sentence of paragraph 10 of Article 6, any anti-dumping duty applied to imports from exporters or producers not included in the examination shall not exceed:

(i) the weighted average margin of dumping established with respect to the selected exporters or producers or,

(ii) where the liability for payment of anti-dumping duties is calculated on the basis of a prospective normal value, the difference between the weighted average normal value of the selected exporters or producers and the export prices of exporters or producers not individually examined,

provided that the authorities shall disregard for the purpose of this paragraph any zero and *de minimis* margins and margins established under the circumstances referred to in paragraph 8 of Article 6. The authorities shall

20. It is understood that the observance of the time-limits mentioned in this subparagraph and in subparagraph 3.2 may not be possible where the product in question is subject to judicial review proceedings.

apply individual duties or normal values to imports from any exporter or producer not included in the examination who has provided the necessary information during the course of the investigation, as provided for in sub-paragraph 10.2 of Article 6.

9.5 If a product is subject to anti-dumping duties in an importing Member, the authorities shall promptly carry out a review for the purpose of determining individual margins of dumping for any exporters or producers in the exporting country in question who have not exported the product to the importing Member during the period of investigation, provided that these exporters or producers can show that they are not related to any of the exporters or producers in the exporting country who are subject to the anti-dumping duties on the product. Such a review shall be initiated and carried out on an accelerated basis, compared to normal duty assessment and review proceedings in the importing Member. No anti-dumping duties shall be levied on imports from such exporters or producers while the review is being carried out. The authorities may, however, withhold appraisement and/or request guarantees to ensure that, should such a review result in a determination of dumping in respect of such producers or exporters, anti-dumping duties can be levied retroactively to the date of the initiation of the review.

Article 10

Retroactivity

10.1 Provisional measures and anti-dumping duties shall only be applied to products which enter for consumption after the time when the decision taken under paragraph 1 of Article 7 and paragraph 1 of Article 9, respectively, enters into force, subject to the exceptions set out in this Article.

10.2 Where a final determination of injury (but not of a threat thereof or of a material retardation of the establishment of an industry) is made or, in the case of a final determination of a threat of injury, where the effect of the dumped imports would, in the absence of the provisional measures, have led to a determination of injury, anti-dumping duties may be levied retroactively for the period for which provisional measures, if any, have been applied.

10.3 If the definitive anti-dumping duty is higher than the provisional duty paid or payable, or the amount estimated for the purpose of the security, the difference shall not be collected. If the definitive duty is lower than the provisional duty paid or payable, or the amount estimated for the purpose of the security, the difference shall be reimbursed or the duty recalculated, as the case may be.

10.4 Except as provided in paragraph 2, where a determination of threat of injury or material retardation is made (but no injury has yet occurred) a definitive anti-dumping duty may be imposed only from the date of the determination of threat of injury or material retardation, and any cash deposit made during the period of the application of provisional measures shall be refunded and any bonds released in an expeditious manner.

10.5 Where a final determination is negative, any cash deposit made during the period of the application of provisional measures shall be refunded and any bonds released in an expeditious manner.

10.6 A definitive anti-dumping duty may be levied on products which were entered for consumption not more than 90 days prior to the date of application of provisional measures, when the authorities determine for the dumped product in question that:

(i) there is a history of dumping which caused injury or that the importer was, or should have been, aware that the exporter practises dumping and that such dumping would cause injury, and

(ii) the injury is caused by massive dumped imports of a product in a relatively short time which in light of the timing and the volume of the dumped imports and other circumstances (such as a rapid build-up of inventories of the imported product) is likely to seriously undermine the remedial effect of the definitive anti-dumping duty to be applied, provided that the importers concerned have been given an opportunity to comment.

10.7 The authorities may, after initiating an investigation, take such measures as the withholding of appraisement or assessment as may be necessary to collect anti-dumping duties retroactively, as provided for in paragraph 6, once they have sufficient evidence that the conditions set forth in that paragraph are satisfied.

10.8 No duties shall be levied retroactively pursuant to paragraph 6 on products entered for consumption prior to the date of initiation of the investigation.

Article 11

Duration and Review of Anti-Dumping Duties and Price Undertakings

11.1 An anti-dumping duty shall remain in force only as long as and to the extent necessary to counteract dumping which is causing injury.

11.2 The authorities shall review the need for the continued imposition of the duty, where warranted, on their own initiative or, provided that a reasonable period of time has elapsed since the imposition of the definitive anti-dumping duty, upon request by any interested party which submits positive information substantiating the need for a review.[21] Interested parties shall have the right to request the authorities to examine whether the continued imposition of the duty is necessary to offset dumping, whether the injury would be likely to continue or recur if the duty were removed or varied, or both. If, as a result of the review under this paragraph, the authorities determine that the anti-dumping duty is no longer warranted, it shall be terminated immediately.

11.3 Notwithstanding the provisions of paragraphs 1 and 2, any definitive anti-dumping duty shall be terminated on a date not later than five years from its imposition (or from the date of the most recent review under paragraph 2 if that review has covered both dumping and injury, or under this paragraph), unless the authorities determine, in a review initiated before that date on their own initiative or upon a duly substantiated request made by or on behalf of the domestic industry within a reasonable period of time prior to that date, that the expiry of the duty would be likely to lead to continuation or recurrence of dumping and injury.[22] The duty may remain in force pending the outcome of such a review.

11.4 The provisions of Article 6 regarding evidence and procedure shall apply to any review carried out under this Article. Any such review shall be carried out expeditiously and shall normally be concluded within 12 months of the date of initiation of the review.

11.5 The provisions of this Article shall apply *mutatis mutandis* to price undertakings accepted under Article 8.

Article 12

Public Notice and Explanation of Determinations

12.1 When the authorities are satisfied that there is sufficient evidence to justify the initiation of an anti-dumping investigation pursuant to Article 5, the Member or Members the products of which are subject to such investigation and other interested parties known to the investigating authorities to have an interest therein shall be notified and a public notice shall be given.

21. A determination of final liability for payment of anti-dumping duties, as provided for in paragraph 3 of Article 9, does not by itself constitute a review within the meaning of this Article.

22. When the amount of the anti-dumping duty is assessed on a retrospective basis, a finding in the most recent assessment proceeding under subparagraph 3.1 of Article 9 that no duty is to be levied shall not by itself require the authorities to terminate the definitive duty.

12.1.1 A public notice of the initiation of an investigation shall contain, or otherwise make available through a separate report[23], adequate information on the following:

(i) the name of the exporting country or countries and the product involved;

(ii) the date of initiation of the investigation;

(iii) the basis on which dumping is alleged in the application;

(iv) a summary of the factors on which the allegation of injury is based;

(v) the address to which representations by interested parties should be directed;

(vi) the time-limits allowed to interested parties for making their views known.

12.2 Public notice shall be given of any preliminary or final determination, whether affirmative or negative, of any decision to accept an undertaking pursuant to Article 8, of the termination of such an undertaking, and of the termination of a definitive anti-dumping duty. Each such notice shall set forth, or otherwise make available through a separate report, in sufficient detail the findings and conclusions reached on all issues of fact and law considered material by the investigating authorities. All such notices and reports shall be forwarded to the Member or Members the products of which are subject to such determination or undertaking and to other interested parties known to have an interest therein.

12.2.1 A public notice of the imposition of provisional measures shall set forth, or otherwise make available through a separate report, sufficiently detailed explanations for the preliminary determinations on dumping and injury and shall refer to the matters of fact and law which have led to arguments being accepted or rejected. Such a notice or report shall, due regard being paid to the requirement for the protection of confidential information, contain in particular:

(i) the names of the suppliers, or when this is impracticable, the supplying countries involved;

23. Where authorities provide information and explanations under the provisions of this Article in a separate report, they shall ensure that such report is readily available to the public.

(ii) a description of the product which is sufficient for customs purposes;

(iii) the margins of dumping established and a full explanation of the reasons for the methodology used in the establishment and comparison of the export price and the normal value under Article 2;

(iv) considerations relevant to the injury determination as set out in Article 3;

(v) the main reasons leading to the determination.

12.2.2 A public notice of conclusion or suspension of an investigation in the case of an affirmative determination providing for the imposition of a definitive duty or the acceptance of a price undertaking shall contain, or otherwise make available through a separate report, all relevant information on the matters of fact and law and reasons which have led to the imposition of final measures or the acceptance of a price undertaking, due regard being paid to the requirement for the protection of confidential information. In particular, the notice or report shall contain the information described in subparagraph 2.1, as well as the reasons for the acceptance or rejection of relevant arguments or claims made by the exporters and importers, and the basis for any decision made under subparagraph 10.2 of Article 6.

12.2.3 A public notice of the termination or suspension of an investigation following the acceptance of an undertaking pursuant to Article 8 shall include, or otherwise make available through a separate report, the non-confidential part of this undertaking.

12.3 The provisions of this Article shall apply *mutatis mutandis* to the initiation and completion of reviews pursuant to Article 11 and to decisions under Article 10 to apply duties retroactively.

Article 13

Judicial Review

Each Member whose national legislation contains provisions on anti-dumping measures shall maintain judicial, arbitral or administrative tribunals or procedures for the purpose, *inter alia*, of the prompt review of administrative actions relating to final determinations and reviews of determinations within the meaning of Article 11. Such tribunals or procedures shall be independent of the authorities responsible for the determination or review in question.

Article 14

Anti-Dumping Action on Behalf of a Third Country

14.1 An application for anti-dumping action on behalf of a third country shall be made by the authorities of the third country requesting action.

14.2 Such an application shall be supported by price information to show that the imports are being dumped and by detailed information to show that the alleged dumping is causing injury to the domestic industry concerned in the third country. The government of the third country shall afford all assistance to the authorities of the importing country to obtain any further information which the latter may require.

14.3 In considering such an application, the authorities of the importing country shall consider the effects of the alleged dumping on the industry concerned as a whole in the third country; that is to say, the injury shall not be assessed in relation only to the effect of the alleged dumping on the industry's exports to the importing country or even on the industry's total exports.

14.4 The decision whether or not to proceed with a case shall rest with the importing country. If the importing country decides that it is prepared to take action, the initiation of the approach to the Council for Trade in Goods seeking its approval for such action shall rest with the importing country.

Article 15

Developing Country Members

It is recognized that special regard must be given by developed country Members to the special situation of developing country Members when considering the application of anti-dumping measures under this Agreement. Possibilities of constructive remedies provided for by this Agreement shall be explored before applying anti-dumping duties where they would affect the essential interests of developing country Members.

Part II

Article 16

Committee on Anti-Dumping Practices

16.1 There is hereby established a Committee on Anti-Dumping Practices (referred to in this Agreement as the "Committee") composed of representatives from each of the Members. The Committee shall elect its own Chairman and shall meet not less than twice a year and otherwise as envisaged by relevant provisions of this Agreement at the request of any Member. The Committee shall carry out responsibilities as assigned to it under this Agreement or by the Members and it shall afford Members the opportunity of consulting on any matters relating to the operation of the Agreement or the furtherance of its objectives. The WTO Secretariat shall act as the secretariat to the Committee.

16.2 The Committee may set up subsidiary bodies as appropriate.

16.3 In carrying out their functions, the Committee and any subsidiary bodies may consult with and seek information from any source they deem appropriate. However, before the Committee or a subsidiary body seeks such information from a source within the jurisdiction of a Member, it shall inform the Member involved. It shall obtain the consent of the Member and any firm to be consulted.

16.4 Members shall report without delay to the Committee all preliminary or final anti-dumping actions taken. Such reports shall be available in the Secretariat for inspection by other Members. Members shall also submit, on a semi-annual basis, reports of any anti-dumping actions taken within the preceding six months. The semi-annual reports shall be submitted on an agreed standard form.

16.5 Each Member shall notify the Committee *(a)* which of its authorities are competent to initiate and conduct investigations referred to in Article 5 and *(b)* its domestic procedures governing the initiation and conduct of such investigations.

Article 17

Consultation and Dispute Settlement

17.1 Except as otherwise provided herein, the Dispute Settlement Understanding is applicable to consultations and the settlement of disputes under this Agreement.

17.2 Each Member shall afford sympathetic consideration to, and shall afford adequate opportunity for consultation regarding, representations made by another Member with respect to any matter affecting the operation of this Agreement.

17.3 If any Member considers that any benefit accruing to it, directly or indirectly, under this Agreement is being nullified or impaired, or that the achievement of any objective is being impeded, by another Member or Members, it may, with a view to reaching a mutually satisfactory resolution of the matter, request in writing consultations with the Member or Members in question. Each Member shall afford sympathetic consideration to any request from another Member for consultation.

17.4 If the Member that requested consultations considers that the consultations pursuant to paragraph 3 have failed to achieve a mutually agreed solution, and if final action has been taken by the administering authorities of the importing Member to levy definitive anti-dumping duties or to accept price undertakings, it may refer the matter to the Dispute Settlement Body ("DSB"). When a provisional measure has a significant impact and the Member that requested consultations considers that the measure was taken contrary to the provisions of paragraph 1 of Article 7, that Member may also refer such matter to the DSB.

17.5 The DSB shall, at the request of the complaining party, establish a panel to examine the matter based upon:

(i) a written statement of the Member making the request indicating how a benefit accruing to it, directly or indirectly, under this Agreement has been nullified or impaired, or that the achieving of the objectives of the Agreement is being impeded, and

(ii) the facts made available in conformity with appropriate domestic procedures to the authorities of the importing Member.

17.6 In examining the matter referred to in paragraph 5:

(i) in its assessment of the facts of the matter, the panel shall determine whether the authorities' establishment of the facts was proper and whether their evaluation of those facts was unbiased and objective. If the establishment of the facts was proper and the evaluation was unbiased and objective, even though the panel might have reached a different conclusion, the evaluation shall not be overturned;

(ii) the panel shall interpret the relevant provisions of the Agreement in accordance with customary rules of interpretation of public international law. Where the panel finds that a relevant provision of the Agreement admits of more than one permissible interpretation, the panel shall find the authorities' measure to be in conformity with the Agreement if it rests upon one of those permissible interpretations.

17.7 Confidential information provided to the panel shall not be disclosed without formal authorization from the person, body or authority providing such information. Where such information is requested from the panel but release of such information by the panel is not authorized, a non-confidential summary of the information, authorized by the person, body or authority providing the information, shall be provided.

Part III

Article 18

Final Provisions

18.1 No specific action against dumping of exports from another Member can be taken except in accordance with the provisions of GATT 1994, as interpreted by this Agreement.[24]

18.2 Reservations may not be entered in respect of any of the provisions of this Agreement without the consent of the other Members.

18.3 Subject to subparagraphs 3.1 and 3.2, the provisions of this Agreement shall apply to investigations, and reviews of existing measures, initiated pursuant to applications which have been made on or after the date of entry into force for a Member of the WTO Agreement.

18.3.1 With respect to the calculation of margins of dumping in refund procedures under paragraph 3 of Article 9, the rules used in the most recent determination or review of dumping shall apply.

18.3.2 For the purposes of paragraph 3 of Article 11, existing anti-dumping measures shall be deemed to be imposed on a date not later than the date of entry into force for a Member of the WTO Agreement, except in cases in which the domestic legislation of a Member in force on that date already included a clause of the type provided for in that paragraph.

18.4 Each Member shall take all necessary steps, of a general or particular character, to ensure, not later than the date of entry into force of the WTO Agreement for it, the conformity of its laws, regulations and administrative procedures with the provisions of this Agreement as they may apply for the Member in question.

18.5 Each Member shall inform the Committee of any changes in its laws and regulations relevant to this Agreement and in the administration of such laws and regulations.

18.6 The Committee shall review annually the implementation and operation of this Agreement taking into account the objectives thereof. The Committee shall inform annually the Council for Trade in Goods of developments during the period covered by such reviews.

18.7 The Annexes to this Agreement constitute an integral part thereof.

24. This is not intended to preclude action under other relevant provisions of GATT 1994, as appropriate.

Annex I

PROCEDURES FOR ON-THE-SPOT INVESTIGATIONS PURSUANT TO PARAGRAPH 7 OF ARTICLE 6

1. Upon initiation of an investigation, the authorities of the exporting Member and the firms known to be concerned should be informed of the intention to carry out on-the-spot investigations.

2. If in exceptional circumstances it is intended to include non-governmental experts in the investigating team, the firms and the authorities of the exporting Member should be so informed. Such non-governmental experts should be subject to effective sanctions for breach of confidentiality requirements.

3. It should be standard practice to obtain explicit agreement of the firms concerned in the exporting Member before the visit is finally scheduled.

4. As soon as the agreement of the firms concerned has been obtained, the investigating authorities should notify the authorities of the exporting Member of the names and addresses of the firms to be visited and the dates agreed.

5. Sufficient advance notice should be given to the firms in question before the visit is made.

6. Visits to explain the questionnaire should only be made at the request of an exporting firm. Such a visit may only be made if *(a)* the authorities of the importing Member notify the representatives of the Member in question and *(b)* the latter do not object to the visit.

7. As the main purpose of the on-the-spot investigation is to verify information provided or to obtain further details, it should be carried out after the response to the questionnaire has been received unless the firm agrees to the contrary and the government of the exporting Member is informed by the investigating authorities of the anticipated visit and does not object to it; further, it should be standard practice prior to the visit to advise the firms concerned of the general nature of the information to be verified and of any further information which needs to be provided, though this should not preclude requests to be made on the spot for further details to be provided in the light of information obtained.

8. Enquiries or questions put by the authorities or firms of the exporting Members and essential to a successful on-the-spot investigation should, whenever possible, be answered before the visit is made.

Annex II

BEST INFORMATION AVAILABLE IN TERMS OF PARAGRAPH 8 OF ARTICLE 6

1. As soon as possible after the initiation of the investigation, the investigating authorities should specify in detail the information required from any interested party, and the manner in which that information should be structured by the interested party in its response. The authorities should also ensure that the party is aware that if information is not supplied within a reasonable time, the authorities will be free to make determinations on the basis of the facts available, including those contained in the application for the initiation of the investigation by the domestic industry.

2. The authorities may also request that an interested party provide its response in a particular medium (e.g. computer tape) or computer language. Where such a request is made, the authorities should consider the reasonable ability of the interested party to respond in the preferred medium or computer language, and should not request the party to use for its response a computer system other than that used by the party. The authority should not maintain a request for a computerized response if the interested party does not maintain computerized accounts and if presenting the response as requested would result in an unreasonable extra burden on the interested party, e.g. it would entail unreasonable additional cost and trouble. The authorities should not maintain a request for a response in a particular medium or computer language if the interested party does not maintain its computerized accounts in such medium or computer language and if presenting the response as requested would result in an unreasonable extra burden on the interested party, e.g. it would entail unreasonable additional cost and trouble.

3. All information which is verifiable, which is appropriately submitted so that it can be used in the investigation without undue difficulties, which is supplied in a timely fashion, and, where applicable, which is supplied in a medium or computer language requested by the authorities, should be taken into account when determinations are made. If a party does not respond in the preferred medium or computer language but the authorities find that the circumstances set out in paragraph 2 have been satisfied, the failure to respond in the preferred medium or computer language should not be considered to significantly impede the investigation.

4. Where the authorities do not have the ability to process information if provided in a particular medium (e.g. computer tape), the information should be supplied in the form of written material or any other form acceptable to the authorities.

5. Even though the information provided may not be ideal in all respects, this should not justify the authorities from disregarding it, provided the interested party has acted to the best of its ability.

6. If evidence or information is not accepted, the supplying party should be informed forthwith of the reasons therefor, and should have an opportunity to provide further explanations within a reasonable period, due account being taken of the time-limits of the investigation. If the explanations are considered by the authorities as not being satisfactory, the reasons for the rejection of such evidence or information should be given in any published determinations.

7. If the authorities have to base their findings, including those with respect to normal value, on information from a secondary source, including the information supplied in the application for the initiation of the investigation, they should do so with special circumspection. In such cases, the authorities should, where practicable, check the information from other independent sources at their disposal, such as published price lists, official import statistics and customs returns, and from the information obtained from other interested parties during the investigation. It is clear, however, that if an interested party does not cooperate and thus relevant information is being withheld from the authorities, this situation could lead to a result which is less favourable to the party than if the party did cooperate.

Document 29

AGREEMENT ON CUSTOMS VALUATION

Official name: Agreement on Implementation of Article VII of the General Agreement on Tariffs and Trade 1994

GENERAL INTRODUCTORY COMMENTARY

1. The primary basis for customs value under this Agreement is "transaction value" as defined in Article 1. Article 1 is to be read together with Article 8 which provides, *inter alia,* for adjustments to the price actually paid or payable in cases where certain specific elements which are considered to form a part of the value for customs purposes are incurred by the buyer but are not included in the price actually paid or payable for the imported goods. Article 8 also provides for the inclusion in the transaction value of certain considerations which may pass from the buyer to the seller in the form of specified goods or services rather than in the form of money. Articles 2 through 7 provide methods of determining the customs value whenever it cannot be determined under the provisions of Article 1.

2. Where the customs value cannot be determined under the provisions of Article 1 there should normally be a process of consultation between the customs administration and importer with a view to arriving at a basis of value under the provisions of Article 2 or 3. It may occur, for example, that the importer has information about the customs value of identical or similar imported goods which is not immediately available to the customs administration in the port of importation. On the other hand, the customs administration may have information about the customs value of identical or similar imported goods which is not readily available to the importer. A process of consultation between the two parties will enable information to be exchanged, subject to the requirements of commercial confidentiality, with a view to determining a proper basis of value for customs purposes.

3. Articles 5 and 6 provide two bases for determining the customs value where it cannot be determined on the basis of the transaction value of the imported goods or of identical or similar imported goods. Under paragraph 1 of Article 5 the customs value is determined on the basis of the price at which the goods are sold in the condition as imported to an unrelated buyer in the country of importation. The importer also has the right to have goods which are further processed after importation valued under the provisions of Article 5 if the importer so requests. Under Article 6 the customs value is determined on the basis of the computed value. Both these methods present certain difficulties and because of this the importer is given the right, under the provisions of Article 4, to choose the order of application of the two methods.

4. Article 7 sets out how to determine the customs value in cases where it cannot be determined under the provisions of any of the preceding Articles.

Members,

Having regard to the Multilateral Trade Negotiations;

Desiring to further the objectives of GATT 1994 and to secure additional benefits for the international trade of developing countries;

Recognizing the importance of the provisions of Article VII of GATT 1994 and desiring to elaborate rules for their application in order to provide greater uniformity and certainty in their implementation;

Recognizing the need for a fair, uniform and neutral system for the valuation of goods for customs purposes that precludes the use of arbitrary or fictitious customs values;

Recognizing that the basis for valuation of goods for customs purposes should, to the greatest extent possible, be the transaction value of the goods being valued;

Recognizing that customs value should be based on simple and equitable criteria consistent with commercial practices and that valuation procedures should be of general application without distinction between sources of supply;

Recognizing that valuation procedures should not be used to combat dumping;

Hereby *agree* as follows:

Part I

RULES ON CUSTOMS VALUATION

Article 1

1. The customs value of imported goods shall be the transaction value, that is the price actually paid or payable for the goods when sold for export to the country of importation adjusted in accordance with the provisions of Article 8, provided:

(a) that there are no restrictions as to the disposition or use of the goods by the buyer other than restrictions which:

(i) are imposed or required by law or by the public authorities in the country of importation;

(ii) limit the geographical area in which the goods may be resold; or

(iii) do not substantially affect the value of the goods;

(b) that the sale or price is not subject to some condition or consideration for which a value cannot be determined with respect to the goods being valued;

(c) that no part of the proceeds of any subsequent resale, disposal or use of the goods by the buyer will accrue directly or indirectly to the seller, unless an appropriate adjustment can be made in accordance with the provisions of Article 8; and

(d) that the buyer and seller are not related, or where the buyer and seller are related, that the transaction value is acceptable for customs purposes under the provisions of paragraph 2.

2. (a) In determining whether the transaction value is acceptable for the purposes of paragraph 1, the fact that the buyer and the seller are related within the meaning of Article 15 shall not in itself be grounds for regarding the transaction value as unacceptable. In such case the circumstances surrounding the sale shall be examined and the transaction value shall be accepted provided that the relationship did not influence the price. If, in the light of information provided by the importer or otherwise, the customs administration has grounds for considering that the relationship influenced the price, it shall communicate its grounds to the importer and the importer shall be given a reasonable opportunity to respond. If the importer so requests, the communication of the grounds shall be in writing.

(b) In a sale between related persons, the transaction value shall be accepted and the goods valued in accordance with the provisions of paragraph 1 whenever the importer demonstrates that such value closely approximates to one of the following occurring at or about the same time:

(i) the transaction value in sales to unrelated buyers of identical or similar goods for export to the same country of importation;

(ii) the customs value of identical or similar goods as determined under the provisions of Article 5;

(iii) the customs value of identical or similar goods as determined under the provisions of Article 6;

In applying the foregoing tests, due account shall be taken of demonstrated differences in commercial levels, quantity levels, the elements enumerated in Article 8 and costs incurred by the seller in sales in which the seller and the buyer are not related that are not incurred by the seller in sales in which the seller and the buyer are related.

(c) The tests set forth in paragraph 2(b) are to be used at the initiative of the importer and only for comparison purposes. Substitute values may not be established under the provisions of paragraph 2(b).

Article 2

1. (a) If the customs value of the imported goods cannot be determined under the provisions of Article 1, the customs value shall be the transaction value of identical goods sold for export to the same country of importation and exported at or about the same time as the goods being valued.

(b) In applying this Article, the transaction value of identical goods in a sale at the same commercial level and in substantially the same quantity as the goods being valued shall be used to determine the customs value. Where no such sale is found, the transaction value of identical goods sold at a different commercial level and/or in different quantities, adjusted to take account of differences attributable to commercial level and/or to quantity, shall be used, provided that such adjustments can be made on the basis of demonstrated evidence which clearly establishes the reasonableness and accuracy of the adjustment, whether the adjustment leads to an increase or a decrease in the value.

2. Where the costs and charges referred to in paragraph 2 of Article 8 are included in the transaction value, an adjustment shall be made to take account of significant differences in such costs and charges between the

imported goods and the identical goods in question arising from differences in distances and modes of transport.

3. If, in applying this Article, more than one transaction value of identical goods is found, the lowest such value shall be used to determine the customs value of the imported goods.

Article 3

1. (a) If the customs value of the imported goods cannot be determined under the provisions of Articles 1 and 2, the customs value shall be the transaction value of similar goods sold for export to the same country of importation and exported at or about the same time as the goods being valued.

(b) In applying this Article, the transaction value of similar goods in a sale at the same commercial level and in substantially the same quantity as the goods being valued shall be used to determine the customs value. Where no such sale is found, the transaction value of similar goods sold at a different commercial level and/or in different quantities, adjusted to take account of differences attributable to commercial level and/or to quantity, shall be used, provided that such adjustments can be made on the basis of demonstrated evidence which clearly establishes the reasonableness and accuracy of the adjustment, whether the adjustment leads to an increase or a decrease in the value.

2. Where the costs and charges referred to in paragraph 2 of Article 8 are included in the transaction value, an adjustment shall be made to take account of significant differences in such costs and charges between the imported goods and the similar goods in question arising from differences in distances and modes of transport.

3. If, in applying this Article, more than one transaction value of similar goods is found, the lowest such value shall be used to determine the customs value of the imported goods.

Article 4

If the customs value of the imported goods cannot be determined under the provisions of Articles 1, 2 and 3, the customs value shall be determined under the provisions of Article 5 or, when the customs value cannot be determined under that Article, under the provisions of Article 6 except that, at the request of the importer, the order of application of Articles 5 and 6 shall be reversed.

Article 5

1. (a) If the imported goods or identical or similar imported goods are sold in the country of importation in the condition as imported, the customs value of the imported goods under the provisions of this Article shall be based on the unit price at which the imported goods or identical or similar imported goods are so sold in the greatest aggregate quantity, at or about the time of the importation of the goods being valued, to persons who are not related to the persons from whom they buy such goods, subject to deductions for the following:

(i) either the commissions usually paid or agreed to be paid or the additions usually made for profit and general expenses in connection with sales in such country of imported goods of the same class or kind;

(ii) the usual costs of transport and insurance and associated costs incurred within the country of importation;

(iii) where appropriate, the costs and charges referred to in paragraph 2 of Article 8; and

(iv) the customs duties and other national taxes payable in the country of importation by reason of the importation or sale of the goods.

(b) If neither the imported goods nor identical nor similar imported goods are sold at or about the time of importation of the goods being valued, the customs value shall, subject otherwise to the provisions of paragraph 1(a), be based on the unit price at which the imported goods or identical or similar imported goods are sold in the country of importation in the condition as imported at the earliest date after the importation of the goods being valued but before the expiration of 90 days after such importation.

2. If neither the imported goods nor identical nor similar imported goods are sold in the country of importation in the condition as imported, then, if the importer so requests, the customs value shall be based on the unit price at which the imported goods, after further processing, are sold in the greatest aggregate quantity to persons in the country of importation who are not related to the persons from whom they buy such goods, due allowance being made for the value added by such processing and the deductions provided for in paragraph 1(a).

Article 6

1. The customs value of imported goods under the provisions of this Article shall be based on a computed value. Computed value shall consist of the sum of:

(a) the cost or value of materials and fabrication or other processing employed in producing the imported goods;

(b) an amount for profit and general expenses equal to that usually reflected in sales of goods of the same class or kind as the goods being valued which are made by producers in the country of exportation for export to the country of importation;

(c) the cost or value of all other expenses necessary to reflect the valuation option chosen by the Member under paragraph 2 of Article 8.

2. No Member may require or compel any person not resident in its own territory to produce for examination, or to allow access to, any account or other record for the purposes of determining a computed value. However, information supplied by the producer of the goods for the purposes of determining the customs value under the provisions of this Article may be verified in another country by the authorities of the country of importation with the agreement of the producer and provided they give sufficient advance notice to the government of the country in question and the latter does not object to the investigation.

Article 7

1. If the customs value of the imported goods cannot be determined under the provisions of Articles 1 through 6, inclusive, the customs value shall be determined using reasonable means consistent with the principles and general provisions of this Agreement and of Article VII of GATT 1994 and on the basis of data available in the country of importation.

2. No customs value shall be determined under the provisions of this Article on the basis of:

(a) the selling price in the country of importation of goods produced in such country;

(b) a system which provides for the acceptance for customs purposes of the higher of two alternative values;

(c) the price of goods on the domestic market of the country of exportation;

(d) the cost of production other than computed values which have been determined for identical or similar goods in accordance with the provisions of Article 6;

(e) the price of the goods for export to a country other than the country of importation;

(f) minimum customs values; or

(g) arbitrary or fictitious values.

3. If the importer so requests, the importer shall be informed in writing of the customs value determined under the provisions of this Article and the method used to determine such value.

Article 8

1. In determining the customs value under the provisions of Article 1, there shall be added to the price actually paid or payable for the imported goods:

(a) the following, to the extent that they are incurred by the buyer but are not included in the price actually paid or payable for the goods:

(i) commissions and brokerage, except buying commissions;

(ii) the cost of containers which are treated as being one for customs purposes with the goods in question;

(iii) the cost of packing whether for labour or materials;

(b) the value, apportioned as appropriate, of the following goods and services where supplied directly or indirectly by the buyer free of charge or at reduced cost for use in connection with the production and sale for export of the imported goods, to the extent that such value has not been included in the price actually paid or payable:

(i) materials, components, parts and similar items incorporated in the imported goods;

(ii) tools, dies, moulds and similar items used in the production of the imported goods;

(iii) materials consumed in the production of the imported goods;

(iv) engineering, development, artwork, design work, and plans and sketches undertaken elsewhere than in the country of importation and necessary for the production of the imported goods;

(c) royalties and licence fees related to the goods being valued that the buyer must pay, either directly or indirectly, as a condition of sale of the goods being valued, to the extent that such royalties and fees are not included in the price actually paid or payable;

(d) the value of any part of the proceeds of any subsequent resale, disposal or use of the imported goods that accrues directly or indirectly to the seller.

2. In framing its legislation, each Member shall provide for the inclusion in or the exclusion from the customs value, in whole or in part, of the following:

(a) the cost of transport of the imported goods to the port or place of importation;

(b) loading, unloading and handling charges associated with the transport of the imported goods to the port or place of importation; and

(c) the cost of insurance.

3. Additions to the price actually paid or payable shall be made under this Article only on the basis of objective and quantifiable data.

4. No additions shall be made to the price actually paid or payable in determining the customs value except as provided in this Article.

Article 9

1. Where the conversion of currency is necessary for the determination of the customs value, the rate of exchange to be used shall be that duly published by the competent authorities of the country of importation concerned and shall reflect as effectively as possible, in respect of the period covered by each such document of publication, the current value of such currency in commercial transactions in terms of the currency of the country of importation.

2. The conversion rate to be used shall be that in effect at the time of exportation or the time of importation, as provided by each Member.

Article 10

All information which is by nature confidential or which is provided on a confidential basis for the purposes of customs valuation shall be treated as strictly confidential by the authorities concerned who shall not disclose it without the specific permission of the person or government providing such information, except to the extent that it may be required to be disclosed in the context of judicial proceedings.

Article 11

1. The legislation of each Member shall provide in regard to a determination of customs value for the right of appeal, without penalty, by the importer or any other person liable for the payment of the duty.

2. An initial right of appeal without penalty may be to an authority within the customs administration or to an independent body, but the legislation of each Member shall provide for the right of appeal without penalty to a judicial authority.

3. Notice of the decision on appeal shall be given to the appellant and the reasons for such decision shall be provided in writing. The appellant shall also be informed of any rights of further appeal.

Article 12

Laws, regulations, judicial decisions and administrative rulings of general application giving effect to this Agreement shall be published in conformity with Article X of GATT 1994 by the country of importation concerned.

Article 13

If, in the course of determining the customs value of imported goods, it becomes necessary to delay the final determination of such customs value, the importer of the goods shall nevertheless be able to withdraw them from customs if, where so required, the importer provides sufficient guarantee in the form of a surety, a deposit or some other appropriate instrument, covering the ultimate payment of customs duties for which the goods may be liable. The legislation of each Member shall make provisions for such circumstances.

Article 14

The notes at Annex I to this Agreement form an integral part of this Agreement and the Articles of this Agreement are to be read and applied in conjunction with their respective notes. Annexes II and III also form an integral part of this Agreement.

Article 15

1. In this Agreement:

(a) "customs value of imported goods" means the value of goods for the purposes of levying ad valorem duties of customs on imported goods;

(b) "country of importation" means country or customs territory of importation; and

(c) "produced" includes grown, manufactured and mined.

2. In this Agreement:

(a) "identical goods" means goods which are the same in all respects, including physical characteristics, quality and reputation. Minor differences in appearance would not preclude goods otherwise conforming to the definition from being regarded as identical;

(b) "similar goods" means goods which, although not alike in all respects, have like characteristics and like component materials which enable them to perform the same functions and to be commercially interchangeable. The quality of the goods, their reputation and the existence of a trademark are among the factors to be considered in determining whether goods are similar;

(c) the terms "identical goods" and "similar goods" do not include, as the case may be, goods which incorporate or reflect engineering, development, artwork, design work, and plans and sketches for which no adjustment has been made under paragraph 1(b)(iv) of Article 8 because such elements were undertaken in the country of importation;

(d) goods shall not be regarded as "identical goods" or "similar goods" unless they were produced in the same country as the goods being valued;

(e) goods produced by a different person shall be taken into account only when there are no identical goods or similar goods, as the case may be, produced by the same person as the goods being valued.

3. In this Agreement "goods of the same class or kind" means goods which fall within a group or range of goods produced by a particular industry or industry sector, and includes identical or similar goods.

4. For the purposes of this Agreement, persons shall be deemed to be related only if:

(a) they are officers or directors of one another's businesses;

(b) they are legally recognized partners in business;

(c) they are employer and employee;

(d) any person directly or indirectly owns, controls or holds 5 per cent or more of the outstanding voting stock or shares of both of them;

(e) one of them directly or indirectly controls the other;

(f) both of them are directly or indirectly controlled by a third person;

(g) together they directly or indirectly control a third person; or

(h) they are members of the same family.

5. Persons who are associated in business with one another in that one is the sole agent, sole distributor or sole concessionaire, however described, of the other shall be deemed to be related for the purposes of this Agreement if they fall within the criteria of paragraph 4.

Article 16

Upon written request, the importer shall have the right to an explanation in writing from the customs administration of the country of importation as to how the customs value of the importer's goods was determined.

Article 17

Nothing in this Agreement shall be construed as restricting or calling into question the rights of customs administrations to satisfy themselves as to the truth or accuracy of any statement, document or declaration presented for customs valuation purposes.

Part II

ADMINISTRATION, CONSULTATIONS AND DISPUTE SETTLEMENT

Article 18

Institutions

1. There is hereby established a Committee on Customs Valuation (referred to in this Agreement as "the Committee") composed of representatives from each of the Members. The Committee shall elect its own Chairman and shall normally meet once a year, or as is otherwise envisaged by the relevant provisions of this Agreement, for the purpose of affording Members the opportunity to consult on matters relating to the administra-

tion of the customs valuation system by any Member as it might affect the operation of this Agreement or the furtherance of its objectives and carrying out such other responsibilities as may be assigned to it by the Members. The WTO Secretariat shall act as the secretariat to the Committee.

2. There shall be established a Technical Committee on Customs Valuation (referred to in this Agreement as "the Technical Committee") under the auspices of the Customs Co-operation Council (referred to in this Agreement as "the CCC"), which shall carry out the responsibilities described in Annex II to this Agreement and shall operate in accordance with the rules of procedure contained therein.

Article 19

Consultations and Dispute Settlement

1. Except as otherwise provided herein, the Dispute Settlement Understanding is applicable to consultations and the settlement of disputes under this Agreement.

2. If any Member considers that any benefit accruing to it, directly or indirectly, under this Agreement is being nullified or impaired, or that the achievement of any objective of this Agreement is being impeded, as a result of the actions of another Member or of other Members, it may, with a view to reaching a mutually satisfactory solution of this matter, request consultations with the Member or Members in question. Each Member shall afford sympathetic consideration to any request from another Member for consultations.

3. The Technical Committee shall provide, upon request, advice and assistance to Members engaged in consultations.

4. At the request of a party to the dispute, or on its own initiative, a panel established to examine a dispute relating to the provisions of this Agreement may request the Technical Committee to carry out an examination of any questions requiring technical consideration. The panel shall determine the terms of reference of the Technical Committee for the particular dispute and set a time period for receipt of the report of the Technical Committee. The panel shall take into consideration the report of the Technical Committee. In the event that the Technical Committee is unable to reach consensus on a matter referred to it pursuant to this paragraph, the panel should afford the parties to the dispute an opportunity to present their views on the matter to the panel.

5. Confidential information provided to the panel shall not be disclosed without formal authorization from the person, body or authority providing

such information. Where such information is requested from the panel but release of such information by the panel is not authorized, a non-confidential summary of this information, authorized by the person, body or authority providing the information, shall be provided.

Part III

SPECIAL AND DIFFERENTIAL TREATMENT

Article 20

1. Developing country Members not party to the Agreement on Implementation of Article VII of the General Agreement on Tariffs and Trade done on 12 April 1979 may delay application of the provisions of this Agreement for a period not exceeding five years from the date of entry into force of the WTO Agreement for such Members. Developing country Members who choose to delay application of this Agreement shall notify the Director-General of the WTO accordingly.

2. In addition to paragraph 1, developing country Members not party to the Agreement on Implementation of Article VII of the General Agreement on Tariffs and Trade done on 12 April 1979 may delay application of paragraph 2(b)(iii) of Article 1 and Article 6 for a period not exceeding three years following their application of all other provisions of this Agreement. Developing country Members that choose to delay application of the provisions specified in this paragraph shall notify the Director- General of the WTO accordingly.

3. Developed country Members shall furnish, on mutually agreed terms, technical assistance to developing country Members that so request. On this basis developed country Members shall draw up programmes of technical assistance which may include, *inter alia,* training of personnel, assistance in preparing implementation measures, access to sources of information regarding customs valuation methodology, and advice on the application of the provisions of this Agreement.

Part IV

FINAL PROVISIONS

Article 21

Reservations

Reservations may not be entered in respect of any of the provisions of this Agreement without the consent of the other Members.

Article 22

National Legislation

1. Each Member shall ensure, not later than the date of application of the provisions of this Agreement for it, the conformity of its laws, regulations and administrative procedures with the provisions of this Agreement.

2. Each Member shall inform the Committee of any changes in its laws and regulations relevant to this Agreement and in the administration of such laws and regulations.

Article 23

Review

The Committee shall review annually the implementation and operation of this Agreement taking into account the objectives thereof. The Committee shall annually inform the Council for Trade in Goods of developments during the period covered by such reviews.

Article 24

Secretariat

This Agreement shall be serviced by the WTO Secretariat except in regard to those responsibilities specifically assigned to the Technical Committee, which will be serviced by the CCC Secretariat.

Annex I

INTERPRETATIVE NOTES

General Note

Sequential Application of Valuation Methods

1. Articles 1 through 7 define how the customs value of imported goods is to be determined under the provisions of this Agreement. The methods of valuation are set out in a sequential order of application. The primary method for customs valuation is defined in Article 1 and imported goods are to be valued in accordance with the provisions of this Article whenever the conditions prescribed therein are fulfilled.

2. Where the customs value cannot be determined under the provisions of Article 1, it is to be determined by proceeding sequentially through the succeeding Articles to the first such Article under which the customs value can be determined. Except as provided in Article 4, it is only when the

customs value cannot be determined under the provisions of a particular Article that the provisions of the next Article in the sequence can be used.

3. If the importer does not request that the order of Articles 5 and 6 be reversed, the normal order of the sequence is to be followed. If the importer does so request but it then proves impossible to determine the customs value under the provisions of Article 6, the customs value is to be determined under the provisions of Article 5, if it can be so determined.

4. Where the customs value cannot be determined under the provisions of Articles 1 through 6 it is to be determined under the provisions of Article 7.

Use of Generally Accepted Accounting Principles

1. "Generally accepted accounting principles" refers to the recognized consensus or substantial authoritative support within a country at a particular time as to which economic resources and obligations should be recorded as assets and liabilities, which changes in assets and liabilities should be recorded, how the assets and liabilities and changes in them should be measured, what information should be disclosed and how it should be disclosed, and which financial statements should be prepared. These standards may be broad guidelines of general application as well as detailed practices and procedures.

2. For the purposes of this Agreement, the customs administration of each Member shall utilize information prepared in a manner consistent with generally accepted accounting principles in the country which is appropriate for the Article in question. For example, the determination of usual profit and general expenses under the provisions of Article 5 would be carried out utilizing information prepared in a manner consistent with generally accepted accounting principles of the country of importation. On the other hand, the determination of usual profit and general expenses under the provisions of Article 6 would be carried out utilizing information prepared in a manner consistent with generally accepted accounting principles of the country of production. As a further example, the determination of an element provided for in paragraph 1(b)(ii) of Article 8 undertaken in the country of importation would be carried out utilizing information in a manner consistent with the generally accepted accounting principles of that country.

Note to Article 1

Price Actually Paid or Payable

1. The price actually paid or payable is the total payment made or to be made by the buyer to or for the benefit of the seller for the imported goods. The payment need not necessarily take the form of a transfer of money.

Payment may be made by way of letters of credit or negotiable instruments. Payment may be made directly or indirectly. An example of an indirect payment would be the settlement by the buyer, whether in whole or in part, of a debt owed by the seller.

2. Activities undertaken by the buyer on the buyer's own account, other than those for which an adjustment is provided in Article 8, are not considered to be an indirect payment to the seller, even though they might be regarded as of benefit to the seller. The costs of such activities shall not, therefore, be added to the price actually paid or payable in determining the customs value.

3. The customs value shall not include the following charges or costs, provided that they are distinguished from the price actually paid or payable for the imported goods:

(a) charges for construction, erection, assembly, maintenance or technical assistance, undertaken after importation on imported goods such as industrial plant, machinery or equipment;

(b) the cost of transport after importation;

(c) duties and taxes of the country of importation.

4. The price actually paid or payable refers to the price for the imported goods. Thus the flow of dividends or other payments from the buyer to the seller that do not relate to the imported goods are not part of the customs value.

Paragraph 1(a)(iii)

Among restrictions which would not render a price actually paid or payable unacceptable are restrictions which do not substantially affect the value of the goods. An example of such restrictions would be the case where a seller requires a buyer of automobiles not to sell or exhibit them prior to a fixed date which represents the beginning of a model year.

Paragraph 1(b)

1. If the sale or price is subject to some condition or consideration for which a value cannot be determined with respect to the goods being valued, the transaction value shall not be acceptable for customs purposes. Some examples of this include:

(a) the seller establishes the price of the imported goods on condition that the buyer will also buy other goods in specified quantities;

(b) the price of the imported goods is dependent upon the price or prices at which the buyer of the imported goods sells other goods to the seller of the imported goods;

(c) the price is established on the basis of a form of payment extraneous to the imported goods, such as where the imported goods are semi-finished goods which have been provided by the seller on condition that the seller will receive a specified quantity of the finished goods.

2. However, conditions or considerations relating to the production or marketing of the imported goods shall not result in rejection of the transaction value. For example, the fact that the buyer furnishes the seller with engineering and plans undertaken in the country of importation shall not result in rejection of the transaction value for the purposes of Article 1. Likewise, if the buyer undertakes on the buyer's own account, even though by agreement with the seller, activities relating to the marketing of the imported goods, the value of these activities is not part of the customs value nor shall such activities result in rejection of the transaction value.

Paragraph 2

1. Paragraphs 2(a) and 2(b) provide different means of establishing the acceptability of a transaction value.

2. Paragraph 2(a) provides that where the buyer and the seller are related, the circumstances surrounding the sale shall be examined and the transaction value shall be accepted as the customs value provided that the relationship did not influence the price. It is not intended that there should be an examination of the circumstances in all cases where the buyer and the seller are related. Such examination will only be required where there are doubts about the acceptability of the price. Where the customs administration have no doubts about the acceptability of the price, it should be accepted without requesting further information from the importer. For example, the customs administration may have previously examined the relationship, or it may already have detailed information concerning the buyer and the seller, and may already be satisfied from such examination or information that the relationship did not influence the price.

3. Where the customs administration is unable to accept the transaction value without further inquiry, it should give the importer an opportunity to supply such further detailed information as may be necessary to enable it to examine the circumstances surrounding the sale. In this context, the customs administration should be prepared to examine relevant aspects of the transaction, including the way in which the buyer and seller organize their commercial relations and the way in which the price in question was arrived at, in order to determine whether the relationship influenced the price.

Where it can be shown that the buyer and seller, although related under the provisions of Article 15, buy from and sell to each other as if they were not related, this would demonstrate that the price had not been influenced by the relationship. As an example of this, if the price had been settled in a manner consistent with the normal pricing practices of the industry in question or with the way the seller settles prices for sales to buyers who are not related to the seller, this would demonstrate that the price had not been influenced by the relationship. As a further example, where it is shown that the price is adequate to ensure recovery of all costs plus a profit which is representative of the firm's overall profit realized over a representative period of time (e.g. on an annual basis) in sales of goods of the same class or kind, this would demonstrate that the price had not been influenced.

4. Paragraph 2(b) provides an opportunity for the importer to demonstrate that the transaction value closely approximates to a "test" value previously accepted by the customs administration and is therefore acceptable under the provisions of Article 1. Where a test under paragraph 2(b) is met, it is not necessary to examine the question of influence under paragraph 2(a). If the customs administration has already sufficient information to be satisfied, without further detailed inquiries, that one of the tests provided in paragraph 2(b) has been met, there is no reason for it to require the importer to demonstrate that the test can be met. In paragraph 2(b) the term "unrelated buyers" means buyers who are not related to the seller in any particular case.

Paragraph 2(b)

A number of factors must be taken into consideration in determining whether one value "closely approximates" to another value. These factors include the nature of the imported goods, the nature of the industry itself, the season in which the goods are imported, and, whether the difference in values is commercially significant. Since these factors may vary from case to case, it would be impossible to apply a uniform standard such as a fixed percentage, in each case. For example, a small difference in value in a case involving one type of goods could be unacceptable while a large difference in a case involving another type of goods might be acceptable in determining whether the transaction value closely approximates to the "test" values set forth in paragraph 2(b) of Article 1.

Note to Article 2

1. In applying Article 2, the customs administration shall, wherever possible, use a sale of identical goods at the same commercial level and in substantially the same quantities as the goods being valued. Where no such sale is found, a sale of identical goods that takes place under any one of the following three conditions may be used:

(a) a sale at the same commercial level but in different quantities;

(b) a sale at a different commercial level but in substantially the same quantities; or

(c) a sale at a different commercial level and in different quantities.

2. Having found a sale under any one of these three conditions adjustments will then be made, as the case may be, for:

(a) quantity factors only;

(b) commercial level factors only; or

(c) both commercial level and quantity factors.

3. The expression "and/or" allows the flexibility to use the sales and make the necessary adjustments in any one of the three conditions described above.

4. For the purposes of Article 2, the transaction value of identical imported goods means a customs value, adjusted as provided for in paragraphs 1(b) and 2, which has already been accepted under Article 1.

5. A condition for adjustment because of different commercial levels or different quantities is that such adjustment, whether it leads to an increase or a decrease in the value, be made only on the basis of demonstrated evidence that clearly establishes the reasonableness and accuracy of the adjustments, e.g. valid price lists containing prices referring to different levels or different quantities. As an example of this, if the imported goods being valued consist of a shipment of 10 units and the only identical imported goods for which a transaction value exists involved a sale of 500 units, and it is recognized that the seller grants quantity discounts, the required adjustment may be accomplished by resorting to the seller's price list and using that price applicable to a sale of 10 units. This does not require that a sale had to have been made in quantities of 10 as long as the price list has been established as being bona fide through sales at other quantities. In the absence of such an objective measure, however, the determination of a customs value under the provisions of Article 2 is not appropriate.

Note to Article 3

1. In applying Article 3, the customs administration shall, wherever possible, use a sale of similar goods at the same commercial level and in substantially the same quantities as the goods being valued. Where no such sale is found, a sale of similar goods that takes place under any one of the following three conditions may be used:

(a) a sale at the same commercial level but in different quantities;

(b) a sale at a different commercial level but in substantially the same quantities; or

(c) a sale at a different commercial level and in different quantities.

2. Having found a sale under any one of these three conditions adjustments will then be made, as the case may be, for:

(a) quantity factors only;

(b) commercial level factors only; or

(c) both commercial level and quantity factors.

3. The expression "and/or" allows the flexibility to use the sales and make the necessary adjustments in any one of the three conditions described above.

4. For the purpose of Article 3, the transaction value of similar imported goods means a customs value, adjusted as provided for in paragraphs 1(b) and 2, which has already been accepted under Article 1.

5. A condition for adjustment because of different commercial levels or different quantities is that such adjustment, whether it leads to an increase or a decrease in the value, be made only on the basis of demonstrated evidence that clearly establishes the reasonableness and accuracy of the adjustment, e. g. valid price lists containing prices referring to different levels or different quantities. As an example of this, if the imported goods being valued consist of a shipment of 10 units and the only similar imported goods for which a transaction value exists involved a sale of 500 units, and it is recognized that the seller grants quantity discounts, the required adjustment may be accomplished by resorting to the seller's price list and using that price applicable to a sale of 10 units. This does not require that a sale had to have been made in quantities of 10 as long as the price list has been established as being bona fide through sales at other quantities. In the absence of such an objective measure, however, the determination of a customs value under the provisions of Article 3 is not appropriate.

Note to Article 5

1. The term "unit price at which . . . goods are sold in the greatest aggregate quantity" means the price at which the greatest number of units is sold in sales to persons who are not related to the persons from whom they buy such goods at the first commercial level after importation at which such sales take place.

2. As an example of this, goods are sold from a price list which grants favourable unit prices for purchases made in larger quantities.

Sale quantity	*Unit price*	*Number of sales*	*Total quantity sold at each price*
1-10 units	100	10 sales of 5 units	65
		5 sales of 3 units	
11-25 units	95	5 sales of 11 units	55
over 25 units	90	1 sale of 30 units	80
		1 sale of 50 units	

The greatest number of units sold at a price is 80; therefore, the unit price in the greatest aggregate quantity is 90.

3. As another example of this, two sales occur. In the first sale 500 units are sold at a price of 95 currency units each. In the second sale 400 units are sold at a price of 90 currency units each. In this example, the greatest number of units sold at a particular price is 500; therefore, the unit price in the greatest aggregate quantity is 95.

4. A third example would be the following situation where various quantities are sold at various prices.

(a) Sales

Sale quantity	*Unit price*
40 units	100
30 units	90
15 units	100
50 units	95
25 units	105
35 units	90
5 units	100

(b) Totals

Total quantity sold	*Unit price*
65	90
50	95
60	100
25	105

In this example, the greatest number of units sold at a particular price is 65; therefore, the unit price in the greatest aggregate quantity is 90.

5. Any sale in the importing country, as described in paragraph 1 above, to a person who supplies directly or indirectly free of charge or at reduced cost for use in connection with the production and sale for export of the imported goods any of the elements specified in paragraph 1(b) of Article 8, should not be taken into account in establishing the unit price for the purposes of Article 5.

6. It should be noted that "profit and general expenses" referred to in paragraph 1 of Article 5 should be taken as a whole. The figure for the purposes of this deduction should be determined on the basis of information supplied by or on behalf of the importer unless the importer's figures are inconsistent with those obtained in sales in the country of importation of imported goods of the same class or kind. Where the importer's figures are inconsistent with such figures, the amount for profit and general expenses may be based upon relevant information other than that supplied by or on behalf of the importer.

7. The "general expenses" include the direct and indirect costs of marketing the goods in question.

8. Local taxes payable by reason of the sale of the goods for which a deduction is not made under the provisions of paragraph 1(a)(iv) of Article 5 shall be deducted under the provisions of paragraph 1(a)(i) of Article 5.

9. In determining either the commissions or the usual profits and general expenses under the provisions of paragraph 1 of Article 5, the question whether certain goods are "of the same class or kind" as other goods must be determined on a case-by-case basis by reference to the circumstances involved. Sales in the country of importation of the narrowest group or range of imported goods of the same class or kind, which includes the goods being valued, for which the necessary information can be provided, should be examined. For the purposes of Article 5, "goods of the same class or kind" includes goods imported from the same country as the goods being valued as well as goods imported from other countries.

10. For the purposes of paragraph 1(b) of Article 5, the "earliest date" shall be the date by which sales of the imported goods or of identical or similar imported goods are made in sufficient quantity to establish the unit price.

11. Where the method in paragraph 2 of Article 5 is used, deductions made for the value added by further processing shall be based on objective and quantifiable data relating to the cost of such work. Accepted industry formulas, recipes, methods of construction, and other industry practices would form the basis of the calculations.

12. It is recognized that the method of valuation provided for in paragraph 2 of Article 5 would normally not be applicable when, as a result of the further processing, the imported goods lose their identity. However, there can be instances where, although the identity of the imported goods is lost, the value added by the processing can be determined accurately without unreasonable difficulty. On the other hand, there can also be instances where the imported goods maintain their identity but form such a minor element in the goods sold in the country of importation that the use of this valuation method would be unjustified. In view of the above, each situation of this type must be considered on a case-by-case basis.

Note to Article 6

1. As a general rule, customs value is determined under this Agreement on the basis of information readily available in the country of importation. In order to determine a computed value, however, it may be necessary to examine the costs of producing the goods being valued and other information which has to be obtained from outside the country of importation. Furthermore, in most cases the producer of the goods will be outside the jurisdiction of the authorities of the country of importation. The use of the computed value method will generally be limited to those cases where the buyer and seller are related, and the producer is prepared to supply to the authorities of the country of importation the necessary costings and to provide facilities for any subsequent verification which may be necessary.

2. The "cost or value" referred to in paragraph 1(a) of Article 6 is to be determined on the basis of information relating to the production of the goods being valued supplied by or on behalf of the producer. It is to be based upon the commercial accounts of the producer, provided that such accounts are consistent with the generally accepted accounting principles applied in the country where the goods are produced.

3. The "cost or value" shall include the cost of elements specified in paragraphs 1(a)(ii) and (iii) of Article 8. It shall also include the value, apportioned as appropriate under the provisions of the relevant note to Article 8, of any element specified in paragraph 1(b) of Article 8 which has been supplied directly or indirectly by the buyer for use in connection with the production of the imported goods. The value of the elements specified in paragraph 1(b)(iv) of Article 8 which are undertaken in the country of importation shall be included only to the extent that such elements are charged to the producer. It is to be understood that no cost or value of the elements referred to in this paragraph shall be counted twice in determining the computed value.

4. The "amount for profit and general expenses" referred to in paragraph 1(b) of Article 6 is to be determined on the basis of information

supplied by or on behalf of the producer unless the producer's figures are inconsistent with those usually reflected in sales of goods of the same class or kind as the goods being valued which are made by producers in the country of exportation for export to the country of importation.

5. It should be noted in this context that the "amount for profit and general expenses" has to be taken as a whole. It follows that if, in any particular case, the producer's profit figure is low and the producer's general expenses are high, the producer's profit and general expenses taken together may nevertheless be consistent with that usually reflected in sales of goods of the same class or kind. Such a situation might occur, for example, if a product were being launched in the country of importation and the producer accepted a nil or low profit to offset high general expenses associated with the launch. Where the producer can demonstrate a low profit on sales of the imported goods because of particular commercial circumstances, the producer's actual profit figures should be taken into account provided that the producer has valid commercial reasons to justify them and the producer's pricing policy reflects usual pricing policies in the branch of industry concerned. Such a situation might occur, for example, where producers have been forced to lower prices temporarily because of an unforeseeable drop in demand, or where they sell goods to complement a range of goods being produced in the country of importation and accept a low profit to maintain competitivity. Where the producer's own figures for profit and general expenses are not consistent with those usually reflected in sales of goods of the same class or kind as the goods being valued which are made by producers in the country of exportation for export to the country of importation, the amount for profit and general expenses may be based upon relevant information other than that supplied by or on behalf of the producer of the goods.

6. Where information other than that supplied by or on behalf of the producer is used for the purposes of determining a computed value, the authorities of the importing country shall inform the importer, if the latter so requests, of the source of such information, the data used and the calculations based upon such data, subject to the provisions of Article 10.

7. The "general expenses" referred to in paragraph 1(b) of Article 6 covers the direct and indirect costs of producing and selling the goods for export which are not included under paragraph 1(a) of Article 6.

8. Whether certain goods are "of the same class or kind" as other goods must be determined on a case-by-case basis with reference to the circumstances involved. In determining the usual profits and general expenses under the provisions of Article 6, sales for export to the country of importation of the narrowest group or range of goods, which includes the goods being valued, for which the necessary information can be provided, should

be examined. For the purposes of Article 6, "goods of the same class or kind" must be from the same country as the goods being valued.

Note to Article 7

1. Customs values determined under the provisions of Article 7 should, to the greatest extent possible, be based on previously determined customs values.

2. The methods of valuation to be employed under Article 7 should be those laid down in Articles 1 through 6 but a reasonable flexibility in the application of such methods would be in conformity with the aims and provisions of Article 7.

3. Some examples of reasonable flexibility are as follows:

(a) *Identical goods*—the requirement that the identical goods should be exported at or about the same time as the goods being valued could be flexibly interpreted; identical imported goods produced in a country other than the country of exportation of the goods being valued could be the basis for customs valuation; customs values of identical imported goods already determined under the provisions of Articles 5 and 6 could be used.

(b) *Similar goods*—the requirement that the similar goods should be exported at or about the same time as the goods being valued could be flexibly interpreted; similar imported goods produced in a country other than the country of exportation of the goods being valued could be the basis for customs valuation; customs values of similar imported goods already determined under the provisions of Articles 5 and 6 could be used.

(c) *Deductive method*—the requirement that the goods shall have been sold in the "condition as imported" in paragraph 1(a) of Article 5 could be flexibly interpreted; the "90 days" requirement could be administered flexibly.

Note to Article 8

Paragraph 1(a)(i)

The term "buying commissions" means fees paid by an importer to the importer's agent for the service of representing the importer abroad in the purchase of the goods being valued.

Paragraph 1(b)(ii)

1. There are two factors involved in the apportionment of the elements specified in paragraph 1(b)(ii) of Article 8 to the imported goods—the value of the element itself and the way in which that value is to be apportioned to the imported goods. The apportionment of these elements should be made in a reasonable manner appropriate to the circumstances and in accordance with generally accepted accounting principles.

2. Concerning the value of the element, if the importer acquires the element from a seller not related to the importer at a given cost, the value of the element is that cost. If the element was produced by the importer or by a person related to the importer, its value would be the cost of producing it. If the element had been previously used by the importer, regardless of whether it had been acquired or produced by such importer, the original cost of acquisition or production would have to be adjusted downward to reflect its use in order to arrive at the value of the element.

3. Once a value has been determined for the element, it is necessary to apportion that value to the imported goods. Various possibilities exist. For example, the value might be apportioned to the first shipment if the importer wishes to pay duty on the entire value at one time. As another example, the importer may request that the value be apportioned over the number of units produced up to the time of the first shipment. As a further example, the importer may request that the value be apportioned over the entire anticipated production where contracts or firm commitments exist for that production. The method of apportionment used will depend upon the documentation provided by the importer.

4. As an illustration of the above, an importer provides the producer with a mould to be used in the production of the imported goods and contracts with the producer to buy 10,000 units. By the time of arrival of the first shipment of 1,000 units, the producer has already produced 4,000 units. The importer may request the customs administration to apportion the value of the mould over 1,000 units, 4,000 units or 10,000 units.

Paragraph 1(b)(iv)

1. Additions for the elements specified in paragraph 1(b)(iv) of Article 8 should be based on objective and quantifiable data. In order to minimize the burden for both the importer and customs administration in determining the values to be added, data readily available in the buyer's commercial record system should be used in so far as possible.

2. For those elements supplied by the buyer which were purchased or leased by the buyer, the addition would be the cost of the purchase or the

lease. No addition shall be made for those elements available in the public domain, other than the cost of obtaining copies of them.

3. The ease with which it may be possible to calculate the values to be added will depend on a particular firm's structure and management practice, as well as its accounting methods.

4. For example, it is possible that a firm which imports a variety of products from several countries maintains the records of its design centre outside the country of importation in such a way as to show accurately the costs attributable to a given product. In such cases, a direct adjustment may appropriately be made under the provisions of Article 8.

5. In another case, a firm may carry the cost of the design centre outside the country of importation as a general overhead expense without allocation to specific products. In this instance, an appropriate adjustment could be made under the provisions of Article 8 with respect to the imported goods by apportioning total design centre costs over total production benefiting from the design centre and adding such apportioned cost on a unit basis to imports.

6. Variations in the above circumstances will, of course, require different factors to be considered in determining the proper method of allocation.

7. In cases where the production of the element in question involves a number of countries and over a period of time, the adjustment should be limited to the value actually added to that element outside the country of importation.

Paragraph 1(c)

1. The royalties and licence fees referred to in paragraph 1(c) of Article 8 may include, among other things, payments in respect to patents, trade marks and copyrights. However, the charges for the right to reproduce the imported goods in the country of importation shall not be added to the price actually paid or payable for the imported goods in determining the customs value.

2. Payments made by the buyer for the right to distribute or resell the imported goods shall not be added to the price actually paid or payable for the imported goods if such payments are not a condition of the sale for export to the country of importation of the imported goods.

Paragraph 3

Where objective and quantifiable data do not exist with regard to the additions required to be made under the provisions of Article 8, the transaction value cannot be determined under the provisions of Article 1. As an illustration of this, a royalty is paid on the basis of the price in a sale in the importing country of a litre of a particular product that was imported by the kilogram and made up into a solution after importation. If the royalty is based partially on the imported goods and partially on other factors which have nothing to do with the imported goods (such as when the imported goods are mixed with domestic ingredients and are no longer separately identifiable, or when the royalty cannot be distinguished from special financial arrangements between the buyer and the seller), it would be inappropriate to attempt to make an addition for the royalty. However, if the amount of this royalty is based only on the imported goods and can be readily quantified, an addition to the price actually paid or payable can be made.

Note to Article 9

For the purposes of Article 9, "time of importation" may include the time of entry for customs purposes.

Note to Article 11

1. Article 11 provides the importer with the right to appeal against a valuation determination made by the customs administration for the goods being valued. Appeal may first be to a higher level in the customs administration, but the importer shall have the right in the final instance to appeal to the judiciary.

2. "Without penalty" means that the importer shall not be subject to a fine or threat of fine merely because the importer chose to exercise the right of appeal. Payment of normal court costs and lawyers' fees shall not be considered to be a fine.

3. However, nothing in Article 11 shall prevent a Member from requiring full payment of assessed customs duties prior to an appeal.

Note to Article 15

Paragraph 4

For the purposes of Article 15, the term "persons" includes a legal person, where appropriate.

Paragraph 4(e)

For the purposes of this Agreement, one person shall be deemed to control another when the former is legally or operationally in a position to exercise restraint or direction over the latter.

Annex II

TECHNICAL COMMITTEE ON CUSTOMS VALUATION

1. In accordance with Article 18 of this Agreement, the Technical Committee shall be established under the auspices of the CCC with a view to ensuring, at the technical level, uniformity in interpretation and application of this Agreement.

2. The responsibilities of the Technical Committee shall include the following:

(a) to examine specific technical problems arising in the day-to-day administration of the customs valuation system of Members and to give advisory opinions on appropriate solutions based upon the facts presented;

(b) to study, as requested, valuation laws, procedures and practices as they relate to this Agreement and to prepare reports on the results of such studies;

(c) to prepare and circulate annual reports on the technical aspects of the operation and status of this Agreement;

(d) to furnish such information and advice on any matters concerning the valuation of imported goods for customs purposes as may be requested by any Member or the Committee. Such information and advice may take the form of advisory opinions, commentaries or explanatory notes;

(e) to facilitate, as requested, technical assistance to Members with a view to furthering the international acceptance of this Agreement;

(f) to carry out an examination of a matter referred to it by a panel under Article 19 of this Agreement; and

(g) to exercise such other responsibilities as the Committee may assign to it.

General

3. The Technical Committee shall attempt to conclude its work on specific matters, especially those referred to it by Members, the Committee or a panel, in a reasonably short period of time. As provided in paragraph 4 of Article 19, a panel shall set a specific time period for receipt of a report of the Technical Committee and the Technical Committee shall provide its report within that period.

4. The Technical Committee shall be assisted as appropriate in its activities by the CCC Secretariat.

Representation

5. Each Member shall have the right to be represented on the Technical Committee. Each Member may nominate one delegate and one or more alternates to be its representatives on the Technical Committee. Such a Member so represented on the Technical Committee is referred to in this Annex as a "member of the Technical Committee". Representatives of members of the Technical Committee may be assisted by advisers. The WTO Secretariat may also attend such meetings with observer status.

6. Members of the CCC which are not Members of the WTO may be represented at meetings of the Technical Committee by one delegate and one or more alternates. Such representatives shall attend meetings of the Technical Committee as observers.

7. Subject to the approval of the Chairman of the Technical Committee, the Secretary-General of the CCC (referred to in this Annex as "the Secretary-General") may invite representatives of governments which are neither Members of the WTO nor members of the CCC and representatives of international governmental and trade organizations to attend meetings of the Technical Committee as observers.

8. Nominations of delegates, alternates and advisers to meetings of the Technical Committee shall be made to the Secretary-General.

Technical Committee Meetings

9. The Technical Committee shall meet as necessary but at least two times a year. The date of each meeting shall be fixed by the Technical Committee at its preceding session. The date of the meeting may be varied either at the request of any member of the Technical Committee concurred in by a simple majority of the members of the Technical Committee or, in cases requiring urgent attention, at the request of the Chairman. Notwithstanding the provisions in sentence 1 of this paragraph, the Technical Committee shall meet as necessary to consider matters referred to it by a panel under the provisions of Article 19 of this Agreement.

10. The meetings of the Technical Committee shall be held at the headquarters of the CCC unless otherwise decided.

11. The Secretary-General shall inform all members of the Technical Committee and those included under paragraphs 6 and 7 at least 30 days in advance, except in urgent cases, of the opening date of each session of the Technical Committee.

Agenda

12. A provisional agenda for each session shall be drawn up by the Secretary-General and circulated to the members of the Technical Committee and to those included under paragraphs 6 and 7 at least 30 days in advance of the session, except in urgent cases. This agenda shall comprise all items whose inclusion has been approved by the Technical Committee during its preceding session, all items included by the Chairman on the Chairman's own initiative, and all items whose inclusion has been requested by the Secretary-General, by the Committee or by any member of the Technical Committee.

13. The Technical Committee shall determine its agenda at the opening of each session. During the session the agenda may be altered at any time by the Technical Committee.

Officers and Conduct of Business

14. The Technical Committee shall elect from among the delegates of its members a Chairman and one or more Vice-Chairmen. The Chairman and Vice-Chairmen shall each hold office for a period of one year. The retiring Chairman and Vice-Chairmen are eligible for re-election. The mandate of a Chairman or Vice-Chairman who no longer represents a member of the Technical Committee shall terminate automatically.

15. If the Chairman is absent from any meeting or part thereof, a Vice-Chairman shall preside. In that event, the latter shall have the same powers and duties as the Chairman.

16. The Chairman of the meeting shall participate in the proceedings of the Technical Committee as such and not as the representative of a member of the Technical Committee.

17. In addition to exercising the other powers conferred upon the Chairman by these rules, the Chairman shall declare the opening and closing of each meeting, direct the discussion, accord the right to speak, and, pursuant to these rules, have control of the proceedings. The Chairman may also call a speaker to order if the speaker's remarks are not relevant.

18. During discussion of any matter a delegation may raise a point of order. In this event, the Chairman shall immediately state a ruling. If this ruling is challenged, the Chairman shall submit it to the meeting for decision and it shall stand unless overruled.

19. The Secretary-General, or officers of the CCC Secretariat designated by the Secretary-General, shall perform the secretarial work of meetings of the Technical Committee.

Quorum and Voting

20. Representatives of a simple majority of the members of the Technical Committee shall constitute a quorum.

21. Each member of the Technical Committee shall have one vote. A decision of the Technical Committee shall be taken by a majority comprising at least two thirds of the members present. Regardless of the outcome of the vote on a particular matter, the Technical Committee shall be free to make a full report to the Committee and to the CCC on that matter indicating the different views expressed in the relevant discussions. Notwithstanding the above provisions of this paragraph, on matters referred to it by a panel, the Technical Committee shall take decisions by consensus. Where no agreement is reached in the Technical Committee on the question referred to it by a panel, the Technical Committee shall provide a report detailing the facts of the matter and indicating the views of the members.

Languages and Records

22. The official languages of the Technical Committee shall be English, French and Spanish. Speeches or statements made in any of these three languages shall be immediately translated into the other official languages unless all delegations agree to dispense with translation. Speeches or statements made in any other language shall be translated into English, French and Spanish, subject to the same conditions, but in that event the delegation concerned shall provide the translation into English, French or Spanish. Only English, French and Spanish shall be used for the official documents of the Technical Committee. Memoranda and correspondence for the consideration of the Technical Committee must be presented in one of the official languages.

23. The Technical Committee shall draw up a report of all its sessions and, if the Chairman considers it necessary, minutes or summary records of its meetings. The Chairman or a designee of the Chairman shall report on the work of the Technical Committee at each meeting of the Committee and at each meeting of the CCC.

Annex III

1. The five-year delay in the application of the provisions of the Agreement by developing country Members provided for in paragraph 1 of Article 20 may, in practice, be insufficient for certain developing country Members. In such cases a developing country Member may request before the end of the period referred to in paragraph 1 of Article 20 an extension of such period, it being understood that the Members will give sympathetic

consideration to such a request in cases where the developing country Member in question can show good cause.

2. Developing countries which currently value goods on the basis of officially established minimum values may wish to make a reservation to enable them to retain such values on a limited and transitional basis under such terms and conditions as may be agreed to by the Members.

3. Developing countries which consider that the reversal of the sequential order at the request of the importer provided for in Article 4 of the Agreement may give rise to real difficulties for them may wish to make a reservation to Article 4 in the following terms:

> "The Government of . . . reserves the right to provide that the relevant provision of Article 4 of the Agreement shall apply only when the customs authorities agree to the request to reverse the order of Articles 5 and 6."

If developing countries make such a reservation, the Members shall consent to it under Article 21 of the Agreement.

4. Developing countries may wish to make a reservation with respect to paragraph 2 of Article 5 of the Agreement in the following terms:

> "The Government ofreserves the right to provide that paragraph 2 of Article 5 of the Agreement shall be applied in accordance with the provisions of the relevant note thereto whether or not the importer so requests."

If developing countries make such a reservation, the Members shall consent to it under Article 21 of the Agreement.

5. Certain developing countries may have problems in the implementation of Article 1 of the Agreement insofar as it relates to importations into their countries by sole agents, sole distributors and sole concessionaires. If such problems arise in practice in developing country Members applying the Agreement, a study of this question shall be made, at the request of such Members, with a view to finding appropriate solutions.

6. Article 17 recognizes that in applying the Agreement, customs administrations may need to make enquiries concerning the truth or accuracy of any statement, document or declaration presented to them for customs valuation purposes. The Article thus acknowledges that enquiries may be made which are, for example, aimed at verifying that the elements of value declared or presented to customs in connection with a determination of customs value are complete and correct. Members, subject to their national laws and procedures, have the right to expect the full cooperation of importers in these enquiries.

7. The price actually paid or payable includes all payments actually made or to be made as a condition of sale of the imported goods, by the buyer to the seller, or by the buyer to a third party to satisfy an obligation of the seller.

Document 30

AGREEMENT ON PRESHIPMENT INSPECTION

Members,

Noting that Ministers on 20 September 1986 agreed that the Uruguay Round of Multilateral Trade Negotiations shall aim to "bring about further liberalization and expansion of world trade", "strengthen the role of GATT" and "increase the responsiveness of the GATT system to the evolving international economic environment";

Noting that a number of developing country Members have recourse to preshipment inspection;

Recognizing the need of developing countries to do so for as long and in so far as it is necessary to verify the quality, quantity or price of imported goods;

Mindful that such programmes must be carried out without giving rise to unnecessary delays or unequal treatment;

Noting that this inspection is by definition carried out on the territory of exporter Members;

Recognizing the need to establish an agreed international framework of rights and obligations of both user Members and exporter Members;

Recognizing that the principles and obligations of GATT 1994 apply to those activities of preshipment inspection entities that are mandated by governments that are Members of the WTO;

Recognizing that it is desirable to provide transparency of the operation of preshipment inspection entities and of laws and regulations relating to preshipment inspection;

Desiring to provide for the speedy, effective and equitable resolution of disputes between exporters and preshipment inspection entities arising under this Agreement;

Hereby *agree* as follows:

Article 1

Coverage—Definitions

1. This Agreement shall apply to all preshipment inspection activities carried out on the territory of Members, whether such activities are contracted or mandated by the government, or any government body, of a Member.

2. The term "user Member" means a Member of which the government or any government body contracts for or mandates the use of preshipment inspection activities.

3. Preshipment inspection activities are all activities relating to the verification of the quality, the quantity, the price, including currency exchange rate and financial terms, and/or the customs classification of goods to be exported to the territory of the user Member.

4. The term "preshipment inspection entity" is any entity contracted or mandated by a Member to carry out preshipment inspection activities.[1]

Article 2

Obligations of User Members

Non-discrimination

1. User Members shall ensure that preshipment inspection activities are carried out in a nondiscriminatory manner, and that the procedures and criteria employed in the conduct of these activities are objective and are applied on an equal basis to all exporters affected by such activities. They shall ensure uniform performance of inspection by all the inspectors of the preshipment inspection entities contracted or mandated by them.

1. It is understood that this provision does not obligate Members to allow government entities of other Members to conduct preshipment inspection activities on their territory.

Governmental Requirements

2. User Members shall ensure that in the course of preshipment inspection activities relating to their laws, regulations and requirements, the provisions of paragraph 4 of Article III of GATT 1994 are respected to the extent that these are relevant.

Site of Inspection

3. User Members shall ensure that all preshipment inspection activities, including the issuance of a Clean Report of Findings or a note of non-issuance, are performed in the customs territory from which the goods are exported or, if the inspection cannot be carried out in that customs territory given the complex nature of the products involved, or if both parties agree, in the customs territory in which the goods are manufactured.

Standards

4. User Members shall ensure that quantity and quality inspections are performed in accordance with the standards defined by the seller and the buyer in the purchase agreement and that, in the absence of such standards, relevant international standards[2] apply.

Transparency

5. User Members shall ensure that preshipment inspection activities are conducted in a transparent manner.

6. User Members shall ensure that, when initially contacted by exporters, preshipment inspection entities provide to the exporters a list of all the information which is necessary for the exporters to comply with inspection requirements. The preshipment inspection entities shall provide the actual information when so requested by exporters. This information shall include a reference to the laws and regulations of user Members relating to preshipment inspection activities, and shall also include the procedures and criteria used for inspection and for price and currency exchange-rate verification purposes, the exporters' rights vis-à-vis the inspection entities, and the appeals procedures set up under paragraph 21. Additional procedural requirements or changes in existing procedures shall not be applied to a shipment unless the exporter concerned is informed of these changes at the time the inspection date is arranged. However, in emergency situations of the types addressed by Articles XX and XXI of GATT 1994, such additional

2. An international standard is a standard adopted by a governmental or non-governmental body whose membership is open to all Members, one of whose recognized activities is in the field of standardization.

requirements or changes may be applied to a shipment before the exporter has been informed. This assistance shall not, however, relieve exporters from their obligations in respect of compliance with the import regulations of the user Members.

7. User Members shall ensure that the information referred to in paragraph 6 is made available to exporters in a convenient manner, and that the preshipment inspection offices maintained by preshipment inspection entities serve as information points where this information is available. 8. User Members shall publish promptly all applicable laws and regulations relating to preshipment inspection activities in such a manner as to enable other governments and traders to become acquainted with them.

Protection of Confidential Business Information

9. User Members shall ensure that preshipment inspection entities treat all information received in the course of the preshipment inspection as business confidential to the extent that such information is not already published, generally available to third parties, or otherwise in the public domain. User Members shall ensure that preshipment inspection entities maintain procedures to this end.

10. User Members shall provide information to Members on request on the measures they are taking to give effect to paragraph 9. The provisions of this paragraph shall not require any Member to disclose confidential information the disclosure of which would jeopardize the effectiveness of the preshipment inspection programmes or would prejudice the legitimate commercial interest of particular enterprises, public or private.

11. User Members shall ensure that preshipment inspection entities do not divulge confidential business information to any third party, except that preshipment inspection entities may share this information with the government entities that have contracted or mandated them. User Members shall ensure that confidential business information which they receive from preshipment inspection entities contracted or mandated by them is adequately safeguarded. Preshipment inspection entities shall share confidential business information with the governments contracting or mandating them only to the extent that such information is customarily required for letters of credit or other forms of payment or for customs, import licensing or exchange control purposes.

12. User Members shall ensure that preshipment inspection entities do not request exporters to provide information regarding:

(a) manufacturing data related to patented, licensed or undisclosed processes, or to processes for which a patent is pending;

(b) unpublished technical data other than data necessary to demonstrate compliance with technical regulations or standards;

(c) internal pricing, including manufacturing costs;

(d) profit levels;

(e) the terms of contracts between exporters and their suppliers unless it is not otherwise possible for the entity to conduct the inspection in question. In such cases, the entity shall only request the information necessary for this purpose.

13. The information referred to in paragraph 12, which preshipment inspection entities shall not otherwise request, may be released voluntarily by the exporter to illustrate a specific case.

Conflicts of Interest

14. User Members shall ensure that preshipment inspection entities, bearing in mind also the provisions on protection of confidential business information in paragraphs 9 through 13, maintain procedures to avoid conflicts of interest:

(a) between preshipment inspection entities and any related entities of the preshipment inspection entities in question, including any entities in which the latter have a financial or commercial interest or any entities which have a financial interest in the preshipment inspection entities in question, and whose shipments the preshipment inspection entities are to inspect;

(b) between preshipment inspection entities and any other entities, including other entities subject to preshipment inspection, with the exception of the government entities contracting or mandating the inspections;

(c) with divisions of preshipment inspection entities engaged in activities other than those required to carry out the inspection process.

Delays

15. User Members shall ensure that preshipment inspection entities avoid unreasonable delays in inspection of shipments. User Members shall ensure that, once a preshipment inspection entity and an exporter agree on an inspection date, the preshipment inspection entity conducts the inspection on that date unless it is rescheduled on a mutually agreed basis between the

exporter and the preshipment inspection entity, or the preshipment inspection entity is prevented from doing so by the exporter or by *force majeure*.[3]

16. User Members shall ensure that, following receipt of the final documents and completion of the inspection, preshipment inspection entities, within five working days, either issue a Clean Report of Findings or provide a detailed written explanation specifying the reasons for non-issuance. User Members shall ensure that, in the latter case, preshipment inspection entities give exporters the opportunity to present their views in writing and, if exporters so request, arrange for re-inspection at the earliest mutually convenient date.

17. User Members shall ensure that, whenever so requested by the exporters, preshipment inspection entities undertake, prior to the date of physical inspection, a preliminary verification of price and, where applicable, of currency exchange rate, on the basis of the contract between exporter and importer, the *pro forma* invoice and, where applicable, the application for import authorization. User Members shall ensure that a price or currency exchange rate that has been accepted by a preshipment inspection entity on the basis of such preliminary verification is not withdrawn, providing the goods conform to the import documentation and/or import licence. They shall ensure that, after a preliminary verification has taken place, preshipment inspection entities immediately inform exporters in writing either of their acceptance or of their detailed reasons for non-acceptance of the price and/or currency exchange rate.

18. User Members shall ensure that, in order to avoid delays in payment, preshipment inspection entities send to exporters or to designated representatives of the exporters a Clean Report of Findings as expeditiously as possible.

19. User Members shall ensure that, in the event of a clerical error in the Clean Report of Findings, preshipment inspection entities correct the error and forward the corrected information to the appropriate parties as expeditiously as possible.

Price Verification

20. User Members shall ensure that, in order to prevent over- and under-invoicing and fraud, preshipment inspection entities conduct price verification[4] according to the following guidelines:

3. It is understood that, for the purposes of this Agreement, "force majeure" shall mean "irresistible compulsion or coercion, unforeseeable course of events excusing from fulfilment of contract".

4. The obligations of user Members with respect to the services of preshipment inspection entities in connection with customs valuation shall be the obligations which they have accepted in GATT 1994 and the other Multilateral Trade Agreements included in Annex 1A of the WTO Agreement.

(a) preshipment inspection entities shall only reject a contract price agreed between an exporter and an importer if they can demonstrate that their findings of an unsatisfactory price are based on a verification process which is in conformity with the criteria set out in subparagraphs (b) through (e);

(b) the preshipment inspection entity shall base its price comparison for the verification of the export price on the price(s) of identical or similar goods offered for export from the same country of exportation at or about the same time, under competitive and comparable conditions of sale, in conformity with customary commercial practices and net of any applicable standard discounts. Such comparison shall be based on the following:

(i) only prices providing a valid basis of comparison shall be used, taking into account the relevant economic factors pertaining to the country of importation and a country or countries used for price comparison;

(ii) the preshipment inspection entity shall not rely upon the price of goods offered for export to different countries of importation to arbitrarily impose the lowest price upon the shipment;

(iii) the preshipment inspection entity shall take into account the specific elements listed in subparagraph (c);

(iv) at any stage in the process described above, the preshipment inspection entity shall provide the exporter with an opportunity to explain the price;

(c) when conducting price verification, preshipment inspection entities shall make appropriate allowances for the terms of the sales contract and generally applicable adjusting factors pertaining to the transaction; these factors shall include but not be limited to the commercial level and quantity of the sale, delivery periods and conditions, price escalation clauses, quality specifications, special design features, special shipping or packing specifications, order size, spot sales, seasonal influences, licence or other intellectual property fees, and services rendered as part of the contract if these are not customarily invoiced separately; they shall also include certain elements relating to the exporter's price, such as the contractual relationship between the exporter and importer;

(d) the verification of transportation charges shall relate only to the agreed price of the mode of transport in the country of exportation as indicated in the sales contract;

(e) the following shall not be used for price verification purposes:

(i) the selling price in the country of importation of goods produced in such country;

(ii) the price of goods for export from a country other than the country of exportation;

(iii) the cost of production;

(iv) arbitrary or fictitious prices or values.

Appeals Procedures

21. User Members shall ensure that preshipment inspection entities establish procedures to receive, consider and render decisions concerning grievances raised by exporters, and that information concerning such procedures is made available to exporters in accordance with the provisions of paragraphs 6 and 7. User Members shall ensure that the procedures are developed and maintained in accordance with the following guidelines:

(a) preshipment inspection entities shall designate one or more officials who shall be available during normal business hours in each city or port in which they maintain a preshipment inspection administrative office to receive, consider and render decisions on exporters' appeals or grievances;

(b) exporters shall provide in writing to the designated official(s) the facts concerning the specific transaction in question, the nature of the grievance and a suggested solution;

(c) the designated official(s) shall afford sympathetic consideration to exporters' grievances and shall render a decision as soon as possible after receipt of the documentation referred to in subparagraph(b).

Derogation

22. By derogation to the provisions of Article 2, user Members shall provide that, with the exception of part shipments, shipments whose value is less than a minimum value applicable to such shipments as defined by the user Member shall not be inspected, except in exceptional circumstances. This minimum value shall form part of the information furnished to exporters under the provisions of paragraph 6.

Article 3

Obligations of Exporter Members Non-discrimination

1. Exporter Members shall ensure that their laws and regulations relating to preshipment inspection activities are applied in a non-discriminatory manner.

Transparency

2. Exporter Members shall publish promptly all applicable laws and regulations relating to preshipment inspection activities in such a manner as to enable other governments and traders to become acquainted with them.

Technical Assistance

3. Exporter Members shall offer to provide to user Members, if requested, technical assistance directed towards the achievement of the objectives of this Agreement on mutually agreed terms.[5]

Article 4

Independent Review Procedure

Members shall encourage preshipment inspection entities and exporters mutually to resolve their disputes. However, two working days after submission of the grievance in accordance with the provisions of paragraph 21 of Article 2, either party may refer the dispute to independent review. Members shall take such reasonable measures as may be available to them to ensure that the following procedures are established and maintained to this end:

(a) these procedures shall be administered by an independent entity constituted jointly by an organization representing preshipment inspection entities and an organization representing exporters for the purposes of this Agreement;

(b) the independent entity referred to in subparagraph (a) shall establish a list of experts as follows:

(i) a section of members nominated by an organization representing preshipment inspection entities;

(ii) a section of members nominated by an organization representing exporters;

5. It is understood that such technical assistance may be given on a bilateral, plurilateral or multilateral basis.

(iii) a section of independent trade experts, nominated by the independent entity referred to in subparagraph (a).

The geographical distribution of the experts on this list shall be such as to enable any disputes raised under these procedures to be dealt with expeditiously. This list shall be drawn up within two months of the entry into force of the WTO Agreement and shall be updated annually. The list shall be publicly available. It shall be notified to the Secretariat and circulated to all Members;

(c) an exporter or preshipment inspection entity wishing to raise a dispute shall contact the independent entity referred to in subparagraph (a) and request the formation of a panel. The independent entity shall be responsible for establishing a panel. This panel shall consist of three members. The members of the panel shall be chosen so as to avoid unnecessary costs and delays. The first member shall be chosen from section (i) of the above list by the preshipment inspection entity concerned, provided that this member is not affiliated to that entity. The second member shall be chosen from section (ii) of the above list by the exporter concerned, provided that this member is not affiliated to that exporter. The third member shall be chosen from section (iii) of the above list by the independent entity referred to in subparagraph (a). No objections shall be made to any independent trade expert drawn from section (iii) of the above list;

(d) the independent trade expert drawn from section (iii) of the above list shall serve as the chairman of the panel. The independent trade expert shall take the necessary decisions to ensure an expeditious settlement of the dispute by the panel, for instance, whether the facts of the case require the panelists to meet and, if so, where such a meeting shall take place, taking into account the site of the inspection in question;

(e) if the parties to the dispute so agree, one independent trade expert could be selected from section (iii) of the above list by the independent entity referred to in subparagraph (a) to review the dispute in question. This expert shall take the necessary decisions to ensure an expeditious settlement of the dispute, for instance taking into account the site of the inspection in question;

(f) the object of the review shall be to establish whether, in the course of the inspection in dispute, the parties to the dispute have complied with the provisions of this Agreement. The procedures shall be expeditious and provide the opportunity for both parties to present their views in person or in writing;

(g) decisions by a three-member panel shall be taken by majority vote. The decision on the dispute shall be rendered within eight working days of the request for independent review and be communicated to the parties to the dispute. This time-limit could be extended upon agreement by the parties to the dispute. The panel or independent trade expert shall apportion the costs, based on the merits of the case;

(h) the decision of the panel shall be binding upon the preshipment inspection entity and the exporter which are parties to the dispute.

Article 5

Notification

Members shall submit to the Secretariat copies of the laws and regulations by which they put this Agreement into force, as well as copies of any other laws and regulations relating to preshipment inspection, when the WTO Agreement enters into force with respect to the Member concerned. No changes in the laws and regulations relating to preshipment inspection shall be enforced before such changes have been officially published. They shall be notified to the Secretariat immediately after their publication. The Secretariat shall inform the Members of the availability of this information.

Article 6

Review

At the end of the second year from the date of entry into force of the WTO Agreement and every three years thereafter, the Ministerial Conference shall review the provisions, implementation and operation of this Agreement, taking into account the objectives thereof and experience gained in its operation. As a result of such review, the Ministerial Conference may amend the provisions of the Agreement.

Article 7

Consultation

Members shall consult with other Members upon request with respect to any matter affecting the operation of this Agreement. In such cases, the provisions of Article XXII of GATT 1994, as elaborated and applied by the Dispute Settlement Understanding, are applicable to this Agreement.

Article 8

Dispute Settlement

Any disputes among Members regarding the operation of this Agreement shall be subject to the provisions of Article XXIII of GATT 1994, as elaborated and applied by the Dispute Settlement Understanding.

Article 9

Final Provisions

1. Members shall take the necessary measures for the implementation of the present Agreement.

2. Members shall ensure that their laws and regulations shall not be contrary to the provisions of this Agreement.

Document 31

AGREEMENT ON RULES OF ORIGIN

Members,

Noting that Ministers on 20 September 1986 agreed that the Uruguay Round of Multilateral Trade Negotiations shall aim to "bring about further liberalization and expansion of world trade," "strengthen the role of GATT" and "increase the responsiveness of the GATT system to the evolving international economic environment";

Desiring to further the objectives of GATT 1994;

Recognizing that clear and predictable rules of origin and their application facilitate the flow of international trade;

Desiring to ensure that rules of origin themselves do not create unnecessary obstacles to trade;

Desiring to ensure that rules of origin do not nullify or impair the rights of Members under GATT 1994;

Recognizing that it is desirable to provide transparency of laws, regulations, and practices regarding rules of origin;

Desiring to ensure that rules of origin are prepared and applied in an impartial, transparent, predictable, consistent and neutral manner;

Recognizing the availability of a consultation mechanism and procedures for the speedy, effective and equitable resolution of disputes arising under this Agreement;

Desiring to harmonize and clarify rules of origin;

Hereby *agree* as follows:

Part I

DEFINITIONS AND COVERAGE

Article 1

Rules of Origin

1. For the purposes of Parts I to IV of this Agreement, rules of origin shall be defined as those laws, regulations and administrative determinations of general application applied by any Member to determine the country of origin of goods provided such rules of origin are not related to contractual or autonomous trade regimes leading to the granting of tariff preferences going beyond the application of paragraph 1 of Article I of GATT 1994.

2. Rules of origin referred to in paragraph 1 shall include all rules of origin used in non-preferential commercial policy instruments, such as in the application of: most-favoured-nation treatment under Articles I, II, III, XI and XIII of GATT 1994; anti-dumping and countervailing duties under Article VI of GATT 1994; safeguard measures under Article XIX of GATT 1994; origin marking requirements under Article IX of GATT 1994; and any discriminatory quantitative restrictions or tariff quotas. They shall also include rules of origin used for government procurement and trade statistics.[1]

Part II

DISCIPLINES TO GOVERN THE APPLICATION OF RULES OF ORIGIN

Article 2

Disciplines During the Transition Period

Until the work programme for the harmonization of rules of origin set out in Part IV is completed, Members shall ensure that:

1. It is understood that this provision is without prejudice to those determinations made for purposes of defining "domestic industry" or "like products of domestic industry" or similar terms wherever they apply.

(a) when they issue administrative determinations of general application, the requirements to be fulfilled are clearly defined. In particular:

(i) in cases where the criterion of change of tariff classification is applied, such a rule of origin, and any exceptions to the rule, must clearly specify the subheadings or headings within the tariff nomenclature that are addressed by the rule;

(ii) in cases where the ad valorem percentage criterion is applied, the method for calculating this percentage shall also be indicated in the rules of origin;

(iii) in cases where the criterion of manufacturing or processing operation is prescribed, the operation that confers origin on the good concerned shall be precisely specified;

(b) notwithstanding the measure or instrument of commercial policy to which they are linked, their rules of origin are not used as instruments to pursue trade objectives directly or indirectly;

(c) rules of origin shall not themselves create restrictive, distorting, or disruptive effects on international trade. They shall not pose unduly strict requirements or require the fulfilment of a certain condition not related to manufacturing or processing, as a prerequisite for the determination of the country of origin. However, costs not directly related to manufacturing or processing may be included for the purposes of the application of an ad valorem percentage criterion consistent with subparagraph (a);

(d) the rules of origin that they apply to imports and exports are not more stringent than the rules of origin they apply to determine whether or not a good is domestic and shall not discriminate between other Members, irrespective of the affiliation of the manufacturers of the good concerned;[2]

(e) their rules of origin are administered in a consistent, uniform, impartial and reasonable manner;

(f) their rules of origin are based on a positive standard. Rules of origin that state what does not confer origin (negative standard) are permissible as part of a clarification of a positive standard or in individual cases where a positive determination of origin is not necessary;

2. With respect to rules of origin applied for the purposes of government procurement, this provision shall not create obligations additional to those already assumed by Members under GATT 1994.

(g) their laws, regulations, judicial decisions and administrative rulings of general application relating to rules of origin are published as if they were subject to, and in accordance with, the provisions of paragraph 1 of Article X of GATT 1994;

(h) upon the request of an exporter, importer or any person with a justifiable cause, assessments of the origin they would accord to a good are issued as soon as possible but no later than 150 days[3] after a request for such an assessment provided that all necessary elements have been submitted. Requests for such assessments shall be accepted before trade in the good concerned begins and may be accepted at any later point in time. Such assessments shall remain valid for three years provided that the facts and conditions, including the rules of origin, under which they have been made remain comparable. Provided that the parties concerned are informed in advance, such assessments will no longer be valid when a decision contrary to the assessment is made in a review as referred to in subparagraph (j). Such assessments shall be made publicly available subject to the provisions of subparagraph (k);

(i) when introducing changes to their rules of origin or new rules of origin, they shall not apply such changes retroactively as defined in, and without prejudice to, their laws or regulations;

(j) any administrative action which they take in relation to the determination of origin is reviewable promptly by judicial, arbitral or administrative tribunals or procedures, independent of the authority issuing the determination, which can effect the modification or reversal of the determination;

(k) all information that is by nature confidential or that is provided on a confidential basis for the purpose of the application of rules of origin is treated as strictly confidential by the authorities concerned, which shall not disclose it without the specific permission of the person or government providing such information, except to the extent that it may be required to be disclosed in the context of judicial proceedings.

Article 3

Disciplines after the Transition Period

Taking into account the aim of all Members to achieve, as a result of the harmonization work programme set out in Part IV, the establishment of

3. In respect of requests made during the first year from the date of entry into force of the WTO Agreement, Members shall only be required to issue these assessments as soon as possible.

harmonized rules of origin, Members shall ensure, upon the implementation of the results of the harmonization work programme, that:

(a) they apply rules of origin equally for all purposes as set out in Article 1;

(b) under their rules of origin, the country to be determined as the origin of a particular good is either the country where the good has been wholly obtained or, when more than one country is concerned in the production of the good, the country where the last substantial transformation has been carried out;

(c) the rules of origin that they apply to imports and exports are not more stringent than the rules of origin they apply to determine whether or not a good is domestic and shall not discriminate between other Members, irrespective of the affiliation of the manufacturers of the good concerned;

(d) the rules of origin are administered in a consistent, uniform, impartial and reasonable manner;

(e) their laws, regulations, judicial decisions and administrative rulings of general application relating to rules of origin are published as if they were subject to, and in accordance with, the provisions of paragraph 1 of Article X of GATT 1994;

(f) upon the request of an exporter, importer or any person with a justifiable cause, assessments of the origin they would accord to a good are issued as soon as possible but no later than 150 days after a request for such an assessment provided that all necessary elements have been submitted. Requests for such assessments shall be accepted before trade in the good concerned begins and may be accepted at any later point in time. Such assessments shall remain valid for three years provided that the facts and conditions, including the rules of origin, under which they have been made remain comparable. Provided that the parties concerned are informed in advance, such assessments will no longer be valid when a decision contrary to the assessment is made in a review as referred to in subparagraph (h). Such assessments shall be made publicly available subject to the provisions of subparagraph (i);

(g) when introducing changes to their rules of origin or new rules of origin, they shall not apply such changes retroactively as defined in, and without prejudice to, their laws or regulations;

(h) any administrative action which they take in relation to the determination of origin is reviewable promptly by judicial, arbitral or administrative tribunals or procedures, independent of the authority issuing the determination, which can effect the modification or reversal of the determination;

(i) all information which is by nature confidential or which is provided on a confidential basis for the purpose of the application of rules of origin is treated as strictly confidential by the authorities concerned, which shall not disclose it without the specific permission of the person or government providing such information, except to the extent that it may be required to be disclosed in the context of judicial proceedings.

Part III

PROCEDURAL ARRANGEMENTS ON NOTIFICATION, REVIEW, CONSULTATION AND DISPUTE SETTLEMENT

Article 4

Institutions

1. There is hereby established a Committee on Rules of Origin (referred to in this Agreement as "the Committee") composed of the representatives from each of the Members. The Committee shall elect its own Chairman and shall meet as necessary, but not less than once a year, for the purpose of affording Members the opportunity to consult on matters relating to the operation of Parts I, II, III and IV or the furtherance of the objectives set out in these Parts and to carry out such other responsibilities assigned to it under this Agreement or by the Council for Trade in Goods. Where appropriate, the Committee shall request information and advice from the Technical Committee referred to in paragraph 2 on matters related to this Agreement. The Committee may also request such other work from the Technical Committee as it considers appropriate for the furtherance of the above-mentioned objectives of this Agreement. The WTO Secretariat shall act as the secretariat to the Committee.

2. There shall be established a Technical Committee on Rules of Origin (referred to in this Agreement as "the Technical Committee") under the auspices of the Customs Co-operation Council (CCC) as set out in Annex I. The Technical Committee shall carry out the technical work called for in Part IV and prescribed in Annex I. Where appropriate, the Technical Committee shall request information and advice from the Committee on matters related to this Agreement. The Technical Committee may also request such other work from the Committee as it considers appropriate for

the furtherance of the above-mentioned objectives of the Agreement. The CCC Secretariat shall act as the secretariat to the Technical Committee.

Article 5

Information and Procedures for Modification and Introduction of New Rules of Origin

1. Each Member shall provide to the Secretariat, within 90 days after the date of entry into force of the WTO Agreement for it, its rules of origin, judicial decisions, and administrative rulings of general application relating to rules of origin in effect on that date. If by inadvertence a rule of origin has not been provided, the Member concerned shall provide it immediately after this fact becomes known. Lists of information received and available with the Secretariat shall be circulated to the Members by the Secretariat.

2. During the period referred to in Article 2, Members introducing modifications, other than *de minimis* modifications, to their rules of origin or introducing new rules of origin, which, for the purpose of this Article, shall include any rule of origin referred to in paragraph 1 and not provided to the Secretariat, shall publish a notice to that effect at least 60 days before the entry into force of the modified or new rule in such a manner as to enable interested parties to become acquainted with the intention to modify a rule of origin or to introduce a new rule of origin, unless exceptional circumstances arise or threaten to arise for a Member. In these exceptional cases, the Member shall publish the modified or new rule as soon as possible.

Article 6

Review

1. The Committee shall review annually the implementation and operation of Parts II and III of this Agreement having regard to its objectives. The Committee shall annually inform the Council for Trade in Goods of developments during the period covered by such reviews.

2. The Committee shall review the provisions of Parts I, II and III and propose amendments as necessary to reflect the results of the harmonization work programme.

3. The Committee, in cooperation with the Technical Committee, shall set up a mechanism to consider and propose amendments to the results of the harmonization work programme, taking into account the objectives and principles set out in Article 9. This may include instances where the rules need to be made more operational or need to be updated to take into account new production processes as affected by any technological change.

Article 7

Consultation

The provisions of Article XXII of GATT 1994, as elaborated and applied by the Dispute Settlement Understanding, are applicable to this Agreement.

Article 8

Dispute Settlement

The provisions of Article XXIII of GATT 1994, as elaborated and applied by the Dispute Settlement Understanding, are applicable to this Agreement.

Part IV

HARMONIZATION OF RULES OF ORIGIN

Article 9

Objectives and Principles

1. With the objectives of harmonizing rules of origin and, *inter alia*, providing more certainty in the conduct of world trade, the Ministerial Conference shall undertake the work programme set out below in conjunction with the CCC, on the basis of the following principles:

(a) rules of origin should be applied equally for all purposes as set out in Article 1;

(b) rules of origin should provide for the country to be determined as the origin of a particular good to be either the country where the good has been wholly obtained or, when more than one country is concerned in the production of the good, the country where the last substantial transformation has been carried out;

(c) rules of origin should be objective, understandable and predictable;

(d) notwithstanding the measure or instrument to which they may be linked, rules of origin should not be used as instruments to pursue trade objectives directly or indirectly. They should not themselves create restrictive, distorting or disruptive effects on international trade. They should not pose unduly strict requirements or require the fulfilment of a certain condition not relating to manufacturing or processing as a prerequisite for the determination of the country of origin. However, costs not directly related to manufacturing or processing may be included for purposes of the application of an ad valorem percentage criterion;

(e) rules of origin should be administrable in a consistent, uniform, impartial and reasonable manner;

(f) rules of origin should be coherent;

(g) rules of origin should be based on a positive standard. Negative standards may be used to clarify a positive standard.

Work Programme

2. (a) The work programme shall be initiated as soon after the entry into force of the WTO Agreement as possible and will be completed within three years of initiation.

(b) The Committee and the Technical Committee provided for in Article 4 shall be the appropriate bodies to conduct this work.

(c) To provide for detailed input by the CCC, the Committee shall request the Technical Committee to provide its interpretations and opinions resulting from the work described below on the basis of the principles listed in paragraph 1. To ensure timely completion of the work programme for harmonization, such work shall be conducted on a product sector basis, as represented by various chapters or sections of the Harmonized System (HS) nomenclature.

(i) *Wholly Obtained and Minimal Operations or Processes*

The Technical Committee shall develop harmonized definitions of:

— the goods that are to be considered as being wholly obtained in one country. This work shall be as detailed as possible;

— minimal operations or processes that do not by themselves confer origin to a good.

The results of this work shall be submitted to the Committee within three months of receipt of the request from the Committee.

(ii) *Substantial Transformation—Change in Tariff Classification*

— The Technical Committee shall consider and elaborate upon, on the basis of the criterion of substantial transformation, the use of change in tariff subheading or heading when developing rules of origin for particular products or a product sector and, if appropriate, the minimum change within the nomenclature that meets this criterion.

—The Technical Committee shall divide the above work on a product basis taking into account the chapters or sections of the HS nomenclature, so as to submit results of its work to the Committee at least on a quarterly basis. The Technical Committee shall complete the above work within one year and three months from receipt of the request of the Committee.

(iii) *Substantial Transformation—Supplementary Criteria*

Upon completion of the work under subparagraph (ii) for each product sector or individual product category where the exclusive use of the HS nomenclature does not allow for the expression of substantial transformation, the Technical Committee:

—shall consider and elaborate upon, on the basis of the criterion of substantial transformation, the use, in a supplementary or exclusive manner, of other requirements, including ad valorem percentages[4] and/or manufacturing or processing operations,[5] when developing rules of origin for particular products or a product sector;

—may provide explanations for its proposals;

—shall divide the above work on a product basis taking into account the chapters or sections of the HS nomenclature, so as to submit results of its work to the Committee at least on a quarterly basis. The Technical Committee shall complete the above work within two years and three months of receipt of the request from the Committee.

Role of the Committee

3. On the basis of the principles listed in paragraph 1:

(a) the Committee shall consider the interpretations and opinions of the Technical Committee periodically in accordance with the time-frames provided in subparagraphs (i), (ii) and (iii) of paragraph 2(c) with a view to endorsing such interpretations and opinions. The Committee may request the Technical Committee to refine or elaborate its work and/or to develop new approaches. To assist the Technical Committee, the

4. If the ad valorem criterion is prescribed, the method for calculating this percentage shall also be indicated in the rules of origin.

5. If the criterion of manufacturing or processing operation is prescribed, the operation that confers origin on the product concerned shall be precisely specified.

Committee should provide its reasons for requests for additional work and, as appropriate, suggest alternative approaches;

(b) upon completion of all the work identified in subparagraphs (i), (ii) and (iii) of paragraph 2(c), the Committee shall consider the results in terms of their overall coherence.

Results of the Harmonization Work Programme and Subsequent Work

4. The Ministerial Conference shall establish the results of the harmonization work programme in an annex as an integral part of this Agreement.[6] The Ministerial Conference shall establish a time-frame for the entry into force of this annex.

Annex I

TECHNICAL COMMITTEE ON RULES OF ORIGIN

Responsibilities

1. The ongoing responsibilities of the Technical Committee shall include the following:

(a) at the request of any member of the Technical Committee, to examine specific technical problems arising in the day-to-day administration of the rules of origin of Members and to give advisory opinions on appropriate solutions based upon the facts presented;

(b) to furnish information and advice on any matters concerning the origin determination of goods as may be requested by any Member or the Committee;

(c) to prepare and circulate periodic reports on the technical aspects of the operation and status of this Agreement; and

(d) to review annually the technical aspects of the implementation and operation of Parts II and III.

2. The Technical Committee shall exercise such other responsibilities as the Committee may request of it.

3. The Technical Committee shall attempt to conclude its work on specific matters, especially those referred to it by Members or the Committee, in a reasonably short period of time.

6. At the same time, consideration shall be given to arrangements concerning the settlement of disputes relating to customs classification.

Representation

4. Each Member shall have the right to be represented on the Technical Committee. Each Member may nominate one delegate and one or more alternates to be its representatives on the Technical Committee. Such a Member so represented on the Technical Committee is hereinafter referred to as a "member" of the Technical Committee. Representatives of members of the Technical Committee may be assisted by advisers at meetings of the Technical Committee. The WTO Secretariat may also attend such meetings with observer status.

5. Members of the CCC which are not Members of the WTO may be represented at meetings of the Technical Committee by one delegate and one or more alternates. Such representatives shall attend meetings of the Technical Committee as observers.

6. Subject to the approval of the Chairman of the Technical Committee, the Secretary-General of the CCC (referred to in this Annex as "the Secretary-General") may invite representatives of governments which are neither Members of the WTO nor members of the CCC and representatives of international governmental and trade organizations to attend meetings of the Technical Committee as observers.

7. Nominations of delegates, alternates and advisers to meetings of the Technical Committee shall be made to the Secretary-General.

Meetings

8. The Technical Committee shall meet as necessary, but not less than once a year.

Procedures

9. The Technical Committee shall elect its own Chairman and shall establish its own procedures.

Annex II

COMMON DECLARATION WITH REGARD TO PREFERENTIAL RULES OF ORIGIN

1. Recognizing that some Members apply preferential rules of origin, distinct from non-preferential rules of origin, the Members hereby *agree* as follows.

2. For the purposes of this Common Declaration, preferential rules of origin shall be defined as those laws, regulations and administrative

determinations of general application applied by any Member to determine whether goods qualify for preferential treatment under contractual or autonomous trade regimes leading to the granting of tariff preferences going beyond the application of paragraph 1 of Article I of GATT 1994.

3. The Members *agree* to ensure that:

(a) when they issue administrative determinations of general application, the requirements to be fulfilled are clearly defined. In particular:

(i) in cases where the criterion of change of tariff classification is applied, such a preferential rule of origin, and any exceptions to the rule, must clearly specify the subheadings or headings within the tariff nomenclature that are addressed by the rule;

(ii) in cases where the ad valorem percentage criterion is applied, the method for calculating this percentage shall also be indicated in the preferential rules of origin;

(iii) in cases where the criterion of manufacturing or processing operation is prescribed, the operation that confers preferential origin shall be precisely specified;

(b) their preferential rules of origin are based on a positive standard. Preferential rules of origin that state what does not confer preferential origin (negative standard) are permissible as part of a clarification of a positive standard or in individual cases where a positive determination of preferential origin is not necessary;

(c) their laws, regulations, judicial decisions and administrative rulings of general application relating to preferential rules of origin are published as if they were subject to, and in accordance with, the provisions of paragraph 1 of Article X of GATT 1994;

(d) upon request of an exporter, importer or any person with a justifiable cause, assessments of the preferential origin they would accord to a good are issued as soon as possible but no later than 150 days[7] after a request for such an assessment provided that all necessary elements have been submitted. Requests for such assessments shall be accepted before trade in the good concerned begins and may be accepted at any later point in time. Such assessments shall remain valid for three years provided that the facts and conditions, including the preferential rules of origin, under which they have been made remain comparable. Provided

7. In respect of requests made during the first year from entry into force of the WTO Agreement, Members shall only be required to issue these assessments as soon as possible.

that the parties concerned are informed in advance, such assessments will no longer be valid when a decision contrary to the assessment is made in a review as referred to in subparagraph (f). Such assessments shall be made publicly available subject to the provisions of subparagraph (g);

(e) when introducing changes to their preferential rules of origin or new preferential rules of origin, they shall not apply such changes retroactively as defined in, and without prejudice to, their laws or regulations;

(f) any administrative action which they take in relation to the determination of preferential origin is reviewable promptly by judicial, arbitral or administrative tribunals or procedures, independent of the authority issuing the determination, which can effect the modification or reversal of the determination;

(g) all information that is by nature confidential or that is provided on a confidential basis for the purpose of the application of preferential rules of origin is treated as strictly confidential by the authorities concerned, which shall not disclose it without the specific permission of the person or government providing such information, except to the extent that it may be required to be disclosed in the context of judicial proceedings.

4. Members *agree* to provide to the Secretariat promptly their preferential rules of origin, including a listing of the preferential arrangements to which they apply, judicial decisions, and administrative rulings of general application relating to their preferential rules of origin in effect on the date of entry into force of the WTO Agreement for the Member concerned. Furthermore, Members agree to provide any modifications to their preferential rules of origin or new preferential rules of origin as soon as possible to the Secretariat. Lists of information received and available with the Secretariat shall be circulated to the Members by the Secretariat.

Document 32

AGREEMENT ON IMPORT LICENSING PROCEDURES

Members,

Having regard to the Multilateral Trade Negotiations;

Desiring to further the objectives of GATT 1994;

Taking into account the particular trade, development and financial needs of developing country Members;

Recognizing the usefulness of automatic import licensing for certain purposes and that such licensing should not be used to restrict trade;

Recognizing that import licensing may be employed to administer measures such as those adopted pursuant to the relevant provisions of GATT 1994;

Recognizing the provisions of GATT 1994 as they apply to import licensing procedures;

Desiring to ensure that import licensing procedures are not utilized in a manner contrary to the principles and obligations of GATT 1994;

Recognizing that the flow of international trade could be impeded by the inappropriate use of import licensing procedures;

Convinced that import licensing, particularly non-automatic import licensing, should be implemented in a transparent and predictable manner;

Recognizing that non-automatic licensing procedures should be no more administratively burdensome than absolutely necessary to administer the relevant measure;

Desiring to simplify, and bring transparency to, the administrative procedures and practices used in international trade, and to ensure the fair and equitable application and administration of such procedures and practices;

Desiring to provide for a consultative mechanism and the speedy, effective and equitable resolution of disputes arising under this Agreement;

Hereby *agree* as follows:

Article 1

General Provisions

1. For the purpose of this Agreement, import licensing is defined as administrative procedures[1] used for the operation of import licensing regimes requiring the submission of an application or other documentation (other than that required for customs purposes) to the relevant administrative body as a prior condition for importation into the customs territory of the importing Member.

2. Members shall ensure that the administrative procedures used to implement import licensing regimes are in conformity with the relevant provisions of GATT 1994 including its annexes and protocols, as interpreted by this Agreement, with a view to preventing trade distortions that may arise from an inappropriate operation of those procedures, taking into account the economic development purposes and financial and trade needs of developing country Members.[2]

3. The rules for import licensing procedures shall be neutral in application and administered in a fair and equitable manner.

4. (a) The rules and all information concerning procedures for the submission of applications, including the eligibility of persons, firms and institutions to make such applications, the administrative body(ies) to be approached, and the lists of products subject to the licensing requirement shall be published, in the sources notified to the Committee on Import

1. Those procedures referred to as "licensing" as well as other similar administrative procedures.

2. Nothing in this Agreement shall be taken as implying that the basis, scope or duration of a measure being implemented by a licensing procedure is subject to question under this Agreement.

Licensing provided for in Article 4 (referred to in this Agreement as "the Committee"), in such a manner as to enable governments[3] and traders to become acquainted with them. Such publication shall take place, whenever practicable, 21 days prior to the effective date of the requirement but in all events not later than such effective date. Any exception, derogations or changes in or from the rules concerning licensing procedures or the list of products subject to import licensing shall also be published in the same manner and within the same time periods as specified above. Copies of these publications shall also be made available to the Secretariat.

(b) Members which wish to make comments in writing shall be provided the opportunity to discuss these comments upon request. The concerned Member shall give due consideration to these comments and results of discussion.

5. Application forms and, where applicable, renewal forms shall be as simple as possible. Such documents and information as are considered strictly necessary for the proper functioning of the licensing regime may be required on application.

6. Application procedures and, where applicable, renewal procedures shall be as simple as possible. Applicants shall be allowed a reasonable period for the submission of licence applications. Where there is a closing date, this period should be at least 21 days with provision for extension in circumstances where insufficient applications have been received within this period. Applicants shall have to approach only one administrative body in connection with an application. Where it is strictly indispensable to approach more than one administrative body, applicants shall not need to approach more than three administrative bodies.

7. No application shall be refused for minor documentation errors which do not alter basic data contained therein. No penalty greater than necessary to serve merely as a warning shall be imposed in respect of any omission or mistake in documentation or procedures which is obviously made without fraudulent intent or gross negligence.

8. Licensed imports shall not be refused for minor variations in value, quantity or weight from the amount designated on the licence due to differences occurring during shipment, differences incidental to bulk loading and other minor differences consistent with normal commercial practice.

3. For the purpose of this Agreement, the term "governments" is deemed to include the competent authorities of the European Communities.

9. The foreign exchange necessary to pay for licensed imports shall be made available to licence holders on the same basis as to importers of goods not requiring import licences.

10. With regard to security exceptions, the provisions of Article XXI of GATT 1994 apply.

11. The provisions of this Agreement shall not require any Member to disclose confidential information which would impede law enforcement or otherwise be contrary to the public interest or would prejudice the legitimate commercial interests of particular enterprises, public or private.

Article 2

Automatic Import Licensing[4]

1. Automatic import licensing is defined as import licensing where approval of the application is granted in all cases, and which is in accordance with the requirements of paragraph 2(a).

2. The following provisions,[5] in addition to those in paragraphs 1 through 11 of Article 1 and paragraph 1 of this Article, shall apply to automatic import licensing procedures:

(a) automatic licensing procedures shall not be administered in such a manner as to have restricting effects on imports subject to automatic licensing. Automatic licensing procedures shall be deemed to have trade-restricting effects unless, *inter alia*:

(i) any person, firm or institution which fulfils the legal requirements of the importing Member for engaging in import operations involving products subject to automatic licensing is equally eligible to apply for and to obtain import licences;

(ii) applications for licences may be submitted on any working day prior to the customs clearance of the goods;

(iii) applications for licences when submitted in appropriate and complete form are approved immediately on receipt, to the extent administratively feasible, but within a maximum of 10 working days;

4. Those import licensing procedures requiring a security which have no restrictive effects on imports are to be considered as falling within the scope of paragraphs 1 and 2.

5. A developing country Member, other than a developing country Member which was a Party to the Agreement on Import Licensing Procedures done on 12 April 1979, which has specific difficulties with the requirements of subparagraphs (a)(ii) and (a)(iii) may, upon notification to the Committee, delay the application of these subparagraphs by not more than two years from the date of entry into force of the WTO Agreement for such Member.

(b) Members recognize that automatic import licensing may be necessary whenever other appropriate procedures are not available. Automatic import licensing may be maintained as long as the circumstances which gave rise to its introduction prevail and as long as its underlying administrative purposes cannot be achieved in a more appropriate way.

Article 3

Non-Automatic Import Licensing

1. The following provisions, in addition to those in paragraphs 1 through 11 of Article 1, shall apply to non-automatic import licensing procedures. Non-automatic import licensing procedures are defined as import licensing not falling within the definition contained in paragraph 1 of Article 2.

2. Non-automatic licensing shall not have trade-restrictive or -distortive effects on imports additional to those caused by the imposition of the restriction. Non-automatic licensing procedures shall correspond in scope and duration to the measure they are used to implement, and shall be no more administratively burdensome than absolutely necessary to administer the measure.

3. In the case of licensing requirements for purposes other than the implementation of quantitative restrictions, Members shall publish sufficient information for other Members and traders to know the basis for granting and/or allocating licences.

4. Where a Member provides the possibility for persons, firms or institutions to request exceptions or derogations from a licensing requirement, it shall include this fact in the information published under paragraph 4 of Article 1 as well as information on how to make such a request and, to the extent possible, an indication of the circumstances under which requests would be considered.

5. (a) Members shall provide, upon the request of any Member having an interest in the trade in the product concerned, all relevant information concerning:

(i) the administration of the restrictions;

(ii) the import licences granted over a recent period;

(iii) the distribution of such licences among supplying countries;

(iv) where practicable, import statistics (i.e. value and/or volume) with respect to the products subject to import licensing. Developing country Members would not be expected to take additional administrative or financial burdens on this account;

(b) Members administering quotas by means of licensing shall publish the overall amount of quotas to be applied by quantity and/or value, the opening and closing dates of quotas, and any change thereof, within the time periods specified in paragraph 4 of Article 1 and in such a manner as to enable governments and traders to become acquainted with them;

(c) in the case of quotas allocated among supplying countries, the Member applying the restrictions shall promptly inform all other Members having an interest in supplying the product concerned of the shares in the quota currently allocated, by quantity or value, to the various supplying countries and shall publish this information within the time periods specified in paragraph 4 of Article 1 and in such a manner as to enable governments and traders to become acquainted with them;

(d) where situations arise which make it necessary to provide for an early opening date of quotas, the information referred to in paragraph 4 of Article 1 should be published within the time-periods specified in paragraph 4 of Article 1 and in such a manner as to enable governments and traders to become acquainted with them;

(e) any person, firm or institution which fulfils the legal and administrative requirements of the importing Member shall be equally eligible to apply and to be considered for a licence. If the licence application is not approved, the applicant shall, on request, be given the reason therefor and shall have a right of appeal or review in accordance with the domestic legislation or procedures of the importing Member;

(f) the period for processing applications shall, except when not possible for reasons outside the control of the Member, not be longer than 30 days if applications are considered as and when received, i.e. on a first-come first-served basis, and no longer than 60 days if all applications are considered simultaneously. In the latter case, the period for processing applications shall be considered to begin on the day following the closing date of the announced application period;

(g) the period of licence validity shall be of reasonable duration and not be so short as to preclude imports. The period of licence validity shall not preclude imports from distant sources, except in special cases where imports are necessary to meet unforeseen short-term requirements;

(h) when administering quotas, Members shall not prevent importation from being effected in accordance with the issued licences, and shall not discourage the full utilization of quotas;

(i) when issuing licences, Members shall take into account the desirability of issuing licences for products in economic quantities;

(j) in allocating licences, the Member should consider the import performance of the applicant. In this regard, consideration should be given as to whether licences issued to applicants in the past have been fully utilized during a recent representative period. In cases where licences have not been fully utilized, the Member shall examine the reasons for this and take these reasons into consideration when allocating new licences. Consideration shall also be given to ensuring a reasonable distribution of licences to new importers, taking into account the desirability of issuing licences for products in economic quantities. In this regard, special consideration should be given to those importers importing products originating in developing country Members and, in particular, the least-developed country Members;

(k) in the case of quotas administered through licences which are not allocated among supplying countries, licence holders[6] shall be free to choose the sources of imports. In the case of quotas allocated among supplying countries, the licence shall clearly stipulate the country or countries;

(*l*) in applying paragraph 8 of Article 1, compensating adjustments may be made in future licence allocations where imports exceeded a previous licence level.

Article 4

Institutions

There is hereby established a Committee on Import Licensing composed of representatives from each of the Members. The Committee shall elect its own Chairman and Vice-Chairman and shall meet as necessary for the purpose of affording Members the opportunity of consulting on any matters relating to the operation of this Agreement or the furtherance of its objectives.

Article 5

Notification

1. Members which institute licensing procedures or changes in these procedures shall notify the Committee of such within 60 days of publication.

6. Sometimes referred to as "quota holders."

2. Notifications of the institution of import licensing procedures shall include the following information:

(a) list of products subject to licensing procedures;

(b) contact point for information on eligibility;

(c) administrative body(ies) for submission of applications;

(d) date and name of publication where licensing procedures are published;

(e) indication of whether the licensing procedure is automatic or non-automatic according to definitions contained in Articles 2 and 3;

(f) in the case of automatic import licensing procedures, their administrative purpose;

(g) in the case of non-automatic import licensing procedures, indication of the measure being implemented through the licensing procedure; and

(h) expected duration of the licensing procedure if this can be estimated with some probability, and if not, reason why this information cannot be provided.

3. Notifications of changes in import licensing procedures shall indicate the elements mentioned above, if changes in such occur.

4. Members shall notify the Committee of the publication(s) in which the information required in paragraph 4 of Article 1 will be published.

5. Any interested Member which considers that another Member has not notified the institution of a licensing procedure or changes therein in accordance with the provisions of paragraphs 1 through 3 may bring the matter to the attention of such other Member. If notification is not made promptly thereafter, such Member may itself notify the licensing procedure or changes therein, including all relevant and available information.

Article 6

Consultation and Dispute Settlement

Consultations and the settlement of disputes with respect to any matter affecting the operation of this Agreement shall be subject to the provisions of

Articles XXII and XXIII of GATT 1994, as elaborated and applied by the Dispute Settlement Understanding.

Article 7

Review

1. The Committee shall review as necessary, but at least once every two years, the implementation and operation of this Agreement, taking into account the objectives thereof, and the rights and obligations contained therein.

2. As a basis for the Committee review, the Secretariat shall prepare a factual report based on information provided under Article 5, responses to the annual questionnaire on import licensing procedures[7] and other relevant reliable information which is available to it. This report shall provide a synopsis of the aforementioned information, in particular indicating any changes or developments during the period under review, and including any other information as agreed by the Committee.

3. Members undertake to complete the annual questionnaire on import licensing procedures promptly and in full.

4. The Committee shall inform the Council for Trade in Goods of developments during the period covered by such reviews.

Article 8

Final Provisions

Reservations

1. Reservations may not be entered in respect of any of the provisions of this Agreement without the consent of the other Members.

Domestic Legislation

2. (a) Each Member shall ensure, not later than the date of entry into force of the WTO Agreement for it, the conformity of its laws, regulations and administrative procedures with the provisions of this Agreement.

(b) Each Member shall inform the Committee of any changes in its laws and regulations relevant to this Agreement and in the administration of such laws and regulations.

7. Originally circulated as GATT 1947 document L/3515 of 23 March 1971.

Document 33

AGREEMENT ON SUBSIDIES AND COUNTERVAILING MEASURES

Members hereby *agree* as follows:

Part I: General Provisions

Article 1

Definition of a Subsidy

1.1 For the purpose of this Agreement, a subsidy shall be deemed to exist if:

(a)(1) there is a financial contribution by a government or any public body within the territory of a Member (referred to in this Agreement as "government"), i.e. where:

(i) a government practice involves a direct transfer of funds (e.g. grants, loans, and equity infusion), potential direct transfers of funds or liabilities (e.g. loan guarantees);

(ii) government revenue that is otherwise due is foregone or not collected (e.g. fiscal incentives such as tax credits);[1]

1. In accordance with the provisions of Article XVI of GATT 1994 (Note to Article XVI) and the provisions of Annexes I through III of this Agreement, the exemption of an exported product from duties or taxes borne by the like product when destined for domestic consumption, or the remission of such duties or taxes in amounts not in excess of those which have accrued, shall not be deemed to be a subsidy.

(iii) a government provides goods or services other than general infrastructure, or purchases goods;

(iv) a government makes payments to a funding mechanism, or entrusts or directs a private body to carry out one or more of the type of functions illustrated in (i) to (iii) above which would normally be vested in the government and the practice, in no real sense, differs from practices normally followed by governments;

or

(a)(2) there is any form of income or price support in the sense of Article XVI of GATT 1994;

and

(b) a benefit is thereby conferred.

1.2 A subsidy as defined in paragraph 1 shall be subject to the provisions of Part II or shall be subject to the provisions of Part III or V only if such a subsidy is specific in accordance with the provisions of Article 2.

Article 2

Specificity

2.1 In order to determine whether a subsidy, as defined in paragraph 1 of Article 1, is specific to an enterprise or industry or group of enterprises or industries (referred to in this Agreement as "certain enterprises") within the jurisdiction of the granting authority, the following principles shall apply:

(a) Where the granting authority, or the legislation pursuant to which the granting authority operates, explicitly limits access to a subsidy to certain enterprises, such subsidy shall be specific.

(b) Where the granting authority, or the legislation pursuant to which the granting authority operates, establishes objective criteria or conditions[2] governing the eligibility for, and the amount of, a subsidy, specificity shall not exist, provided that the eligibility is automatic and that such criteria and conditions are strictly adhered to. The criteria or conditions must be clearly spelled out in law, regulation, or other official document, so as to be capable of verification.

2. Objective criteria or conditions, as used herein, mean criteria or conditions which are neutral, which do not favour certain enterprises over others, and which are economic in nature and horizontal in application, such as number of employees or size of enterprise.

(c) If, notwithstanding any appearance of non-specificity resulting from the application of the principles laid down in subparagraphs (a) and (b), there are reasons to believe that the subsidy may in fact be specific, other factors may be considered. Such factors are: use of a subsidy programme by a limited number of certain enterprises, predominant use by certain enterprises, the granting of disproportionately large amounts of subsidy to certain enterprises, and the manner in which discretion has been exercised by the granting authority in the decision to grant a subsidy.[3] In applying this subparagraph, account shall be taken of the extent of diversification of economic activities within the jurisdiction of the granting authority, as well as of the length of time during which the subsidy programme has been in operation.

2.2 A subsidy which is limited to certain enterprises located within a designated geographical region within the jurisdiction of the granting authority shall be specific. It is understood that the setting or change of generally applicable tax rates by all levels of government entitled to do so shall not be deemed to be a specific subsidy for the purposes of this Agreement.

2.3 Any subsidy falling under the provisions of Article 3 shall be deemed to be specific.

2.4 Any determination of specificity under the provisions of this Article shall be clearly substantiated on the basis of positive evidence.

Part II: Prohibited Subsidies

Article 3

Prohibition

3.1 Except as provided in the Agreement on Agriculture, the following subsidies, within the meaning of Article 1, shall be prohibited:

(a) subsidies contingent, in law or in fact,[4] whether solely or as one of several other conditions, upon export performance, including those illustrated in Annex I;[5]

3. In this regard, in particular, information on the frequency with which applications for a subsidy are refused or approved and the reasons for such decisions shall be considered.

4. This standard is met when the facts demonstrate that the granting of a subsidy, without having been made legally contingent upon export performance, is in fact tied to actual or anticipated exportation or export earnings. The mere fact that a subsidy is granted to enterprises which export shall not for that reason alone be considered to be an export subsidy within the meaning of this provision.

5. Measures referred to in Annex I as not constituting export subsidies shall not be prohibited under this or any other provision of this Agreement.

(b) subsidies contingent, whether solely or as one of several other conditions, upon the use of domestic over imported goods.

3.2 A Member shall neither grant nor maintain subsidies referred to in paragraph 1.

Article 4

Remedies

4.1 Whenever a Member has reason to believe that a prohibited subsidy is being granted or maintained by another Member, such Member may request consultations with such other Member.

4.2 A request for consultations under paragraph 1 shall include a statement of available evidence with regard to the existence and nature of the subsidy in question.

4.3 Upon request for consultations under paragraph 1, the Member believed to be granting or maintaining the subsidy in question shall enter into such consultations as quickly as possible. The purpose of the consultations shall be to clarify the facts of the situation and to arrive at a mutually agreed solution.

4.4 If no mutually agreed solution has been reached within 30 days[6] of the request for consultations, any Member party to such consultations may refer the matter to the Dispute Settlement Body ("DSB") for the immediate establishment of a panel, unless the DSB decides by consensus not to establish a panel.

4.5 Upon its establishment, the panel may request the assistance of the Permanent Group of Experts[7] (referred to in this Agreement as the "PGE") with regard to whether the measure in question is a prohibited subsidy. If so requested, the PGE shall immediately review the evidence with regard to the existence and nature of the measure in question and shall provide an opportunity for the Member applying or maintaining the measure to demonstrate that the measure in question is not a prohibited subsidy. The PGE shall report its conclusions to the panel within a time-limit determined by the panel. The PGE's conclusions on the issue of whether or not the measure in question is a prohibited subsidy shall be accepted by the panel without modification.

6. Any time-periods mentioned in this Article may be extended by mutual agreement.
7. As established in Article 24.

4.6 The panel shall submit its final report to the parties to the dispute. The report shall be circulated to all Members within 90 days of the date of the composition and the establishment of the panel's terms of reference.

4.7 If the measure in question is found to be a prohibited subsidy, the panel shall recommend that the subsidizing Member withdraw the subsidy without delay. In this regard, the panel shall specify in its recommendation the time-period within which the measure must be withdrawn.

4.8 Within 30 days of the issuance of the panel's report to all Members, the report shall be adopted by the DSB unless one of the parties to the dispute formally notifies the DSB of its decision to appeal or the DSB decides by consensus not to adopt the report.

4.9 Where a panel report is appealed, the Appellate Body shall issue its decision within 30 days from the date when the party to the dispute formally notifies its intention to appeal. When the Appellate Body considers that it cannot provide its report within 30 days, it shall inform the DSB in writing of the reasons for the delay together with an estimate of the period within which it will submit its report. In no case shall the proceedings exceed 60 days. The appellate report shall be adopted by the DSB and unconditionally accepted by the parties to the dispute unless the DSB decides by consensus not to adopt the appellate report within 20 days following its issuance to the Members.[8]

4.10 In the event the recommendation of the DSB is not followed within the time-period specified by the panel, which shall commence from the date of adoption of the panel's report or the Appellate Body's report, the DSB shall grant authorization to the complaining Member to take appropriate[9] countermeasures, unless the DSB decides by consensus to reject the request.

4.11 In the event a party to the dispute requests arbitration under paragraph 6 of Article 22 of the Dispute Settlement Understanding ("DSU"), the arbitrator shall determine whether the countermeasures are appropriate.[10]

4.12 For purposes of disputes conducted pursuant to this Article, except for time-periods specifically prescribed in this Article, time-periods

8. If a meeting of the DSB is not scheduled during this period, such a meeting shall be held for this purpose.

9. This expression is not meant to allow countermeasures that are disproportionate in light of the fact that the subsidies dealt with under these provisions are prohibited.

10. This expression is not meant to allow countermeasures that are disproportionate in light of the fact that the subsidies dealt with under these provisions are prohibited.

applicable under the DSU for the conduct of such disputes shall be half the time prescribed therein.

Part III: Actionable Subsidies

Article 5

Adverse Effects

No Member should cause, through the use of any subsidy referred to in paragraphs 1 and 2 of Article 1, adverse effects to the interests of other Members, i.e.:

(a) injury to the domestic industry of another Member;[11]

(b) nullification or impairment of benefits accruing directly or indirectly to other Members under GATT 1994 in particular the benefits of concessions bound under Article II of GATT 1994;[12]

(c) serious prejudice to the interests of another Member.[13]

This Article does not apply to subsidies maintained on agricultural products as provided in Article 13 of the Agreement on Agriculture.

Article 6

Serious Prejudice

6.1 Serious prejudice in the sense of paragraph (c) of Article 5 shall be deemed to exist in the case of:

(a) the total ad valorem subsidization[14] of a product exceeding 5 per cent;[15]

11. The term "injury to the domestic industry" is used here in the same sense as it is used in Part V.

12. The term "nullification or impairment" is used in this Agreement in the same sense as it is used in the relevant provisions of GATT 1994, and the existence of such nullification or impairment shall be established in accordance with the practice of application of these provisions.

13. The term "serious prejudice to the interests of another Member" is used in this Agreement in the same sense as it is used in paragraph 1 of Article XVI of GATT 1994, and includes threat of serious prejudice.

14. The total ad valorem subsidization shall be calculated in accordance with the provisions of Annex IV.

15. Since it is anticipated that civil aircraft will be subject to specific multilateral rules, the threshold in this subparagraph does not apply to civil aircraft.

(b) subsidies to cover operating losses sustained by an industry;

(c) subsidies to cover operating losses sustained by an enterprise, other than one-time measures which are non-recurrent and cannot be repeated for that enterprise and which are given merely to provide time for the development of long-term solutions and to avoid acute social problems;

(d) direct forgiveness of debt, i.e. forgiveness of government-held debt, and grants to cover debt repayment.[16]

6.2 Notwithstanding the provisions of paragraph 1, serious prejudice shall not be found if the subsidizing Member demonstrates that the subsidy in question has not resulted in any of the effects enumerated in paragraph 3.

6.3 Serious prejudice in the sense of paragraph (c) of Article 5 may arise in any case where one or several of the following apply:

(a) the effect of the subsidy is to displace or impede the imports of a like product of another Member into the market of the subsidizing Member;

(b) the effect of the subsidy is to displace or impede the exports of a like product of another Member from a third country market;

(c) the effect of the subsidy is a significant price undercutting by the subsidized product as compared with the price of a like product of another Member in the same market or significant price suppression, price depression or lost sales in the same market;

(d) the effect of the subsidy is an increase in the world market share of the subsidizing Member in a particular subsidized primary product or commodity[17] as compared to the average share it had during the previous period of three years and this increase follows a consistent trend over a period when subsidies have been granted.

6.4 For the purpose of paragraph 3(b), the displacement or impeding of exports shall include any case in which, subject to the provisions of paragraph 7, it has been demonstrated that there has been a change in relative shares of the market to the disadvantage of the non-subsidized like product

16. Members recognize that where royalty-based financing for a civil aircraft programme is not being fully repaid due to the level of actual sales falling below the level of forecast sales, this does not in itself constitute serious prejudice for the purposes of this subparagraph.

17. Unless other multilaterally agreed specific rules apply to the trade in the product or commodity in question.

(over an appropriately representative period sufficient to demonstrate clear trends in the development of the market for the product concerned, which, in normal circumstances, shall be at least one year). "Change in relative shares of the market" shall include any of the following situations: *(a)* there is an increase in the market share of the subsidized product; *(b)* the market share of the subsidized product remains constant in circumstances in which, in the absence of the subsidy, it would have declined; *(c)* the market share of the subsidized product declines, but at a slower rate than would have been the case in the absence of the subsidy.

6.5 For the purpose of paragraph 3(c), price undercutting shall include any case in which such price undercutting has been demonstrated through a comparison of prices of the subsidized product with prices of a non-subsidized like product supplied to the same market. The comparison shall be made at the same level of trade and at comparable times, due account being taken of any other factor affecting price comparability. However, if such a direct comparison is not possible, the existence of price undercutting may be demonstrated on the basis of export unit values.

6.6 Each Member in the market of which serious prejudice is alleged to have arisen shall, subject to the provisions of paragraph 3 of Annex V, make available to the parties to a dispute arising under Article 7, and to the panel established pursuant to paragraph 4 of Article 7, all relevant information that can be obtained as to the changes in market shares of the parties to the dispute as well as concerning prices of the products involved.

6.7 Displacement or impediment resulting in serious prejudice shall not arise under paragraph 3 where any of the following circumstances exist[18] during the relevant period:

(a) prohibition or restriction on exports of the like product from the complaining Member or on imports from the complaining Member into the third country market concerned;

(b) decision by an importing government operating a monopoly of trade or state trading in the product concerned to shift, for non-commercial reasons, imports from the complaining Member to another country or countries;

(c) natural disasters, strikes, transport disruptions or other *force majeure* substantially affecting production, qualities, quantities or prices of the product available for export from the complaining Member;

18. The fact that certain circumstances are referred to in this paragraph does not, in itself, confer upon them any legal status in terms of either GATT 1994 or this Agreement. These circumstances must not be isolated, sporadic or otherwise insignificant.

(d) existence of arrangements limiting exports from the complaining Member;

(e) voluntary decrease in the availability for export of the product concerned from the complaining Member (including, *inter alia*, a situation where firms in the complaining Member have been autonomously reallocating exports of this product to new markets);

(f) failure to conform to standards and other regulatory requirements in the importing country.

6.8 In the absence of circumstances referred to in paragraph 7, the existence of serious prejudice should be determined on the basis of the information submitted to or obtained by the panel, including information submitted in accordance with the provisions of Annex V.

6.9 This Article does not apply to subsidies maintained on agricultural products as provided in Article 13 of the Agreement on Agriculture.

Article 7

Remedies

7.1 Except as provided in Article 13 of the Agreement on Agriculture, whenever a Member has reason to believe that any subsidy referred to in Article 1, granted or maintained by another Member, results in injury to its domestic industry, nullification or impairment or serious prejudice, such Member may request consultations with such other Member.

7.2 A request for consultations under paragraph 1 shall include a statement of available evidence with regard to *(a)* the existence and nature of the subsidy in question, and *(b)* the injury caused to the domestic industry, or the nullification or impairment, or serious prejudice[19] caused to the interests of the Member requesting consultations.

7.3 Upon request for consultations under paragraph 1, the Member believed to be granting or maintaining the subsidy practice in question shall enter into such consultations as quickly as possible. The purpose of the consultations shall be to clarify the facts of the situation and to arrive at a mutually agreed solution.

19. In the event that the request relates to a subsidy deemed to result in serious prejudice in terms of paragraph 1 of Article 6, the available evidence of serious prejudice may be limited to the available evidence as to whether the conditions of paragraph 1 of Article 6 have been met or not.

7.4 If consultations do not result in a mutually agreed solution within 60 days,[20] any Member party to such consultations may refer the matter to the DSB for the establishment of a panel, unless the DSB decides by consensus not to establish a panel. The composition of the panel and its terms of reference shall be established within 15 days from the date when it is established.

7.5 The panel shall review the matter and shall submit its final report to the parties to the dispute. The report shall be circulated to all Members within 120 days of the date of the composition and establishment of the panel's terms of reference.

7.6 Within 30 days of the issuance of the panel's report to all Members, the report shall be adopted by the DSB[21] unless one of the parties to the dispute formally notifies the DSB of its decision to appeal or the DSB decides by consensus not to adopt the report.

7.7 Where a panel report is appealed, the Appellate Body shall issue its decision within 60 days from the date when the party to the dispute formally notifies its intention to appeal. When the Appellate Body considers that it cannot provide its report within 60 days, it shall inform the DSB in writing of the reasons for the delay together with an estimate of the period within which it will submit its report. In no case shall the proceedings exceed 90 days. The appellate report shall be adopted by the DSB and unconditionally accepted by the parties to the dispute unless the DSB decides by consensus not to adopt the appellate report within 20 days following its issuance to the Members.[22]

7.8 Where a panel report or an Appellate Body report is adopted in which it is determined that any subsidy has resulted in adverse effects to the interests of another Member within the meaning of Article 5, the Member granting or maintaining such subsidy shall take appropriate steps to remove the adverse effects or shall withdraw the subsidy.

7.9 In the event the Member has not taken appropriate steps to remove the adverse effects of the subsidy or withdraw the subsidy within six months from the date when the DSB adopts the panel report or the Appellate Body report, and in the absence of agreement on compensation, the DSB shall grant authorization to the complaining Member to take countermeasures,

20. Any time-periods mentioned in this Article may be extended by mutual agreement.

21. If a meeting of the DSB is not scheduled during this period, such a meeting shall be held for this purpose.

22. If a meeting of the DSB is not scheduled during this period, such a meeting shall be held for this purpose.

commensurate with the degree and nature of the adverse effects determined to exist, unless the DSB decides by consensus to reject the request.

7.10 In the event that a party to the dispute requests arbitration under paragraph 6 of Article 22 of the DSU, the arbitrator shall determine whether the countermeasures are commensurate with the degree and nature of the adverse effects determined to exist.

Part IV: Non-Actionable Subsidies

Article 8

Identification of Non-Actionable Subsidies

8.1 The following subsidies shall be considered as non-actionable:[23]

(a) subsidies which are not specific within the meaning of Article 2;

(b) subsidies which are specific within the meaning of Article 2 but which meet all of the conditions provided for in paragraphs 2(a), 2(b) or 2(c) below.

8.2 Notwithstanding the provisions of Parts III and V, the following subsidies shall be non-actionable:

(a) assistance for research activities conducted by firms or by higher education or research establishments on a contract basis with firms if:[24,25,26]

23. It is recognized that government assistance for various purposes is widely provided by Members and that the mere fact that such assistance may not qualify for non-actionable treatment under the provisions of this Article does not in itself restrict the ability of Members to provide such assistance.

24. Since it is anticipated that civil aircraft will be subject to specific multilateral rules, the provisions of this subparagraph do not apply to that product.

25. Not later than 18 months after the date of entry into force of the WTO Agreement, the Committee on Subsidies and Countervailing Measures provided for in Article 24 (referred to in this Agreement as "the Committee") shall review the operation of the provisions of subparagraph 2(a) with a view to making all necessary modifications to improve the operation of these provisions. In its consideration of possible modifications, the Committee shall carefully review the definitions of the categories set forth in this subparagraph in the light of the experience of Members in the operation of research programmes and the work in other relevant international institutions.

26. The provisions of this Agreement do not apply to fundamental research activities independently conducted by higher education or research establishments. The term "fundamental research" means an enlargement of general scientific and technical knowledge not linked to industrial or commercial objectives.

the assistance covers[27] not more than 75 per cent of the costs of industrial research[28] or 50 per cent of the costs of pre-competitive development activity[29,30]; and provided that such assistance is limited exclusively to:

(i) costs of personnel (researchers, technicians and other supporting staff employed exclusively in the research activity);

(ii) costs of instruments, equipment, land and buildings used exclusively and permanently (except when disposed of on a commercial basis) for the research activity;

(iii) costs of consultancy and equivalent services used exclusively for the research activity, including bought-in research, technical knowledge, patents, etc.;

(iv) additional overhead costs incurred directly as a result of the research activity;

(v) other running costs (such as those of materials, supplies and the like), incurred directly as a result of the research activity.

(b) assistance to disadvantaged regions within the territory of a Member given pursuant to a general framework of regional development[31] and non-specific (within the meaning of Article 2) within eligible regions provided that:

27. The allowable levels of non-actionable assistance referred to in this subparagraph shall be established by reference to the total eligible costs incurred over the duration of an individual project.

28. The term "industrial research" means planned search or critical investigation aimed at discovery of new knowledge, with the objective that such knowledge may be useful in developing new products, processes or services, or in bringing about a significant improvement to existing products, processes or services.

29. The term "pre-competitive development activity" means the translation of industrial research findings into a plan, blueprint or design for new, modified or improved products, processes or services whether intended for sale or use, including the creation of a first prototype which would not be capable of commercial use. It may further include the conceptual formulation and design of products, processes or services alternatives and initial demonstration or pilot projects, provided that these same projects cannot be converted or used for industrial application or commercial exploitation. It does not include routine or periodic alterations to existing products, production lines, manufacturing processes, services, and other on-going operations even though those alterations may represent improvements.

30. In the case of programmes which span industrial research and pre-competitive development activity, the allowable level of non-actionable assistance shall not exceed the simple average of the allowable levels of non-actionable assistance applicable to the above two categories, calculated on the basis of all eligible costs as set forth in items (i) to (v) of this subparagraph.

31. A "general framework of regional development" means that regional subsidy programmes are part of an internally consistent and generally applicable regional development policy and that regional development subsidies are not granted in isolated geographical points having no, or virtually no, influence on the development of a region.

(i) each disadvantaged region must be a clearly designated contiguous geographical area with a definable economic and administrative identity;

(ii) the region is considered as disadvantaged on the basis of neutral and objective criteria,[32] indicating that the region's difficulties arise out of more than temporary circumstances; such criteria must be clearly spelled out in law, regulation, or other official document, so as to be capable of verification;

(iii) the criteria shall include a measurement of economic development which shall be based on at least one of the following factors:

— one of either income per capita or household income per capita, or GDP per capita, which must not be above 85 per cent of the average for the territory concerned;

— unemployment rate, which must be at least 110 per cent of the average for the territory concerned;

as measured over a three-year period; such measurement, however, may be a composite one and may include other factors.

(c) assistance to promote adaptation of existing facilities[33] to new environmental requirements imposed by law and/or regulations which result in greater constraints and financial burden on firms, provided that the assistance:

(i) is a one-time non-recurring measure; and

(ii) is limited to 20 per cent of the cost of adaptation; and

(iii) does not cover the cost of replacing and operating the assisted investment, which must be fully borne by firms; and

32. "Neutral and objective criteria" means criteria which do not favour certain regions beyond what is appropriate for the elimination or reduction of regional disparities within the framework of the regional development policy. In this regard, regional subsidy programmes shall include ceilings on the amount of assistance which can be granted to each subsidized project. Such ceilings must be differentiated according to the different levels of development of assisted regions and must be expressed in terms of investment costs or cost of job creation. Within such ceilings, the distribution of assistance shall be sufficiently broad and even to avoid the predominant use of a subsidy by, or the granting of disproportionately large amounts of subsidy to, certain enterprises as provided for in Article 2.

33. The term "existing facilities" means facilities which have been in operation for at least two years at the time when new environmental requirements are imposed.

(iv) is directly linked to and proportionate to a firm's planned reduction of nuisances and pollution, and does not cover any manufacturing cost savings which may be achieved; and

(v) is available to all firms which can adopt the new equipment and/or production processes.

8.3 A subsidy programme for which the provisions of paragraph 2 are invoked shall be notified in advance of its implementation to the Committee in accordance with the provisions of Part VII. Any such notification shall be sufficiently precise to enable other Members to evaluate the consistency of the programme with the conditions and criteria provided for in the relevant provisions of paragraph 2. Members shall also provide the Committee with yearly updates of such notifications, in particular by supplying information on global expenditure for each programme, and on any modification of the programme. Other Members shall have the right to request information about individual cases of subsidization under a notified programme.[34]

8.4 Upon request of a Member, the Secretariat shall review a notification made pursuant to paragraph 3 and, where necessary, may require additional information from the subsidizing Member concerning the notified programme under review. The Secretariat shall report its findings to the Committee. The Committee shall, upon request, promptly review the findings of the Secretariat (or, if a review by the Secretariat has not been requested, the notification itself), with a view to determining whether the conditions and criteria laid down in paragraph 2 have not been met. The procedure provided for in this paragraph shall be completed at the latest at the first regular meeting of the Committee following the notification of a subsidy programme, provided that at least two months have elapsed between such notification and the regular meeting of the Committee. The review procedure described in this paragraph shall also apply, upon request, to substantial modifications of a programme notified in the yearly updates referred to in paragraph 3.

8.5 Upon the request of a Member, the determination by the Committee referred to in paragraph 4, or a failure by the Committee to make such a determination, as well as the violation, in individual cases, of the conditions set out in a notified programme, shall be submitted to binding arbitration. The arbitration body shall present its conclusions to the Members within 120 days from the date when the matter was referred to the arbitration body. Except as otherwise provided in this paragraph, the DSU shall apply to arbitrations conducted under this paragraph.

34. It is recognized that nothing in this notification provision requires the provision of confidential information, including confidential business information.

Article 9

Consultations and Authorized Remedies

9.1 If, in the course of implementation of a programme referred to in paragraph 2 of Article 8, notwithstanding the fact that the programme is consistent with the criteria laid down in that paragraph, a Member has reasons to believe that this programme has resulted in serious adverse effects to the domestic industry of that Member, such as to cause damage which would be difficult to repair, such Member may request consultations with the Member granting or maintaining the subsidy.

9.2 Upon request for consultations under paragraph 1, the Member granting or maintaining the subsidy programme in question shall enter into such consultations as quickly as possible. The purpose of the consultations shall be to clarify the facts of the situation and to arrive at a mutually acceptable solution.

9.3 If no mutually acceptable solution has been reached in consultations under paragraph 2 within 60 days of the request for such consultations, the requesting Member may refer the matter to the Committee.

9.4 Where a matter is referred to the Committee, the Committee shall immediately review the facts involved and the evidence of the effects referred to in paragraph 1. If the Committee determines that such effects exist, it may recommend to the subsidizing Member to modify this programme in such a way as to remove these effects. The Committee shall present its conclusions within 120 days from the date when the matter is referred to it under paragraph 3. In the event the recommendation is not followed within six months, the Committee shall authorize the requesting Member to take appropriate countermeasures commensurate with the nature and degree of the effects determined to exist.

Part V: Countervailing Measures

Article 10

Application of Article VI of GATT 1994[35]

Members shall take all necessary steps to ensure that the imposition of a

35. The provisions of Part II or III may be invoked in parallel with the provisions of Part V; however, with regard to the effects of a particular subsidy in the domestic market of the importing Member, only one form of relief (either a countervailing duty, if the requirements of Part V are met, or a countermeasure under Articles 4 or 7) shall be available. The provisions of Parts III and V shall not be invoked regarding measures considered non-actionable in

countervailing duty[36] on any product of the territory of any Member imported into the territory of another Member is in accordance with the provisions of Article VI of GATT 1994 and the terms of this Agreement. Countervailing duties may only be imposed pursuant to investigations initiated[37] and conducted in accordance with the provisions of this Agreement and the Agreement on Agriculture.

Article 11

Initiation and Subsequent Investigation

11.1 Except as provided in paragraph 6, an investigation to determine the existence, degree and effect of any alleged subsidy shall be initiated upon a written application by or on behalf of the domestic industry.

11.2 An application under paragraph 1 shall include sufficient evidence of the existence of *(a)* a subsidy and, if possible, its amount, *(b)* injury within the meaning of Article VI of GATT 1994 as interpreted by this Agreement, and *(c)* a causal link between the subsidized imports and the alleged injury. Simple assertion, unsubstantiated by relevant evidence, cannot be considered sufficient to meet the requirements of this paragraph. The application shall contain such information as is reasonably available to the applicant on the following:

(i) the identity of the applicant and a description of the volume and value of the domestic production of the like product by the applicant. Where a written application is made on behalf of the domestic industry, the application shall identify the industry on behalf of which the application is made by a list of all known domestic producers of the like product (or associations of domestic producers of the like product) and, to the extent possible, a description of the volume and value of domestic production of the like product accounted for by such producers;

(ii) a complete description of the allegedly subsidized product, the names of the country or countries of origin or export in question, the

---

accordance with the provisions of Part IV. However, measures referred to in paragraph 1(a) of Article 8 may be investigated in order to determine whether or not they are specific within the meaning of Article 2. In addition, in the case of a subsidy referred to in paragraph 2 of Article 8 conferred pursuant to a programme which has not been notified in accordance with paragraph 3 of Article 8, the provisions of Part III or V may be invoked, but such subsidy shall be treated as non-actionable if it is found to conform to the standards set forth in paragraph 2 of Article 8.

36. The term "countervailing duty" shall be understood to mean a special duty levied for the purpose of offsetting any subsidy bestowed directly or indirectly upon the manufacture, production or export of any merchandise, as provided for in paragraph 3 of Article VI of GATT 1994.

37. The term "initiated" as used hereinafter means procedural action by which a Member formally commences an investigation as provided in Article 11.

identity of each known exporter or foreign producer and a list of known persons importing the product in question;

(iii) evidence with regard to the existence, amount and nature of the subsidy in question;

(iv) evidence that alleged injury to a domestic industry is caused by subsidized imports through the effects of the subsidies; this evidence includes information on the evolution of the volume of the allegedly subsidized imports, the effect of these imports on prices of the like product in the domestic market and the consequent impact of the imports on the domestic industry, as demonstrated by relevant factors and indices having a bearing on the state of the domestic industry, such as those listed in paragraphs 2 and 4 of Article 15.

11.3 The authorities shall review the accuracy and adequacy of the evidence provided in the application to determine whether the evidence is sufficient to justify the initiation of an investigation.

11.4 An investigation shall not be initiated pursuant to paragraph 1 unless the authorities have determined, on the basis of an examination of the degree of support for, or opposition to, the application expressed[38] by domestic producers of the like product, that the application has been made by or on behalf of the domestic industry.[39] The application shall be considered to have been made "by or on behalf of the domestic industry" if it is supported by those domestic producers whose collective output constitutes more than 50 per cent of the total production of the like product produced by that portion of the domestic industry expressing either support for or opposition to the application. However, no investigation shall be initiated when domestic producers expressly supporting the application account for less than 25 per cent of total production of the like product produced by the domestic industry.

11.5 The authorities shall avoid, unless a decision has been made to initiate an investigation, any publicizing of the application for the initiation of an investigation.

11.6 If, in special circumstances, the authorities concerned decide to initiate an investigation without having received a written application by or

38. In the case of fragmented industries involving an exceptionally large number of producers, authorities may determine support and opposition by using statistically valid sampling techniques.

39. Members are aware that in the territory of certain Members employees of domestic producers of the like product or representatives of those employees may make or support an application for an investigation under paragraph 1.

on behalf of a domestic industry for the initiation of such investigation, they shall proceed only if they have sufficient evidence of the existence of a subsidy, injury and causal link, as described in paragraph 2, to justify the initiation of an investigation.

11.7 The evidence of both subsidy and injury shall be considered simultaneously *(a)* in the decision whether or not to initiate an investigation and *(b)* thereafter, during the course of the investigation, starting on a date not later than the earliest date on which in accordance with the provisions of this Agreement provisional measures may be applied.

11.8 In cases where products are not imported directly from the country of origin but are exported to the importing Member from an intermediate country, the provisions of this Agreement shall be fully applicable and the transaction or transactions shall, for the purposes of this Agreement, be regarded as having taken place between the country of origin and the importing Member.

11.9 An application under paragraph 1 shall be rejected and an investigation shall be terminated promptly as soon as the authorities concerned are satisfied that there is not sufficient evidence of either subsidization or of injury to justify proceeding with the case. There shall be immediate termination in cases where the amount of a subsidy is *de minimis*, or where the volume of subsidized imports, actual or potential, or the injury, is negligible. For the purpose of this paragraph, the amount of the subsidy shall be considered to be *de minimis* if the subsidy is less than 1 per cent ad valorem.

11.10 An investigation shall not hinder the procedures of customs clearance.

11.11 Investigations shall, except in special circumstances, be concluded within one year, and in no case more than 18 months, after their initiation.

Article 12

Evidence

12.1 Interested Members and all interested parties in a countervailing duty investigation shall be given notice of the information which the authorities require and ample opportunity to present in writing all evidence which they consider relevant in respect of the investigation in question.

12.1.1 Exporters, foreign producers or interested Members receiving questionnaires used in a countervailing duty investigation shall be given at least 30 days for reply.[40] Due consideration should be given to any request for an extension of the 30-day period and, upon cause shown, such an extension should be granted whenever practicable.

12.1.2 Subject to the requirement to protect confidential information, evidence presented in writing by one interested Member or interested party shall be made available promptly to other interested Members or interested parties participating in the investigation.

12.1.3 As soon as an investigation has been initiated, the authorities shall provide the full text of the written application received under paragraph 1 of Article 11 to the known exporters[41] and to the authorities of the exporting Member and shall make it available, upon request, to other interested parties involved. Due regard shall be paid to the protection of confidential information, as provided for in paragraph 4.

12.2. Interested Members and interested parties also shall have the right, upon justification, to present information orally. Where such information is provided orally, the interested Members and interested parties subsequently shall be required to reduce such submissions to writing. Any decision of the investigating authorities can only be based on such information and arguments as were on the written record of this authority and which were available to interested Members and interested parties participating in the investigation, due account having been given to the need to protect confidential information.

12.3 The authorities shall whenever practicable provide timely opportunities for all interested Members and interested parties to see all information that is relevant to the presentation of their cases, that is not confidential as defined in paragraph 4, and that is used by the authorities in a countervailing duty investigation, and to prepare presentations on the basis of this information.

12.4 Any information which is by nature confidential (for example, because its disclosure would be of significant competitive advantage to a competitor or because its disclosure would have a significantly adverse effect upon a person supplying the information or upon a person from whom the

40. As a general rule, the time-limit for exporters shall be counted from the date of receipt of the questionnaire, which for this purpose shall be deemed to have been received one week from the date on which it was sent to the respondent or transmitted to the appropriate diplomatic representatives of the exporting Member or, in the case of a separate customs territory Member of the WTO, an official representative of the exporting territory.

41. It being understood that where the number of exporters involved is particularly high, the full text of the application should instead be provided only to the authorities of the exporting Member or to the relevant trade association who then should forward copies to the exporters concerned.

supplier acquired the information), or which is provided on a confidential basis by parties to an investigation shall, upon good cause shown, be treated as such by the authorities. Such information shall not be disclosed without specific permission of the party submitting it.[42]

12.4.1 The authorities shall require interested Members or interested parties providing confidential information to furnish non-confidential summaries thereof. These summaries shall be in sufficient detail to permit a reasonable understanding of the substance of the information submitted in confidence. In exceptional circumstances, such Members or parties may indicate that such information is not susceptible of summary. In such exceptional circumstances, a statement of the reasons why summarization is not possible must be provided.

12.4.2 If the authorities find that a request for confidentiality is not warranted and if the supplier of the information is either unwilling to make the information public or to authorize its disclosure in generalized or summary form, the authorities may disregard such information unless it can be demonstrated to their satisfaction from appropriate sources that the information is correct.[43]

12.5 Except in circumstances provided for in paragraph 7, the authorities shall during the course of an investigation satisfy themselves as to the accuracy of the information supplied by interested Members or interested parties upon which their findings are based.

12.6 The investigating authorities may carry out investigations in the territory of other Members as required, provided that they have notified in good time the Member in question and unless that Member objects to the investigation. Further, the investigating authorities may carry out investigations on the premises of a firm and may examine the records of a firm if *(a)* the firm so agrees and *(b)* the Member in question is notified and does not object. The procedures set forth in Annex VI shall apply to investigations on the premises of a firm. Subject to the requirement to protect confidential information, the authorities shall make the results of any such investigations available, or shall provide disclosure thereof pursuant to paragraph 8, to the firms to which they pertain and may make such results available to the applicants.

42. Members are aware that in the territory of certain Members disclosure pursuant to a narrowly-drawn protective order may be required.

43. Members agree that requests for confidentiality should not be arbitrarily rejected. Members further agree that the investigating authority may request the waiving of confidentiality only regarding information relevant to the proceedings.

12.7 In cases in which any interested Member or interested party refuses access to, or otherwise does not provide, necessary information within a reasonable period or significantly impedes the investigation, preliminary and final determinations, affirmative or negative, may be made on the basis of the facts available.

12.8 The authorities shall, before a final determination is made, inform all interested Members and interested parties of the essential facts under consideration which form the basis for the decision whether to apply definitive measures. Such disclosure should take place in sufficient time for the parties to defend their interests.

12.9 For the purposes of this Agreement, "interested parties" shall include:

(i) an exporter or foreign producer or the importer of a product subject to investigation, or a trade or business association a majority of the members of which are producers, exporters or importers of such product; and

(ii) a producer of the like product in the importing Member or a trade and business association a majority of the members of which produce the like product in the territory of the importing Member.

This list shall not preclude Members from allowing domestic or foreign parties other than those mentioned above to be included as interested parties.

12.10 The authorities shall provide opportunities for industrial users of the product under investigation, and for representative consumer organizations in cases where the product is commonly sold at the retail level, to provide information which is relevant to the investigation regarding subsidization, injury and causality.

12.11 The authorities shall take due account of any difficulties experienced by interested parties, in particular small companies, in supplying information requested, and shall provide any assistance practicable.

12.12 The procedures set out above are not intended to prevent the authorities of a Member from proceeding expeditiously with regard to initiating an investigation, reaching preliminary or final determinations, whether affirmative or negative, or from applying provisional or final measures, in accordance with relevant provisions of this Agreement.

Article 13

Consultations

13.1 As soon as possible after an application under Article 11 is accepted, and in any event before the initiation of any investigation, Members the products of which may be subject to such investigation shall be invited for consultations with the aim of clarifying the situation as to the matters referred to in paragraph 2 of Article 11 and arriving at a mutually agreed solution.

13.2 Furthermore, throughout the period of investigation, Members the products of which are the subject of the investigation shall be afforded a reasonable opportunity to continue consultations, with a view to clarifying the factual situation and to arriving at a mutually agreed solution.[44]

13.3 Without prejudice to the obligation to afford reasonable opportunity for consultation, these provisions regarding consultations are not intended to prevent the authorities of a Member from proceeding expeditiously with regard to initiating the investigation, reaching preliminary or final determinations, whether affirmative or negative, or from applying provisional or final measures, in accordance with the provisions of this Agreement.

13.4 The Member which intends to initiate any investigation or is conducting such an investigation shall permit, upon request, the Member or Members the products of which are subject to such investigation access to non-confidential evidence, including the non-confidential summary of confidential data being used for initiating or conducting the investigation.

Article 14

Calculation of the Amount of a Subsidy in Terms of the Benefit to the Recipient

For the purpose of Part V, any method used by the investigating authority to calculate the benefit to the recipient conferred pursuant to paragraph 1 of Article 1 shall be provided for in the national legislation or implementing regulations of the Member concerned and its application to each particular case shall be transparent and adequately explained. Furthermore, any such method shall be consistent with the following guidelines:

(a) government provision of equity capital shall not be considered as conferring a benefit, unless the investment decision can be regarded as

44. It is particularly important, in accordance with the provisions of this paragraph, that no affirmative determination whether preliminary or final be made without reasonable opportunity for consultations having been given. Such consultations may establish the basis for proceeding under the provisions of Part II, III or X.

inconsistent with the usual investment practice (including for the provision of risk capital) of private investors in the territory of that Member;

(b) a loan by a government shall not be considered as conferring a benefit, unless there is a difference between the amount that the firm receiving the loan pays on the government loan and the amount the firm would pay on a comparable commercial loan which the firm could actually obtain on the market. In this case the benefit shall be the difference between these two amounts;

(c) a loan guarantee by a government shall not be considered as conferring a benefit, unless there is a difference between the amount that the firm receiving the guarantee pays on a loan guaranteed by the government and the amount that the firm would pay on a comparable commercial loan absent the government guarantee. In this case the benefit shall be the difference between these two amounts adjusted for any differences in fees;

(d) the provision of goods or services or purchase of goods by a government shall not be considered as conferring a benefit unless the provision is made for less than adequate remuneration, or the purchase is made for more than adequate remuneration. The adequacy of remuneration shall be determined in relation to prevailing market conditions for the good or service in question in the country of provision or purchase (including price, quality, availability, marketability, transportation and other conditions of purchase or sale).

Article 15

Determination of Injury[45]

15.1 A determination of injury for purposes of Article VI of GATT 1994 shall be based on positive evidence and involve an objective examination of both *(a)* the volume of the subsidized imports and the effect of the subsidized imports on prices in the domestic market for like products[46] and *(b)* the consequent impact of these imports on the domestic producers of such products.

45. Under this Agreement the term "injury" shall, unless otherwise specified, be taken to mean material injury to a domestic industry, threat of material injury to a domestic industry or material retardation of the establishment of such an industry and shall be interpreted in accordance with the provisions of this Article.

46. Throughout this Agreement the term "like product" ("produit similaire") shall be interpreted to mean a product which is identical, i.e. alike in all respects to the product under consideration, or in the absence of such a product, another product which, although not alike in all respects, has characteristics closely resembling those of the product under consideration.

15.2 With regard to the volume of the subsidized imports, the investigating authorities shall consider whether there has been a significant increase in subsidized imports, either in absolute terms or relative to production or consumption in the importing Member. With regard to the effect of the subsidized imports on prices, the investigating authorities shall consider whether there has been a significant price undercutting by the subsidized imports as compared with the price of a like product of the importing Member, or whether the effect of such imports is otherwise to depress prices to a significant degree or to prevent price increases, which otherwise would have occurred, to a significant degree. No one or several of these factors can necessarily give decisive guidance.

15.3 Where imports of a product from more than one country are simultaneously subject to countervailing duty investigations, the investigating authorities may cumulatively assess the effects of such imports only if they determine that *(a)* the amount of subsidization established in relation to the imports from each country is more than *de minimis* as defined in paragraph 9 of Article 11 and the volume of imports from each country is not negligible and *(b)* a cumulative assessment of the effects of the imports is appropriate in light of the conditions of competition between the imported products and the conditions of competition between the imported products and the like domestic product.

15.4 The examination of the impact of the subsidized imports on the domestic industry shall include an evaluation of all relevant economic factors and indices having a bearing on the state of the industry, including actual and potential decline in output, sales, market share, profits, productivity, return on investments, or utilization of capacity; factors affecting domestic prices; actual and potential negative effects on cash flow, inventories, employment, wages, growth, ability to raise capital or investments and, in the case of agriculture, whether there has been an increased burden on government support programmes. This list is not exhaustive, nor can one or several of these factors necessarily give decisive guidance.

15.5 It must be demonstrated that the subsidized imports are, through the effects[47] of subsidies, causing injury within the meaning of this Agreement. The demonstration of a causal relationship between the subsidized imports and the injury to the domestic industry shall be based on an examination of all relevant evidence before the authorities. The authorities shall also examine any known factors other than the subsidized imports which at the same time are injuring the domestic industry, and the injuries caused by these other factors must not be attributed to the subsidized imports. Factors which may be relevant in this respect include, *inter alia*, the volumes and prices of non-subsidized imports of the product in question,

47. As set forth in paragraphs 2 and 4.

contraction in demand or changes in the patterns of consumption, trade restrictive practices of and competition between the foreign and domestic producers, developments in technology and the export performance and productivity of the domestic industry.

15.6 The effect of the subsidized imports shall be assessed in relation to the domestic production of the like product when available data permit the separate identification of that production on the basis of such criteria as the production process, producers' sales and profits. If such separate identification of that production is not possible, the effects of the subsidized imports shall be assessed by the examination of the production of the narrowest group or range of products, which includes the like product, for which the necessary information can be provided.

15.7 A determination of a threat of material injury shall be based on facts and not merely on allegation, conjecture or remote possibility. The change in circumstances which would create a situation in which the subsidy would cause injury must be clearly foreseen and imminent. In making a determination regarding the existence of a threat of material injury, the investigating authorities should consider, *inter alia*, such factors as:

(i) nature of the subsidy or subsidies in question and the trade effects likely to arise therefrom;

(ii) a significant rate of increase of subsidized imports into the domestic market indicating the likelihood of substantially increased importation;

(iii) sufficient freely disposable, or an imminent, substantial increase in, capacity of the exporter indicating the likelihood of substantially increased subsidized exports to the importing Member's market, taking into account the availability of other export markets to absorb any additional exports;

(iv) whether imports are entering at prices that will have a significant depressing or suppressing effect on domestic prices, and would likely increase demand for further imports; and

(v) inventories of the product being investigated.

No one of these factors by itself can necessarily give decisive guidance but the totality of the factors considered must lead to the conclusion that further subsidized exports are imminent and that, unless protective action is taken, material injury would occur.

15.8 With respect to cases where injury is threatened by subsidized imports, the application of countervailing measures shall be considered and decided with special care.

Article 16

Definition of Domestic Industry

16.1 For the purposes of this Agreement, the term "domestic industry" shall, except as provided in paragraph 2, be interpreted as referring to the domestic producers as a whole of the like products or to those of them whose collective output of the products constitutes a major proportion of the total domestic production of those products, except that when producers are related[48] to the exporters or importers or are themselves importers of the allegedly subsidized product or a like product from other countries, the term "domestic industry" may be interpreted as referring to the rest of the producers.

16.2. In exceptional circumstances, the territory of a Member may, for the production in question, be divided into two or more competitive markets and the producers within each market may be regarded as a separate industry if *(a)* the producers within such market sell all or almost all of their production of the product in question in that market, and *(b)* the demand in that market is not to any substantial degree supplied by producers of the product in question located elsewhere in the territory. In such circumstances, injury may be found to exist even where a major portion of the total domestic industry is not injured, provided there is a concentration of subsidized imports into such an isolated market and provided further that the subsidized imports are causing injury to the producers of all or almost all of the production within such market.

16.3 When the domestic industry has been interpreted as referring to the producers in a certain area, i.e. a market as defined in paragraph 2, countervailing duties shall be levied only on the products in question consigned for final consumption to that area. When the constitutional law of the importing Member does not permit the levying of countervailing duties on such a basis, the importing Member may levy the countervailing duties without limitation only if *(a)* the exporters shall have been given an opportunity to cease exporting at subsidized prices to the area concerned or

48. For the purpose of this paragraph, producers shall be deemed to be related to exporters or importers only if *(a)* one of them directly or indirectly controls the other; or *(b)* both of them are directly or indirectly controlled by a third person; or *(c)* together they directly or indirectly control a third person, provided that there are grounds for believing or suspecting that the effect of the relationship is such as to cause the producer concerned to behave differently from non-related producers. For the purpose of this paragraph, one shall be deemed to control another when the former is legally or operationally in a position to exercise restraint or direction over the latter.

otherwise give assurances pursuant to Article 18, and adequate assurances in this regard have not been promptly given, and *(b)* such duties cannot be levied only on products of specific producers which supply the area in question.

16.4 Where two or more countries have reached under the provisions of paragraph 8(a) of Article XXIV of GATT 1994 such a level of integration that they have the characteristics of a single, unified market, the industry in the entire area of integration shall be taken to be the domestic industry referred to in paragraphs 1 and 2.

16.5 The provisions of paragraph 6 of Article 15 shall be applicable to this Article.

Article 17

Provisional Measures

17.1 Provisional measures may be applied only if:

(a) an investigation has been initiated in accordance with the provisions of Article 11, a public notice has been given to that effect and interested Members and interested parties have been given adequate opportunities to submit information and make comments;

(b) a preliminary affirmative determination has been made that a subsidy exists and that there is injury to a domestic industry caused by subsidized imports; and

(c) the authorities concerned judge such measures necessary to prevent injury being caused during the investigation.

17.2 Provisional measures may take the form of provisional countervailing duties guaranteed by cash deposits or bonds equal to the amount of the provisionally calculated amount of subsidization.

17.3 Provisional measures shall not be applied sooner than 60 days from the date of initiation of the investigation.

17.4 The application of provisional measures shall be limited to as short a period as possible, not exceeding four months.

17.5 The relevant provisions of Article 19 shall be followed in the application of provisional measures.

Article 18

Undertakings

18.1 Proceedings may[49] be suspended or terminated without the imposition of provisional measures or countervailing duties upon receipt of satisfactory voluntary undertakings under which:

(a) the government of the exporting Member agrees to eliminate or limit the subsidy or take other measures concerning its effects; or

(b) the exporter agrees to revise its prices so that the investigating authorities are satisfied that the injurious effect of the subsidy is eliminated. Price increases under such undertakings shall not be higher than necessary to eliminate the amount of the subsidy. It is desirable that the price increases be less than the amount of the subsidy if such increases would be adequate to remove the injury to the domestic industry.

18.2 Undertakings shall not be sought or accepted unless the authorities of the importing Member have made a preliminary affirmative determination of subsidization and injury caused by such subsidization and, in case of undertakings from exporters, have obtained the consent of the exporting Member.

18.3 Undertakings offered need not be accepted if the authorities of the importing Member consider their acceptance impractical, for example if the number of actual or potential exporters is too great, or for other reasons, including reasons of general policy. Should the case arise and where practicable, the authorities shall provide to the exporter the reasons which have led them to consider acceptance of an undertaking as inappropriate, and shall, to the extent possible, give the exporter an opportunity to make comments thereon.

18.4 If an undertaking is accepted, the investigation of subsidization and injury shall nevertheless be completed if the exporting Member so desires or the importing Member so decides. In such a case, if a negative determination of subsidization or injury is made, the undertaking shall automatically lapse, except in cases where such a determination is due in large part to the existence of an undertaking. In such cases, the authorities concerned may require that an undertaking be maintained for a reasonable period consistent with the provisions of this Agreement. In the event that an affirmative determination of subsidization and injury is made, the undertaking shall continue consistent with its terms and the provisions of this Agreement.

49. The word "may" shall not be interpreted to allow the simultaneous continuation of proceedings with the implementation of undertakings, except as provided in paragraph 4.

18.5 Price undertakings may be suggested by the authorities of the importing Member, but no exporter shall be forced to enter into such undertakings. The fact that governments or exporters do not offer such undertakings, or do not accept an invitation to do so, shall in no way prejudice the consideration of the case. However, the authorities are free to determine that a threat of injury is more likely to be realized if the subsidized imports continue.

18.6 Authorities of an importing Member may require any government or exporter from whom an undertaking has been accepted to provide periodically information relevant to the fulfilment of such an undertaking, and to permit verification of pertinent data. In case of violation of an undertaking, the authorities of the importing Member may take, under this Agreement in conformity with its provisions, expeditious actions which may constitute immediate application of provisional measures using the best information available. In such cases, definitive duties may be levied in accordance with this Agreement on products entered for consumption not more than 90 days before the application of such provisional measures, except that any such retroactive assessment shall not apply to imports entered before the violation of the undertaking.

Article 19

Imposition and Collection of Countervailing Duties

19.1 If, after reasonable efforts have been made to complete consultations, a Member makes a final determination of the existence and amount of the subsidy and that, through the effects of the subsidy, the subsidized imports are causing injury, it may impose a countervailing duty in accordance with the provisions of this Article unless the subsidy or subsidies are withdrawn.

19.2 The decision whether or not to impose a countervailing duty in cases where all requirements for the imposition have been fulfilled, and the decision whether the amount of the countervailing duty to be imposed shall be the full amount of the subsidy or less, are decisions to be made by the authorities of the importing Member. It is desirable that the imposition should be permissive in the territory of all Members, that the duty should be less than the total amount of the subsidy if such lesser duty would be adequate to remove the injury to the domestic industry, and that procedures should be established which would allow the authorities concerned to take due account of representations made by domestic interested parties[50] whose

50. For the purpose of this paragraph, the term "domestic interested parties" shall include consumers and industrial users of the imported product subject to investigation.

interests might be adversely affected by the imposition of a countervailing duty.

19.3 When a countervailing duty is imposed in respect of any product, such countervailing duty shall be levied, in the appropriate amounts in each case, on a non-discriminatory basis on imports of such product from all sources found to be subsidized and causing injury, except as to imports from those sources which have renounced any subsidies in question or from which undertakings under the terms of this Agreement have been accepted. Any exporter whose exports are subject to a definitive countervailing duty but who was not actually investigated for reasons other than a refusal to cooperate, shall be entitled to an expedited review in order that the investigating authorities promptly establish an individual countervailing duty rate for that exporter.

19.4 No countervailing duty shall be levied[51] on any imported product in excess of the amount of the subsidy found to exist, calculated in terms of subsidization per unit of the subsidized and exported product.

Article 20

Retroactivity

20.1 Provisional measures and countervailing duties shall only be applied to products which enter for consumption after the time when the decision under paragraph 1 of Article 17 and paragraph 1 of Article 19, respectively, enters into force, subject to the exceptions set out in this Article.

20.2 Where a final determination of injury (but not of a threat thereof or of a material retardation of the establishment of an industry) is made or, in the case of a final determination of a threat of injury, where the effect of the subsidized imports would, in the absence of the provisional measures, have led to a determination of injury, countervailing duties may be levied retroactively for the period for which provisional measures, if any, have been applied.

20.3 If the definitive countervailing duty is higher than the amount guaranteed by the cash deposit or bond, the difference shall not be collected. If the definitive duty is less than the amount guaranteed by the cash deposit or bond, the excess amount shall be reimbursed or the bond released in an expeditious manner.

51. As used in this Agreement "levy" shall mean the definitive or final legal assessment or collection of a duty or tax.

20.4 Except as provided in paragraph 2, where a determination of threat of injury or material retardation is made (but no injury has yet occurred) a definitive countervailing duty may be imposed only from the date of the determination of threat of injury or material retardation, and any cash deposit made during the period of the application of provisional measures shall be refunded and any bonds released in an expeditious manner.

20.5 Where a final determination is negative, any cash deposit made during the period of the application of provisional measures shall be refunded and any bonds released in an expeditious manner.

20.6 In critical circumstances where for the subsidized product in question the authorities find that injury which is difficult to repair is caused by massive imports in a relatively short period of a product benefiting from subsidies paid or bestowed inconsistently with the provisions of GATT 1994 and of this Agreement and where it is deemed necessary, in order to preclude the recurrence of such injury, to assess countervailing duties retroactively on those imports, the definitive countervailing duties may be assessed on imports which were entered for consumption not more than 90 days prior to the date of application of provisional measures.

Article 21

Duration and Review of Countervailing Duties and Undertakings

21.1 A countervailing duty shall remain in force only as long as and to the extent necessary to counteract subsidization which is causing injury.

21.2 The authorities shall review the need for the continued imposition of the duty, where warranted, on their own initiative or, provided that a reasonable period of time has elapsed since the imposition of the definitive countervailing duty, upon request by any interested party which submits positive information substantiating the need for a review. Interested parties shall have the right to request the authorities to examine whether the continued imposition of the duty is necessary to offset subsidization, whether the injury would be likely to continue or recur if the duty were removed or varied, or both. If, as a result of the review under this paragraph, the authorities determine that the countervailing duty is no longer warranted, it shall be terminated immediately.

21.3 Notwithstanding the provisions of paragraphs 1 and 2, any definitive countervailing duty shall be terminated on a date not later than five years from its imposition (or from the date of the most recent review under paragraph 2 if that review has covered both subsidization and injury, or under this paragraph), unless the authorities determine, in a review initiated before that date on their own initiative or upon a duly substantiated request made by or on behalf of the domestic industry within a reasonable period of time prior to that date, that the expiry of the duty would be likely to lead to continuation or recurrence of subsidization and injury.[52] The duty may remain in force pending the outcome of such a review.

21.4 The provisions of Article 12 regarding evidence and procedure shall apply to any review carried out under this Article. Any such review shall be carried out expeditiously and shall normally be concluded within 12 months of the date of initiation of the review.

21.5 The provisions of this Article shall apply *mutatis mutandis* to undertakings accepted under Article 18.

Article 22

Public Notice and Explanation of Determinations

22.1 When the authorities are satisfied that there is sufficient evidence to justify the initiation of an investigation pursuant to Article 11, the Member or Members the products of which are subject to such investigation and other interested parties known to the investigating authorities to have an interest therein shall be notified and a public notice shall be given.

22.2 A public notice of the initiation of an investigation shall contain, or otherwise make available through a separate report,[53] adequate information on the following:

(i) the name of the exporting country or countries and the product involved;

(ii) the date of initiation of the investigation;

(iii) a description of the subsidy practice or practices to be investigated;

(iv) a summary of the factors on which the allegation of injury is based;

(v) the address to which representations by interested Members and interested parties should be directed; and

52. When the amount of the countervailing duty is assessed on a retrospective basis, a finding in the most recent assessment proceeding that no duty is to be levied shall not by itself require the authorities to terminate the definitive duty.

53. Where authorities provide information and explanations under the provisions of this Article in a separate report, they shall ensure that such report is readily available to the public.

(vi) the time-limits allowed to interested Members and interested parties for making their views known.

22.3 Public notice shall be given of any preliminary or final determination, whether affirmative or negative, of any decision to accept an undertaking pursuant to Article 18, of the termination of such an undertaking, and of the termination of a definitive countervailing duty. Each such notice shall set forth, or otherwise make available through a separate report, in sufficient detail the findings and conclusions reached on all issues of fact and law considered material by the investigating authorities. All such notices and reports shall be forwarded to the Member or Members the products of which are subject to such determination or undertaking and to other interested parties known to have an interest therein.

22.4 A public notice of the imposition of provisional measures shall set forth, or otherwise make available through a separate report, sufficiently detailed explanations for the preliminary determinations on the existence of a subsidy and injury and shall refer to the matters of fact and law which have led to arguments being accepted or rejected. Such a notice or report shall, due regard being paid to the requirement for the protection of confidential information, contain in particular:

(i) the names of the suppliers or, when this is impracticable, the supplying countries involved;

(ii) a description of the product which is sufficient for customs purposes;

(iii) the amount of subsidy established and the basis on which the existence of a subsidy has been determined;

(iv) considerations relevant to the injury determination as set out in Article 15;

(v) the main reasons leading to the determination.

22.5 A public notice of conclusion or suspension of an investigation in the case of an affirmative determination providing for the imposition of a definitive duty or the acceptance of an undertaking shall contain, or otherwise make available through a separate report, all relevant information on the matters of fact and law and reasons which have led to the imposition of final measures or the acceptance of an undertaking, due regard being paid to the requirement for the protection of confidential information. In particular, the notice or report shall contain the information described in paragraph 4, as well as the reasons for the acceptance or rejection of relevant arguments or claims made by interested Members and by the exporters and importers.

22.6 A public notice of the termination or suspension of an investigation following the acceptance of an undertaking pursuant to Article 18 shall include, or otherwise make available through a separate report, the non-confidential part of this undertaking.

22.7 The provisions of this Article shall apply *mutatis mutandis* to the initiation and completion of reviews pursuant to Article 21 and to decisions under Article 20 to apply duties retroactively.

Article 23

Judicial Review

Each Member whose national legislation contains provisions on countervailing duty measures shall maintain judicial, arbitral or administrative tribunals or procedures for the purpose, *inter alia*, of the prompt review of administrative actions relating to final determinations and reviews of determinations within the meaning of Article 21. Such tribunals or procedures shall be independent of the authorities responsible for the determination or review in question, and shall provide all interested parties who participated in the administrative proceeding and are directly and individually affected by the administrative actions with access to review.

Part VI: Institutions

Article 24

Committee on Subsidies and Countervailing Measures and Subsidiary Bodies

24.1 There is hereby established a Committee on Subsidies and Countervailing Measures composed of representatives from each of the Members. The Committee shall elect its own Chairman and shall meet not less than twice a year and otherwise as envisaged by relevant provisions of this Agreement at the request of any Member. The Committee shall carry out responsibilities as assigned to it under this Agreement or by the Members and it shall afford Members the opportunity of consulting on any matter relating to the operation of the Agreement or the furtherance of its objectives. The WTO Secretariat shall act as the secretariat to the Committee.

24.2 The Committee may set up subsidiary bodies as appropriate.

24.3 The Committee shall establish a Permanent Group of Experts composed of five independent persons, highly qualified in the fields of subsidies and trade relations. The experts will be elected by the Committee and one of them will be replaced every year. The PGE may be requested to assist a panel, as provided for in paragraph 5 of Article 4. The Committee may also seek an advisory opinion on the existence and nature of any subsidy.

24.4 The PGE may be consulted by any Member and may give advisory opinions on the nature of any subsidy proposed to be introduced or currently maintained by that Member. Such advisory opinions will be confidential and may not be invoked in proceedings under Article 7.

24.5 In carrying out their functions, the Committee and any subsidiary bodies may consult with and seek information from any source they deem appropriate. However, before the Committee or a subsidiary body seeks such information from a source within the jurisdiction of a Member, it shall inform the Member involved.

Part VII: Notification and Surveillance

Article 25

Notifications

25.1 Members agree that, without prejudice to the provisions of paragraph 1 of Article XVI of GATT 1994, their notifications of subsidies shall be submitted not later than 30 June of each year and shall conform to the provisions of paragraphs 2 through 6.

25.2 Members shall notify any subsidy as defined in paragraph 1 of Article 1, which is specific within the meaning of Article 2, granted or maintained within their territories.

25.3 The content of notifications should be sufficiently specific to enable other Members to evaluate the trade effects and to understand the operation of notified subsidy programmes. In this connection, and without prejudice to the contents and form of the questionnaire on subsidies,[54] Members shall ensure that their notifications contain the following information:

(i) form of a subsidy (i.e. grant, loan, tax concession, etc.);

(ii) subsidy per unit or, in cases where this is not possible, the total amount or the annual amount budgeted for that subsidy (indicating, if possible, the average subsidy per unit in the previous year);

54. The Committee shall establish a Working Party to review the contents and form of the questionnaire as contained in BISD 9S/193-194.

(iii) policy objective and/or purpose of a subsidy;

(iv) duration of a subsidy and/or any other time-limits attached to it;

(v) statistical data permitting an assessment of the trade effects of a subsidy.

25.4 Where specific points in paragraph 3 have not been addressed in a notification, an explanation shall be provided in the notification itself.

25.5 If subsidies are granted to specific products or sectors, the notifications should be organized by product or sector.

25.6 Members which consider that there are no measures in their territories requiring notification under paragraph 1 of Article XVI of GATT 1994 and this Agreement shall so inform the Secretariat in writing.

25.7 Members recognize that notification of a measure does not prejudge either its legal status under GATT 1994 and this Agreement, the effects under this Agreement, or the nature of the measure itself.

25.8 Any Member may, at any time, make a written request for information on the nature and extent of any subsidy granted or maintained by another Member (including any subsidy referred to in Part IV), or for an explanation of the reasons for which a specific measure has been considered as not subject to the requirement of notification.

25.9 Members so requested shall provide such information as quickly as possible and in a comprehensive manner, and shall be ready, upon request, to provide additional information to the requesting Member. In particular, they shall provide sufficient details to enable the other Member to assess their compliance with the terms of this Agreement. Any Member which considers that such information has not been provided may bring the matter to the attention of the Committee.

25.10 Any Member which considers that any measure of another Member having the effects of a subsidy has not been notified in accordance with the provisions of paragraph 1 of Article XVI of GATT 1994 and this Article may bring the matter to the attention of such other Member. If the alleged subsidy is not thereafter notified promptly, such Member may itself bring the alleged subsidy in question to the notice of the Committee.

25.11 Members shall report without delay to the Committee all preliminary or final actions taken with respect to countervailing duties. Such reports shall be available in the Secretariat for inspection by other Members. Members shall also submit, on a semi-annual basis, reports on any countervailing duty actions taken within the preceding six months. The semi-annual reports shall be submitted on an agreed standard form.

25.12 Each Member shall notify the Committee *(a)* which of its authorities are competent to initiate and conduct investigations referred to in Article 11 and *(b)* its domestic procedures governing the initiation and conduct of such investigations.

Article 26

Surveillance

26.1 The Committee shall examine new and full notifications submitted under paragraph 1 of Article XVI of GATT 1994 and paragraph 1 of Article 25 of this Agreement at special sessions held every third year. Notifications submitted in the intervening years (updating notifications) shall be examined at each regular meeting of the Committee.

26.2 The Committee shall examine reports submitted under paragraph 11 of Article 25 at each regular meeting of the Committee.

Part VIII: Developing Country Members

Article 27

Special and Differential Treatment of Developing Country Members

27.1 Members recognize that subsidies may play an important role in economic development programmes of developing country Members.

27.2 The prohibition of paragraph 1(a) of Article 3 shall not apply to:

(a) developing country Members referred to in Annex VII.

(b) other developing country Members for a period of eight years from the date of entry into force of the WTO Agreement, subject to compliance with the provisions in paragraph 4.

27.3 The prohibition of paragraph 1(b) of Article 3 shall not apply to developing country Members for a period of five years, and shall not apply to least developed country Members for a period of eight years, from the date of entry into force of the WTO Agreement.

27.4 Any developing country Member referred to in paragraph 2(b) shall phase out its export subsidies within the eight-year period, preferably in a progressive manner. However, a developing country Member shall not increase the level of its export subsidies[55], and shall eliminate them within a period shorter than that provided for in this paragraph when the use of such export subsidies is inconsistent with its development needs. If a developing country Member deems it necessary to apply such subsidies beyond the 8-year period, it shall not later than one year before the expiry of this period enter into consultation with the Committee, which will determine whether an extension of this period is justified, after examining all the relevant economic, financial and development needs of the developing country Member in question. If the Committee determines that the extension is justified, the developing country Member concerned shall hold annual consultations with the Committee to determine the necessity of maintaining the subsidies. If no such determination is made by the Committee, the developing country Member shall phase out the remaining export subsidies within two years from the end of the last authorized period.

27.5 A developing country Member which has reached export competitiveness in any given product shall phase out its export subsidies for such product(s) over a period of two years. However, for a developing country Member which is referred to in Annex VII and which has reached export competitiveness in one or more products, export subsidies on such products shall be gradually phased out over a period of eight years.

27.6 Export competitiveness in a product exists if a developing country Member's exports of that product have reached a share of at least 3.25 per cent in world trade of that product for two consecutive calendar years. Export competitiveness shall exist either *(a)* on the basis of notification by the developing country Member having reached export competitiveness, or *(b)* on the basis of a computation undertaken by the Secretariat at the request of any Member. For the purpose of this paragraph, a product is defined as a section heading of the Harmonized System Nomenclature. The Committee shall review the operation of this provision five years from the date of the entry into force of the WTO Agreement.

27.7 The provisions of Article 4 shall not apply to a developing country Member in the case of export subsidies which are in conformity with the provisions of paragraphs 2 through 5. The relevant provisions in such a case shall be those of Article 7.

27.8 There shall be no presumption in terms of paragraph 1 of Article 6 that a subsidy granted by a developing country Member results in serious prejudice, as defined in this Agreement. Such serious prejudice, where applicable under the terms of paragraph 9, shall be demonstrated by positive evidence, in accordance with the provisions of paragraphs 3 through 8 of Article 6.

55. For a developing country Member not granting export subsidies as of the date of entry into force of the WTO Agreement, this paragraph shall apply on the basis of the level of export subsidies granted in 1986.

27.9 Regarding actionable subsidies granted or maintained by a developing country Member other than those referred to in paragraph 1 of Article 6, action may not be authorized or taken under Article 7 unless nullification or impairment of tariff concessions or other obligations under GATT 1994 is found to exist as a result of such a subsidy, in such a way as to displace or impede imports of a like product of another Member into the market of the subsidizing developing country Member or unless injury to a domestic industry in the market of an importing Member occurs.

27.10 Any countervailing duty investigation of a product originating in a developing country Member shall be terminated as soon as the authorities concerned determine that:

(a) the overall level of subsidies granted upon the product in question does not exceed 2 per cent of its value calculated on a per unit basis; or

(b) the volume of the subsidized imports represents less than 4 per cent of the total imports of the like product in the importing Member, unless imports from developing country Members whose individual shares of total imports represent less than 4 per cent collectively account for more than 9 per cent of the total imports of the like product in the importing Member.

27.11 For those developing country Members within the scope of paragraph 2(b) which have eliminated export subsidies prior to the expiry of the period of eight years from the date of entry into force of the WTO Agreement, and for those developing country Members referred to in Annex VII, the number in paragraph 10(a) shall be 3 per cent rather than 2 per cent. This provision shall apply from the date that the elimination of export subsidies is notified to the Committee, and for so long as export subsidies are not granted by the notifying developing country Member. This provision shall expire eight years from the date of entry into force of the WTO Agreement.

27.12 The provisions of paragraphs 10 and 11 shall govern any determination of *de minimis* under paragraph 3 of Article 15.

27.13 The provisions of Part III shall not apply to direct forgiveness of debts, subsidies to cover social costs, in whatever form, including relinquishment of government revenue and other transfer of liabilities when such subsidies are granted within and directly linked to a privatization programme of a developing country Member, provided that both such programme and the subsidies involved are granted for a limited period and notified to the Committee and that the programme results in eventual privatization of the enterprise concerned.

27.14 The Committee shall, upon request by an interested Member, undertake a review of a specific export subsidy practice of a developing country Member to examine whether the practice is in conformity with its development needs.

27.15 The Committee shall, upon request by an interested developing country Member, undertake a review of a specific countervailing measure to examine whether it is consistent with the provisions of paragraphs 10 and 11 as applicable to the developing country Member in question.

Part IX: Transitional Arrangements

Article 28

Existing Programmes

28.1 Subsidy programmes which have been established within the territory of any Member before the date on which such a Member signed the WTO Agreement and which are inconsistent with the provisions of this Agreement shall be:

(a) notified to the Committee not later than 90 days after the date of entry into force of the WTO Agreement for such Member; and

(b) brought into conformity with the provisions of this Agreement within three years of the date of entry into force of the WTO Agreement for such Member and until then shall not be subject to Part II.

28.2 No Member shall extend the scope of any such programme, nor shall such a programme be renewed upon its expiry.

Article 29

Transformation into a Market Economy

29.1 Members in the process of transformation from a centrally-planned into a market, free-enterprise economy may apply programmes and measures necessary for such a transformation.

29.2 For such Members, subsidy programmes falling within the scope of Article 3, and notified according to paragraph 3, shall be phased out or brought into conformity with Article 3 within a period of seven years from the date of entry into force of the WTO Agreement. In such a case, Article 4 shall not apply. In addition during the same period:

(a) Subsidy programmes falling within the scope of paragraph 1(d) of Article 6 shall not be actionable under Article 7;

(b) With respect to other actionable subsidies, the provisions of paragraph 9 of Article 27 shall apply.

29.3 Subsidy programmes falling within the scope of Article 3 shall be notified to the Committee by the earliest practicable date after the date of entry into force of the WTO Agreement. Further notifications of such subsidies may be made up to two years after the date of entry into force of the WTO Agreement.

29.4 In exceptional circumstances Members referred to in paragraph 1 may be given departures from their notified programmes and measures and their time-frame by the Committee if such departures are deemed necessary for the process of transformation.

Part X: Dispute Settlement

Article 30

The provisions of Articles XXII and XXIII of GATT 1994 as elaborated and applied by the Dispute Settlement Understanding shall apply to consultations and the settlement of disputes under this Agreement, except as otherwise specifically provided herein.

Part XI: Final Provisions

Article 31

Provisional Application

The provisions of paragraph 1 of Article 6 and the provisions of Article 8 and Article 9 shall apply for a period of five years, beginning with the date of entry into force of the WTO Agreement. Not later than 180 days before the end of this period, the Committee shall review the operation of those provisions, with a view to determining whether to extend their application, either as presently drafted or in a modified form, for a further period.

Article 32

Other Final Provisions

32.1 No specific action against a subsidy of another Member can be taken except in accordance with the provisions of GATT 1994, as interpreted by this Agreement.[56]

56. This paragraph is not intended to preclude action under other relevant provisions of GATT 1994, where appropriate.

32.2 Reservations may not be entered in respect of any of the provisions of this Agreement without the consent of the other Members.

32.3 Subject to paragraph 4, the provisions of this Agreement shall apply to investigations, and reviews of existing measures, initiated pursuant to applications which have been made on or after the date of entry into force for a Member of the WTO Agreement.

32.4 For the purposes of paragraph 3 of Article 21, existing countervailing measures shall be deemed to be imposed on a date not later than the date of entry into force for a Member of the WTO Agreement, except in cases in which the domestic legislation of a Member in force at that date already included a clause of the type provided for in that paragraph.

32.5 Each Member shall take all necessary steps, of a general or particular character, to ensure, not later than the date of entry into force of the WTO Agreement for it, the conformity of its laws, regulations and administrative procedures with the provisions of this Agreement as they may apply to the Member in question.

32.6 Each Member shall inform the Committee of any changes in its laws and regulations relevant to this Agreement and in the administration of such laws and regulations.

32.7 The Committee shall review annually the implementation and operation of this Agreement, taking into account the objectives thereof. The Committee shall inform annually the Council for Trade in Goods of developments during the period covered by such reviews.

32.8 The Annexes to this Agreement constitute an integral part thereof.

Annex I

ILLUSTRATIVE LIST OF EXPORT SUBSIDIES

(a) The provision by governments of direct subsidies to a firm or an industry contingent upon export performance.

(b) Currency retention schemes or any similar practices which involve a bonus on exports.

(c) Internal transport and freight charges on export shipments, provided or mandated by governments, on terms more favourable than for domestic shipments.

(d) The provision by governments or their agencies either directly or indirectly through government-mandated schemes, of imported or domestic products or services for use in the production of exported goods, on terms or conditions more favourable than for provision of like or directly competitive products or services for use in the production of goods for domestic consumption, if (in the case of products) such terms or conditions are more favourable than those commercially available[57] on world markets to their exporters.

(e) The full or partial exemption remission, or deferral specifically related to exports, of direct taxes[58] or social welfare charges paid or payable by industrial or commercial enterprises.[59]

(f) The allowance of special deductions directly related to exports or export performance, over and above those granted in respect to production for domestic consumption, in the calculation of the base on which direct taxes are charged.

57. The term "commercially available" means that the choice between domestic and imported products is unrestricted and depends only on commercial considerations.

58. For the purpose of this Agreement:

The term "direct taxes" shall mean taxes on wages, profits, interests, rents, royalties, and all other forms of income, and taxes on the ownership of real property;

The term "import charges" shall mean tariffs, duties, and other fiscal charges not elsewhere enumerated in this note that are levied on imports;

The term "indirect taxes" shall mean sales, excise, turnover, value added, franchise, stamp, transfer, inventory and equipment taxes, border taxes and all taxes other than direct taxes and import charges;

"Prior-stage" indirect taxes are those levied on goods or services used directly or indirectly in making the product;

"Cumulative" indirect taxes are multi-staged taxes levied where there is no mechanism for subsequent crediting of the tax if the goods or services subject to tax at one stage of production are used in a succeeding stage of production;

"Remission" of taxes includes the refund or rebate of taxes;

"Remission or drawback" includes the full or partial exemption or deferral of import charges.

59. The Members recognize that deferral need not amount to an export subsidy where, for example, appropriate interest charges are collected. The Members reaffirm the principle that prices for goods in transactions between exporting enterprises and foreign buyers under their or under the same control should for tax purposes be the prices which would be charged between independent enterprises acting at arm's length. Any Member may draw the attention of another Member to administrative or other practices which may contravene this principle and which result in a significant saving of direct taxes in export transactions. In such circumstances the Members shall normally attempt to resolve their differences using the facilities of existing bilateral tax treaties or other specific international mechanisms, without prejudice to the rights and obligations of Members under GATT 1994, including the right of consultation created in the preceding sentence.

(g) The exemption or remission, in respect of the production and distribution of exported products, of indirect taxes[58] in excess of those levied in respect of the production and distribution of like products when sold for domestic consumption.

(h) The exemption, remission or deferral of prior-stage cumulative indirect taxes[58] on goods or services used in the production of exported products in excess of the exemption, remission or deferral of like prior-stage cumulative indirect taxes on goods or services used in the production of like products when sold for domestic consumption; provided, however, that prior-stage cumulative indirect taxes may be exempted, remitted or deferred on exported products even when not exempted, remitted or deferred on like products when sold for domestic consumption, if the prior-stage cumulative indirect taxes are levied on inputs that are consumed in the production of the exported product (making normal allowance for waste).[60] This item shall be interpreted in accordance with the guidelines on consumption of inputs in the production process contained in Annex II.

(i) The remission or drawback of import charges[58] in excess of those levied on imported inputs that are consumed in the production of the exported product (making normal allowance for waste); provided, however, that in particular cases a firm may use a quantity of home market inputs equal to, and having the same quality and characteristics as, the imported inputs as a substitute for them in order to benefit from this provision if the import and the corresponding export operations both occur within a reasonable time period, not to exceed two years. This item shall be interpreted in accordance with the guidelines on consumption of inputs in the production process contained in Annex II and the guidelines in the determination of substitution drawback systems as export subsidies contained in Annex III.

(j) The provision by governments (or special institutions controlled by governments) of export credit guarantee or insurance programmes, of insurance or guarantee programmes against increases in the cost of exported products or of exchange risk programmes, at premium rates which are inadequate to cover the long-term operating costs and losses of the programmes.

(k) The grant by governments (or special institutions controlled by and/or acting under the authority of governments) of export credits at rates below those which they actually have to pay for the funds so

60. Paragraph (h) does not apply to value-added tax systems and border-tax adjustment in lieu thereof; the problem of the excessive remission of value-added taxes is exclusively covered by paragraph (g).

employed (or would have to pay if they borrowed on international capital markets in order to obtain funds of the same maturity and other credit terms and denominated in the same currency as the export credit), or the payment by them of all or part of the costs incurred by exporters or financial institutions in obtaining credits, in so far as they are used to secure a material advantage in the field of export credit terms.

Provided, however, that if a Member is a party to an international undertaking on official export credits to which at least twelve original Members to this Agreement are parties as of 1 January 1979 (or a successor undertaking which has been adopted by those original Members), or if in practice a Member applies the interest rates provisions of the relevant undertaking, an export credit practice which is in conformity with those provisions shall not be considered an export subsidy prohibited by this Agreement.

(l) Any other charge on the public account constituting an export subsidy in the sense of Article XVI of GATT 1994.

Annex II

GUIDELINES ON CONSUMPTION OF INPUTS IN THE PRODUCTION PROCESS[61]

I

1. Indirect tax rebate schemes can allow for exemption, remission or deferral of prior-stage cumulative indirect taxes levied on inputs that are consumed in the production of the exported product (making normal allowance for waste). Similarly, drawback schemes can allow for the remission or drawback of import charges levied on inputs that are consumed in the production of the exported product (making normal allowance for waste).

2. The Illustrative List of Export Subsidies in Annex I of this Agreement makes reference to the term "inputs that are consumed in the production of the exported product" in paragraphs (h) and (i). Pursuant to paragraph (h), indirect tax rebate schemes can constitute an export subsidy to the extent that they result in exemption, remission or deferral of prior-stage cumulative indirect taxes in excess of the amount of such taxes actually levied on

61. Inputs consumed in the production process are inputs physically incorporated, energy, fuels and oil used in the production process and catalysts which are consumed in the course of their use to obtain the exported product.

inputs that are consumed in the production of the exported product. Pursuant to paragraph (i), drawback schemes can constitute an export subsidy to the extent that they result in a remission or drawback of import charges in excess of those actually levied on inputs that are consumed in the production of the exported product. Both paragraphs stipulate that normal allowance for waste must be made in findings regarding consumption of inputs in the production of the exported product. Paragraph (i) also provides for substitution, where appropriate.

II

In examining whether inputs are consumed in the production of the exported product, as part of a countervailing duty investigation pursuant to this Agreement, investigating authorities should proceed on the following basis:

1. Where it is alleged that an indirect tax rebate scheme, or a drawback scheme, conveys a subsidy by reason of over-rebate or excess drawback of indirect taxes or import charges on inputs consumed in the production of the exported product, the investigating authorities should first determine whether the government of the exporting Member has in place and applies a system or procedure to confirm which inputs are consumed in the production of the exported product and in what amounts. Where such a system or procedure is determined to be applied, the investigating authorities should then examine the system or procedure to see whether it is reasonable, effective for the purpose intended, and based on generally accepted commercial practices in the country of export. The investigating authorities may deem it necessary to carry out, in accordance with paragraph 6 of Article 12, certain practical tests in order to verify information or to satisfy themselves that the system or procedure is being effectively applied.

2. Where there is no such system or procedure, where it is not reasonable, or where it is instituted and considered reasonable but is found not to be applied or not to be applied effectively, a further examination by the exporting Member based on the actual inputs involved would need to be carried out in the context of determining whether an excess payment occurred. If the investigating authorities deemed it necessary, a further examination would be carried out in accordance with paragraph 1.

3. Investigating authorities should treat inputs as physically incorporated if such inputs are used in the production process and are physically present in the product exported. The Members note that an input need not be present in the final product in the same form in which it entered the production process.

4. In determining the amount of a particular input that is consumed in the production of the exported product, a "normal allowance for waste" should be taken into account, and such waste should be treated as consumed in the production of the exported product. The term "waste" refers to that portion of a given input which does not serve an independent function in the production process, is not consumed in the production of the exported product (for reasons such as inefficiencies) and is not recovered, used or sold by the same manufacturer.

5. The investigating authority's determination of whether the claimed allowance for waste is "normal" should take into account the production process, the average experience of the industry in the country of export, and other technical factors, as appropriate. The investigating authority should bear in mind that an important question is whether the authorities in the exporting Member have reasonably calculated the amount of waste, when such an amount is intended to be included in the tax or duty rebate or remission.

Annex III

GUIDELINES IN THE DETERMINATION OF SUBSTITUTION DRAWBACK SYSTEMS AS EXPORT SUBSIDIES

I

Drawback systems can allow for the refund or drawback of import charges on inputs which are consumed in the production process of another product and where the export of this latter product contains domestic inputs having the same quality and characteristics as those substituted for the imported inputs. Pursuant to paragraph (i) of the Illustrative List of Export Subsidies in Annex I, substitution drawback systems can constitute an export subsidy to the extent that they result in an excess drawback of the import charges levied initially on the imported inputs for which drawback is being claimed.

II

In examining any substitution drawback system as part of a countervailing duty investigation pursuant to this Agreement, investigating authorities should proceed on the following basis:

1. Paragraph (i) of the Illustrative List stipulates that home market inputs may be substituted for imported inputs in the production of a product for export provided such inputs are equal in quantity to, and have the same quality and characteristics as, the imported inputs being substituted. The existence of a verification system or procedure is important because it enables the government of the exporting Member to ensure and demonstrate that the quantity of inputs for which drawback is claimed does not exceed the quantity of similar products exported, in whatever form, and that there is not drawback of import charges in excess of those originally levied on the imported inputs in question.

2. Where it is alleged that a substitution drawback system conveys a subsidy, the investigating authorities should first proceed to determine whether the government of the exporting Member has in place and applies a verification system or procedure. Where such a system or procedure is determined to be applied, the investigating authorities should then examine the verification procedures to see whether they are reasonable, effective for the purpose intended, and based on generally accepted commercial practices in the country of export. To the extent that the procedures are determined to meet this test and are effectively applied, no subsidy should be presumed to exist. It may be deemed necessary by the investigating authorities to carry out, in accordance with paragraph 6 of Article 12, certain practical tests in order to verify information or to satisfy themselves that the verification procedures are being effectively applied.

3. Where there are no verification procedures, where they are not reasonable, or where such procedures are instituted and considered reasonable but are found not to be actually applied or not applied effectively, there may be a subsidy. In such cases a further examination by the exporting Member based on the actual transactions involved would need to be carried out to determine whether an excess payment occurred. If the investigating authorities deemed it necessary, a further examination would be carried out in accordance with paragraph 2.

4. The existence of a substitution drawback provision under which exporters are allowed to select particular import shipments on which drawback is claimed should not of itself be considered to convey a subsidy.

5. An excess drawback of import charges in the sense of paragraph (i) would be deemed to exist where governments paid interest on any monies refunded under their drawback schemes, to the extent of the interest actually paid or payable.

Annex IV

CALCULATION OF THE TOTAL AD VALOREM SUBSIDIZATION (PARAGRAPH 1(A) OF ARTICLE 6)[62]

1. Any calculation of the amount of a subsidy for the purpose of paragraph 1(a) of Article 6 shall be done in terms of the cost to the granting government.

2. Except as provided in paragraphs 3 through 5, in determining whether the overall rate of subsidization exceeds 5 per cent of the value of the product, the value of the product shall be calculated as the total value of the recipient firm's[63] sales in the most recent 12-month period, for which sales data is available, preceding the period in which the subsidy is granted.[64]

3. Where the subsidy is tied to the production or sale of a given product, the value of the product shall be calculated as the total value of the recipient firm's sales of that product in the most recent 12-month period, for which sales data is available, preceding the period in which the subsidy is granted.

4. Where the recipient firm is in a start-up situation, serious prejudice shall be deemed to exist if the overall rate of subsidization exceeds 15 per cent of the total funds invested. For purposes of this paragraph, a start-up period will not extend beyond the first year of production.[65]

5. Where the recipient firm is located in an inflationary economy country, the value of the product shall be calculated as the recipient firm's total sales (or sales of the relevant product, if the subsidy is tied) in the preceding calendar year indexed by the rate of inflation experienced in the 12 months preceding the month in which the subsidy is to be given.

6. In determining the overall rate of subsidization in a given year, subsidies given under different programmes and by different authorities in the territory of a Member shall be aggregated.

62. An understanding among Members should be developed, as necessary, on matters which are not specified in this Annex or which need further clarification for the purposes of paragraph 1(a) of Article 6.

63. The recipient firm is a firm in the territory of the subsidizing Member.

64. In the case of tax-related subsidies the value of the product shall be calculated as the total value of the recipient firm's sales in the fiscal year in which the tax-related measure was earned.

65. Start-up situations include instances where financial commitments for product development or construction of facilities to manufacture products benefiting from the subsidy have been made, even though production has not begun.

7. Subsidies granted prior to the date of entry into force of the WTO Agreement, the benefits of which are allocated to future production, shall be included in the overall rate of subsidization.

8. Subsidies which are non-actionable under relevant provisions of this Agreement shall not be included in the calculation of the amount of a subsidy for the purpose of paragraph 1(a) of Article 6.

Annex V

PROCEDURES FOR DEVELOPING INFORMATION CONCERNING SERIOUS PREJUDICE

1. Every Member shall cooperate in the development of evidence to be examined by a panel in procedures under paragraphs 4 through 6 of Article 7. The parties to the dispute and any third-country Member concerned shall notify to the DSB, as soon as the provisions of paragraph 4 of Article 7 have been invoked, the organization responsible for administration of this provision within its territory and the procedures to be used to comply with requests for information.

2. In cases where matters are referred to the DSB under paragraph 4 of Article 7, the DSB shall, upon request, initiate the procedure to obtain such information from the government of the subsidizing Member as necessary to establish the existence and amount of subsidization, the value of total sales of the subsidized firms, as well as information necessary to analyze the adverse effects caused by the subsidized product.[66] This process may include, where appropriate, presentation of questions to the government of the subsidizing Member and of the complaining Member to collect information, as well as to clarify and obtain elaboration of information available to the parties to a dispute through the notification procedures set forth in Part VII.[67]

3. In the case of effects in third-country markets, a party to a dispute may collect information, including through the use of questions to the government of the third-country Member, necessary to analyse adverse effects, which is not otherwise reasonably available from the complaining Member or the subsidizing Member. This requirement should be administered in such a way as not to impose an unreasonable burden on the third-country Member. In particular, such a Member is not expected to make a market or price analysis specially for that purpose. The information to be

66. In cases where the existence of serious prejudice has to be demonstrated.

67. The information-gathering process by the DSB shall take into account the need to protect information which is by nature confidential or which is provided on a confidential basis by any Member involved in this process.

supplied is that which is already available or can be readily obtained by this Member (e.g. most recent statistics which have already been gathered by relevant statistical services but which have not yet been published, customs data concerning imports and declared values of the products concerned, etc.). However, if a party to a dispute undertakes a detailed market analysis at its own expense, the task of the person or firm conducting such an analysis shall be facilitated by the authorities of the third-country Member and such a person or firm shall be given access to all information which is not normally maintained confidential by the government.

4. The DSB shall designate a representative to serve the function of facilitating the information-gathering process. The sole purpose of the representative shall be to ensure the timely development of the information necessary to facilitate expeditious subsequent multilateral review of the dispute. In particular, the representative may suggest ways to most efficiently solicit necessary information as well as encourage the cooperation of the parties.

5. The information-gathering process outlined in paragraphs 2 through 4 shall be completed within 60 days of the date on which the matter has been referred to the DSB under paragraph 4 of Article 7. The information obtained during this process shall be submitted to the panel established by the DSB in accordance with the provisions of Part X. This information should include, *inter alia*, data concerning the amount of the subsidy in question (and, where appropriate, the value of total sales of the subsidized firms), prices of the subsidized product, prices of the non-subsidized product, prices of other suppliers to the market, changes in the supply of the subsidized product to the market in question and changes in market shares. It should also include rebuttal evidence, as well as such supplemental information as the panel deems relevant in the course of reaching its conclusions.

6. If the subsidizing and/or third-country Member fail to cooperate in the information-gathering process, the complaining Member will present its case of serious prejudice, based on evidence available to it, together with facts and circumstances of the non-cooperation of the subsidizing and/or third-country Member. Where information is unavailable due to non-cooperation by the subsidizing and/or third-country Member, the panel may complete the record as necessary relying on best information otherwise available.

7. In making its determination, the panel should draw adverse inferences from instances of non- cooperation by any party involved in the information-gathering process.

8. In making a determination to use either best information available or adverse inferences, the panel shall consider the advice of the DSB repre-

sentative nominated under paragraph 4 as to the reasonableness of any requests for information and the efforts made by parties to comply with these requests in a cooperative and timely manner.

9. Nothing in the information-gathering process shall limit the ability of the panel to seek such additional information it deems essential to a proper resolution to the dispute, and which was not adequately sought or developed during that process. However, ordinarily the panel should not request additional information to complete the record where the information would support a particular party's position and the absence of that information in the record is the result of unreasonable non-cooperation by that party in the information-gathering process.

Annex VI

PROCEDURES FOR ON-THE-SPOT INVESTIGATIONS PURSUANT TO PARAGRAPH 6 OF ARTICLE 12

1. Upon initiation of an investigation, the authorities of the exporting Member and the firms known to be concerned should be informed of the intention to carry out on-the-spot investigations.

2. If in exceptional circumstances it is intended to include non-governmental experts in the investigating team, the firms and the authorities of the exporting Member should be so informed. Such non-governmental experts should be subject to effective sanctions for breach of confidentiality requirements.

3. It should be standard practice to obtain explicit agreement of the firms concerned in the exporting Member before the visit is finally scheduled.

4. As soon as the agreement of the firms concerned has been obtained, the investigating authorities should notify the authorities of the exporting Member of the names and addresses of the firms to be visited and the dates agreed.

5. Sufficient advance notice should be given to the firms in question before the visit is made.

6. Visits to explain the questionnaire should only be made at the request of an exporting firm. In case of such a request the investigating authorities may place themselves at the disposal of the firm; such a visit may only be made if *(a)* the authorities of the importing Member notify the representatives of the government of the Member in question and *(b)* the latter do not object to the visit.

7. As the main purpose of the on-the-spot investigation is to verify information provided or to obtain further details, it should be carried out after the response to the questionnaire has been received unless the firm agrees to the contrary and the government of the exporting Member is informed by the investigating authorities of the anticipated visit and does not object to it; further, it should be standard practice prior to the visit to advise the firms concerned of the general nature of the information to be verified and of any further information which needs to be provided, though this should not preclude requests to be made on the spot for further details to be provided in the light of information obtained.

8. Enquiries or questions put by the authorities or firms of the exporting Members and essential to a successful on-the-spot investigation should, whenever possible, be answered before the visit is made.

Annex VII

DEVELOPING COUNTRY MEMBERS REFERRED TO IN PARAGRAPH 2(A) OF ARTICLE 27

The developing country Members not subject to the provisions of paragraph 1(a) of Article 3 under the terms of paragraph 2(a) of Article 27 are:

(a) Least-developed countries designated as such by the United Nations which are Members of the WTO.

(b) Each of the following developing countries which are Members of the WTO shall be subject to the provisions which are applicable to other developing country Members according to paragraph 2(b) of Article 27 when GNP per capita has reached $1,000 per annum:[68] Bolivia, Cameroon, Congo, Côte d'Ivoire, Dominican Republic, Egypt, Ghana, Guatemala, Guyana, India, Indonesia, Kenya, Morocco, Nicaragua, Nigeria, Pakistan, Philippines, Senegal, Sri Lanka and Zimbabwe.

68. The inclusion of developing country Members in the list in paragraph (b) is based on the most recent data from the World Bank on GNP per capita.

Document 34

AGREEMENT ON SAFEGUARDS

Members,

Having in mind the overall objective of the Members to improve and strengthen the international trading system based on GATT 1994;

Recognizing the need to clarify and reinforce the disciplines of GATT 1994, and specifically those of its Article XIX (Emergency Action on Imports of Particular Products), to re-establish multilateral control over safeguards and eliminate measures that escape such control;

Recognizing the importance of structural adjustment and the need to enhance rather than limit competition in international markets; and

Recognizing further that, for these purposes, a comprehensive agreement, applicable to all Members and based on the basic principles of GATT 1994, is called for;

Hereby *agree* as follows:

Article 1

General Provision

This Agreement establishes rules for the application of safeguard measures which shall be understood to mean those measures provided for in Article XIX of GATT 1994.

Article 2

Conditions

1. A Member[1] may apply a safeguard measure to a product only if that Member has determined, pursuant to the provisions set out below, that such product is being imported into its territory in such increased quantities, absolute or relative to domestic production, and under such conditions as to cause or threaten to cause serious injury to the domestic industry that produces like or directly competitive products.

2. Safeguard measures shall be applied to a product being imported irrespective of its source.

Article 3

Investigation

1. A Member may apply a safeguard measure only following an investigation by the competent authorities of that Member pursuant to procedures previously established and made public in consonance with Article X of GATT 1994. This investigation shall include reasonable public notice to all interested parties and public hearings or other appropriate means in which importers, exporters and other interested parties could present evidence and their views, including the opportunity to respond to the presentations of other parties and to submit their views, *inter alia,* as to whether or not the application of a safeguard measure would be in the public interest. The competent authorities shall publish a report setting forth their findings and reasoned conclusions reached on all pertinent issues of fact and law.

2. Any information which is by nature confidential or which is provided on a confidential basis shall, upon cause being shown, be treated as such by the competent authorities. Such information shall not be disclosed without permission of the party submitting it. Parties providing confidential information may be requested to furnish non-confidential summaries thereof or, if such parties indicate that such information cannot be summarized, the reasons why a summary cannot be provided. However, if the competent authorities find that a request for confidentiality is not warranted and if the party concerned is either unwilling to make the information public or to

1. A customs union may apply a safeguard measure as a single unit or on behalf of a member State. When a customs union applies a safeguard measure as a single unit, all the requirements for the determination of serious injury or threat thereof under this Agreement shall be based on the conditions existing in the customs union as a whole. When a safeguard measure is applied on behalf of a member State, all the requirements for the determination of serious injury or threat thereof shall be based on the conditions existing in that member State and the measure shall be limited to that member State. Nothing in this Agreement prejudges the interpretation of the relationship between Article XIX and paragraph 8 of Article XXIV of GATT 1994.

authorize its disclosure in generalized or summary form, the authorities may disregard such information unless it can be demonstrated to their satisfaction from appropriate sources that the information is correct.

Article 4

Determination of Serious Injury or Threat Thereof

1. For the purposes of this Agreement:

(a) "serious injury" shall be understood to mean a significant overall impairment in the position of a domestic industry;

(b) "threat of serious injury" shall be understood to mean serious injury that is clearly imminent, in accordance with the provisions of paragraph 2. A determination of the existence of a threat of serious injury shall be based on facts and not merely on allegation, conjecture or remote possibility; and

(c) in determining injury or threat thereof, a "domestic industry" shall be understood to mean the producers as a whole of the like or directly competitive products operating within the territory of a Member, or those whose collective output of the like or directly competitive products constitutes a major proportion of the total domestic production of those products.

2. (a) In the investigation to determine whether increased imports have caused or are threatening to cause serious injury to a domestic industry under the terms of this Agreement, the competent authorities shall evaluate all relevant factors of an objective and quantifiable nature having a bearing on the situation of that industry, in particular, the rate and amount of the increase in imports of the product concerned in absolute and relative terms, the share of the domestic market taken by increased imports, changes in the level of sales, production, productivity, capacity utilization, profits and losses, and employment.

(b) The determination referred to in subparagraph (a) shall not be made unless this investigation demonstrates, on the basis of objective evidence, the existence of the causal link between increased imports of the product concerned and serious injury or threat thereof. When factors other than increased imports are causing injury to the domestic industry at the same time, such injury shall not be attributed to increased imports.

(c) The competent authorities shall publish promptly, in accordance with the provisions of Article 3, a detailed analysis of the case under investigation as well as a demonstration of the relevance of the factors examined.

Article 5

Application of Safeguard Measures

1. A Member shall apply safeguard measures only to the extent necessary to prevent or remedy serious injury and to facilitate adjustment. If a quantitative restriction is used, such a measure shall not reduce the quantity of imports below the level of a recent period which shall be the average of imports in the last three representative years for which statistics are available, unless clear justification is given that a different level is necessary to prevent or remedy serious injury. Members should choose measures most suitable for the achievement of these objectives.

2. (a) In cases in which a quota is allocated among supplying countries, the Member applying the restrictions may seek agreement with respect to the allocation of shares in the quota with all other Members having a substantial interest in supplying the product concerned. In cases in which this method is not reasonably practicable, the Member concerned shall allot to Members having a substantial interest in supplying the product shares based upon the proportions, supplied by such Members during a previous representative period, of the total quantity or value of imports of the product, due account being taken of any special factors which may have affected or may be affecting the trade in the product.

(b) A Member may depart from the provisions in subparagraph (a) provided that consultations under paragraph 3 of Article 12 are conducted under the auspices of the Committee on Safeguards provided for in paragraph 1 of Article 13 and that clear demonstration is provided to the Committee that (*i*) imports from certain Members have increased in disproportionate percentage in relation to the total increase of imports of the product concerned in the representative period, (*ii*) the reasons for the departure from the provisions in subparagraph (a) are justified, and (*iii*) the conditions of such departure are equitable to all suppliers of the product concerned. The duration of any such measure shall not be extended beyond the initial period under paragraph 1 of Article 7. The departure referred to above shall not be permitted in the case of threat of serious injury.

Article 6

Provisional Safeguard Measures

In critical circumstances where delay would cause damage which it would be difficult to repair, a Member may take a provisional safeguard measure pursuant to a preliminary determination that there is clear evidence that increased imports have caused or are threatening to cause serious injury. The duration of the provisional measure shall not exceed 200 days, during which period the pertinent requirements of Articles 2 through 7 and 12 shall be met. Such measures should take the form of tariff increases to be promptly refunded if the subsequent investigation referred to in paragraph 2 of Article 4 does not determine that increased imports have caused or threatened to cause serious injury to a domestic industry. The duration of any such provisional measure shall be counted as a part of the initial period and any extension referred to in paragraphs 1, 2 and 3 of Article 7.

Article 7

Duration and Review of Safeguard Measures

1. A Member shall apply safeguard measures only for such period of time as may be necessary to prevent or remedy serious injury and to facilitate adjustment. The period shall not exceed four years, unless it is extended under paragraph 2.

2. The period mentioned in paragraph 1 may be extended provided that the competent authorities of the importing Member have determined, in conformity with the procedures set out in Articles 2, 3, 4 and 5, that the safeguard measure continues to be necessary to prevent or remedy serious injury and that there is evidence that the industry is adjusting, and provided that the pertinent provisions of Articles 8 and 12 are observed.

3. The total period of application of a safeguard measure including the period of application of any provisional measure, the period of initial application and any extension thereof, shall not exceed eight years.

4. In order to facilitate adjustment in a situation where the expected duration of a safeguard measure as notified under the provisions of paragraph 1 of Article 12 is over one year, the Member applying the measure shall progressively liberalize it at regular intervals during the period of application. If the duration of the measure exceeds three years, the Member applying such a measure shall review the situation not later than the mid-term of the measure and, if appropriate, withdraw it or increase the pace of liberalization. A measure extended under paragraph 2 shall not be more restrictive than it was at the end of the initial period, and should continue to be liberalized.

5. No safeguard measure shall be applied again to the import of a product which has been subject to such a measure, taken after the date of entry into force of the WTO Agreement, for a period of time equal to that during which such measure had been previously applied, provided that the period of non-application is at least two years.

6. Notwithstanding the provisions of paragraph 5, a safeguard measure with a duration of 180 days or less may be applied again to the import of a product if:

(a) at least one year has elapsed since the date of introduction of a safeguard measure on the import of that product; and

(b) such a safeguard measure has not been applied on the same product more than twice in the five-year period immediately preceding the date of introduction of the measure.

Article 8

Level of Concessions and Other Obligations

1. A Member proposing to apply a safeguard measure or seeking an extension of a safeguard measure shall endeavour to maintain a substantially equivalent level of concessions and other obligations to that existing under GATT 1994 between it and the exporting Members which would be affected by such a measure, in accordance with the provisions of paragraph 3 of Article 12. To achieve this objective, the Members concerned may agree on any adequate means of trade compensation for the adverse effects of the measure on their trade.

2. If no agreement is reached within 30 days in the consultations under paragraph 3 of Article 12, then the affected exporting Members shall be free, not later than 90 days after the measure is applied, to suspend, upon the expiration of 30 days from the day on which written notice of such suspension is received by the Council for Trade in Goods, the application of substantially equivalent concessions or other obligations under GATT 1994, to the trade of the Member applying the safeguard measure, the suspension of which the Council for Trade in Goods does not disapprove.

3. The right of suspension referred to in paragraph 2 shall not be exercised for the first three years that a safeguard measure is in effect, provided that the safeguard measure has been taken as a result of an absolute increase in imports and that such a measure conforms to the provisions of this Agreement.

Article 9

Developing Country Members

1. Safeguard measures shall not be applied against a product originating in a developing country Member as long as its share of imports of the product concerned in the importing Member does not exceed 3 per cent, provided that developing country Members with less than 3 per cent import

share collectively account for not more than 9 per cent of total imports of the product concerned.[2]

2. A developing country Member shall have the right to extend the period of application of a safeguard measure for a period of up to two years beyond the maximum period provided for in paragraph 3 of Article 7. Notwithstanding the provisions of paragraph 5 of Article 7, a developing country Member shall have the right to apply a safeguard measure again to the import of a product which has been subject to such a measure, taken after the date of entry into force of the WTO Agreement, after a period of time equal to half that during which such a measure has been previously applied, provided that the period of non-application is at least two years.

Article 10

Pre-Existing Article XIX Measures

Members shall terminate all safeguard measures taken pursuant to Article XIX of GATT 1947 that were in existence on the date of entry into force of the WTO Agreement not later than eight years after the date on which they were first applied or five years after the date of entry into force of the WTO Agreement, whichever comes later.

Article 11

Prohibition and Elimination of Certain Measures

1. (a) A Member shall not take or seek any emergency action on imports of particular products as set forth in Article XIX of GATT 1994 unless such action conforms with the provisions of that Article applied in accordance with this Agreement.

(b) Furthermore, a Member shall not seek, take or maintain any voluntary export restraints, orderly marketing arrangements or any other similar measures on the export or the import side.[3,4] These include actions taken by a single Member as well as actions under agreements, arrangements and understandings entered into by two or more Members. Any such measure in effect on the date of entry into force of the WTO

2. A Member shall immediately notify an action taken under paragraph 1 of Article 9 to the Committee on Safeguards.

3. An import quota applied as a safeguard measure in conformity with the relevant provisions of GATT 1994 and this Agreement may, by mutual agreement, be administered by the exporting Member.

4. Examples of similar measures include export moderation, export-price or import-price monitoring systems, export or import surveillance, compulsory import cartels and discretionary export or import licensing schemes, any of which afford protection.

Agreement shall be brought into conformity with this Agreement or phased out in accordance with paragraph 2.

(c) This Agreement does not apply to measures sought, taken or maintained by a Member pursuant to provisions of GATT 1994 other than Article XIX, and Multilateral Trade Agreements in Annex 1A other than this Agreement, or pursuant to protocols and agreements or arrangements concluded within the framework of GATT 1994.

2. The phasing out of measures referred to in paragraph 1(b) shall be carried out according to timetables to be presented to the Committee on Safeguards by the Members concerned not later than 180 days after the date of entry into force of the WTO Agreement. These timetables shall provide for all measures referred to in paragraph 1 to be phased out or brought into conformity with this Agreement within a period not exceeding four years after the date of entry into force of the WTO Agreement, subject to not more than one specific measure per importing Member[5], the duration of which shall not extend beyond 31 December 1999. Any such exception must be mutually agreed between the Members directly concerned and notified to the Committee on Safeguards for its review and acceptance within 90 days of the entry into force of the WTO Agreement. The Annex to this Agreement indicates a measure which has been agreed as falling under this exception.

3. Members shall not encourage or support the adoption or maintenance by public and private enterprises of non-governmental measures equivalent to those referred to in paragraph 1.

Article 12

Notification and Consultation

1. A Member shall immediately notify the Committee on Safeguards upon:

(a) initiating an investigatory process relating to serious injury or threat thereof and the reasons for it;

(b) making a finding of serious injury or threat thereof caused by increased imports; and

(c) taking a decision to apply or extend a safeguard measure.

5. The only such exception to which the European Communities is entitled is indicated in the Annex to this Agreement.

2. In making the notifications referred to in paragraphs 1(b) and 1(c), the Member proposing to apply or extend a safeguard measure shall provide the Committee on Safeguards with all pertinent information, which shall include evidence of serious injury or threat thereof caused by increased imports, precise description of the product involved and the proposed measure, proposed date of introduction, expected duration and timetable for progressive liberalization. In the case of an extension of a measure, evidence that the industry concerned is adjusting shall also be provided. The Council for Trade in Goods or the Committee on Safeguards may request such additional information as they may consider necessary from the Member proposing to apply or extend the measure.

3. A Member proposing to apply or extend a safeguard measure shall provide adequate opportunity for prior consultations with those Members having a substantial interest as exporters of the product concerned, with a view to, *inter alia,* reviewing the information provided under paragraph 2, exchanging views on the measure and reaching an understanding on ways to achieve the objective set out in paragraph 1 of Article 8.

4. A Member shall make a notification to the Committee on Safeguards before taking a provisional safeguard measure referred to in Article 6. Consultations shall be initiated immediately after the measure is taken.

5. The results of the consultations referred to in this Article, as well as the results of mid-term reviews referred to in paragraph 4 of Article 7, any form of compensation referred to in paragraph 1 of Article 8, and proposed suspensions of concessions and other obligations referred to in paragraph 2 of Article 8, shall be notified immediately to the Council for Trade in Goods by the Members concerned.

6. Members shall notify promptly the Committee on Safeguards of their laws, regulations and administrative procedures relating to safeguard measures as well as any modifications made to them.

7. Members maintaining measures described in Article 10 and paragraph 1 of Article 11 which exist on the date of entry into force of the WTO Agreement shall notify such measures to the Committee on Safeguards not later than 60 days after the date of entry into force of the WTO Agreement.

8. Any Member may notify the Committee on Safeguards of all laws, regulations, administrative procedures and any measures or actions dealt with in this Agreement that have not been notified by other Members that are required by this Agreement to make such notifications.

9. Any Member may notify the Committee on Safeguards of any non-governmental measures referred to in paragraph 3 of Article 11.

10. All notifications to the Council for Trade in Goods referred to in this Agreement shall normally be made through the Committee on Safeguards.

11. The provisions on notification in this Agreement shall not require any Member to disclose confidential information the disclosure of which would impede law enforcement or otherwise be contrary to the public interest or would prejudice the legitimate commercial interests of particular enterprises, public or private.

Article 13

Surveillance

1. A Committee on Safeguards is hereby established, under the authority of the Council for Trade in Goods, which shall be open to the participation of any Member indicating its wish to serve on it. The Committee will have the following functions:

(a) to monitor, and report annually to the Council for Trade in Goods on, the general implementation of this Agreement and make recommendations towards its improvement;

(b) to find, upon request of an affected Member, whether or not the procedural requirements of this Agreement have been complied with in connection with a safeguard measure, and report its findings to the Council for Trade in Goods;

(c) to assist Members, if they so request, in their consultations under the provisions of this Agreement;

(d) to examine measures covered by Article 10 and paragraph 1 of Article 11, monitor the phase-out of such measures and report as appropriate to the Council for Trade in Goods;

(e) to review, at the request of the Member taking a safeguard measure, whether proposals to suspend concessions or other obligations are "substantially equivalent," and report as appropriate to the Council for Trade in Goods;

(f) to receive and review all notifications provided for in this Agreement and report as appropriate to the Council for Trade in Goods; and

(g) to perform any other function connected with this Agreement that the Council for Trade in Goods may determine.

2. To assist the Committee in carrying out its surveillance function, the Secretariat shall prepare annually a factual report on the operation of

this Agreement based on notifications and other reliable information available to it.

Article 14

Dispute Settlement

The provisions of Articles XXII and XXIII of GATT 1994 as elaborated and applied by the Dispute Settlement Understanding shall apply to consultations and the settlement of disputes arising under this Agreement.

Annex

EXCEPTION REFERRED TO IN PARAGRAPH 2 OF ARTICLE 11

Members concerned	Product	Termination
EC/Japan	Passenger cars, off road vehicles, light commercial vehicles, light trucks (up to 5 tonnes), and the same vehicles in wholly knocked-down form (CKD sets).	31 December 1999

Document 35

INFORMATION TECHNOLOGY AGREEMENT

Official name: Ministerial Declaration on Trade in Information Technology Products

Singapore, 13 December 1996

Ministers,

Representing the following Members of the World Trade Organization ("WTO"), and States or separate customs territories in the process of acceding to the WTO, which have agreed in Singapore on the expansion of world trade in information technology products and which account for well over 80 per cent of world trade in these products ("parties"):*

Australia
Canada
European Communities
Hong Kong
Iceland
Norway
Separate Customs Territory of Taiwan, Penghu, Kinmen and Matsu
Singapore
Switzerland[1]

* List of signatories as of May 2012: Albania, Australia, Bahrain, Bulgaria, Canada, China, Columbia, Costa Rica, Croatia, Dominican Republic, Egypt, El Salvador, European Communities (including its member states), Georgia, Guatemala, Honduras, Hong Kong, Iceland, India, Indonesia, Israel, Japan, Jordan, Korea, Kuwait, Kyrgys Republic, Macao, Malaysia, Mauritius, Moldova, Morocco, New Zealand, Nicaragua, Norway, Oman, Panama, Peru, Philippines, Saudi Arabia, Singapore, Switzerland (on behalf of the Switzerland and Liechtenstein customs union), Chinese Taipei, Thailand, Turkey, Ukraine, United Arab Emirates, United States, Vietnam.

1. On behalf of the customs union Switzerland and Liechtenstein.

Indonesia	Turkey
Japan	United States
Korea	

Considering the key role of trade in information technology products in the development of information industries and in the dynamic expansion of the world economy,

Recognizing the goals of raising standards of living and expanding the production of and trade in goods;

Desiring to achieve maximum freedom of world trade in information technology products;

Desiring to encourage the continued technological development of the information technology industry on a world-wide basis;

Mindful of the positive contribution information technology makes to global economic growth and welfare;

Having agreed to put into effect the results of these negotiations which involve concessions additional to those included in the Schedules attached to the Marrakesh Protocol to the General Agreement on Tariffs and Trade 1994, and

Recognizing that the results of these negotiations also involve some concessions offered in negotiations leading to the establishment of Schedules annexed to the Marrakesh Protocol,

Declare as follows:

1. Each party's trade regime should evolve in a manner that enhances market access opportunities for information technology products.

2. Pursuant to the modalities set forth in the Annex to this Declaration, each party shall bind and eliminate customs duties and other duties and charges of any kind, within the meaning of Article II:1(b) of the General Agreement on Tariffs and Trade 1994, with respect to the following:

(a) all products classified (or classifiable) with Harmonized System (1996) ("HS") headings listed in Attachment A to the Annex to this Declaration; and

(b) all products specified in Attachment B to the Annex to this Declaration, whether or not they are included in Attachment A;

through equal rate reductions of customs duties beginning in 1997 and concluding in 2000, recognizing that extended staging of reductions and, before implementation, expansion of product coverage may be necessary in limited circumstances.

3. Ministers express satisfaction about the large product coverage outlined in the Attachments to the Annex to this Declaration. They instruct their respective officials to make good faith efforts to finalize plurilateral technical discussions in Geneva on the basis of these modalities, and instruct these officials to complete this work by 31 January 1997, so as to ensure the implementation of this Declaration by the largest number of participants.

4. Ministers invite the Ministers of other Members of the WTO, and States or separate customs territories in the process of acceding to the WTO, to provide similar instructions to their respective officials, so that they may participate in the technical discussions referred to in paragraph 3 above and participate fully in the expansion of world trade in information technology products.

Annex: Modalities and Product Coverage

Attachment A: list of HS headings

Attachment B: list of products

ANNEX

Modalities and Product Coverage

Any Member of the World Trade Organization, or State or separate customs territory in the process of acceding to the WTO, may participate in the expansion of world trade in information technology products in accordance with the following modalities:

1. Each participant shall incorporate the measures described in paragraph 2 of the Declaration into its schedule to the General Agreement on Tariffs and Trade 1994, and, in addition, at either its own tariff line level or the Harmonized System (1996) ("HS") 6-digit level in either its official tariff or any other published versions of the tariff schedule, whichever is ordinarily used by importers and exporters. Each participant that is not a Member of the WTO shall implement these measures on an autonomous basis, pending completion of its WTO accession, and shall incorporate these measures into its WTO market access schedule for goods.

2. To this end, as early as possible and no later than 1 March 1997 each participant shall provide all other participants a document containing (a) the

details concerning how the appropriate duty treatment will be provided in its WTO schedule of concessions, and (b) a list of the detailed HS headings involved for products specified in Attachment B. These documents will be reviewed and approved on a consensus basis and this review process shall be completed no later than 1 April 1997. As soon as this review process has been completed for any such document, that document shall be submitted as a modification to the Schedule of the participant concerned, in accordance with the Decision of 26 March 1980 on Procedures for Modification and Rectification of Schedules of Tariff Concessions (BISD 27S/25).

(a) The concessions to be proposed by each participant as modifications to its Schedule shall bind and eliminate all customs duties and other duties and charges of any kind on information technology products as follows:

(i) elimination of such customs duties shall take place through rate reductions in equal steps, except as may be otherwise agreed by the participants. Unless otherwise agreed by the participants, each participant shall bind all tariffs on items listed in the Attachments no later than 1 July 1997, and shall make the first such rate reduction effective no later than 1 July 1997, the second such rate reduction no later than 1 January 1998, and the third such rate reduction no later than 1 January 1999, and the elimination of customs duties shall be completed effective no later than 1 January 2000. The participants agree to encourage autonomous elimination of customs duties prior to these dates. The reduced rate should in each stage be rounded off to the first decimal; and

(ii) elimination of such other duties and charges of any kind, within the meaning of Article II:1(b) of the General Agreement, shall be completed by 1 July 1997, except as may be otherwise specified in the participant's document provided to other participants for review.

(b) The modifications to its Schedule to be proposed by a participant in order to implement its binding and elimination of customs duties on information technology products shall achieve this result:

(i) in the case of the HS headings listed in Attachment A, by creating, where appropriate, sub-divisions in its Schedule at the national tariff line level; and

(ii) in the case of the products specified in Attachment B, by attaching an annex to its Schedule including all products in Attachment B, which is to specify the detailed HS headings for those products at either the national tariff line level or the HS 6-digit level.

Each participant shall promptly modify its national tariff schedule to reflect the modifications it has proposed, as soon as they have entered into effect.

3. Participants shall meet periodically under the auspices of the Council on Trade in Goods to review the product coverage specified in the Attachments, with a view to agreeing, by consensus, whether in the light of technological developments, experience in applying the tariff concessions, or changes to the HS nomenclature, the Attachments should be modified to incorporate additional products, and to consult on non-tariff barriers to trade in information technology products. Such consultations shall be without prejudice to rights and obligations under the WTO Agreement.

4. Participants shall meet as soon as practicable and in any case no later than 1 April 1997 to review the state of acceptances received and to assess the conclusions to be drawn therefrom. Participants will implement the actions foreseen in the Declaration provided that participants representing approximately 90 per cent of world trade[2] in information technology products have by then notified their acceptance, and provided that the staging has been agreed to the participants' satisfaction. In assessing whether to implement actions foreseen in the Declaration, if the percentage of world trade represented by participants falls somewhat short of 90 per cent of world trade in information technology products, participants may take into account the extent of the participation of States or separate customs territories representing for them the substantial bulk of their own trade in such products. At this meeting the participants will establish whether these criteria have been met.

5. Participants shall meet as often as necessary and no later than 30 September 1997 to consider any divergence among them in classifying information technology products, beginning with the products specified in Attachment B. Participants agree on the common objective of achieving, where appropriate, a common classification for these products within existing HS nomenclature, giving consideration to interpretations and rulings of the Customs Co-operation Council (also known as the World Customs Organization or "WCO"). In any instance in which a divergence in classification remains, participants will consider whether a joint suggestion could be made to the WCO with regard to updating existing HS nomenclature or resolving divergence in interpretation of the HS nomenclature.

6. The participants understand that Article XXIII of the General Agreement will address nullification or impairment of benefits accruing directly or indirectly to a WTO Member participant through the implementation of

2. This percentage shall be calculated by the WTO Secretariat on the basis of the most recent data available at the time of the meeting.

this Declaration as a result of the application by another WTO Member participant of any measure, whether or not that measure conflicts with the provisions of the General Agreement.

7. Each participant shall afford sympathetic consideration to any request for consultation from any other participant concerning the undertakings set out above. Such consultations shall be without prejudice to rights and obligations under the WTO Agreement.

8. Participants acting under the auspices of the Council for Trade in Goods shall inform other Members of the WTO and States or separate customs territories in the process of acceding to the WTO of these modalities and initiate consultations with a view to facilitate their participation in the expansion of trade in information technology products on the basis of the Declaration.

9. As used in these modalities, the term "participant" shall mean those Members of the WTO, or States or separate customs territories in the process of acceding to the WTO, that provide the document described in paragraph 2 no later than 1 March 1997.

10. This Annex shall be open for acceptance by all Members of the WTO and any State or any separate customs territory in the process of acceding to the WTO. Acceptances shall be notified in writing to the Director-General who shall communicate them to all participants.

There are two attachments to the Annex.

Attachment A lists the HS headings or parts thereof to be covered.

Attachment B lists specific products to be covered by an ITA wherever they are classified in the HS.

Attachment A, Section 1

	HS96		*HS description*
	3818		**Chemical elements doped for use in electronics, in form of discs, wafers or similar forms; chemical compounds doped for use in electronics**
	8469	**11**	**Word processing machines**
	8470		**Calculating machines and pocket-size data recording, reproducing and displaying machines with a calculating function; accounting machines,**

	HS96		*HS description*
			postage franking machines, ticket-issuing machines and similar machines, incorporating a calculating devices; cash registers:
	8470	10	Electronic calculators capable of operating without an external source of electric power and pocket size data recording, reproducing and displaying machines with calculating functions
	8470	21	Other electronic calculating machines incorporating a printing device
	8470	29	Other
	8470	30	Other calculating machines
	8470	40	Accounting machines
	8470	50	Cash registers
	8470	90	Other
	8471		**Automatic data processing machines and units thereof; magnetic or optical readers, machines for transcribing data onto data media in coded form and machines for processing such data, not elsewhere specified or included:**
	8471	10	Analogue or hybrid automatic data processing machines
	8471	30	Portable digital automatic data processing machines, weighing no more than 10 kg, consisting of at least a central processing unit, a keyboard and a display
	8471	41	Other digital automatic data processing machines comprising in the same housing at least a central processing unit and an input and output unit, whether or not combined
	8471	49	Other digital automatic data processing machines presented in the form of systems
	8471	50	Digital processing units other than those of subheading 8471 41 and 8471 49, whether or not in the same housing one or two of the following types of units : storage units, input units, output units

	HS96		*HS description*
	8471	60	Input or output units, whether or not containing storage units in the same housing
	8471	70	Storage units, including central storage units, optical disk storage units, hard disk drives and magnetic tape storage units
	8471	80	Other units of automatic data processing machines
	8471	90	Other
ex	**8472**	**90**	**Automatic teller machines**
	8473	**21**	**Parts and accessories of the machines of heading No 8470 of the electronic calculating machines of subheading 8470 10, 8470 21 and 8470 29**
	8473	**29**	**Parts and accessories of the machines of heading No 8470 other than the electronic calculating machines of subheading 8470 10, 8470 21 and 8470 29**
	8473	**30**	**Parts and accessories of the machines of heading No 8471**
	8473	**50**	**Parts and accessories equally suitable for use with machines of two or more of the headings Nos. 8469 to 8472**
ex	**8504**	**40**	**Static converters for automatic data processing machines and units thereof, and telecommunication apparatus**
ex	**8504**	**50**	**Other inductors for power supplies for automatic data processing machines and units thereof, and telecommunication apparatus**
	8517		**Electrical apparatus for line telephony or line telegraphy, including line telephone sets with cordless handsets and telecommunication apparatus for carrier-current line systems or for digital line systems; videophones:**
	8517	11	Line telephone sets with cordless handsets
	8517	19	Other telephone sets and videophones
	8517	21	Facsimile machines

	HS96		*HS description*
	8517	22	Teleprinters
	8517	30	Telephonic or telegraphic switching apparatus
	8517	50	Other apparatus, for carrier-current line systems or for digital line systems
	8517	80	Other apparatus including entry-phone systems
	8517	90	Parts of apparatus of heading 8517
ex	**8518**	**10**	**Microphones having a frequency range of 300 Hz to 3,4 KHz with a diameter of not exceeding 10 mm and a height not exceeding 3 mm, for telecommunication use**
ex	**8518**	**30**	**Line telephone handsets**
ex	**8518**	**29**	**Loudspeakers, without housing, having a frequency range of 300 Hz to 3,4 KHz with a diameter of not exceeding 50 mm, for telecommunication use**
	8520	**20**	**Telephone answering machines**
	8523	**11**	**Magnetic tapes of a width not exceeding 4 mm**
	8523	**12**	**Magnetic tapes of a width exceeding 4 mm but not exceeding 6,5 mm**
	8523	**13**	**Magnetic tapes of a width exceeding 6,5 mm**
	8523	**20**	**Magnetic discs**
	8523	**90**	**Other**
	8524	**31**	**Discs for laser reading systems for reproducing phenomena other than sound or image**
ex	**8524**	**39**	**Other :** **— for reproducing representations of instructions, data, sound, and image, recorded in a machine readable binary form, and capable of being manipulated or providing interactivity to a user, by means of an automatic data processing machine**
	8524	**40**	**Magnetic tapes for reproducing phenomena other than sound or image**

	HS96		*HS description*
	8524	**91**	**Media for reproducing phenomena other than sound or image**
ex	**8424**	**99**	**Other :** **— for reproducing representations of instructions, data, sound, and image, recorded in a machine readable binary form, and capable of being manipulated or providing interactivity to a user, by means of an automatic data processing machine**
ex	**8525**	**10**	**Transmission apparatus other than apparatus for radio-broadcasting or television**
	8525	**20**	**Transmission apparatus incorporating reception apparatus**
ex	**8525**	**40**	**Digital still image video cameras**
ex	**8527**	**90**	**Portable receivers for calling, alerting or paging**
ex	**8529**	**10**	**Aerials or antennae of a kind used with apparatus for radio-telephony and radio-telegraphy**
ex	**8529**	**90**	**Parts of:** **transmission apparatus other than apparatus for radio-broadcasting or television** **transmission apparatus incorporating reception apparatus** **digital still image video cameras,** **portable receivers for calling, alerting or paging**
	8531	**20**	**Indicator panels incorporating liquid crystal devices (LCD) or light emitting diodes (LED)**
ex	**8531**	**90**	**Parts of apparatus of subheading 8531 20**
	8532		**Electrical capacitors, fixed, variable or adjustable (pre-set):**
	8532	10	Fixed capacitors designed for use in 50/60 Hz circuits and having a reactive power handling capacity of not less than 0,5 kvar (power capacitors)
	8532	21	Tantalum fixed capacitors
	8532	22	Aluminium electrolytic fixed capacitors
	8532	23	Ceramic dielectric, single layer fixed capacitors

	HS96		*HS description*
	8532	24	Ceramic dielectric, multilayer fixed capacitors
	8532	25	Dielectric fixed capacitors of paper or plastics
	8532	29	Other fixed capacitors
	8532	30	Variable or adjustable (pre-set) capacitors
	8532	90	Parts
	8533		**Electrical resistors (including rheostats and potentiometers), other than heating resistors:**
	8533	10	Fixed carbon resistors, composition or film types
	8533	21	Other fixed resistors for a power handling capacity not exceeding 20 W
	8533	29	Other fixed resistors for a power handling capacity of 20 W or more
	8533	31	Wirewound variable resistors, including rheostats and potentiometers, for a power handling capacity not exceeding 20 W
	8533	39	Wirewound variable resistors, including rheostats and potentiometers, for a power handling capacity of 20 W or more
	8533	40	Other variable resistors, including rheostats and potentiometers
	8533	90	Parts
	8534		**Printed circuits**
ex	**8536**	**50**	**Electronic AC switches consisting of optically coupled input and output circuits (Insulated thyristor AC switches)**
ex	**8536**	**50**	**Electronic switches, including temperature protected electronic switches, consisting of a transistor and a logic chip (chip-on-chip technology) for a voltage not exceeding 1000 volts**
ex	**8536**	**50**	**Electromechanical snap-action switches for a current not exceeding 11 amps**
ex	**8536**	**69**	**Plugs and sockets for co-axial cables and printed circuits**

	HS96		*HS description*
ex	**8536**	**90**	**Connection and contact elements for wires and cables**
	8541		**Diodes, transistors and similar semiconductor devices; photosensitive semiconductor devices, including photovoltaic cells whether or not assembled in modules or made up into panels; light-emitting diodes; mounted piezo-electric crystals:**
	8541	10	Diodes, other than photosensitive or light-emitting diodes
	8541	21	Transistors, other than photosensitive transistors, with a dissipation rate of less than 1 W
	8541	29	Transistors, other than photosensitive transistors, with a dissipation rate of 1 W or more
	8541	30	Thyristors, diacs and triacs, other than photosensitive devices
	8541	40	Photosensitive semiconductor devices, including photovoltaic cells whether or not assembled in modules or made up into panels; light emitting diodes
	8541	50	Other semiconductor devices
	8541	60	Mounted piezo-electric crystals
	8541	90	Parts
	8542		**Electronic integrated circuits and microassemblies**
	8542	12	Cards incorporating an electronic integrated circuit ("smart" cards)
	8542	13	Metal oxide semiconductors (MOS technology)
	8542	14	Circuits obtained by bipolar technology
	8542	19	Other monolithic digital integrated circuits, including circuits obtained by a combination of bipolar and MOS technologies (BIMOS technology)
	8542	30	Other monolithic integrated circuits
	8542	40	Hybrid integrated circuits

	HS96		*HS description*
	8542	50	Electronic microassemblies
	8542	90	Part
	8543	**81**	**Proximity cards and tags**
ex	**8543**	**89**	**Electrical machines with translation or dictionary functions**
ex	**8544**	**41**	**Other electric conductors, for a voltage not exceeding 80 V, fitted with connectors, of a kind used for telecommunications**
ex	**8544**	**49**	**Other electric conductors, for a voltage not exceeding 80 V, not fitted with connectors, of a kind used for telecommunications**
ex	**8544**	**51**	**Other electric conductors, for a voltage exceeding 80 V but not exceeding 1000 V, fitted with connectors, of a kind used for telecommunications**
	8544	**70**	**Optical fibre cables**
	9009	**11**	**Electrostatic photocopying apparatus, operating by reproducing the original image directly onto the copy (direct process)]**
	9009	**21**	**Other photocopying apparatus, incorporating an optical system**
	9009	**90**	**Parts and accessories**
	9026		**Instruments and apparatus for measuring or checking the flow, level, pressure or other variables of liquids or gases (for example, flow meters, level gauges, manometers, heat meters), excluding instruments and apparatus of heading No 9014, 9015, 9028 or 9032:**
	9026	10	Instruments for measuring or checking the flow or level of liquids
	9026	20	Instruments and apparatus for measuring or checking pressure
	9026	80	Other instruments and apparatus for measuring or checking of heading 9026

	HS96		*HS description*
	9026	90	Parts and accessories of instruments and apparatus of heading 9026
	9027	**20**	**Chromatographs and electrophoresis instruments**
	9027	**30**	**Spectrometers, spectrophotometers and spectrographs using optical radiations (UV, visible, IR)**
	9027	**50**	**Other instruments and apparatus using optical radiations (UV, visible, IR) of heading No 9027**
	9027	**80**	**Other instruments and apparatus of heading No 9027 (other than those of heading No 9027 10)**
ex	**9027**	**90**	**Parts and accessories of products of heading 9027, other than for gas or smoke analysis apparatus and microtomes**
	9030	**40**	**Instruments and apparatus for measuring and checking, specially designed for telecommunications (for example, cross-talk meters, gain measuring instruments, distorsion factor meters, psophometers)**

Attachment A, Section 2
Semiconductor manufacturing and testing equipment and parts thereof

	HS Code		*Description*	*Comments*
ex	7017	10	Quartz reactor tubes and holders designed for insertion into diffusion and oxidation furnaces for production of semiconductor wafers	For Attachment B
ex	8419	89	Chemical vapor deposition apparatus for semiconductor production	For Attachment B
ex	8419	90	Parts of chemical vapor deposition apparatus for semiconductor production	For Attachment B
ex	8421	19	Spin dryers for semiconductor wafer processing	

	HS Code	*Description*	*Comments*
ex	8421 91	Parts of spin dryers for semiconductor wafer processing	
ex	8424 89	Deflash machines for cleaning and removing contaminants from the metal leads of semiconductor packages prior to the electroplating process	
ex	8424 89	Spraying appliances for etching, stripping or cleaning semiconductor wafers	
ex	8424 90	Parts of spraying appliances for etching, stripping or cleaning semiconductor wafers	
ex	8456 10	Machines for working any material by removal of material, by laser or other light or photo beam in the production of semiconductor wafers	
ex	8456 91	Apparatus for stripping or cleaning semiconductor wafers	For Attachment B
	8456 91	Machines for dry-etching patterns on semiconductor materials	
ex	8456 99	Focused ion beam milling machines to produce or repair masks and reticles for patterns on semiconductor devices	
ex	8456 99	Lasercutters for cutting contacting tracks in semiconductor production by laser beam	For Attachment B
ex	8464 10	Machines for sawing monocrystal semiconductor boules into slices, or wafers into chips	For Attachment B
ex	8464 20	Grinding, polishing and lapping machines for processing of semiconductor wafers	
ex	8464 90	Dicing machines for scribing or scoring semiconductor wafers	
ex	8466 91	Parts for machines for sawing monocrystal semiconductor boules into slices, or wafers into chips	For Attachment B

	HS Code	*Description*	*Comments*
ex	8466 91	Parts of dicing machines for scribing or scoring semiconductor wafers	For Attachment B
ex	8466 91	Parts of grinding, polishing and lapping machines for processing of semiconductor wafers	
ex	8466 93	Parts of focused ion beam milling machines to produce or repair masks and reticles for patterns on semiconductor devices	
ex	8466 93	Parts of lasercutters for cutting contacting tracks in semiconductor production by laser beam	For Attachment B
ex	8466 93	Parts of machines for working any material by removal of material, by laser or other light or photo beam in the production of semiconductor wafers	
ex	8456 93	Parts of apparatus for stripping or cleaning semiconductor wafers	For Attachment B
ex	8466 93	Parts of machines for dry-etching patterns on semiconductor materials	
ex	8477 10	Encapsulation equipment for assembly of semiconductors	For Attachment B
ex	8477 90	Parts of encapsulation equipment	For Attachment B
ex	8479 50	Automated machines for transport, handling and storage of semiconductor wafers, wafer cassettes, wafer boxes and other material for semiconductor devices	For Attachment B
ex	8479 89	Apparatus for growing or pulling monocrystal semiconductor boules	
ex	8479 89	Apparatus for physical deposition by sputtering on semiconductor wafers	For Attachment B

	HS Code	Description	Comments
ex	8479 89	Apparatus for wet etching, developing, stripping or cleaning semiconductor wafers and flat panel displays	For Attachment B
ex	8479 89	Die attach apparatus, tape automated bonders, and wire bonders for assembly of semiconductors	For Attachment B
ex	8479 89	Encapsulation equipment for assembly of semiconductors	For Attachment B
ex	8479 89	Epitaxial deposition machines for semiconductor wafers	
ex	8479 89	Machines for bending, folding and straightening semiconductor leads	For Attachment B
ex	8479 89	Physical deposition apparatus for for semiconductor production	For Attachment B
ex	8479 89	Spinners for coating photographic emulsions on semiconductor wafers	For Attachment B
ex	8479 90	Part of apparatus for physical deposition by sputtering on semiconductor wafers	For Attachment B
ex	8479 90	Parts for die attach apparatus, tape automated bonders, and wire bonders for assembly of semiconductors	For Attachment B
ex	8479 90	Parts for spinners for coating photographic emulsions on semiconductor wafers	For Attachment B
ex	8479 90	Parts of apparatus for growing or pulling monocrystal semiconductor boules	
ex	8479 90	Parts of apparatus for wet etching, developing, stripping or cleaning semiconductor wafers and flat panel displays	For Attachment B

	HS Code	*Description*	*Comments*
ex	8479 90	Parts of automated machines for transport, handling and storage of semiconductor wafers, wafer cassettes, wafer boxes and other material for semiconductor devices	For Attachment B
ex	8479 90	Parts of encapsulation equipment for assembly of semiconductors	For Attachment B
ex	8479 90	Parts of epitaxial deposition machines for semiconductor wafers	
ex	8479 90	Parts of machines for bending, folding and straightening semiconductor leads	For Attachment B
ex	8479 90	Parts of physical deposition apparatus for for semiconductor production	For Attachment B
ex	8480 71	Injection and compression moulds for the manufacture of semiconductor devices	
ex	8514 10	Resistance heated furnaces and ovens for the manufacture of semiconductor devices on semiconductor wafers	
ex	8514 20	Inductance or dielectric furnaces and ovens for the manufacture of semiconductor devices on semiconductors wafers	
ex	8514 30	Apparatus for rapid heating of semiconductor wafers	For Attachment B
ex	8514 30	Parts of resistance heated furnaces and ovens for the manufacture of semiconductor devices on semiconductor wafers	
ex	8514 90	Parts of apparatus for rapid heating of wafers	For Attachment B
ex	8514 90	Parts of furnaces and ovens of Headings No 8514 10 to No 8514 30	

	HS Code	*Description*	*Comments*
ex	8536 90	Wafer probers	For Attachment B
	8543 11	Ion implanters for doping semiconductor materials	
ex	8543 30	Apparatus for wet etching, developing, stripping or cleaning semiconductor wafers and flat panel displays	For Attachment B
ex	8543 90	Parts of apparatus for wet etching, developing, stripping or cleaning semiconductor wafers and flat panel displays	For Attachment B
ex	8543 90	Parts of ion implanters for doping semiconductor materials	
	9010 41 to 9010 49	Apparatus for projection, drawing or plating circuit patterns on sensitized semiconductor materials and flat panel displays	
ex	9010 90	Parts and accessories of the apparatus of Headings No 9010 41 to 9010 49	
ex	9011 10	Optical stereoscopic microscopes fitted with equipment specifically designed for the handling and transport of semiconductor wafers or reticles	For Attachment B
ex	9011 20	Photomicrographic microscopes fitted with equipment specifically designed for the handling and transport of semiconductor wafers or reticles	For Attachment B
ex	9011 90	Parts and accessories of optical stereoscopic microscopes fitted with equipment specifically designed for the handling and transport of semiconductor wafers or reticles	For Attachment B
ex	9011 90	Parts and accessories of photomicrographic microscopes fitted with equipment specifically designed for the handling and transport of	For Attachment B

	HS Code	*Description*	*Comments*
		semiconductor wafers or reticles	
ex	9012 10	Electron beam microscopes fitted with equipment specifically designed for the handling and transport of semiconductor wafers or reticles	For Attachment B
ex	9012 90	Parts and accessories of electron beam microscopes fitted with equipment specifically designed for the handling and transport of semiconductor wafers or reticles	For Attachment B
ex	9017 20	Pattern generating apparatus of a kind used for producing masks or reticles from photoresist coated substrates	For Attachment B
ex	9017 90	Parts and accessories for pattern generating apparatus of a kind used for producing masks or reticles from photoresist coated substrates	For Attachment B
ex	9017 90	Parts of such pattern generating apparatus	For Attachment B
	9030 82	Instruments and apparatus for measuring or checking semiconductor wafers or devices	
ex	9030 90	Parts and accessories of instruments and apparatus for measuring or checking semiconductor wafers or devices	
ex	9030 90	Parts of instruments and appliances for measuring or checking semiconductor wafers or devices	
	9031 41	Optical instruments and appliances for inspecting semiconductor wafers or devices or for inspecting masks, photomasks or reticles used in manufacturing semiconductor devices	
ex	9031 49	Optical instruments and appliances for measuring surface particulate contamination on semiconductor wafers	

	HS Code	*Description*	*Comments*
ex	9031 90	Parts and accessories of optical instruments and appliances for inspecting semiconductor wafers or devices or for inspecting masks, photomasks or reticles used in manufacturing semiconductor devices	
ex	9031 90	Parts and accessories of optical instruments and appliances for measuring surface particulate contamination on semiconductor wafers	

Attachment B

Positive list of specific products to be covered by this agreement wherever they are classified in the HS.

Where parts are specified, they are to be covered in accordance with HS Notes 2(b) to Section XVI and Chapter 90, respectively.

Computers: automatic data processing machines capable of 1) storing the processing program or programs and at least the data immediately necessary for the execution of the program; 2) being freely programmed in accordance with the requirements of the user; 3) performing arithmetical computations specified by the user; and 4) executing, without human intervention, a processing program which requires them to modify their execution, by logical decision during the processing run. The agreement covers such automatic data processing machines whether or not they are able to receive and process with the assistance of central processing unit telephony signals, television signals, or other analogue or digitally processed audio or video signals. Machines performing a specific function other than data processing, or incorporating or working in conjunction with an automatic data processing machine, and not otherwise specified under Attachment A or B, are not covered by this agreement.
Electric amplifiers when used as repeaters in line telephony products falling within this agreement, and parts thereof
Flat panel displays (including LCD, Electro Luminescence, Plasma and other technologies) for products falling within this agreement, and parts thereof.
Network equipment: Local Area Network (LAN) and Wide Area Network (WAN) apparatus, including those products dedicated for use solely or

principally to permit the interconnection of automatic data processing machines and units thereof for a network that is used primarily for the sharing of resources such as central processor units, data storage devices and input or output units-including adapters, hubs, in-line repeaters, converters, concentrators, bridges and routers, and printed circuit assemblies for physical incorporation into automatic data processing machines and units thereof.
Monitors: display units of automatic data processing machines with a cathode ray tube with a dot screen pitch smaller than 0,4 mm not capable of receiving and processing television signals or other analogue or digitally processed audio or video signals without assistance of a central processing unit of a computer as defined in this agreement. The agreement does not, therefore, cover televisions, including high definition televisions.[3]
Optical disc storage units, for automatic data processing machines (including CD drives and DVD-drives), whether or not having the capability of writing/recording as well as reading, whether or not in their own housings.
Paging alert devices, and parts thereof.
Plotters whether input or output units of HS heading No 8471 or drawing or drafting machines of HS heading No 9017.
Printed Circuit Assemblies for products falling within this agreement, including such assemblies for external connections such as cards that conform to the PCMCIA standard. Such printed circuit assemblies consist of one or more printed circuits of heading 8534 with one or more active elements assembled thereon, with or without passive elements "Active elements" means diodes, transistors, and similar semiconductor devices, whether or not photosensitive, of heading 8541, and integrated circuits and micro assemblies of heading 8542.
Projection type flat panel display units used with automatic data processing machines which can display digital information generated by the central processing unit.
Proprietary format storage devices including media therefor for automatic data processing machines, with or without removable media and whether magnetic, optical or other technology, including Bernoulli Box, Syquest, or Zipdrive cartridge storage units.

3. Participants will conduct a review of this product description in January 1999 under the consultation provisions of paragraph 3 of the Declaration.

Multimedia upgrade kits for automatic data processing machines, and units thereof, put up for retail sale, consisting of, at least, speakers and/or microphones as well as a printed circuit assembly that enables the ADP machines and units thereof to process audio signals (sound cards).
Set top boxes which have a communication function: a microprocessor-based device incorporating a modem for gaining access to the Internet, and having a function of interactive information exchange

Document 36

WAIVER—GENERALIZED SYSTEM OF PREFERENCES*

The CONTRACTING PARTIES to the General Agreement on Tariffs and Trade,

Recognizing that a principal aim of the CONTRACTING PARTIES is promotion of the trade and export earnings of developing countries for the furtherance of their economic development;

Recognizing further that individual and joint action is essential to further the development of the economies of developing countries;

Recalling that at the Second UNCTAD, unanimous agreement was reached in favour of the early establishment of a mutually acceptable system of generalized, non-reciprocal and non-discriminatory preferences beneficial to the developing countries in order to increase the export earnings, to promote the industrialization, and to accelerate the rates of economic growth of these countries;

Considering that mutually acceptable arrangements have been drawn up in the UNCTAD concerning the establishment of generalized, non-discriminatory, non-reciprocal preferential tariff treatment in the markets of developed countries for products originating in developing countries;

Noting the statement of developed contracting parties that the grant of tariff preferences does not constitute a binding commitment and that they are temporary in nature;

*Decision of 25 June 1971, BISD 18S/24.

Recognizing fully that the proposed preferential arrangements do not constitute an impediment to the reduction of tariffs on a most-favoured-nation basis,

Decide:

(a) That without prejudice to any other Article of the General Agreement, the provisions of Article I shall be waived for a period of ten years to the extent necessary to permit developed contracting parties, subject to the procedures set out hereunder, to accord preferential tariff treatment to products originating in developing countries and territories with a view to extending to such countries and territories generally the preferential tariff treatment referred to in the Preamble to this Decision, without according such treatment to like products of other contracting parties

Provided that any such preferential tariff arrangements shall be designed to facilitate trade from developing countries and territories and not to raise barriers to the trade of other contracting parties;

(b) That they will, without duplicating the work of other international organizations, keep under review the operation of this Decision and decide, before its expiry and in the light of the considerations outlined in the Preamble, whether the Decision should be renewed and if so, what its terms should be;

(c) That any contracting party which introduces a preferential tariff arrangement under the terms of the present Decision or later modifies such arrangement, shall notify the CONTRACTING PARTIES and furnish them with all useful information relating to the actions taken pursuant to the present Decision;

(d) That such contracting party shall afford adequate opportunity for consultations at the request of any other contracting party which considers that any benefit accruing to it under the General Agreement may be or is being impaired unduly as a result of the preferential arrangement;

(e) That any contracting party which considers that the arrangement or its later extension is not consistent with the present Decision or that any benefit accruing to it under the General Agreement may be or is being impaired unduly as a result of the arrangement or its subsequent extension and that consultations have proved unsatisfactory, may bring the matter before the CONTRACTING PARTIES which will examine it promptly and will formulate any recommendations that they judge appropriate.

Document 37

"ENABLING CLAUSE"*

Official name: Differential and More Favourable Treatment. Reciprocity and Fuller Participation of Developing Countries

Following negotiations within the framework of the Multilateral Trade Negotiations, the CONTRACTING PARTIES *decide* as follows:

1. Notwithstanding the provisions of Article I of the General Agreement, contracting parties may accord differential and more favourable treatment to developing countries,[1] without according such treatment to other contracting parties.

2. The provisions of paragraph 1 apply to the following:[2]

(a) Preferential tariff treatment accorded by developed contracting parties to products originating in developing countries in accordance with the Generalized System of Preferences,[3]

(b) Differential and more favourable treatment with respect to the provisions of the General Agreement concerning non-tariff measures

*Decision of 28 November 1974, GATT Document L/4903.

1. The words "developing countries" as used in this text are to be understood to refer also to developing territories.

2. It would remain open for the CONTRACTING PARTIES to consider on an *ad hoc* basis under the GATT provisions for joint action any proposals for differential and more favourable treatment not falling within the scope of this paragraph.

3. As described in the Decision of the CONTRACTING PARTIES of 25 June 1971, relating to the establishment of "generalized, non-reciprocal and non discriminatory preferences beneficial to the developing countries" (BISD 18S/24).

governed by the provisions of instruments multilaterally negotiated under the auspices of the GATT;

(c) Regional or global arrangements entered into amongst less-developed contracting parties for the mutual reduction or elimination of tariffs and, in accordance with criteria or conditions which may be prescribed by the CONTRACTING PARTIES, for the mutual reduction or elimination of non-tariff measures, on products imported from one another;

(d) Special treatment on the least developed among the developing countries in the context of any general or specific measures in favour of developing countries.

3. Any differential and more favourable treatment provided under this clause:

(a) shall be designed to facilitate and promote the trade of developing countries and not to raise barriers to or create undue difficulties for the trade of any other contracting parties;

(b) shall not constitute an impediment to the reduction or elimination of tariffs and other restrictions to trade on a most-favoured-nation basis;

(c) shall in the case of such treatment accorded by developed contracting parties to developing countries be designed and, if necessary, modified, to respond positively to the development, financial and trade needs of developing countries.

4. Any contracting party taking action to introduce an arrangement pursuant to paragraphs 1, 2 and 3 above or subsequently taking action to introduce modification or withdrawal of the differential and more favourable treatment so provided shall:[4]

(a) notify the CONTRACTING PARTIES and furnish them with all the information they may deem appropriate relating to such action;

(b) afford adequate opportunity for prompt consultations at the request of any interested contracting party with respect to any difficulty or matter that may arise. The CONTRACTING PARTIES shall, if requested to do so by such contracting party, consult with all contracting parties concerned with respect to the matter with a view to reaching solutions satisfactory to all such contracting parties.

4. Nothing in these provisions shall affect the rights of contracting parties under the General Agreement.

5. The developed countries do not expect reciprocity for commitments made by them in trade negotiations to reduce or remove tariffs and other barriers to the trade of developing countries, i.e., the developed countries do not expect the developing countries, in the course of trade negotiations, to make contributions which are inconsistent with their individual development, financial and trade needs. Developed contracting parties shall therefore not seek, neither shall less-developed contracting parties be required to make, concessions that are inconsistent with the latter's development, financial and trade needs.

6. Having regard to the special economic difficulties and the particular development, financial and trade needs of the least-developed countries, the developed countries shall exercise the utmost restraint in seeking any concessions or contributions for commitments made by them to reduce or remove tariffs and other barriers to the trade of such countries, and the least-developed countries shall not be expected to make concessions or contributions that are inconsistent with the recognition of their particular situation and problems.

7. The concessions and contributions made and the obligations assumed by developed and less-developed contracting parties under the provisions of the General Agreement should promote the basic objectives of the Agreement, including those embodied in the Preamble and in Article XXXVI. Less-developed contracting parties expect that their capacity to make contributions or negotiated concessions or take other mutually agreed action under the provisions and procedures of the General Agreement would improve with the progressive development of their economies and improvement in their trade situation and they would accordingly expect to participate more fully in the framework of rights and obligations under the General Agreement.

8. Particular account shall be taken of the serious difficulty of the least-developed countries in making concessions and contributions in view of their special economic situation and their development, financial and trade needs.

9. The contracting parties will collaborate in arrangements for review of the operation of these provisions, bearing in mind the need for individual and joint efforts by contracting parties to meet the development needs of developing countries and the objectives of the General Agreement.

Document 38

PREFERENTIAL TARIFF TREATMENT FOR LEAST-DEVELOPED COUNTRIES*

Decision on Waiver, adopted on 15 June 1999[1]

Considering that the Parties to the World Trade Organization Agreement have recognized the need for positive efforts designed to ensure that developing countries, and especially the least-developed among them, secure a share in the growth in international trade commensurate with the needs of their economic development;

Considering the statements contained in the Comprehensive and Integrated WTO Plan of Action for the Least-Developed Countries adopted at the Singapore Ministerial Conference on 13 December 1996 and in the Ministerial Declaration of 20 May 1998 concerning integration of least-developed countries into the world trading system and providing predictable and favourable market access conditions for the products of such countries;

Considering the 1979 Decision on Differential and More Favourable Treatment, Reciprocity and Fuller Participation of Developing Countries and the 1994 Decision on Measures in Favour of Least-Developed Countries, and without prejudice to rights of Members to continue to act pursuant to the provisions contained in those Decisions;

Desiring to provide an additional means for developing country Members to offer preferential tariff treatment to products of least-developed

* WTO Document WT/L/304.

1. Adopted in accordance with the Decision-Making Procedures under Articles IX and XII of the WTO Agreement agreed by the General Council (WT/L/93).

countries notwithstanding the obligations of paragraph 1 of Article I of the General Agreement;

Having regard to the Guiding Principles to be followed in considering applications for waivers adopted on 1 November 1956, the Understanding in Respect of Waivers of Obligations under the General Agreement on Tariffs and Trade 1994, and paragraphs 3 and 4 of Article IX of the Marrakesh Agreement Establishing the World Trade Organization (the "WTO Agreement");

Members, acting pursuant to the provisions of paragraph 3 of Article IX of the WTO Agreement,

Decide that:

1. Subject to the terms and conditions set out hereunder, the provisions of paragraph 1 of Article I of the GATT 1994 shall be waived until 30 June 2009, to the extent necessary to allow developing country Members to provide preferential tariff treatment to products of least-developed countries, designated as such by the United Nations, without being required to extend the same tariff rates to like products of any other Member.

2. Developing country Members wishing to take actions pursuant to the provisions of this Waiver shall notify to the Council on Trade in Goods the list of all products of least-developed countries for which preferential tariff treatment is to be provided on a generalized, non-reciprocal and non-discriminatory basis and the preference margins to be accorded. Subsequent modifications to the preferences shall similarly be notified.

3. Any preferential tariff treatment implemented pursuant to this Waiver shall be designed to facilitate and promote the trade of least-developed countries and not to raise barriers or create undue difficulties for the trade of any other Member. Such preferential tariff treatment shall not constitute an impediment to the reduction or elimination of tariffs on a most-favoured-nation basis.

4. In accordance with the provisions of paragraph 4 of Article IX of the WTO Agreement, the General Council shall review annually whether the exceptional circumstances justifying the Waiver still exist and whether the terms and conditions attached to the Waiver have been met.

5. The government of any Member providing preferential tariff treatment pursuant to this Waiver shall, upon request, promptly enter into consultations with any interested Member with respect to any difficulty or any matter that may arise as a result of the implementation of programmes authorized by this Waiver. Where a Member considers that any benefit

accruing to it under GATT 1994 may be or is being impaired unduly as a result of such implementation, such consultation shall examine the possibility of action for a satisfactory adjustment of the matter. This Waiver does not affect Members' rights as set forth in the Understanding in Respect of Waivers of Obligations under GATT 1994.

6. This waiver does not affect in any way and is without prejudice to rights of Members in their actions pursuant to the provisions of the 1979 Decision on Differential and More Favourable Treatment, Reciprocity and Fuller Participation of Developing Countries.

PART VI

Trade in Services

Document 39

GENERAL AGREEMENT ON TRADE IN SERVICES

Annex 1B—Agreement Establishing the World Trade Organization

General Agreement on Trade in Services

Members,

Recognizing the growing importance of trade in services for the growth and development of the world economy;

Wishing to establish a multilateral framework of principles and rules for trade in services with a view to the expansion of such trade under conditions of transparency and progressive liberalization and as a means of promoting the economic growth of all trading partners and the development of developing countries;

Desiring the early achievement of progressively higher levels of liberalization of trade in services through successive rounds of multilateral negotiations aimed at promoting the interests of all participants on a mutually advantageous basis and at securing an overall balance of rights and obligations, while giving due respect to national policy objectives;

Recognizing the right of Members to regulate, and to introduce new regulations, on the supply of services within their territories in order to meet national policy objectives and, given asymmetries existing with respect to the degree of development of services regulations in different countries, the particular need of developing countries to exercise this right;

Desiring to facilitate the increasing participation of developing countries in trade in services and the expansion of their service exports including, *inter alia*, through the strengthening of their domestic services capacity and its efficiency and competitiveness;

Taking particular account of the serious difficulty of the least-developed countries in view of their special economic situation and their development, trade and financial needs;

Hereby *agree* as follows:

Part I

SCOPE AND DEFINITION

Article I

Scope and Definition

1. This Agreement applies to measures by Members affecting trade in services.

2. For the purposes of this Agreement, trade in services is defined as the supply of a service:

(a) from the territory of one Member into the territory of any other Member;

(b) in the territory of one Member to the service consumer of any other Member;

(c) by a service supplier of one Member, through commercial presence in the territory of any other Member;

(d) by a service supplier of one Member, through presence of natural persons of a Member in the territory of any other Member.

3. For the purposes of this Agreement:

(a) "measures by Members" means measures taken by:

(i) central, regional or local governments and authorities; and

(ii) non-governmental bodies in the exercise of powers delegated by central, regional or local governments or authorities;

In fulfilling its obligations and commitments under the Agreement, each Member shall take such reasonable measures as may be available to it to ensure their observance by regional and local governments and authorities and non-governmental bodies within its territory;

(b) "services" includes any service in any sector except services supplied in the exercise of governmental authority;

(c) "a service supplied in the exercise of governmental authority" means any service which is supplied neither on a commercial basis, nor in competition with one or more service suppliers.

Part II

GENERAL OBLIGATIONS AND DISCIPLINES

Article II

Most-Favoured-Nation Treatment

1. With respect to any measure covered by this Agreement, each Member shall accord immediately and unconditionally to services and service suppliers of any other Member treatment no less favourable than that it accords to like services and service suppliers of any other country.

2. A Member may maintain a measure inconsistent with paragraph 1 provided that such a measure is listed in, and meets the conditions of, the Annex on Article II Exemptions.

3. The provisions of this Agreement shall not be so construed as to prevent any Member from conferring or according advantages to adjacent countries in order to facilitate exchanges limited to contiguous frontier zones of services that are both locally produced and consumed.

Article III

Transparency

1. Each Member shall publish promptly and, except in emergency situations, at the latest by the time of their entry into force, all relevant measures of general application which pertain to or affect the operation of

this Agreement. International agreements pertaining to or affecting trade in services to which a Member is a signatory shall also be published.

2. Where publication as referred to in paragraph 1 is not practicable, such information shall be made otherwise publicly available.

3. Each Member shall promptly and at least annually inform the Council for Trade in Services of the introduction of any new, or any changes to existing, laws, regulations or administrative guidelines which significantly affect trade in services covered by its specific commitments under this Agreement.

4. Each Member shall respond promptly to all requests by any other Member for specific information on any of its measures of general application or international agreements within the meaning of paragraph 1. Each Member shall also establish one or more enquiry points to provide specific information to other Members, upon request, on all such matters as well as those subject to the notification requirement in paragraph 3. Such enquiry points shall be established within two years from the date of entry into force of the Agreement Establishing the WTO (referred to in this Agreement as the "WTO Agreement"). Appropriate flexibility with respect to the time-limit within which such enquiry points are to be established may be agreed upon for individual developing country Members. Enquiry points need not be depositories of laws and regulations.

5. Any Member may notify to the Council for Trade in Services any measure, taken by any other Member, which it considers affects the operation of this Agreement.

Article III bis

Disclosure of Confidential Information

Nothing in this Agreement shall require any Member to provide confidential information, the disclosure of which would impede law enforcement, or otherwise be contrary to the public interest, or which would prejudice legitimate commercial interests of particular enterprises, public or private.

Article IV

Increasing Participation of Developing Countries

1. The increasing participation of developing country Members in world trade shall be facilitated through negotiated specific commitments, by different Members pursuant to Parts III and IV of this Agreement, relating to:

(a) the strengthening of their domestic services capacity and its efficiency and competitiveness, *inter alia* through access to technology on a commercial basis;

(b) the improvement of their access to distribution channels and information networks; and

(c) the liberalization of market access in sectors and modes of supply of export interest to them.

2. Developed country Members, and to the extent possible other Members, shall establish contact points within two years from the date of entry into force of the WTO Agreement to facilitate the access of developing country Members' service suppliers to information, related to their respective markets, concerning:

(a) commercial and technical aspects of the supply of services;

(b) registration, recognition and obtaining of professional qualifications; and

(c) the availability of services technology.

3. Special priority shall be given to the least-developed country Members in the implementation of paragraphs 1 and 2. Particular account shall be taken of the serious difficulty of the least-developed countries in accepting negotiated specific commitments in view of their special economic situation and their development, trade and financial needs.

Article V

Economic Integration

1. This Agreement shall not prevent any of its Members from being a party to or entering into an agreement liberalizing trade in services between or among the parties to such an agreement, provided that such an agreement:

(a) has substantial sectoral coverage,[1] and

1. This condition is understood in terms of number of sectors, volume of trade affected and modes of supply. In order to meet this condition, agreements should not provide for the *a priori* exclusion of any mode of supply.

(b) provides for the absence or elimination of substantially all discrimination, in the sense of Article XVII, between or among the parties, in the sectors covered under subparagraph (a), through:

(i) elimination of existing discriminatory measures, and/or

(ii) prohibition of new or more discriminatory measures, either at the entry into force of that agreement or on the basis of a reasonable time-frame, except for measures permitted under Articles XI, XII, XIV and XIV bis.

2. In evaluating whether the conditions under paragraph 1(b) are met, consideration may be given to the relationship of the agreement to a wider process of economic integration or trade liberalization among the countries concerned.

3. (a) Where developing countries are parties to an agreement of the type referred to in paragraph 1, flexibility shall be provided for regarding the conditions set out in paragraph 1, particularly with reference to subparagraph (b) thereof, in accordance with the level of development of the countries concerned, both overall and in individual sectors and subsectors.

(b) Notwithstanding paragraph 6, in the case of an agreement of the type referred to in paragraph 1 involving only developing countries, more favourable treatment may be granted to juridical persons owned or controlled by natural persons of the parties to such an agreement.

4. Any agreement referred to in paragraph 1 shall be designed to facilitate trade between the parties to the agreement and shall not in respect of any Member outside the agreement raise the overall level of barriers to trade in services within the respective sectors or subsectors compared to the level applicable prior to such an agreement.

5. If, in the conclusion, enlargement or any significant modification of any agreement under paragraph 1, a Member intends to withdraw or modify a specific commitment inconsistently with the terms and conditions set out in its Schedule, it shall provide at least 90 days advance notice of such modification or withdrawal and the procedure set forth in paragraphs 2, 3 and 4 of Article XXI shall apply.

6. A service supplier of any other Member that is a juridical person constituted under the laws of a party to an agreement referred to in paragraph 1 shall be entitled to treatment granted under such agreement, provided that it engages in substantive business operations in the territory of the parties to such agreement.

7. (a) Members which are parties to any agreement referred to in paragraph 1 shall promptly notify any such agreement and any enlargement or any significant modification of that agreement to the Council for Trade in Services. They shall also make available to the Council such relevant information as may be requested by it. The Council may establish a working party to examine such an agreement or enlargement or modification of that agreement and to report to the Council on its consistency with this Article.

(b) Members which are parties to any agreement referred to in paragraph 1 which is implemented on the basis of a time-frame shall report periodically to the Council for Trade in Services on its implementation. The Council may establish a working party to examine such reports if it deems such a working party necessary.

(c) Based on the reports of the working parties referred to in subparagraphs (a) and (b), the Council may make recommendations to the parties as it deems appropriate.

8. A Member which is a party to any agreement referred to in paragraph 1 may not seek compensation for trade benefits that may accrue to any other Member from such agreement.

Article V bis

Labour Markets Integration Agreements

This Agreement shall not prevent any of its Members from being a party to an agreement establishing full integration[2] of the labour markets between or among the parties to such an agreement, provided that such an agreement:

(a) exempts citizens of parties to the agreement from requirements concerning residency and work permits;

(b) is notified to the Council for Trade in Services.

Article VI

Domestic Regulation

1. In sectors where specific commitments are undertaken, each Member shall ensure that all measures of general application affecting trade in services are administered in a reasonable, objective and impartial manner.

2. Typically, such integration provides citizens of the parties concerned with a right of free entry to the employment markets of the parties and includes measures concerning conditions of pay, other conditions of employment and social benefits.

2. (a) Each Member shall maintain or institute as soon as practicable judicial, arbitral or administrative tribunals or procedures which provide, at the request of an affected service supplier, for the prompt review of, and where justified, appropriate remedies for, administrative decisions affecting trade in services. Where such procedures are not independent of the agency entrusted with the administrative decision concerned, the Member shall ensure that the procedures in fact provide for an objective and impartial review.

(b) The provisions of subparagraph (a) shall not be construed to require a Member to institute such tribunals or procedures where this would be inconsistent with its constitutional structure or the nature of its legal system.

3. Where authorization is required for the supply of a service on which a specific commitment has been made, the competent authorities of a Member shall, within a reasonable period of time after the submission of an application considered complete under domestic laws and regulations, inform the applicant of the decision concerning the application. At the request of the applicant, the competent authorities of the Member shall provide, without undue delay, information concerning the status of the application.

4. With a view to ensuring that measures relating to qualification requirements and procedures, technical standards and licensing requirements do not constitute unnecessary barriers to trade in services, the Council for Trade in Services shall, through appropriate bodies it may establish, develop any necessary disciplines. Such disciplines shall aim to ensure that such requirements are, *inter alia*:

(a) based on objective and transparent criteria, such as competence and the ability to supply the service;

(b) not more burdensome than necessary to ensure the quality of the service;

(c) in the case of licensing procedures, not in themselves a restriction on the supply of the service.

5. (a) In sectors in which a Member has undertaken specific commitments, pending the entry into force of disciplines developed in these sectors pursuant to paragraph 4, the Member shall not apply licensing and qualification requirements and technical standards that nullify or impair such specific commitments in a manner which:

(i) does not comply with the criteria outlined in subparagraphs 4(a), (b) or (c); and

(ii) could not reasonably have been expected of that Member at the time the specific commitments in those sectors were made.

(b) In determining whether a Member is in conformity with the obligation under paragraph 5(a), account shall be taken of international standards of relevant international organizations[3] applied by that Member.

6. In sectors where specific commitments regarding professional services are undertaken, each Member shall provide for adequate procedures to verify the competence of professionals of any other Member.

Article VII

Recognition

1. For the purposes of the fulfilment, in whole or in part, of its standards or criteria for the authorization, licensing or certification of services suppliers, and subject to the requirements of paragraph 3, a Member may recognize the education or experience obtained, requirements met, or licenses or certifications granted in a particular country. Such recognition, which may be achieved through harmonization or otherwise, may be based upon an agreement or arrangement with the country concerned or may be accorded autonomously.

2. A Member that is a party to an agreement or arrangement of the type referred to in paragraph 1, whether existing or future, shall afford adequate opportunity for other interested Members to negotiate their accession to such an agreement or arrangement or to negotiate comparable ones with it. Where a Member accords recognition autonomously, it shall afford adequate opportunity for any other Member to demonstrate that education, experience, licenses, or certifications obtained or requirements met in that other Member's territory should be recognized.

3. A Member shall not accord recognition in a manner which would constitute a means of discrimination between countries in the application of its standards or criteria for the authorization, licensing or certification of services suppliers, or a disguised restriction on trade in services.

4. Each Member shall:

(a) within 12 months from the date on which the WTO Agreement takes effect for it, inform the Council for Trade in Services of its existing

3. The term "relevant international organizations" refers to international bodies whose membership is open to the relevant bodies of at least all Members of the WTO.

recognition measures and state whether such measures are based on agreements or arrangements of the type referred to in paragraph 1;

(b) promptly inform the Council for Trade in Services as far in advance as possible of the opening of negotiations on an agreement or arrangement of the type referred to in paragraph 1 in order to provide adequate opportunity to any other Member to indicate their interest in participating in the negotiations before they enter a substantive phase;

(c) promptly inform the Council for Trade in Services when it adopts new recognition measures or significantly modifies existing ones and state whether the measures are based on an agreement or arrangement of the type referred to in paragraph 1.

5. Wherever appropriate, recognition should be based on multilaterally agreed criteria. In appropriate cases, Members shall work in cooperation with relevant intergovernmental and non-governmental organizations towards the establishment and adoption of common international standards and criteria for recognition and common international standards for the practice of relevant services trades and professions.

Article VIII

Monopolies and Exclusive Service Suppliers

1. Each Member shall ensure that any monopoly supplier of a service in its territory does not, in the supply of the monopoly service in the relevant market, act in a manner inconsistent with that Member's obligations under Article II and specific commitments.

2. Where a Member's monopoly supplier competes, either directly or through an affiliated company, in the supply of a service outside the scope of its monopoly rights and which is subject to that Member's specific commitments, the Member shall ensure that such a supplier does not abuse its monopoly position to act in its territory in a manner inconsistent with such commitments.

3. The Council for Trade in Services may, at the request of a Member which has a reason to believe that a monopoly supplier of a service of any other Member is acting in a manner inconsistent with paragraph 1 or 2, request the Member establishing, maintaining or authorizing such supplier to provide specific information concerning the relevant operations.

4. If, after the date of entry into force of the WTO Agreement, a Member grants monopoly rights regarding the supply of a service covered by its specific commitments, that Member shall notify the Council for Trade

in Services no later than three months before the intended implementation of the grant of monopoly rights and the provisions of paragraphs 2, 3 and 4 of Article XXI shall apply.

5. The provisions of this Article shall also apply to cases of exclusive service suppliers, where a Member, formally or in effect, (*a*) authorizes or establishes a small number of service suppliers and (*b*) substantially prevents competition among those suppliers in its territory.

Article IX

Business Practices

1. Members recognize that certain business practices of service suppliers, other than those falling under Article VIII, may restrain competition and thereby restrict trade in services.

2. Each Member shall, at the request of any other Member, enter into consultations with a view to eliminating practices referred to in paragraph 1. The Member addressed shall accord full and sympathetic consideration to such a request and shall cooperate through the supply of publicly available non-confidential information of relevance to the matter in question. The Member addressed shall also provide other information available to the requesting Member, subject to its domestic law and to the conclusion of satisfactory agreement concerning the safeguarding of its confidentiality by the requesting Member.

Article X

Emergency Safeguard Measures

1. There shall be multilateral negotiations on the question of emergency safeguard measures based on the principle of non-discrimination. The results of such negotiations shall enter into effect on a date not later than three years from the date of entry into force of the WTO Agreement.

2. In the period before the entry into effect of the results of the negotiations referred to in paragraph 1, any Member may, notwithstanding the provisions of paragraph 1 of Article XXI, notify the Council on Trade in Services of its intention to modify or withdraw a specific commitment after a period of one year from the date on which the commitment enters into force; provided that the Member shows cause to the Council that the modification or withdrawal cannot await the lapse of the three-year period provided for in paragraph 1 of Article XXI.

3. The provisions of paragraph 2 shall cease to apply three years after the date of entry into force of the WTO Agreement.

Article XI

Payments and Transfers

1. Except under the circumstances envisaged in Article XII, a Member shall not apply restrictions on international transfers and payments for current transactions relating to its specific commitments.

2. Nothing in this Agreement shall affect the rights and obligations of the members of the International Monetary Fund under the Articles of Agreement of the Fund, including the use of exchange actions which are in conformity with the Articles of Agreement, provided that a Member shall not impose restrictions on any capital transactions inconsistently with its specific commitments regarding such transactions, except under Article XII or at the request of the Fund.

Article XII

Restrictions to Safeguard the Balance of Payments

1. In the event of serious balance-of-payments and external financial difficulties or threat thereof, a Member may adopt or maintain restrictions on trade in services on which it has undertaken specific commitments, including on payments or transfers for transactions related to such commitments. It is recognized that particular pressures on the balance of payments of a Member in the process of economic development or economic transition may necessitate the use of restrictions to ensure, *inter alia*, the maintenance of a level of financial reserves adequate for the implementation of its programme of economic development or economic transition.

2. The restrictions referred to in paragraph 1:

(a) shall not discriminate among Members;

(b) shall be consistent with the Articles of Agreement of the International Monetary Fund;

(c) shall avoid unnecessary damage to the commercial, economic and financial interests of any other Member;

(d) shall not exceed those necessary to deal with the circumstances described in paragraph 1;

(e) shall be temporary and be phased out progressively as the situation specified in paragraph 1 improves.

3. In determining the incidence of such restrictions, Members may give priority to the supply of services which are more essential to their economic

or development programmes. However, such restrictions shall not be adopted or maintained for the purpose of protecting a particular service sector.

4. Any restrictions adopted or maintained under paragraph 1, or any changes therein, shall be promptly notified to the General Council.

5. (a) Members applying the provisions of this Article shall consult promptly with the Committee on Balance-of-Payments Restrictions on restrictions adopted under this Article.

(b) The Ministerial Conference shall establish procedures[4] for periodic consultations with the objective of enabling such recommendations to be made to the Member concerned as it may deem appropriate.

(c) Such consultations shall assess the balance-of-payment situation of the Member concerned and the restrictions adopted or maintained under this Article, taking into account, *inter alia,* such factors as:

(i) the nature and extent of the balance-of-payments and the external financial difficulties;

(ii) the external economic and trading environment of the consulting Member;

(iii) alternative corrective measures which may be available.

(d) The consultations shall address the compliance of any restrictions with paragraph 2, in particular the progressive phaseout of restrictions in accordance with paragraph 2(e).

(e) In such consultations, all findings of statistical and other facts presented by the International Monetary Fund relating to foreign exchange, monetary reserves and balance of payments, shall be accepted and conclusions shall be based on the assessment by the Fund of the balance-of-payments and the external financial situation of the consulting Member.

6. If a Member which is not a member of the International Monetary Fund wishes to apply the provisions of this Article, the Ministerial Conference shall establish a review procedure and any other procedures necessary.

4. It is understood that the procedures under paragraph 5 shall be the same as the GATT 1994 procedures.

Article XIII

Government Procurement

1. Articles II, XVI and XVII shall not apply to laws, regulations or requirements governing the procurement by governmental agencies of services purchased for governmental purposes and not with a view to commercial resale or with a view to use in the supply of services for commercial sale.

2. There shall be multilateral negotiations on government procurement in services under this Agreement within two years from the date of entry into force of the WTO Agreement.

Article XIV

General Exceptions

Subject to the requirement that such measures are not applied in a manner which would constitute a means of arbitrary or unjustifiable discrimination between countries where like conditions prevail, or a disguised restriction on trade in services, nothing in this Agreement shall be construed to prevent the adoption or enforcement by any Member of measures:

(a) necessary to protect public morals or to maintain public order;[5]

(b) necessary to protect human, animal or plant life or health;

(c) necessary to secure compliance with laws or regulations which are not inconsistent with the provisions of this Agreement including those relating to:

(i) the prevention of deceptive and fraudulent practices or to deal with the effects of a default on services contracts;

(ii) the protection of the privacy of individuals in relation to the processing and dissemination of personal data and the protection of confidentiality of individual records and accounts;

(iii) safety;

(d) inconsistent with Article XVII, provided that the difference in treatment is aimed at ensuring the equitable or effective[6] imposition or

5. The public order exception may be invoked only where a genuine and sufficiently serious threat is posed to one of the fundamental interests of society.

6. Measures that are aimed at ensuring the equitable or effective imposition or collection of direct taxes include measures taken by a Member under its taxation system which:

collection of direct taxes in respect of services or service suppliers of other Members;

(e) inconsistent with Article II, provided that the difference in treatment is the result of an agreement on the avoidance of double taxation or provisions on the avoidance of double taxation in any other international agreement or arrangement by which the Member is bound.

Article XIV bis

Security Exceptions

1. Nothing in this Agreement shall be construed:

(a) to require any Member to furnish any information, the disclosure of which it considers contrary to its essential security interests; or

(b) to prevent any Member from taking any action which it considers necessary for the protection of its essential security interests:

(i) relating to the supply of services as carried out directly or indirectly for the purpose of provisioning a military establishment;

(ii) relating to fissionable and fusionable materials or the materials from which they are derived;

(iii) taken in time of war or other emergency in international relations; or

---

(i) apply to non-resident service suppliers in recognition of the fact that the tax obligation of non-residents is determined with respect to taxable items sourced or located in the Member's territory; or

(ii) apply to non-residents in order to ensure the imposition or collection of taxes in the Member's territory; or

(iii) apply to non-residents or residents in order to prevent the avoidance or evasion of taxes, including compliance measures; or

(iv) apply to consumers of services supplied in or from the territory of another Member in order to ensure the imposition or collection of taxes on such consumers derived from sources in the Member's territory; or

(v) distinguish service suppliers subject to tax on worldwide taxable items from other service suppliers, in recognition of the difference in the nature of the tax base between them; or

(vi) determine, allocate or apportion income, profit, gain, loss, deduction or credit of resident persons or branches, or between related persons or branches of the same person, in order to safeguard the Member's tax base.

Tax terms or concepts in paragraph (d) of Article XIV and in this footnote are determined according to tax definitions and concepts, or equivalent or similar definitions and concepts, under the domestic law of the Member taking the measure.

(c) to prevent any Member from taking any action in pursuance of its obligations under the United Nations Charter for the maintenance of international peace and security.

2. The Council for Trade in Services shall be informed to the fullest extent possible of measures taken under paragraphs 1(b) and (c) and of their termination.

Article XV

Subsidies

1. Members recognize that, in certain circumstances, subsidies may have distortive effects on trade in services. Members shall enter into negotiations with a view to developing the necessary multilateral disciplines to avoid such trade-distortive effects.[7] The negotiations shall also address the appropriateness of countervailing procedures. Such negotiations shall recognize the role of subsidies in relation to the development programmes of developing countries and take into account the needs of Members, particularly developing country Members, for flexibility in this area. For the purpose of such negotiations, Members shall exchange information concerning all subsidies related to trade in services that they provide to their domestic service suppliers.

2. Any Member which considers that it is adversely affected by a subsidy of another Member may request consultations with that Member on such matters. Such requests shall be accorded sympathetic consideration.

Part III

SPECIFIC COMMITMENTS

Article XVI

Market Access

1. With respect to market access through the modes of supply identified in Article I, each Member shall accord services and service suppliers of any other Member treatment no less favourable than that provided for under the terms, limitations and conditions agreed and specified in its Schedule.[8]

7. A future work programme shall determine how, and in what time-frame, negotiations on such multilateral disciplines will be conducted.

8. If a Member undertakes a market-access commitment in relation to the supply of a service through the mode of supply referred to in subparagraph 2(a) of Article I and if the cross-border movement of capital is an essential part of the service itself, that Member is thereby committed to allow such movement of capital. If a Member undertakes a market-access

2. In sectors where market-access commitments are undertaken, the measures which a Member shall not maintain or adopt either on the basis of a regional subdivision or on the basis of its entire territory, unless otherwise specified in its Schedule, are defined as:

(a) limitations on the number of service suppliers whether in the form of numerical quotas, monopolies, exclusive service suppliers or the requirements of an economic needs test;

(b) limitations on the total value of service transactions or assets in the form of numerical quotas or the requirement of an economic needs test;

(c) limitations on the total number of service operations or on the total quantity of service output expressed in terms of designated numerical units in the form of quotas or the requirement of an economic needs test;[9]

(d) limitations on the total number of natural persons that may be employed in a particular service sector or that a service supplier may employ and who are necessary for, and directly related to, the supply of a specific service in the form of numerical quotas or the requirement of an economic needs test;

(e) measures which restrict or require specific types of legal entity or joint venture through which a service supplier may supply a service; and

(f) limitations on the participation of foreign capital in terms of maximum percentage limit on foreign shareholding or the total value of individual or aggregate foreign investment.

Article XVII

National Treatment

1. In the sectors inscribed in its Schedule, and subject to any conditions and qualifications set out therein, each Member shall accord to services and service suppliers of any other Member, in respect of all measures affecting the supply of services, treatment no less favourable than that it accords to its own like services and service suppliers.[10]

---

commitment in relation to the supply of a service through the mode of supply referred to in subparagraph 2(c) of Article I, it is thereby committed to allow related transfers of capital into its territory.

9. Subparagraph 2(c) does not cover measures of a Member which limit inputs for the supply of services.

10. Specific commitments assumed under this Article shall not be construed to require any Member to compensate for any inherent competitive disadvantages which result from the foreign character of the relevant services or service suppliers.

2. A Member may meet the requirement of paragraph 1 by according to services and service suppliers of any other Member, either formally identical treatment or formally different treatment to that it accords to its own like services and service suppliers.

3. Formally identical or formally different treatment shall be considered to be less favourable if it modifies the conditions of competition in favour of services or service suppliers of the Member compared to like services or service suppliers of any other Member.

Article XVIII

Additional Commitments

Members may negotiate commitments with respect to measures affecting trade in services not subject to scheduling under Articles XVI or XVII, including those regarding qualifications, standards or licensing matters. Such commitments shall be inscribed in a Member's Schedule.

Part IV

PROGRESSIVE LIBERALIZATION

Article XIX

Negotiation of Specific Commitments

1. In pursuance of the objectives of this Agreement, Members shall enter into successive rounds of negotiations, beginning not later than five years from the date of entry into force of the WTO Agreement and periodically thereafter, with a view to achieving a progressively higher level of liberalization. Such negotiations shall be directed to the reduction or elimination of the adverse effects on trade in services of measures as a means of providing effective market access. This process shall take place with a view to promoting the interests of all participants on a mutually advantageous basis and to securing an overall balance of rights and obligations.

2. The process of liberalization shall take place with due respect for national policy objectives and the level of development of individual Members, both overall and in individual sectors. There shall be appropriate flexibility for individual developing country Members for opening fewer sectors, liberalizing fewer types of transactions, progressively extending market access in line with their development situation and, when making access to their markets available to foreign service suppliers, attaching to such access conditions aimed at achieving the objectives referred to in Article IV.

3. For each round, negotiating guidelines and procedures shall be established. For the purposes of establishing such guidelines, the Council for Trade in Services shall carry out an assessment of trade in services in overall terms and on a sectoral basis with reference to the objectives of this Agreement, including those set out in paragraph 1 of Article IV. Negotiating guidelines shall establish modalities for the treatment of liberalization undertaken autonomously by Members since previous negotiations, as well as for the special treatment for least-developed country Members under the provisions of paragraph 3 of Article IV.

4. The process of progressive liberalization shall be advanced in each such round through bilateral, plurilateral or multilateral negotiations directed towards increasing the general level of specific commitments undertaken by Members under this Agreement.

Article XX

Schedules of Specific Commitments

1. Each Member shall set out in a schedule the specific commitments it undertakes under Part III of this Agreement. With respect to sectors where such commitments are undertaken, each Schedule shall specify:

(a) terms, limitations and conditions on market access;

(b) conditions and qualifications on national treatment;

(c) undertakings relating to additional commitments;

(d) where appropriate the time-frame for implementation of such commitments; and

(e) the date of entry into force of such commitments.

2. Measures inconsistent with both Articles XVI and XVII shall be inscribed in the column relating to Article XVI. In this case the inscription will be considered to provide a condition or qualification to Article XVII as well.

3. Schedules of specific commitments shall be annexed to this Agreement and shall form an integral part thereof.

Article XXI

Modification of Schedules

1. (a) A Member (referred to in this Article as the "modifying Member") may modify or withdraw any commitment in its Schedule, at any time after

three years have elapsed from the date on which that commitment entered into force, in accordance with the provisions of this Article.

(b) A modifying Member shall notify its intent to modify or withdraw a commitment pursuant to this Article to the Council for Trade in Services no later than three months before the intended date of implementation of the modification or withdrawal.

2. (a) At the request of any Member the benefits of which under this Agreement may be affected (referred to in this Article as an "affected Member") by a proposed modification or withdrawal notified under subparagraph 1(b), the modifying Member shall enter into negotiations with a view to reaching agreement on any necessary compensatory adjustment. In such negotiations and agreement, the Members concerned shall endeavour to maintain a general level of mutually advantageous commitments not less favourable to trade than that provided for in Schedules of specific commitments prior to such negotiations.

(b) Compensatory adjustments shall be made on a most-favoured-nation basis.

3. (a) If agreement is not reached between the modifying Member and any affected Member before the end of the period provided for negotiations, such affected Member may refer the matter to arbitration. Any affected Member that wishes to enforce a right that it may have to compensation must participate in the arbitration.

(b) If no affected Member has requested arbitration, the modifying Member shall be free to implement the proposed modification or withdrawal.

4. (a) The modifying Member may not modify or withdraw its commitment until it has made compensatory adjustments in conformity with the findings of the arbitration.

(b) If the modifying Member implements its proposed modification or withdrawal and does not comply with the findings of the arbitration, any affected Member that participated in the arbitration may modify or withdraw substantially equivalent benefits in conformity with those findings. Notwithstanding Article II, such a modification or withdrawal may be implemented solely with respect to the modifying Member.

5. The Council for Trade in Services shall establish procedures for rectification or modification of Schedules. Any Member which has modified or withdrawn scheduled commitments under this Article shall modify its Schedule according to such procedures.

Part V

INSTITUTIONAL PROVISIONS

Article XXII

Consultation

1. Each Member shall accord sympathetic consideration to, and shall afford adequate opportunity for, consultation regarding such representations as may be made by any other Member with respect to any matter affecting the operation of this Agreement. The Dispute Settlement Understanding (DSU) shall apply to such consultations.

2. The Council for Trade in Services or the Dispute Settlement Body (DSB) may, at the request of a Member, consult with any Member or Members in respect of any matter for which it has not been possible to find a satisfactory solution through consultation under paragraph 1.

3. A Member may not invoke Article XVII, either under this Article or Article XXIII, with respect to a measure of another Member that falls within the scope of an international agreement between them relating to the avoidance of double taxation. In case of disagreement between Members as to whether a measure falls within the scope of such an agreement between them, it shall be open to either Member to bring this matter before the Council for Trade in Services.[11] The Council shall refer the matter to arbitration. The decision of the arbitrator shall be final and binding on the Members.

Article XXIII

Dispute Settlement and Enforcement

1. If any Member should consider that any other Member fails to carry out its obligations or specific commitments under this Agreement, it may with a view to reaching a mutually satisfactory resolution of the matter have recourse to the DSU.

2. If the DSB considers that the circumstances are serious enough to justify such action, it may authorize a Member or Members to suspend the application to any other Member or Members of obligations and specific commitments in accordance with Article 22 of the DSU.

11. With respect to agreements on the avoidance of double taxation which exist on the date of entry into force of the WTO Agreement, such a matter may be brought before the Council for Trade in Services only with the consent of both parties to such an agreement.

3. If any Member considers that any benefit it could reasonably have expected to accrue to it under a specific commitment of another Member under Part III of this Agreement is being nullified or impaired as a result of the application of any measure which does not conflict with the provisions of this Agreement, it may have recourse to the DSU. If the measure is determined by the DSB to have nullified or impaired such a benefit, the Member affected shall be entitled to a mutually satisfactory adjustment on the basis of paragraph 2 of Article XXI, which may include the modification or withdrawal of the measure. In the event an agreement cannot be reached between the Members concerned, Article 22 of the DSU shall apply.

Article XXIV

Council for Trade in Services

1. The Council for Trade in Services shall carry out such functions as may be assigned to it to facilitate the operation of this Agreement and further its objectives. The Council may establish such subsidiary bodies as it considers appropriate for the effective discharge of its functions.

2. The Council and, unless the Council decides otherwise, its subsidiary bodies shall be open to participation by representatives of all Members.

3. The Chairman of the Council shall be elected by the Members.

Article XXV

Technical Cooperation

1. Service suppliers of Members which are in need of such assistance shall have access to the services of contact points referred to in paragraph 2 of Article IV.

2. Technical assistance to developing countries shall be provided at the multilateral level by the Secretariat and shall be decided upon by the Council for Trade in Services.

Article XXVI

Relationship with Other International Organizations

The General Council shall make appropriate arrangements for consultation and cooperation with the United Nations and its specialized agencies as well as with other intergovernmental organizations concerned with services.

Part VI

FINAL PROVISIONS

Article XXVII

Denial of Benefits

A Member may deny the benefits of this Agreement:

(a) to the supply of a service, if it establishes that the service is supplied from or in the territory of a non-Member or of a Member to which the denying Member does not apply the WTO Agreement;

(b) in the case of the supply of a maritime transport service, if it establishes that the service is supplied:

(i) by a vessel registered under the laws of a non-Member or of a Member to which the denying Member does not apply the WTO Agreement, and

(ii) by a person which operates and/or uses the vessel in whole or in part but which is of a non-Member or of a Member to which the denying Member does not apply the WTO Agreement;

(c) to a service supplier that is a juridical person, if it establishes that it is not a service supplier of another Member, or that it is a service supplier of a Member to which the denying Member does not apply the WTO Agreement.

Article XXVIII

Definitions

For the purpose of this Agreement:

(a) "measure" means any measure by a Member, whether in the form of a law, regulation, rule, procedure, decision, administrative action, or any other form;

(b) "supply of a service" includes the production, distribution, marketing, sale and delivery of a service;

(c) "measures by Members affecting trade in services" include measures in respect of

(i) the purchase, payment or use of a service;

(ii) the access to and use of, in connection with the supply of a service, services which are required by those Members to be offered to the public generally;

(iii) the presence, including commercial presence, of persons of a Member for the supply of a service in the territory of another Member;

(d) "commercial presence" means any type of business or professional establishment, including through

(i) the constitution, acquisition or maintenance of a juridical person, or

(ii) the creation or maintenance of a branch or a representative office, within the territory of a Member for the purpose of supplying a service;

(e) "sector" of a service means,

(i) with reference to a specific commitment, one or more, or all, subsectors of that service, as specified in a Member's Schedule,

(ii) otherwise, the whole of that service sector, including all of its subsectors;

(f) "service of another Member" means a service which is supplied,

(i) from or in the territory of that other Member, or in the case of maritime transport, by a vessel registered under the laws of that other Member, or by a person of that other Member which supplies the service through the operation of a vessel and/or its use in whole or in part; or

(ii) in the case of the supply of a service through commercial presence or through the presence of natural persons, by a service supplier of that other Member;

(g) "service supplier" means any person that supplies a service;[12]

12. Where the service is not supplied directly by a juridical person but through other forms of commercial presence such as a branch or a representative office, the service supplier (i.e. the juridical person) shall, nonetheless, through such presence be accorded the treatment provided for service suppliers under the Agreement. Such treatment shall be extended to the presence through which the service is supplied and need not be extended to any other parts of the supplier located outside the territory where the service is supplied.

(h) "monopoly supplier of a service" means any person, public or private, which in the relevant market of the territory of a Member is authorized or established formally or in effect by that Member as the sole supplier of that service;

(i) "service consumer" means any person that receives or uses a service;

(j) "person" means either a natural person or a juridical person;

(k) "natural person of another Member" means a natural person who resides in the territory of that other Member or any other Member, and who under the law of that other Member:

(i) is a national of that other Member; or

(ii) has the right of permanent residence in that other Member, in the case of a Member which:

1. does not have nationals; or

2. accords substantially the same treatment to its permanent residents as it does to its nationals in respect of measures affecting trade in services, as notified in its acceptance of or accession to the WTO Agreement, provided that no Member is obligated to accord to such permanent residents treatment more favourable than would be accorded by that other Member to such permanent residents. Such notification shall include the assurance to assume, with respect to those permanent residents, in accordance with its laws and regulations, the same responsibilities that other Member bears with respect to its nationals;

(l) "juridical person" means any legal entity duly constituted or otherwise organized under applicable law, whether for profit or otherwise, and whether privately-owned or governmentally-owned, including any corporation, trust, partnership, joint venture, sole proprietorship or association;

(m) "juridical person of another Member" means a juridical person which is either:

(i) constituted or otherwise organized under the law of that other Member, and is engaged in substantive business operations in the territory of that Member or any other Member; or

(ii) in the case of the supply of a service through commercial presence, owned or controlled by:

1. natural persons of that Member; or

2. juridical persons of that other Member identified under subparagraph (i);

(n) a juridical person is:

(i) "owned" by persons of a Member if more than 50 per cent of the equity interest in it is beneficially owned by persons of that Member;

(ii) "controlled" by persons of a Member if such persons have the power to name a majority of its directors or otherwise to legally direct its actions;

(iii) "affiliated" with another person when it controls, or is controlled by, that other person; or when it and the other person are both controlled by the same person;

(o) "direct taxes" comprise all taxes on total income, on total capital or on elements of income or of capital, including taxes on gains from the alienation of property, taxes on estates, inheritances and gifts, and taxes on the total amounts of wages or salaries paid by enterprises, as well as taxes on capital appreciation.

Article XXIX

Annexes

The Annexes to this Agreement are an integral part of this Agreement.

Annex on Article II Exemptions

Scope

1. This Annex specifies the conditions under which a Member, at the entry into force of this Agreement, is exempted from its obligations under paragraph 1 of Article II.

2. Any new exemptions applied for after the date of entry into force of the WTO Agreement shall be dealt with under paragraph 3 of Article IX of that Agreement.

Review

3. The Council for Trade in Services shall review all exemptions granted for a period of more than 5 years. The first such review shall take place no more than 5 years after the entry into force of the WTO Agreement.

4. The Council for Trade in Services in a review shall:

(a) examine whether the conditions which created the need for the exemption still prevail; and

(b) determine the date of any further review.

Termination

5. The exemption of a Member from its obligations under paragraph 1 of Article II of the Agreement with respect to a particular measure terminates on the date provided for in the exemption.

6. In principle, such exemptions should not exceed a period of 10 years. In any event, they shall be subject to negotiation in subsequent trade liberalizing rounds.

7. A Member shall notify the Council for Trade in Services at the termination of the exemption period that the inconsistent measure has been brought into conformity with paragraph 1 of Article II of the Agreement.

Lists of Article II Exemptions

[The agreed lists of exemptions under paragraph 2 of Article II will be annexed here in the treaty copy of the WTO Agreement.]

Annex on Movement of Natural Persons supplying Services Under the Agreement

1. This Annex applies to measures affecting natural persons who are service suppliers of a Member, and natural persons of a Member who are employed by a service supplier of a Member, in respect of the supply of a service.

2. The Agreement shall not apply to measures affecting natural persons seeking access to the employment market of a Member, nor shall it apply to measures regarding citizenship, residence or employment on a permanent basis.

3. In accordance with Parts III and IV of the Agreement, Members may negotiate specific commitments applying to the movement of all categories of natural persons supplying services under the Agreement. Natural persons covered by a specific commitment shall be allowed to supply the service in accordance with the terms of that commitment.

4. The Agreement shall not prevent a Member from applying measures to regulate the entry of natural persons into, or their temporary stay in, its territory, including those measures necessary to protect the integrity of, and to ensure the orderly movement of natural persons across, its borders, provided that such measures are not applied in such a manner as to nullify or impair the benefits accruing to any Member under the terms of a specific commitment.[13]

Annex on AIR Transport Services

1. This Annex applies to measures affecting trade in air transport services, whether scheduled or non-scheduled, and ancillary services. It is confirmed that any specific commitment or obligation assumed under this Agreement shall not reduce or affect a Member's obligations under bilateral or multilateral agreements that are in effect on the date of entry into force of the WTO Agreement.

2. The Agreement, including its dispute settlement procedures, shall not apply to measures affecting:

(a) traffic rights, however granted; or

(b) services directly related to the exercise of traffic rights, except as provided in paragraph 3 of this Annex.

3. The Agreement shall apply to measures affecting:

(a) aircraft repair and maintenance services;

(b) the selling and marketing of air transport services;

(c) computer reservation system (CRS) services.

4. The dispute settlement procedures of the Agreement may be invoked only where obligations or specific commitments have been assumed by the concerned Members and where dispute settlement procedures in bilateral and other multilateral agreements or arrangements have been exhausted.

5. The Council for Trade in Services shall review periodically, and at least every five years, developments in the air transport sector and the

13. The sole fact of requiring a visa for natural persons of certain Members and not for those of others shall not be regarded as nullifying or impairing benefits under a specific commitment.

operation of this Annex with a view to considering the possible further application of the Agreement in this sector.

6. Definitions:

(a) "Aircraft repair and maintenance services" mean such activities when undertaken on an aircraft or a part thereof while it is withdrawn from service and do not include so-called line maintenance.

(b) "Selling and marketing of air transport services" mean opportunities for the air carrier concerned to sell and market freely its air transport services including all aspects of marketing such as market research, advertising and distribution. These activities do not include the pricing of air transport services nor the applicable conditions.

(c) "Computer reservation system (CRS) services" mean services provided by computerised systems that contain information about air carriers' schedules, availability, fares and fare rules, through which reservations can be made or tickets may be issued.

(d) "Traffic rights" mean the right for scheduled and non-scheduled services to operate and/or to carry passengers, cargo and mail for remuneration or hire from, to, within, or over the territory of a Member, including points to be served, routes to be operated, types of traffic to be carried, capacity to be provided, tariffs to be charged and their conditions, and criteria for designation of airlines, including such criteria as number, ownership, and control.

Annex on Financial Services

1. *Scope and Definition*

(a) This Annex applies to measures affecting the supply of financial services. Reference to the supply of a financial service in this Annex shall mean the supply of a service as defined in paragraph 2 of Article I of the Agreement.

(b) For the purposes of subparagraph 3(b) of Article I of the Agreement, "services supplied in the exercise of governmental authority" means the following:

(i) activities conducted by a central bank or monetary authority or by any other public entity in pursuit of monetary or exchange rate policies;

(ii) activities forming part of a statutory system of social security or public retirement plans; and

(iii) other activities conducted by a public entity for the account or with the guarantee or using the financial resources of the Government.

(c) For the purposes of subparagraph 3(b) of Article I of the Agreement, if a Member allows any of the activities referred to in subparagraphs (b)(ii) or (b)(iii) of this paragraph to be conducted by its financial service suppliers in competition with a public entity or a financial service supplier, "services" shall include such activities.

(d) Subparagraph 3(c) of Article I of the Agreement shall not apply to services covered by this Annex.

2. *Domestic Regulation*

(a) Notwithstanding any other provisions of the Agreement, a Member shall not be prevented from taking measures for prudential reasons, including for the protection of investors, depositors, policy holders or persons to whom a fiduciary duty is owed by a financial service supplier, or to ensure the integrity and stability of the financial system. Where such measures do not conform with the provisions of the Agreement, they shall not be used as a means of avoiding the Member's commitments or obligations under the Agreement.

(b) Nothing in the Agreement shall be construed to require a Member to disclose information relating to the affairs and accounts of individual customers or any confidential or proprietary information in the possession of public entities.

3. *Recognition*

(a) A Member may recognize prudential measures of any other country in determining how the Member's measures relating to financial services shall be applied. Such recognition, which may be achieved through harmonization or otherwise, may be based upon an agreement or arrangement with the country concerned or may be accorded autonomously.

(b) A Member that is a party to such an agreement or arrangement referred to in subparagraph (a), whether future or existing, shall afford adequate opportunity for other interested Members to negotiate their accession to such agreements or arrangements, or to negotiate comparable ones with it, under circumstances in which there would be equivalent regulation, oversight, implementation of such regulation, and, if appropriate, procedures concerning the sharing of information between the parties to the agreement or arrangement. Where a Member accords recognition autonomously, it shall afford adequate opportunity for any other Member to demonstrate that such circumstances exist.

(c) Where a Member is contemplating according recognition to prudential measures of any other country, paragraph 4(b) of Article VII shall not apply.

4. *Dispute Settlement*

Panels for disputes on prudential issues and other financial matters shall have the necessary expertise relevant to the specific financial service under dispute.

5. *Definitions*

For the purposes of this Annex:

(a) A financial service is any service of a financial nature offered by a financial service supplier of a Member. Financial services include all insurance and insurance-related services, and all banking and other financial services (excluding insurance). Financial services include the following activities:

Insurance and insurance-related services

(i) Direct insurance (including co-insurance):

(A) life

(B) non-life

(ii) Reinsurance and retrocession;

(iii) Insurance intermediation, such as brokerage and agency;

(iv) Services auxiliary to insurance, such as consultancy, actuarial, risk assessment and claim settlement services.

Banking and other financial services (excluding insurance)

(v) Acceptance of deposits and other repayable funds from the public;

(vi) Lending of all types, including consumer credit, mortgage credit, factoring and financing of commercial transaction;

(vii) Financial leasing;

(viii) All payment and money transmission services, including credit, charge and debit cards, travellers cheques and bankers drafts;

(ix) Guarantees and commitments;

(x) Trading for own account or for account of customers, whether on an exchange, in an over-the-counter market or otherwise, the following:

(A) money market instruments (including cheques, bills, certificates of deposits);

(B) foreign exchange;

(C) derivative products including, but not limited to, futures and options;

(D) exchange rate and interest rate instruments, including products such as swaps, forward rate agreements;

(E) transferable securities;

(F) other negotiable instruments and financial assets, including bullion.

(xi) Participation in issues of all kinds of securities, including underwriting and placement as agent (whether publicly or privately) and provision of services related to such issues;

(xii) Money broking;

(xiii) Asset management, such as cash or portfolio management, all forms of collective investment management, pension fund management, custodial, depository and trust services;

(xiv) Settlement and clearing services for financial assets, including securities, derivative products, and other negotiable instruments;

(xv) Provision and transfer of financial information, and financial data processing and related software by suppliers of other financial services;

(xvi) Advisory, intermediation and other auxiliary financial services on all the activities listed in subparagraphs (v) through (xv), including credit reference and analysis, investment and portfolio research and advice, advice on acquisitions and on corporate restructuring and strategy.

(b) A financial service supplier means any natural or juridical person of a Member wishing to supply or supplying financial services but the term "financial service supplier" does not include a public entity.

(c) "Public entity" means:

(i) a government, a central bank or a monetary authority, of a Member, or an entity owned or controlled by a Member, that is principally engaged in carrying out governmental functions or activities for governmental purposes, not including an entity principally engaged in supplying financial services on commercial terms; or

(ii) a private entity, performing functions normally performed by a central bank or monetary authority, when exercising those functions.

Second Annex on Financial Services

1. Notwithstanding Article II of the Agreement and paragraphs 1 and 2 of the Annex on Article II Exemptions, a Member may, during a period of 60 days beginning four months after the date of entry into force of the WTO Agreement, list in that Annex measures relating to financial services which are inconsistent with paragraph 1 of Article II of the Agreement.

2. Notwithstanding Article XXI of the Agreement, a Member may, during a period of 60 days beginning four months after the date of entry into force of the WTO Agreement, improve, modify or withdraw all or part of the specific commitments on financial services inscribed in its Schedule.

3. The Council for Trade in Services shall establish any procedures necessary for the application of paragraphs 1 and 2.

Annex on Negotiations on Maritime Transport Services

1. Article II and the Annex on Article II Exemptions, including the requirement to list in the Annex any measure inconsistent with most-favoured-nation treatment that a Member will maintain, shall enter into force for international shipping, auxiliary services and access to and use of port facilities only on:

(a) the implementation date to be determined under paragraph 4 of the Ministerial Decision on Negotiations on Maritime Transport Services; or,

(b) should the negotiations not succeed, the date of the final report of the Negotiating Group on Maritime Transport Services provided for in that Decision.

2. Paragraph 1 shall not apply to any specific commitment on maritime transport services which is inscribed in a Member's Schedule.

3. From the conclusion of the negotiations referred to in paragraph 1, and before the implementation date, a Member may improve, modify or withdraw all or part of its specific commitments in this sector without offering compensation, notwithstanding the provisions of Article XXI.

Annex on Telecommunications

1. *Objectives*

Recognizing the specificities of the telecommunications services sector and, in particular, its dual role as a distinct sector of economic activity and as the underlying transport means for other economic activities, the Members have agreed to the following Annex with the objective of elaborating upon the provisions of the Agreement with respect to measures affecting access to and use of public telecommunications transport networks and services. Accordingly, this Annex provides notes and supplementary provisions to the Agreement.

2. *Scope*

(a) This Annex shall apply to all measures of a Member that affect access to and use of public telecommunications transport networks and services.[14]

(b) This Annex shall not apply to measures affecting the cable or broadcast distribution of radio or television programming.

(c) Nothing in this Annex shall be construed:

14. This paragraph is understood to mean that each Member shall ensure that the obligations of this Annex are applied with respect to suppliers of public telecommunications transport networks and services by whatever measures are necessary.

(i) to require a Member to authorize a service supplier of any other Member to establish, construct, acquire, lease, operate, or supply telecommunications transport networks or services, other than as provided for in its Schedule; or

(ii) to require a Member (or to require a Member to oblige service suppliers under its jurisdiction) to establish, construct, acquire, lease, operate or supply telecommunications transport networks or services not offered to the public generally.

3. *Definitions*

For the purposes of this Annex:

(a) "Telecommunications" means the transmission and reception of signals by any electromagnetic means.

(b) "Public telecommunications transport service" means any telecommunications transport service required, explicitly or in effect, by a Member to be offered to the public generally. Such services may include, *inter alia*, telegraph, telephone, telex, and data transmission typically involving the real-time transmission of customer-supplied information between two or more points without any end-to-end change in the form or content of the customer's information.

(c) "Public telecommunications transport network" means the public telecommunications infrastructure which permits telecommunications between and among defined network termination points.

(d) "Intra-corporate communications" means telecommunications through which a company communicates within the company or with or among its subsidiaries, branches and, subject to a Member's domestic laws and regulations, affiliates. For these purposes, "subsidiaries," "branches" and, where applicable, "affiliates" shall be as defined by each Member. "Intra-corporate communications" in this Annex excludes commercial or non-commercial services that are supplied to companies that are not related subsidiaries, branches or affiliates, or that are offered to customers or potential customers.

(e) Any reference to a paragraph or subparagraph of this Annex includes all subdivisions thereof.

4. *Transparency*

In the application of Article III of the Agreement, each Member shall ensure that relevant information on conditions affecting access to and use of public telecommunications transport networks and services is publicly available, including: tariffs and other terms and conditions of service; specifications of technical interfaces with such networks and services; information on bodies responsible for the preparation and adoption of standards affecting such access and use; conditions applying to attachment of terminal or other equipment; and notifications, registration or licensing requirements, if any.

5. *Access to and use of Public Telecommunications Transport Networks and Services*

(a) Each Member shall ensure that any service supplier of any other Member is accorded access to and use of public telecommunications transport networks and services on reasonable and non-discriminatory terms and conditions, for the supply of a service included in its Schedule. This obligation shall be applied, *inter alia*, through paragraphs (b) through (f).[15]

(b) Each Member shall ensure that service suppliers of any other Member have access to and use of any public telecommunications transport network or service offered within or across the border of that Member, including private leased circuits, and to this end shall ensure, subject to paragraphs (e) and (f), that such suppliers are permitted:

(i) to purchase or lease and attach terminal or other equipment which interfaces with the network and which is necessary to supply a supplier's services;

(ii) to interconnect private leased or owned circuits with public telecommunications transport networks and services or with circuits leased or owned by another service supplier; and

(iii) to use operating protocols of the service supplier's choice in the supply of any service, other than as necessary to ensure the availability of telecommunications transport networks and services to the public generally.

(c) Each Member shall ensure that service suppliers of any other Member may use public telecommunications transport networks and services for the movement of information within and across borders, including for intra-corporate communications of such service suppliers, and for access to information contained in data bases or otherwise stored in

15. The term "non-discriminatory" is understood to refer to most-favoured-nation and national treatment as defined in the Agreement, as well as to reflect sector-specific usage of the term to mean "terms and conditions no less favourable than those accorded to any other user of like public telecommunications transport networks or services under like circumstances."

machine-readable form in the territory of any Member. Any new or amended measures of a Member significantly affecting such use shall be notified and shall be subject to consultation, in accordance with relevant provisions of the Agreement.

(d) Notwithstanding the preceding paragraph, a Member may take such measures as are necessary to ensure the security and confidentiality of messages, subject to the requirement that such measures are not applied in a manner which would constitute a means of arbitrary or unjustifiable discrimination or a disguised restriction on trade in services.

(e) Each Member shall ensure that no condition is imposed on access to and use of public telecommunications transport networks and services other than as necessary:

(i) to safeguard the public service responsibilities of suppliers of public telecommunications transport networks and services, in particular their ability to make their networks or services available to the public generally;

(ii) to protect the technical integrity of public telecommunications transport networks or services; or

(iii) to ensure that service suppliers of any other Member do not supply services unless permitted pursuant to commitments in the Member's Schedule.

(f) Provided that they satisfy the criteria set out in paragraph (e), conditions for access to and use of public telecommunications transport networks and services may include:

(i) restrictions on resale or shared use of such services;

(ii) a requirement to use specified technical interfaces, including interface protocols, for inter-connection with such networks and services;

(iii) requirements, where necessary, for the inter-operability of such services and to encourage the achievement of the goals set out in paragraph 7(a);

(iv) type approval of terminal or other equipment which interfaces with the network and technical requirements relating to the attachment of such equipment to such networks;

(v) restrictions on inter-connection of private leased or owned circuits with such networks or services or with circuits leased or owned by another service supplier; or

(vi) notification, registration and licensing.

(g) Notwithstanding the preceding paragraphs of this section, a developing country Member may, consistent with its level of development, place reasonable conditions on access to and use of public telecommunications transport networks and services necessary to strengthen its domestic telecommunications infrastructure and service capacity and to increase its participation in international trade in telecommunications services. Such conditions shall be specified in the Member's Schedule.

6. *Technical Cooperation*

(a) Members recognize that an efficient, advanced telecommunications infrastructure in countries, particularly developing countries, is essential to the expansion of their trade in services. To this end, Members endorse and encourage the participation, to the fullest extent practicable, of developed and developing countries and their suppliers of public telecommunications transport networks and services and other entities in the development programmes of international and regional organizations, including the International Telecommunication Union, the United Nations Development Programme, and the International Bank for Reconstruction and Development.

(b) Members shall encourage and support telecommunications cooperation among developing countries at the international, regional and sub-regional levels.

(c) In cooperation with relevant international organizations, Members shall make available, where practicable, to developing countries information with respect to telecommunications services and developments in telecommunications and information technology to assist in strengthening their domestic telecommunications services sector.

(d) Members shall give special consideration to opportunities for the least-developed countries to encourage foreign suppliers of telecommunications services to assist in the transfer of technology, training and other activities that support the development of their telecommunications infrastructure and expansion of their telecommunications services trade.

7. *Relation to International Organizations and Agreements*

(a) Members recognize the importance of international standards for global compatibility and inter-operability of telecommunication networks and services and undertake to promote such standards through the work of relevant international bodies, including the International Telecommunication Union and the International Organization for Standardization.

(b) Members recognize the role played by intergovernmental and non-governmental organizations and agreements in ensuring the efficient operation of domestic and global telecommunications services, in particular the International Telecommunication Union. Members shall make appropriate arrangements, where relevant, for consultation with such organizations on matters arising from the implementation of this Annex.

Annex on Negotiations on Basic Telecommunications

1. Article II and the Annex on Article II Exemptions, including the requirement to list in the Annex any measure inconsistent with most-favoured-nation treatment that a Member will maintain, shall enter into force for basic telecommunications only on:

(a) the implementation date to be determined under paragraph 5 of the Ministerial Decision on Negotiations on Basic Telecommunications; or,

(b) should the negotiations not succeed, the date of the final report of the Negotiating Group on Basic Telecommunications provided for in that Decision.

2. Paragraph 1 shall not apply to any specific commitment on basic telecommunications which is inscribed in a Member's Schedule.

Document 40

UNDERSTANDING ON COMMITMENTS IN FINANCIAL SERVICES

Participants in the Uruguay Round have been enabled to take on specific commitments with respect to financial services under the General Agreement on Trade in Services (hereinafter referred to as the "Agreement") on the basis of an alternative approach to that covered by the provisions of Part III of the Agreement. It was agreed that this approach could be applied subject to the following understanding:

(i) it does not conflict with the provisions of the Agreement;

(ii) it does not prejudice the right of any Member to schedule its specific commitments in accordance with the approach under Part III of the Agreement;

(iii) resulting specific commitments shall apply on a most-favoured-nation basis;

(iv) no presumption has been created as to the degree of liberalization to which a Member is committing itself under the Agreement.

Interested Members, on the basis of negotiations, and subject to conditions and qualifications where specified, have inscribed in their schedule specific commitments conforming to the approach set out below.

A. *Standstill*

Any conditions, limitations and qualifications to the commitments noted below shall be limited to existing non-conforming measures.

B. *Market Access*

Monopoly Rights

1. In addition to Article VIII of the Agreement, the following shall apply:

Each Member shall list in its schedule pertaining to financial services existing monopoly rights and shall endeavour to eliminate them or reduce their scope. Notwithstanding subparagraph 1(b) of the Annex on Financial Services, this paragraph applies to the activities referred to in subparagraph 1(b)(iii) of the Annex.

Financial Services purchased by Public Entities

2. Notwithstanding Article XIII of the Agreement, each Member shall ensure that financial service suppliers of any other Member established in its territory are accorded most-favoured-nation treatment and national treatment as regards the purchase or acquisition of financial services by public entities of the Member in its territory.

Cross-border Trade

3. Each Member shall permit non-resident suppliers of financial services to supply, as a principal, through an intermediary or as an intermediary, and under terms and conditions that accord national treatment, the following services:

(a) insurance of risks relating to:

(i) maritime shipping and commercial aviation and space launching and freight (including satellites), with such insurance to cover any or all of the following: the goods being transported, the vehicle transporting the goods and any liability arising therefrom; and

(ii) goods in international transit;

(b) reinsurance and retrocession and the services auxiliary to insurance as referred to in subparagraph 5(a)(iv) of the Annex;

(c) provision and transfer of financial information and financial data processing as referred to in subparagraph 5(a)(xv) of the Annex and advisory and other auxiliary services, excluding intermediation, relating to banking and other financial services as referred to in subparagraph 5(a)(xvi) of the Annex.

4. Each Member shall permit its residents to purchase in the territory of any other Member the financial services indicated in:

(a) subparagraph 3(a);

(b) subparagraph 3(b); and

(c) subparagraphs 5(a)(v) to (xvi) of the Annex.

Commercial Presence

5. Each Member shall grant financial service suppliers of any other Member the right to establish or expand within its territory, including through the acquisition of existing enterprises, a commercial presence.

6. A Member may impose terms, conditions and procedures for authorization of the establishment and expansion of a commercial presence in so far as they do not circumvent the Member's obligation under paragraph 5 and they are consistent with the other obligations of the Agreement.

New Financial Services

7. A Member shall permit financial service suppliers of any other Member established in its territory to offer in its territory any new financial service.

Transfers of Information and Processing of Information

8. No Member shall take measures that prevent transfers of information or the processing of financial information, including transfers of data by electronic means, or that, subject to importation rules consistent with international agreements, prevent transfers of equipment, where such transfers of information, processing of financial information or transfers of equipment are necessary for the conduct of the ordinary business of a financial service supplier. Nothing in this paragraph restricts the right of a Member to protect personal data, personal privacy and the confidentiality of individual records and accounts so long as such right is not used to circumvent the provisions of the Agreement.

Temporary Entry of Personnel

9. (a) Each Member shall permit temporary entry into its territory of the following personnel of a financial service supplier of any other Member that is establishing or has established a commercial presence in the territory of the Member:

(i) senior managerial personnel possessing proprietary information essential to the establishment, control and operation of the services of the financial service supplier; and

(ii) specialists in the operation of the financial service supplier.

(b) Each Member shall permit, subject to the availability of qualified personnel in its territory, temporary entry into its territory of the following personnel associated with a commercial presence of a financial service supplier of any other Member:

(i) specialists in computer services, telecommunication services and accounts of the financial service supplier; and

(ii) actuarial and legal specialists.

Non-discriminatory Measures

10. Each Member shall endeavour to remove or to limit any significant adverse effects on financial service suppliers of any other Member of:

(a) non-discriminatory measures that prevent financial service suppliers from offering in the Member's territory, in the form determined by the Member, all the financial services permitted by the Member;

(b) non-discriminatory measures that limit the expansion of the activities of financial service suppliers into the entire territory of the Member;

(c) measures of a Member, when such a Member applies the same measures to the supply of both banking and securities services, and a financial service supplier of any other Member concentrates its activities in the provision of securities services; and

(d) other measures that, although respecting the provisions of the Agreement, affect adversely the ability of financial service suppliers of any other Member to operate, compete or enter the Member's market;

provided that any action taken under this paragraph would not unfairly discriminate against financial service suppliers of the Member taking such action.

11. With respect to the non-discriminatory measures referred to in subparagraphs 10(a) and (b), a Member shall endeavour not to limit or restrict the present degree of market opportunities nor the benefits already enjoyed by financial service suppliers of all other Members as a class in the

territory of the Member, provided that this commitment does not result in unfair discrimination against financial service suppliers of the Member applying such measures.

C. National Treatment

1. Under terms and conditions that accord national treatment, each Member shall grant to financial service suppliers of any other Member established in its territory access to payment and clearing systems operated by public entities, and to official funding and refinancing facilities available in the normal course of ordinary business. This paragraph is not intended to confer access to the Member's lender of last resort facilities.

2. When membership or participation in, or access to, any self-regulatory body, securities or futures exchange or market, clearing agency, or any other organization or association, is required by a Member in order for financial service suppliers of any other Member to supply financial services on an equal basis with financial service suppliers of the Member, or when the Member provides directly or indirectly such entities, privileges or advantages in supplying financial services, the Member shall ensure that such entities accord national treatment to financial service suppliers of any other Member resident in the territory of the Member.

D. Definitions

For the purposes of this approach:

1. A non-resident supplier of financial services is a financial service supplier of a Member which supplies a financial service into the territory of another Member from an establishment located in the territory of another Member, regardless of whether such a financial service supplier has or has not a commercial presence in the territory of the Member in which the financial service is supplied.

2. "Commercial presence" means an enterprise within a Member's territory for the supply of financial services and includes wholly- or partly-owned subsidiaries, joint ventures, partnerships, sole proprietorships, franchising operations, branches, agencies, representative offices or other organizations.

3. A new financial service is a service of a financial nature, including services related to existing and new products or the manner in which a product is delivered, that is not supplied by any financial service supplier in the territory of a particular Member but which is supplied in the territory of another Member.

PART VII

Intellectual Property Rights

Document 41

AGREEMENT ON TRADE-RELATED ASPECTS OF INTELLECTUAL PROPERTY RIGHTS

Members,

Desiring to reduce distortions and impediments to international trade, and taking into account the need to promote effective and adequate protection of intellectual property rights, and to ensure that measures and procedures to enforce intellectual property rights do not themselves become barriers to legitimate trade;

Recognizing, to this end, the need for new rules and disciplines concerning:

(a) the applicability of the basic principles of GATT 1994 and of relevant international intellectual property agreements or conventions;

(b) the provision of adequate standards and principles concerning the availability, scope and use of trade-related intellectual property rights;

(c) the provision of effective and appropriate means for the enforcement of trade-related intellectual property rights, taking into account differences in national legal systems;

(d) the provision of effective and expeditious procedures for the multilateral prevention and settlement of disputes between governments; and

(e) transitional arrangements aiming at the fullest participation in the results of the negotiations;

Recognizing the need for a multilateral framework of principles, rules and disciplines dealing with international trade in counterfeit goods;

Recognizing that intellectual property rights are private rights;

Recognizing the underlying public policy objectives of national systems for the protection of intellectual property, including developmental and technological objectives;

Recognizing also the special needs of the least-developed country Members in respect of maximum flexibility in the domestic implementation of laws and regulations in order to enable them to create a sound and viable technological base;

Emphasizing the importance of reducing tensions by reaching strengthened commitments to resolve disputes on trade-related intellectual property issues through multilateral procedures;

Desiring to establish a mutually supportive relationship between the WTO and the World Intellectual Property Organization (referred to in this Agreement as "WIPO") as well as other relevant international organizations;

Hereby agree as follows:

Part I

GENERAL PROVISIONS AND BASIC PRINCIPLES

Article 1

Nature and Scope of Obligations

1. Members shall give effect to the provisions of this Agreement. Members may, but shall not be obliged to, implement in their law more extensive protection than is required by this Agreement, provided that such protection does not contravene the provisions of this Agreement. Members shall be free to determine the appropriate method of implementing the provisions of this Agreement within their own legal system and practice.

2. For the purposes of this Agreement, the term "intellectual property" refers to all categories of intellectual property that are the subject of Sections 1 through 7 of Part II.

3. Members shall accord the treatment provided for in this Agreement to the nationals of other Members.[1] In respect of the relevant intellectual property right, the nationals of other Members shall be understood as those natural or legal persons that would meet the criteria for eligibility for protection provided for in the Paris Convention (1967), the Berne Convention (1971), the Rome Convention and the Treaty on Intellectual Property in Respect of Integrated Circuits, were all Members of the WTO members of those conventions.[2] Any Member availing itself of the possibilities provided in paragraph 3 of Article 5 or paragraph 2 of Article 6 of the Rome Convention shall make a notification as foreseen in those provisions to the Council for Trade-Related Aspects of Intellectual Property Rights (the "Council for TRIPS").

Article 2

Intellectual Property Conventions

1. In respect of Parts II, III and IV of this Agreement, Members shall comply with Articles 1 through 12, and Article 19, of the Paris Convention (1967).

2. Nothing in Parts I to IV of this Agreement shall derogate from existing obligations that Members may have to each other under the Paris Convention, the Berne Convention, the Rome Convention and the Treaty on Intellectual Property in Respect of Integrated Circuits.

Article 3

National Treatment

1. Each Member shall accord to the nationals of other Members treatment no less favourable than that it accords to its own nationals with regard to the protection[3] of intellectual property, subject to the exceptions

1. When "nationals" are referred to in this Agreement, they shall be deemed, in the case of a separate customs territory Member of the WTO, to mean persons, natural or legal, who are domiciled or who have a real and effective industrial or commercial establishment in that customs territory.

2. In this Agreement, "Paris Convention" refers to the Paris Convention for the Protection of Industrial Property; "Paris Convention (1967)" refers to the Stockholm Act of this Convention of 14 July 1967. "Berne Convention" refers to the Berne Convention for the Protection of Literary and Artistic Works; "Berne Convention (1971)" refers to the Paris Act of this Convention of 24 July 1971. "Rome Convention" refers to the International Convention for the Protection of Performers, Producers of Phonograms and Broadcasting Organizations, adopted at Rome on 26 October 1961. "Treaty on Intellectual Property in Respect of Integrated Circuits" (IPIC Treaty) refers to the Treaty on Intellectual Property in Respect of Integrated Circuits, adopted at Washington on 26 May 1989. "WTO Agreement" refers to the Agreement Establishing the WTO.

3. For the purposes of Articles 3 and 4, "protection" shall include matters affecting the availability, acquisition, scope, maintenance and enforcement of intellectual property rights as

already provided in, respectively, the Paris Convention (1967), the Berne Convention (1971), the Rome Convention or the Treaty on Intellectual Property in Respect of Integrated Circuits. In respect of performers, producers of phonograms and broadcasting organizations, this obligation only applies in respect of the rights provided under this Agreement. Any Member availing itself of the possibilities provided in Article 6 of the Berne Convention (1971) or paragraph 1(b) of Article 16 of the Rome Convention shall make a notification as foreseen in those provisions to the Council for TRIPS.

2. Members may avail themselves of the exceptions permitted under paragraph 1 in relation to judicial and administrative procedures, including the designation of an address for service or the appointment of an agent within the jurisdiction of a Member, only where such exceptions are necessary to secure compliance with laws and regulations which are not inconsistent with the provisions of this Agreement and where such practices are not applied in a manner which would constitute a disguised restriction on trade.

Article 4

Most-Favoured-Nation Treatment

With regard to the protection of intellectual property, any advantage, favour, privilege or immunity granted by a Member to the nationals of any other country shall be accorded immediately and unconditionally to the nationals of all other Members. Exempted from this obligation are any advantage, favour, privilege or immunity accorded by a Member:

(a) deriving from international agreements on judicial assistance or law enforcement of a general nature and not particularly confined to the protection of intellectual property;

(b) granted in accordance with the provisions of the Berne Convention (1971) or the Rome Convention authorizing that the treatment accorded be a function not of national treatment but of the treatment accorded in another country;

(c) in respect of the rights of performers, producers of phonograms and broadcasting organizations not provided under this Agreement;

---

well as those matters affecting the use of intellectual property rights specifically addressed in this Agreement.

(d) deriving from international agreements related to the protection of intellectual property which entered into force prior to the entry into force of the WTO Agreement, provided that such agreements are notified to the Council for TRIPS and do not constitute an arbitrary or unjustifiable discrimination against nationals of other Members.

Article 5

Multilateral Agreements on Acquisition or Maintenance of Protection

The obligations under Articles 3 and 4 do not apply to procedures provided in multilateral agreements concluded under the auspices of WIPO relating to the acquisition or maintenance of intellectual property rights.

Article 6

Exhaustion

For the purposes of dispute settlement under this Agreement, subject to the provisions of Articles 3 and 4 nothing in this Agreement shall be used to address the issue of the exhaustion of intellectual property rights.

Article 7

Objectives

The protection and enforcement of intellectual property rights should contribute to the promotion of technological innovation and to the transfer and dissemination of technology, to the mutual advantage of producers and users of technological knowledge and in a manner conducive to social and economic welfare, and to a balance of rights and obligations.

Article 8

Principles

1. Members may, in formulating or amending their laws and regulations, adopt measures necessary to protect public health and nutrition, and to promote the public interest in sectors of vital importance to their socio-economic and technological development, provided that such measures are consistent with the provisions of this Agreement.

2. Appropriate measures, provided that they are consistent with the provisions of this Agreement, may be needed to prevent the abuse of intellectual property rights by right holders or the resort to practices which unreasonably restrain trade or adversely affect the international transfer of technology.

Part II

STANDARDS CONCERNING THE AVAILABILITY, SCOPE AND USE OF INTELLECTUAL PROPERTY RIGHTS

SECTION 1: COPYRIGHT AND RELATED RIGHTS

Article 9

Relation to the Berne Convention

1. Members shall comply with Articles 1 through 21 of the Berne Convention (1971) and the Appendix thereto. However, Members shall not have rights or obligations under this Agreement in respect of the rights conferred under Article 6*bis* of that Convention or of the rights derived therefrom.

2. Copyright protection shall extend to expressions and not to ideas, procedures, methods of operation or mathematical concepts as such.

Article 10

Computer Programs and Compilations of Data

1. Computer programs, whether in source or object code, shall be protected as literary works under the Berne Convention (1971).

2. Compilations of data or other material, whether in machine readable or other form, which by reason of the selection or arrangement of their contents constitute intellectual creations shall be protected as such. Such protection, which shall not extend to the data or material itself, shall be without prejudice to any copyright subsisting in the data or material itself.

Article 11

Rental Rights

In respect of at least computer programs and cinematographic works, a Member shall provide authors and their successors in title the right to authorize or to prohibit the commercial rental to the public of originals or copies of their copyright works. A Member shall be excepted from this obligation in respect of cinematographic works unless such rental has led to widespread copying of such works which is materially impairing the exclusive right of reproduction conferred in that Member on authors and their successors in title. In respect of computer programs, this obligation does not apply to rentals where the program itself is not the essential object of the rental.

Article 12

Term of Protection

Whenever the term of protection of a work, other than a photographic work or a work of applied art, is calculated on a basis other than the life of a natural person, such term shall be no less than 50 years from the end of the calendar year of authorized publication, or, failing such authorized publication within 50 years from the making of the work, 50 years from the end of the calendar year of making.

Article 13

Limitations and Exceptions

Members shall confine limitations or exceptions to exclusive rights to certain special cases which do not conflict with a normal exploitation of the work and do not unreasonably prejudice the legitimate interests of the right holder.

Article 14

Protection of Performers, Producers of Phonograms (Sound Recordings) and Broadcasting Organizations

1. In respect of a fixation of their performance on a phonogram, performers shall have the possibility of preventing the following acts when undertaken without their authorization: the fixation of their unfixed performance and the reproduction of such fixation. Performers shall also have the possibility of preventing the following acts when undertaken without their authorization: the broadcasting by wireless means and the communication to the public of their live performance.

2. Producers of phonograms shall enjoy the right to authorize or prohibit the direct or indirect reproduction of their phonograms.

3. Broadcasting organizations shall have the right to prohibit the following acts when undertaken without their authorization: the fixation, the reproduction of fixations, and the rebroadcasting by wireless means of broadcasts, as well as the communication to the public of television broadcasts of the same. Where Members do not grant such rights to broadcasting organizations, they shall provide owners of copyright in the subject matter of broadcasts with the possibility of preventing the above acts, subject to the provisions of the Berne Convention (1971).

4. The provisions of Article 11 in respect of computer programs shall apply *mutatis mutandis* to producers of phonograms and any other right

holders in phonograms as determined in a Member's law. If on 15 April 1994 a Member has in force a system of equitable remuneration of right holders in respect of the rental of phonograms, it may maintain such system provided that the commercial rental of phonograms is not giving rise to the material impairment of the exclusive rights of reproduction of right holders.

5. The term of the protection available under this Agreement to performers and producers of phonograms shall last at least until the end of a period of 50 years computed from the end of the calendar year in which the fixation was made or the performance took place. The term of protection granted pursuant to paragraph 3 shall last for at least 20 years from the end of the calendar year in which the broadcast took place.

6. Any Member may, in relation to the rights conferred under paragraphs 1, 2 and 3, provide for conditions, limitations, exceptions and reservations to the extent permitted by the Rome Convention. However, the provisions of Article 18 of the Berne Convention (1971) shall also apply, *mutatis mutandis*, to the rights of performers and producers of phonograms in phonograms.

SECTION 2: TRADEMARKS

Article 15

Protectable Subject Matter

1. Any sign, or any combination of signs, capable of distinguishing the goods or services of one undertaking from those of other undertakings, shall be capable of constituting a trademark. Such signs, in particular words including personal names, letters, numerals, figurative elements and combinations of colours as well as any combination of such signs, shall be eligible for registration as trademarks. Where signs are not inherently capable of distinguishing the relevant goods or services, Members may make registrability depend on distinctiveness acquired through use. Members may require, as a condition of registration, that signs be visually perceptible.

2. Paragraph 1 shall not be understood to prevent a Member from denying registration of a trademark on other grounds, provided that they do not derogate from the provisions of the Paris Convention (1967).

3. Members may make registrability depend on use. However, actual use of a trademark shall not be a condition for filing an application for registration. An application shall not be refused solely on the ground that intended use has not taken place before the expiry of a period of three years from the date of application.

4. The nature of the goods or services to which a trademark is to be applied shall in no case form an obstacle to registration of the trademark.

5. Members shall publish each trademark either before it is registered or promptly after it is registered and shall afford a reasonable opportunity for petitions to cancel the registration. In addition, Members may afford an opportunity for the registration of a trademark to be opposed.

Article 16

Rights Conferred

1. The owner of a registered trademark shall have the exclusive right to prevent all third parties not having the owner's consent from using in the course of trade identical or similar signs for goods or services which are identical or similar to those in respect of which the trademark is registered where such use would result in a likelihood of confusion. In case of the use of an identical sign for identical goods or services, a likelihood of confusion shall be presumed. The rights described above shall not prejudice any existing prior rights, nor shall they affect the possibility of Members making rights available on the basis of use.

2. Article 6*bis* of the Paris Convention (1967) shall apply, *mutatis mutandis*, to services. In determining whether a trademark is well-known, Members shall take account of the knowledge of the trademark in the relevant sector of the public, including knowledge in the Member concerned which has been obtained as a result of the promotion of the trademark.

3. Article 6*bis* of the Paris Convention (1967) shall apply, *mutatis mutandis*, to goods or services which are not similar to those in respect of which a trademark is registered, provided that use of that trademark in relation to those goods or services would indicate a connection between those goods or services and the owner of the registered trademark and provided that the interests of the owner of the registered trademark are likely to be damaged by such use.

Article 17

Exceptions

Members may provide limited exceptions to the rights conferred by a trademark, such as fair use of descriptive terms, provided that such exceptions take account of the legitimate interests of the owner of the trademark and of third parties.

Article 18

Term of Protection

Initial registration, and each renewal of registration, of a trademark shall be for a term of no less than seven years. The registration of a trademark shall be renewable indefinitely.

Article 19

Requirement of Use

1. If use is required to maintain a registration, the registration may be cancelled only after an uninterrupted period of at least three years of non-use, unless valid reasons based on the existence of obstacles to such use are shown by the trademark owner. Circumstances arising independently of the will of the owner of the trademark which constitute an obstacle to the use of the trademark, such as import restrictions on or other government requirements for goods or services protected by the trademark, shall be recognized as valid reasons for non-use.

2. When subject to the control of its owner, use of a trademark by another person shall be recognized as use of the trademark for the purpose of maintaining the registration.

Article 20

Other Requirements

The use of a trademark in the course of trade shall not be unjustifiably encumbered by special requirements, such as use with another trademark, use in a special form or use in a manner detrimental to its capability to distinguish the goods or services of one undertaking from those of other undertakings. This will not preclude a requirement prescribing the use of the trademark identifying the undertaking producing the goods or services along with, but without linking it to, the trademark distinguishing the specific goods or services in question of that undertaking.

Article 21

Licensing and Assignment

Members may determine conditions on the licensing and assignment of trademarks, it being understood that the compulsory licensing of trademarks shall not be permitted and that the owner of a registered trademark shall have the right to assign the trademark with or without the transfer of the business to which the trademark belongs.

Section 3: Geographical Indications

Article 22

Protection of Geographical Indications

1. Geographical indications are, for the purposes of this Agreement, indications which identify a good as originating in the territory of a Member, or a region or locality in that territory, where a given quality, reputation or other characteristic of the good is essentially attributable to its geographical origin.

2. In respect of geographical indications, Members shall provide the legal means for interested parties to prevent:

(a) the use of any means in the designation or presentation of a good that indicates or suggests that the good in question originates in a geographical area other than the true place of origin in a manner which misleads the public as to the geographical origin of the good;

(b) any use which constitutes an act of unfair competition within the meaning of Article 10*bis* of the Paris Convention (1967).

3. A Member shall, *ex officio* if its legislation so permits or at the request of an interested party, refuse or invalidate the registration of a trademark which contains or consists of a geographical indication with respect to goods not originating in the territory indicated, if use of the indication in the trademark for such goods in that Member is of such a nature as to mislead the public as to the true place of origin.

4. The protection under paragraphs 1, 2 and 3 shall be applicable against a geographical indication which, although literally true as to the territory, region or locality in which the goods originate, falsely represents to the public that the goods originate in another territory.

Article 23

Additional Protection for Geographical Indications for Wines and Spirits

1. Each Member shall provide the legal means for interested parties to prevent use of a geographical indication identifying wines for wines not originating in the place indicated by the geographical indication in question or identifying spirits for spirits not originating in the place indicated by the geographical indication in question, even where the true origin of the goods is indicated or the geographical indication is used in translation or accompanied by expressions such as "kind," "type," "style," "imitation" or the like.[4]

4. Notwithstanding the first sentence of Article 42, Members may, with respect to these obligations, instead provide for enforcement by administrative action.

2. The registration of a trademark for wines which contains or consists of a geographical indication identifying wines or for spirits which contains or consists of a geographical indication identifying spirits shall be refused or invalidated, *ex officio* if a Member's legislation so permits or at the request of an interested party, with respect to such wines or spirits not having this origin.

3. In the case of homonymous geographical indications for wines, protection shall be accorded to each indication, subject to the provisions of paragraph 4 of Article 22. Each Member shall determine the practical conditions under which the homonymous indications in question will be differentiated from each other, taking into account the need to ensure equitable treatment of the producers concerned and that consumers are not misled.

4. In order to facilitate the protection of geographical indications for wines, negotiations shall be undertaken in the Council for TRIPS concerning the establishment of a multilateral system of notification and registration of geographical indications for wines eligible for protection in those Members participating in the system.

Article 24

International Negotiations; Exceptions

1. Members agree to enter into negotiations aimed at increasing the protection of individual geographical indications under Article 23. The provisions of paragraphs 4 through 8 below shall not be used by a Member to refuse to conduct negotiations or to conclude bilateral or multilateral agreements. In the context of such negotiations, Members shall be willing to consider the continued applicability of these provisions to individual geographical indications whose use was the subject of such negotiations.

2. The Council for TRIPS shall keep under review the application of the provisions of this Section; the first such review shall take place within two years of the entry into force of the WTO Agreement. Any matter affecting the compliance with the obligations under these provisions may be drawn to the attention of the Council, which, at the request of a Member, shall consult with any Member or Members in respect of such matter in respect of which it has not been possible to find a satisfactory solution through bilateral or plurilateral consultations between the Members concerned. The Council shall take such action as may be agreed to facilitate the operation and further the objectives of this Section.

3. In implementing this Section, a Member shall not diminish the protection of geographical indications that existed in that Member immediately prior to the date of entry into force of the WTO Agreement.

4. Nothing in this Section shall require a Member to prevent continued and similar use of a particular geographical indication of another Member identifying wines or spirits in connection with goods or services by any of its nationals or domiciliaries who have used that geographical indication in a continuous manner with regard to the same or related goods or services in the territory of that Member either (*a*) for at least 10 years preceding 15 April 1994 or (*b*) in good faith preceding that date.

5. Where a trademark has been applied for or registered in good faith, or where rights to a trademark have been acquired through use in good faith either:

(a) before the date of application of these provisions in that Member as defined in Part VI; or

(b) before the geographical indication is protected in its country of origin;

measures adopted to implement this Section shall not prejudice eligibility for or the validity of the registration of a trademark, or the right to use a trademark, on the basis that such a trademark is identical with, or similar to, a geographical indication.

6. Nothing in this Section shall require a Member to apply its provisions in respect of a geographical indication of any other Member with respect to goods or services for which the relevant indication is identical with the term customary in common language as the common name for such goods or services in the territory of that Member. Nothing in this Section shall require a Member to apply its provisions in respect of a geographical indication of any other Member with respect to products of the vine for which the relevant indication is identical with the customary name of a grape variety existing in the territory of that Member as of the date of entry into force of the WTO Agreement.

7. A Member may provide that any request made under this Section in connection with the use or registration of a trademark must be presented within five years after the adverse use of the protected indication has become generally known in that Member or after the date of registration of the trademark in that Member provided that the trademark has been published by that date, if such date is earlier than the date on which the adverse use became generally known in that Member, provided that the geographical indication is not used or registered in bad faith.

8. The provisions of this Section shall in no way prejudice the right of any person to use, in the course of trade, that person's name or the name of that person's predecessor in business, except where such name is used in such a manner as to mislead the public.

9. There shall be no obligation under this Agreement to protect geographical indications which are not or cease to be protected in their country of origin, or which have fallen into disuse in that country.

Section 4: Industrial Designs

Article 25

Requirements for Protection

1. Members shall provide for the protection of independently created industrial designs that are new or original. Members may provide that designs are not new or original if they do not significantly differ from known designs or combinations of known design features. Members may provide that such protection shall not extend to designs dictated essentially by technical or functional considerations.

2. Each Member shall ensure that requirements for securing protection for textile designs, in particular in regard to any cost, examination or publication, do not unreasonably impair the opportunity to seek and obtain such protection. Members shall be free to meet this obligation through industrial design law or through copyright law.

Article 26

Protection

1. The owner of a protected industrial design shall have the right to prevent third parties not having the owner's consent from making, selling or importing articles bearing or embodying a design which is a copy, or substantially a copy, of the protected design, when such acts are undertaken for commercial purposes.

2. Members may provide limited exceptions to the protection of industrial designs, provided that such exceptions do not unreasonably conflict with the normal exploitation of protected industrial designs and do not unreasonably prejudice the legitimate interests of the owner of the protected design, taking account of the legitimate interests of third parties.

3. The duration of protection available shall amount to at least 10 years.

Section 5: Patents

Article 27

Patentable Subject Matter

1. Subject to the provisions of paragraphs 2 and 3, patents shall be available for any inventions, whether products or processes, in all fields of

technology, provided that they are new, involve an inventive step and are capable of industrial application.[5] Subject to paragraph 4 of Article 65, paragraph 8 of Article 70 and paragraph 3 of this Article, patents shall be available and patent rights enjoyable without discrimination as to the place of invention, the field of technology and whether products are imported or locally produced.

2. Members may exclude from patentability inventions, the prevention within their territory of the commercial exploitation of which is necessary to protect *ordre public* or morality, including to protect human, animal or plant life or health or to avoid serious prejudice to the environment, provided that such exclusion is not made merely because the exploitation is prohibited by their law.

3. Members may also exclude from patentability:

(a) diagnostic, therapeutic and surgical methods for the treatment of humans or animals;

(b) plants and animals other than micro-organisms, and essentially biological processes for the production of plants or animals other than non-biological and microbiological processes. However, Members shall provide for the protection of plant varieties either by patents or by an effective *sui generis* system or by any combination thereof. The provisions of this subparagraph shall be reviewed four years after the date of entry into force of the WTO Agreement.

Article 28

Rights Conferred

1. A patent shall confer on its owner the following exclusive rights:

(a) where the subject matter of a patent is a product, to prevent third parties not having the owner's consent from the acts of: making, using, offering for sale, selling, or importing[6] for these purposes that product;

(b) where the subject matter of a patent is a process, to prevent third parties not having the owner's consent from the act of using the process, and from the acts of: using, offering for sale, selling, or importing for these purposes at least the product obtained directly by that process.

5. For the purposes of this Article, the terms "inventive step" and "capable of industrial application" may be deemed by a Member to be synonymous with the terms "non-obvious" and "useful" respectively.

6. This right, like all other rights conferred under this Agreement in respect of the use, sale, importation or other distribution of goods, is subject to the provisions of Article 6.

2. Patent owners shall also have the right to assign, or transfer by succession, the patent and to conclude licensing contracts.

Article 29

Conditions on Patent Applicants

1. Members shall require that an applicant for a patent shall disclose the invention in a manner sufficiently clear and complete for the invention to be carried out by a person skilled in the art and may require the applicant to indicate the best mode for carrying out the invention known to the inventor at the filing date or, where priority is claimed, at the priority date of the application.

2. Members may require an applicant for a patent to provide information concerning the applicant's corresponding foreign applications and grants.

Article 30

Exceptions to Rights Conferred

Members may provide limited exceptions to the exclusive rights conferred by a patent, provided that such exceptions do not unreasonably conflict with a normal exploitation of the patent and do not unreasonably prejudice the legitimate interests of the patent owner, taking account of the legitimate interests of third parties.

Article 31

Other Use Without Authorization of the Right Holder

Where the law of a Member allows for other use[7] of the subject matter of a patent without the authorization of the right holder, including use by the government or third parties authorized by the government, the following provisions shall be respected:

(a) authorization of such use shall be considered on its individual merits;

(b) such use may only be permitted if, prior to such use, the proposed user has made efforts to obtain authorization from the right holder on reasonable commercial terms and conditions and that such efforts have not been successful within a reasonable period of time. This requirement may be waived by a Member in the case of a national emergency or other

7. "Other use" refers to use other than that allowed under Article 30.

circumstances of extreme urgency or in cases of public non-commercial use. In situations of national emergency or other circumstances of extreme urgency, the right holder shall, nevertheless, be notified as soon as reasonably practicable. In the case of public non-commercial use, where the government or contractor, without making a patent search, knows or has demonstrable grounds to know that a valid patent is or will be used by or for the government, the right holder shall be informed promptly;

(c) the scope and duration of such use shall be limited to the purpose for which it was authorized, and in the case of semi-conductor technology shall only be for public non-commercial use or to remedy a practice determined after judicial or administrative process to be anti-competitive;

(d) such use shall be non-exclusive;

(e) such use shall be non-assignable, except with that part of the enterprise or goodwill which enjoys such use;

(f) any such use shall be authorized predominantly for the supply of the domestic market of the Member authorizing such use;

(g) authorization for such use shall be liable, subject to adequate protection of the legitimate interests of the persons so authorized, to be terminated if and when the circumstances which led to it cease to exist and are unlikely to recur. The competent authority shall have the authority to review, upon motivated request, the continued existence of these circumstances;

(h) the right holder shall be paid adequate remuneration in the circumstances of each case, taking into account the economic value of the authorization;

(i) the legal validity of any decision relating to the authorization of such use shall be subject to judicial review or other independent review by a distinct higher authority in that Member;

(j) any decision relating to the remuneration provided in respect of such use shall be subject to judicial review or other independent review by a distinct higher authority in that Member;

(k) Members are not obliged to apply the conditions set forth in subparagraphs (b) and (f) where such use is permitted to remedy a practice determined after judicial or administrative process to be anti-competitive. The need to correct anti-competitive practices may be taken into account in determining the amount of remuneration in such cases. Competent authorities shall have the authority to refuse termination of authorization if and when the conditions which led to such authorization are likely to recur;

(*l*) where such use is authorized to permit the exploitation of a patent ("the second patent") which cannot be exploited without infringing another patent ("the first patent"), the following additional conditions shall apply:

(i) the invention claimed in the second patent shall involve an important technical advance of considerable economic significance in relation to the invention claimed in the first patent;

(ii) the owner of the first patent shall be entitled to a cross-licence on reasonable terms to use the invention claimed in the second patent; and

(iii) the use authorized in respect of the first patent shall be non-assignable except with the assignment of the second patent.

Article 32

Revocation/Forfeiture

An opportunity for judicial review of any decision to revoke or forfeit a patent shall be available.

Article 33

Term of Protection

The term of protection available shall not end before the expiration of a period of twenty years counted from the filing date.[8]

Article 34

Process Patents: Burden of Proof

1. For the purposes of civil proceedings in respect of the infringement of the rights of the owner referred to in paragraph 1(b) of Article 28, if the subject matter of a patent is a process for obtaining a product, the judicial authorities shall have the authority to order the defendant to prove that the process to obtain an identical product is different from the patented process. Therefore, Members shall provide, in at least one of the following circumstances, that any identical product when produced without the consent of the

8. It is understood that those Members which do not have a system of original grant may provide that the term of protection shall be computed from the filing date in the system of original grant.

patent owner shall, in the absence of proof to the contrary, be deemed to have been obtained by the patented process:

(a) if the product obtained by the patented process is new;

(b) if there is a substantial likelihood that the identical product was made by the process and the owner of the patent has been unable through reasonable efforts to determine the process actually used.

2. Any Member shall be free to provide that the burden of proof indicated in paragraph 1 shall be on the alleged infringer only if the condition referred to in subparagraph (a) is fulfilled or only if the condition referred to in subparagraph (b) is fulfilled.

3. In the adduction of proof to the contrary, the legitimate interests of defendants in protecting their manufacturing and business secrets shall be taken into account.

SECTION 6: LAYOUT-DESIGNS (TOPOGRAPHIES) OF INTEGRATED CIRCUITS

Article 35

Relation to the IPIC Treaty

Members agree to provide protection to the layout-designs (topographies) of integrated circuits (referred to in this Agreement as "layout-designs") in accordance with Articles 2 through 7 (other than paragraph 3 of Article 6), Article 12 and paragraph 3 of Article 16 of the Treaty on Intellectual Property in Respect of Integrated Circuits and, in addition, to comply with the following provisions.

Article 36

Scope of the Protection

Subject to the provisions of paragraph 1 of Article 37, Members shall consider unlawful the following acts if performed without the authorization of the right holder:[9] importing, selling, or otherwise distributing for commercial purposes a protected layout-design, an integrated circuit in which a protected layout-design is incorporated, or an article incorporating such an integrated circuit only in so far as it continues to contain an unlawfully reproduced layout-design.

9. The term "right holder" in this Section shall be understood as having the same meaning as the term "holder of the right" in the IPIC Treaty.

Article 37

Acts Not Requiring the Authorization of the Right Holder

1. Notwithstanding Article 36, no Member shall consider unlawful the performance of any of the acts referred to in that Article in respect of an integrated circuit incorporating an unlawfully reproduced layout-design or any article incorporating such an integrated circuit where the person performing or ordering such acts did not know and had no reasonable ground to know, when acquiring the integrated circuit or article incorporating such an integrated circuit, that it incorporated an unlawfully reproduced layout-design. Members shall provide that, after the time that such person has received sufficient notice that the layout-design was unlawfully reproduced, that person may perform any of the acts with respect to the stock on hand or ordered before such time, but shall be liable to pay to the right holder a sum equivalent to a reasonable royalty such as would be payable under a freely negotiated licence in respect of such a layout-design.

2. The conditions set out in subparagraphs (a) through (k) of Article 31 shall apply *mutatis mutandis* in the event of any non-voluntary licensing of a layout-design or of its use by or for the government without the authorization of the right holder.

Article 38

Term of Protection

1. In Members requiring registration as a condition of protection, the term of protection of layout-designs shall not end before the expiration of a period of 10 years counted from the date of filing an application for registration or from the first commercial exploitation wherever in the world it occurs.

2. In Members not requiring registration as a condition for protection, layout-designs shall be protected for a term of no less than 10 years from the date of the first commercial exploitation wherever in the world it occurs.

3. Notwithstanding paragraphs 1 and 2, a Member may provide that protection shall lapse 15 years after the creation of the layout-design.

SECTION 7: PROTECTION OF UNDISCLOSED INFORMATION

Article 39

1. In the course of ensuring effective protection against unfair competition as provided in Article 10*bis* of the Paris Convention (1967), Members shall protect undisclosed information in accordance with paragraph 2 and data submitted to governments or governmental agencies in accordance with paragraph 3.

2. Natural and legal persons shall have the possibility of preventing information lawfully within their control from being disclosed to, acquired by, or used by others without their consent in a manner contrary to honest commercial practices[10] so long as such information:

(a) is secret in the sense that it is not, as a body or in the precise configuration and assembly of its components, generally known among or readily accessible to persons within the circles that normally deal with the kind of information in question;

(b) has commercial value because it is secret; and

(c) has been subject to reasonable steps under the circumstances, by the person lawfully in control of the information, to keep it secret.

3. Members, when requiring, as a condition of approving the marketing of pharmaceutical or of agricultural chemical products which utilize new chemical entities, the submission of undisclosed test or other data, the origination of which involves a considerable effort, shall protect such data against unfair commercial use. In addition, Members shall protect such data against disclosure, except where necessary to protect the public, or unless steps are taken to ensure that the data are protected against unfair commercial use.

SECTION 8: CONTROL OF ANTI-COMPETITIVE PRACTICES IN CONTRACTUAL LICENCES

Article 40

1. Members agree that some licensing practices or conditions pertaining to intellectual property rights which restrain competition may have adverse effects on trade and may impede the transfer and dissemination of technology.

2. Nothing in this Agreement shall prevent Members from specifying in their legislation licensing practices or conditions that may in particular cases constitute an abuse of intellectual property rights having an adverse effect on competition in the relevant market. As provided above, a Member may adopt, consistently with the other provisions of this Agreement, appropriate measures to prevent or control such practices, which may include for example exclusive grantback conditions, conditions preventing challenges to

10. For the purpose of this provision, "a manner contrary to honest commercial practices" shall mean at least practices such as breach of contract, breach of confidence and inducement to breach, and includes the acquisition of undisclosed information by third parties who knew, or were grossly negligent in failing to know, that such practices were involved in the acquisition.

validity and coercive package licensing, in the light of the relevant laws and regulations of that Member.

3. Each Member shall enter, upon request, into consultations with any other Member which has cause to believe that an intellectual property right owner that is a national or domiciliary of the Member to which the request for consultations has been addressed is undertaking practices in violation of the requesting Member's laws and regulations on the subject matter of this Section, and which wishes to secure compliance with such legislation, without prejudice to any action under the law and to the full freedom of an ultimate decision of either Member. The Member addressed shall accord full and sympathetic consideration to, and shall afford adequate opportunity for, consultations with the requesting Member, and shall cooperate through supply of publicly available non-confidential information of relevance to the matter in question and of other information available to the Member, subject to domestic law and to the conclusion of mutually satisfactory agreements concerning the safeguarding of its confidentiality by the requesting Member.

4. A Member whose nationals or domiciliaries are subject to proceedings in another Member concerning alleged violation of that other Member's laws and regulations on the subject matter of this Section shall, upon request, be granted an opportunity for consultations by the other Member under the same conditions as those foreseen in paragraph 3.

Part III

ENFORCEMENT OF INTELLECTUAL PROPERTY RIGHTS

Section 1: General Obligations

Article 41

1. Members shall ensure that enforcement procedures as specified in this Part are available under their law so as to permit effective action against any act of infringement of intellectual property rights covered by this Agreement, including expeditious remedies to prevent infringements and remedies which constitute a deterrent to further infringements. These procedures shall be applied in such a manner as to avoid the creation of barriers to legitimate trade and to provide for safeguards against their abuse.

2. Procedures concerning the enforcement of intellectual property rights shall be fair and equitable. They shall not be unnecessarily complicated or costly, or entail unreasonable time-limits or unwarranted delays.

3. Decisions on the merits of a case shall preferably be in writing and reasoned. They shall be made available at least to the parties to the pro-

ceeding without undue delay. Decisions on the merits of a case shall be based only on evidence in respect of which parties were offered the opportunity to be heard.

4. Parties to a proceeding shall have an opportunity for review by a judicial authority of final administrative decisions and, subject to jurisdictional provisions in a Member's law concerning the importance of a case, of at least the legal aspects of initial judicial decisions on the merits of a case. However, there shall be no obligation to provide an opportunity for review of acquittals in criminal cases.

5. It is understood that this Part does not create any obligation to put in place a judicial system for the enforcement of intellectual property rights distinct from that for the enforcement of law in general, nor does it affect the capacity of Members to enforce their law in general. Nothing in this Part creates any obligation with respect to the distribution of resources as between enforcement of intellectual property rights and the enforcement of law in general.

SECTION 2: CIVIL AND ADMINISTRATIVE PROCEDURES AND REMEDIES

Article 42

Fair and Equitable Procedures

Members shall make available to right holders[11] civil judicial procedures concerning the enforcement of any intellectual property right covered by this Agreement. Defendants shall have the right to written notice which is timely and contains sufficient detail, including the basis of the claims. Parties shall be allowed to be represented by independent legal counsel, and procedures shall not impose overly burdensome requirements concerning mandatory personal appearances. All parties to such procedures shall be duly entitled to substantiate their claims and to present all relevant evidence. The procedure shall provide a means to identify and protect confidential information, unless this would be contrary to existing constitutional requirements.

Article 43

Evidence

1. The judicial authorities shall have the authority, where a party has presented reasonably available evidence sufficient to support its claims and has specified evidence relevant to substantiation of its claims which lies in

11. For the purpose of this Part, the term "right holder" includes federations and associations having legal standing to assert such rights.

the control of the opposing party, to order that this evidence be produced by the opposing party, subject in appropriate cases to conditions which ensure the protection of confidential information.

2. In cases in which a party to a proceeding voluntarily and without good reason refuses access to, or otherwise does not provide necessary information within a reasonable period, or significantly impedes a procedure relating to an enforcement action, a Member may accord judicial authorities the authority to make preliminary and final determinations, affirmative or negative, on the basis of the information presented to them, including the complaint or the allegation presented by the party adversely affected by the denial of access to information, subject to providing the parties an opportunity to be heard on the allegations or evidence.

Article 44

Injunctions

1. The judicial authorities shall have the authority to order a party to desist from an infringement, *inter alia* to prevent the entry into the channels of commerce in their jurisdiction of imported goods that involve the infringement of an intellectual property right, immediately after customs clearance of such goods. Members are not obliged to accord such authority in respect of protected subject matter acquired or ordered by a person prior to knowing or having reasonable grounds to know that dealing in such subject matter would entail the infringement of an intellectual property right.

2. Notwithstanding the other provisions of this Part and provided that the provisions of Part II specifically addressing use by governments, or by third parties authorized by a government, without the authorization of the right holder are complied with, Members may limit the remedies available against such use to payment of remuneration in accordance with subparagraph (h) of Article 31. In other cases, the remedies under this Part shall apply or, where these remedies are inconsistent with a Member's law, declaratory judgments and adequate compensation shall be available.

Article 45

Damages

1. The judicial authorities shall have the authority to order the infringer to pay the right holder damages adequate to compensate for the injury the right holder has suffered because of an infringement of that person's intellectual property right by an infringer who knowingly, or with reasonable grounds to know, engaged in infringing activity.

2. The judicial authorities shall also have the authority to order the infringer to pay the right holder expenses, which may include appropriate attorney's fees. In appropriate cases, Members may authorize the judicial authorities to order recovery of profits and/or payment of pre-established damages even where the infringer did not knowingly, or with reasonable grounds to know, engage in infringing activity.

Article 46

Other Remedies

In order to create an effective deterrent to infringement, the judicial authorities shall have the authority to order that goods that they have found to be infringing be, without compensation of any sort, disposed of outside the channels of commerce in such a manner as to avoid any harm caused to the right holder, or, unless this would be contrary to existing constitutional requirements, destroyed. The judicial authorities shall also have the authority to order that materials and implements the predominant use of which has been in the creation of the infringing goods be, without compensation of any sort, disposed of outside the channels of commerce in such a manner as to minimize the risks of further infringements. In considering such requests, the need for proportionality between the seriousness of the infringement and the remedies ordered as well as the interests of third parties shall be taken into account. In regard to counterfeit trademark goods, the simple removal of the trademark unlawfully affixed shall not be sufficient, other than in exceptional cases, to permit release of the goods into the channels of commerce.

Article 47

Right of Information

Members may provide that the judicial authorities shall have the authority, unless this would be out of proportion to the seriousness of the infringement, to order the infringer to inform the right holder of the identity of third persons involved in the production and distribution of the infringing goods or services and of their channels of distribution.

Article 48

Indemnification of the Defendant

1. The judicial authorities shall have the authority to order a party at whose request measures were taken and who has abused enforcement procedures to provide to a party wrongfully enjoined or restrained adequate compensation for the injury suffered because of such abuse. The judicial authorities shall also have the authority to order the applicant to pay the defendant expenses, which may include appropriate attorney's fees.

2. In respect of the administration of any law pertaining to the protection or enforcement of intellectual property rights, Members shall only exempt both public authorities and officials from liability to appropriate remedial measures where actions are taken or intended in good faith in the course of the administration of that law.

Article 49

Administrative Procedures

To the extent that any civil remedy can be ordered as a result of administrative procedures on the merits of a case, such procedures shall conform to principles equivalent in substance to those set forth in this Section.

SECTION 3: PROVISIONAL MEASURES

Article 50

1. The judicial authorities shall have the authority to order prompt and effective provisional measures:

(a) to prevent an infringement of any intellectual property right from occurring, and in particular to prevent the entry into the channels of commerce in their jurisdiction of goods, including imported goods immediately after customs clearance;

(b) to preserve relevant evidence in regard to the alleged infringement.

2. The judicial authorities shall have the authority to adopt provisional measures *inaudita altera parte* where appropriate, in particular where any delay is likely to cause irreparable harm to the right holder, or where there is a demonstrable risk of evidence being destroyed.

3. The judicial authorities shall have the authority to require the applicant to provide any reasonably available evidence in order to satisfy themselves with a sufficient degree of certainty that the applicant is the right holder and that the applicant's right is being infringed or that such infringement is imminent, and to order the applicant to provide a security or equivalent assurance sufficient to protect the defendant and to prevent abuse.

4. Where provisional measures have been adopted *inaudita altera parte*, the parties affected shall be given notice, without delay after the execution of the measures at the latest. A review, including a right to be heard, shall take place upon request of the defendant with a view to deciding, within a reasonable period after the notification of the measures, whether these measures shall be modified, revoked or confirmed.

5. The applicant may be required to supply other information necessary for the identification of the goods concerned by the authority that will execute the provisional measures.

6. Without prejudice to paragraph 4, provisional measures taken on the basis of paragraphs 1 and 2 shall, upon request by the defendant, be revoked or otherwise cease to have effect, if proceedings leading to a decision on the merits of the case are not initiated within a reasonable period, to be determined by the judicial authority ordering the measures where a Member's law so permits or, in the absence of such a determination, not to exceed 20 working days or 31 calendar days, whichever is the longer.

7. Where the provisional measures are revoked or where they lapse due to any act or omission by the applicant, or where it is subsequently found that there has been no infringement or threat of infringement of an intellectual property right, the judicial authorities shall have the authority to order the applicant, upon request of the defendant, to provide the defendant appropriate compensation for any injury caused by these measures.

8. To the extent that any provisional measure can be ordered as a result of administrative procedures, such procedures shall conform to principles equivalent in substance to those set forth in this Section.

Section 4: Special Requirements Related to Border Measures[12]

Article 51

Suspension of Release by Customs Authorities

Members shall, in conformity with the provisions set out below, adopt procedures[13] to enable a right holder, who has valid grounds for suspecting that the importation of counterfeit trademark or pirated copyright goods[14]

12. Where a Member has dismantled substantially all controls over movement of goods across its border with another Member with which it forms part of a customs union, it shall not be required to apply the provisions of this Section at that border.

13. It is understood that there shall be no obligation to apply such procedures to imports of goods put on the market in another country by or with the consent of the right holder, or to goods in transit.

14. For the purposes of this Agreement:

(a) "counterfeit trademark goods" shall mean any goods, including packaging, bearing without authorization a trademark which is identical to the trademark validly registered in respect of such goods, or which cannot be distinguished in its essential aspects from such a trademark, and which thereby infringes the rights of the owner of the trademark in question under the law of the country of importation;

(b) "pirated copyright goods" shall mean any goods which are copies made without the consent of the right holder or person duly authorized by the right holder in the country of production and which are made directly or indirectly from an article where the making of

may take place, to lodge an application in writing with competent authorities, administrative or judicial, for the suspension by the customs authorities of the release into free circulation of such goods. Members may enable such an application to be made in respect of goods which involve other infringements of intellectual property rights, provided that the requirements of this Section are met. Members may also provide for corresponding procedures concerning the suspension by the customs authorities of the release of infringing goods destined for exportation from their territories.

Article 52

Application

Any right holder initiating the procedures under Article 51 shall be required to provide adequate evidence to satisfy the competent authorities that, under the laws of the country of importation, there is *prima facie* an infringement of the right holder's intellectual property right and to supply a sufficiently detailed description of the goods to make them readily recognizable by the customs authorities. The competent authorities shall inform the applicant within a reasonable period whether they have accepted the application and, where determined by the competent authorities, the period for which the customs authorities will take action.

Article 53

Security or Equivalent Assurance

1. The competent authorities shall have the authority to require an applicant to provide a security or equivalent assurance sufficient to protect the defendant and the competent authorities and to prevent abuse. Such security or equivalent assurance shall not unreasonably deter recourse to these procedures.

2. Where pursuant to an application under this Section the release of goods involving industrial designs, patents, layout-designs or undisclosed information into free circulation has been suspended by customs authorities on the basis of a decision other than by a judicial or other independent authority, and the period provided for in Article 55 has expired without the granting of provisional relief by the duly empowered authority, and provided that all other conditions for importation have been complied with, the owner, importer, or consignee of such goods shall be entitled to their release on the posting of a security in an amount sufficient to protect the right holder for any infringement. Payment of such security shall not prejudice any other remedy available to the right holder, it being understood that the

---

that copy would have constituted an infringement of a copyright or a related right under the law of the country of importation.

security shall be released if the right holder fails to pursue the right of action within a reasonable period of time.

Article 54

Notice of Suspension

The importer and the applicant shall be promptly notified of the suspension of the release of goods according to Article 51.

Article 55

Duration of Suspension

If, within a period not exceeding 10 working days after the applicant has been served notice of the suspension, the customs authorities have not been informed that proceedings leading to a decision on the merits of the case have been initiated by a party other than the defendant, or that the duly empowered authority has taken provisional measures prolonging the suspension of the release of the goods, the goods shall be released, provided that all other conditions for importation or exportation have been complied with; in appropriate cases, this time-limit may be extended by another 10 working days. If proceedings leading to a decision on the merits of the case have been initiated, a review, including a right to be heard, shall take place upon request of the defendant with a view to deciding, within a reasonable period, whether these measures shall be modified, revoked or confirmed. Notwithstanding the above, where the suspension of the release of goods is carried out or continued in accordance with a provisional judicial measure, the provisions of paragraph 6 of Article 50 shall apply.

Article 56

Indemnification of the Importer and of the Owner of the Goods

Relevant authorities shall have the authority to order the applicant to pay the importer, the consignee and the owner of the goods appropriate compensation for any injury caused to them through the wrongful detention of goods or through the detention of goods released pursuant to Article 55.

Article 57

Right of Inspection and Information

Without prejudice to the protection of confidential information, Members shall provide the competent authorities the authority to give the right holder sufficient opportunity to have any goods detained by the customs authorities inspected in order to substantiate the right holder's claims. The competent authorities shall also have authority to give the importer an equivalent opportunity to have any such goods inspected. Where a positive determination has been made on the merits of a case, Members may provide the competent authorities the authority to inform the right holder of the names and addresses of the consignor, the importer and the consignee and of the quantity of the goods in question.

Article 58

Ex Officio Action

Where Members require competent authorities to act upon their own initiative and to suspend the release of goods in respect of which they have acquired *prima facie* evidence that an intellectual property right is being infringed:

(a) the competent authorities may at any time seek from the right holder any information that may assist them to exercise these powers;

(b) the importer and the right holder shall be promptly notified of the suspension. Where the importer has lodged an appeal against the suspension with the competent authorities, the suspension shall be subject to the conditions, *mutatis mutandis*, set out at Article 55;

(c) Members shall only exempt both public authorities and officials from liability to appropriate remedial measures where actions are taken or intended in good faith.

Article 59

Remedies

Without prejudice to other rights of action open to the right holder and subject to the right of the defendant to seek review by a judicial authority, competent authorities shall have the authority to order the destruction or disposal of infringing goods in accordance with the principles set out in Article 46. In regard to counterfeit trademark goods, the authorities shall not allow the re-exportation of the infringing goods in an unaltered state or subject them to a different customs procedure, other than in exceptional circumstances.

Article 60

De Minimis Imports

Members may exclude from the application of the above provisions small quantities of goods of a non-commercial nature contained in travellers' personal luggage or sent in small consignments.

Section 5: Criminal Procedures

Article 61

Members shall provide for criminal procedures and penalties to be applied at least in cases of wilful trademark counterfeiting or copyright piracy on a commercial scale. Remedies available shall include imprisonment and/or monetary fines sufficient to provide a deterrent, consistently with the level of penalties applied for crimes of a corresponding gravity. In appropriate cases, remedies available shall also include the seizure, forfeiture and destruction of the infringing goods and of any materials and implements the predominant use of which has been in the commission of the offence. Members may provide for criminal procedures and penalties to be applied in other cases of infringement of intellectual property rights, in particular where they are committed wilfully and on a commercial scale.

Part IV

ACQUISITION AND MAINTENANCE OF INTELLECTUAL PROPERTY RIGHTS AND RELATED INTER-PARTES PROCEDURES

Article 62

1. Members may require, as a condition of the acquisition or maintenance of the intellectual property rights provided for under Sections 2 through 6 of Part II, compliance with reasonable procedures and formalities. Such procedures and formalities shall be consistent with the provisions of this Agreement.

2. Where the acquisition of an intellectual property right is subject to the right being granted or registered, Members shall ensure that the procedures for grant or registration, subject to compliance with the substantive conditions for acquisition of the right, permit the granting or registration of the right within a reasonable period of time so as to avoid unwarranted curtailment of the period of protection.

3. Article 4 of the Paris Convention (1967) shall apply *mutatis mutandis* to service marks.

4. Procedures concerning the acquisition or maintenance of intellectual property rights and, where a Member's law provides for such procedures, administrative revocation and *inter partes* procedures such as opposition, revocation and cancellation, shall be governed by the general principles set out in paragraphs 2 and 3 of Article 41.

5. Final administrative decisions in any of the procedures referred to under paragraph 4 shall be subject to review by a judicial or quasi-judicial authority. However, there shall be no obligation to provide an opportunity for such review of decisions in cases of unsuccessful opposition or administrative revocation, provided that the grounds for such procedures can be the subject of invalidation procedures.

Part V

DISPUTE PREVENTION AND SETTLEMENT

Article 63

Transparency

1. Laws and regulations, and final judicial decisions and administrative rulings of general application, made effective by a Member pertaining to the subject matter of this Agreement (the availability, scope, acquisition, enforcement and prevention of the abuse of intellectual property rights) shall be published, or where such publication is not practicable made publicly available, in a national language, in such a manner as to enable governments and right holders to become acquainted with them. Agreements concerning the subject matter of this Agreement which are in force between the government or a governmental agency of a Member and the government or a governmental agency of another Member shall also be published.

2. Members shall notify the laws and regulations referred to in paragraph 1 to the Council for TRIPS in order to assist that Council in its review of the operation of this Agreement. The Council shall attempt to minimize the burden on Members in carrying out this obligation and may decide to waive the obligation to notify such laws and regulations directly to the Council if consultations with WIPO on the establishment of a common register containing these laws and regulations are successful. The Council shall also consider in this connection any action required regarding notifications pursuant to the obligations under this Agreement stemming from the provisions of Article 6*ter* of the Paris Convention (1967).

3. Each Member shall be prepared to supply, in response to a written request from another Member, information of the sort referred to in paragraph 1. A Member, having reason to believe that a specific judicial decision or administrative ruling or bilateral agreement in the area of intellectual property rights affects its rights under this Agreement, may also request in writing to be given access to or be informed in sufficient detail of such specific judicial decisions or administrative rulings or bilateral agreements.

4. Nothing in paragraphs 1, 2 and 3 shall require Members to disclose confidential information which would impede law enforcement or otherwise

be contrary to the public interest or would prejudice the legitimate commercial interests of particular enterprises, public or private.

Article 64

Dispute Settlement

1. The provisions of Articles XXII and XXIII of GATT 1994 as elaborated and applied by the Dispute Settlement Understanding shall apply to consultations and the settlement of disputes under this Agreement except as otherwise specifically provided herein.

2. Subparagraphs 1(b) and 1(c) of Article XXIII of GATT 1994 shall not apply to the settlement of disputes under this Agreement for a period of five years from the date of entry into force of the WTO Agreement.

3. During the time period referred to in paragraph 2, the Council for TRIPS shall examine the scope and modalities for complaints of the type provided for under subparagraphs 1(b) and 1(c) of Article XXIII of GATT 1994 made pursuant to this Agreement, and submit its recommendations to the Ministerial Conference for approval. Any decision of the Ministerial Conference to approve such recommendations or to extend the period in paragraph 2 shall be made only by consensus, and approved recommendations shall be effective for all Members without further formal acceptance process.

Part VI

TRANSITIONAL ARRANGEMENTS

Article 65

Transitional Arrangements

1. Subject to the provisions of paragraphs 2, 3 and 4, no Member shall be obliged to apply the provisions of this Agreement before the expiry of a general period of one year following the date of entry into force of the WTO Agreement.

2. A developing country Member is entitled to delay for a further period of four years the date of application, as defined in paragraph 1, of the provisions of this Agreement other than Articles 3, 4 and 5.

3. Any other Member which is in the process of transformation from a centrally-planned into a market, free-enterprise economy and which is undertaking structural reform of its intellectual property system and facing special problems in the preparation and implementation of intellectual

property laws and regulations, may also benefit from a period of delay as foreseen in paragraph 2.

4. To the extent that a developing country Member is obliged by this Agreement to extend product patent protection to areas of technology not so protectable in its territory on the general date of application of this Agreement for that Member, as defined in paragraph 2, it may delay the application of the provisions on product patents of Section 5 of Part II to such areas of technology for an additional period of five years.

5. A Member availing itself of a transitional period under paragraphs 1, 2, 3 or 4 shall ensure that any changes in its laws, regulations and practice made during that period do not result in a lesser degree of consistency with the provisions of this Agreement.

Article 66

Least-Developed Country Members

1. In view of the special needs and requirements of least-developed country Members, their economic, financial and administrative constraints, and their need for flexibility to create a viable technological base, such Members shall not be required to apply the provisions of this Agreement, other than Articles 3, 4 and 5, for a period of 10 years from the date of application as defined under paragraph 1 of Article 65. The Council for TRIPS shall, upon duly motivated request by a least-developed country Member, accord extensions of this period.

2. Developed country Members shall provide incentives to enterprises and institutions in their territories for the purpose of promoting and encouraging technology transfer to least-developed country Members in order to enable them to create a sound and viable technological base.

Article 67

Technical Cooperation

In order to facilitate the implementation of this Agreement, developed country Members shall provide, on request and on mutually agreed terms and conditions, technical and financial cooperation in favour of developing and least-developed country Members. Such cooperation shall include assistance in the preparation of laws and regulations on the protection and enforcement of intellectual property rights as well as on the prevention of their abuse, and shall include support regarding the establishment or reinforcement of domestic offices and agencies relevant to these matters, including the training of personnel.

Part VII

INSTITUTIONAL ARRANGEMENTS; FINAL PROVISIONS

Article 68

Council for Trade-Related Aspects of Intellectual Property Rights

The Council for TRIPS shall monitor the operation of this Agreement and, in particular, Members' compliance with their obligations hereunder, and shall afford Members the opportunity of consulting on matters relating to the trade-related aspects of intellectual property rights. It shall carry out such other responsibilities as assigned to it by the Members, and it shall, in particular, provide any assistance requested by them in the context of dispute settlement procedures. In carrying out its functions, the Council for TRIPS may consult with and seek information from any source it deems appropriate. In consultation with WIPO, the Council shall seek to establish, within one year of its first meeting, appropriate arrangements for cooperation with bodies of that Organization.

Article 69

International Cooperation

Members agree to cooperate with each other with a view to eliminating international trade in goods infringing intellectual property rights. For this purpose, they shall establish and notify contact points in their administrations and be ready to exchange information on trade in infringing goods. They shall, in particular, promote the exchange of information and cooperation between customs authorities with regard to trade in counterfeit trademark goods and pirated copyright goods.

Article 70

Protection of Existing Subject Matter

1. This Agreement does not give rise to obligations in respect of acts which occurred before the date of application of the Agreement for the Member in question.

2. Except as otherwise provided for in this Agreement, this Agreement gives rise to obligations in respect of all subject matter existing at the date of application of this Agreement for the Member in question, and which is protected in that Member on the said date, or which meets or comes subsequently to meet the criteria for protection under the terms of this Agreement. In respect of this paragraph and paragraphs 3 and 4, copyright obligations with respect to existing works shall be solely determined under Article 18 of the Berne Convention (1971), and obligations with respect to the rights of

producers of phonograms and performers in existing phonograms shall be determined solely under Article 18 of the Berne Convention (1971) as made applicable under paragraph 6 of Article 14 of this Agreement.

3. There shall be no obligation to restore protection to subject matter which on the date of application of this Agreement for the Member in question has fallen into the public domain.

4. In respect of any acts in respect of specific objects embodying protected subject matter which become infringing under the terms of legislation in conformity with this Agreement, and which were commenced, or in respect of which a significant investment was made, before the date of acceptance of the WTO Agreement by that Member, any Member may provide for a limitation of the remedies available to the right holder as to the continued performance of such acts after the date of application of this Agreement for that Member. In such cases the Member shall, however, at least provide for the payment of equitable remuneration.

5. A Member is not obliged to apply the provisions of Article 11 and of paragraph 4 of Article 14 with respect to originals or copies purchased prior to the date of application of this Agreement for that Member.

6. Members shall not be required to apply Article 31, or the requirement in paragraph 1 of Article 27 that patent rights shall be enjoyable without discrimination as to the field of technology, to use without the authorization of the right holder where authorization for such use was granted by the government before the date this Agreement became known.

7. In the case of intellectual property rights for which protection is conditional upon registration, applications for protection which are pending on the date of application of this Agreement for the Member in question shall be permitted to be amended to claim any enhanced protection provided under the provisions of this Agreement. Such amendments shall not include new matter.

8. Where a Member does not make available as of the date of entry into force of the WTO Agreement patent protection for pharmaceutical and agricultural chemical products commensurate with its obligations under Article 27, that Member shall:

(a) notwithstanding the provisions of Part VI, provide as from the date of entry into force of the WTO Agreement a means by which applications for patents for such inventions can be filed;

(b) apply to these applications, as of the date of application of this Agreement, the criteria for patentability as laid down in this Agreement as if those criteria were being applied on the date of filing in that Member or, where priority is available and claimed, the priority date of the application; and

(c) provide patent protection in accordance with this Agreement as from the grant of the patent and for the remainder of the patent term, counted from the filing date in accordance with Article 33 of this Agreement, for those of these applications that meet the criteria for protection referred to in subparagraph (b).

9. Where a product is the subject of a patent application in a Member in accordance with paragraph 8(a), exclusive marketing rights shall be granted, notwithstanding the provisions of Part VI, for a period of five years after obtaining marketing approval in that Member or until a product patent is granted or rejected in that Member, whichever period is shorter, provided that, subsequent to the entry into force of the WTO Agreement, a patent application has been filed and a patent granted for that product in another Member and marketing approval obtained in such other Member.

Article 71

Review and Amendment

1. The Council for TRIPS shall review the implementation of this Agreement after the expiration of the transitional period referred to in paragraph 2 of Article 65. The Council shall, having regard to the experience gained in its implementation, review it two years after that date, and at identical intervals thereafter. The Council may also undertake reviews in the light of any relevant new developments which might warrant modification or amendment of this Agreement.

2. Amendments merely serving the purpose of adjusting to higher levels of protection of intellectual property rights achieved, and in force, in other multilateral agreements and accepted under those agreements by all Members of the WTO may be referred to the Ministerial Conference for action in accordance with paragraph 6 of Article X of the WTO Agreement on the basis of a consensus proposal from the Council for TRIPS.

Article 72

Reservations

Reservations may not be entered in respect of any of the provisions of this Agreement without the consent of the other Members.

Article 73

Security Exceptions

Nothing in this Agreement shall be construed:

(a) to require a Member to furnish any information the disclosure of which it considers contrary to its essential security interests; or

(b) to prevent a Member from taking any action which it considers necessary for the protection of its essential security interests;

(i) relating to fissionable materials or the materials from which they are derived;

(ii) relating to the traffic in arms, ammunition and implements of war and to such traffic in other goods and materials as is carried on directly or indirectly for the purpose of supplying a military establishment;

(iii) taken in time of war or other emergency in international relations; or

(c) to prevent a Member from taking any action in pursuance of its obligations under the United Nations Charter for the maintenance of international peace and security.

Document 42

Paris Convention for the Protection of Industrial Property

Article 2.1 of the TRIPS Agreement incorporates Articles 1 through 12, and Article 19, of the Paris Convention. These articles are reproduced below.

Article 1

[Establishment of the Union; Scope of Industrial Property][1])

(1) The countries to which this Convention applies constitute a Union for the protection of industrial property.

(2) The protection of industrial property has as its object patents, utility models, industrial designs, trademarks, service marks, trade names, indications of source or appellations of origin, and the repression of unfair competition.

(3) Industrial property shall be understood in the broadest sense and shall apply not only to industry and commerce proper, but likewise to agricultural and extractive industries and to all manufactured or natural products, for example, wines, grain, tobacco leaf, fruit, cattle, minerals, mineral waters, beer, flowers, and flour.

(4) Patents shall include the various kinds of industrial patents recognized by the laws of the countries of the Union, such as patents of importation, patents of improvement, patents and certificates of addition, etc.

1. Articles have been given titles to facilitate their identification. There are no titles in the signed (French) text.

Article 2

[National Treatment for Nationals of Countries of the Union]

(1) Nationals of any country of the Union shall, as regards the protection of industrial property, enjoy in all the other countries of the Union the advantages that their respective laws now grant, or may hereafter grant, to nationals; all without prejudice to the rights specially provided for by this Convention. Consequently, they shall have the same protection as the latter, and the same legal remedy against any infringement of their rights, provided that the conditions and formalities imposed upon nationals are complied with.

(2) However, no requirement as to domicile or establishment in the country where protection is claimed may be imposed upon nationals of countries of the Union for the enjoyment of any industrial property rights.

(3) The provisions of the laws of each of the countries of the Union relating to judicial and administrative procedure and to jurisdiction, and to the designation of an address for service or the appointment of an agent, which may be required by the laws on industrial property are expressly reserved.

Article 3

[Same Treatment for Certain Categories of Persons as for Nationals of Countries of the Union]

Nationals of countries outside the Union who are domiciled or who have real and effective industrial or commercial establishments in the territory of one of the countries of the Union shall be treated in the same manner as nationals of the countries of the Union.

Article 4

[A to I. *Patents, Utility Models, Industrial Designs, Marks, Inventors' Certificates:* Right of Priority.—G. *Patents:* Division of the Application]

A.—

(1) Any person who has duly filed an application for a patent, or for the registration of a utility model, or of an industrial design, or of a trademark, in one of the countries of the Union, or his successor in title, shall enjoy, for the purpose of filing in the other countries, a right of priority during the periods hereinafter fixed.

(2) Any filing that is equivalent to a regular national filing under the domestic legislation of any country of the Union or under bilateral

or multilateral treaties concluded between countries of the Union shall be recognized as giving rise to the right of priority.

(3) By a regular national filing is meant any filing that is adequate to establish the date on which the application was filed in the country concerned, whatever may be the subsequent fate of the application.

B.—Consequently, any subsequent filing in any of the other countries of the Union before the expiration of the periods referred to above shall not be invalidated by reason of any acts accomplished in the interval, in particular, another filing, the publication or exploitation of the invention, the putting on sale of copies of the design, or the use of the mark, and such acts cannot give rise to any third–party right or any right of personal possession. Rights acquired by third parties before the date of the first application that serves as the basis for the right of priority are reserved in accordance with the domestic legislation of each country of the Union

C.—

(1) The periods of priority referred to above shall be twelve months for patents and utility models, and six months for industrial designs and trademarks.

(2) These periods shall start from the date of filing of the first application; the day of filing shall not be included in the period.

(3) If the last day of the period is an official holiday, or a day when the Office is not open for the filing of applications in the country where protection is claimed, the period shall be extended until the first following working day.

(4) A subsequent application concerning the same subject as a previous first application within the meaning of paragraph (2), above, filed in the same country of the Union shall be considered as the first application, of which the filing date shall be the starting point of the period of priority, if, at the time of filing the subsequent application, the said previous application has been withdrawn, abandoned, or refused, without having been laid open to public inspection and without leaving any rights outstanding, and if it has not yet served as a basis for claiming a right of priority. The previous application may not thereafter serve as a basis for claiming a right of priority.

D.—

(1) Any person desiring to take advantage of the priority of a previous filing shall be required to make a declaration indicating the

date of such filing and the country in which it was made. Each country shall determine the latest date on which such declaration must be made.

(2) These particulars shall be mentioned in the publications issued by the competent authority, and in particular in the patents and the specifications relating thereto.

(3) The countries of the Union may require any person making a declaration of priority to produce a copy of the application (description, drawings, etc.) previously filed. The copy, certified as correct by the authority which received such application, shall not require any authentication, and may in any case be filed, without fee, at any time within three months of the filing of the subsequent application. They may require it to be accompanied by a certificate from the same authority showing the date of filing, and by a translation.

(4) No other formalities may be required for the declaration of priority at the time of filing the application. Each country of the Union shall determine the consequences of failure to comply with the formalities prescribed by this Article, but such consequences shall in no case go beyond the loss of the right of priority.

(5) Subsequently, further proof may be required. Any person who avails himself of the priority of a previous application shall be required to specify the number of that application; this number shall be published as provided for by paragraph (2), above.

E.—

(1) Where an industrial design is filed in a country by virtue of a right of priority based on the filing of a utility model, the period of priority shall be the same as that fixed for industrial designs

(2) Furthermore, it is permissible to file a utility model in a country by virtue of a right of priority based on the filing of a patent application, and vice versa.

F.—No country of the Union may refuse a priority or a patent application on the ground that the applicant claims multiple priorities, even if they originate in different countries, or on the ground that an application claiming one or more priorities contains one or more elements that were not included in the application or applications whose priority is claimed, provided that, in both cases, there is unity of invention within the meaning of the law of the country.

With respect to the elements not included in the application or applications whose priority is claimed, the filing of the subsequent application shall give rise to a right of priority under ordinary conditions.

G.—

(1) If the examination reveals that an application for a patent contains more than one invention, the applicant may divide the application into a certain number of divisional applications and preserve as the date of each the date of the initial application and the benefit of the right of priority, if any.

(2) The applicant may also, on his own initiative, divide a patent application and preserve as the date of each divisional application the date of the initial application and the benefit of the right of priority, if any. Each country of the Union shall have the right to determine the conditions under which such division shall be authorized.

H.—Priority may not be refused on the ground that certain elements of the invention for which priority is claimed do not appear among the claims formulated in the application in the country of origin, provided that the application documents as a whole specifically disclose such elements.

I.—

(1) Applications for inventors' certificates filed in a country in which applicants have the right to apply at their own option either for a patent or for an inventor's certificate shall give rise to the right of priority provided for by this Article, under the same conditions and with the same effects as applications for patents.

(2) In a country in which applicants have the right to apply at their own option either for a patent or for an inventor's certificate, an applicant for an inventor's certificate shall, in accordance with the provisions of this Article relating to patent applications, enjoy a right of priority based on an application for a patent, a utility model, or an inventor's certificate.

Article 4 bis

[*Patents:* Independence of Patents Obtained for the Same Invention in Different Countries]

(1) Patents applied for in the various countries of the Union by nationals of countries of the Union shall be independent of patents obtained

for the same invention in other countries, whether members of the Union or not.

(2) The foregoing provision is to be understood in an unrestricted sense, in particular, in the sense that patents applied for during the period of priority are independent, both as regards the grounds for nullity and forfeiture, and as regards their normal duration.

(3) The provision shall apply to all patents existing at the time when it comes into effect.

(4) Similarly, it shall apply, in the case of the accession of new countries, to patents in existence on either side at the time of accession.

(5) Patents obtained with the benefit of priority shall, in the various countries of the Union, have a duration equal to that which they would have, had they been applied for or granted without the benefit of priority.

Article 4 ter

[*Patents:* Mention of the Inventor in the Patent]

The inventor shall have the right to be mentioned as such in the patent.

Article 4 quater

[*Patents:* Patentability in Case of Restrictions of Sale by Law]

The grant of a patent shall not be refused and a patent shall not be invalidated on the ground that the sale of the patented product or of a product obtained by means of a patented process is subject to restrictions or limitations resulting from the domestic law.

Article 5

[A. *Patents:* Importation of Articles; Failure to Work or Insufficient Working; Compulsory Licenses.—B. *Industrial Designs:* Failure to Work; Importation of Articles.—C. *Marks:* Failure to Use; Different Forms; Use by Co–proprietors.—D. *Patents, Utility Models, Marks, Industrial Designs:* Marking]

A.—

(1) Importation by the patentee into the country where the patent has been granted of articles manufactured in any of the countries of the Union shall not entail forfeiture of the patent.

(2) Each country of the Union shall have the right to take legislative measures providing for the grant of compulsory licenses to prevent the abuses which might result from the exercise of the exclusive rights conferred by the patent, for example, failure to work.

(3) Forfeiture of the patent shall not be provided for except in cases where the grant of compulsory licenses would not have been sufficient to prevent the said abuses. No proceedings for the forfeiture or revocation of a patent may be instituted before the expiration of two years from the grant of the first compulsory license.

(4) A compulsory license may not be applied for on the ground of failure to work or insufficient working before the expiration of a period of four years from the date of filing of the patent application or three years from the date of the grant of the patent, whichever period expires last; it shall be refused if the patentee justifies his inaction by legitimate reasons. Such a compulsory license shall be non–exclusive and shall not be transferable, even in the form of the grant of a sub–license, except with that part of the enterprise or goodwill which exploits such license.

(5) The foregoing provisions shall be applicable, mutatis mutandis, to utility models.

B.—The protection of industrial designs shall not, under any circumstance, be subject to any forfeiture, either by reason of failure to work or by reason of the importation of articles corresponding to those which are protected.

C.—

(1) If, in any country, use of the registered mark is compulsory, the registration may be cancelled only after a reasonable period, and then only if the person concerned does not justify his inaction.

(2) Use of a trademark by the proprietor in a form differing in elements which do not alter the distinctive character of the mark in the form in which it was registered in one of the countries of the Union shall not entail invalidation of the registration and shall not diminish the protection granted to the mark.

(3) Concurrent use of the same mark on identical or similar goods by industrial or commercial establishments considered as co–proprietors of the mark according to the provisions of the domestic law of the

country where protection is claimed shall not prevent registration or diminish in any way the protection granted to the said mark in any country of the Union, provided that such use does not result in misleading the public and is not contrary to the public interest.

D.—No indication or mention of the patent, of the utility model, of the registration of the trademark, or of the deposit of the industrial design, shall be required upon the goods as a condition of recognition of the right to protection.

Article 5 bis

[*All Industrial Property Rights:* Period of Grace for the Payment of Fees for the Maintenance of Rights; *Patents:* Restoration]

(1) A period of grace of not less than six months shall be allowed for the payment of the fees prescribed for the maintenance of industrial property rights, subject, if the domestic legislation so provides, to the payment of a surcharge.

(2) The countries of the Union shall have the right to provide for the restoration of patents which have lapsed by reason of non–payment of fees.

Article 5 ter

[*Patents:* Patented Devices Forming Part of Vessels, Aircraft, or Land Vehicles]

In any country of the Union the following shall not be considered as infringements of the rights of a patentee:

1. the use on board vessels of other countries of the Union of devices forming the subject of his patent in the body of the vessel, in the machinery, tackle, gear and other accessories, when such vessels temporarily or accidentally enter the waters of the said country, provided that such devices are used there exclusively for the needs of the vessel;
2. the use of devices forming the subject of the patent in the construction or operation of aircraft or land vehicles of other countries of the Union, or of accessories of such aircraft or land vehicles, when those aircraft or land vehicles temporarily or accidentally enter the said country.

Article 5 quater

[*Patents:* Importation of Products Manufactured by a Process Patented in the Importing Country]

When a product is imported into a country of the Union where there exists a patent protecting a process of manufacture of the said product, the patentee shall have all the rights, with regard to the imported product, that are accorded to him by the legislation of the country of importation, on the basis of the process patent, with respect to products manufactured in that country.

Article 5 quinquies

[*Industrial Designs*]

Industrial designs shall be protected in all the countries of the Union.

Article 6

[*Marks:* Conditions of Registration; Independence of Protection of Same Mark in Different Countries]

(1) The conditions for the filing and registration of trademarks shall be determined in each country of the Union by its domestic legislation.

(2) However, an application for the registration of a mark filed by a national of a country of the Union in any country of the Union may not be refused, nor may a registration be invalidated, on the ground that filing, registration, or renewal, has not been effected in the country of origin.

(3) A mark duly registered in a country of the Union shall be regarded as independent of marks registered in the other countries of the Union, including the country of origin.

Article 6 bis

[*Marks:* Well–Known Marks]

(1) The countries of the Union undertake, ex officio if their legislation so permits, or at the request of an interested party, to refuse or to cancel the registration, and to prohibit the use, of a trademark which constitutes a reproduction, an imitation, or a translation, liable to create confusion, of a mark considered by the competent authority of the country of registration or use to be well known in that country as being already the mark of a person entitled to the benefits of this Convention and used for identical or similar

goods. These provisions shall also apply when the essential part of the mark constitutes a reproduction of any such well-known mark or an imitation liable to create confusion therewith.

(2) A period of at least five years from the date of registration shall be allowed for requesting the cancellation of such a mark. The countries of the Union may provide for a period within which the prohibition of use must be requested.

(3) No time limit shall be fixed for requesting the cancellation or the prohibition of the use of marks registered or used in bad faith.

Article 6 ter

[*Marks:* Prohibitions concerning State Emblems, Official Hallmarks, and Emblems of Intergovernmental Organizations]

(1)

(a) The countries of the Union agree to refuse or to invalidate the registration, and to prohibit by appropriate measures the use, without authorization by the competent authorities, either as trademarks or as elements of trademarks, of armorial bearings, flags, and other State emblems, of the countries of the Union, official signs and hallmarks indicating control and warranty adopted by them, and any imitation from a heraldic point of view.

(b) The provisions of subparagraph *(a)*, above, shall apply equally to armorial bearings, flags, other emblems, abbreviations, and names, of international intergovernmental organizations of which one or more countries of the Union are members, with the exception of armorial bearings, flags, other emblems, abbreviations, and names, that are already the subject of international agreements in force, intended to ensure their protection.

(c) No country of the Union shall be required to apply the provisions of subparagraph *(b)*, above, to the prejudice of the owners of rights acquired in good faith before the entry into force, in that country, of this Convention. The countries of the Union shall not be required to apply the said provisions when the use or registration referred to in subparagraph *(a)*, above, is not of such a nature as to suggest to the public that a connection exists between the organization concerned and the armorial bearings, flags, emblems, abbreviations, and names, or if such use or registration is probably not of such a nature as to mislead the public as to the existence of a connection between the user and the organization.

(2) Prohibition of the use of official signs and hallmarks indicating control and warranty shall apply solely in cases where the marks in which they are incorporated are intended to be used on goods of the same or a similar kind.

(3)

(a) For the application of these provisions, the countries of the Union agree to communicate reciprocally, through the intermediary of the International Bureau, the list of State emblems, and official signs and hallmarks indicating control and warranty, which they desire, or may hereafter desire, to place wholly or within certain limits under the protection of this Article, and all subsequent modifications of such list. Each country of the Union shall in due course make available to the public the lists so communicated. Nevertheless such communication is not obligatory in respect of flags of States.

(b) The provisions of subparagraph *(b)* of paragraph (1) of this Article shall apply only to such armorial bearings, flags, other emblems, abbreviations, and names, of international intergovernmental organizations as the latter have communicated to the countries of the Union through the intermediary of the International Bureau.

(4) Any country of the Union may, within a period of twelve months from the receipt of the notification, transmit its objections, if any, through the intermediary of the International Bureau, to the country or international intergovernmental organization concerned.

(5) In the case of State flags, the measures prescribed by paragraph (1), above, shall apply solely to marks registered after November 6, 1925.

(6) In the case of State emblems other than flags, and of official signs and hallmarks of the countries of the Union, and in the case of armorial bearings, flags, other emblems, abbreviations, and names, of international intergovernmental organizations, these provisions shall apply only to marks registered more than two months after receipt of the communication provided for in paragraph (3), above.

(7) In cases of bad faith, the countries shall have the right to cancel even those marks incorporating State emblems, signs, and hallmarks, which were registered before November 6, 1925.

(8) Nationals of any country who are authorized to make use of the State emblems, signs, and hallmarks, of their country may use them even if they are similar to those of another country.

(9) The countries of the Union undertake to prohibit the unauthorized use in trade of the State armorial bearings of the other countries of the Union, when the use is of such a nature as to be misleading as to the origin of the goods.

(10) The above provisions shall not prevent the countries from exercising the right given in paragraph (3) of Article 6[quinquies], Section B, to refuse or to invalidate the registration of marks incorporating, without authorization, armorial bearings, flags, other State emblems, or official signs and hallmarks adopted by a country of the Union, as well as the distinctive signs of international intergovernmental organizations referred to in paragraph (1), above.

Article 6 quater

[*Marks:* Assignment of Marks]

(1) When, in accordance with the law of a country of the Union, the assignment of a mark is valid only if it takes place at the same time as the transfer of the business or goodwill to which the mark belongs, it shall suffice for the recognition of such validity that the portion of the business or goodwill located in that country be transferred to the assignee, together with the exclusive right to manufacture in the said country, or to sell therein, the goods bearing the mark assigned.

(2) The foregoing provision does not impose upon the countries of the Union any obligation to regard as valid the assignment of any mark the use of which by the assignee would, in fact, be of such a nature as to mislead the public, particularly as regards the origin, nature, or essential qualities, of the goods to which the mark is applied.

Article 6 quinquies

[*Marks:* Protection of Marks Registered in One Country of the Union in the Other Countries of the Union]

A.—

(1) Every trademark duly registered in the country of origin shall be accepted for filing and protected as is in the other countries of the Union, subject to the reservations indicated in this Article. Such countries may, before proceeding to final registration, require the production of a certificate of registration in the country of origin, issued by the competent authority. No authentication shall be required for this certificate.

(2) Shall be considered the country of origin the country of the Union where the applicant has a real and effective industrial or commercial establishment, or, if he has no such establishment within the Union, the country of the Union where he has his domicile, or, if he has no domicile within the Union but is a national of a country of the Union, the country of which he is a national.

B.—Trademarks covered by this Article may be neither denied registration nor invalidated except in the following cases:

1. when they are of such a nature as to infringe rights acquired by third parties in the country where protection is claimed;
2. when they are devoid of any distinctive character, or consist exclusively of signs or indications which may serve, in trade, to designate the kind, quality, quantity, intended purpose, value, place of origin, of the goods, or the time of production, or have become customary in the current language or in the bona fide and established practices of the trade of the country where protection is claimed;
3. when they are contrary to morality or public order and, in particular, of such a nature as to deceive the public. It is understood that a mark may not be considered contrary to public order for the sole reason that it does not conform to a provision of the legislation on marks, except if such provision itself relates to public order.

This provision is subject, however, to the application of Article 10bis.

C.—

(1) In determining whether a mark is eligible for protection, all the factual circumstances must be taken into consideration, particularly the length of time the mark has been in use.

(2) No trademark shall be refused in the other countries of the Union for the sole reason that it differs from the mark protected in the country of origin only in respect of elements that do not alter its distinctive character and do not affect its identity in the form in which it has been registered in the said country of origin.

D.—No person may benefit from the provisions of this Article if the mark for which he claims protection is not registered in the country of origin.

E.—However, in no case shall the renewal of the registration of the mark in the country of origin involve an obligation to renew the registration in the other countries of the Union in which the mark has been registered.

F.—The benefit of priority shall remain unaffected for applications for the registration of marks filed within the period fixed by Article 4, even if registration in the country of origin is effected after the expiration of such period.

Article 6 sexies

[*Marks:* Service Marks]

The countries of the Union undertake to protect service marks. They shall not be required to provide for the registration of such marks.

Article 6 septies

[*Marks:* Registration in the Name of the Agent or Representative of the Proprietor Without the Latter's Authorization]

(1) If the agent or representative of the person who is the proprietor of a mark in one of the countries of the Union applies, without such proprietor's authorization, for the registration of the mark in his own name, in one or more countries of the Union, the proprietor shall be entitled to oppose the registration applied for or demand its cancellation or, if the law of the country so allows, the assignment in his favor of the said registration, unless such agent or representative justifies his action.

(2) The proprietor of the mark shall, subject to the provisions of paragraph (1), above, be entitled to oppose the use of his mark by his agent or representative if he has not authorized such use.

(3) Domestic legislation may provide an equitable time limit within which the proprietor of a mark must exercise the rights provided for in this Article.

Article 7

[*Marks:* Nature of the Goods to which the Mark Is Applied]

The nature of the goods to which a trademark is to be applied shall in no case form an obstacle to the registration of the mark.

Article 7 bis

[*Marks:* Collective Marks]

(1) The countries of the Union undertake to accept for filing and to protect collective marks belonging to associations the existence of which is not contrary to the law of the country of origin, even if such associations do not possess an industrial or commercial establishment.

(2) Each country shall be the judge of the particular conditions under which a collec tive mark shall be protected and may refuse protection if the mark is contrary to the public interest.

(3) Nevertheless, the protection of these marks shall not be refused to any association the existence of which is not contrary to the law of the country of origin, on the ground that such association is not established in the country where protection is sought or is not constituted according to the law of the latter country.

Article 8

[*Trade Names*]

A trade name shall be protected in all the countries of the Union without the obligation of filing or registration, whether or not it forms part of a trademark.

Article 9

[*Marks, Trade Names:* Seizure, on Importation, etc., of Goods Unlawfully Bearing a Mark or Trade Name]

(1) All goods unlawfully bearing a trademark or trade name shall be seized on importation into those countries of the Union where such mark or trade name is entitled to legal protection.

(2) Seizure shall likewise be effected in the country where the unlawful affixation occurred or in the country into which the goods were imported.

(3) Seizure shall take place at the request of the public prosecutor, or any other competent authority, or any interested party, whether a natural person or a legal entity, in conformity with the domestic legislation of each country.

(4) The authorities shall not be bound to effect seizure of goods in transit.

(5) If the legislation of a country does not permit seizure on importation, seizure shall be replaced by prohibition of importation or by seizure inside the country.

(6) If the legislation of a country permits neither seizure on importation nor prohibition of importation nor seizure inside the country, then, until such time as the legislation is modified accordingly, these measures shall be replaced by the actions and remedies available in such cases to nationals under the law of such country.

Article 10

[*False Indications:* Seizure, on Importation, etc., of Goods Bearing False Indications as to their Source or the Identity of the Producer]

(1) The provisions of the preceding Article shall apply in cases of direct or indirect use of a false indication of the source of the goods or the identity of the producer, manufacturer, or merchant.

(2) Any producer, manufacturer, or merchant, whether a natural person or a legal entity, engaged in the production or manufacture of or trade in such goods and established either in the locality falsely indicated as the source, or in the region where such locality is situated, or in the country falsely indicated, or in the country where the false indication of source is used, shall in any case be deemed an interested party.

Article 10 bis

[*Unfair Competition*]

(1) The countries of the Union are bound to assure to nationals of such countries effective protection against unfair competition.

(2) Any act of competition contrary to honest practices in industrial or commercial matters constitutes an act of unfair competition.

(3) The following in particular shall be prohibited:

1. all acts of such a nature as to create confusion by any means whatever with the establishment, the goods, or the industrial or commercial activities, of a competitor;
2. false allegations in the course of trade of such a nature as to discredit the establishment, the goods, or the industrial or commercial activities, of a competitor;

3. indications or allegations the use of which in the course of trade is liable to mislead the public as to the nature, the manufacturing process, the characteristics, the suitability for their purpose, or the quantity, of the goods.

Article 10 ter

[*Marks, Trade Names, False Indications, Unfair Competition:* Remedies, Right to Sue]

(1) The countries of the Union undertake to assure to nationals of the other countries of the Union appropriate legal remedies effectively to repress all the acts referred to in Articles 9, 10, and 10bis.

(2) They undertake, further, to provide measures to permit federations and associations representing interested industrialists, producers, or merchants, provided that the existence of such federations and associations is not contrary to the laws of their countries, to take action in the courts or before the administrative authorities, with a view to the repression of the acts referred to in Articles 9, 10, and 10bis, in so far as the law of the country in which protection is claimed allows such action by federations and associations of that country.

Article 11

[*Inventions, Utility Models, Industrial Designs, Marks:* Temporary Protection at Certain International Exhibitions]

(1) The countries of the Union shall, in conformity with their domestic legislation, grant temporary protection to patentable inventions, utility models, industrial designs, and trademarks, in respect of goods exhibited at official or officially recognized international exhibitions held in the territory of any of them.

(2) Such temporary protection shall not extend the periods provided by Article 4. If, later, the right of priority is invoked, the authorities of any country may provide that the period shall start from the date of introduction of the goods into the exhibition.

(3) Each country may require, as proof of the identity of the article exhibited and of the date of its introduction, such documentary evidence as it considers necessary.

Article 12

[Special National Industrial Property Services]

(1) Each country of the Union undertakes to establish a special industrial property service and a central office for the communication to the public of patents, utility models, industrial designs, and trademarks.

(2) This service shall publish an official periodical journal. It shall publish regularly:

(a) the names of the proprietors of patents granted, with a brief designation of the inventions patented;

(b) the reproductions of registered trademarks.

Article 19

[Special Agreements]

It is understood that the countries of the Union reserve the right to make separately between themselves special agreements for the protection of industrial property, in so far as these agreements do not contravene the provisions of this Convention.

Document 43

Berne Convention for the Protection of Literary and Artistic Works

Article 9.1 of the TRIPS Agreement incorporates Articles 1 through 21 of the Berne Convention and the Appendix thereto (not reproduced below). It adds that "Members shall not have rights or obligations under this [TRIPS] Agreement in respect of the rights conferred under Article 6bis of that [Berne] Convention or of the rights derived therefrom."

The countries of the Union, being equally animated by the desire to protect, in as effective and uniform a manner as possible, the rights of authors in their literary and artistic works,

Recognizing the importance of the work of the Revision Conference held at Stockholm in 1967,

Have resolved to revise the Act adopted by the Stockholm Conference, while maintaining without change Articles 1 to 20 and 22 to 26 of that Act. Consequently, the undersigned Plenipotentiaries, having presented their full powers, recognized as in good and due form, have agreed as follows:

Article 1

[*Establishment of a Union*][1]

The countries to which this Convention applies constitute a Union for the protection of the rights of authors in their literary and artistic works.

1. Each Article and the Appendix have been given titles to facilitate their identification. There are no titles in the signed (English) text.

Article 2

[*Protected Works:* 1. "Literary and artistic works"; 2. Possible requirement of fixation; 3. Derivative works; 4. Official texts; 5. Collections; 6. Obligation to protect; beneficiaries of protection; 7. Works of applied art and industrial designs; 8. News]

(1) The expression "literary and artistic works" shall include every production in the literary, scientific and artistic domain, whatever may be the mode or form of its expression, such as books, pamphlets and other writings; lectures, addresses, sermons and other works of the same nature; dramatic or dramaticomusical works; choreographic works and entertainments in dumb show; musical compositions with or without words; cinematographic works to which are assimilated works expressed by a process analogous to cinematography; works of drawing, painting, architecture, sculpture, engraving and lithography; photographic works to which are assimilated works expressed by a process analogous to photography; works of applied art; illustrations, maps, plans, sketches and three-dimensional works relative to geography, topography, architecture or science.

(2) It shall, however, be a matter for legislation in the countries of the Union to prescribe that works in general or any specified categories of works shall not be protected unless they have been fixed in some material form.

(3) Translations, adaptations, arrangements of music and other alterations of a literary or artistic work shall be protected as original works without prejudice to the copyright in the original work.

(4) It shall be a matter for legislation in the countries of the Union to determine the protection to be granted to official texts of a legislative, administrative and legal nature, and to official translations of such texts.

(5) Collections of literary or artistic works such as encyclopaedias and anthologies which, by reason of the selection and arrangement of their contents, constitute intellectual creations shall be protected as such, without prejudice to the copyright in each of the works forming part of such collections.

(6) The works mentioned in this Article shall enjoy protection in all countries of the Union. This protection shall operate for the benefit of the author and his successors in title.

(7) Subject to the provisions of Article 7(4) of this Convention, it shall be a matter for legislation in the countries of the Union to determine the extent of the application of their laws to works of applied art and industrial designs and models, as well as the conditions under which such works, designs and

models shall be protected. Works protected in the country of origin solely as designs and models shall be entitled in another country of the Union only to such special protection as is granted in that country to designs and models; however, if no such special protection is granted in that country, such works shall be protected as artistic works.

(8) The protection of this Convention shall not apply to news of the day or to miscellaneous facts having the character of mere items of press information.

Article 2 bis

[*Possible Limitation of Protection of Certain Works:* 1. Certain speeches; 2. Certain uses of lectures and addresses; 3. Right to make collections of such works]

(1) It shall be a matter for legislation in the countries of the Union to exclude, wholly or in part, from the protection provided by the preceding Article political speeches and speeches delivered in the course of legal proceedings.

(2) It shall also be a matter for legislation in the countries of the Union to determine the conditions under which lectures, addresses and other works of the same nature which are delivered in public may be reproduced by the press, broadcast, communicated to the public by wire and made the subject of public communication as envisaged in Article $11^{bis}(1)$ of this Convention, when such use is justified by the informatory purpose.

(3) Nevertheless, the author shall enjoy the exclusive right of making a collection of his works mentioned in the preceding paragraphs.

Article 3

[*Criteria of Eligibility for Protection:* 1. Nationality of author; place of publication of work; 2. Residence of author; 3. "Published" works; 4. "Simultaneously published" works]

(1) The protection of this Convention shall apply to:

(a) authors who are nationals of one of the countries of the Union, for their works, whether published or not;
(b) authors who are not nationals of one of the countries of the Union, for their works first published in one of those countries, or simultaneously in a country outside the Union and in a country of the Union.

(2) Authors who are not nationals of one of the countries of the Union but who have their habitual residence in one of them shall, for the purposes of this Convention, be assimilated to nationals of that country.

(3) The expression "published works" means works published with the consent of their authors, whatever may be the means of manufacture of the copies, provided that the availability of such copies has been such as to satisfy the reasonable requirements of the public, having regard to the nature of the work. The performance of a dramatic, dramatico-musical, cinematographic or musical work, the public recitation of a literary work, the communication by wire or the broadcasting of literary or artistic works, the exhibition of a work of art and the construction of a work of architecture shall not constitute publication.

(4) A work shall be considered as having been published simultaneously in several countries if it has been published in two or more countries within thirty days of its first publication.

Article 4

[*Criteria of Eligibility for Protection of Cinematographic Works, Works of Architecture and Certain Artistic Works*]

The protection of this Convention shall apply, even if the conditions of Article 3 are not fulfilled, to:

(a) authors of cinematographic works the maker of which has his headquarters or habitual residence in one of the countries of the Union;
(b) authors of works of architecture erected in a country of the Union or of other artistic works incorporated in a building or other structure located in a country of the Union.

Article 5

[*Rights Guaranteed:* 1. and 2. Outside the country of origin; 3. In the country of origin; 4. "Country of origin"]

(1) Authors shall enjoy, in respect of works for which they are protected under this Convention, in countries of the Union other than the country of origin, the rights which their respective laws do now or may hereafter grant to their nationals, as well as the rights specially granted by this Convention.

(2) The enjoyment and the exercise of these rights shall not be subject to any formality; such enjoyment and such exercise shall be independent of the

existence of protection in the country of origin of the work. Consequently, apart from the provisions of this Convention, the extent of protection, as well as the means of redress afforded to the author to protect his rights, shall be governed exclusively by the laws of the country where protection is claimed.

(3) Protection in the country of origin is governed by domestic law. However, when the author is not a national of the country of origin of the work for which he is protected under this Convention, he shall enjoy in that country the same rights as national authors.

(4) The country of origin shall be considered to be:

(a) in the case of works first published in a country of the Union, that country; in the case of works published simultaneously in several countries of the Union which grant different terms of protection, the country whose legislation grants the shortest term of protection;
(b) in the case of works published simultaneously in a country outside the Union and in a country of the Union, the latter country;
(c) in the case of unpublished works or of works first published in a country outside the Union, without simultaneous publication in a country of the Union, the country of the Union of which the author is a national, provided that:

(i) when these are cinematographic works the maker of which has his headquarters or his habitual residence in a country of the Union, the country of origin shall be that country, and
(ii) when these are works of architecture erected in a country of the Union or other artistic works incorporated in a building or other structure located in a country of the Union, the country of origin shall be that country.

Article 6

[*Possible Restriction of Protection in Respect of Certain Works of Nationals of Certain Countries Outside the Union:* 1. In the country of the first publication and in other countries; 2. No retroactivity; 3. Notice]

(1) Where any country outside the Union fails to protect in an adequate manner the works of authors who are nationals of one of the countries of the Union, the latter country may restrict the protection given to the works of authors who are, at the date of the first publication thereof, nationals of the

other country and are not habitually resident in one of the countries of the Union. If the country of first publication avails itself of this right, the other countries of the Union shall not be required to grant to works thus subjected to special treatment a wider protection than that granted to them in the country of first publication.

(2) No restrictions introduced by virtue of the preceding paragraph shall affect the rights which an author may have acquired in respect of a work published in a country of the Union before such restrictions were put into force.

(3) The countries of the Union which restrict the grant of copyright in accordance with this Article shall give notice thereof to the Director General of the World Intellectual Property Organization (hereinafter designated as "the Director General") by a written declaration specifying the countries in regard to which protection is restricted, and the restrictions to which rights of authors who are nationals of those countries are subjected. The Director General shall immediately communicate this declaration to all the countries of the Union.

Article 6 bis

[*Moral Rights:* 1. To claim authorship; to object to certain modifications and other derogatory actions; 2. After the author's death; 3. Means of redress]

(1) Independently of the author's economic rights, and even after the transfer of the said rights, the author shall have the right to claim authorship of the work and to object to any distortion, mutilation or other modification of, or other derogatory action in relation to, the said work, which would be prejudicial to his honor or reputation.

(2) The rights granted to the author in accordance with the preceding paragraph shall, after his death, be maintained, at least until the expiry of the economic rights, and shall be exercisable by the persons or institutions authorized by the legislation of the country where protection is claimed. However, those countries whose legislation, at the moment of their ratification of or accession to this Act, does not provide for the protection after the death of the author of all the rights set out in the preceding paragraph may provide that some of these rights may, after his death, cease to be maintained.

(3) The means of redress for safeguarding the rights granted by this Article shall be governed by the legislation of the country where protection is claimed.

Article 7

[*Term of Protection:* 1. Generally; 2. For cinematographic works; 3. For anonymous and pseudonymous works; 4. For photographic works and works of applied art; 5. Starting date of computation; 6. Longer terms; 7. Shorter terms; 8. Applicable law; "comparison" of terms]

(1) The term of protection granted by this Convention shall be the life of the author and fifty years after his death.

(2) However, in the case of cinematographic works, the countries of the Union may provide that the term of protection shall expire fifty years after the work has been made available to the public with the consent of the author, or, failing such an event within fifty years from the making of such a work, fifty years after the making.

(3) In the case of anonymous or pseudonymous works, the term of protection granted by this Convention shall expire fifty years after the work has been lawfully made available to the public. However, when the pseudonym adopted by the author leaves no doubt as to his identity, the term of protection shall be that provided in paragraph (1). If the author of an anonymous or pseudonymous work discloses his identity during the above-mentioned period, the term of protection applicable shall be that provided in paragraph (1). The countries of the Union shall not be required to protect anonymous or pseudonymous works in respect of which it is reasonable to presume that their author has been dead for fifty years.

(4) It shall be a matter for legislation in the countries of the Union to determine the term of protection of photographic works and that of works of applied art in so far as they are protected as artistic works; however, this term shall last at least until the end of a period of twenty-five years from the making of such a work.

(5) The term of protection subsequent to the death of the author and the terms provided by paragraphs (2), (3) and (4) shall run from the date of death or of the event referred to in those paragraphs, but such terms shall always be deemed to begin on the first of January of the year following the death or such event.

(6) The countries of the Union may grant a term of protection in excess of those provided by the preceding paragraphs.

(7) Those countries of the Union bound by the Rome Act of this Convention which grant, in their national legislation in force at the time of signature of the present Act, shorter terms of protection than those provided for in the preceding paragraphs shall have the right to maintain such terms when ratifying or acceding to the present Act.

(8) In any case, the term shall be governed by the legislation of the country where protection is claimed; however, unless the legislation of that country otherwise provides, the term shall not exceed the term fixed in the country of origin of the work.

Article 7bis

[*Term of Protection for Works of Joint Authorship*]

The provisions of the preceding Article shall also apply in the case of a work of joint authorship, provided that the terms measured from the death of the author shall be calculated from the death of the last surviving author.

Article 8

[*Right of Translation*]

Authors of literary and artistic works protected by this Convention shall enjoy the exclusive right of making and of authorizing the translation of their works throughout the term of protection of their rights in the original works.

Article 9

[*Right of Reproduction:* 1. Generally; 2. Possible exceptions; 3. Sound and visual recordings]

(1) Authors of literary and artistic works protected by this Convention shall have the exclusive right of authorizing the reproduction of these works, in any manner or form.

(2) It shall be a matter for legislation in the countries of the Union to permit the reproduction of such works in certain special cases, provided that such reproduction does not conflict with a normal exploitation of the work and does not unreasonably prejudice the legitimate interests of the author.

(3) Any sound or visual recording shall be considered as a reproduction for the purposes of this Convention.

Article 10

[*Certain Free Uses of Works:* 1. Quotations; 2. Illustrations for teaching; 3. Indication of source and author]

(1) It shall be permissible to make quotations from a work which has already been lawfully made available to the public, provided that their

making is compatible with fair practice, and their extent does not exceed that justified by the purpose, including quotations from newspaper articles and periodicals in the form of press summaries.

(2) It shall be a matter for legislation in the countries of the Union, and for special agreements existing or to be concluded between them, to permit the utilization, to the extent justified by the purpose, of literary or artistic works by way of illustration in publications, broadcasts or sound or visual recordings for teaching, provided such utilization is compatible with fair practice.

(3) Where use is made of works in accordance with the preceding paragraphs of this Article, mention shall be made of the source, and of the name of the author if it appears thereon.

*Article 10bis*

[*Further Possible Free Uses of Works:* 1. Of certain articles and broadcast works; 2. Of works seen or heard in connection with current events]

(1) It shall be a matter for legislation in the countries of the Union to permit the reproduction by the press, the broadcasting or the communication to the public by wire of articles published in newspapers or periodicals on current economic, political or religious topics, and of broadcast works of the same character, in cases in which the reproduction, broadcasting or such communication thereof is not expressly reserved. Nevertheless, the source must always be clearly indicated; the legal consequences of a breach of this obligation shall be determined by the legislation of the country where protection is claimed.

(2) It shall also be a matter for legislation in the countries of the Union to determine the conditions under which, for the purpose of reporting current events by means of photography, cinematography, broadcasting or communication to the public by wire, literary or artistic works seen or heard in the course of the event may, to the extent justified by the informatory purpose, be reproduced and made available to the public.

Article 11

[*Certain Rights in Dramatic and Musical Works:* 1. Right of public performance and of communication to the public of a performance; 2. In respect of translations]

(1) Authors of dramatic, dramatico-musical and musical works shall enjoy the exclusive right of authorizing:

(i) the public performance of their works, including such public performance by any means or process;

(ii) any communication to the public of the performance of their works.

(2) Authors of dramatic or dramatico-musical works shall enjoy, during the full term of their rights in the original works, the same rights with respect to translations thereof.

Article 11 bis

[*Broadcasting and Related Rights:* 1. Broadcasting and other wireless communications, public communication of broadcast by wire or rebroadcast, public communication of broadcast by loudspeaker or analogous instruments; 2. Compulsory licenses; 3. Recording; ephemeral recordings]

(1) Authors of literary and artistic works shall enjoy the exclusive right of authorizing:

(i) the broadcasting of their works or the communication thereof to the public by any other means of wireless diffusion of signs, sounds or images;

(ii) any communication to the public by wire or by rebroadcasting of the broadcast of the work, when this communication is made by an organization other than the original one;

(iii) the public communication by loudspeaker or any other analogous instrument transmitting, by signs, sounds or images, the broadcast of the work.

(2) It shall be a matter for legislation in the countries of the Union to determine the conditions under which the rights mentioned in the preceding paragraph may be exercised, but these conditions shall apply only in the countries where they have been prescribed. They shall not in any circumstances be prejudicial to the moral rights of the author, nor to his right to obtain equitable remuneration which, in the absence of agreement, shall be fixed by competent authority.

(3) In the absence of any contrary stipulation, permission granted in accordance with paragraph (1) of this Article shall not imply permission to record, by means of instruments recording sounds or images, the work broadcast. It shall, however, be a matter for legislation in the countries of the Union to determine the regulations for ephemeral recordings made by a broadcasting organization by means of its own facilities and used for its own broadcasts. The preservation of these recordings in official archives may, on the ground of their exceptional documentary character, be authorized by such legislation.

Article 11 ter

[*Certain Rights in Literary Works:* 1. Right of public recitation and of communication to the public of a recitation; 2. In respect of translations]

(1) Authors of literary works shall enjoy the exclusive right of authorizing:

(i) the public recitation of their works, including such public recitation by any means or process;

(ii) any communication to the public of the recitation of their works.

(2) Authors of literary works shall enjoy, during the full term of their rights in the original works, the same rights with respect to translations thereof.

Article 12

[*Right of Adaptation, Arrangement and Other Alteration*]

Authors of literary or artistic works shall enjoy the exclusive right of authorizing adaptations, arrangements and other alterations of their works.

Article 13

[*Possible Limitation of the Right of Recording of Musical Works and Any Words Pertaining Thereto:* 1. Compulsory licenses; 2. Transitory measures; 3. Seizure on importation of copies made without the author's permission]

(1) Each country of the Union may impose for itself reservations and conditions on the exclusive right granted to the author of a musical work and to the author of any words, the recording of which together with the musical work has already been authorized by the latter, to authorize the sound recording of that musical work, together with such words, if any; but all such reservations and conditions shall apply only in the countries which have imposed them and shall not, in any circumstances, be prejudicial to the rights of these authors to obtain equitable remuneration which, in the absence of agreement, shall be fixed by competent authority.

(2) Recordings of musical works made in a country of the Union in accordance with Article 13(3) of the Conventions signed at Rome on June 2, 1928, and at Brussels on June 26, 1948, may be reproduced in that country without the permission of the author of the musical work until a date two years after that country becomes bound by this Act.

(3) Recordings made in accordance with paragraphs (1) and (2) of this Article and imported without permission from the parties concerned into a

country where they are treated as infringing recordings shall be liable to seizure.

Article 14

[*Cinematographic and Related Rights:* 1. Cinematographic adaptation and reproduction; distribution; public performance and public communication by wire of works thus adapted or reproduced; 2. Adaptation of cinematographic productions; 3. No compulsory licenses]

(1) Authors of literary or artistic works shall have the exclusive right of authorizing:

(i) the cinematographic adaptation and reproduction of these works, and the distribution of the works thus adapted or reproduced;

(ii) the public performance and communication to the public by wire of the works thus adapted or reproduced.

(2) The adaptation into any other artistic form of a cinematographic production derived from literary or artistic works shall, without prejudice to the authorization of the author of the cinematographic production, remain subject to the authorization of the authors of the original works.

(3) The provisions of Article 13(1) shall not apply.

Article 14 bis

[*Special Provisions Concerning Cinematographic Works:* 1. Assimilation to "original" works; 2. Ownership; limitation of certain rights of certain contributors; 3. Certain other contributors]

(1) Without prejudice to the copyright in any work which may have been adapted or reproduced, a cinematographic work shall be protected as an original work. The owner of copyright in a cinematographic work shall enjoy the same rights as the author of an original work, including the rights referred to in the preceding Article.

(2)

(a) Ownership of copyright in a cinematographic work shall be a matter for legislation in the country where protection is claimed.

(b) However, in the countries of the Union which, by legislation, include among the owners of copyright in a cinematographic work authors who have brought contributions to the making of the work, such authors, if they have undertaken to bring such contributions, may not, in the absence of any contrary or special stipulation, object to the reproduction, distribution, public performance, communication to the public by wire, broadcasting or any other communication to the public, or to the subtitling or dubbing of texts, of the work.

(c) The question whether or not the form of the undertaking referred to above should, for the application of the preceding subparagraph *(b)*, be in a written agreement or a written act of the same effect shall be a matter for the legislation of the country where the maker of the cinematographic work has his headquarters or habitual residence. However, it shall be a matter for the legislation of the country of the Union where protection is claimed to provide that the said undertaking shall be in a written agreement or a written act of the same effect. The countries whose legislation so provides shall notify the Director General by means of a written declaration, which will be immediately communicated by him to all the other countries of the Union.

(d) By "contrary or special stipulation" is meant any restrictive condition which is relevant to the aforesaid undertaking.

(3) Unless the national legislation provides to the contrary, the provisions of paragraph (2)*(b)* above shall not be applicable to authors of scenarios, dialogues and musical works created for the making of the cinematographic work, or to the principal director thereof. However, those countries of the Union whose legislation does not contain rules providing for the application of the said paragraph (2)*(b)* to such director shall notify the Director General by means of a written declaration, which will be immediately communicated by him to all the other countries of the Union.

Article 14 ter

[*"Droit de suite" in Works of Art and Manuscripts:* 1. Right to an interest in resales; 2. Applicable law; 3. Procedure]

(1) The author, or after his death the persons or institutions authorized by national legislation, shall, with respect to original works of art and original manuscripts of writers and composers, enjoy the inalienable right to an interest in any sale of the work subsequent to the first transfer by the author of the work.

(2) The protection provided by the preceding paragraph may be claimed in a country of the Union only if legislation in the country to which the author belongs so permits, and to the extent permitted by the country where this protection is claimed.

(3) The procedure for collection and the amounts shall be matters for determination by national legislation.

Article 15

[*Right to Enforce Protected Rights:* 1. Where author's name is indicated or where pseudonym leaves no doubt as to author's identity; 2. In the case of cinematographic works; 3. In the case of anonymous and pseudonymous works; 4. In the case of certain unpublished works of unknown authorship]

(1) In order that the author of a literary or artistic work protected by this Convention shall, in the absence of proof to the contrary, be regarded as such, and consequently be entitled to institute infringement proceedings in the countries of the Union, it shall be sufficient for his name to appear on the work in the usual manner. This paragraph shall be applicable even if this name is a pseudonym, where the pseudonym adopted by the author leaves no doubt as to his identity.

(2) The person or body corporate whose name appears on a cinematographic work in the usual manner shall, in the absence of proof to the contrary, be presumed to be the maker of the said work.

(3) In the case of anonymous and pseudonymous works, other than those referred to in paragraph (1) above, the publisher whose name appears on the work shall, in the absence of proof to the contrary, be deemed to represent the author, and in this capacity he shall be entitled to protect and enforce the author's rights. The provisions of this paragraph shall cease to apply when the author reveals his identity and establishes his claim to authorship of the work.

(4)

(a) In the case of unpublished works where the identity of the author is unknown, but where there is every ground to presume that he is a national of a country of the Union, it shall be a matter for legislation in that country to designate the competent authority which shall represent the author and shall be entitled to protect and enforce his rights in the countries of the Union.

(b) Countries of the Union which make such designation under the terms of this provision shall notify the Director General by means of a

written declaration giving full information concerning the authority thus designated. The Director General shall at once communicate this declaration to all other countries of the Union.

Article 16

[*Infringing Copies:* 1. Seizure; 2. Seizure on importation; 3. Applicable law]

(1) Infringing copies of a work shall be liable to seizure in any country of the Union where the work enjoys legal protection.

(2) The provisions of the preceding paragraph shall also apply to reproductions coming from a country where the work is not protected, or has ceased to be protected.

(3) The seizure shall take place in accordance with the legislation of each country.

Article 17

[*Possibility of Control of Circulation, Presentation and Exhibition of Works*]

The provisions of this Convention cannot in any way affect the right of the Government of each country of the Union to permit, to control, or to prohibit, by legislation or regulation, the circulation, presentation, or exhibition of any work or production in regard to which the competent authority may find it necessary to exercise that right.

Article 18

[*Works Existing on Convention's Entry Into Force:* 1. Protectable where protection not yet expired in country of origin; 2. Non-protectable where protection already expired in country where it is claimed; 3. Application of these principles; 4. Special cases]

(1) This Convention shall apply to all works which, at the moment of its coming into force, have not yet fallen into the public domain in the country of origin through the expiry of the term of protection. fallen into the public domain of the country where protection is claimed, that work shall not be protected anew.

(2) If, however, through the expiry of the term of protection which was previously granted, a work has fallen into the public domain of the country where protection is claimed, that work shall not be protected anew.

(3) The application of this principle shall be subject to any provisions contained in special conventions to that effect existing or to be concluded between countries of the Union. In the absence of such provisions, the respective countries shall determine, each in so far as it is concerned, the conditions of application of this principle.

(4) The preceding provisions shall also apply in the case of new accessions to the Union and to cases in which protection is extended by the application of Article 7 or by the abandonment of reservations.

Article 19

[*Protection Greater than Resulting from Convention*]

The provisions of this Convention shall not preclude the making of a claim to the benefit of any greater protection which may be granted by legislation in a country of the Union.

Article 20

[*Special Agreements Among Countries of the Union*]

The Governments of the countries of the Union reserve the right to enter into special agreements among themselves, in so far as such agreements grant to authors more extensive rights than those granted by the Convention, or contain other provisions not contrary to this Convention. The provisions of existing agreements which satisfy these conditions shall remain applicable.

Article 21

[*Special Provisions Regarding Developing Countries:* 1. Reference to Appendix; 2. Appendix part of Act]

(1) Special provisions regarding developing countries are included in the Appendix.

(2) Subject to the provisions of Article 28(1)*(b)*, the Appendix forms an integral part of this Act.

Document 44

DECLARATION ON THE TRIPS AGREEMENT AND PUBLIC HEALTH*

1. We recognize the gravity of the public health problems afflicting many developing and least-developed countries, especially those resulting from HIV/AIDS, tuberculosis, malaria and other epidemics.

2. We stress the need for the WTO Agreement on Trade-Related Aspects of Intellectual Property Rights (TRIPS Agreement) to be part of the wider national and international action to address these problems.

3. We recognize that intellectual property protection is important for the development of new medicines. We also recognize the concerns about its effects on prices.

4. We agree that the TRIPS Agreement does not and should not prevent Members from taking measures to protect public health. Accordingly, while reiterating our commitment to the TRIPS Agreement, we affirm that the Agreement can and should be interpreted and implemented in a manner supportive of WTO Members' right to protect public health and, in particular, to promote access to medicines for all.

In this connection, we reaffirm the right of WTO Members to use, to the full, the provisions in the TRIPS Agreement, which provide flexibility for this purpose.

*WTO Document WT/MIN(01)/DEC/2, adopted on 14 November 2001.

5. Accordingly and in the light of paragraph 4 above, while maintaining our commitments in the TRIPS Agreement, we recognize that these flexibilities include:

(a) In applying the customary rules of interpretation of public international law, each provision of the TRIPS Agreement shall be read in the light of the object and purpose of the Agreement as expressed, in particular, in its objectives and principles.

(b) Each Member has the right to grant compulsory licences and the freedom to determine the grounds upon which such licences are granted.

(c) Each Member has the right to determine what constitutes a national emergency or other circumstances of extreme urgency, it being understood that public health crises, including those relating to HIV/AIDS, tuberculosis, malaria and other epidemics, can represent a national emergency or other circumstances of extreme urgency.

(d) The effect of the provisions in the TRIPS Agreement that are relevant to the exhaustion of intellectual property rights is to leave each Member free to establish its own regime for such exhaustion without challenge, subject to the MFN and national treatment provisions of Articles 3 and 4.

6. We recognize that WTO Members with insufficient or no manufacturing capacities in the pharmaceutical sector could face difficulties in making effective use of compulsory licensing under the TRIPS Agreement. We instruct the Council for TRIPS to find an expeditious solution to this problem and to report to the General Council before the end of 2002.

7. We reaffirm the commitment of developed-country Members to provide incentives to their enterprises and institutions to promote and encourage technology transfer to least-developed country Members pursuant to Article 66.2. We also agree that the least-developed country Members will not be obliged, with respect to pharmaceutical products, to implement or apply Sections 5 and 7 of Part II of the TRIPS Agreement or to enforce rights provided for under these Sections until 1 January 2016, without prejudice to the right of least-developed country Members to seek other extensions of the transition periods as provided for in Article 66.1 of the TRIPS Agreement. We instruct the Council for TRIPS to take the necessary action to give effect to this pursuant to Article 66.1 of the TRIPS Agreement.

Document 45

AMENDMENT OF THE TRIPS AGREEMENT*

The General Council;

Having regard to paragraph 1 of Article X of the Marrakesh Agreement Establishing the World Trade Organization ("the WTO Agreement");

Conducting the functions of the Ministerial Conference in the interval between meetings pursuant to paragraph 2 of Article IV of the WTO Agreement;

Noting the Declaration on the TRIPS Agreement and Public Health (WT/MIN(01)/DEC/2) and, in particular, the instruction of the Ministerial Conference to the Council for TRIPS contained in paragraph 6 of the Declaration to find an expeditious solution to the problem of the difficulties that WTO Members with insufficient or no manufacturing capacities in the pharmaceutical sector could face in making effective use of compulsory licensing under the TRIPS Agreement;

Recognizing, where eligible importing Members seek to obtain supplies under the system set out in the proposed amendment of the TRIPS Agreement, the importance of a rapid response to those needs consistent with the provisions of the proposed amendment of the TRIPS Agreement;

*WTO Document WT/L/641, adopted 6 December 2005. The amendment will be formally built into the TRIPS Agreement when two thirds of the WTO's members have accepted the change. They originally set themselves until 1 December 2007 to do so, but the deadline was extended to 31 December 2009 under a decision by the General Council on 18 December 2007. Once two thirds of members have formally accepted the amendment, it will take effect in those members and will replace the 2003 waiver for them. For each of the remaining members: the waiver will continue to apply until that member accepts the amendment and it takes effect. The waiver is reproduced in Document 46.

Recalling paragraph 11 of the General Council Decision of 30 August 2003 on the Implementation of Paragraph 6 of the Doha Declaration on the TRIPS Agreement and Public Health;

Having considered the proposal to amend the TRIPS Agreement submitted by the Council for TRIPS (IP/C/41);

Noting the consensus to submit this proposed amendment to the Members for acceptance;

Decides as follows:

1. The Protocol amending the TRIPS Agreement attached to this Decision is hereby adopted and submitted to the Members for acceptance.
2. The Protocol shall be open for acceptance by Members until 1 December 2007 or such later date as may be decided by the Ministerial Conference.
3. The Protocol shall take effect in accordance with the provisions of paragraph 3 of Article X of the WTO Agreement.

Attachment

PROTOCOL AMENDING THE TRIPS AGREEMENT

Members of the World Trade Organization;

Having regard to the Decision of the General Council in document WT/L/641, adopted pursuant to paragraph 1 of Article X of the Marrakesh Agreement Establishing the World Trade Organization ("the WTO Agreement");

Hereby agree as follows:

1. The Agreement on Trade-Related Aspects of Intellectual Property Rights (the "TRIPS Agreement") shall, upon the entry into force of the Protocol pursuant to paragraph 4, be amended as set out in the Annex to this Protocol, by inserting Article 31*bis* after Article 31 and by inserting the Annex to the TRIPS Agreement after Article 73.

2. Reservations may not be entered in respect of any of the provisions of this Protocol without the consent of the other Members.

3. This Protocol shall be open for acceptance by Members until 1 December 2007 or such later date as may be decided by the Ministerial Conference.

4. This Protocol shall enter into force in accordance with paragraph 3 of Article X of the WTO Agreement.

5. This Protocol shall be deposited with the Director-General of the World Trade Organization who shall promptly furnish to each Member a certified copy thereof and a notification of each acceptance thereof pursuant to paragraph 3.

6. This Protocol shall be registered in accordance with the provisions of Article 102 of the Charter of the United Nations.

Done at Geneva this sixth day of December two thousand and five, in a single copy in the English, French and Spanish languages, each text being authentic.

Annex to the Protocol Amending the Trips Agreement

Article 31bis

1. The obligations of an exporting Member under Article 31(f) shall not apply with respect to the grant by it of a compulsory licence to the extent necessary for the purposes of production of a pharmaceutical product(s) and its export to an eligible importing Member(s) in accordance with the terms set out in paragraph 2 of the Annex to this Agreement.

2. Where a compulsory licence is granted by an exporting Member under the system set out in this Article and the Annex to this Agreement, adequate remuneration pursuant to Article 31(h) shall be paid in that Member taking into account the economic value to the importing Member of the use that has been authorized in the exporting Member. Where a compulsory licence is granted for the same products in the eligible importing Member, the obligation of that Member under Article 31(h) shall not apply in respect of those products for which remuneration in accordance with the first sentence of this paragraph is paid in the exporting Member.

3. With a view to harnessing economies of scale for the purposes of enhancing purchasing power for, and facilitating the local production of, pharmaceutical products: where a developing or least-developed country WTO Member is a party to a regional trade agreement within the meaning of Article XXIV of the GATT 1994 and the Decision of 28 November 1979 on Differential and More Favourable Treatment Reciprocity and Fuller Participation of Developing Countries (L/4903), at least half of the current membership of which is made up of countries presently on the United Nations list of least-developed countries, the obligation of that Member under Article 31(f) shall not apply to the extent necessary to enable a

pharmaceutical product produced or imported under a compulsory licence in that Member to be exported to the markets of those other developing or least-developed country parties to the regional trade agreement that share the health problem in question. It is understood that this will not prejudice the territorial nature of the patent rights in question.

4. Members shall not challenge any measures taken in conformity with the provisions of this Article and the Annex to this Agreement under sub-paragraphs 1(b) and 1(c) of Article XXIII of GATT 1994.

5. This Article and the Annex to this Agreement are without prejudice to the rights, obligations and flexibilities that Members have under the provisions of this Agreement other than paragraphs (f) and (h) of Article 31, including those reaffirmed by the Declaration on the TRIPS Agreement and Public Health (WT/MIN(01)/DEC/2), and to their interpretation. They are also without prejudice to the extent to which pharmaceutical products produced under a compulsory licence can be exported under the provisions of Article 31(f).

Annex to the TRIPS Agreement

1. For the purposes of Article 31*bis* and this Annex:

(a) "pharmaceutical product" means any patented product, or product manufactured through a patented process, of the pharmaceutical sector needed to address the public health problems as recognized in paragraph 1 of the Declaration on the TRIPS Agreement and Public Health (WT/MIN(01)/DEC/2). It is understood that active ingredients necessary for its manufacture and diagnostic kits needed for its use would be included[1];

(b) "eligible importing Member" means any least-developed country Member, and any other Member that has made a notification[2] to the Council for TRIPS of its intention to use the system set out in Article 31*bis* and this Annex ("system") as an importer, it being understood that a Member may notify at any time that it will use the system in whole or in a limited way, for example only in the case of a national emergency or other circumstances of extreme urgency or in cases of public non-commercial use. It is noted that some Members will not use the system as importing Members[3] and that some other Members have stated that, if they use the

1. This subparagraph is without prejudice to subparagraph 1(b).

2. It is understood that this notification does not need to be approved by a WTO body in order to use the system.

3. Australia, Canada, the European Communities with, for the purposes of Article 31*bis* and this Annex, its member States, Iceland, Japan, New Zealand, Norway, Switzerland, and the United States.

system, it would be in no more than situations of national emergency or other circumstances of extreme urgency;

(c) "exporting Member" means a Member using the system to produce pharmaceutical products for, and export them to, an eligible importing Member.

2. The terms referred to in paragraph 1 of Article 31*bis* are that:

(a) the eligible importing Member(s)[4] has made a notification[2] to the Council for TRIPS, that:

(i) specifies the names and expected quantities of the product(s) needed[5];

(ii) confirms that the eligible importing Member in question, other than a least-developed country Member, has established that it has insufficient or no manufacturing capacities in the pharmaceutical sector for the product(s) in question in one of the ways set out in the Appendix to this Annex; and

(iii) confirms that, where a pharmaceutical product is patented in its territory, it has granted or intends to grant a compulsory licence in accordance with Articles 31 and 31*bis* of this Agreement and the provisions of this Annex[6];

(b) the compulsory licence issued by the exporting Member under the system shall contain the following conditions:

(i) only the amount necessary to meet the needs of the eligible importing Member(s) may be manufactured under the licence and the entirety of this production shall be exported to the Member(s) which has notified its needs to the Council for TRIPS;

(ii) products produced under the licence shall be clearly identified as being produced under the system through specific labelling or marking. Suppliers should distinguish such products through special packaging and/or special colouring/shaping of the products themselves, provided that such distinction is feasible and does not have a significant impact on price; and

4. Joint notifications providing the information required under this subparagraph may be made by the regional organizations referred to in paragraph 3 of Article 31*bis* on behalf of eligible importing Members using the system that are parties to them, with the agreement of those parties.

5. The notification will be made available publicly by the WTO Secretariat through a page on the WTO website dedicated to the system.

6. This subparagraph is without prejudice to Article 66.1 of this Agreement.

(iii) before shipment begins, the licensee shall post on a website[7] the following information:

— the quantities being supplied to each destination as referred to in indent (i) above; and
— the distinguishing features of the product(s) referred to in indent (ii) above;

(c) the exporting Member shall notify[8] the Council for TRIPS of the grant of the licence, including the conditions attached to it.[9] The information provided shall include the name and address of the licensee, the product(s) for which the licence has been granted, the quantity(ies) for which it has been granted, the country(ies) to which the product(s) is (are) to be supplied and the duration of the licence. The notification shall also indicate the address of the website referred to in subparagraph (b)(iii) above.

3. In order to ensure that the products imported under the system are used for the public health purposes underlying their importation, eligible importing Members shall take reasonable measures within their means, proportionate to their administrative capacities and to the risk of trade diversion to prevent re-exportation of the products that have actually been imported into their territories under the system. In the event that an eligible importing Member that is a developing country Member or a least-developed country Member experiences difficulty in implementing this provision, developed country Members shall provide, on request and on mutually agreed terms and conditions, technical and financial cooperation in order to facilitate its implementation.

4. Members shall ensure the availability of effective legal means to prevent the importation into, and sale in, their territories of products produced under the system and diverted to their markets inconsistently with its provisions, using the means already required to be available under this Agreement. If any Member considers that such measures are proving insufficient for this purpose, the matter may be reviewed in the Council for TRIPS at the request of that Member.

5. With a view to harnessing economies of scale for the purposes of enhancing purchasing power for, and facilitating the local production of, pharmaceutical products, it is recognized that the development of systems

7. The licensee may use for this purpose its own website or, with the assistance of the WTO Secretariat, the page on the WTO website dedicated to the system.

8. It is understood that this notification does not need to be approved by a WTO body in order to use the system.

9. The notification will be made available publicly by the WTO Secretariat through a page on the WTO website dedicated to the system.

providing for the grant of regional patents to be applicable in the Members described in paragraph 3 of Article 31*bis* should be promoted. To this end, developed country Members undertake to provide technical cooperation in accordance with Article 67 of this Agreement, including in conjunction with other relevant intergovernmental organizations.

6. Members recognize the desirability of promoting the transfer of technology and capacity building in the pharmaceutical sector in order to overcome the problem faced by Members with insufficient or no manufacturing capacities in the pharmaceutical sector. To this end, eligible importing Members and exporting Members are encouraged to use the system in a way which would promote this objective. Members undertake to cooperate in paying special attention to the transfer of technology and capacity building in the pharmaceutical sector in the work to be undertaken pursuant to Article 66.2 of this Agreement, paragraph 7 of the Declaration on the TRIPS Agreement and Public Health and any other relevant work of the Council for TRIPS.

7. The Council for TRIPS shall review annually the functioning of the system with a view to ensuring its effective operation and shall annually report on its operation to the General Council.

Appendix to the Annex to the TRIPS Agreement

Assessment of Manufacturing Capacities in the Pharmaceutical Sector

Least-developed country Members are deemed to have insufficient or no manufacturing capacities in the pharmaceutical sector.

For other eligible importing Members insufficient or no manufacturing capacities for the product(s) in question may be established in either of the following ways:

(i) the Member in question has established that it has no manufacturing capacity in the pharmaceutical sector;

or

(ii) where the Member has some manufacturing capacity in this sector, it has examined this capacity and found that, excluding any capacity owned or controlled by the patent owner, it is currently insufficient for the purposes of meeting its needs. When it is established that such capacity has become sufficient to meet the Member's needs, the system shall no longer apply.

Document 46

TRIPS WAIVER OF 2003*

Official name: Implementation of paragraph 6 of the Doha Declaration on the TRIPS Agreement and Public Health

Decision of 30 August 2003

The General Council,

Having regard to paragraphs 1, 3 and 4 of Article IX of the Marrakesh Agreement Establishing the World Trade Organization ("the WTO Agreement");

Conducting the functions of the Ministerial Conference in the interval between meetings pursuant to paragraph 2 of Article IV of the WTO Agreement;

Noting the Declaration on the TRIPS Agreement and Public Health (WT/MIN(01)/DEC/2) (the "Declaration") and, in particular, the instruction of the Ministerial Conference to the Council for TRIPS contained in paragraph 6 of the Declaration to find an expeditious solution to the problem of the difficulties that WTO Members with insufficient or no manufacturing capacities in the pharmaceutical sector could face in making effective use of compulsory licensing under the TRIPS Agreement and to report to the General Council before the end of 2002;

*WTO Document WT/L/540, decision of 30 August 2003. In the original document, an asterisked note at the bottom of page 1, as corrected by WTO document WT/L/540/Corr.1, states: Secretariat note for information purposes only and without prejudice to Members' legal rights and obligations: This Decision was adopted by the General Council in the light of a statement read out by the Chairman, which can be found in JOB(03)/177. This statement will be reproduced in the minutes of the General Council to be issued as WT/GC/M/82.

Recognizing, where eligible importing Members seek to obtain supplies under the system set out in this Decision, the importance of a rapid response to those needs consistent with the provisions of this Decision;

Noting that, in the light of the foregoing, exceptional circumstances exist justifying waivers from the obligations set out in paragraphs (f) and (h) of Article 31 of the TRIPS Agreement with respect to pharmaceutical products;

Decides as follows:

1. For the purposes of this Decision:

(a) "pharmaceutical product" means any patented product, or product manufactured through a patented process, of the pharmaceutical sector needed to address the public health problems as recognized in paragraph 1 of the Declaration. It is understood that active ingredients necessary for its manufacture and diagnostic kits needed for its use would be included[1];

(b) "eligible importing Member" means any least-developed country Member, and any other Member that has made a notification[2] to the Council for TRIPS of its intention to use the system as an importer, it being understood that a Member may notify at any time that it will use the system in whole or in a limited way, for example only in the case of a national emergency or other circumstances of extreme urgency or in cases of public non-commercial use. It is noted that some Members will not use the system set out in this Decision as importing Members[3] and that some other Members have stated that, if they use the system, it would be in no more than situations of national emergency or other circumstances of extreme urgency;

(c) "exporting Member" means a Member using the system set out in this Decision to produce pharmaceutical products for, and export them to, an eligible importing Member.

2. The obligations of an exporting Member under Article 31(f) of the TRIPS Agreement shall be waived with respect to the grant by it of a compulsory licence to the extent necessary for the purposes of production of a pharmaceutical product(s) and its export to an eligible importing Member(s) in accordance with the terms set out below in this paragraph:

1. This subparagraph is without prejudice to subparagraph 1(b).

2. It is understood that this notification does not need to be approved by a WTO body in order to use the system set out in this Decision.

3. Australia, Austria, Belgium, Canada, Denmark, Finland, France, Germany, Greece, Iceland, Ireland, Italy, Japan, Luxembourg, the Netherlands, New Zealand, Norway, Portugal, Spain, Sweden, Switzerland, the United Kingdom and the United States.

(a) the eligible importing Member(s)[4] has made a notification[2] to the Council for TRIPS, that:

(i) specifies the names and expected quantities of the product(s) needed;[5]

(ii) confirms that the eligible importing Member in question, other than a least-developed country Member, has established that it has insufficient or no manufacturing capacities in the pharmaceutical sector for the product(s) in question in one of the ways set out in the Annex to this Decision; and

(iii) confirms that, where a pharmaceutical product is patented in its territory, it has granted or intends to grant a compulsory licence in accordance with Article 31 of the TRIPS Agreement and the provisions of this Decision;[6]

(b) the compulsory licence issued by the exporting Member under this Decision shall contain the following conditions:

(i) only the amount necessary to meet the needs of the eligible importing Member(s) may be manufactured under the licence and the entirety of this production shall be exported to the Member(s) which has notified its needs to the Council for TRIPS;

(ii) products produced under the licence shall be clearly identified as being produced under the system set out in this Decision through specific labelling or marking. Suppliers should distinguish such products through special packaging and/or special colouring/shaping of the products themselves, provided that such distinction is feasible and does not have a significant impact on price; and

(iii) before shipment begins, the licensee shall post on a website[7] the following information:

— the quantities being supplied to each destination as referred to in indent (i) above; and

4. Joint notifications providing the information required under this subparagraph may be made by the regional organizations referred to in paragraph 6 of this Decision on behalf of eligible importing Members using the system that are parties to them, with the agreement of those parties.

5. The notification will be made available publicly by the WTO Secretariat through a page on the WTO website dedicated to this Decision.

6. This subparagraph is without prejudice to Article 66.1 of the TRIPS Agreement.

7. The licensee may use for this purpose its own website or, with the assistance of the WTO Secretariat, the page on the WTO website dedicated to this Decision.

— the distinguishing features of the product(s) referred to in indent (ii) above;

(c) the exporting Member shall notify[8] the Council for TRIPS of the grant of the licence, including the conditions attached to it.[9] The information provided shall include the name and address of the licensee, the product(s) for which the licence has been granted, the quantity(ies) for which it has been granted, the country(ies) to which the product(s) is (are) to be supplied and the duration of the licence. The notification shall also indicate the address of the website referred to in subparagraph (b)(iii) above.

3. Where a compulsory licence is granted by an exporting Member under the system set out in this Decision, adequate remuneration pursuant to Article 31(h) of the TRIPS Agreement shall be paid in that Member taking into account the economic value to the importing Member of the use that has been authorized in the exporting Member. Where a compulsory licence is granted for the same products in the eligible importing Member, the obligation of that Member under Article 31(h) shall be waived in respect of those products for which remuneration in accordance with the first sentence of this paragraph is paid in the exporting Member.

4. In order to ensure that the products imported under the system set out in this Decision are used for the public health purposes underlying their importation, eligible importing Members shall take reasonable measures within their means, proportionate to their administrative capacities and to the risk of trade diversion to prevent re-exportation of the products that have actually been imported into their territories under the system. In the event that an eligible importing Member that is a developing country Member or a least-developed country Member experiences difficulty in implementing this provision, developed country Members shall provide, on request and on mutually agreed terms and conditions, technical and financial cooperation in order to facilitate its implementation.

5. Members shall ensure the availability of effective legal means to prevent the importation into, and sale in, their territories of products produced under the system set out in this Decision and diverted to their markets inconsistently with its provisions, using the means already required to be available under the TRIPS Agreement. If any Member considers that such measures are proving insufficient for this purpose, the matter may be reviewed in the Council for TRIPS at the request of that Member.

8. It is understood that this notification does not need to be approved by a WTO body in order to use the system set out in this Decision.

9. The notification will be made available publicly by the WTO Secretariat through a page on the WTO website dedicated to this Decision.

6. With a view to harnessing economies of scale for the purposes of enhancing purchasing power for, and facilitating the local production of, pharmaceutical products:

(i) where a developing or least-developed country WTO Member is a party to a regional trade agreement within the meaning of Article XXIV of the GATT 1994 and the Decision of 28 November 1979 on Differential and More Favourable Treatment Reciprocity and Fuller Participation of Developing Countries (L/4903), at least half of the current membership of which is made up of countries presently on the United Nations list of least-developed countries, the obligation of that Member under Article 31(f) of the TRIPS Agreement shall be waived to the extent necessary to enable a pharmaceutical product produced or imported under a compulsory licence in that Member to be exported to the markets of those other developing or least-developed country parties to the regional trade agreement that share the health problem in question. It is understood that this will not prejudice the territorial nature of the patent rights in question;

(ii) it is recognized that the development of systems providing for the grant of regional patents to be applicable in the above Members should be promoted. To this end, developed country Members undertake to provide technical cooperation in accordance with Article 67 of the TRIPS Agreement, including in conjunction with other relevant intergovernmental organizations.

7. Members recognize the desirability of promoting the transfer of technology and capacity building in the pharmaceutical sector in order to overcome the problem identified in paragraph 6 of the Declaration. To this end, eligible importing Members and exporting Members are encouraged to use the system set out in this Decision in a way which would promote this objective. Members undertake to cooperate in paying special attention to the transfer of technology and capacity building in the pharmaceutical sector in the work to be undertaken pursuant to Article 66.2 of the TRIPS Agreement, paragraph 7 of the Declaration and any other relevant work of the Council for TRIPS.

8. The Council for TRIPS shall review annually the functioning of the system set out in this Decision with a view to ensuring its effective operation and shall annually report on its operation to the General Council. This review shall be deemed to fulfil the review requirements of Article IX:4 of the WTO Agreement.

9. This Decision is without prejudice to the rights, obligations and flexibilities that Members have under the provisions of the TRIPS Agreement other than paragraphs (f) and (h) of Article 31, including those reaffirmed by

the Declaration, and to their interpretation. It is also without prejudice to the extent to which pharmaceutical products produced under a compulsory licence can be exported under the present provisions of Article 31(f) of the TRIPS Agreement.

10. Members shall not challenge any measures taken in conformity with the provisions of the waivers contained in this Decision under subparagraphs 1(b) and 1(c) of Article XXIII of GATT 1994.

This Decision, including the waivers granted in it, shall terminate for each Member on the date on which an amendment to the TRIPS Agreement replacing its provisions takes effect for that Member. The TRIPS Council shall initiate by the end of 2003 work on the preparation of such an amendment with a view to its adoption within six months, on the understanding that the amendment will be based, where appropriate, on this Decision and on the further understanding that it will not be part of the negotiations referred to in paragraph 45 of the Doha Ministerial Declaration (WT/MIN(01)/DEC/1).

Annex

Assessment of Manufacturing Capacities in the Pharmaceutical Sector

Least-developed country Members are deemed to have insufficient or no manufacturing capacities in the pharmaceutical sector.

For other eligible importing Members insufficient or no manufacturing capacities for the product(s) in question may be established in either of the following ways:

(i) the Member in question has established that it has no manufacturing capacity in the pharmaceutical sector;

OR

(ii) where the Member has some manufacturing capacity in this sector, it has examined this capacity and found that, excluding any capacity owned or controlled by the patent owner, it is currently insufficient for the purposes of meeting its needs. When it is established that such capacity has become sufficient to meet the Member's needs, the system shall no longer apply.

PART VIII

Government Procurement

Document 47

AGREEMENT ON GOVERNMENT PROCUREMENT

Parties to this Agreement (hereinafter referred to as "Parties"),*

Recognizing the need for an effective multilateral framework of rights and obligations with respect to laws, regulations, procedures and practices regarding government procurement with a view to achieving greater liberalization and expansion of world trade and improving the international framework for the conduct of world trade;

Recognizing that laws, regulations, procedures and practices regarding government procurement should not be prepared, adopted or applied to foreign or domestic products and services and to foreign or domestic suppliers so as to afford protection to domestic products or services or domestic suppliers and should not discriminate among foreign products or services or among foreign suppliers;

Recognizing that it is desirable to provide transparency of laws, regulations, procedures and practices regarding government procurement;

Recognizing the need to establish international procedures on notification, consultation, surveillance and dispute settlement with a view to ensuring a fair, prompt and effective enforcement of the international provisions on

*List of members: Armenia; Canada; Chinese Taipei; the European Communities, including its 27 member States; Hong Kong; Iceland; Israel; Japan; Korea; Liechtenstein; the Kingdom of the Netherlands with respect to Aruba; Norway; Singapore; Switzerland and the United States.

government procurement and to maintain the balance of rights and obligations at the highest possible level;

Recognizing the need to take into account the development, financial and trade needs of developing countries, in particular the least-developed countries;

Desiring, in accordance with paragraph 6(b) of Article IX of the Agreement on Government Procurement done on 12 April 1979, as amended on 2 February 1987, to broaden and improve the Agreement on the basis of mutual reciprocity and to expand the coverage of the Agreement to include service contracts;

Desiring to encourage acceptance of and accession to this Agreement by governments not party to it;

Having undertaken further negotiations in pursuance of these objectives;

Hereby *agree* as follows:

Article I

Scope and Coverage

1. This Agreement applies to any law, regulation, procedure or practice regarding any procurement by entities covered by this Agreement, as specified in Appendix I.[1]

2. This Agreement applies to procurement by any contractual means, including through such methods as purchase or as lease, rental or hire purchase, with or without an option to buy, including any combination of products and services.

3. Where entities, in the context of procurement covered under this Agreement, require enterprises not included in Appendix I to award contracts in accordance with particular requirements, Article III shall apply *mutatis mutandis* to such requirements.

1. For each Party, Appendix I is divided into five Annexes:

— Annex 1 contains central government entities.
— Annex 2 contains sub-central government entities.
— Annex 3 contains all other entities that procure in accordance with the provisions of this Agreement.
— Annex 4 specifies services, whether listed positively or negatively, covered by this Agreement.
— Annex 5 specifies covered construction services.

Relevant thresholds are specified in each Party's Annexes.

4. This Agreement applies to any procurement contract of a value of not less than the relevant threshold specified in Appendix I.

Article II

Valuation of Contracts

1. The following provisions shall apply in determining the value of contracts[2] for purposes of implementing this Agreement.

2. Valuation shall take into account all forms of remuneration, including any premiums, fees, commissions and interest receivable.

3. The selection of the valuation method by the entity shall not be used, nor shall any procurement requirement be divided, with the intention of avoiding the application of this Agreement.

4. If an individual requirement for a procurement results in the award of more than one contract, or in contracts being awarded in separate parts, the basis for valuation shall be either:

(a) the actual value of similar recurring contracts concluded over the previous fiscal year or 12 months adjusted, where possible, for anticipated changes in quantity and value over the subsequent 12 months; or

(b) the estimated value of recurring contracts in the fiscal year or 12 months subsequent to the initial contract.

5. In cases of contracts for the lease, rental or hire purchase of products or services, or in the case of contracts which do not specify a total price, the basis for valuation shall be:

(a) in the case of fixed-term contracts, where their term is 12 months or less, the total contract value for their duration, or, where their term exceeds 12 months, their total value including the estimated residual value;

(b) in the case of contracts for an indefinite period, the monthly instalment multiplied by 48.

If there is any doubt, the second basis for valuation, namely (b), is to be used.

2. This Agreement shall apply to any procurement contract for which the contract value is estimated to equal or exceed the threshold at the time of publication of the notice in accordance with Article IX.

6. In cases where an intended procurement specifies the need for option clauses, the basis for valuation shall be the total value of the maximum permissible procurement, inclusive of optional purchases.

Article III

National Treatment and Non-discrimination

1. With respect to all laws, regulations, procedures and practices regarding government procurement covered by this Agreement, each Party shall provide immediately and unconditionally to the products, services and suppliers of other Parties offering products or services of the Parties, treatment no less favourable than:

(a) that accorded to domestic products, services and suppliers; and

(b) that accorded to products, services and suppliers of any other Party.

2. With respect to all laws, regulations, procedures and practices regarding government procurement covered by this Agreement, each Party shall ensure:

(a) that its entities shall not treat a locally-established supplier less favourably than another locally-established supplier on the basis of degree of foreign affiliation or ownership; and

(b) that its entities shall not discriminate against locally-established suppliers on the basis of the country of production of the good or service being supplied, provided that the country of production is a Party to the Agreement in accordance with the provisions of Article IV.

3. The provisions of paragraphs 1 and 2 shall not apply to customs duties and charges of any kind imposed on or in connection with importation, the method of levying such duties and charges, other import regulations and formalities, and measures affecting trade in services other than laws, regulations, procedures and practices regarding government procurement covered by this Agreement.

Article IV

Rules of Origin

1. A Party shall not apply rules of origin to products or services imported or supplied for purposes of government procurement covered by this Agreement from other Parties, which are different from the rules of origin applied in the normal course of trade and at the time of the transaction in

question to imports or supplies of the same products or services from the same Parties.

2. Following the conclusion of the work programme for the harmonization of rules of origin for goods to be undertaken under the Agreement on Rules of Origin in Annex 1A of the Agreement Establishing the World Trade Organization (hereinafter referred to as "WTO Agreement") and negotiations regarding trade in services, Parties shall take the results of that work programme and those negotiations into account in amending paragraph 1 as appropriate.

Article V

Special and Differential Treatment for Developing Countries

Objectives

1. Parties shall, in the implementation and administration of this Agreement, through the provisions set out in this Article, duly take into account the development, financial and trade needs of developing countries, in particular least-developed countries, in their need to:

(a) safeguard their balance-of-payments position and ensure a level of reserves adequate for the implementation of programmes of economic development;

(b) promote the establishment or development of domestic industries including the development of small-scale and cottage industries in rural or backward areas; and economic development of other sectors of the economy;

(c) support industrial units so long as they are wholly or substantially dependent on government procurement; and

(d) encourage their economic development through regional or global arrangements among developing countries presented to the Ministerial Conference of the World Trade Organization (hereinafter referred to as the "WTO") and not disapproved by it.

2. Consistently with the provisions of this Agreement, each Party shall, in the preparation and application of laws, regulations and procedures affecting government procurement, facilitate increased imports from developing countries, bearing in mind the special problems of least-developed countries and of those countries at low stages of economic development.

Coverage

3. With a view to ensuring that developing countries are able to adhere to this Agreement on terms consistent with their development, financial and trade needs, the objectives listed in paragraph 1 shall be duly taken into account in the course of negotiations with respect to the procurement of developing countries to be covered by the provisions of this Agreement. Developed countries, in the preparation of their coverage lists under the provisions of this Agreement, shall endeavour to include entities procuring products and services of export interest to developing countries.

Agreed Exclusions

4. A developing country may negotiate with other participants in negotiations under this Agreement mutually acceptable exclusions from the rules on national treatment with respect to certain entities, products or services that are included in its coverage lists, having regard to the particular circumstances of each case. In such negotiations, the considerations mentioned in subparagraphs 1(a) through 1(c) shall be duly taken into account. A developing country participating in regional or global arrangements among developing countries referred to in subparagraph 1(d) may also negotiate exclusions to its lists, having regard to the particular circumstances of each case, taking into account, *inter alia*, the provisions on government procurement provided for in the regional or global arrangements concerned and, in particular, products or services which may be subject to common industrial development programmes.

5. After entry into force of this Agreement, a developing country Party may modify its coverage lists in accordance with the provisions for modification of such lists contained in paragraph 6 of Article XXIV, having regard to its development, financial and trade needs, or may request the Committee on Government Procurement (hereinafter referred to as "the Committee") to grant exclusions from the rules on national treatment for certain entities, products or services that are included in its coverage lists, having regard to the particular circumstances of each case and taking duly into account the provisions of subparagraphs 1(a) through 1(c). After entry into force of this Agreement, a developing country Party may also request the Committee to grant exclusions for certain entities, products or services that are included in its coverage lists in the light of its participation in regional or global arrangements among developing countries, having regard to the particular circumstances of each case and taking duly into account the provisions of subparagraph 1(d). Each request to the Committee by a developing country Party relating to modification of a list shall be accompanied by documentation relevant to the request or by such information as may be necessary for consideration of the matter.

6. Paragraphs 4 and 5 shall apply *mutatis mutandis* to developing countries acceding to this Agreement after its entry into force.

7. Such agreed exclusions as mentioned in paragraphs 4, 5 and 6 shall be subject to review in accordance with the provisions of paragraph 14 below.

Technical Assistance for Developing Country Parties

8. Each developed country Party shall, upon request, provide all technical assistance which it may deem appropriate to developing country Parties in resolving their problems in the field of government procurement.

9. This assistance, which shall be provided on the basis of non-discrimination among developing country Parties, shall relate, *inter alia*, to:

— the solution of particular technical problems relating to the award of a specific contract; and
— any other problem which the Party making the request and another Party agree to deal with in the context of this assistance.

10. Technical assistance referred to in paragraphs 8 and 9 would include translation of qualification documentation and tenders made by suppliers of developing country Parties into an official language of the WTO designated by the entity, unless developed country Parties deem translation to be burdensome, and in that case explanation shall be given to developing country Parties upon their request addressed either to the developed country Parties or to their entities.

Information Centres

11. Developed country Parties shall establish, individually or jointly, information centres to respond to reasonable requests from developing country Parties for information relating to, *inter alia*, laws, regulations, procedures and practices regarding government procurement, notices about intended procurements which have been published, addresses of the entities covered by this Agreement, and the nature and volume of products or services procured or to be procured, including available information about future tenders. The Committee may also set up an information centre.

Special Treatment for Least-Developed Countries

12. Having regard to paragraph 6 of the Decision of the CONTRACTING PARTIES to GATT 1947 of 28 November 1979 on Differential and More Favourable Treatment, Reciprocity and Fuller Participation of Developing Countries (BISD 26S/203-205), special treatment shall be

granted to least-developed country Parties and to the suppliers in those Parties with respect to products or services originating in those Parties, in the context of any general or specific measures in favour of developing country Parties. A Party may also grant the benefits of this Agreement to suppliers in least-developed countries which are not Parties, with respect to products or services originating in those countries.

13. Each developed country Party shall, upon request, provide assistance which it may deem appropriate to potential tenderers in least-developed countries in submitting their tenders and selecting the products or services which are likely to be of interest to its entities as well as to suppliers in least-developed countries, and likewise assist them to comply with technical regulations and standards relating to products or services which are the subject of the intended procurement.

Review

14. The Committee shall review annually the operation and effectiveness of this Article and, after each three years of its operation on the basis of reports to be submitted by Parties, shall carry out a major review in order to evaluate its effects. As part of the three-yearly reviews and with a view to achieving the maximum implementation of the provisions of this Agreement, including in particular Article III, and having regard to the development, financial and trade situation of the developing countries concerned, the Committee shall examine whether exclusions provided for in accordance with the provisions of paragraphs 4 through 6 of this Article shall be modified or extended.

15. In the course of further rounds of negotiations in accordance with the provisions of paragraph 7 of Article XXIV, each developing country Party shall give consideration to the possibility of enlarging its coverage lists, having regard to its economic, financial and trade situation.

Article VI

Technical Specifications

1. Technical specifications laying down the characteristics of the products or services to be procured, such as quality, performance, safety and dimensions, symbols, terminology, packaging, marking and labelling, or the processes and methods for their production and requirements relating to conformity assessment procedures prescribed by procuring entities, shall not be prepared, adopted or applied with a view to, or with the effect of, creating unnecessary obstacles to international trade.

2. Technical specifications prescribed by procuring entities shall, where appropriate:

(a) be in terms of performance rather than design or descriptive characteristics; and

(b) be based on international standards, where such exist; otherwise, on national technical regulations,[3] recognized national standards,[4] or building codes.

3. There shall be no requirement or reference to a particular trademark or trade name, patent, design or type, specific origin, producer or supplier, unless there is no sufficiently precise or intelligible way of describing the procurement requirements and provided that words such as "or equivalent" are included in the tender documentation.

4. Entities shall not seek or accept, in a manner which would have the effect of precluding competition, advice which may be used in the preparation of specifications for a specific procurement from a firm that may have a commercial interest in the procurement.

Article VII

Tendering Procedures

1. Each Party shall ensure that the tendering procedures of its entities are applied in a non-discriminatory manner and are consistent with the provisions contained in Articles VII through XVI.

2. Entities shall not provide to any supplier information with regard to a specific procurement in a manner which would have the effect of precluding competition.

3. For the purposes of this Agreement:

3. For the purpose of this Agreement, a technical regulation is a document which lays down characteristics of a product or a service or their related processes and production methods, including the applicable administrative provisions, with which compliance is mandatory. It may also include or deal exclusively with terminology, symbols, packaging, marking or labelling requirements as they apply to a product, service, process or production method.

4. For the purpose of this Agreement, a standard is a document approved by a recognized body, that provides, for common and repeated use, rules, guidelines or characteristics for products or services or related processes and production methods, with which compliance is not mandatory. It may also include or deal exclusively with terminology, symbols, packaging, marking or labelling requirements as they apply to a product, service, process or production method.

(a) Open tendering procedures are those procedures under which all interested suppliers may submit a tender.

(b) Selective tendering procedures are those procedures under which, consistent with paragraph 3 of Article X and other relevant provisions of this Agreement, those suppliers invited to do so by the entity may submit a tender.

(c) Limited tendering procedures are those procedures where the entity contacts suppliers individually, only under the conditions specified in Article XV.

Article VIII

Qualification of Suppliers

In the process of qualifying suppliers, entities shall not discriminate among suppliers of other Parties or between domestic suppliers and suppliers of other Parties. Qualification procedures shall be consistent with the following:

(a) any conditions for participation in tendering procedures shall be published in adequate time to enable interested suppliers to initiate and, to the extent that it is compatible with efficient operation of the procurement process, complete the qualification procedures;

(b) any conditions for participation in tendering procedures shall be limited to those which are essential to ensure the firm's capability to fulfil the contract in question. Any conditions for participation required from suppliers, including financial guarantees, technical qualifications and information necessary for establishing the financial, commercial and technical capacity of suppliers, as well as the verification of qualifications, shall be no less favourable to suppliers of other Parties than to domestic suppliers and shall not discriminate among suppliers of other Parties. The financial, commercial and technical capacity of a supplier shall be judged on the basis both of that supplier's global business activity as well as of its activity in the territory of the procuring entity, taking due account of the legal relationship between the supply organizations;

(c) the process of, and the time required for, qualifying suppliers shall not be used in order to keep suppliers of other Parties off a suppliers' list or from being considered for a particular intended procurement. Entities shall recognize as qualified suppliers such domestic suppliers or suppliers of other Parties who meet the conditions for participation in a particular intended procurement. Suppliers requesting to participate in a particular intended procurement who may not yet be qualified shall also be considered, provided there is sufficient time to complete the qualification procedure;

(d) entities maintaining permanent lists of qualified suppliers shall ensure that suppliers may apply for qualification at any time; and that all qualified suppliers so requesting are included in the lists within a reasonably short time;

(e) if, after publication of the notice under paragraph 1 of Article IX, a supplier not yet qualified requests to participate in an intended procurement, the entity shall promptly start procedures for qualification;

(f) any supplier having requested to become a qualified supplier shall be advised by the entities concerned of the decision in this regard. Qualified suppliers included on permanent lists by entities shall also be notified of the termination of any such lists or of their removal from them;

(g) each Party shall ensure that:

(i) each entity and its constituent parts follow a single qualification procedure, except in cases of duly substantiated need for a different procedure; and

(ii) efforts be made to minimize differences in qualification procedures between entities.

(h) nothing in subparagraphs (a) through (g) shall preclude the exclusion of any supplier on grounds such as bankruptcy or false declarations, provided that such an action is consistent with the national treatment and non-discrimination provisions of this Agreement.

Article IX

Invitation to Participate Regarding Intended Procurement

1. In accordance with paragraphs 2 and 3, entities shall publish an invitation to participate for all cases of intended procurement, except as otherwise provided for in Article XV (limited tendering). The notice shall be published in the appropriate publication listed in Appendix II.

2. The invitation to participate may take the form of a notice of proposed procurement, as provided for in paragraph 6.

3. Entities in Annexes 2 and 3 may use a notice of planned procurement, as provided for in paragraph 7, or a notice regarding a qualification system, as provided for in paragraph 9, as an invitation to participate.

4. Entities which use a notice of planned procurement as an invitation to participate shall subsequently invite all suppliers who have expressed an

interest to confirm their interest on the basis of information which shall include at least the information referred to in paragraph 6.

5. Entities which use a notice regarding a qualification system as an invitation to participate shall provide, subject to the considerations referred to in paragraph 4 of Article XVIII and in a timely manner, information which allows all those who have expressed an interest to have a meaningful opportunity to assess their interest in participating in the procurement. This information shall include the information contained in the notices referred to in paragraphs 6 and 8, to the extent such information is available. Information provided to one interested supplier shall be provided in a non-discriminatory manner to the other interested suppliers.

6. Each notice of proposed procurement, referred to in paragraph 2, shall contain the following information:

(a) the nature and quantity, including any options for further procurement and, if possible, an estimate of the timing when such options may be exercised; in the case of recurring contracts the nature and quantity and, if possible, an estimate of the timing of the subsequent tender notices for the products or services to be procured;

(b) whether the procedure is open or selective or will involve negotiation;

(c) any date for starting delivery or completion of delivery of goods or services;

(d) the address and final date for submitting an application to be invited to tender or for qualifying for the suppliers' lists, or for receiving tenders, as well as the language or languages in which they must be submitted;

(e) the address of the entity awarding the contract and providing any information necessary for obtaining specifications and other documents;

(f) any economic and technical requirements, financial guarantees and information required from suppliers;

(g) the amount and terms of payment of any sum payable for the tender documentation; and

(h) whether the entity is inviting offers for purchase, lease, rental or hire purchase, or more than one of these methods.

7. Each notice of planned procurement referred to in paragraph 3 shall contain as much of the information referred to in paragraph 6 as is available. It shall in any case include the information referred to in paragraph 8 and:

(a) a statement that interested suppliers should express their interest in the procurement to the entity;

(b) a contact point with the entity from which further information may be obtained.

8. For each case of intended procurement, the entity shall publish a summary notice in one of the official languages of the WTO. The notice shall contain at least the following information:

(a) the subject matter of the contract;

(b) the time-limits set for the submission of tenders or an application to be invited to tender; and

(c) the addresses from which documents relating to the contracts may be requested.

9. In the case of selective tendering procedures, entities maintaining permanent lists of qualified suppliers shall publish annually in one of the publications listed in Appendix III a notice of the following:

(a) the enumeration of the lists maintained, including their headings, in relation to the products or services or categories of products or services to be procured through the lists;

(b) the conditions to be fulfilled by suppliers with a view to their inscription on those lists and the methods according to which each of those conditions will be verified by the entity concerned; and

(c) the period of validity of the lists, and the formalities for their renewal.

When such a notice is used as an invitation to participate in accordance with paragraph 3, the notice shall, in addition, include the following information:

(d) the nature of the products or services concerned;

(e) a statement that the notice constitutes an invitation to participate.

However, when the duration of the qualification system is three years or less, and if the duration of the system is made clear in the notice and it is also made clear that further notices will not be published, it shall be sufficient to publish the notice once only, at the beginning of the system. Such a system shall not be used in a manner which circumvents the provisions of this Agreement.

10. If, after publication of an invitation to participate in any case of intended procurement, but before the time set for opening or receipt of tenders as specified in the notices or the tender documentation, it becomes necessary to amend or re-issue the notice, the amendment or the re-issued notice shall be given the same circulation as the original documents upon which the amendment is based. Any significant information given to one supplier with respect to a particular intended procurement shall be given simultaneously to all other suppliers concerned in adequate time to permit the suppliers to consider such information and to respond to it.

11. Entities shall make clear, in the notices referred to in this Article or in the publication in which the notices appear, that the procurement is covered by the Agreement.

Article X

Selection Procedures

1. To ensure optimum effective international competition under selective tendering procedures, entities shall, for each intended procurement, invite tenders from the maximum number of domestic suppliers and suppliers of other Parties, consistent with the efficient operation of the procurement system. They shall select the suppliers to participate in the procedure in a fair and non-discriminatory manner.

2. Entities maintaining permanent lists of qualified suppliers may select suppliers to be invited to tender from among those listed. Any selection shall allow for equitable opportunities for suppliers on the lists.

3. Suppliers requesting to participate in a particular intended procurement shall be permitted to submit a tender and be considered, provided, in the case of those not yet qualified, there is sufficient time to complete the qualification procedure under Articles VIII and IX. The number of additional suppliers permitted to participate shall be limited only by the efficient operation of the procurement system.

4. Requests to participate in selective tendering procedures may be submitted by telex, telegram or facsimile.

Article XI

Time-Limits for Tendering and Delivery

General

1. (a) Any prescribed time-limit shall be adequate to allow suppliers of other Parties as well as domestic suppliers to prepare and submit tenders before the closing of the tendering procedures. In determining any such time-limit, entities shall, consistent with their own reasonable needs, take into account such factors as the complexity of the intended procurement, the extent of subcontracting anticipated and the normal time for transmitting tenders by mail from foreign as well as domestic points.

(b) Each Party shall ensure that its entities shall take due account of publication delays when setting the final date for receipt of tenders or of applications to be invited to tender.

Deadlines

2. Except in so far as provided in paragraph 3,

(a) in open procedures, the period for the receipt of tenders shall not be less than 40 days from the date of publication referred to in paragraph 1 of Article IX;

(b) in selective procedures not involving the use of a permanent list of qualified supplier, the period for submitting an application to be invited to tender shall not be less than 25 days from the date of publication referred to in paragraph 1 of Article IX; the period for receipt of tenders shall in no case be less than 40 days from the date of issuance of the invitation to tender;

(c) in selective procedures involving the use of a permanent list of qualified suppliers, the period for receipt of tenders shall not be less than 40 days from the date of the initial issuance of invitations to tender, whether or not the date of initial issuance of invitations to tender coincides with the date of the publication referred to in paragraph 1 of Article IX.

3. The periods referred to in paragraph 2 may be reduced in the circumstances set out below:

(a) if a separate notice has been published 40 days and not more than 12 months in advance and the notice contains at least:

(i) as much of the information referred to in paragraph 6 of Article IX as is available;

(ii) the information referred to in paragraph 8 of Article IX;

(iii) a statement that interested suppliers should express their interest in the procurement to the entity; and

(iv) a contact point with the entity from which further information may be obtained, the 40-day limit for receipt of tenders may be replaced by a period sufficiently long to enable responsive tendering, which, as a general rule, shall not be less than 24 days, but in any case not less than 10 days;

(b) in the case of the second or subsequent publications dealing with contracts of a recurring nature within the meaning of paragraph 6 of Article IX, the 40-day limit for receipt of tenders may be reduced to not less than 24 days;

(c) where a state of urgency duly substantiated by the entity renders impracticable the periods in question, the periods specified in paragraph 2 may be reduced but shall in no case be less than 10 days from the date of the publication referred to in paragraph 1 of Article IX; or

(d) the period referred to in paragraph 2(c) may, for procurements by entities listed in Annexes 2 and 3, be fixed by mutual agreement between the entity and the selected suppliers. In the absence of agreement, the entity may fix periods which shall be sufficiently long to enable responsive tendering and shall in any case not be less than 10 days.

4. Consistent with the entity's own reasonable needs, any delivery date shall take into account such factors as the complexity of the intended procurement, the extent of subcontracting anticipated and the realistic time required for production, de-stocking and transport of goods from the points of supply or for supply of services.

Article XII

Tender Documentation

1. If, in tendering procedures, an entity allows tenders to be submitted in several languages, one of those languages shall be one of the official languages of the WTO.

2. Tender documentation provided to suppliers shall contain all information necessary to permit them to submit responsive tenders, including information required to be published in the notice of intended procurement, except for paragraph 6(g) of Article IX, and the following:

(a) the address of the entity to which tenders should be sent;

(b) the address where requests for supplementary information should be sent;

(c) the language or languages in which tenders and tendering documents must be submitted;

(d) the closing date and time for receipt of tenders and the length of time during which any tender should be open for acceptance;

(e) the persons authorized to be present at the opening of tenders and the date, time and place of this opening;

(f) any economic and technical requirement, financial guarantees and information or documents required from suppliers;

(g) a complete description of the products or services required or of any requirements including technical specifications, conformity certification to be fulfilled, necessary plans, drawings and instructional materials;

(h) the criteria for awarding the contract, including any factors other than price that are to be considered in the evaluation of tenders and the cost elements to be included in evaluating tender prices, such as transport, insurance and inspection costs, and in the case of products or services of other Parties, customs duties and other import charges, taxes and currency of payment;

(i) the terms of payment;

(j) any other terms or conditions;

(k) in accordance with Article XVII the terms and conditions, if any, under which tenders from countries not Parties to this Agreement, but which apply the procedures of that Article, will be entertained.

Forwarding of Tender Documentation by the Entities

3. (a) In open procedures, entities shall forward the tender documentation at the request of any supplier participating in the procedure, and shall reply promptly to any reasonable request for explanations relating thereto.

(b) In selective procedures, entities shall forward the tender documentation at the request of any supplier requesting to participate, and shall reply promptly to any reasonable request for explanations relating thereto.

(c) Entities shall reply promptly to any reasonable request for relevant information submitted by a supplier participating in the tendering procedure, on condition that such information does not give that supplier an advantage over its competitors in the procedure for the award of the contract.

Article XIII

Submission, Receipt and Opening of Tenders and Awarding of Contracts

1. The submission, receipt and opening of tenders and awarding of contracts shall be consistent with the following:

(a) tenders shall normally be submitted in writing directly or by mail. If tenders by telex, telegram or facsimile are permitted, the tender made thereby must include all the information necessary for the evaluation of the tender, in particular the definitive price proposed by the tenderer and a statement that the tenderer agrees to all the terms, conditions and provisions of the invitation to tender. The tender must be confirmed promptly by letter or by the despatch of a signed copy of the telex, telegram or facsimile. Tenders presented by telephone shall not be permitted. The content of the telex, telegram or facsimile shall prevail where there is a difference or conflict between that content and any documentation received after the time-limit; and

(b) the opportunities that may be given to tenderers to correct unintentional errors of form between the opening of tenders and the awarding of the contract shall not be permitted to give rise to any discriminatory practice.

Receipt of Tenders

2. A supplier shall not be penalized if a tender is received in the office designated in the tender documentation after the time specified because of delay due solely to mishandling on the part of the entity. Tenders may also be considered in other exceptional circumstances if the procedures of the entity concerned so provide.

Opening of Tenders

3. All tenders solicited under open or selective procedures by entities shall be received and opened under procedures and conditions guaranteeing the regularity of the openings. The receipt and opening of tenders shall also be consistent with the national treatment and non-discrimination provisions of this Agreement. Information on the opening of tenders shall remain with the entity concerned at the disposal of the government authorities

responsible for the entity in order that it may be used if required under the procedures of Articles XVIII, XIX, XX and XXII.

Award of Contracts

4. (a) To be considered for award, a tender must, at the time of opening, conform to the essential requirements of the notices or tender documentation and be from a supplier which complies with the conditions for participation. If an entity has received a tender abnormally lower than other tenders submitted, it may enquire with the tenderer to ensure that it can comply with the conditions of participation and be capable of fulfilling the terms of the contract.

(b) Unless in the public interest an entity decides not to issue the contract, the entity shall make the award to the tenderer who has been determined to be fully capable of undertaking the contract and whose tender, whether for domestic products or services, or products or services of other Parties, is either the lowest tender or the tender which in terms of the specific evaluation criteria set forth in the notices or tender documentation is determined to be the most advantageous.

(c) Awards shall be made in accordance with the criteria and essential requirements specified in the tender documentation.

Option Clauses

5. Option clauses shall not be used in a manner which circumvents the provisions of the Agreement.

Article XIV

Negotiation

1. A Party may provide for entities to conduct negotiations:

(a) in the context of procurements in which they have indicated such intent, namely in the notice referred to in paragraph 2 of Article IX (the invitation to suppliers to participate in the procedure for the proposed procurement); or

(b) when it appears from evaluation that no one tender is obviously the most advantageous in terms of the specific evaluation criteria set forth in the notices or tender documentation.

2. Negotiations shall primarily be used to identify the strengths and weaknesses in tenders.

3. Entities shall treat tenders in confidence. In particular, they shall not provide information intended to assist particular participants to bring their tenders up to the level of other participants.

4. Entities shall not, in the course of negotiations, discriminate between different suppliers. In particular, they shall ensure that:

(a) any elimination of participants is carried out in accordance with the criteria set forth in the notices and tender documentation;

(b) all modifications to the criteria and to the technical requirements are transmitted in writing to all remaining participants in the negotiations;

(c) all remaining participants are afforded an opportunity to submit new or amended submissions on the basis of the revised requirements; and

(d) when negotiations are concluded, all participants remaining in the negotiations shall be permitted to submit final tenders in accordance with a common deadline.

Article XV

Limited Tendering

1. The provisions of Articles VII through XIV governing open and selective tendering procedures need not apply in the following conditions, provided that limited tendering is not used with a view to avoiding maximum possible competition or in a manner which would constitute a means of discrimination among suppliers of other Parties or protection to domestic producers or suppliers:

(a) in the absence of tenders in response to an open or selective tender, or when the tenders submitted have been collusive, or not in conformity with the essential requirements in the tender, or from suppliers who do not comply with the conditions for participation provided for in accordance with this Agreement, on condition, however, that the requirements of the initial tender are not substantially modified in the contract as awarded;

(b) when, for works of art or for reasons connected with protection of exclusive rights, such as patents or copyrights, or in the absence of competition for technical reasons, the products or services can be supplied only by a particular supplier and no reasonable alternative or substitute exists;

(c) in so far as is strictly necessary when, for reasons of extreme urgency brought about by events unforeseeable by the entity, the products or services could not be obtained in time by means of open or selective tendering procedures;

(d) for additional deliveries by the original supplier which are intended either as parts replacement for existing supplies, or installations, or as the extension of existing supplies, services, or installations where a change of supplier would compel the entity to procure equipment or services not meeting requirements of interchangeability with already existing equipment or services;[5]

(e) when an entity procures prototypes or a first product or service which are developed at its request in the course of, and for, a particular contract for research, experiment, study or original development. When such contracts have been fulfilled, subsequent procurements of products or services shall be subject to Articles VII through XIV;[6]

(f) when additional construction services which were not included in the initial contract but which were within the objectives of the original tender documentation have, through unforeseeable circumstances, become necessary to complete the construction services described therein, and the entity needs to award contracts for the additional construction services to the contractor carrying out the construction services concerned since the separation of the additional construction services from the initial contract would be difficult for technical or economic reasons and cause significant inconvenience to the entity. However, the total value of contracts awarded for the additional construction services may not exceed 50 per cent of the amount of the main contract;

(g) for new construction services consisting of the repetition of similar construction services which conform to a basic project for which an initial contract was awarded in accordance with Articles VII through XIV and for which the entity has indicated in the notice of intended procurement concerning the initial construction service, that limited tendering procedures might be used in awarding contracts for such new construction services;

(h) for products purchased on a commodity market;

5. It is the understanding that "existing equipment" includes software to the extent that the initial procurement of the software was covered by the Agreement.

6. Original development of a first product or service may include limited production or supply in order to incorporate the results of field testing and to demonstrate that the product or service is suitable for production or supply in quantity to acceptable quality standards. It does not extend to quantity production or supply to establish commercial viability or to recover research and development costs.

(i) for purchases made under exceptionally advantageous conditions which only arise in the very short term. This provision is intended to cover unusual disposals by firms which are not normally suppliers, or disposal of assets of businesses in liquidation or receivership. It is not intended to cover routine purchases from regular suppliers;

(j) in the case of contracts awarded to the winner of a design contest provided that the contest has been organized in a manner which is consistent with the principles of this Agreement, notably as regards the publication, in the sense of Article IX, of an invitation to suitably qualified suppliers, to participate in such a contest which shall be judged by an independent jury with a view to design contracts being awarded to the winners.

2. Entities shall prepare a report in writing on each contract awarded under the provisions of paragraph 1. Each report shall contain the name of the procuring entity, value and kind of goods or services procured, country of origin, and a statement of the conditions in this Article which prevailed. This report shall remain with the entities concerned at the disposal of the government authorities responsible for the entity in order that it may be used if required under the procedures of Articles XVIII, XIX, XX and XXII.

Article XVI

Offsets

1. Entities shall not, in the qualification and selection of suppliers, products or services, or in the evaluation of tenders and award of contracts, impose, seek or consider offsets.[7]

2. Nevertheless, having regard to general policy considerations, including those relating to development, a developing country may at the time of accession negotiate conditions for the use of offsets, such as requirements for the incorporation of domestic content. Such requirements shall be used only for qualification to participate in the procurement process and not as criteria for awarding contracts. Conditions shall be objective, clearly defined and non-discriminatory. They shall be set forth in the country's Appendix I and may include precise limitations on the imposition of offsets in any contract subject to this Agreement. The existence of such conditions shall be notified to the Committee and included in the notice of intended procurement and other documentation.

7. Offsets in government procurement are measures used to encourage local development or improve the balance-of payments accounts by means of domestic content, licensing of technology, investment requirements, counter-trade or similar requirements.

Article XVII

Transparency

1. Each Party shall encourage entities to indicate the terms and conditions, including any deviations from competitive tendering procedures or access to challenge procedures, under which tenders will be entertained from suppliers situated in countries not Parties to this Agreement but which, with a view to creating transparency in their own contract awards, nevertheless:

(a) specify their contracts in accordance with Article VI (technical specifications);

(b) publish the procurement notices referred to in Article IX, including, in the version of the notice referred to in paragraph 8 of Article IX (summary of the notice of intended procurement) which is published in an official language of the WTO, an indication of the terms and conditions under which tenders shall be entertained from suppliers situated in countries Parties to this Agreement;

(c) are willing to ensure that their procurement regulations shall not normally change during a procurement and, in the event that such change proves unavoidable, to ensure the availability of a satisfactory means of redress.

2. Governments not Parties to the Agreement which comply with the conditions specified in paragraphs 1(a) through 1(c), shall be entitled if they so inform the Parties to participate in the Committee as observers.

Article XVIII

Information and Review as Regards Obligations of Entities

1. Entities shall publish a notice in the appropriate publication listed in Appendix II not later than 72 days after the award of each contract under Articles XIII through XV. These notices shall contain:

(a) the nature and quantity of products or services in the contract award;

(b) the name and address of the entity awarding the contract;

(c) the date of award;

(d) the name and address of winning tenderer;

(e) the value of the winning award or the highest and lowest offer taken into account in the award of the contract;

(f) where appropriate, means of identifying the notice issued under paragraph 1 of Article IX or justification according to Article XV for the use of such procedure; and

(g) the type of procedure used.

2. Each entity shall, on request from a supplier of a Party, promptly provide:

(a) an explanation of its procurement practices and procedures;

(b) pertinent information concerning the reasons why the supplier's application to qualify was rejected, why its existing qualification was brought to an end and why it was not selected; and

(c) to an unsuccessful tenderer, pertinent information concerning the reasons why its tender was not selected and on the characteristics and relative advantages of the tender selected as well as the name of the winning tenderer.

3. Entities shall promptly inform participating suppliers of decisions on contract awards and, upon request, in writing.

4. However, entities may decide that certain information on the contract award, contained in paragraphs 1 and 2(c), be withheld where release of such information would impede law enforcement or otherwise be contrary to the public interest or would prejudice the legitimate commercial interest of particular enterprises, public or private, or might prejudice fair competition between suppliers.

Article XIX

Information and Review as Regards Obligations of Parties

1. Each Party shall promptly publish any law, regulation, judicial decision, administrative ruling of general application, and any procedure (including standard contract clauses) regarding government procurement covered by this Agreement, in the appropriate publications listed in Appendix IV and in such a manner as to enable other Parties and suppliers to become acquainted with them. Each Party shall be prepared, upon request, to explain to any other Party its government procurement procedures.

2. The government of an unsuccessful tenderer which is a Party to this Agreement may seek, without prejudice to the provisions under Article

XXII, such additional information on the contract award as may be necessary to ensure that the procurement was made fairly and impartially. To this end, the procuring government shall provide information on both the characteristics and relative advantages of the winning tender and the contract price. Normally this latter information may be disclosed by the government of the unsuccessful tenderer provided it exercises this right with discretion. In cases where release of this information would prejudice competition in future tenders, this information shall not be disclosed except after consultation with and agreement of the Party which gave the information to the government of the unsuccessful tenderer.

3. Available information concerning procurement by covered entities and their individual contract awards shall be provided, upon request, to any other Party.

4. Confidential information provided to any Party which would impede law enforcement or otherwise be contrary to the public interest or would prejudice the legitimate commercial interest of particular enterprises, public or private, or might prejudice fair competition between suppliers shall not be revealed without formal authorization from the party providing the information.

5. Each Party shall collect and provide to the Committee on an annual basis statistics on its procurements covered by this Agreement. Such reports shall contain the following information with respect to contracts awarded by all procurement entities covered under this Agreement:

(a) for entities in Annex 1, statistics on the estimated value of contracts awarded, both above and below the threshold value, on a global basis and broken down by entities; for entities in Annexes 2 and 3, statistics on the estimated value of contracts awarded above the threshold value on a global basis and broken down by categories of entities;

(b) for entities in Annex 1, statistics on the number and total value of contracts awarded above the threshold value, broken down by entities and categories of products and services according to uniform classification systems; for entities in Annexes 2 and 3, statistics on the estimated value of contracts awarded above the threshold value broken down by categories of entities and categories of products and services;

(c) for entities in Annex 1, statistics, broken down by entity and by categories of products and services, on the number and total value of contracts awarded under each of the cases of Article XV; for categories of entities in Annexes 2 and 3, statistics on the total value of contracts awarded above the threshold value under each of the cases of Article XV; and

(d) for entities in Annex 1, statistics, broken down by entities, on the number and total value of contracts awarded under derogations to the Agreement contained in the relevant Annexes; for categories of entities in Annexes 2 and 3, statistics on the total value of contracts awarded under derogations to the Agreement contained in the relevant Annexes.

To the extent that such information is available, each Party shall provide statistics on the country of origin of products and services purchased by its entities. With a view to ensuring that such statistics are comparable, the Committee shall provide guidance on methods to be used. With a view to ensuring effective monitoring of procurement covered by this Agreement, the Committee may decide unanimously to modify the requirements of subparagraphs (a) through (d) as regards the nature and the extent of statistical information to be provided and the breakdowns and classifications to be used.

Article XX

Challenge Procedures

Consultations

1. In the event of a complaint by a supplier that there has been a breach of this Agreement in the context of a procurement, each Party shall encourage the supplier to seek resolution of its complaint in consultation with the procuring entity. In such instances the procuring entity shall accord impartial and timely consideration to any such complaint, in a manner that is not prejudicial to obtaining corrective measures under the challenge system.

Challenge

2. Each Party shall provide non-discriminatory, timely, transparent and effective procedures enabling suppliers to challenge alleged breaches of the Agreement arising in the context of procurements in which they have, or have had, an interest.

3. Each Party shall provide its challenge procedures in writing and make them generally available.

4. Each Party shall ensure that documentation relating to all aspects of the process concerning procurements covered by this Agreement shall be retained for three years.

5. The interested supplier may be required to initiate a challenge procedure and notify the procuring entity within specified time-limits from

the time when the basis of the complaint is known or reasonably should have been known, but in no case within a period of less than 10 days.

6. Challenges shall be heard by a court or by an impartial and independent review body with no interest in the outcome of the procurement and the members of which are secure from external influence during the term of appointment. A review body which is not a court shall either be subject to judicial review or shall have procedures which provide that:

(a) participants can be heard before an opinion is given or a decision is reached;

(b) participants can be represented and accompanied;

(c) participants shall have access to all proceedings;

(d) proceedings can take place in public;

(e) opinions or decisions are given in writing with a statement describing the basis for theopinions or decisions;

(f) witnesses can be presented;

(g) documents are disclosed to the review body.

7. Challenge procedures shall provide for:

(a) rapid interim measures to correct breaches of the Agreement and to preserve commercial opportunities. Such action may result in suspension of the procurement process. However, procedures may provide that overriding adverse consequences for the interests concerned, including the public interest, may be taken into account in deciding whether such measures should be applied. In such circumstances, just cause for not acting shall be provided in writing;

(b) an assessment and a possibility for a decision on the justification of the challenge;

(c) correction of the breach of the Agreement or compensation for the loss or damages suffered, which may be limited to costs for tender preparation or protest.

8. With a view to the preservation of the commercial and other interests involved, the challenge procedure shall normally be completed in a timely fashion.

Article XXI

Institutions

1. A Committee on Government Procurement composed of representatives from each of the Parties shall be established. This Committee shall elect its own Chairman and Vice-Chairman and shall meet as necessary but not less than once a year for the purpose of affording Parties the opportunity to consult on any matters relating to the operation of this Agreement or the furtherance of its objectives, and to carry out such other responsibilities as may be assigned to it by the Parties.

2. The Committee may establish working parties or other subsidiary bodies which shall carry out such functions as may be given to them by the Committee.

Article XXII

Consultations and Dispute Settlement

1. The provisions of the Understanding on Rules and Procedures Governing the Settlement of Disputes under the WTO Agreement (hereinafter referred to as the "Dispute Settlement Understanding") shall be applicable except as otherwise specifically provided below.

2. If any Party considers that any benefit accruing to it, directly or indirectly, under this Agreement is being nullified or impaired, or that the attainment of any objective of this Agreement is being impeded as the result of the failure of another Party or Parties to carry out its obligations under this Agreement, or the application by another Party or Parties of any measure, whether or not it conflicts with the provisions of this Agreement, it may with a view to reaching a mutually satisfactory resolution of the matter, make written representations or proposals to the other Party or Parties which it considers to be concerned. Such action shall be promptly notified to the Dispute Settlement Body established under the Dispute Settlement Understanding (hereinafter referred to as "DSB"), as specified below. Any Party thus approached shall give sympathetic consideration to the representations or proposals made to it.

3. The DSB shall have the authority to establish panels, adopt panel and Appellate Body reports, make recommendations or give rulings on the matter, maintain surveillance of implementation of rulings and recommendations, and authorize suspension of concessions and other obligations under this Agreement or consultations regarding remedies when withdrawal of measures found to be in contravention of the Agreement is not possible, provided that only Members of the WTO Party to this Agreement shall participate in decisions or actions taken by the DSB with respect to disputes under this Agreement.

4. Panels shall have the following terms of reference unless the parties to the dispute agree otherwise within 20 days of the establishment of the panel: "To examine, in the light of the relevant provisions of this Agreement and of (name of any other covered Agreement cited by the parties to the dispute), the matter referred to the DSB by (name of party) in document . . . and to make such findings as will assist the DSB in making the recommendations or in giving the rulings provided for in this Agreement." In the case of a dispute in which provisions both of this Agreement and of one or more other Agreements listed in Appendix 1 of the Dispute Settlement Understanding are invoked by one of the parties to the dispute, paragraph 3 shall apply only to those parts of the panel report concerning the interpretation and application of this Agreement.

5. Panels established by the DSB to examine disputes under this Agreement shall include persons qualified in the area of government procurement.

6. Every effort shall be made to accelerate the proceedings to the greatest extent possible. Notwithstanding the provisions of paragraphs 8 and 9 of Article 12 of the Dispute Settlement Understanding, the panel shall attempt to provide its final report to the parties to the dispute not later than four months, and in case of delay not later than seven months, after the date on which the composition and terms of reference of the panel are agreed. Consequently, every effort shall be made to reduce also the periods foreseen in paragraph 1 of Article 20 and paragraph 4 of Article 21 of the Dispute Settlement Understanding by two months. Moreover, notwithstanding the provisions of paragraph 5 of Article 21 of the Dispute Settlement Understanding, the panel shall attempt to issue its decision, in case of a disagreement as to the existence or consistency with a covered Agreement of measures taken to comply with the recommendations and rulings, within 60 days.

7. Notwithstanding paragraph 2 of Article 22 of the Dispute Settlement Understanding, any dispute arising under any Agreement listed in Appendix 1 to the Dispute Settlement Understanding other than this Agreement shall not result in the suspension of concessions or other obligations under this Agreement, and any dispute arising under this Agreement shall not result in the suspension of concessions or other obligations under any other Agreement listed in the said Appendix 1.

Article XXIII

Exceptions to the Agreement

1. Nothing in this Agreement shall be construed to prevent any Party from taking any action or not disclosing any information which it considers necessary for the protection of its essential security interests relating to the

procurement of arms, ammunition or war materials, or to procurement indispensable for national security or for national defence purposes.

2. Subject to the requirement that such measures are not applied in a manner which would constitute a means of arbitrary or unjustifiable discrimination between countries where the same conditions prevail or a disguised restriction on international trade, nothing in this Agreement shall be construed to prevent any Party from imposing or enforcing measures: necessary to protect public morals, order or safety, human, animal or plant life or health or intellectual property; or relating to the products or services of handicapped persons, of philanthropic institutions or of prison labour.

Article XXIV

Final Provisions

1. *Acceptance and Entry into Force*

This Agreement shall enter into force on 1 January 1996 for those governments[8] whose agreed coverage is contained in Annexes 1 through 5 of Appendix I of this Agreement and which have, by signature, accepted the Agreement on 15 April 1994 or have, by that date, signed the Agreement subject to ratification and subsequently ratified the Agreement before 1 January 1996.

2. *Accession*

Any government which is a Member of the WTO, or prior to the date of entry into force of the WTO Agreement which is a contracting party to GATT 1947, and which is not a Party to this Agreement may accede to this Agreement on terms to be agreed between that government and the Parties. Accession shall take place by deposit with the Director-General of the WTO of an instrument of accession which states the terms so agreed. The Agreement shall enter into force for an acceding government on the 30th day following the date of its accession to the Agreement.

3. *Transitional Arrangements*

(a) Hong Kong and Korea may delay application of the provisions of this Agreement, except Articles XXI and XXII, to a date not later than 1 January 1997. The commencement date of their application of the provisions, if prior to 1 January 1997, shall be notified to the Director-General of the WTO 30 days in advance.

8. For the purpose of this Agreement, the term "government" is deemed to include the competent authorities of the European Communities.

(b) During the period between the date of entry into force of this Agreement and the date of its application by Hong Kong, the rights and obligations between Hong Kong and all other Parties to this Agreement which were on 15 April 1994 Parties to the Agreement on Government Procurement done at Geneva on 12 April 1979 as amended on 2 February 1987 (the "1988 Agreement") shall be governed by the substantive[9] provisions of the 1988 Agreement, including its Annexes as modified or rectified, which provisions are incorporated herein by reference for that purpose and shall remain in force until 31 December 1996.

(c) Between Parties to this Agreement which are also Parties to the 1988 Agreement, the rights and obligations of this Agreement shall supersede those under the 1988 Agreement.

(d) Article XXII shall not enter into force until the date of entry into force of the WTO Agreement. Until such time, the provisions of Article VII of the 1988 Agreement shall apply to consultations and dispute settlement under this Agreement, which provisions are hereby incorporated in the Agreement by reference for that purpose. These provisions shall be applied under the auspices of the Committee under this Agreement.

(e) Prior to the date of entry into force of the WTO Agreement, references to WTO bodies shall be construed as referring to the corresponding GATT body and references to the Director-General of the WTO and to the WTO Secretariat shall be construed as references to, respectively, the Director-General to the CONTRACTING PARTIES to GATT 1947 and to the GATT Secretariat.

4. *Reservations*

Reservations may not be entered in respect of any of the provisions of this Agreement.

5. *National Legislation*

(a) Each government accepting or acceding to this Agreement shall ensure, not later than the date of entry into force of this Agreement for it, the conformity of its laws, regulations and administrative procedures, and the rules, procedures and practices applied by the entities contained in its lists annexed hereto, with the provisions of this Agreement.

(b) Each Party shall inform the Committee of any changes in its laws and regulations relevant to this Agreement and in the administration of

9. All provisions of the 1988 Agreement except the Preamble, Article VII and Article IX other than paragraphs 5(a) and (b) and paragraph 10.

such laws and regulations.

6. *Rectifications or Modifications*

(a) Rectifications, transfers of an entity from one Annex to another or, in exceptional cases, other modifications relating to Appendices I through IV shall be notified to the Committee, along with information as to the likely consequences of the change for the mutually agreed coverage provided in this Agreement. If the rectifications, transfers or other modifications are of a purely formal or minor nature, they shall become effective provided there is no objection within 30 days. In other cases, the Chairman of the Committee shall promptly convene a meeting of the Committee. The Committee shall consider the proposal and any claim for compensatory adjustments, with a view to maintaining a balance of rights and obligations and a comparable level of mutually agreed coverage provided in this Agreement prior to such notification. In the event of agreement not being reached, the matter may be pursued in accordance with the provisions contained in Article XXII.

(b) Where a Party wishes, in exercise of its rights, to withdraw an entity from Appendix I on the grounds that government control or influence over it has been effectively eliminated, that Party shall notify the Committee. Such modification shall become effective the day after the end of the following meeting of the Committee, provided that the meeting is no sooner than 30 days from the date of notification and no objection has been made. In the event of an objection, the matter may be pursued in accordance with the procedures on consultations and dispute settlement contained in Article XXII. In considering the proposed modification to Appendix I and any consequential compensatory adjustment, allowance shall be made for the market-opening effects of the removal of government control or influence.

7. *Reviews, Negotiations and Future Work*

(a) The Committee shall review annually the implementation and operation of this Agreement taking into account the objectives thereof. The Committee shall annually inform the General Council of the WTO of developments during the periods covered by such reviews.

(b) Not later than the end of the third year from the date of entry into force of this Agreement and periodically thereafter, the Parties thereto shall undertake further negotiations, with a view to improving this Agreement and achieving the greatest possible extension of its coverage among all Parties on the basis of mutual reciprocity, having regard to the provisions of Article V relating to developing countries.

(c) Parties shall seek to avoid introducing or prolonging discriminatory measures and practices which distort open procurement and shall, in the context of negotiations under subparagraph (b), seek to eliminate those which remain on the date of entry into force of this Agreement.

8. *Information Technology*

With a view to ensuring that the Agreement does not constitute an unnecessary obstacle to technical progress, Parties shall consult regularly in the Committee regarding developments in the use of information technology in government procurement and shall, if necessary, negotiate modifications to the Agreement. These consultations shall in particular aim to ensure that the use of information technology promotes the aims of open, non-discriminatory and efficient government procurement through transparent procedures, that contracts covered under the Agreement are clearly identified and that all available information relating to a particular contract can be identified. When a Party intends to innovate, it shall endeavour to take into account the views expressed by other Parties regarding any potential problems.

9. *Amendments*

Parties may amend this Agreement having regard, *inter alia*, to the experience gained in its implementation. Such an amendment, once the Parties have concurred in accordance with the procedures established by the Committee, shall not enter into force for any Party until it has been accepted by such Party.

10. *Withdrawal*

(a) Any Party may withdraw from this Agreement. The withdrawal shall take effect upon the expiration of 60 days from the date on which written notice of withdrawal is received by the Director-General of the WTO. Any Party may upon such notification request an immediate meeting of the Committee.

(b) If a Party to this Agreement does not become a Member of the WTO within one year of the date of entry into force of the WTO Agreement or ceases to be a Member of the WTO, it shall cease to be a Party to this Agreement with effect from the same date.

11. *Non-application of this Agreement between Particular Parties*

This Agreement shall not apply as between any two Parties if either of the Parties, at the time either accepts or accedes to this Agreement, does not consent to such application.

12. *Notes, Appendices and Annexes*

The Notes, Appendices and Annexes to this Agreement constitute an integral part thereof.

13. *Secretariat*

This Agreement shall be serviced by the WTO Secretariat.

14. *Deposit*

This Agreement shall be deposited with the Director-General of the WTO, who shall promptly furnish to each Party a certified true copy of this Agreement, of each rectification or modification thereto pursuant to paragraph 6 and of each amendment thereto pursuant to paragraph 9, and a notification of each acceptance thereof or accession thereto pursuant to paragraphs 1 and 2 and of each withdrawal therefrom pursuant to paragraph 10 of this Article.

15. *Registration*

This Agreement shall be registered in accordance with the provisions of Article 102 of the Charter of the United Nations.

Done at Marrakesh this fifteenth day of April one thousand nine hundred and ninety-four in a single copy, in the English, French and Spanish languages, each text being authentic, except as otherwise specified with respect to the Appendices hereto.

NOTES

The terms "country" or "countries" as used in this Agreement, including the Appendices, are to be understood to include any separate customs territory Party to this Agreement.

In the case of a separate customs territory Party to this Agreement, where an expression in this Agreement is qualified by the term "national", such expression shall be read as pertaining to that customs territory, unless otherwise specified.

Article 1, paragraph 1

Having regard to general policy considerations relating to tied aid, including the objective of developing countries with respect to the untying of such aid, this Agreement does not apply to procurement made in furtherance of tied aid to developing countries so long as it is practised by Parties.

Document 48

DECISION ON THE OUTCOMES OF THE NEGOTIATIONS UNDER ARTICLE XXIV:7 OF THE AGREEMENT ON GOVERNMENT PROCUREMENT

Decision of 30 March 2012

1. We, the Parties to the WTO Agreement on Government Procurement ("the Agreement"), meeting at Ambassadorial level in Geneva, having completed the final verification and legal review of the results of the negotiations under Article XXIV:7 of the Agreement, are pleased to adopt the elements of the results of the negotiations under Article XXIV:7 of the Agreement, which are set out in two Appendices to this Decision:

(a) Appendix 1 is comprised of the Decision of the Committee on Government Procurement on Adoption of "The Protocol Amending the Agreement on Government Procurement" ("the Protocol"), which includes the Revised Text of the Agreement and its Appendices; and

(b) Appendix 2 is comprised of the following Decisions of the Committee:

(i) Decision of the Committee on Government Procurement on Notification Requirements under Articles XIX and XXII of the Agreement (Annex A);

(ii) Decision of the Committee on Government Procurement on Adoption of Work Programmes (Annex B);

(iii) Decision of the Committee on Government Procurement on a Work Programme on SMEs (Annex C);

(iv) Decision of the Committee on Government Procurement on a Work Programme on the Collection and Reporting of Statistical Data (Annex D);

(v) Decision of the Committee on Government Procurement on a Work Programme on Sustainable Procurement (Annex E);

(vi) Decision of the Committee on Government Procurement on a Work Programme on Exclusions and Restrictions in Parties' Annexes (Annex F); and

(vii) Decision of the Committee on Government Procurement on a Work Programme on Safety Standards in International Procurement (Annex G).

2. We agree that the Decisions set out in Paragraph 1(b) shall enter into effect at the same time as the Protocol. The Committee at its first meeting after the entry into force of the Protocol shall make a statement confirming that the Decisions have been adopted and entered into effect on the date the Protocol entered into force.

3. We also reiterate the commitment made by our respective Ministers in GPA/112 to seek prompt acceptance and implementation of the Protocol within our respective jurisdictions.

Document 49

ADOPTION OF THE TEXT OF "THE PROTOCOL AMENDING THE AGREEMENT ON GOVERNMENT PROCUREMENT"

Decision of 30 March 2012

The Committee on Government Procurement,

Having regard to paragraph 9 of Article XXIV of the WTO Agreement on Government Procurement done at Marrakesh on 15 April 1994 ("the 1994 Agreement");

Having undertaken further negotiations pursuant to Article XXIV:7(b) and (c) of the 1994 Agreement and reached agreement on amendments to improve the 1994 Agreement;

Noting the consensus among the Parties to the 1994 Agreement, all of whom are participating in this Decision, to adopt the text of the Protocol Amending the Agreement on Government Procurement ("the Protocol") attached to this Decision and to submit the Protocol to their respective Governments for acceptance in accordance with their respective internal procedures;

Considering that not all the Parties to the 1994 Agreement may be able to conclude their domestic procedures for acceptance of the Protocol by the time the Protocol has entered into force and that therefore, there may be a period when not all the Parties to the 1994 Agreement are Parties to the Protocol;

Decides as follows:

1. The text of the Protocol Amending the Agreement on Government Procurement attached to this Decision is hereby adopted, and open for acceptance by Parties to the 1994 Agreement.

2. Pursuant to paragraph 3 of the Protocol and consistent with paragraph 9 of Article XXIV of the 1994 Agreement, the Protocol shall enter into force for those Parties to the 1994 Agreement that have deposited their respective instruments of acceptance thereof, on the 30th day following such deposit by two thirds of the Parties to the 1994 Agreement. Thereafter the Protocol shall enter into force for each Party to the 1994 Agreement that has deposited its instrument of acceptance thereof, on the 30th day following the date of such deposit.

3. Upon the entry into force of the Protocol,

(a) as between a Party to the 1994 Agreement, which is also a Party to the Protocol, and a Party only to the 1994 Agreement, the 1994 Agreement shall apply, including Appendix I of the 1994 Agreement; and

(b) a Party that has accepted the Protocol shall only be required to provide access to the procurement that it covers under Appendix I attached to the Protocol to the other Parties that have accepted the Protocol.

4. Any terms of accession to the 1994 Agreement agreed after the date of this Decision, pursuant to paragraph 2 of Article XXIV of the 1994 Agreement, shall provide that, upon entry into force of the Protocol, the acceding WTO Member shall be bound by the Protocol.

Document 50

PROTOCOL AMENDING THE AGREEMENT ON GOVERNMENT PROCUREMENT

The Parties to the *Agreement on Government Procurement*, done at Marrakesh on 15 April 1994, (hereinafter referred to as "the 1994 Agreement"),

Having undertaken further negotiations pursuant to Article XXIV:7(b) and (c) of the 1994 Agreement;

Hereby *agree* as follows:

1. The Preamble, Articles I through XXIV, and Appendices to the 1994 Agreement shall be deleted and replaced by the provisions as set forth in the Annex hereto.

2. This Protocol shall be open for acceptance by the Parties to the 1994 Agreement.

3. This Protocol shall enter into force for those Parties to the 1994 Agreement that have deposited their respective instruments of acceptance of this Protocol, on the 30th day following such deposit by two thirds of the Parties to the 1994 Agreement. Thereafter this Protocol shall enter into force for each Party to the 1994 Agreement which has deposited its instrument of acceptance of this Protocol, on the 30th day following the date of such deposit.

4. This Protocol shall be deposited with the Director-General of the WTO, who shall promptly furnish to each Party to the 1994 Agreement a certified true copy of this Protocol, and a notification of each acceptance thereof.

5. This Protocol shall be registered in accordance with the provisions of Article 102 of the Charter of the United Nations.

Done at Geneva this 30th day of March two thousand and twelve in a single copy, in the English, French and Spanish languages, each text being authentic, except as otherwise specified with respect to the Appendices hereto.

Annex to the Protocol Amending the Agreement on Government Procurement

Preamble

The Parties to this Agreement (hereinafter referred to as "the Parties"),

Recognizing the need for an effective multilateral framework for government procurement, with a view to achieving greater liberalization and expansion of, and improving the framework for, the conduct of international trade;

Recognizing that measures regarding government procurement should not be prepared, adopted or applied so as to afford protection to domestic suppliers, goods or services, or to discriminate among foreign suppliers, goods or services;

Recognizing that the integrity and predictability of government procurement systems are integral to the efficient and effective management of public resources, the performance of the Parties' economies and the functioning of the multilateral trading system;

Recognizing that the procedural commitments under this Agreement should be sufficiently flexible to accommodate the specific circumstances of each Party;

Recognizing the need to take into account the development, financial and trade needs of developing countries, in particular the least developed countries;

Recognizing the importance of transparent measures regarding government procurement, of carrying out procurements in a transparent and impartial manner and of avoiding conflicts of interest and corrupt practices, in accordance with applicable international instruments, such as the United Nations Convention Against Corruption;

Recognizing the importance of using, and encouraging the use of, electronic means for procurement covered by this Agreement;

Desiring to encourage acceptance of and accession to this Agreement by WTO Members not party to it;

Hereby *agree* as follows:

Article I Definitions

For purposes of this Agreement:

(a) **commercial goods or services** means goods or services of a type generally sold or offered for sale in the commercial marketplace to, and customarily purchased by, non-governmental buyers for non-governmental purposes;

(b) **Committee** means the Committee on Government Procurement established by Article XXI:1;

(c) **construction service** means a service that has as its objective the realization by whatever means of civil or building works, based on Division 51 of the United Nations Provisional Central Product Classification (CPC);

(d) **country** includes any separate customs territory that is a Party to this Agreement. In the case of a separate customs territory that is a Party to this Agreement, where an expression in this Agreement is qualified by the term "national", such expression shall be read as pertaining to that customs territory, unless otherwise specified;

(e) **days** means calendar days;

(f) **electronic auction** means an iterative process that involves the use of electronic means for the presentation by suppliers of either new prices, or new values for quantifiable non-price elements of the tender related to the evaluation criteria, or both, resulting in a ranking or re-ranking of tenders;

(g) **in writing** or **written** means any worded or numbered expression that can be read, reproduced and later communicated. It may include electronically transmitted and stored information;

(h) **limited tendering** means a procurement method whereby the procuring entity contacts a supplier or suppliers of its choice;

(i) **measure** means any law, regulation, procedure, administrative guidance or practice, or any action of a procuring entity relating to a covered procurement;

(j) **multi-use list** means a list of suppliers that a procuring entity has determined satisfy the conditions for participation in that list, and that the procuring entity intends to use more than once;

(k) **notice of intended procurement** means a notice published by a procuring entity inviting interested suppliers to submit a request for participation, a tender, or both;

(*l*) **offset** means any condition or undertaking that encourages local development or improves a Party's balance-of-payments accounts, such as the use of domestic content, the licensing of technology, investment, counter-trade and similar action or requirement;

(m) **open tendering** means a procurement method whereby all interested suppliers may submit a tender;

(n) **person** means a natural person or a juridical person;

(o) **procuring entity** means an entity covered under a Party's Annex 1, 2 or 3 to Appendix I;

(p) **qualified supplier** means a supplier that a procuring entity recognizes as having satisfied the conditions for participation;

(q) **selective tendering** means a procurement method whereby only qualified suppliers are invited by the procuring entity to submit a tender;

(r) **services** includes construction services, unless otherwise specified;

(s) **standard** means a document approved by a recognized body that provides for common and repeated use, rules, guidelines or characteristics for goods or services, or related processes and production methods, with which compliance is not mandatory. It may also include or deal exclusively with terminology, symbols, packaging, marking or labelling requirements as they apply to a good, service, process or production method;

(t) **supplier** means a person or group of persons that provides or could provide goods or services; and

(u) **technical specification** means a tendering requirement that:

(i) lays down the characteristics of goods or services to be procured, including quality, performance, safety and dimensions, or the processes and methods for their production or provision; or

(ii) addresses terminology, symbols, packaging, marking or labelling requirements, as they apply to a good or service.

Article II Scope and Coverage

Application of Agreement

1. This Agreement applies to any measure regarding covered procurement, whether or not it is conducted exclusively or partially by electronic means.

2. For the purposes of this Agreement, covered procurement means procurement for governmental purposes:

(a) of goods, services, or any combination thereof:

(i) as specified in each Party's annexes to Appendix I; and

(ii) not procured with a view to commercial sale or resale, or for use in the production or supply of goods or services for commercial sale or resale;

(b) by any contractual means, including: purchase; lease; and rental or hire purchase, with or without an option to buy;

(c) for which the value, as estimated in accordance with paragraphs 6 through 8, equals or exceeds the relevant threshold specified in a Party's annexes to Appendix I, at the time of publication of a notice in accordance with Article VII;

(d) by a procuring entity; and

(e) that is not otherwise excluded from coverage in paragraph 3 or a Party's annexes to Appendix I.

3. Except where provided otherwise in a Party's annexes to Appendix I, this Agreement does not apply to:

(a) the acquisition or rental of land, existing buildings or other immovable property or the rights thereon;

(b) non-contractual agreements or any form of assistance that a Party provides, including cooperative agreements, grants, loans, equity infusions, guarantees and fiscal incentives;

(c) the procurement or acquisition of fiscal agency or depository services, liquidation and management services for regulated financial institutions or services related to the sale, redemption and distribution of public debt, including loans and government bonds, notes and other securities;

(d) public employment contracts;

(e) procurement conducted:

(i) for the specific purpose of providing international assistance, including development aid;

(ii) under the particular procedure or condition of an international agreement relating to the stationing of troops or relating to the joint implementation by the signatory countries of a project; or

(iii) under the particular procedure or condition of an international organization, or funded by international grants, loans or other assistance where the applicable procedure or condition would be inconsistent with this Agreement.

4. Each Party shall specify the following information in its annexes to Appendix I:

(a) in Annex 1, the central government entities whose procurement is covered by this Agreement;

(b) in Annex 2, the sub-central government entities whose procurement is covered by this Agreement;

(c) in Annex 3, all other entities whose procurement is covered by this Agreement;

(d) in Annex 4, the goods covered by this Agreement;

(e) in Annex 5, the services, other than construction services, covered by this Agreement;

(f) in Annex 6, the construction services covered by this Agreement; and

(g) in Annex 7, any General Notes.

5. Where a procuring entity, in the context of covered procurement, requires persons not covered under a Party's annexes to Appendix I to procure in accordance with particular requirements, Article IV shall apply *mutatis mutandis* to such requirements.

Valuation

6. In estimating the value of a procurement for the purpose of ascertaining whether it is a covered procurement, a procuring entity shall:

(a) neither divide a procurement into separate procurements nor select or use a particular valuation method for estimating the value of a procurement with the intention of totally or partially excluding it from the application of this Agreement; and

(b) include the estimated maximum total value of the procurement over its entire duration, whether awarded to one or more suppliers, taking into account all forms of remuneration, including:

(i) premiums, fees, commissions and interest; and

(ii) where the procurement provides for the possibility of options, the total value of such options.

7. Where an individual requirement for a procurement results in the award of more than one contract, or in the award of contracts in separate parts (hereinafter referred to as "recurring contracts"), the calculation of the estimated maximum total value shall be based on:

(a) the value of recurring contracts of the same type of good or service awarded during the preceding 12 months or the procuring entity's preceding fiscal year, adjusted, where possible, to take into account anticipated changes in the quantity or value of the good or service being procured over the following 12 months; or

(b) the estimated value of recurring contracts of the same type of good or service to be awarded during the 12 months following the initial contract award or the procuring entity's fiscal year.

8. In the case of procurement by lease, rental or hire purchase of goods or services, or procurement for which a total price is not specified, the basis for valuation shall be:

(a) in the case of a fixed-term contract:

(i) where the term of the contract is 12 months or less, the total estimated maximum value for its duration; or

(ii) where the term of the contract exceeds 12 months, the total estimated maximum value, including any estimated residual value;

(b) where the contract is for an indefinite period, the estimated monthly instalment multiplied by 48; and

(c) where it is not certain whether the contract is to be a fixed-term contract, subparagraph (b) shall be used.

Article III Security and General Exceptions

1. Nothing in this Agreement shall be construed to prevent any Party from taking any action or not disclosing any information that it considers necessary for the protection of its essential security interests relating to the procurement of arms, ammunition or war materials, or to procurement indispensable for national security or for national defence purposes.

2. Subject to the requirement that such measures are not applied in a manner that would constitute a means of arbitrary or unjustifiable discrimination between Parties where the same conditions prevail or a disguised restriction on international trade, nothing in this Agreement shall be construed to prevent any Party from imposing or enforcing measures:

(a) necessary to protect public morals, order or safety;

(b) necessary to protect human, animal or plant life or health;

(c) necessary to protect intellectual property; or

(d) relating to goods or services of persons with disabilities, philanthropic institutions or prison labour.

Article IV General Principles

Non-Discrimination

1. With respect to any measure regarding covered procurement, each Party, including its procuring entities, shall accord immediately and unconditionally to the goods and services of any other Party and to the suppliers of any other Party offering the goods or services of any Party, treatment no less favourable than the treatment the Party, including its procuring entities, accords to:

(a) domestic goods, services and suppliers; and

(b) goods, services and suppliers of any other Party.

2. With respect to any measure regarding covered procurement, a Party, including its procuring entities, shall not:

(a) treat a locally established supplier less favourably than another locally established supplier on the basis of the degree of foreign affiliation or ownership; or

(b) discriminate against a locally established supplier on the basis that the goods or services offered by that supplier for a particular procurement are goods or services of any other Party.

Use of Electronic Means

3. When conducting covered procurement by electronic means, a procuring entity shall:

(a) ensure that the procurement is conducted using information technology systems and software, including those related to authentication and encryption of information, that are generally available and interoperable with other generally available information technology systems and software; and

(b) maintain mechanisms that ensure the integrity of requests for participation and tenders, including establishment of the time of receipt and the prevention of inappropriate access.

Conduct of Procurement

4. A procuring entity shall conduct covered procurement in a transparent and impartial manner that:

(a) is consistent with this Agreement, using methods such as open tendering, selective tendering and limited tendering;

(b) avoids conflicts of interest; and

(c) prevents corrupt practices.

Rules of Origin

5. For purposes of covered procurement, a Party shall not apply rules of origin to goods or services imported from or supplied from another Party that are different from the rules of origin the Party applies at the same time in the normal course of trade to imports or supplies of the same goods or services from the same Party.

Offsets

6. With regard to covered procurement, a Party, including its procuring entities, shall not seek, take account of, impose or enforce any offset.

Measures Not Specific to Procurement

7. Paragraphs 1 and 2 shall not apply to: customs duties and charges of any kind imposed on, or in connection with, importation; the method of levying such duties and charges; other import regulations or formalities and measures affecting trade in services other than measures governing covered procurement.

Article V Developing Countries

1. In negotiations on accession to, and in the implementation and administration of, this Agreement, the Parties shall give special consideration to the development, financial and trade needs and circumstances of developing countries and least developed countries (collectively referred to hereinafter as "developing countries", unless specifically identified otherwise), recognizing that these may differ significantly from country to country. As provided for in this Article and on request, the Parties shall accord special and differential treatment to:

(a) least developed countries; and

(b) any other developing country, where and to the extent that this special and differential treatment meets its development needs.

2. Upon accession by a developing country to this Agreement, each Party shall provide immediately to the goods, services and suppliers of that country the most favourable coverage that the Party provides under its annexes to Appendix I to any other Party to this Agreement, subject to any terms negotiated between the Party and the developing country in order to maintain an appropriate balance of opportunities under this Agreement.

3. Based on its development needs, and with the agreement of the Parties, a developing country may adopt or maintain one or more of the

following transitional measures, during a transition period and in accordance with a schedule, set out in its relevant annexes to Appendix I, and applied in a manner that does not discriminate among the other Parties:

(a) a price preference programme, provided that the programme:

(i) provides a preference only for the part of the tender incorporating goods or services originating in the developing country applying the preference or goods or services originating in other developing countries in respect of which the developing country applying the preference has an obligation to provide national treatment under a preferential agreement, provided that where the other developing country is a Party to this Agreement, such treatment would be subject to any conditions set by the Committee; and

(ii) is transparent, and the preference and its application in the procurement are clearly described in the notice of intended procurement;

(b) an offset, provided that any requirement for, or consideration of, the imposition of the offset is clearly stated in the notice of intended procurement;

(c) the phased-in addition of specific entities or sectors; and

(d) a threshold that is higher than its permanent threshold.

4. In negotiations on accession to this Agreement, the Parties may agree to the delayed application of any specific obligation in this Agreement, other than Article IV:1(b), by the acceding developing country while that country implements the obligation. The implementation period shall be:

(a) for a least developed country, five years after its accession to this Agreement; and

(b) for any other developing country, only the period necessary to implement the specific obligation and not to exceed three years.

5. Any developing country that has negotiated an implementation period for an obligation under paragraph 4 shall list in its Annex 7 to Appendix I the agreed implementation period, the specific obligation subject to the implementation period and any interim obligation with which it has agreed to comply during the implementation period.

6. After this Agreement has entered into force for a developing country, the Committee, on request of the developing country, may:

(a) extend the transition period for a measure adopted or maintained under paragraph 3 or any implementation period negotiated under paragraph 4; or

(b) approve the adoption of a new transitional measure under paragraph 3, in special circumstances that were unforeseen during the accession process.

7. A developing country that has negotiated a transitional measure under paragraph 3 or 6, an implementation period under paragraph 4 or any extension under paragraph 6 shall take such steps during the transition period or implementation period as may be necessary to ensure that it is in compliance with this Agreement at the end of any such period. The developing country shall promptly notify the Committee of each step.

8. The Parties shall give due consideration to any request by a developing country for technical cooperation and capacity building in relation to that country's accession to, or implementation of, this Agreement.

9. The Committee may develop procedures for the implementation of this Article. Such procedures may include provisions for voting on decisions relating to requests under paragraph 6.

10. The Committee shall review the operation and effectiveness of this Article every five years.

Article VI Information on the Procurement System

1. Each Party shall:

(a) promptly publish any law, regulation, judicial decision, administrative ruling of general application, standard contract clause mandated by law or regulation and incorporated by reference in notices or tender documentation and procedure regarding covered procurement, and any modifications thereof, in an officially designated electronic or paper medium that is widely disseminated and remains readily accessible to the public; and

(b) provide an explanation thereof to any Party, on request.

2. Each Party shall list:

(a) in Appendix II, the electronic or paper media in which the Party publishes the information described in paragraph 1;

(b) in Appendix III, the electronic or paper media in which the Party publishes the notices required by Articles VII, IX:7 and XVI:2; and

(c) in Appendix IV, the website address or addresses where the Party publishes:

(i) its procurement statistics pursuant to Article XVI:5; or

(ii) its notices concerning awarded contracts pursuant to Article XVI:6.

3. Each Party shall promptly notify the Committee of any modification to the Party's information listed in Appendix II, III or IV.

Article VII Notices

Notice of Intended Procurement

1. For each covered procurement, a procuring entity shall publish a notice of intended procurement in the appropriate paper or electronic medium listed in Appendix III, except in the circumstances described in Article XIII. Such medium shall be widely disseminated and such notices shall remain readily accessible to the public, at least until expiration of the time-period indicated in the notice. The notices shall:

(a) for procuring entities covered under Annex 1, be accessible by electronic means free of charge through a single point of access, for at least any minimum period of time specified in Appendix III; and

(b) for procuring entities covered under Annex 2 or 3, where accessible by electronic means, be provided, at least, through links in a gateway electronic site that is accessible free of charge.

Parties, including their procuring entities covered under Annex 2 or 3, are encouraged to publish their notices by electronic means free of charge through a single point of access.

2. Except as otherwise provided in this Agreement, each notice of intended procurement shall include:

(a) the name and address of the procuring entity and other information necessary to contact the procuring entity and obtain all relevant documents relating to the procurement, and their cost and terms of payment, if any;

(b) a description of the procurement, including the nature and the quantity of the goods or services to be procured or, where the quantity is not known, the estimated quantity;

(c) for recurring contracts, an estimate, if possible, of the timing of subsequent notices of intended procurement;

(d) a description of any options;

(e) the time-frame for delivery of goods or services or the duration of the contract;

(f) the procurement method that will be used and whether it will involve negotiation or electronic auction;

(g) where applicable, the address and any final date for the submission of requests for participation in the procurement;

(h) the address and the final date for the submission of tenders;

(i) the language or languages in which tenders or requests for participation may be submitted, if they may be submitted in a language other than an official language of the Party of the procuring entity;

(j) a list and brief description of any conditions for participation of suppliers, including any requirements for specific documents or certifications to be provided by suppliers in connection therewith, unless such requirements are included in tender documentation that is made available to all interested suppliers at the same time as the notice of intended procurement;

(k) where, pursuant to Article IX, a procuring entity intends to select a limited number of qualified suppliers to be invited to tender, the criteria that will be used to select them and, where applicable, any limitation on the number of suppliers that will be permitted to tender; and

(l) an indication that the procurement is covered by this Agreement.

Summary Notice

3. For each case of intended procurement, a procuring entity shall publish a summary notice that is readily accessible, at the same time as the publication of the notice of intended procurement, in one of the WTO languages. The summary notice shall contain at least the following information:

(a) the subject-matter of the procurement;

(b) the final date for the submission of tenders or, where applicable, any final date for the submission of requests for participation in the procurement or for inclusion on a multi-use list; and

(c) the address from which documents relating to the procurement may be requested.

Notice of Planned Procurement

4. Procuring entities are encouraged to publish in the appropriate paper or electronic medium listed in Appendix III as early as possible in each fiscal year a notice regarding their future procurement plans (hereinafter referred to as "notice of planned procurement"). The notice of planned procurement should include the subject-matter of the procurement and the planned date of the publication of the notice of intended procurement.

5. A procuring entity covered under Annex 2 or 3 may use a notice of planned procurement as a notice of intended procurement provided that the notice of planned procurement includes as much of the information referred to in paragraph 2 as is available to the entity and a statement that interested suppliers should express their interest in the procurement to the procuring entity.

Article VIII Conditions for Participation

1. A procuring entity shall limit any conditions for participation in a procurement to those that are essential to ensure that a supplier has the legal and financial capacities and the commercial and technical abilities to undertake the relevant procurement.

2. In establishing the conditions for participation, a procuring entity:

(a) shall not impose the condition that, in order for a supplier to participate in a procurement, the supplier has previously been awarded one or more contracts by a procuring entity of a given Party; and

(b) may require relevant prior experience where essential to meet the requirements of the procurement.

3. In assessing whether a supplier satisfies the conditions for participation, a procuring entity:

(a) shall evaluate the financial capacity and the commercial and technical abilities of a supplier on the basis of that supplier's business activities both inside and outside the territory of the Party of the procuring entity; and

(b) shall base its evaluation on the conditions that the procuring entity has specified in advance in notices or tender documentation.

4. Where there is supporting evidence, a Party, including its procuring entities, may exclude a supplier on grounds such as:

(a) bankruptcy;

(b) false declarations;

(c) significant or persistent deficiencies in performance of any substantive requirement or obligation under a prior contract or contracts;

(d) final judgments in respect of serious crimes or other serious offences;

(e) professional misconduct or acts or omissions that adversely reflect on the commercial integrity of the supplier; or

(f) failure to pay taxes.

Article IX Qualification of Suppliers

Registration Systems and Qualification Procedures

1. A Party, including its procuring entities, may maintain a supplier registration system under which interested suppliers are required to register and provide certain information.

2. Each Party shall ensure that:

(a) its procuring entities make efforts to minimize differences in their qualification procedures; and

(b) where its procuring entities maintain registration systems, the entities make efforts to minimize differences in their registration systems.

3. A Party, including its procuring entities, shall not adopt or apply any registration system or qualification procedure with the purpose or the effect of creating unnecessary obstacles to the participation of suppliers of another Party in its procurement.

Selective Tendering

4. Where a procuring entity intends to use selective tendering, the entity shall:

(a) include in the notice of intended procurement at least the information specified in Article VII:2(a), (b), (f), (g), (j), (k) and (l) and invite suppliers to submit a request for participation; and

(b) provide, by the commencement of the time-period for tendering, at least the information in Article VII:2 (c), (d), (e), (h) and (i) to the qualified suppliers that it notifies as specified in Article XI:3(b).

5. A procuring entity shall allow all qualified suppliers to participate in a particular procurement, unless the procuring entity states in the notice of intended procurement any limitation on the number of suppliers that will be permitted to tender and the criteria for selecting the limited number of suppliers.

6. Where the tender documentation is not made publicly available from the date of publication of the notice referred to in paragraph 4, a procuring entity shall ensure that those documents are made available at the same time to all the qualified suppliers selected in accordance with paragraph 5.

Multi-Use Lists

7. A procuring entity may maintain a multi-use list of suppliers, provided that a notice inviting interested suppliers to apply for inclusion on the list is:

(a) published annually; and

(b) where published by electronic means, made available continuously, in the appropriate medium listed in Appendix III.

8. The notice provided for in paragraph 7 shall include:

(a) a description of the goods or services, or categories thereof, for which the list may be used;

(b) the conditions for participation to be satisfied by suppliers for inclusion on the list and the methods that the procuring entity will use to verify that a supplier satisfies the conditions;

(c) the name and address of the procuring entity and other information necessary to contact the entity and obtain all relevant documents relating to the list;

(d) the period of validity of the list and the means for its renewal or termination, or where the period of validity is not provided, an indication of the method by which notice will be given of the termination of use of the list; and

(e) an indication that the list may be used for procurement covered by this Agreement.

9. Notwithstanding paragraph 7, where a multi-use list will be valid for three years or less, a procuring entity may publish the notice referred to in paragraph 7 only once, at the beginning of the period of validity of the list, provided that the notice:

(a) states the period of validity and that further notices will not be published; and

(b) is published by electronic means and is made available continuously during the period of its validity.

10. A procuring entity shall allow suppliers to apply at any time for inclusion on a multi-use list and shall include on the list all qualified suppliers within a reasonably short time.

11. Where a supplier that is not included on a multi-use list submits a request for participation in a procurement based on a multi-use list and all required documents, within the time-period provided for in Article XI:2, a procuring entity shall examine the request. The procuring entity shall not exclude the supplier from consideration in respect of the procurement on the grounds that the entity has insufficient time to examine the request, unless, in exceptional cases, due to the complexity of the procurement, the entity is not able to complete the examination of the request within the time-period allowed for the submission of tenders.

Annex 2 and Annex 3 Entities

12. A procuring entity covered under Annex 2 or 3 may use a notice inviting suppliers to apply for inclusion on a multi-use list as a notice of intended procurement, provided that:

(a) the notice is published in accordance with paragraph 7 and includes the information required under paragraph 8, as much of the information required under Article VII:2 as is available and a statement that it constitutes a notice of intended procurement or that only the suppliers on the multi-use list will receive further notices of procurement covered by the multi-use list; and

(b) the entity promptly provides to suppliers that have expressed an interest in a given procurement to the entity, sufficient information to permit them to assess their interest in the procurement, including all remaining information required in Article VII:2, to the extent such information is available.

13. A procuring entity covered under Annex 2 or 3 may allow a supplier that has applied for inclusion on a multi-use list in accordance with para-

graph 10 to tender in a given procurement, where there is sufficient time for the procuring entity to examine whether the supplier satisfies the conditions for participation.

Information on Procuring Entity Decisions

14. A procuring entity shall promptly inform any supplier that submits a request for participation in a procurement or application for inclusion on a multi-use list of the procuring entity's decision with respect to the request or application.

15. Where a procuring entity rejects a supplier's request for participation in a procurement or application for inclusion on a multi-use list, ceases to recognize a supplier as qualified, or removes a supplier from a multi-use list, the entity shall promptly inform the supplier and, on request of the supplier, promptly provide the supplier with a written explanation of the reasons for its decision.

Article X Technical Specifications and Tender Documentation

Technical Specifications

1. A procuring entity shall not prepare, adopt or apply any technical specification or prescribe any conformity assessment procedure with the purpose or the effect of creating unnecessary obstacles to international trade.

2. In prescribing the technical specifications for the goods or services being procured, a procuring entity shall, where appropriate:

(a) set out the technical specification in terms of performance and functional requirements, rather than design or descriptive characteristics; and

(b) base the technical specification on international standards, where such exist; otherwise, on national technical regulations, recognized national standards or building codes.

3. Where design or descriptive characteristics are used in the technical specifications, a procuring entity should indicate, where appropriate, that it will consider tenders of equivalent goods or services that demonstrably fulfil the requirements of the procurement by including words such as "or equivalent" in the tender documentation.

4. A procuring entity shall not prescribe technical specifications that require or refer to a particular trademark or trade name, patent, copyright, design, type, specific origin, producer or supplier, unless there is no other

sufficiently precise or intelligible way of describing the procurement requirements and provided that, in such cases, the entity includes words such as "or equivalent" in the tender documentation.

5. A procuring entity shall not seek or accept, in a manner that would have the effect of precluding competition, advice that may be used in the preparation or adoption of any technical specification for a specific procurement from a person that may have a commercial interest in the procurement.

6. For greater certainty, a Party, including its procuring entities, may, in accordance with this Article, prepare, adopt or apply technical specifications to promote the conservation of natural resources or protect the environment.

Tender Documentation

7. A procuring entity shall make available to suppliers tender documentation that includes all information necessary to permit suppliers to prepare and submit responsive tenders. Unless already provided in the notice of intended procurement, such documentation shall include a complete description of:

(a) the procurement, including the nature and the quantity of the goods or services to be procured or, where the quantity is not known, the estimated quantity and any requirements to be fulfilled, including any technical specifications, conformity assessment certification, plans, drawings or instructional materials;

(b) any conditions for participation of suppliers, including a list of information and documents that suppliers are required to submit in connection with the conditions for participation;

(c) all evaluation criteria the entity will apply in the awarding of the contract, and, except where price is the sole criterion, the relative importance of such criteria;

(d) where the procuring entity will conduct the procurement by electronic means, any authentication and encryption requirements or other requirements related to the submission of information by electronic means;

(e) where the procuring entity will hold an electronic auction, the rules, including identification of the elements of the tender related to the evaluation criteria, on which the auction will be conducted;

(f) where there will be a public opening of tenders, the date, time and place for the opening and, where appropriate, the persons authorized to be present;

(g) any other terms or conditions, including terms of payment and any limitation on the means by which tenders may be submitted, such as whether on paper or by electronic means; and

(h) any dates for the delivery of goods or the supply of services.

8. In establishing any date for the delivery of goods or the supply of services being procured, a procuring entity shall take into account such factors as the complexity of the procurement, the extent of subcontracting anticipated and the realistic time required for production, de-stocking and transport of goods from the point of supply or for supply of services.

9. The evaluation criteria set out in the notice of intended procurement or tender documentation may include, among others, price and other cost factors, quality, technical merit, environmental characteristics and terms of delivery.

10. A procuring entity shall promptly:

(a) make available tender documentation to ensure that interested suppliers have sufficient time to submit responsive tenders;

(b) provide, on request, the tender documentation to any interested supplier; and

(c) reply to any reasonable request for relevant information by any interested or participating supplier, provided that such information does not give that supplier an advantage over other suppliers.

Modifications

11. Where, prior to the award of a contract, a procuring entity modifies the criteria or requirements set out in the notice of intended procurement or tender documentation provided to participating suppliers, or amends or reissues a notice or tender documentation, it shall transmit in writing all such modifications or amended or re-issued notice or tender documentation:

(a) to all suppliers that are participating at the time of the modification, amendment or re-issuance, where such suppliers are known to the entity, and in all other cases, in the same manner as the original information was made available; and

(b) in adequate time to allow such suppliers to modify and re-submit amended tenders, as appropriate.

Article XI Time-Periods

General

1. A procuring entity shall, consistent with its own reasonable needs, provide sufficient time for suppliers to prepare and submit requests for participation and responsive tenders, taking into account such factors as:

(a) the nature and complexity of the procurement;

(b) the extent of subcontracting anticipated; and

(c) the time necessary for transmitting tenders by non-electronic means from foreign as well as domestic points where electronic means are not used.

Such time-periods, including any extension of the time-periods, shall be the same for all interested or participating suppliers.

Deadlines

2. A procuring entity that uses selective tendering shall establish that the final date for the submission of requests for participation shall not, in principle, be less than 25 days from the date of publication of the notice of intended procurement. Where a state of urgency duly substantiated by the procuring entity renders this time-period impracticable, the time-period may be reduced to not less than 10 days.

3. Except as provided for in paragraphs 4, 5, 7 and 8 a procuring entity shall establish that the final date for the submission of tenders shall not be less than 40 days from the date on which:

(a) in the case of open tendering, the notice of intended procurement is published; or

(b) in the case of selective tendering, the entity notifies suppliers that they will be invited to submit tenders, whether or not it uses a multi-use list.

4. A procuring entity may reduce the time-period for tendering established in accordance with paragraph 3 to not less than 10 days where:

(a) the procuring entity has published a notice of planned procurement as described in Article VII:4 at least 40 days and not more than 12 months in advance of the publication of the notice of intended procurement, and the notice of planned procurement contains:

(i) a description of the procurement;

(ii) the approximate final dates for the submission of tenders or requests for participation;

(iii) a statement that interested suppliers should express their interest in the procurement to the procuring entity;

(iv) the address from which documents relating to the procurement may be obtained; and

(v) as much of the information that is required for the notice of intended procurement under Article VII:2, as is available;

(b) the procuring entity, for recurring contracts, indicates in an initial notice of intended procurement that subsequent notices will provide time-periods for tendering based on this paragraph; or

(c) a state of urgency duly substantiated by the procuring entity renders the time-period for tendering established in accordance with paragraph 3 impracticable.

5. A procuring entity may reduce the time-period for tendering established in accordance with paragraph 3 by five days for each one of the following circumstances:

(a) the notice of intended procurement is published by electronic means;

(b) all the tender documentation is made available by electronic means from the date of the publication of the notice of intended procurement; and

(c) the entity accepts tenders by electronic means.

6. The use of paragraph 5, in conjunction with paragraph 4, shall in no case result in the reduction of the time-period for tendering established in accordance with paragraph 3 to less than 10 days from the date on which the notice of intended procurement is published.

7. Notwithstanding any other provision in this Article, where a procuring entity purchases commercial goods or services, or any combination thereof, it may reduce the time-period for tendering established in accordance with paragraph 3 to not less than 13 days, provided that it publishes by electronic means, at the same time, both the notice of intended procurement and the tender documentation. In addition, where the entity accepts tenders for commercial goods or services by electronic means, it may reduce the time-period established in accordance with paragraph 3 to not less than 10 days.

8. Where a procuring entity covered under Annex 2 or 3 has selected all or a limited number of qualified suppliers, the time-period for tendering may be fixed by mutual agreement between the procuring entity and the selected suppliers. In the absence of agreement, the period shall not be less than 10 days.

Article XII Negotiation

1. A Party may provide for its procuring entities to conduct negotiations:

(a) where the entity has indicated its intent to conduct negotiations in the notice of intended procurement required under Article VII:2; or

(b) where it appears from the evaluation that no tender is obviously the most advantageous in terms of the specific evaluation criteria set out in the notice of intended procurement or tender documentation.

2. A procuring entity shall:

(a) ensure that any elimination of suppliers participating in negotiations is carried out in accordance with the evaluation criteria set out in the notice of intended procurement or tender documentation; and

(b) where negotiations are concluded, provide a common deadline for the remaining participating suppliers to submit any new or revised tenders.

Article XIII Limited Tendering

1. Provided that it does not use this provision for the purpose of avoiding competition among suppliers or in a manner that discriminates against suppliers of any other Party or protects domestic suppliers, a procuring entity may use limited tendering and may choose not to apply Articles VII through IX, X (paragraphs 7 through 11), XI, XII, XIV and XV only under any of the following circumstances:

(a) where:

(i) no tenders were submitted or no suppliers requested participation;

(ii) no tenders that conform to the essential requirements of the tender documentation were submitted;

(iii) no suppliers satisfied the conditions for participation; or

(iv) the tenders submitted have been collusive, provided that the requirements of the tender documentation are not substantially modified;

(b) where the goods or services can be supplied only by a particular supplier and no reasonable alternative or substitute goods or services exist for any of the following reasons:

(i) the requirement is for a work of art;

(ii) the protection of patents, copyrights or other exclusive rights; or

(iii) due to an absence of competition for technical reasons;

(c) for additional deliveries by the original supplier of goods or services that were not included in the initial procurement where a change of supplier for such additional goods or services:

(i) cannot be made for economic or technical reasons such as requirements of interchangeability or interoperability with existing equipment, software, services or installations procured under the initial procurement; and

(ii) would cause significant inconvenience or substantial duplication of costs for the procuring entity;

(d) insofar as is strictly necessary where, for reasons of extreme urgency brought about by events unforeseeable by the procuring entity, the goods or services could not be obtained in time using open tendering or selective tendering;

(e) for goods purchased on a commodity market;

(f) where a procuring entity procures a prototype or a first good or service that is developed at its request in the course of, and for, a particular contract for research, experiment, study or original development. Original development of a first good or service may include limited production or supply in order to incorporate the results of field testing and to demonstrate that the good or service is suitable for production or supply in quantity to acceptable quality standards, but does not include quantity production or supply to establish commercial viability or to recover research and development costs;

(g) for purchases made under exceptionally advantageous conditions that only arise in the very short term in the case of unusual disposals such as those arising from liquidation, receivership or bankruptcy, but not for routine purchases from regular suppliers; or

(h) where a contract is awarded to a winner of a design contest provided that:

(i) the contest has been organized in a manner that is consistent with the principles of this Agreement, in particular relating to the publication of a notice of intended procurement; and

(ii) the participants are judged by an independent jury with a view to a design contract being awarded to a winner.

2. A procuring entity shall prepare a report in writing on each contract awarded under paragraph 1. The report shall include the name of the procuring entity, the value and kind of goods or services procured and a statement indicating the circumstances and conditions described in paragraph 1 that justified the use of limited tendering.

Article XIV Electronic Auctions

Where a procuring entity intends to conduct a covered procurement using an electronic auction, the entity shall provide each participant, before commencing the electronic auction, with:

(a) the automatic evaluation method, including the mathematical formula, that is based on the evaluation criteria set out in the tender documentation and that will be used in the automatic ranking or reranking during the auction;

(b) the results of any initial evaluation of the elements of its tender where the contract is to be awarded on the basis of the most advantageous tender; and

(c) any other relevant information relating to the conduct of the auction.

Article XV Treatment of Tenders and Awarding of Contracts

Treatment of Tenders

1. A procuring entity shall receive, open and treat all tenders under procedures that guarantee the fairness and impartiality of the procurement process, and the confidentiality of tenders.

2. A procuring entity shall not penalize any supplier whose tender is received after the time specified for receiving tenders if the delay is due solely to mishandling on the part of the procuring entity.

3. Where a procuring entity provides a supplier with an opportunity to correct unintentional errors of form between the opening of tenders and the awarding of the contract, the procuring entity shall provide the same opportunity to all participating suppliers.

Awarding of Contracts

4. To be considered for an award, a tender shall be submitted in writing and shall, at the time of opening, comply with the essential requirements set out in the notices and tender documentation and be from a supplier that satisfies the conditions for participation.

5. Unless a procuring entity determines that it is not in the public interest to award a contract, the entity shall award the contract to the supplier that the entity has determined to be capable of fulfilling the terms of the contract and that, based solely on the evaluation criteria specified in the notices and tender documentation, has submitted:

(a) the most advantageous tender; or

(b) where price is the sole criterion, the lowest price.

6. Where a procuring entity receives a tender with a price that is abnormally lower than the prices in other tenders submitted, it may verify with the supplier that it satisfies the conditions for participation and is capable of fulfilling the terms of the contract.

7. A procuring entity shall not use options, cancel a procurement or modify awarded contracts in a manner that circumvents the obligations under this Agreement.

Article XVI Transparency of Procurement Information

Information Provided to Suppliers

1. A procuring entity shall promptly inform participating suppliers of the entity's contract award decisions and, on the request of a supplier, shall do so in writing. Subject to paragraphs 2 and 3 of Article XVII, a procuring entity shall, on request, provide an unsuccessful supplier with an explanation of the reasons why the entity did not select its tender and the relative advantages of the successful supplier's tender.

Publication of Award Information

2. Not later than 72 days after the award of each contract covered by this Agreement, a procuring entity shall publish a notice in the appropriate paper or electronic medium listed in Appendix III. Where the entity publishes the notice only in an electronic medium, the information shall remain readily accessible for a reasonable period of time. The notice shall include at least the following information:

(a) a description of the goods or services procured;

(b) the name and address of the procuring entity;

(c) the name and address of the successful supplier;

(d) the value of the successful tender or the highest and lowest offers taken into account in the award of the contract;

(e) the date of award; and

(f) the type of procurement method used, and in cases where limited tendering was used in accordance with Article XIII, a description of the circumstances justifying the use of limited tendering.

Maintenance of Documentation, Reports and Electronic Traceability

3. Each procuring entity shall, for a period of at least three years from the date it awards a contract, maintain:

(a) the documentation and reports of tendering procedures and contract awards relating to covered procurement, including the reports required under Article XIII; and

(b) data that ensure the appropriate traceability of the conduct of covered procurement by electronic means.

Collection and Reporting of Statistics

4. Each Party shall collect and report to the Committee statistics on its contracts covered by this Agreement. Each report shall cover one year and be submitted within two years of the end of the reporting period, and shall contain:

(a) for Annex 1 procuring entities:

(i) the number and total value, for all such entities, of all contracts covered by this Agreement;

(ii) the number and total value of all contracts covered by this Agreement awarded by each such entity, broken down by categories of goods and services according to an internationally recognized uniform classification system; and

(iii) the number and total value of all contracts covered by this Agreement awarded by each such entity under limited tendering;

(b) for Annex 2 and 3 procuring entities, the number and total value of contracts covered by this Agreement awarded by all such entities, broken down by Annex; and

(c) estimates for the data required under subparagraphs (a) and (b), with an explanation of the methodology used to develop the estimates, where it is not feasible to provide the data.

5. Where a Party publishes its statistics on an official website, in a manner that is consistent with the requirements of paragraph 4, the Party may substitute a notification to the Committee of the website address for the submission of the data under paragraph 4, with any instructions necessary to access and use such statistics.

6. Where a Party requires notices concerning awarded contracts, pursuant to paragraph 2, to be published electronically and where such notices are accessible to the public through a single database in a form permitting analysis of the covered contracts, the Party may substitute a notification to the Committee of the website address for the submission of the data under paragraph 4, with any instructions necessary to access and use such data.

Article XVII Disclosure of Information

Provision of Information to Parties

1. On request of any other Party, a Party shall provide promptly any information necessary to determine whether a procurement was conducted fairly, impartially and in accordance with this Agreement, including infor-

mation on the characteristics and relative advantages of the successful tender. In cases where release of the information would prejudice competition in future tenders, the Party that receives the information shall not disclose it to any supplier, except after consulting with, and obtaining the agreement of, the Party that provided the information.

Non-Disclosure of Information

2. Notwithstanding any other provision of this Agreement, a Party, including its procuring entities, shall not provide to any particular supplier information that might prejudice fair competition between suppliers.

3. Nothing in this Agreement shall be construed to require a Party, including its procuring entities, authorities and review bodies, to disclose confidential information where disclosure:

(a) would impede law enforcement;

(b) might prejudice fair competition between suppliers;

(c) would prejudice the legitimate commercial interests of particular persons, including the protection of intellectual property; or

(d) would otherwise be contrary to the public interest.

Article XVIII Domestic Review Procedures

1. Each Party shall provide a timely, effective, transparent and non-discriminatory administrative or judicial review procedure through which a supplier may challenge:

(a) a breach of the Agreement; or

(b) where the supplier does not have a right to challenge directly a breach of the Agreement under the domestic law of a Party, a failure to comply with a Party's measures implementing this Agreement, arising in the context of a covered procurement, in which the supplier has, or has had, an interest. The procedural rules for all challenges shall be in writing and made generally available.

2. In the event of a complaint by a supplier, arising in the context of covered procurement in which the supplier has, or has had, an interest, that there has been a breach or a failure as referred to in paragraph 1, the Party of the procuring entity conducting the procurement shall encourage the entity and the supplier to seek resolution of the complaint through con-

sultations. The entity shall accord impartial and timely consideration to any such complaint in a manner that is not prejudicial to the supplier's participation in ongoing or future procurement or its right to seek corrective measures under the administrative or judicial review procedure.

3. Each supplier shall be allowed a sufficient period of time to prepare and submit a challenge, which in no case shall be less than 10 days from the time when the basis of the challenge became known or reasonably should have become known to the supplier.

4. Each Party shall establish or designate at least one impartial administrative or judicial authority that is independent of its procuring entities to receive and review a challenge by a supplier arising in the context of a covered procurement.

5. Where a body other than an authority referred to in paragraph 4 initially reviews a challenge, the Party shall ensure that the supplier may appeal the initial decision to an impartial administrative or judicial authority that is independent of the procuring entity whose procurement is the subject of the challenge.

6. Each Party shall ensure that a review body that is not a court shall have its decision subject to judicial review or have procedures that provide that:

(a) the procuring entity shall respond in writing to the challenge and disclose all relevant documents to the review body;

(b) the participants to the proceedings (hereinafter referred to as "participants") shall have the right to be heard prior to a decision of the review body being made on the challenge;

(c) the participants shall have the right to be represented and accompanied;

(d) the participants shall have access to all proceedings;

(e) the participants shall have the right to request that the proceedings take place in public and that witnesses may be presented; and

(f) the review body shall make its decisions or recommendations in a timely fashion, in writing, and shall include an explanation of the basis for each decision or recommendation.

7. Each Party shall adopt or maintain procedures that provide for:

(a) rapid interim measures to preserve the supplier's opportunity to participate in the procurement. Such interim measures may result in suspension of the procurement process. The procedures may provide that overriding adverse consequences for the interests concerned, including the public interest, may be taken into account when deciding whether such measures should be applied. Just cause for not acting shall be provided in writing; and

(b) where a review body has determined that there has been a breach or a failure as referred to in paragraph 1, corrective action or compensation for the loss or damages suffered, which may be limited to either the costs for the preparation of the tender or the costs relating to the challenge, or both.

Article XIX Modifications and Rectifications to Coverage

Notification of Proposed Modification

1. A Party shall notify the Committee of any proposed rectification, transfer of an entity from one annex to another, withdrawal of an entity or other modification of its annexes to Appendix I (any of which is hereinafter referred to as "modification"). The Party proposing the modification (hereinafter referred to as "modifying Party") shall include in the notification:

(a) for any proposed withdrawal of an entity from its annexes to Appendix I in exercise of its rights on the grounds that government control or influence over the entity's covered procurement has been effectively eliminated, evidence of such elimination; or

(b) for any other proposed modification, information as to the likely consequences of the change for the mutually agreed coverage provided for in this Agreement.

Objection to Notification

2. Any Party whose rights under this Agreement may be affected by a proposed modification notified under paragraph 1 may notify the Committee of any objection to the proposed modification. Such objections shall be made within 45 days from the date of the circulation to the Parties of the notification, and shall set out reasons for the objection.

Consultations

3. The modifying Party and any Party making an objection (hereinafter referred to as "objecting Party") shall make every attempt to resolve the objection through consultations. In such consultations, the modifying and objecting Parties shall consider the proposed modification:

(a) in the case of a notification under paragraph 1(a), in accordance with any indicative criteria adopted pursuant to paragraph 8(b), indicating the effective elimination of government control or influence over an entity's covered procurement; and

(b) in the case of a notification under paragraph 1(b), in accordance with any criteria adopted pursuant to paragraph 8(c), relating to the level of compensatory adjustments to be offered for modifications, with a view to maintaining a balance of rights and obligations and a comparable level of mutually agreed coverage provided in this Agreement.

Revised Modification

4. Where the modifying Party and any objecting Party resolve the objection through consultations, and the modifying Party revises its proposed modification as a result of those consultations, the modifying Party shall notify the Committee in accordance with paragraph 1, and any such revised modification shall only be effective after fulfilling the requirements of this Article.

Implementation of Modifications

5. A proposed modification shall become effective only where:

(a) no Party submits to the Committee a written objection to the proposed modification within 45 days from the date of circulation of the notification of the proposed modification under paragraph 1;

(b) all objecting Parties have notified the Committee that they withdraw their objections to the proposed modification; or

(c) 150 days from the date of circulation of the notification of the proposed modification under paragraph 1 have elapsed, and the modifying Party has informed the Committee in writing of its intention to implement the modification.

Withdrawal of Substantially Equivalent Coverage

6. Where a modification becomes effective pursuant to paragraph 5(c), any objecting Party may withdraw substantially equivalent coverage.

Notwithstanding Article IV:1(b), a withdrawal pursuant to this paragraph may be implemented solely with respect to the modifying Party. Any objecting Party shall inform the Committee in writing of any such withdrawal at least 30 days before the withdrawal becomes effective. A withdrawal pursuant to this paragraph shall be consistent with any criteria relating to the level of compensatory adjustment adopted by the Committee pursuant to paragraph 8(c).

Arbitration Procedures to Facilitate Resolution of Objections

7. Where the Committee has adopted arbitration procedures to facilitate the resolution of objections pursuant to paragraph 8, a modifying or any objecting Party may invoke the arbitration procedures within 120 days of circulation of the notification of the proposed modification:

(a) Where no Party has invoked the arbitration procedures within the time-period:

(i) notwithstanding paragraph 5(c), the proposed modification shall become effective where 130 days from the date of circulation of the notification of the proposed modification under paragraph 1 have elapsed, and the modifying Party has informed the Committee in writing of its intention to implement the modification; and

(ii) no objecting Party may withdraw coverage pursuant to paragraph 6.

(b) Where a modifying Party or objecting Party has invoked the arbitration procedures:

(i) notwithstanding paragraph 5(c), the proposed modification shall not become effective before the completion of the arbitration procedures;

(ii) any objecting Party that intends to enforce a right to compensation, or to withdraw substantially equivalent coverage pursuant to paragraph 6, shall participate in the arbitration proceedings;

(iii) a modifying Party should comply with the results of the arbitration procedures in making any modification effective pursuant to paragraph 5(c); and

(iv) where a modifying Party does not comply with the results of the arbitration procedures in making any modification effective pursuant to paragraph 5(c), any objecting Party may withdraw substantially equivalent coverage pursuant to paragraph 6, provided that any such withdrawal is consistent with the result of the arbitration procedures.

Committee Responsibilities

8. The Committee shall adopt:

(a) arbitration procedures to facilitate resolution of objections under paragraph 2;

(b) indicative criteria that demonstrate the effective elimination of government control or influence over an entity's covered procurement; and

(c) criteria for determining the level of compensatory adjustment to be offered for modifications made pursuant to paragraph 1(b) and of substantially equivalent coverage under paragraph 6.

Article XX Consultations and Dispute Settlement

1. Each Party shall accord sympathetic consideration to and shall afford adequate opportunity for consultation regarding any representation made by another Party with respect to any matter affecting the operation of this Agreement.

2. Where any Party considers that any benefit accruing to it, directly or indirectly, under this Agreement is being nullified or impaired, or that the attainment of any objective of this Agreement is being impeded as the result of:

(a) the failure of another Party or Parties to carry out its obligations under this Agreement; or

(b) the application by another Party or Parties of any measure, whether or not it conflicts with the provisions of this Agreement, it may, with a view to reaching a mutually satisfactory solution to the matter, have recourse to the provisions of the Understanding on Rules and Procedures Governing the Settlement of Disputes (hereinafter referred to as "the Dispute Settlement Understanding").

3. The Dispute Settlement Understanding shall apply to consultations and the settlement of disputes under this Agreement, with the exception that, notwithstanding paragraph 3 of Article 22 of the Dispute Settlement Understanding, any dispute arising under any Agreement listed in Appendix 1 to the Dispute Settlement Understanding other than this Agreement shall not result in the suspension of concessions or other obligations under this Agreement, and any dispute arising under this Agreement shall not result in the suspension of concessions or other obligations under any other Agreement listed in Appendix 1 of the Dispute Settlement Understanding.

Article XXI Institutions

Committee on Government Procurement

1. There shall be a Committee on Government Procurement composed of representatives from each of the Parties. This Committee shall elect its own Chairman and shall meet as necessary, but not less than once a year, for the purpose of affording Parties the opportunity to consult on any matters relating to the operation of this Agreement or the furtherance of its objectives, and to carry out such other responsibilities as may be assigned to it by the Parties.

2. The Committee may establish working parties or other subsidiary bodies that shall carry out such functions as may be given to them by the Committee.

3. The Committee shall annually:

(a) review the implementation and operation of this Agreement; and

(b) inform the General Council of its activities, pursuant to Article IV:8 of the Marrakesh Agreement Establishing the World Trade Organization (hereinafter referred to as "WTO Agreement"), and of developments relating to the implementation and operation of this Agreement.

Observers

4. Any WTO Member that is not a Party to this Agreement shall be entitled to participate in the Committee as an observer by submitting a written notice to the Committee. Any WTO observer may submit a written request to the Committee to participate in the Committee as an observer, and may be accorded observer status by the Committee.

Article XXII Final Provisions

Acceptance and Entry into Force

1. This Agreement shall enter into force on 1 January 1996 for those governments[1] whose agreed coverage is contained in the Annexes of Appendix I of this Agreement, and which have, by signature, accepted the Agreement on 15 April 1994, or have, by that date, signed the Agreement subject to ratification and have subsequently ratified the Agreement before 1 January 1996.

1. For the purpose of this Agreement, the term "government" is deemed to include the competent authorities of the European Union.

Accession

2. Any Member of the WTO may accede to this Agreement on terms to be agreed between that Member and the Parties, with such terms stated in a decision of the Committee. Accession shall take place by deposit with the Director-General of the WTO of an instrument of accession that states the terms so agreed. This Agreement shall enter into force for a Member acceding to it on the 30th day following the deposit of its instrument of accession.

Reservations

3. No Party may enter a reservation in respect of any provision of this Agreement.

Domestic Legislation

4. Each Party shall ensure, not later than the date of entry into force of this Agreement for it, the conformity of its laws, regulations and administrative procedures, and the rules, procedures and practices applied by its procuring entities, with the provisions of this Agreement.

5. Each Party shall inform the Committee of any changes to its laws and regulations relevant to this Agreement and in the administration of such laws and regulations.

Future Negotiations and Future Work Programmes

6. Each Party shall seek to avoid introducing or continuing discriminatory measures that distort open procurement.

7. Not later than the end of three years from the date of entry into force of the Protocol Amending the Agreement on Government Procurement, adopted on 30 March 2012, and periodically thereafter, the Parties shall undertake further negotiations, with a view to improving this Agreement, progressively reducing and eliminating discriminatory measures, and achieving the greatest possible extension of its coverage among all Parties on the basis of mutual reciprocity, taking into consideration the needs of developing countries.

8. (a) The Committee shall undertake further work to facilitate the implementation of this Agreement and the negotiations provided for in paragraph 7, through the adoption of work programmes for the following items:

(i) the treatment of small and medium-sized enterprises;

(ii) the collection and dissemination of statistical data;

(iii) the treatment of sustainable procurement;

(iv) exclusions and restrictions in Parties' Annexes; and

(v) safety standards in international procurement.

(b) The Committee:

(i) may adopt a decision that contains a list of work programmes on additional items, which may be reviewed and updated periodically; and

(ii) shall adopt a decision setting out the work to be undertaken on each particular work programme under subparagraph (a) and any work programme adopted under subparagraph (b)(i).

9. Following the conclusion of the work programme to harmonize rules of origin for goods being undertaken under the Agreement on Rules of Origin in Annex 1A to the WTO Agreement and negotiations regarding trade in services, the Parties shall take the results of that work programme and those negotiations into account in amending Article IV:5, as appropriate.

10. Not later than the end of the fifth year from the date of entry into force of the Protocol Amending the Agreement on Government Procurement, the Committee shall examine the applicability of Article XX:2(b).

Amendments

11. The Parties may amend this Agreement. A decision to adopt an amendment and to submit it for acceptance by the Parties shall be taken by consensus. An amendment shall enter into force:

(a) except as provided for in subparagraph (b), in respect of those Parties that accept it, upon acceptance by two thirds of the Parties and thereafter for each other Party upon acceptance by it;

(b) for all Parties upon acceptance by two thirds of the Parties if it is an amendment that the Committee, by consensus, has determined to be of a nature that would not alter the rights and obligations of the Parties.

Withdrawal

12. Any Party may withdraw from this Agreement. The withdrawal shall take effect upon the expiration of 60 days from the date the Director-Gen-

eral of the WTO receives written notice of the withdrawal. Any Party may, upon such notification, request an immediate meeting of the Committee.

13. Where a Party to this Agreement ceases to be a Member of the WTO, it shall cease to be a Party to this Agreement with effect on the date on which it ceases to be a Member of the WTO.

Non-application of this Agreement between Particular Parties

14. This Agreement shall not apply as between any two Parties where either Party, at the time either Party accepts or accedes to this Agreement, does not consent to such application.

Appendices

15. The Appendices to this Agreement constitute an integral part thereof.

Secretariat

16. This Agreement shall be serviced by the WTO Secretariat.

Deposit

17. This Agreement shall be deposited with the Director-General of the WTO, who shall promptly furnish to each Party a certified true copy of this Agreement, of each rectification or modification thereto pursuant to Article XIX and of each amendment pursuant to paragraph 11, and a notification of each accession thereto pursuant to paragraph 2 and of each withdrawal pursuant to paragraphs 12 or 13.

Registration

18. This Agreement shall be registered in accordance with the provisions of Article 102 of the Charter of the United Nations.

PART IX

Selected Accession Documents and Protocols

Document 51

ACCESSION OF THE PEOPLE'S REPUBLIC OF CHINA*

Decision of 10 November 2001

The Ministerial Conference,

Having regard to paragraph 2 of Article XII and paragraph 1 of Article IX of the Marrakesh Agreement Establishing the World Trade Organization, and the Decision-Making Procedures under Articles IX and XII of the Marrakesh Agreement Establishing the World Trade Organization agreed by the General Council (WT/L/93),

Taking note of the application of the People's Republic of China for accession to the Marrakesh Agreement Establishing the World Trade Organization dated 7 December 1995,

Noting the results of the negotiations directed toward the establishment of the terms of accession of the People's Republic of China to the Marrakesh Agreement Establishing the World Trade Organization and having prepared a Protocol on the Accession of the People's Republic of China,

Decides as follows:

The People's Republic of China may accede to the Marrakesh Agreement Establishing the World Trade Organization on the terms and conditions set out in the Protocol annexed to this decision.

---

*WTO Document WT/L/432, adopted on 23 November 2001.

Protocol on the Accession of the People's Republic of China

Preamble

The World Trade Organization ("WTO"), pursuant to the approval of the Ministerial Conference of the WTO accorded under Article XII of the Marrakesh Agreement Establishing the World Trade Organization ("WTO Agreement"), and the People's Republic of China ("China"),

Recalling that China was an original contracting party to the General Agreement on Tariffs and Trade 1947,

Taking note that China is a signatory to the Final Act Embodying the Results of the Uruguay Round of Multilateral Trade Negotiations,

Taking note of the Report of the Working Party on the Accession of China in document WT/ACC/CHN/49 ("Working Party Report"),

Having regard to the results of the negotiations concerning China's membership in the WTO,

Agree as follows:

Part I—General Provisions

1. General

1. Upon accession, China accedes to the WTO Agreement pursuant to Article XII of that Agreement and thereby becomes a Member of the WTO.

2. The WTO Agreement to which China accedes shall be the WTO Agreement as rectified, amended or otherwise modified by such legal instruments as may have entered into force before the date of accession. This Protocol, which shall include the commitments referred to in paragraph 342 of the Working Party Report, shall be an integral part of the WTO Agreement.

3. Except as otherwise provided for in this Protocol, those obligations in the Multilateral Trade Agreements annexed to the WTO Agreement that are to be implemented over a period of time starting with entry into force of that Agreement shall be implemented by China as if it had accepted that Agreement on the date of its entry into force.

4. China may maintain a measure inconsistent with paragraph 1of Article II of the General Agreement on Trade in Services ("GATS") provided that such a measure is recorded in the List of Article II Exemptions annexed to this Protocol and meets the conditions of the Annex to the GATS on Article II Exemptions.

2. Administration of the Trade Regime

(A) Uniform Administration

1. The provisions of the WTO Agreement and this Protocol shall apply to the entire customs territory of China, including border trade regions and minority autonomous areas, Special Economic Zones, open coastal cities, economic and technical development zones and other areas where special regimes for tariffs, taxes and regulations are established (collectively referred to as "special economic areas").

2. China shall apply and administer in a uniform, impartial and reasonable manner all its laws, regulations and other measures of the central government as well as local regulations, rules and other measures issued or applied at the sub-national level (collectively referred to as "laws, regulations and other measures") pertaining to or affecting trade in goods, services, trade-related aspects of intellectual property rights ("TRIPS") or the control of foreign exchange.

3. China's local regulations, rules and other measures of local governments at the sub-national level shall conform to the obligations undertaken in the WTO Agreement and this Protocol.

4. China shall establish a mechanism under which individuals and enterprises can bring to the attention of the national authorities cases of non-uniform application of the trade regime.

(B) Special Economic Areas

1. China shall notify to the WTO all the relevant laws, regulations and other measures relating to its special economic areas, listing these areas by name and indicating the geographic boundaries that define them. China shall notify the WTO promptly, but in any case within 60 days, of any additions or modifications to its special economic areas, including notification of the laws, regulations and other measures relating thereto.

2. China shall apply to imported products, including physically incorporated components, introduced into the other parts of China's customs territory from the special economic areas, all taxes, charges and measures affecting imports, including import restrictions and customs and tariff charges, that are normally applied to imports into the other parts of China's customs territory.

3. Except as otherwise provided for in this Protocol, in providing preferential arrangements for enterprises within such special economic areas, WTO provisions on non-discrimination and national treatment shall be fully observed.

(C) Transparency

1. China undertakes that only those laws, regulations and other measures pertaining to or affecting trade in goods, services, TRIPS or the control of foreign exchange that are published and readily available to other WTO Members, individuals and enterprises, shall be enforced. In addition, China shall make available to WTO Members, upon request, all laws, regulations and other measures pertaining to or affecting trade in goods, services, TRIPS or the control of foreign exchange before such measures are implemented or enforced. In emergency situations, laws, regulations and other measures shall be made available at the latest when they are implemented or enforced.

2. China shall establish or designate an official journal dedicated to the publication of all laws, regulations and other measures pertaining to or affecting trade in goods, services, TRIPS or the control of foreign exchange and, after publication of its laws, regulations or other measures in such journal, shall provide a reasonable period for comment to the appropriate authorities before such measures are implemented, except for those laws, regulations and other measures involving national security, specific measures setting foreign exchange rates or monetary policy and other measures the publication of which would impede law enforcement. China shall publish this journal on a regular basis and make copies of all issues of this journal readily available to individuals and enterprises.

3. China shall establish or designate an enquiry point where, upon request of any individual, enterprise or WTO Member all information relating to the measures required to be published under paragraph 2(C)1 of this Protocol may be obtained. Replies to requests for information shall generally be provided within 30 days after receipt of a request. In exceptional cases, replies may be provided within 45 days after receipt of a request. Notice of the delay and the reasons therefor shall be provided in writing to the interested party. Replies to WTO Members shall be complete and shall represent the authoritative view of the Chinese government. Accurate and reliable information shall be provided to individuals and enterprises.

(D) Judicial Review

1. China shall establish, or designate, and maintain tribunals, contact points and procedures for the prompt review of all administrative actions relating to the implementation of laws, regulations, judicial decisions and administrative rulings of general application referred to in Article X:1 of the

GATT 1994, Article VI of the GATS and the relevant provisions of the TRIPS Agreement. Such tribunals shall be impartial and independent of the agency entrusted with administrative enforcement and shall not have any substantial interest in the outcome of the matter.

2. Review procedures shall include the opportunity for appeal, without penalty, by individuals or enterprises affected by any administrative action subject to review. If the initial right of appeal is to an administrative body, there shall in all cases be the opportunity to choose to appeal the decision to a judicial body. Notice of the decision on appeal shall be given to the appellant and the reasons for such decision shall be provided in writing. The appellant shall also be informed of any right to further appeal.

3. Non-discrimination

Except as otherwise provided for in this Protocol, foreign individuals and enterprises and foreign-funded enterprises shall be accorded treatment no less favourable than that accorded to other individuals and enterprises in respect of:

(a) the procurement of inputs and goods and services necessary for production and the conditions under which their goods are produced, marketed or sold, in the domestic market and for export; and

(b) the prices and availability of goods and services supplied by national and sub-national authorities and public or state enterprises, in areas including transportation, energy, basic telecommunications, other utilities and factors of production.

4. Special Trade Arrangements

Upon accession, China shall eliminate or bring into conformity with the WTO Agreement all special trade arrangements, including barter trade arrangements, with third countries and separate customs territories, which are not in conformity with the WTO Agreement.

5. Right to Trade

1. Without prejudice to China's right to regulate trade in a manner consistent with the WTO Agreement, China shall progressively liberalize the availability and scope of the right to trade, so that, within three years after accession, all enterprises in China shall have the right to trade in all goods throughout the customs territory of China, except for those goods listed in Annex 2A which continue to be subject to state trading in accordance with this Protocol. Such right to trade shall be the right to import and export goods. All such goods shall be accorded national treatment under Article III

of the GATT 1994, especially paragraph 4 thereof, in respect of their internal sale, offering for sale, purchase, transportation, distribution or use, including their direct access to end-users. For those goods listed in Annex 2B, China shall phase out limitation on the grant of trading rights pursuant to the schedule in that Annex. China shall complete all necessary legislative procedures to implement these provisions during the transition period.

2. Except as otherwise provided for in this Protocol, all foreign individuals and enterprises, including those not invested or registered in China, shall be accorded treatment no less favourable than that accorded to enterprises in China with respect to the right to trade.

6. State Trading

1. China shall ensure that import purchasing procedures of state trading enterprises are fully transparent, and in compliance with the WTO Agreement, and shall refrain from taking any measure to influence or direct state trading enterprises as to the quantity, value, or country of origin of goods purchased or sold, except in accordance with the WTO Agreement.

2. As part of China's notification under the GATT 1994 and the Understanding on the Interpretation of Article XVII of the GATT 1994, China shall also provide full information on the pricing mechanisms of its state trading enterprises for exported goods.

7. Non-Tariff Measures

1. China shall implement the schedule for phased elimination of the measures contained in Annex 3. During the periods specified in Annex 3, the protection afforded by the measures listed in that Annex shall not be increased or expanded in size, scope or duration, nor shall any new measures be applied, unless in conformity with the provisions of the WTO Agreement.

2. In implementing the provisions of Articles III and XI of the GATT 1994 and the Agreement on Agriculture, China shall eliminate and shall not introduce, re-introduce or apply non-tariff measures that cannot be justified under the provisions of the WTO Agreement. For all non-tariff measures, whether or not referred to in Annex 3, that are applied after the date of accession, consistent with the WTO Agreement or this Protocol, China shall allocate and otherwise administer such measures in strict conformity with the provisions of the WTO Agreement, including GATT 1994 and Article XIII thereof, and the Agreement on Import Licensing Procedures, including notification requirements.

3. China shall, upon accession, comply with the TRIMs Agreement, without recourse to the provisions of Article 5 of the TRIMs Agreement.

China shall eliminate and cease to enforce trade and foreign exchange balancing requirements, local content and export or performance requirements made effective through laws, regulations or other measures. Moreover, China will not enforce provisions of contracts imposing such requirements. Without prejudice to the relevant provisions of this Protocol, China shall ensure that the distribution of import licences, quotas, tariff-rate quotas, or any other means of approval for importation, the right of importation or investment by national and sub-national authorities, is not conditioned on: whether competing domestic suppliers of such products exist; or performance requirements of any kind, such as local content, offsets, the transfer of technology, export performance or the conduct of research and development in China.

4. Import and export prohibitions and restrictions, and licensing requirements affecting imports and exports shall only be imposed and enforced by the national authorities or by sub-national authorities with authorization from the national authorities. Such measures which are not imposed by the national authorities or by sub-national authorities with authorization from the national authorities, shall not be implemented or enforced.

8. Import and Export Licensing

1. In implementing the WTO Agreement and provisions of the Agreement on Import Licensing Procedures, China shall undertake the following measures to facilitate compliance with these agreements:

(a) China shall publish on a regular basis the following in the official journal referred to in paragraph 2(C)2 of this Protocol:

- by product, the list of all organizations, including those organizations delegated such authority by the national authorities, that are responsible for authorizing or approving imports or exports, whether through grant of licence or other approval;
- procedures and criteria for obtaining such import or export licences or other approvals, and the conditions for deciding whether they should be granted;
- a list of all products, by tariff number, that are subject to tendering requirements, including information on products subject to such tendering requirements and any changes, pursuant to the Agreement on Import Licensing Procedures;
- a list of all goods and technologies whose import or export are restricted or prohibited; these goods shall also be notified to the Committee on Import Licensing;
- any changes to the list of goods and technologies whose import and export are restricted or prohibited.

Copies of these submissions in one or more official languages of the WTO shall be forwarded to the WTO for circulation to WTO Members and for submission to the Committee on Import Licensing within 75 days of each publication.

(b) China shall notify the WTO of all licensing and quota requirements remaining in effect after accession, listed separately by HS tariff line and with the quantities associated with the restriction, if any, and the justification for maintaining the restriction or its scheduled date of termination.

(c) China shall submit the notification of its import licensing procedures to the Committee on Import Licensing. China shall report annually to the Committee on Import Licensing on its automatic import licensing procedures, explaining the circumstances which give rise to these requirements and justifying the need for their continuation. This report shall also provide the information listed in Article 3 of the Agreement on Import Licensing Procedures.

(d) China shall issue import licences for a minimum duration of validity of six months, except where exceptional circumstances make this impossible. In such cases, China shall promptly notify the Committee on Import Licensing of the exceptional circumstances requiring the shorter period of licence validity.

2. Except as otherwise provided for in this Protocol, foreign individuals and enterprises and foreign-funded enterprises shall be accorded treatment no less favourable than that accorded to other individuals and enterprises in respect of the distribution of import and export licences and quotas.

9. Price Controls

1. China shall, subject to paragraph 2 below, allow prices for traded goods and services in every sector to be determined by market forces, and multi-tier pricing practices for such goods and services shall be eliminated.

2. The goods and services listed in Annex 4 may be subject to price controls, consistent with the WTO Agreement, in particular Article III of the GATT 1994 and Annex 2, paragraphs 3 and 4 of the Agreement on Agriculture. Except in exceptional circumstances, and subject to notification to the WTO, price controls shall not be extended to goods or services beyond those listed in Annex 4, and China shall make best efforts to reduce and eliminate these controls.

3. China shall publish in the official journal the list of goods and services subject to state pricing and changes thereto.

10. Subsidies

1. China shall notify the WTO of any subsidy within the meaning of Article 1 of the Agreement on Subsidies and Countervailing Measures ("SCM Agreement"), granted or maintained in its territory, organized by specific product, including those subsidies defined in Article 3 of the SCM Agreement. The information provided should be as specific as possible, following the requirements of the questionnaire on subsidies as noted in Article 25 of the SCM Agreement.

2. For purposes of applying Articles 1.2 and 2 of the SCM Agreement, subsidies provided to state-owned enterprises will be viewed as specific if, inter alia, state-owned enterprises are the predominant recipients of such subsidies or state-owned enterprises receive disproportionately large amounts of such subsidies.

3. China shall eliminate all subsidy programmes falling within the scope of Article 3 of the SCM Agreement upon accession.

11. Taxes and Charges Levied on Imports and Exports

1. China shall ensure that customs fees or charges applied or administered by national or sub-national authorities, shall be in conformity with the GATT 1994.

2. China shall ensure that internal taxes and charges, including value-added taxes, applied or administered by national or sub-national authorities shall be in conformity with the GATT 1994.

3. China shall eliminate all taxes and charges applied to exports unless specifically provided for in Annex 6 of this Protocol or applied in conformity with the provisions of Article VIII of the GATT 1994.

4. Foreign individuals and enterprises and foreign-funded enterprises shall, upon accession, be accorded treatment no less favourable than that accorded to other individuals and enterprises in respect of the provision of border tax adjustments.

12. Agriculture

1. China shall implement the provisions contained in China's Schedule of Concessions and Commitments on Goods and, as specifically provided in this Protocol, those of the Agreement on Agriculture. In this context, China shall not maintain or introduce any export subsidies on agricultural products.

2. China shall, under the Transitional Review Mechanism, notify fiscal and other transfers between or among state-owned enterprises in the agricultural sector (whether national or sub-national) and other enterprises that operate as state trading enterprises in the agricultural sector.

13. Technical Barriers to Trade

1. China shall publish in the official journal all criteria, whether formal or informal, that are the basis for a technical regulation, standard or conformity assessment procedure.

2. China shall, upon accession, bring into conformity with the TBT Agreement all technical regulations, standards and conformity assessment procedures.

3. China shall apply conformity assessment procedures to imported products only to determine compliance with technical regulations and standards that are consistent with the provisions of this Protocol and the WTO Agreement. Conformity assessment bodies will determine the conformity of imported products with commercial terms of contracts only if authorized by the parties to such contract. China shall ensure that such inspection of products for compliance with the commercial terms of contracts does not affect customs clearance or the granting of import licences for such products.

4. (a) Upon accession, China shall ensure that the same technical regulations, standards and conformity assessment procedures are applied to both imported and domestic products. In order to ensure a smooth transition from the current system, China shall ensure that, upon accession, all certification, safety licensing, and quality licensing bodies and agencies are authorized to undertake these activities for both imported and domestic products, and that, one year after accession, all conformity assessment bodies and agencies are authorized to undertake conformity assessment for both imported and domestic products. The choice of body or agency shall be at the discretion of the applicant. For imported and domestic products, all bodies and agencies shall issue the same mark and charge the same fee. They shall also provide the same processing periods and complaint procedures. Imported products shall not be subject to more than one conformity assessment. China shall publish and make readily available to other WTO Members, individuals, and enterprises full information on the respective responsibilities of its conformity assessment bodies and agencies.

(b) No later than 18 months after accession, China shall assign the respective responsibilities of its conformity assessment bodies solely on the basis of the scope of work and type of product without any consideration of the origin of a product. The respective responsibilities that will be assigned to China's conformity assessment bodies will be notified to the TBT Committee 12 months after accession.

14. Sanitary and Phytosanitary Measures

China shall notify to the WTO all laws, regulations and other measures relating to its sanitary and phytosanitary measures, including product coverage and relevant international standards, guidelines and recommendations, within 30 days after accession.

15. Price Comparability in Determining Subsidies and Dumping

Article VI of the GATT 1994, the Agreement on Implementation of Article VI of the General Agreement on Tariffs and Trade 1994 ("Anti-Dumping Agreement") and the SCM Agreement shall apply in proceedings involving imports of Chinese origin into a WTO Member consistent with the following:

(a) In determining price comparability under Article VI of the GATT 1994 and the Anti-Dumping Agreement, the importing WTO Member shall use either Chinese prices or costs for the industry under investigation or a methodology that is not based on a strict comparison with domestic prices or costs in China based on the following rules:

(i) If the producers under investigation can clearly show that market economy conditions prevail in the industry producing the like product with regard to the manufacture, production and sale of that product, the importing WTO Member shall use Chinese prices or costs for the industry under investigation in determining price comparability;

(ii) The importing WTO Member may use a methodology that is not based on a strict comparison with domestic prices or costs in China if the producers under investigation cannot clearly show that market economy conditions prevail in the industry producing the like product with regard to manufacture, production and sale of that product.

(b) In proceedings under Parts II, III and V of the SCM Agreement, when addressing subsidies described in Articles 14(a), 14(b), 14(c) and 14(d), relevant provisions of the SCM Agreement shall apply; however, if there are special difficulties in that application, the importing WTO Member may then use methodologies for identifying and measuring the subsidy benefit which take into account the possibility that prevailing terms and conditions in China may not always be available as appropriate benchmarks. In applying such methodologies, where practicable, the importing WTO Member should adjust such prevailing terms and conditions before considering the use of terms and conditions prevailing outside China.

(c) The importing WTO Member shall notify methodologies used in accordance with subparagraph (a) to the Committee on Anti-Dumping Practices and shall notify methodologies used in accordance with subparagraph (b) to the Committee on Subsidies and Countervailing Measures.

(d) Once China has established, under the national law of the importing WTO Member, that it is a market economy, the provisions of subparagraph (a) shall be terminated provided that the importing Member's national law contains market economy criteria as of the date of accession. In any event, the provisions of subparagraph (a)(ii) shall expire 15 years after the date of accession. In addition, should China establish, pursuant to the national law of the importing WTO Member, that market economy conditions prevail in a particular industry or sector, the non-market economy provisions of subparagraph (a) shall no longer apply to that industry or sector.

16. Transitional Product-Specific Safeguard Mechanism

1. In cases where products of Chinese origin are being imported into the territory of any WTO Member in such increased quantities or under such conditions as to cause or threaten to cause market disruption to the domestic producers of like or directly competitive products, the WTO Member so affected may request consultations with China with a view to seeking a mutually satisfactory solution, including whether the affected WTO Member should pursue application of a measure under the Agreement on Safeguards. Any such request shall be notified immediately to the Committee on Safeguards.

2. If, in the course of these bilateral consultations, it is agreed that imports of Chinese origin are such a cause and that action is necessary, China shall take such action as to prevent or remedy the market disruption. Any such action shall be notified immediately to the Committee on Safeguards.

3. If consultations do not lead to an agreement between China and the WTO Member concerned within 60 days of the receipt of a request for consultations, the WTO Member affected shall be free, in respect of such products, to withdraw concessions or otherwise to limit imports only to the extent necessary to prevent or remedy such market disruption. Any such action shall be notified immediately to the Committee on Safeguards.

4. Market disruption shall exist whenever imports of an article, like or directly competitive with an article produced by the domestic industry, are increasing rapidly, either absolutely or relatively, so as to be a significant cause of material injury, or threat of material injury to the domestic industry. In determining if market disruption exists, the affected WTO Member shall consider objective factors, including the volume of imports, the effect of imports on prices for like or directly competitive articles, and the effect of such imports on the domestic industry producing like or directly competitive products.

5. Prior to application of a measure pursuant to paragraph 3, the WTO Member taking such action shall provide reasonable public notice to all interested parties and provide adequate opportunity for importers, exporters and other interested parties to submit their views and evidence on the appropriateness of the proposed measure and whether it would be in the public interest. The WTO Member shall provide written notice of the decision to apply a measure, including the reasons for such measure and its scope and duration.

6. A WTO Member shall apply a measure pursuant to this Section only for such period of time as may be necessary to prevent or remedy the market disruption. If a measure is taken as a result of a relative increase in the level of imports, China has the right to suspend the application of substantially equivalent concessions or obligations under the GATT 1994 to the trade of the WTO Member applying the measure, if such measure remains in effect more than two years. However, if a measure is taken as a result of an absolute increase in imports, China has a right to suspend the application of substantially equivalent concessions or obligations under the GATT 1994 to the trade of the WTO Member applying the measure, if such measure remains in effect more than three years. Any such action by China shall be notified immediately to the Committee on Safeguards.

7. In critical circumstances, where delay would cause damage which it would be difficult to repair, the WTO Member so affected may take a provisional safeguard measure pursuant to a preliminary determination that imports have caused or threatened to cause market disruption. In this case, notification of the measures taken to the Committee on Safeguards and a request for bilateral consultations shall be effected immediately thereafter. The duration of the provisional measure shall not exceed 200 days during which the pertinent requirements of paragraphs 1, 2 and 5 shall be met. The duration of any provisional measure shall be counted toward the period provided for under paragraph 6.

8. If a WTO Member considers that an action taken under paragraphs 2, 3 or 7 causes or threatens to cause significant diversions of trade into its market, it may request consultations with China and/or the WTO Member

concerned. Such consultations shall be held within 30 days after the request is notified to the Committee on Safeguards. If such consultations fail to lead to an agreement between China and the WTO Member or Members concerned within 60 days after the notification, the requesting WTO Member shall be free, in respect of such product, to withdraw concessions accorded to or otherwise limit imports from China, to the extent necessary to prevent or remedy such diversions. Such action shall be notified immediately to the Committee on Safeguards.

9. Application of this Section shall be terminated 12 years after the date of accession.

17. Reservations by WTO Members

All prohibitions, quantitative restrictions and other measures maintained by WTO Members against imports from China in a manner inconsistent with the WTO Agreement are listed in Annex 7. All such prohibitions, quantitative restrictions and other measures shall be phased out or dealt with in accordance with mutually agreed terms and timetables as specified in the said Annex.

18. Transitional Review Mechanism

1. Those subsidiary bodies[1] of the WTO which have a mandate covering China's commitments under the WTO Agreement or this Protocol shall, within one year after accession and in accordance with paragraph 4 below, review, as appropriate to their mandate, the implementation by China of the WTO Agreement and of the related provisions of this Protocol. China shall provide relevant information, including information specified in Annex 1A, to each subsidiary body in advance of the review. China can also raise issues relating to any reservations under Section 17 or to any other specific commitments made by other Members in this Protocol, in those subsidiary bodies which have a relevant mandate. Each subsidiary body shall report the results of such review promptly to the relevant Council established by paragraph 5 of Article IV of the WTO Agreement, if applicable, which shall in turn report promptly to the General Council.

2. The General Council shall, within one year after accession, and in accordance with paragraph 4 below, review the implementation by China of the WTO Agreement and the provisions of this Protocol. The General

1. Council for Trade in Goods, Council for Trade-Related Aspects of Intellectual Property Rights, Council for Trade in Services, Committees on Balance-of-Payments Restrictions, Market Access (covering also ITA), Agriculture, Sanitary and Phytosanitary Measures, Technical Barriers to Trade, Subsidies and Countervailing Measures, Anti-Dumping Measures, Customs Valuation, Rules of Origin, Import Licensing, Trade-Related Investment Measures, Safeguards, Trade in Financial Services.

Council shall conduct such review in accordance with the framework set out in Annex 1B and in the light of the results of any reviews held pursuant to paragraph 1. China also can raise issues relating to any reservations under Section 17 or to any other specific commitments made by other Members in this Protocol. The General Council may make recommendations to China and to other Members in these respects.

3. Consideration of issues pursuant to this Section shall be without prejudice to the rights and obligations of any Member, including China, under the WTO Agreement or any Plurilateral Trade Agreement, and shall not preclude or be a precondition to recourse to consultation or other provisions of the WTO Agreement or this Protocol.

4. The review provided for in paragraphs 1 and 2 will take place after accession in each year for eight years. Thereafter there will be a final review in year 10 or at an earlier date decided by the General Council.

Part II—Schedules

1. The Schedules annexed to this Protocol shall become the Schedule of Concessions and Commitments annexed to the GATT 1994 and the Schedule of Specific Commitments annexed to the GATS relating to China. The staging of concessions and commitments listed in the Schedules shall be implemented as specified in the relevant parts of the relevant Schedules.

2. For the purpose of the reference in paragraph 6(a) of Article II of the GATT 1994 to the date of that Agreement, the applicable date in respect of the Schedules of Concessions and Commitments annexed to this Protocol shall be the date of accession.

Part III—Final Provisions

1. This Protocol shall be open for acceptance, by signature or otherwise, by China until 1 January 2002.

2. This Protocol shall enter into force on the thirtieth day following the day of its acceptance.

3. This Protocol shall be deposited with the Director-General of the WTO. The Director-General shall promptly furnish a certified copy of this Protocol and a notification of acceptance by China thereof, pursuant to paragraph 1 of Part III of this Protocol, to each WTO Member and to China.

4. This Protocol shall be registered in accordance with the provisions of Article 102 of the Charter of the United Nations.

Done at Doha this tenth day of November two thousand and one, in a single copy, in the English, French and Spanish languages, each text being authentic, except that a Schedule annexed hereto may specify that it is authentic in only one or more of these languages.

[Annexes omitted]

Document 52

DECISION ACCESSION OF THE RUSSIAN FEDERATION

Decision of 16 December 2011

The Ministerial Conference,

Having regard to paragraph 2 of Article XII and paragraph 1 of Article IX of the Marrakesh Agreement Establishing the World Trade Organization (the "WTO Agreement"), and the Decision-Making Procedures under Articles IX and XII of the Marrakesh Agreement Establishing the World Trade Organization agreed by the General Council (WT/L/93);

Taking note of the application of the Russian Federation for accession to the Marrakesh Agreement Establishing the World Trade Organization dated 14 June 1993 (L/7243);

Noting the results of the negotiations directed toward the establishment of the terms of accession of the Russian Federation to the WTO Agreement and having prepared a Draft Protocol on the Accession of the Russian Federation;

Decides as follows:

The Russian Federation may accede to the WTO Agreement on the terms and conditions set-out in the Protocol annexed to this Decision.

Protocol on the Accession of the Russian Federation

Preamble

The World Trade Organization (hereinafter referred to as the "WTO"), pursuant to the approval of the Ministerial Conference accorded under Article XII of the Marrakesh Agreement Establishing the World Trade Organization (hereinafter referred to as the "WTO Agreement"), and the Russian Federation,

Taking note of the Report of the Working Party on the Accession of the Russian Federation to the WTO Agreement reproduced in document WT/ACC/RUS/70, dated 17 November 2011 (hereinafter referred to as the "Working Party Report"),

Having regard to the results of the negotiations on the accession of the Russian Federation to the WTO Agreement,

Agree as follows:

Part I—General

1. Upon entry into force of this Protocol pursuant to paragraph 8, the Russian Federation accedes to the WTO Agreement pursuant to Article XII of that Agreement and thereby becomes a Member of the WTO.

2. The WTO Agreement to which the Russian Federation accedes shall be the WTO Agreement, including the Explanatory Notes to that Agreement, as rectified, amended or otherwise modified by such legal instruments as may have entered into force before the date of entry into force of this Protocol. This Protocol, which shall include the commitments referred to in paragraph 1450 of the Working Party Report, shall be an integral part of the WTO Agreement.

3. Except as otherwise provided for in paragraph 1450 of the Working Party Report, those obligations in the Multilateral Trade Agreements annexed to the WTO Agreement that are to be implemented over a period of time starting with the entry into force of that Agreement shall be implemented by the Russian Federation as if it had accepted that Agreement on the date of its entry into force.

4. The Russian Federation may maintain a measure inconsistent with paragraph 1 of Article II of the General Agreement on Trade in Services

(hereinafter referred to as "GATS") provided that such a measure was recorded in the list of Article II Exemptions annexed to this Protocol and meets the conditions of the Annex to the GATS on Article II Exemptions.

Part II—Schedules

5. The Schedules reproduced in Annex I to this Protocol shall become the Schedule of Concessions and Commitments annexed to the General Agreement on Tariffs and Trade 1994 (hereinafter referred to as the "GATT 1994") and the Schedule of Specific Commitments annexed to the GATS relating to the Russian Federation. The staging of the concessions and commitments listed in the Schedules shall be implemented as specified in the relevant parts of the respective Schedules.

6. For the purpose of the reference in paragraph 6(a) of Article II of the GATT 1994 to the date of that Agreement, the applicable date in respect of the Schedules of Concessions and Commitments annexed to this Protocol shall be the date of entry into force of this Protocol.

Part III—Final Provisions

7. This Protocol shall be open for acceptance, by signature or otherwise, by the Russian Federation within a period of 220 days from the approval of the Protocol of Accession of the Russian Federation.

8. This Protocol shall enter into force on the thirtieth day following the day upon which it shall have been accepted by the Russian Federation.

9. This Protocol shall be deposited with the Director-General of the WTO. The Director-General of the WTO shall promptly furnish a certified copy of this Protocol and a notification of acceptance by the Russian Federation thereto pursuant to paragraph 7 to each Member of the WTO and to the Russian Federation.

10. This Protocol shall be registered in accordance with the provisions of Article 102 of the Charter of the United Nations.

Done at Geneva this [sixteenth] day of [December two thousand and eleven], in a single copy in the English, French and Spanish languages, each text being authentic, except that a Schedule annexed hereto may specify that it its authentic in only one of these languages.

[Annexes omitted]

PART X

Selected Post-1994 Declarations and Decisions

Document 53

SINGAPORE DECLARATION

Purpose

1. We, the Ministers, have met in Singapore from 9 to 13 December 1996 for the first regular biennial meeting of the WTO at Ministerial level, as called for in Article IV of the Agreement Establishing the World Trade Organization, to further strengthen the WTO as a forum for negotiation, the continuing liberalization of trade within a rule-based system, and the multilateral review and assessment of trade policies, and in particular to:

- assess the implementation of our commitments under the WTO Agreements and decisions;
- review the ongoing negotiations and Work Programme;
- examine developments in world trade; and
- address the challenges of an evolving world economy.

Trade and Economic Growth

2. For nearly 50 years Members have sought to fulfil, first in the GATT and now in the WTO, the objectives reflected in the preamble to the WTO Agreement of conducting our trade relations with a view to raising standards of living worldwide. The rise in global trade facilitated by trade liberalization within the rules-based system has created more and better-paid jobs in many countries. The achievements of the WTO during its first two years bear witness to our desire to work together to make the most of the possibilities that the multilateral system provides to promote sustainable growth and development while contributing to a more stable and secure climate in international relations.

Integration of Economies; Opportunities and Challenges

3. We believe that the scope and pace of change in the international economy, including the growth in trade in services and direct investment, and the increasing integration of economies offer unprecedented opportunities for improved growth, job creation, and development. These developments require adjustment by economies and societies. They also pose challenges to the trading system. We commit ourselves to address these challenges.

Core Labour Standards

4. We renew our commitment to the observance of internationally recognized core labour standards. The International Labour Organization (ILO) is the competent body to set and deal with these standards, and we affirm our support for its work in promoting them. We believe that economic growth and development fostered by increased trade and further trade liberalization contribute to the promotion of these standards. We reject the use of labour standards for protectionist purposes, and agree that the comparative advantage of countries, particularly low-wage developing countries, must in no way be put into question. In this regard, we note that the WTO and ILO Secretariats will continue their existing collaboration.

Marginalization

5. We commit ourselves to address the problem of marginalization for least-developed countries, and the risk of it for certain developing countries. We will also continue to work for greater coherence in international economic policy-making and for improved coordination between the WTO and other agencies in providing technical assistance.

Role of WTO

6. In pursuit of the goal of sustainable growth and development for the common good, we envisage a world where trade flows freely. To this end we renew our commitment to:

- a fair, equitable and more open rule-based system;
- progressive liberalization and elimination of tariff and non-tariff barriers to trade in goods;
- progressive liberalization of trade in services;
- rejection of all forms of protectionism;
- elimination of discriminatory treatment in international trade relations;
- integration of developing and least-developed countries and economies in transition into the multilateral system; and
- the maximum possible level of transparency.

Regional Agreements

7. We note that trade relations of WTO Members are being increasingly influenced by regional trade agreements, which have expanded vastly in number, scope and coverage. Such initiatives can promote further liberalization and may assist least-developed, developing and transition economies in integrating into the international trading system. In this context, we note the importance of existing regional arrangements involving developing and least-developed countries. The expansion and extent of regional trade agreements make it important to analyse whether the system of WTO rights and obligations as it relates to regional trade agreements needs to be further clarified. We reaffirm the primacy of the multilateral trading system, which includes a framework for the development of regional trade agreements, and we renew our commitment to ensure that regional trade agreements are complementary to it and consistent with its rules. In this regard, we welcome the establishment and endorse the work of the new Committee on Regional Trade Agreements. We shall continue to work through progressive liberalization in the WTO as we are committed in the WTO Agreement and Decisions adopted at Marrakesh, and in so doing facilitate mutually supportive processes of global and regional trade liberalization.

Accessions

8. It is important that the 28 applicants now negotiating accession contribute to completing the accession process by accepting the WTO rules and by offering meaningful market access commitments. We will work to bring these applicants expeditiously into the WTO system.

Dispute Settlement

9. The Dispute Settlement Understanding (DSU) offers a means for the settlement of disputes among Members that is unique in international agreements. We consider its impartial and transparent operation to be of fundamental importance in assuring the resolution of trade disputes, and in fostering the implementation and application of the WTO agreements. The Understanding, with its predictable procedures, including the possibility of appeal of panel decisions to an Appellate Body and provisions on implementation of recommendations, has improved Members' means of resolving their differences. We believe that the DSU has worked effectively during its first two years. We also note the role that several WTO bodies have played in helping to avoid disputes. We renew our determination to abide by the rules and procedures of the DSU and other WTO agreements in the conduct of our trade relations and the settlement of disputes. We are confident that longer experience with the DSU, including the implementation of panel and appellate recommendations, will further enhance the effectiveness and credibility of the dispute settlement system.

Implementation

10. We attach high priority to full and effective implementation of the WTO Agreement in a manner consistent with the goal of trade liberalization. Implementation thus far has been generally satisfactory, although some Members have expressed dissatisfaction with certain aspects. It is clear that further effort in this area is required, as indicated by the relevant WTO bodies in their reports. Implementation of the specific commitments scheduled by Members with respect to market access in industrial goods and trade in services appears to be proceeding smoothly. With respect to industrial market access, monitoring of implementation would be enhanced by the timely availability of trade and tariff data. Progress has been made also in advancing the WTO reform programme in agriculture, including in implementation of agreed market access concessions and domestic subsidy and export subsidy commitments.

Notifications and Legislation

11. Compliance with notification requirements has not been fully satisfactory. Because the WTO system relies on mutual monitoring as a means to assess implementation, those Members which have not submitted notifications in a timely manner, or whose notifications are not complete, should renew their efforts. At the same time, the relevant bodies should take appropriate steps to promote full compliance while considering practical proposals for simplifying the notification process.

12. Where legislation is needed to implement WTO rules, Members are mindful of their obligations to complete their domestic legislative process without further delay. Those Members entitled to transition periods are urged to take steps as they deem necessary to ensure timely implementation of obligations as they come into effect. Each Member should carefully review all its existing or proposed legislation, programmes and measures to ensure their full compatibility with the WTO obligations, and should carefully consider points made during review in the relevant WTO bodies regarding the WTO consistency of legislation, programmes and measures, and make appropriate changes where necessary.

Developing Countries

13. The integration of developing countries in the multilateral trading system is important for their economic development and for global trade expansion. In this connection, we recall that the WTO Agreement embodies provisions conferring differential and more favourable treatment for developing countries, including special attention to the particular situation of least-developed countries. We acknowledge the fact that developing country Members have undertaken significant new commitments, both substantive

and procedural, and we recognize the range and complexity of the efforts that they are making to comply with them. In order to assist them in these efforts, including those with respect to notification and legislative requirements, we will improve the availability of technical assistance under the agreed guidelines. We have also agreed to recommendations relative to the decision we took at Marrakesh concerning the possible negative effects of the agricultural reform programme on least-developed and net food-importing developing countries.

Least-Developed Countries

14. We remain concerned by the problems of the least-developed countries and have agreed to:

- a Plan of Action, including provision for taking positive measures, for example duty-free access, on an autonomous basis, aimed at improving their overall capacity to respond to the opportunities offered by the trading system;
- seek to give operational content to the Plan of Action, for example, by enhancing conditions for investment and providing predictable and favourable market access conditions for LLDCs' products, to foster the expansion and diversification of their exports to the markets of all developed countries; and in the case of relevant developing countries in the context of the Global System of Trade Preferences; and
- organize a meeting with UNCTAD and the International Trade Centre as soon as possible in 1997, with the participation of aid agencies, multilateral financial institutions and least-developed countries to foster an integrated approach to assisting these countries in enhancing their trading opportunities.

Textiles and Clothing

15. We confirm our commitment to full and faithful implementation of the provisions of the Agreement on Textiles and Clothing (ATC). We stress the importance of the integration of textile products, as provided for in the ATC, into GATT 1994 under its strengthened rules and disciplines because of its systemic significance for the rule-based, non-discriminatory trading system and its contribution to the increase in export earnings of developing countries. We attach importance to the implementation of this Agreement so as to ensure an effective transition to GATT 1994 by way of integration which is progressive in character. The use of safeguard measures in accordance with ATC provisions should be as sparing as possible. We note concerns regarding the use of other trade distortive measures and circumvention. We reiterate the importance of fully implementing the provisions of the ATC relating to small suppliers, new entrants and least-developed

country Members, as well as those relating to cotton-producing exporting Members. We recognize the importance of wool products for some developing country Members. We reaffirm that as part of the integration process and with reference to the specific commitments undertaken by the Members as a result of the Uruguay Round, all Members shall take such action as may be necessary to abide by GATT 1994 rules and disciplines so as to achieve improved market access for textiles and clothing products. We agree that, keeping in view its quasi-judicial nature, the Textiles Monitoring Body (TMB) should achieve transparency in providing rationale for its findings and recommendations. We expect that the TMB shall make findings and recommendations whenever called upon to do so under the Agreement. We emphasize the responsibility of the Goods Council in overseeing, in accordance with Article IV:5 of the WTO Agreement and Article 8 of the ATC, the functioning of the ATC, whose implementation is being supervised by the TMB.

Trade and Environment

16. The Committee on Trade and Environment has made an important contribution towards fulfilling its Work Programme. The Committee has been examining and will continue to examine, inter alia, the scope of the complementarities between trade liberalization, economic development and environmental protection. Full implementation of the WTO Agreements will make an important contribution to achieving the objectives of sustainable development. The work of the Committee has underlined the importance of policy coordination at the national level in the area of trade and environment. In this connection, the work of the Committee has been enriched by the participation of environmental as well as trade experts from Member governments and the further participation of such experts in the Committee's deliberations would be welcomed. The breadth and complexity of the issues covered by the Committee's Work Programme shows that further work needs to be undertaken on all items of its agenda, as contained in its report. We intend to build on the work accomplished thus far, and therefore direct the Committee to carry out its work, reporting to the General Council, under its existing terms of reference.

Services Negotiations

17. The fulfilment of the objectives agreed at Marrakesh for negotiations on the improvement of market access in services—in financial services, movement of natural persons, maritime transport services and basic telecommunications—has proved to be difficult. The results have been below expectations. In three areas, it has been necessary to prolong negotiations beyond the original deadlines. We are determined to obtain a progressively higher level of liberalization in services on a mutually advantageous basis with appropriate flexibility for individual developing country Members, as

envisaged in the Agreement, in the continuing negotiations and those scheduled to begin no later than 1 January 2000. In this context, we look forward to full MFN agreements based on improved market access commitments and national treatment. Accordingly, we will:

- achieve a successful conclusion to the negotiations on basic telecommunications in February 1997; and
- resume financial services negotiations in April 1997 with the aim of achieving significantly improved market access commitments with a broader level of participation in the agreed time frame.
- With the same broad objectives in mind, we also look forward to a successful conclusion of the negotiations on Maritime Transport Services in the next round of negotiations on services liberalization.

In professional services, we shall aim at completing the work on the accountancy sector by the end of 1997, and will continue to develop multilateral disciplines and guidelines. In this connection, we encourage the successful completion of international standards in the accountancy sector by IFAC, IASC, and IOSCO. With respect to GATS rules, we shall undertake the necessary work with a view to completing the negotiations on safeguards by the end of 1997. We also note that more analytical work will be needed on emergency safeguards measures, government procurement in services and subsidies.

ITA and Pharmaceuticals

18. Taking note that a number of Members have agreed on a Declaration on Trade in Information Technology Products, we welcome the initiative taken by a number of WTO Members and other States or separate customs territories which have applied to accede to the WTO, who have agreed to tariff elimination for trade in information technology products on an MFN basis as well as the addition by a number of Members of over 400 products to their lists of tariff-free products in pharmaceuticals.

Work Programme and Built-In Agenda

19. Bearing in mind that an important aspect of WTO activities is a continuous overseeing of the implementation of various agreements, a periodic examination and updating of the WTO Work Programme is a key to enable the WTO to fulfil its objectives. In this context, we endorse the reports of the various WTO bodies. A major share of the Work Programme stems from the WTO Agreement and decisions adopted at Marrakesh. As part of these Agreements and decisions we agreed to a number of provisions calling for future negotiations on Agriculture, Services and aspects of TRIPS, or reviews and other work on Anti-Dumping, Customs Valuation, Dispute Settlement Understanding, Import Licensing, Preshipment Inspection,

Rules of Origin, Sanitary and Phyto-Sanitary Measures, Safeguards, Subsidies and Countervailing Measures, Technical Barriers to Trade, Textiles and Clothing, Trade Policy Review Mechanism, Trade-Related Aspects of Intellectual Property Rights and Trade-Related Investment Measures. We agree to a process of analysis and exchange of information, where provided for in the conclusions and recommendations of the relevant WTO bodies, on the Built-in Agenda issues, to allow Members to better understand the issues involved and identify their interests before undertaking the agreed negotiations and reviews. We agree that:

- the time frames established in the Agreements will be respected in each case;
- the work undertaken shall not prejudge the scope of future negotiations where such negotiations are called for; and
- the work undertaken shall not prejudice the nature of the activity agreed upon (i.e. negotiation or review).

Investment and Competition

20. Having regard to the existing WTO provisions on matters related to investment and competition policy and the built-in agenda in these areas, including under the TRIMs Agreement, and on the understanding that the work undertaken shall not prejudge whether negotiations will be initiated in the future, we also agree to:

- establish a working group to examine the relationship between trade and investment; and
- establish a working group to study issues raised by Members relating to the interaction between trade and competition policy, including anti-competitive practices, in order to identify any areas that may merit further consideration in the WTO framework.

These groups shall draw upon each other's work if necessary and also draw upon and be without prejudice to the work in UNCTAD and other appropriate intergovernmental fora. As regards UNCTAD, we welcome the work under way as provided for in the Midrand Declaration and the contribution it can make to the understanding of issues. In the conduct of the work of the working groups, we encourage cooperation with the above organizations to make the best use of available resources and to ensure that the development dimension is taken fully into account. The General Council will keep the work of each body under review, and will determine after two years how the work of each body should proceed. It is clearly understood that future negotiations, if any, regarding multilateral disciplines in these areas, will take place only after an explicit consensus decision is taken among WTO Members regarding such negotiations.

Transparency in Government Procurement

21. We further agree to:

- establish a working group to conduct a study on transparency in government procurement practices, taking into account national policies, and, based on this study, to develop elements for inclusion in an appropriate agreement; and
- direct the Council for Trade in Goods to undertake exploratory and analytical work, drawing on the work of other relevant international organizations, on the simplification of trade procedures in order to assess the scope for WTO rules in this area.

Trade Facilitation

22. In the organization of the work referred to in paragraphs 20 and 21, careful attention will be given to minimizing the burdens on delegations, especially those with more limited resources, and to coordinating meetings with those of relevant UNCTAD bodies. The technical cooperation programme of the Secretariat will be available to developing and, in particular, least-developed country Members to facilitate their participation in this work.

23. Noting that the 50th anniversary of the multilateral trading system will occur early in 1998, we instruct the General Council to consider how this historic event can best be commemorated.

Finally, we express our warmest thanks to the Chairman of the Ministerial Conference, Mr. Yeo Cheow Tong, for his personal contribution to the success of this Ministerial Conference. We also want to express our sincere gratitude to Prime Minister Goh Chok Tong, his colleagues in the Government of Singapore and the people of Singapore for their warm hospitality and the excellent organization they have provided. The fact that this first Ministerial Conference of the WTO has been held at Singapore is an additional manifestation of Singapore's commitment to an open world trading system.

Document 54

DOHA DECLARATION*

1. The multilateral trading system embodied in the World Trade Organization has contributed significantly to economic growth, development and employment throughout the past fifty years. We are determined, particularly in the light of the global economic slowdown, to maintain the process of reform and liberalization of trade policies, thus ensuring that the system plays its full part in promoting recovery, growth and development. We therefore strongly reaffirm the principles and objectives set out in the Marrakesh Agreement Establishing the World Trade Organization, and pledge to reject the use of protectionism.

2. International trade can play a major role in the promotion of economic development and the alleviation of poverty. We recognize the need for all our peoples to benefit from the increased opportunities and welfare gains that the multilateral trading system generates. The majority of WTO Members are developing countries. We seek to place their needs and interests at the heart of the Work Programme adopted in this Declaration. Recalling the Preamble to the Marrakesh Agreement, we shall continue to make positive efforts designed to ensure that developing countries, and especially the least-developed among them, secure a share in the growth of world trade commensurate with the needs of their economic development. In this context, enhanced market access, balanced rules, and well targeted, sustainably financed technical assistance and capacity-building programmes have important roles to play.

3. We recognize the particular vulnerability of the least-developed countries and the special structural difficulties they face in the global economy.

*Ministerial Declaration, adopted on 14 November 2001, WTO document WT/MIN(01)/DEC/1.

We are committed to addressing the marginalization of least-developed countries in international trade and to improving their effective participation in the multilateral trading system. We recall the commitments made by Ministers at our meetings in Marrakesh, Singapore and Geneva, and by the international community at the Third UN Conference on Least-Developed Countries in Brussels, to help least-developed countries secure beneficial and meaningful integration into the multilateral trading system and the global economy. We are determined that the WTO will play its part in building effectively on these commitments under the Work Programme we are establishing.

4. We stress our commitment to the WTO as the unique forum for global trade rule-making and liberalization, while also recognizing that regional trade agreements can play an important role in promoting the liberalization and expansion of trade and in fostering development.

5. We are aware that the challenges Members face in a rapidly changing international environment cannot be addressed through measures taken in the trade field alone. We shall continue to work with the Bretton Woods institutions for greater coherence in global economic policy-making.

6. We strongly reaffirm our commitment to the objective of sustainable development, as stated in the Preamble to the Marrakesh Agreement. We are convinced that the aims of upholding and safeguarding an open and non-discriminatory multilateral trading system, and acting for the protection of the environment and the promotion of sustainable development can and must be mutually supportive. We take note of the efforts by Members to conduct national environmental assessments of trade policies on a voluntary basis. We recognize that under WTO rules no country should be prevented from taking measures for the protection of human, animal or plant life or health, or of the environment at the levels it considers appropriate, subject to the requirement that they are not applied in a manner which would constitute a means of arbitrary or unjustifiable discrimination between countries where the same conditions prevail, or a disguised restriction on international trade, and are otherwise in accordance with the provisions of the WTO Agreements. We welcome the WTO's continued cooperation with UNEP and other inter-governmental environmental organizations. We encourage efforts to promote cooperation between the WTO and relevant international environmental and developmental organizations, especially in the lead-up to the World Summit on Sustainable Development to be held in Johannesburg, South Africa, in September 2002.

7. We reaffirm the right of Members under the General Agreement on Trade in Services to regulate, and to introduce new regulations on, the supply of services.

8. We reaffirm our declaration made at the Singapore Ministerial Conference regarding internationally recognized core labour standards. We take note of work under way in the International Labour Organization (ILO) on the social dimension of globalization.

9. We note with particular satisfaction that this Conference has completed the WTO accession procedures for China and Chinese Taipei. We also welcome the accession as new Members, since our last Session, of Albania, Croatia, Georgia, Jordan, Lithuania, Moldova and Oman, and note the extensive market-access commitments already made by these countries on accession. These accessions will greatly strengthen the multilateral trading system, as will those of the 28 countries now negotiating their accession. We therefore attach great importance to concluding accession proceedings as quickly as possible. In particular, we are committed to accelerating the accession of least-developed countries.

10. Recognizing the challenges posed by an expanding WTO membership, we confirm our collective responsibility to ensure internal transparency and the effective participation of all Members. While emphasizing the intergovernmental character of the organization, we are committed to making the WTO's operations more transparent, including through more effective and prompt dissemination of information, and to improve dialogue with the public. We shall therefore at the national and multilateral levels continue to promote a better public understanding of the WTO and to communicate the benefits of a liberal, rules-based multilateral trading system.

11. In view of these considerations, we hereby agree to undertake the broad and balanced Work Programme set out below. This incorporates both an expanded negotiating agenda and other important decisions and activities necessary to address the challenges facing the multilateral trading system.

Work Programme

Implementation-Related Issues and Concerns

12. We attach the utmost importance to the implementation-related issues and concerns raised by Members and are determined to find appropriate solutions to them. In this connection, and having regard to the General Council Decisions of 3 May and 15 December 2000, we further adopt the Decision on Implementation-Related Issues and Concerns in document WT/MIN(01)/17 to address a number of implementation problems faced by Members. We agree that negotiations on outstanding implementation issues shall be an integral part of the Work Programme we are establishing, and that agreements reached at an early stage in these negotiations shall be treated in accordance with the provisions of paragraph 47 below. In this regard, we shall proceed as follows: (a) where we provide a

specific negotiating mandate in this Declaration, the relevant implementation issues shall be addressed under that mandate; (b) the other outstanding implementation issues shall be addressed as a matter of priority by the relevant WTO bodies, which shall report to the Trade Negotiations Committee, established under paragraph 46 below, by the end of 2002 for appropriate action.

Agriculture

13. We recognize the work already undertaken in the negotiations initiated in early 2000 under Article 20 of the Agreement on Agriculture, including the large number of negotiating proposals submitted on behalf of a total of 121 Members. We recall the long-term objective referred to in the Agreement to establish a fair and market-oriented trading system through a programme of fundamental reform encompassing strengthened rules and specific commitments on support and protection in order to correct and prevent restrictions and distortions in world agricultural markets. We reconfirm our commitment to this programme. Building on the work carried out to date and without prejudging the outcome of the negotiations we commit ourselves to comprehensive negotiations aimed at: substantial improvements in market access; reductions of, with a view to phasing out, all forms of export subsidies; and substantial reductions in trade-distorting domestic support. We agree that special and differential treatment for developing countries shall be an integral part of all elements of the negotiations and shall be embodied in the Schedules of concessions and commitments and as appropriate in the rules and disciplines to be negotiated, so as to be operationally effective and to enable developing countries to effectively take account of their development needs, including food security and rural development. We take note of the non-trade concerns reflected in the negotiating proposals submitted by Members and confirm that non-trade concerns will be taken into account in the negotiations as provided for in the Agreement on Agriculture.

14. Modalities for the further commitments, including provisions for special and differential treatment, shall be established no later than 31 March 2003. Participants shall submit their comprehensive draft Schedules based on these modalities no later than the date of the Fifth Session of the Ministerial Conference. The negotiations, including with respect to rules and disciplines and related legal texts, shall be concluded as part and at the date of conclusion of the negotiating agenda as a whole.

Services

15. The negotiations on trade in services shall be conducted with a view to promoting the economic growth of all trading partners and the development of developing and least-developed countries. We recognize the work

already undertaken in the negotiations, initiated in January 2000 under Article XIX of the General Agreement on Trade in Services, and the large number of proposals submitted by Members on a wide range of sectors and several horizontal issues, as well as on movement of natural persons. We reaffirm the Guidelines and Procedures for the Negotiations adopted by the Council for Trade in Services on 28 March 2001 as the basis for continuing the negotiations, with a view to achieving the objectives of the General Agreement on Trade in Services, as stipulated in the Preamble, Article IV and Article XIX of that Agreement. Participants shall submit initial requests for specific commitments by 30 June 2002 and initial offers by 31 March 2003.

Market Access for Non-Agricultural Products

16. We agree to negotiations which shall aim, by modalities to be agreed, to reduce or as appropriate eliminate tariffs, including the reduction or elimination of tariff peaks, high tariffs, and tariff escalation, as well as non-tariff barriers, in particular on products of export interest to developing countries. Product coverage shall be comprehensive and without *a priori* exclusions. The negotiations shall take fully into account the special needs and interests of developing and least-developed country participants, including through less than full reciprocity in reduction commitments, in accordance with the relevant provisions of Article XXVIII *bis* of GATT 1994 and the provisions cited in paragraph 50 below. To this end, the modalities to be agreed will include appropriate studies and capacity-building measures to assist least-developed countries to participate effectively in the negotiations.

Trade-Related Aspects of Intellectual Property Rights

17. We stress the importance we attach to implementation and interpretation of the Agreement on Trade-Related Aspects of Intellectual Property Rights (TRIPS Agreement) in a manner supportive of public health, by promoting both access to existing medicines and research and development into new medicines and, in this connection, are adopting a separate Declaration.

18. With a view to completing the work started in the Council for Trade-Related Aspects of Intellectual Property Rights (Council for TRIPS) on the implementation of Article 23.4, we agree to negotiate the establishment of a multilateral system of notification and registration of geographical indications for wines and spirits by the Fifth Session of the Ministerial Conference. We note that issues related to the extension of the protection of geographical indications provided for in Article 23 to products other than wines and spirits will be addressed in the Council for TRIPS pursuant to paragraph 12 of this Declaration.

19. We instruct the Council for TRIPS, in pursuing its work programme including under the review of Article 27.3(b), the review of the implementation of the TRIPS Agreement under Article 71.1 and the work foreseen pursuant to paragraph 12 of this Declaration, to examine, *inter alia*, the relationship between the TRIPS Agreement and the Convention on Biological Diversity, the protection of traditional knowledge and folklore, and other relevant new developments raised by Members pursuant to Article 71.1. In undertaking this work, the TRIPS Council shall be guided by the objectives and principles set out in Articles 7 and 8 of the TRIPS Agreement and shall take fully into account the development dimension.

Relationship Between Trade and Investment

20. Recognizing the case for a multilateral framework to secure transparent, stable and predictable conditions for long-term cross-border investment, particularly foreign direct investment, that will contribute to the expansion of trade, and the need for enhanced technical assistance and capacity-building in this area as referred to in paragraph 21, we agree that negotiations will take place after the Fifth Session of the Ministerial Conference on the basis of a decision to be taken, by explicit consensus, at that Session on modalities of negotiations.

21. We recognize the needs of developing and least-developed countries for enhanced support for technical assistance and capacity building in this area, including policy analysis and development so that they may better evaluate the implications of closer multilateral cooperation for their development policies and objectives, and human and institutional development. To this end, we shall work in cooperation with other relevant intergovernmental organisations, including UNCTAD, and through appropriate regional and bilateral channels, to provide strengthened and adequately resourced assistance to respond to these needs.

22. In the period until the Fifth Session, further work in the Working Group on the Relationship Between Trade and Investment will focus on the clarification of: scope and definition; transparency; non-discrimination; modalities for pre-establishment commitments based on a GATS-type, positive list approach; development provisions; exceptions and balance-of-payments safeguards; consultation and the settlement of disputes between Members. Any framework should reflect in a balanced manner the interests of home and host countries, and take due account of the development policies and objectives of host governments as well as their right to regulate in the public interest. The special development, trade and financial needs of developing and least-developed countries should be taken into account as an integral part of any framework, which should enable Members to undertake obligations and commitments commensurate with their individual needs and circumstances. Due regard should be paid to other relevant WTO

provisions. Account should be taken, as appropriate, of existing bilateral and regional arrangements on investment.

Interaction Between Trade and Competition Policy

23. Recognizing the case for a multilateral framework to enhance the contribution of competition policy to international trade and development, and the need for enhanced technical assistance and capacity-building in this area as referred to in paragraph 24, we agree that negotiations will take place after the Fifth Session of the Ministerial Conference on the basis of a decision to be taken, by explicit consensus, at that Session on modalities of negotiations.

24. We recognize the needs of developing and least-developed countries for enhanced support for technical assistance and capacity building in this area, including policy analysis and development so that they may better evaluate the implications of closer multilateral cooperation for their development policies and objectives, and human and institutional development. To this end, we shall work in cooperation with other relevant intergovernmental organisations, including UNCTAD, and through appropriate regional and bilateral channels, to provide strengthened and adequately resourced assistance to respond to these needs.

25. In the period until the Fifth Session, further work in the Working Group on the Interaction between Trade and Competition Policy will focus on the clarification of: core principles, including transparency, non-discrimination and procedural fairness, and provisions on hardcore cartels; modalities for voluntary cooperation; and support for progressive reinforcement of competition institutions in developing countries through capacity building. Full account shall be taken of the needs of developing and least-developed country participants and appropriate flexibility provided to address them.

Transparency in Government Procurement

26. Recognizing the case for a multilateral agreement on transparency in government procurement and the need for enhanced technical assistance and capacity building in this area, we agree that negotiations will take place after the Fifth Session of the Ministerial Conference on the basis of a decision to be taken, by explicit consensus, at that Session on modalities of negotiations. These negotiations will build on the progress made in the Working Group on Transparency in Government Procurement by that time and take into account participants' development priorities, especially those of least-developed country participants. Negotiations shall be limited to the transparency aspects and therefore will not restrict the scope for countries to give preferences to domestic supplies and suppliers. We commit ourselves to

ensuring adequate technical assistance and support for capacity building both during the negotiations and after their conclusion.

Trade Facilitation

27. Recognizing the case for further expediting the movement, release and clearance of goods, including goods in transit, and the need for enhanced technical assistance and capacity building in this area, we agree that negotiations will take place after the Fifth Session of the Ministerial Conference on the basis of a decision to be taken, by explicit consensus, at that Session on modalities of negotiations. In the period until the Fifth Session, the Council for Trade in Goods shall review and as appropriate, clarify and improve relevant aspects of Articles V, VIII and X of the GATT 1994 and identify the trade facilitation needs and priorities of Members, in particular developing and least-developed countries. We commit ourselves to ensuring adequate technical assistance and support for capacity building in this area.

WTO Rules

28. In the light of experience and of the increasing application of these instruments by Members, we agree to negotiations aimed at clarifying and improving disciplines under the Agreements on Implementation of Article VI of the GATT 1994 and on Subsidies and Countervailing Measures, while preserving the basic concepts, principles and effectiveness of these Agreements and their instruments and objectives, and taking into account the needs of developing and least-developed participants. In the initial phase of the negotiations, participants will indicate the provisions, including disciplines on trade distorting practices, that they seek to clarify and improve in the subsequent phase. In the context of these negotiations, participants shall also aim to clarify and improve WTO disciplines on fisheries subsidies, taking into account the importance of this sector to developing countries. We note that fisheries subsidies are also referred to in paragraph 31.

29. We also agree to negotiations aimed at clarifying and improving disciplines and procedures under the existing WTO provisions applying to regional trade agreements. The negotiations shall take into account the developmental aspects of regional trade agreements.

Dispute Settlement Understanding

30. We agree to negotiations on improvements and clarifications of the Dispute Settlement Understanding. The negotiations should be based on the work done thus far as well as any additional proposals by Members, and aim to agree on improvements and clarifications not later than May 2003, at which time we will take steps to ensure that the results enter into force as soon as possible thereafter.

Trade and Environment

31. With a view to enhancing the mutual supportiveness of trade and environment, we agree to negotiations, without prejudging their outcome, on:

(i) the relationship between existing WTO rules and specific trade obligations set out in multilateral environmental agreements (MEAs). The negotiations shall be limited in scope to the applicability of such existing WTO rules as among parties to the MEA in question. The negotiations shall not prejudice the WTO rights of any Member that is not a party to the MEA in question;

(ii) procedures for regular information exchange between MEA Secretariats and the relevant WTO committees, and the criteria for the granting of observer status;

(iii) the reduction or, as appropriate, elimination of tariff and non-tariff barriers to environmental goods and services.

We note that fisheries subsidies form part of the negotiations provided for in paragraph 28.

32. We instruct the Committee on Trade and Environment, in pursuing work on all items on its agenda within its current terms of reference, to give particular attention to:

(i) the effect of environmental measures on market access, especially in relation to developing countries, in particular the least-developed among them, and those situations in which the elimination or reduction of trade restrictions and distortions would benefit trade, the environment and development;

(ii) the relevant provisions of the Agreement on Trade-Related Aspects of Intellectual Property Rights; and

(iii) labelling requirements for environmental purposes.

Work on these issues should include the identification of any need to clarify relevant WTO rules. The Committee shall report to the Fifth Session of the Ministerial Conference, and make recommendations, where appropriate, with respect to future action, including the desirability of negotiations. The outcome of this work as well as the negotiations carried out under paragraph 31(i) and (ii) shall be compatible with the open and non-discriminatory nature of the multilateral trading system, shall not add to or diminish the rights and obligations of Members under existing WTO agreements, in particular the Agreement on the Application of Sanitary and Phytosanitary

Measures, nor alter the balance of these rights and obligations, and will take into account the needs of developing and least-developed countries.

33. We recognize the importance of technical assistance and capacity building in the field of trade and environment to developing countries, in particular the least-developed among them. We also encourage that expertise and experience be shared with Members wishing to perform environmental reviews at the national level. A report shall be prepared on these activities for the Fifth Session.

Electronic Commerce

34. We take note of the work which has been done in the General Council and other relevant bodies since the Ministerial Declaration of 20 May 1998 and agree to continue the Work Programme on Electronic Commerce. The work to date demonstrates that electronic commerce creates new challenges and opportunities for trade for Members at all stages of development, and we recognize the importance of creating and maintaining an environment which is favourable to the future development of electronic commerce. We instruct the General Council to consider the most appropriate institutional arrangements for handling the Work Programme, and to report on further progress to the Fifth Session of the Ministerial Conference. We declare that Members will maintain their current practice of not imposing customs duties on electronic transmissions until the Fifth Session.

Small Economies

35. We agree to a work programme, under the auspices of the General Council, to examine issues relating to the trade of small economies. The objective of this work is to frame responses to the trade-related issues identified for the fuller integration of small, vulnerable economies into the multilateral trading system, and not to create a sub-category of WTO Members. The General Council shall review the work programme and make recommendations for action to the Fifth Session of the Ministerial Conference.

Trade, Debt and Finance

36. We agree to an examination, in a Working Group under the auspices of the General Council, of the relationship between trade, debt and finance, and of any possible recommendations on steps that might be taken within the mandate and competence of the WTO to enhance the capacity of the multilateral trading system to contribute to a durable solution to the problem of external indebtedness of developing and least-developed countries, and to strengthen the coherence of international trade and financial policies, with a view to safeguarding the multilateral trading system from the effects of financial and monetary instability. The General Council shall

report to the Fifth Session of the Ministerial Conference on progress in the examination.

Trade and Transfer of Technology

37. We agree to an examination, in a Working Group under the auspices of the General Council, of the relationship between trade and transfer of technology, and of any possible recommendations on steps that might be taken within the mandate of the WTO to increase flows of technology to developing countries. The General Council shall report to the Fifth Session of the Ministerial Conference on progress in the examination.

Technical Cooperation and Capacity Building

38. We confirm that technical cooperation and capacity building are core elements of the development dimension of the multilateral trading system, and we welcome and endorse the New Strategy for WTO Technical Cooperation for Capacity Building, Growth and Integration. We instruct the Secretariat, in coordination with other relevant agencies, to support domestic efforts for mainstreaming trade into national plans for economic development and strategies for poverty reduction. The delivery of WTO technical assistance shall be designed to assist developing and least-developed countries and low-income countries in transition to adjust to WTO rules and disciplines, implement obligations and exercise the rights of membership, including drawing on the benefits of an open, rules-based multilateral trading system. Priority shall also be accorded to small, vulnerable, and transition economies, as well as to Members and Observers without representation in Geneva. We reaffirm our support for the valuable work of the International Trade Centre, which should be enhanced.

39. We underscore the urgent necessity for the effective coordinated delivery of technical assistance with bilateral donors, in the OECD Development Assistance Committee and relevant international and regional intergovernmental institutions, within a coherent policy framework and timetable. In the coordinated delivery of technical assistance, we instruct the Director-General to consult with the relevant agencies, bilateral donors and beneficiaries, to identify ways of enhancing and rationalizing the Integrated Framework for Trade-Related Technical Assistance to Least-Developed Countries and the Joint Integrated Technical Assistance Programme (JITAP).

40. We agree that there is a need for technical assistance to benefit from secure and predictable funding. We therefore instruct the Committee on Budget, Finance and Administration to develop a plan for adoption by the General Council in December 2001 that will ensure long-term funding for WTO technical assistance at an overall level no lower than that of the current year and commensurate with the activities outlined above.

41. We have established firm commitments on technical cooperation and capacity building in various paragraphs in this Ministerial Declaration. We reaffirm these specific commitments contained in paragraphs 16, 21, 24, 26, 27, 33, 38-40, 42 and 43, and also reaffirm the understanding in paragraph 2 on the important role of sustainably financed technical assistance and capacity-building programmes. We instruct the Director-General to report to the Fifth Session of the Ministerial Conference, with an interim report to the General Council in December 2002 on the implementation and adequacy of these commitments in the identified paragraphs.

Least-Developed Countries

42. We acknowledge the seriousness of the concerns expressed by the least-developed countries (LDCs) in the Zanzibar Declaration adopted by their Ministers in July 2001. We recognize that the integration of the LDCs into the multilateral trading system requires meaningful market access, support for the diversification of their production and export base, and trade-related technical assistance and capacity building. We agree that the meaningful integration of LDCs into the trading system and the global economy will involve efforts by all WTO Members. We commit ourselves to the objective of duty-free, quota-free market access for products originating from LDCs. In this regard, we welcome the significant market access improvements by WTO Members in advance of the Third UN Conference on LDCs (LDC-III), in Brussels, May 2001. We further commit ourselves to consider additional measures for progressive improvements in market access for LDCs. Accession of LDCs remains a priority for the Membership. We agree to work to facilitate and accelerate negotiations with acceding LDCs. We instruct the Secretariat to reflect the priority we attach to LDCs' accessions in the annual plans for technical assistance. We reaffirm the commitments we undertook at LDC-III, and agree that the WTO should take into account, in designing its work programme for LDCs, the trade-related elements of the Brussels Declaration and Programme of Action, consistent with the WTO's mandate, adopted at LDC-III. We instruct the Sub-Committee for Least-Developed Countries to design such a work programme and to report on the agreed work programme to the General Council at its first meeting in 2002.

43. We endorse the Integrated Framework for Trade-Related Technical Assistance to Least-Developed Countries (IF) as a viable model for LDCs' trade development. We urge development partners to significantly increase contributions to the IF Trust Fund and WTO extra-budgetary trust funds in favour of LDCs. We urge the core agencies, in coordination with development partners, to explore the enhancement of the IF with a view to addressing the supply-side constraints of LDCs and the extension of the model to all LDCs, following the review of the IF and the appraisal of the ongoing Pilot Scheme in selected LDCs. We request the Director-General,

following coordination with heads of the other agencies, to provide an interim report to the General Council in December 2002 and a full report to the Fifth Session of the Ministerial Conference on all issues affecting LDCs.

Special and Differential Treatment

44. We reaffirm that provisions for special and differential treatment are an integral part of the WTO Agreements. We note the concerns expressed regarding their operation in addressing specific constraints faced by developing countries, particularly least-developed countries. In that connection, we also note that some Members have proposed a Framework Agreement on Special and Differential Treatment (WT/GC/W/442). We therefore agree that all special and differential treatment provisions shall be reviewed with a view to strengthening them and making them more precise, effective and operational. In this connection, we endorse the work programme on special and differential treatment set out in the Decision on Implementation-Related Issues and Concerns.

Organization and Management of the Work Programme

45. The negotiations to be pursued under the terms of this Declaration shall be concluded not later than 1 January 2005. The Fifth Session of the Ministerial Conference will take stock of progress in the negotiations, provide any necessary political guidance, and take decisions as necessary. When the results of the negotiations in all areas have been established, a Special Session of the Ministerial Conference will be held to take decisions regarding the adoption and implementation of those results.

46. The overall conduct of the negotiations shall be supervised by a Trade Negotiations Committee under the authority of the General Council. The Trade Negotiations Committee shall hold its first meeting not later than 31 January 2002. It shall establish appropriate negotiating mechanisms as required and supervise the progress of the negotiations.

47. With the exception of the improvements and clarifications of the Dispute Settlement Understanding, the conduct, conclusion and entry into force of the outcome of the negotiations shall be treated as parts of a single undertaking. However, agreements reached at an early stage may be implemented on a provisional or a definitive basis. Early agreements shall be taken into account in assessing the overall balance of the negotiations.

48. Negotiations shall be open to:

(i) all Members of the WTO; and

(ii) States and separate customs territories currently in the process of accession and those that inform Members, at a regular meeting of the General Council, of their intention to negotiate the terms of their membership and for whom an accession working party is established.

Decisions on the outcomes of the negotiations shall be taken only by WTO Members.

49. The negotiations shall be conducted in a transparent manner among participants, in order to facilitate the effective participation of all. They shall be conducted with a view to ensuring benefits to all participants and to achieving an overall balance in the outcome of the negotiations.

50. The negotiations and the other aspects of the Work Programme shall take fully into account the principle of special and differential treatment for developing and least-developed countries embodied in: Part IV of the GATT 1994; the Decision of 28 November 1979 on Differential and More Favourable Treatment, Reciprocity and Fuller Participation of Developing Countries; the Uruguay Round Decision on Measures in Favour of Least-Developed Countries; and all other relevant WTO provisions.

51. The Committee on Trade and Development and the Committee on Trade and Environment shall, within their respective mandates, each act as a forum to identify and debate developmental and environmental aspects of the negotiations, in order to help achieve the objective of having sustainable development appropriately reflected.

52. Those elements of the Work Programme which do not involve negotiations are also accorded a high priority. They shall be pursued under the overall supervision of the General Council, which shall report on progress to the Fifth Session of the Ministerial Conference.

Document 55

DOHA DECISION ON IMPLEMENTATION*

Official name: Implementation—Related Issues and Concerns, Decision of 14 November 2001

The Ministerial Conference,

Having regard to Articles IV.1, IV.5 and IX of the Marrakesh Agreement Establishing the World Trade Organization (WTO);

Mindful of the importance that Members attach to the increased participation of developing countries in the multilateral trading system, and of the need to ensure that the system responds fully to the needs and interests of all participants;

Determined to take concrete action to address issues and concerns that have been raised by many developing-country Members regarding the implementation of some WTO Agreements and Decisions, including the difficulties and resource constraints that have been encountered in the implementation of obligations in various areas;

Recalling the 3 May 2000 Decision of the General Council to meet in special sessions to address outstanding implementation issues, and to assess the existing difficulties, identify ways needed to resolve them, and take decisions for appropriate action not later than the Fourth Session of the Ministerial Conference;

Noting the actions taken by the General Council in pursuance of this mandate at its Special Sessions in October and December 2000 (WT/L/384),

*WTO Document WT/MIN(01)/17.

as well as the review and further discussion undertaken at the Special Sessions held in April, July and October 2001, including the referral of additional issues to relevant WTO bodies or their chairpersons for further work;

Noting also the reports on the issues referred to the General Council from subsidiary bodies and their chairpersons and from the Director-General, and the discussions as well as the clarifications provided and understandings reached on implementation issues in the intensive informal and formal meetings held under this process since May 2000;

Decides as follows:

1. General Agreement on Tariffs and Trade 1994 (GATT 1994)

1.1 Reaffirms that Article XVIII of the GATT 1994 is a special and differential treatment provision for developing countries and that recourse to it should be less onerous than to Article XII of the GATT 1994.

1.2 Noting the issues raised in the report of the Chairperson of the Committee on Market Access (WT/GC/50) concerning the meaning to be given to the phrase "substantial interest" in paragraph 2(d) of Article XIII of the GATT 1994, the Market Access Committee is directed to give further consideration to the issue and make recommendations to the General Council as expeditiously as possible but in any event not later than the end of 2002.

2. Agreement on Agriculture

2.1 Urges Members to exercise restraint in challenging measures notified under the green box by developing countries to promote rural development and adequately address food security concerns.

2.2 Takes note of the report of the Committee on Agriculture (G/AG/11) regarding the implementation of the Decision on Measures Concerning the Possible Negative Effects of the Reform Programme on Least-Developed and Net Food-Importing Developing Countries, and approves the recommendations contained therein regarding (i) food aid; (ii) technical and financial assistance in the context of aid programmes to improve agricultural productivity and infrastructure; (iii) financing normal levels of commercial imports of basic foodstuffs; and (iv) review of follow-up.

2.3 Takes note of the report of the Committee on Agriculture (G/AG/11) regarding the implementation of Article 10.2 of the Agreement on Agriculture, and approves the recommendations and reporting requirements contained therein.

2.4 Takes note of the report of the Committee on Agriculture (G/AG/11) regarding the administration of tariff rate quotas and the submission by Members of addenda to their notifications, and endorses the decision by the Committee to keep this matter under review.

3. Agreement on the Application of Sanitary and Phytosanitary Measures

3.1 Where the appropriate level of sanitary and phytosanitary protection allows scope for the phased introduction of new sanitary and phytosanitary measures, the phrase "longer time-frame for compliance" referred to in Article 10.2 of the Agreement on the Application of Sanitary and Phytosanitary Measures, shall be understood to mean normally a period of not less than 6 months. Where the appropriate level of sanitary and phytosanitary protection does not allow scope for the phased introduction of a new measure, but specific problems are identified by a Member, the Member applying the measure shall upon request enter into consultations with the country with a view to finding a mutually satisfactory solution to the problem while continuing to achieve the importing Member's appropriate level of protection.

3.2 Subject to the conditions specified in paragraph 2 of Annex B to the Agreement on the Application of Sanitary and Phytosanitary Measures, the phrase "reasonable interval" shall be understood to mean normally a period of not less than 6 months. It is understood that time-frames for specific measures have to be considered in the context of the particular circumstances of the measure and actions necessary to implement it. The entry into force of measures which contribute to the liberalization of trade should not be unnecessarily delayed.

3.3 Takes note of the Decision of the Committee on Sanitary and Phytosanitary Measures (G/SPS/19) regarding equivalence, and instructs the Committee to develop expeditiously the specific programme to further the implementation of Article 4 of the Agreement on the Application of Sanitary and Phytosanitary Measures.

3.4 Pursuant to the provisions of Article 12.7 of the Agreement on the Application of Sanitary and Phytosanitary Measures, the Committee on Sanitary and Phytosanitary Measures is instructed to review the operation and implementation of the Agreement on Sanitary and Phytosanitary Measures at least once every four years.

3.5 (i) Takes note of the actions taken to date by the Director-General to facilitate the increased participation of Members at different levels of development in the work of the relevant international standard setting organizations as well as his efforts to coordinate with these organizations and financial institutions in identifying SPS-related technical assistance needs and how best to address them; and

(ii) urges the Director-General to continue his cooperative efforts with these organizations and institutions in this regard, including with a view to according priority to the effective participation of least-developed countries and facilitating the provision of technical and financial assistance for this purpose.

3.6 (i) Urges Members to provide, to the extent possible, the financial and technical assistance necessary to enable least-developed countries to respond adequately to the introduction of any new SPS measures which may have significant negative effects on their trade; and

(ii) urges Members to ensure that technical assistance is provided to least-developed countries with a view to responding to the special problems faced by them in implementing the Agreement on the Application of Sanitary and Phytosanitary Measures.

4. Agreement on Textiles and Clothing

Reaffirms the commitment to full and faithful implementation of the Agreement on Textiles and Clothing, and agrees:

4.1 that the provisions of the Agreement relating to the early integration of products and the elimination of quota restrictions should be effectively utilised.

4.2 that Members will exercise particular consideration before initiating investigations in the context of antidumping remedies on textile and clothing exports from developing countries previously subject to quantitative restrictions under the Agreement for a period of two years following full integration of this Agreement into the WTO.

4.3 that without prejudice to their rights and obligations, Members shall notify any changes in their rules of origin concerning products falling under the coverage of the Agreement to the Committee on Rules of Origin which may decide to examine them.

Requests the Council for Trade in Goods to examine the following proposals:

4.4 that when calculating the quota levels for small suppliers for the remaining years of the Agreement, Members will apply the most favourable methodology available in respect of those Members under the growth-on-growth provisions from the beginning of the implementation period; extend the same treatment to least-developed countries; and, where possible, eliminate quota restrictions on imports of such Members;

4.5 that Members will calculate the quota levels for the remaining years of the Agreement with respect to other restrained Members as if implementation of the growth-on-growth provision for stage 3 had been advanced to 1 January 2000;

and make recommendations to the General Council by 31 July 2002 for appropriate action.

5. Agreement on Technical Barriers to Trade

5.1 Confirms the approach to technical assistance being developed by the Committee on Technical Barriers to Trade, reflecting the results of the triennial review work in this area, and mandates this work to continue.

5.2 Subject to the conditions specified in paragraph 12 of Article 2 of the Agreement on Technical Barriers to Trade, the phrase "reasonable interval" shall be understood to mean normally a period of not less than 6 months, except when this would be ineffective in fulfilling the legitimate objectives pursued.

5.3 (i) Takes note of the actions taken to date by the Director-General to facilitate the increased participation of Members at different levels of development in the work of the relevant international standard setting organizations as well as his efforts to coordinate with these organizations and financial institutions in identifying TBT-related technical assistance needs and how best to address them; and

(ii) urges the Director-General to continue his cooperative efforts with these organizations and institutions, including with a view to according priority to the effective participation of least-developed countries and facilitating the provision of technical and financial assistance for this purpose.

5.4 (i) Urges Members to provide, to the extent possible, the financial and technical assistance necessary to enable least-developed countries to respond adequately to the introduction of any new TBT measures which may have significant negative effects on their trade; and

(ii) urges Members to ensure that technical assistance is provided to least-developed countries with a view to responding to the special problems faced by them in implementing the Agreement on Technical Barriers to Trade.

6. Agreement on Trade-Related Investment Measures

6.1 Takes note of the actions taken by the Council for Trade in Goods in regard to requests from some developing-country Members for the extension of the five-year transitional period provided for in Article 5.2 of Agreement on Trade-Related Investment Measures.

6.2 Urges the Council for Trade in Goods to consider positively requests that may be made by least-developed countries under Article 5.3 of the TRIMs Agreement or Article IX.3 of the WTO Agreement, as well as to take into consideration the particular circumstances of least-developed countries when setting the terms and conditions including time-frames.

7. Agreement on the Implementation of Article VI of the General Agreement on Tariffs and Trade 1994

7.1 Agrees that investigating authorities shall examine with special care any application for the initiation of an anti-dumping investigation where an investigation of the same product from the same Member resulted in a negative finding within the 365 days prior to the filing of the application and that, unless this pre-initiation examination indicates that circumstances have changed, the investigation shall not proceed.

7.2 Recognizes that, while Article 15 of the Agreement on the Implementation of Article VI of the General Agreement on Tariffs and Trade 1994 is a mandatory provision, the modalities for its application would benefit from clarification. Accordingly, the Committee on Anti-Dumping Practices is instructed, through its working group on Implementation, to examine this issue and to draw up appropriate recommendations within twelve months on how to operationalize this provision.

7.3 Takes note that Article 5.8 of the Agreement on the Implementation of Article VI of the General Agreement on Tariffs and Trade 1994 does not specify the time-frame to be used in determining the volume of dumped imports, and that this lack of specificity creates uncertainties in the implementation of the provision. The Committee on Anti-Dumping Practices is instructed, through its working group on Implementation, to study this issue and draw up recommendations within 12 months, with a view to ensuring the maximum possible predictability and objectivity in the application of time frames.

7.4 Takes note that Article 18.6 of the Agreement on the Implementation of Article VI of the General Agreement on Tariffs and Trade 1994 requires the Committee on Anti-Dumping Practices to review annually the implementation and operation of the Agreement taking into account the objectives thereof. The Committee on Anti-dumping Practices is instructed to draw up guidelines for the improvement of annual reviews and to report its views and recommendations to the General Council for subsequent decision within 12 months.

8. Agreement on the Implementation of Article VII of the General Agreement on Tariffs and Trade 1994

8.1 Takes note of the actions taken by the Committee on Customs Valuation in regard to the requests from a number of developing-country Members for the extension of the five-year transitional period provided for in Article 20.1 of Agreement on the Implementation of Article VII of the General Agreement on Tariffs and Trade 1994.

8.2 Urges the Council for Trade in Goods to give positive consideration to requests that may be made by least-developed country Members under paragraphs 1 and 2 of Annex III of the Customs Valuation Agreement or under Article IX.3 of the WTO Agreement, as well as to take into consideration the particular circumstances of least-developed countries when setting the terms and conditions including time-frames.

8.3 Underlines the importance of strengthening cooperation between the customs administrations of Members in the prevention of customs fraud. In this regard, it is agreed that, further to the 1994 Ministerial Decision Regarding Cases Where Customs Administrations Have Reasons to Doubt the Truth or Accuracy of the Declared Value, when the customs administration of an importing Member has reasonable grounds to doubt the truth or accuracy of the declared value, it may seek assistance from the customs administration of an exporting Member on the value of the good concerned. In such cases, the exporting Member shall offer cooperation and assistance, consistent with its domestic laws and procedures, including furnishing information on the export value of the good concerned. Any information provided in this context shall be treated in accordance with Article 10 of the Customs Valuation Agreement. Furthermore, recognizing the legitimate concerns expressed by the customs administrations of several importing Members on the accuracy of the declared value, the Committee on Customs Valuation is directed to identify and assess practical means to address such concerns, including the exchange of information on export values and to report to the General Council by the end of 2002 at the latest.

9. Agreement on Rules of Origin

9.1 Takes note of the report of the Committee on Rules of Origin (G/RO/48) regarding progress on the harmonization work programme, and urges the Committee to complete its work by the end of 2001.

9.2 Agrees that any interim arrangements on rules of origin implemented by Members in the transitional period before the entry into force of the results of the harmonisation work programme shall be consistent with the Agreement on Rules of Origin, particularly Articles 2 and 5 thereof. Without prejudice to Members' rights and obligations, such arrangements may be examined by the Committee on Rules of Origin.

10. Agreement on Subsidies and Countervailing Measures

10.1 Agrees that Annex VII(b) to the Agreement on Subsidies and Countervailing Measures includes the Members that are listed therein until their GNP per capita reaches US $1,000 in constant 1990 dollars for three consecutive years. This decision will enter into effect upon the adoption by the Committee on Subsidies and Countervailing Measures of an appropriate methodology for calculating constant 1990 dollars. If, however, the Committee on Subsidies and Countervailing Measures does not reach a consensus agreement on an appropriate methodology by 1 January 2003, the methodology proposed by the Chairman of the Committee set forth in G/SCM/38, Appendix 2 shall be applied. A Member shall not leave Annex VII(b) so long as its GNP per capita in current dollars has not reached US $1000 based upon the most recent data from the World Bank.

10.2 Takes note of the proposal to treat measures implemented by developing countries with a view to achieving legitimate development goals, such as regional growth, technology research and development funding, production diversification and development and implementation of environmentally sound methods of production as non-actionable subsidies, and agrees that this issue be addressed in accordance with paragraph 13 below. During the course of the negotiations, Members are urged to exercise due restraint with respect to challenging such measures.

10.3 Agrees that the Committee on Subsidies and Countervailing Measures shall continue its review of the provisions of the Agreement on Subsidies and Countervailing Measures regarding countervailing duty investigations and report to the General Council by 31 July 2002.

10.4 Agrees that if a Member has been excluded from the list in paragraph (b) of Annex VII to the Agreement on Subsidies and Countervailing Measures, it shall be re-included in it when its GNP per capita falls back below US$ 1,000.

10.5 Subject to the provisions of Articles 27.5 and 27.6, it is reaffirmed that least-developed country Members are exempt from the prohibition on export subsidies set forth in Article 3.1(a) of the Agreement on Subsidies and Countervailing Measures, and thus have flexibility to finance their exporters, consistent with their development needs. It is understood that the eight-year period in Article 27.5 within which a least-developed country Member must phase out its export subsidies in respect of a product in which it is export-competitive begins from the date export competitiveness exists within the meaning of Article 27.6.

10.6 Having regard to the particular situation of certain developing-country Members, directs the Committee on Subsidies and Countervailing Measures to extend the transition period, under the rubric of Article 27.4 of the Agreement on Subsidies and Countervailing Measures, for certain export subsidies provided by such Members, pursuant to the procedures set forth in document G/SCM/39. Furthermore, when considering a request for an extension of the transition period under the rubric of Article 27.4 of the Agreement on Subsidies and Countervailing Measures, and in order to avoid that Members at similar stages of development and having a similar order of magnitude of share in world trade are treated differently in terms of receiving such extensions for the same eligible programmes and the length of such extensions, directs the Committee to extend the transition period for those developing countries, after taking into account the relative competitiveness in relation to other developing-country Members who have requested extension of the transition period following the procedures set forth in document G/SCM/39.

11. Agreement on Trade-Related Aspects of Intellectual Property Rights (TRIPS)

11.1 The TRIPS Council is directed to continue its examination of the scope and modalities for complaints of the types provided for under subparagraphs 1(b) and 1(c) of Article XXIII of GATT 1994 and make recommendations to the Fifth Session of the Ministerial Conference. It is agreed that, in the meantime, Members will not initiate such complaints under the TRIPS Agreement.

11.2 Reaffirming that the provisions of Article 66.2 of the TRIPS Agreement are mandatory, it is agreed that the TRIPS Council shall put in place a mechanism for ensuring the monitoring and full implementation of the obligations in question. To this end, developed-country Members shall submit prior to the end of 2002 detailed reports on the functioning in practice of the incentives provided to their enterprises for the transfer of technology in pursuance of their commitments under Article 66.2. These submissions shall be subject to a review in the TRIPS Council and information shall be updated by Members annually.

12. Cross-Cutting Issues

12.1 The Committee on Trade and Development is instructed:

(i) to identify those special and differential treatment provisions that are already mandatory in nature and those that are non-binding in character, to consider the legal and practical implications for developed and developing Members of converting special and differential treatment measures into mandatory provisions, to identify those that Members consider should be made mandatory, and to report to the General Council with clear recommendations for a decision by July 2002;

(ii) to examine additional ways in which special and differential treatment provisions can be made more effective, to consider ways, including improved information flows, in which developing countries, in particular the least-developed countries, may be assisted to make best use of special and differential treatment provisions, and to report to the General Council with clear recommendations for a decision by July 2002; and

(iii) to consider, in the context of the work programme adopted at the Fourth Session of the Ministerial Conference, how special and differential treatment may be incorporated into the architecture of WTO rules.

The work of the Committee on Trade and Development in this regard shall take fully into consideration previous work undertaken as noted in WT/COMTD/W/77/Rev.1. It will also be without prejudice to work in respect of implementation of WTO Agreements in the General Council and in other Councils and Committees.

12.2 Reaffirms that preferences granted to developing countries pursuant to the Decision of the Contracting Parties of 28 November 1979 ("Enabling Clause")[1] should be generalised, non-reciprocal and non-discriminatory.

13. Outstanding Implementation Issues[2]

Agrees that outstanding implementation issues be addressed in accordance with paragraph 12 of the Ministerial Declaration (WT/MIN(01)/DEC/1).

14. Final Provisions

Requests the Director-General, consistent with paragraphs 38 to 43 of the Ministerial Declaration (WT/MIN(01)/DEC/1), to ensure that WTO technical assistance focuses, on a priority basis, on assisting developing

1. BISD 26S/203.
2. A list of these issues is compiled in document Job(01)/152/Rev.1.

countries to implement existing WTO obligations as well as on increasing their capacity to participate more effectively in future multilateral trade negotiations. In carrying out this mandate, the WTO Secretariat should cooperate more closely with international and regional intergovernmental organisations so as to increase efficiency and synergies and avoid duplication of programmes.

Document 56

TRANSPARENCY MECHANISM FOR REGIONAL TRADE AGREEMENTS*

Decision of 14 December 2006

The General Council,

Having regard to paragraph 1 of Article IX of the Marrakesh Agreement Establishing the World Trade Organization ("WTO Agreement");

Conducting the functions of the Ministerial Conference in the interval between meetings pursuant to paragraph 2 of Article IV of the WTO Agreement;

Noting that trade agreements of a mutually preferential nature ("regional trade agreements" or "RTAs") have greatly increased in number and have become an important element in Members' trade policies and developmental strategies;

Convinced that enhancing transparency in, and understanding of, RTAs and their effects is of systemic interest and will be of benefit to all Members;

Having regard also to the transparency provisions of Article XXIV of GATT 1994, the Understanding on the Interpretation of Article XXIV of GATT 1994 ("GATT Understanding"), Article V of GATS and the 1979 Decision on Differential and More Favourable Treatment, Reciprocity and Fuller Participation of Developing Countries ("Enabling Clause");

*WTO Document WT/L/671.

Recognizing the resource and technical constraints of developing country Members;

Recalling that in the negotiations pursued under the terms of the Doha Ministerial Declaration,[1] in accordance with paragraph 47 of that Declaration, agreements reached at an early stage may be implemented on a provisional basis;

Decides:

A. Early Announcement

1. Without prejudging the substance and the timing of the notification required under Article XXIV of the GATT 1994, Article V of the GATS or the Enabling Clause, nor affecting Members' rights and obligations under the WTO agreements in any way:

(a) Members participating in new negotiations aimed at the conclusion of an RTA shall endeavour to so inform the WTO.

(b) Members parties to a newly signed RTA shall convey to the WTO, in so far as and when it is publicly available, information on the RTA, including its official name, scope and date of signature, any foreseen timetable for its entry into force or provisional application, relevant contact points and/or website addresses, and any other relevant unrestricted information.

2. The information referred to in paragraph 1 above is to be forwarded to the WTO Secretariat, which will post it on the WTO website and will periodically provide Members with a synopsis of the communications received.

B. Notification

3. The required notification of an RTA by Members that are party to it shall take place as early as possible. As a rule, it will occur no later than directly following the parties' ratification of the RTA or any party's decision on application of the relevant parts of an agreement, and before the application of preferential treatment between the parties.

4. In notifying their RTA, the parties shall specify under which provision(s) of the WTO agreements it is notified. They will also provide the full text of the RTA (or those parts they have decided to apply) and any related schedules, annexes and protocols, in one of the WTO official languages; if available, these shall also be submitted in an electronically exploitable format. Reference to related official Internet links shall also be supplied.

1. WT/MIN(01)/DEC/1.

C. Procedures to Enhance Transparency

5. Upon notification, and without affecting Members' rights and obligations under the WTO agreements under which it has been notified, the RTA shall be considered by Members under the procedures established in paragraphs 6 to 13 below.

6. The consideration by Members of a notified RTA shall be normally concluded in a period not exceeding one year after the date of notification. A precise timetable for the consideration of the RTA shall be drawn by the WTO Secretariat in consultation with the parties at the time of the notification.

7. To assist Members in their consideration of a notified RTA:

(a) the parties shall make available to the WTO Secretariat data as specified in the Annex, if possible in an electronically exploitable format; and

(b) the WTO Secretariat, on its own responsibility and in full consultation with the parties, shall prepare a factual presentation of the RTA.

8. The data referred to in paragraph 7(a) shall be made available as soon as possible. Normally, the timing of the data submission shall not exceed ten weeks—or 20 weeks in the case of RTAs involving only developing countries—after the date of notification of the agreement.

9. The factual presentation provided for in paragraph 7(b) shall be primarily based on the information provided by the parties; if necessary, the WTO Secretariat may also use data available from other sources, taking into account the views of the parties in furtherance of factual accuracy. In preparing the factual presentation, the WTO Secretariat shall refrain from any value judgement.

10. The WTO Secretariat's factual presentation shall not be used as a basis for dispute settlement procedures or to create new rights and obligations for Members.

11. As a rule, a single formal meeting will be devoted to consider each notified RTA; any additional exchange of information should take place in written form.

12. The WTO Secretariat's factual presentation, as well as any additional information submitted by the parties, shall be circulated in all WTO official languages not less than eight weeks in advance of the meeting devoted to the consideration of the RTA. Members' written questions or comments on the

RTA under consideration shall be transmitted to the parties through the WTO Secretariat at least four weeks before the corresponding meeting; they shall be distributed, together with replies, to all Members at least three working days before the corresponding meeting.

13. All written material submitted, as well as the minutes of the meeting devoted to the consideration of a notified agreement will be promptly circulated in all WTO official languages and made available on the WTO website.

D. Subsequent Notification and Reporting

14. The required notification of changes affecting the implementation of an RTA, or the operation of an already implemented RTA, shall take place as soon as possible after the changes occur. Changes to be notified include, *inter alia*, modifications to the preferential treatment between the parties and to the RTA's disciplines. The parties shall provide a summary of the changes made, as well as any related texts, schedules, annexes and protocols, in one of the WTO official languages and, if available, in electronically exploitable format.[2]

15. At the end of the RTA's implementation period, the parties shall submit to the WTO a short written report on the realization of the liberalization commitments in the RTA as originally notified.

16. Upon request, the relevant WTO body shall provide an adequate opportunity for an exchange of views on the communications submitted under paragraphs 14 and 15.

17. The communications submitted under paragraphs 14 and 15 will be promptly made available on the WTO website and a synopsis will be periodically circulated by the WTO Secretariat to Members.

E. Bodies Entrusted with the Implementation of the Mechanism

18. The Committee on Regional Trade Agreements ("CRTA") and the Committee on Trade and Development ("CTD") are instructed to implement this Transparency Mechanism.[3] The CRTA shall do so for RTAs falling under Article XXIV of GATT 1994 and Article V of GATS, while the CTD shall do so for RTAs falling under paragraph 2(c) of the Enabling Clause.

2. In their notification, Members may refer to official Internet links related to the agreement where the relevant information can be consulted in full, in one of the WTO official languages.

3. The Director-General is invited to ensure consistency in the preparation of the WTO Secretariat factual presentations for the different types of RTAs, taking into account the variations in data provided by different Members.

For purposes of performing the functions established under this Mechanism, the CTD shall convene in dedicated session.

F. *Technical Support for Developing Countries*

19. Upon request, the WTO Secretariat shall provide technical support to developing country Members, and especially least-developed countries, in the implementation of this Transparency Mechanism, in particular—but not limited to—with respect to the preparation of RTA-related data and other information to be submitted to the WTO Secretariat.

G. *Other Provisions*

20. Any Member may, at any time, bring to the attention of the relevant WTO body information on any RTA that it considers ought to have been submitted to Members in the framework of this Transparency Mechanism.

21. The WTO Secretariat shall establish and maintain an updated electronic database on individual RTAs. This database shall include relevant tariff and trade-related information, and give access to all written material related to announced or notified RTAs available at the WTO. The RTA database should be structured so as to be easily accessible to the public.

H. *Provisional Application of the Transparency Mechanism*

22. This Decision shall apply, on a provisional basis, to all RTAs. With respect to RTAs already notified under the relevant WTO transparency provisions and in force, this Decision shall apply as follows:

(a) RTAs for which a working party report has been adopted by the GATT Council and those RTAs notified to the GATT under the Enabling Clause will be subject to the procedures under Sections D to G above.

(b) RTAs for which the CRTA has concluded the "factual examination" prior to the adoption of this Decision and those for which the "factual examination" will have been concluded by 31 December 2006, and RTAs notified to the WTO under the Enabling Clause will be subject to the procedures under Sections D to G above. In addition, for each of these RTAs, the WTO Secretariat shall prepare a factual abstract presenting the features of the agreement.

(c) Any RTA notified prior to the adoption of this Decision and not referred to in subparagraphs (a) or (b) will be subject to the procedures under Sections C to G above.

I. *Reappraisal of the Mechanism*

23. Members will review, and if necessary modify, this Decision, in light of the experience gained from its provisional operation, and replace it by a permanent mechanism adopted as part of the overall results of the Round, in accordance with paragraph 47 of the Doha Declaration. Members will also review the legal relationship between this Mechanism and relevant WTO provisions related to RTAs.

Annex

Submission of Data by RTA Parties

1. RTA parties shall not be expected to make available the information required below if the corresponding data has already been submitted to the Integrated Data Base (IDB),[4] or has otherwise been provided to the Secretariat in an adequate format.[5]

2. For the goods aspects in RTAs, the parties shall submit the following data, at the tariff-line level:[6]

(a) Tariff concessions under the agreement:

(i) a full listing of each party's preferential duties applied in the year of entry into force of the agreement; and

(ii) when the agreement is to be implemented by stages, a full listing of each party's preferential duties to be applied over the transition period.

4. Trade and tariff data submissions in the context of an RTA notification can subsequently be included in the IDB, provided that their key features are appropriate. In this respect, see document G/MA/IDB/W/6 (dated 15 June 2000) for the Guidelines for Supplying PC IDB Submissions and documents G/MA/115 (dated 17 June 2002) and G/MA/115/Add.5 (dated 13 January 2005) for WTO Policy regarding the dissemination of IDB data.

5. Data submissions can be furnished in PC database formats, spreadsheet formats, or text-delimited formats; the use of word-processing formats should be avoided, if possible.

6. References to "tariff-line level" shall be understood to mean the detailed breakdown of the national customs nomenclature (HS codes with, for example, 8, 10 or more digits). It is crucial that all data elements supplied use the same national customs nomenclature or are associated with corresponding conversion tables.

(b) MFN duty rates:

(i) a full tariff listing of each RTA party's MFN duties applied on the year of entry into force of the agreement;[7] and

(ii) a full tariff listing of each RTA party's MFN duties applied on the year preceding the entry into force of the agreement.

(c) Where applicable, other data (e.g., preferential margins, tariff-rate quotas, seasonal restrictions, special safeguards and, if available, *ad valorem* equivalents for non-*ad valorem* duties).

(d) Product-specific preferential rules of origin as defined in the agreement.

(e) Import statistics, for the most recent three years preceding the notification for which they are available:

(i) each party's imports from each of the other parties, in value; and

(ii) each party's imports from the rest of the world, broken down by country of origin, in value.

3. For the services aspects in RTAs, the parties shall submit the following data, if available, for the three most recent years preceding the notification: trade or balance of payments statistics (by services sector/subsector and partner), gross domestic product data or production statistics (by services sector/subsector), and relevant statistics on foreign direct investment and on movement of natural persons (by country and, if possible, by services sector/subsector).

4. For RTAs involving only developing countries, in particular when these comprise least-developed countries, the data requirements specified above will take into account the technical constraints of the parties to the agreement.

7. In the case of a customs union, the MFN applied common external tariff.